Guatemala

El Petén
p225

The Highlands
p89

Central & Eastern
Guatemala
p176

Antigua
p62

Guatemala City
p42

The Pacific Slope
p156

THIS EDITION WRITTEN AND RESEARCHED BY
Lucas Vidgen, Daniel C Schechter

Contents

PLAN YOUR TRIP

ON THE ROAD

STREET VENDOR,
CHICHICASTENANGO P118

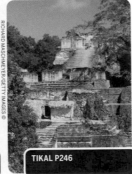

TIKAL P246

ANTIGUA P62

MARKET,
QUETZALTENANGO P130

CULTURA TRAVEL/BEN PIPE PHOTOGRAPHY/GETTY IMAGES ©

RICHARD MASCHMEYER/GETTY IMAGES ©

CULTURA TRAVEL/BEN PIPE PHOTOGRAPHY/GETTY IMAGES ©

RICHARD I'ANSON/GETTY IMAGES ©

Contents

Welcome to Guatemala

Mysterious and often challenging, Central America's most diverse country offers landscapes and experiences that have been captivating travelers for centuries.

Colonial Grandeur

Say what you like about the Spanish in Latin America, you have to agree that they left behind some stunning architecture. From Antigua's crumbling ruins to the stately cathedral in Guatemala City's central plaza, there are plenty of opportunities to get snap-happy. In even the smallest towns you can find picturesque buildings – the small coastal town of Retalhuleu has a charming central plaza, while larger coffee-boom towns like Cobán and Quetzaltenango maintain vestiges of their glory days in their cathedrals, town halls and other public buildings.

The Timeless Maya

While many ask whatever happened to the Maya, the simple answer is nothing – they're still here, and some traditions continue to thrive. If you're interested in archaeology, the must-see sites are Tikal, Copán (in Honduras), and Guatemala City's superb selection of museums.

Living Maya culture can be witnessed in its 'pure' form in towns like Rabinal and sacred sites such as Laguna Chicabal. And the Maya themselves? Well, they're everywhere. But the most traditional villages are in the highlands – the Ixil Triangle is a good place to start.

Adventure Awaits

Active souls tend to find their agenda very full once they get to Guatemala. Stunning trekking routes through the jungles and up volcanoes, world class white-water rafting, more miles of caves than you could possibly explore in one vacation, and what seems like a zipline strung between every two trees in the country are just the beginning. Like to take things up a notch? How about paragliding into a volcanic crater at Lago de Atitlán? Or scuba diving in the same place? You might even luck onto some good swell on the Pacific coast. Or you could just find a hammock and think about doing all that. Your call.

Natural Highs

With not even 2% of its landmass urbanized, it's not surprising that Guatemala offers some superb natural scenery. National parks are few but impressive, particularly in the Petén region and the lush canyons of the Río Dulce make for an unforgettable boat ride. The natural beauty of the volcano-ringed Lago de Atitlán has been captivating travelers for centuries, while the swimming hole that launched a thousand postcards, Semuc Champey, has to be seen to be believed.

Why I Love Guatemala

By Lucas Vidgen, Author

Having lived here for nearly 10 years, I've found my love for the country change and develop over time. The first, obvious infatuation was visual – the dramatic landscapes of jungles and volcanoes, the little cultural jolts of traditionally dressed Maya women toting the latest model cell phones. But over time what I really came to admire was the Guatemalan spirit, the idea that tragedies happen – wars, earthquakes, floods and hurricanes – but the simple things abide. A meal with the family, a joke with some friends – as crazy as everything else gets, these are the things to treasure.

For more about our authors, see p328

Above: Mam Maya locals, highlands (p89)

Guatemala

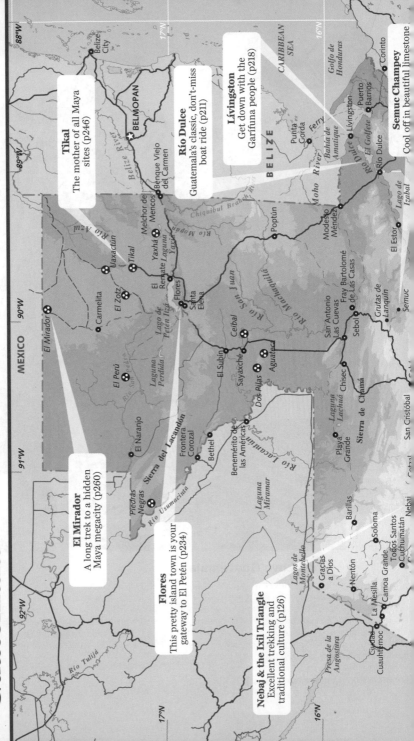

El Mirador
A long trek to a hidden Maya megacity (p260)

Flores
This pretty island town is your gateway to El Petén (p234)

Nebaj & the Ixil Triangle
Excellent trekking and traditional culture (p126)

Tikal
The mother of all Maya sites (p246)

Río Dulce
Guatemala's classic, don't-miss boat ride (p211)

Livingston
Get down with the Garifuna people (p218)

Semuc Champey
Cool off in beautiful limestone

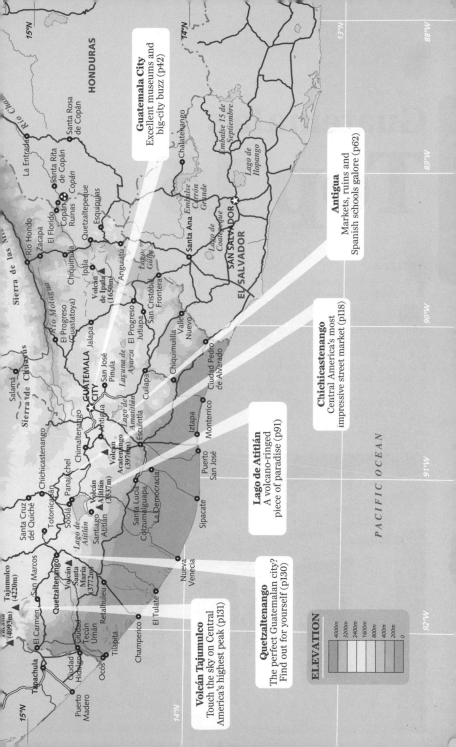

Guatemala City
Excellent museums and big-city buzz (p42)

Antigua
Markets, ruins and Spanish schools galore (p62)

Chichicastenango
Central America's most impressive street market (p118)

Lago de Atitlán
A volcano-ringed piece of paradise (p91)

Volcán Tajumulco
Touch the sky on Central America's highest peak (p131)

Quetzaltenango
The perfect Guatemalan city? Find out for yourself (p130)

ELEVATION

4000m
3200m
2400m
1600m
800m
400m
200m
0

PACIFIC OCEAN

Guatemala's
Top 15

Antigua

1 With mammoth volcanic peaks and coffee-covered slopes as a backdrop for the scattered remnants of Spanish occupation, the former capital of Guatemala (p62) makes an appealing setting for learning Spanish, and a globally varied population come here to study at such quality institutes as Escuela de Español San José el Viejo (p74). This influx fuels a surprisingly sophisticated culinary panorama and bubbly nightlife scene, best represented by the rowdily literate Café No Sé (p82).

Tikal

2 The remarkably restored temples (p246) that stand in this partially cleared corner the jungle astonish for both their monumenta size and architectural brilliance, as an early morning arrival at the Gran Plaza proves. Occupied for some 16 centuries, it's an amazing testament to the cultural and artistic heights scaled by this jungle civilization. A highlight is the helicopter-like vantage from towering Temple IV on the west edge of the precinct. Equally compelling is the abundance of wildli which can be appreciated strolling ancient causeways between ceremonial centers.

Lago de Atitlán

3 Possibly the single worthiest destination in Guatemala, Atitlán (p91) elicits poetic outbursts from even the most seasoned traveler. Of volcanic origin, the alternately placid and turbulent lake is ringed by volcanoes and villages like Santiago Atitlán, with a thriving indigenous culture, and San Marcos, a haven for seekers who plug into the lake's cosmic energy. And there are enough activities – paragliding from Santa Catarina Palopó, kayaking around Santa Cruz La Laguna or hiking the glorious lakeshore trails – to make a longer stay viable.

Chichicastenango

4 More than a place to shop, the twice-weekly market (p118) here is a vivid window on indigenous tradition, an ancient crossroads for the area's K'iche' Maya–speaking inhabitants and a spiritually charged site. At Santo Tomás (p120) church in the center of town and the hill of Pascual Abaj (p120) on its southern edge, shamans overlay Maya rituals upon Christian iconography. And it's a good place to shop too, especially if you're after finely woven textiles.

3

Volcanoes

5 Sacred to the Maya and integral to the country's history, Guatemala's volcanoes dominate the skylines of the country's west, and are one of its emblematic features. You can gaze upon their domed beauty from the comfort of a cafe in Antigua or on Lago de Atitlán, or get up close and personal by climbing (at least) one. Favorites include the lava-spewing Pacaya (p70), Tajumulco (p131), which forms Central America's highest point, and San Pedro (p97), for its sweeping views over picturesque Lago de Atitlán. Pacaya volcano

Sweet River

6 The Río Dulce (literally, sweet river) connects Guatemala's largest lake with the Caribbean coast, and winding along it, through a steep-walled valley, surrounded by lush vegetation, bird calls and the (very occasional) manatee is Guatemala's classic, don't-miss boat ride (p219). This is no tourist cruise – the river is a way of life and a means of transportation around here – but you get to stop at a couple of places to visit river-dwelling communities and natural hot springs, making for a magical, unforgettable experience.

KELLY CHENG TRAVEL PHOTOGRAPHY/GETTY IMAGES ©

Handicrafts & Textiles

7 Inextricably woven into the country's heritage, Guatemalan fabrics are much more than just tourist tat. The designs tell the stories of the wearer's community and beliefs. Likewise, handicraft production has always been a part of life. Fine examples of craftwork and weaving can be seen on the streets all over the country, but if you're looking to take some home (or even just get some priceless pics), you'll find the best selections in the markets in Guatemala City (p57), Antigua (p83), Panajachel (p102) and Chichicastenango (p118).

Guatemala City

8 Vibrant and raw, often confronting and occasionally surprising, the nation's capital (p42) is very much a love it or leave it proposition. Many choose the latter – and as fast as they can – but those who hang around and look behind the drab architecture and scruffy edges find a city teeming with life. For culture vultures, fine diners, mall rats, live-music lovers and city people in general, the capital has a buzz that's unmatched in the rest of the country.

Semuc Champey

9 Guatemala doesn't have that many freshwater swimming holes that you'd really want to dive into, but the jungle-shrouded oasis of Semuc Champey (p188) is definitely an exception. Turquoise-colored water cascades down a series of limestone pools, creating an idyllic setting that many call the most beautiful place in the country. You can make it out here on a rushed day tour, but you'd be mad to – Semuc and surrounds are rural Guatemala at its finest.

Quetzaltenango

10 Quetzaltenango (p130) is a kinder, gentler urban experience than the capital, and its blend of mountain scenery, highlands indigenous life, handsome architecture and urban sophistication attracts outsiders after an authentic slice of city life in Guatemala. Come here to study Spanish at the numerous language institutes, such as the well-regarded Celas Maya (p133), or make it a base for excursions to high-altitude destinations such as Laguna Chicabal (p147), a crater lake/Maya pilgrimage site, or Fuentes Georginas (p144), a hot-springs resort ensconced in a verdant valley. Local girl

R FOX PHOTOGRAPHY/GETTY IMAGES ©

El Mirador

11 For true adventurers, the trek to El Mirador (p260) is a thrilling chance to explore the origins of Maya history; it is still being uncovered by archaeologists whom you're likely to meet at the site. Among the hundreds of vegetation-shrouded temples is the tallest pyramid in the Maya world, La Danta, which can be climbed for panoramic views of the jungle canopy. It's at least a six-day hike there and back through the mud and mosquitoes, unless you hop a chopper to the site. La Danta

Garífuna Culture in Lívingston

12 Descended from Carib, Arawak and West African people, the Garífuna are probably the most strikingly different of Guatemala's 23 indigenous language groups. They have their own religion, (delicious) cuisine and (funky) dance and music styles and a strong cultural identity that has survived despite direct and indirect attempts to quash it. The Garífuna are historically coastal dwellers – their heritage is strongly linked to the Caribbean – and the best place in Guatemala to immerse yourself in Garífuna culture is in the accessible-by-boat-only enclave of Lívingston (p218).

KONRAD WOTHE/GETTY IMAGES ©

JAMIE MARSHALL – TRIBALEYE IMAGES/GETTY IMAGES ©

Flores

13 An isle of calm at the threshold of a vast jungle reserve, Flores (p234) is both a base for exploring El Petén and a stunning spot to recharge your rambling batteries. Unwinding at the numerous dining and drinking terraces that look across Lago de Petén Ixtá, or cruising in a weathered long boat to even smaller islets, you're likely to find companions for forays to Tikal or more remote places. But the picturesqueness of the town, with its captivating tableau of distant villages, is reason enough to head here. Street scene in Flores

Wildlife-Watching

14 While Guatemala's jungles, rivers, oceans and mountains don't exactly teem with life, there are several species that are worth keeping an eye out for. The Pacific coast (p156) is popular for whale-watching and turtle-spotting and there are manatees around the Río Dulce (p211) region. The Verapaces (p177) are popular birding spots – you might even see an endangered Quetzal – as are the jungles of the Petén region (p225), where you also stand a chance of spotting jaguars, howler monkeys, armadillos and agoutis, among others. Quetzal

Nebaj & the Ixil Triangle

15 A pocket of indigenous culture in a remote (though easily accessed) alpine setting, Nebaj (p126) is little visited, yet it's essential Guatemala. Homeland of the Ixil Maya people, with their own language and vivid clothing, it's also a crossroads for hikes through the spectacular Cuchumatanes mountain range, with dozens of intensely traditional villages such as Cocop (p128) and Chajul (p129), where community-run lodging and meals are amiably provided. Ixil Maya locals

Need to Know

For more information, see Survival Guide (p295)

Currency
Quetzal (Q)

Language
Spanish (official)
Maya languages (K'iche',
Kaqchiquel and Mam
most widespread)
Garífuna

Visas
Generally not required
for stays of up to three
months.

Money
ATMs widely available.
Credit cards accepted in
most higher-end hotels
and restaurants.

Cell Phones
Roaming is available but
expensive. Most travel-
ers buy a local SIM card
on arrival.

Time
North American Central
Standard Time (GMT/
UTC minus six hours)

When to Go

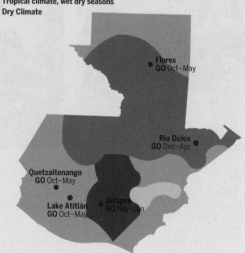

■ Warm to hot summers, mild winters
■ Tropical climate, rain year around
■ Tropical climate, wet dry seasons
■ Dry Climate

Flores
GO Oct–May

Río Dulce
GO Dec–Apr

Quetzaltenango
GO Oct–May

Lake Atitlán
GO Oct–May

Antigua
GO Nov–Jun

High Season
(Dec–May)

➡ Around key times
(Christmas, New
Year, Easter) hotel
prices can be at their
highest.

➡ Accommodation
should be booked
well in advance for
Easter in Antigua.

➡ Another peak
occurs in June and
July.

Shoulder
(Oct–Nov)

➡ Rains begin to
ease up, but October
is peak hurricane
season.

➡ Mild temperatures
and clear days make
this a good time to be
traveling and hiking
in the highlands.

Low Season
(Apr–Sep)

➡ Prices drop,
crowds thin out
at archaeological
sites, and booking
accommodation is
rarely necessary.

➡ Daily afternoon
rains can make
traveling chilly in the
highlands and muddy
in the jungle.

Websites

➡ **Lanic Guatemala** (www .lanic.utexas.edu/la/ca/ guatemala) Excellent collection of Guatemala links.

➡ **Entre Mundos** (www .entremundos.org) Guatemalan social and political issues and NGO database.

➡ **Lonely Planet** (www .lonelyplanet.com/guatemala) Information, hotel bookings, traveler forum and more.

➡ **Mostly Maya** (www.mostly maya.com) Extensive info on remote Maya sites.

➡ **Xela Pages** (www.xelapages .com) Information on the highlands and coast, plus forum.

Important Numbers

Guatemala has no regional, area or city codes; just dial the eight-digit number from anywhere in the country.

Guatemala country code	☑502
International access code	☑00
International collect calls	☑147120
Proatur (24hr tourist information & assistance)	☑1500

Exchange Rates

Australia	A$1	Q7.91
Canada	C$1	Q7.50
Euro zone	€1	Q10
Japan	¥100	Q7.84
New Zealand	NZ$1	Q6.50
UK	UK£1	Q11.70
US	US$1	Q7.64

For current exchange rates, see xe.com.

Daily Costs

Budget: Less than Q350

➡ Dorm bed: Q60–100

➡ Double room in budget hotel: Q120–180

➡ Set meal in *comedor*: Q25–40

➡ Three-hour chicken-bus ride: Q20

Midrange: Q350–Q1000

➡ Double room in decent hotel: Q300–500

➡ À la carte meal in comfortable restaurant: Q90–130

➡ Admission to archaeological site: Q50–150

➡ Three-hour shuttle bus ride: Q150

Top End: More than Q1000

➡ Double room in hotel: Q500 or more

➡ Meal in elegant restaurant: Q130 or more

➡ Tour guide at archaeological site: up to Q450

➡ 4WD car hire, per day: Q560

Opening Hours

Cafes and restaurants tend to close earlier in smaller towns and later in larger cities.

Banks 9am-5pm Monday-Friday, 9am-1pm Saturday

Cafes 7.30am-8pm

Restaurants 7am-9pm (many close Sunday)

Shops 8am-noon & 2-6pm Monday-Saturday

Bars and clubs until 1am

Arriving in Guatemala

Aeropuerto La Aurora (p58) Authorized taxis wait out the front of departures. Buy a coupon (Q80 for Zona 1) at the booth before the exit. Shuttle buses to Antigua (Q80) wait out the front, too – just listen for someone yelling 'Antigua, Antigua'.

Getting Around

Pullman Bus Running only on major highways, these are the most comfortable choice, although quality ranges from recycled Greyhounds to brand-new Mercedes. You get your own numbered seat and they run either semidirect or direct.

Shuttle Bus Booked through travel agents, hotels etc, these nonstop minibuses run between major tourist destinations offering door-to-door service.

Chicken Bus Recycled US school buses, these ones are cheap, go everywhere, stop for everybody and have no maximum capacity.

Pickup Truck In rural areas where there is no bus service this is a common way to get around. Flag one down wherever, climb in the back and hang on. Fares are equivalent to chicken buses.

Car If you're accustomed to crazy Latino traffic, driving is a great way to get off the beaten track.

Tuk-tuk These little three-wheelers are great for short hops around town at a fraction of a taxi fare.

For much more on transport, see p305

First Time Guatemala

For more information, see Survival Guide (p295)

Checklist

➡ Check the validity of your passport

➡ Check the visa situation (p304)

➡ Organize travel insurance (p299)

➡ Inform your bank/credit card company that you'll be making foreign transactions

➡ Get necessary immunizations

➡ Check your government's Guatemala travel advisories (p302)

What to Pack

➡ International adapter (for non-US appliances)

➡ Phrasebook

➡ Small medical kit

➡ Flashlight (torch)

➡ Money belt

➡ Good walking shoes

➡ Warm clothes if going to the highlands

➡ Padlock (if staying in dorms)

➡ Driver's license (if driving)

➡ Sunscreen and insect repellent

➡ Sunglasses

➡ Pocketknife

Top Tips for Your Trip

➡ Try to learn some Spanish before you arrive and some more when you get here – Guatemalans are extremely patient and will love you for just giving it a go.

➡ Pack as lightly as possible. Anything that locals use on a day-to-day basis can be bought cheaply. Anything remotely luxurious (electronics, imported goods etc) will be cheaper at home.

➡ Be aware of your surroundings (but not paranoid). If your gut tells you something is not right, it probably isn't.

What to Wear

Regardless of their economic status, Guatemalans do their best to look neat at all times, and you should do the same. This goes double when dealing with officialdom. The general look is neat-casual – pants and jeans are fine for both sexes, skirts should be (at least) below the knee. The only places you're really going to want to dress up are in fancy restaurants or Guatemala City discos.

Shorts and sleeveless tops are OK for the beach and coastal towns. In the highlands people tend to cover up more – a sensible move, considering the climate.

Dress conservatively when entering churches and visiting rural communities.

Sleeping

It's generally not necessary to book your accommodation in advance. However, if you're planning on being in Antigua or at the beach during Easter, the sooner you book the better. See p296 for more accommodation information.

➡ **Hotels** From desperate dives out by the bus terminal to fancy-pants boutique numbers, there are no shortage of options here.

➡ **Hostels** Starting to make a dent in the budget accommodation scene, especially in backpacker-favored destinations like Antigua, Quetzaltenango and around Lago de Atitlán.

➡ **Homestays** Generally organized through Spanish schools, these are a great way to connect with local culture.

Money

While everybody accepts dollars, you will almost always get a better deal by paying in quetzals. A small cash reserve in US dollars can be handy if ATMs are down. Paying with credit card can attract a service charge of up to 5% – be sure to ask. Banks change cash and (sometimes) travelers checks, but *casas de cambio* (exchange houses) are usually quicker and may offer better rates. For a note on ATM security, see p302.

For more information, see p300.

Bargaining

Haggling is pretty much a national pastime in Guatemala and everything from a banana in the market to a speeding fine is negotiable to locals. Treat it as a game and if you feel you're getting ripped off, just walk away. Places not to haggle include small stores and restaurants. Always haggle in markets and with taxi drivers.

Tipping

Tips are always welcome, but rarely expected. Tip based on service, not a sense of obligation.

➡ **Restaurants** 10% maximum (if not already included)

➡ **Taxi drivers** Not customary

➡ **Hotel porters** Q10 per bag

➡ **Homestays** Better to buy a present than give cash

➡ **Trekking and tour guides** Q50 per person per day (extremely optional)

Street vendor, Sololá (p92)

Language

The main language of Guatemala is Spanish, although in very rural destinations it may be a distant second language to the local Maya dialect. Highly educated Guatemalans, tourism industry workers and the many Guatemalans who have spent time working in the US are likely to speak at least some English. It's useful and polite to know at least some Spanish, and even a hearty *'buenos días'* can go a long way to getting an interaction off on the right foot. See Language (p310) for more information.

Etiquette

For more on Guatemalan customs, see p277.

➡ **Greetings** When meeting someone personally, men shake hands with men, women air-kiss women and men and women may air-kiss or shake – wait to see if she offers her hand, fellas.

➡ **Photos** The Maya can be very touchy about being photographed. Always ask permission before taking pictures.

➡ **Maya Women** Many Maya women avoid contact with foreign men, as virtuous Maya women don't talk with strange men. Male travelers in need of information should ask another man.

➡ **Entering a Room** In public places such as a restaurant or waiting room, make a general greeting to everyone – *buenos días* or *buenas tardes* will do.

➡ **Dress** General standards of modesty in dress have relaxed somewhat. Coastal dwellers tend to show a lot more skin than highland types, but not all locals appreciate this type of attire.

If You Like

Colonial Architecture

Antigua Guatemala's colonial showpony is a riot of gorgeous cobblestoned streetscapes, crumbling ruins and noble churches. (p64)

Quetzaltenango The country's second city has some great old buildings, especially around the Parque Central. (p131)

Guatemala City While most of the city is fabulously ugly, there are some real gems here, centered around the Centro Historico. (p44)

Cobán This cute hilltop town has a couple of real lookers, some of which have been converted into charming hotels. (p181)

Volcanoes

Tajumulco Central America's highest point is a relatively easy climb, particularly if you take two days and camp overnight. (p131)

Pacaya An easy day trip from Antigua, this smoking, lava-dribbling peak is an all-time favorite for hikers. (p70)

Santa María Get an early start and catch the sunrise and views that stretch from Mexico to Antigua and out to the Pacific. (p131)

San Pedro A moderate half-day hike rewards you with some of the best views of Lago de Atitlán and surrounds. (p108)

Ruins

Tikal This regional superstar is well on the tourist trail but totally worth the visit for its soaring, jungle-shrouded temples. (p246)

El Mirador A little hard to get to (unless you pony up for the helicopter ride), you can watch archaeologists at work at this former megacity. (p260)

Copán Just over the border in Honduras, this site hosts some of the finest carvings and stonework in the region. (p200)

Quiriguá Snuggled among the banana plantations, this little-visited site has some impressively sized carved stelae. (p198)

Off-the-Beaten-Track Places

Chajul Step back in time and experience life as it has been lived for hundreds of years in this intensely traditional town. (p129)

Laguna Magdalena Saddle up and take a two-day horse ride out to this turquoise lagoon nestled in the Cuchamatanes mountain range. (p151)

San Mateo Ixtatán Up near the Mexican border, this cute village is surrounded by spectacular scenery. (p154)

Laguna Lachuá It's well worth the effort to get out to this crystal-clear lagoon that's surrounded by thick jungle. (p186)

Wildlife

Monterrico Save a turtle, spot a whale or go bird-watching in the mangroves from this Pacific coast village. (p171)

Alta Verapaz The cloud forests around Cobán are home to a plethora of bird species, including the national bird, the resplendent quetzal. (p180)

IF YOU LIKE STUDYING SPANISH

Rock-bottom prices and high-quality instruction make Guatemala a magnet for Spanish students. Antigua (p73), Lago de Atitlán (p97) and Quetzaltenango (p133) are the main centers, but there are schools all over the country.

Río Dulce If you're very quiet and very lucky, you might just spot a manatee or a crocodile near the banks of this jungle-shrouded river. (p211)

Petén The jungles to the north teem with life – from big cats like the jaguar to creepy crawlies and hummingbirds. (p260)

Handicrafts & Textiles

Chichicastenango Central America's oldest and largest handicrafts market is a visual feast and souvenir heaven. (p118)

Antigua For a tourist-town market, prices are reasonable and shopping is reasonably hassle-free. (p83)

Panajachel A cruise down the main street will give you a glance at just about every style of handicraft and textile made in the country. (p102)

Totonicapan Tour around this artisan town and see the woodworkers, weavers and tinsmiths at work. (p145)

Doing Nothing

San Pedro La Laguna Taking it easy is pretty much a way of life in Guatemala's consummate chill zone. (p108)

Lanquín Sure there are caves to explore and rivers to tube... tomorrow... (p187)

Monterrico The ultimate in hammock swinging, no shoes, no shirt, no worries Guatemalan beach towns. (p171)

Río Dulce Kick back riverside for a few days in a secluded jungle lodge. (p211)

Top: Arco de Santa Catalina (p71), Antigua
Bottom: Santiaguito (p131), on Volcán Santa María's southwest flank

Month by Month

January

Generally cooler temperatures make this a good time to be traveling. The first couple of weeks you're bound to meet plenty of Guatemalan families taking advantage of school holidays.

✈ El Cristo Negro de Esquipulas

Pilgrims in their thousands flock to the town of Esqui-pulas in the days leading up to January 15 to pay homage to the Black Christ. Why shouldn't you?

✈ Rabinal Acha

In the highly traditional Baja Verapaz town of Rab-inal pre-Colombian dances are performed during the fiesta de San Pedro (p177) from the 19th to the 25th.

March

The European spring break sees a mini high season – nothing books out, but things start to get a little more lively.

✈ Desfile de Bufos (The Parade of Fools)

On the Friday before Good Friday, this 100+ year old tradition sees thousands of hooded Guatemala City university students take to the streets in floats and costumes to mock the government.

April

On average the warmest month. All the foreigners want to be in Antigua and all the Guatemalans want to be at the beach – accommodation in both places should be booked well in advance.

✈ Semana Santa

While there are Easter pro-cessions all over the coun-try, the most atmospheric are in Antigua (p75) and the most elaborate floats are in Guatemala City.

May

The semi-official start of the rainy season (although this is starting to vary wildly) sees afternoon showers across the country until the end of October (or thereabouts).

✈ Día del Trabajo (Labor Day)

On the first day of May there are celebrations, parades and protests throughout the country, the largest being in Guatemala City.

June

The end of the US college year sees a large influx of students arriving to study Spanish, volunteer and travel. The rainy season continues.

✈ Turtle Nesting Season

Running until November, the main nesting season on the Pacific coast sees thousands of turtles come ashore to lay eggs. The best place to spot them is around Monterrico (p171).

July

The college break continues, with many Spanish students finishing their studies and starting to travel. This is the depths of the rainy season, with the most rain and least sunshine.

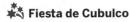 Fiesta de Cubulco

This small town (see the boxed text, p117) is one of the few places left in the country to keep the *palo volador* (literally, flying pole) tradition alive. It happens on the last day of their five-day festival, on July 25.

Rabin Ajau

In the last week of July Cobán (p181) hosts this festival which showcases pre-Colombian traditions, including Maya ceremonies, traditional handicrafts, and much music and dance.

August

Crowds start to thin out as college students return home. Often in this month there is a phenomenon called the *Canicula* (dog days in English) which sees a warm, sunny break in the rains.

Fiesta de la Virgen de la Asunción

Peaking on August 15, this fiesta is celebrated with folk dances and parades in Sololá, Guatemala City and Jocotenango.

September

Temperatures start to cool and rains begin to ease up. This is the start of the real low season, and if you're into haggling on accommodation, now's a good time to start.

Independence Day

The 15th of September marks Guatemala's anniversary of independence. There are celebrations all over the country, but being that it coincides with Quetzaltenango's week-long festival, you'll find the most activity there, with loads of concerts and other cultural activities.

October

As the rains peter out, this month marks the start of volcano trekking season, with spectacular cloud formations until mid-November.

Fiesta de San José Petén

On the night of the 31st a very curious ceremony takes place, as one of three skulls (thought to be of the village's founding fathers) is removed from the town church and paraded through this small town.

November

Día de Todos los Santos

All Saints' Day (November 1) is celebrated with particular rigor in Santiago Sacatepéquez and Sumpango (p87), where celebrations include the flying of huge, technicolor kites.

Todos Santos Cuchumatán

On All Saints' Day, this tiny highlands town hosts drunken horse races (see the boxed text, p152) through the main streets of town. Some love it, others find it a rather disturbing spectacle.

Garífuna Day

The Garífuna enclave of Lívingston celebrates its heritage with live music, dancing, parades, typical food and other lively celebrations.

December

Orchid Festival

The misty hill country around Cobán makes for perfect orchid habitat and this annual festival, held in the first week of December, showcases the variety of species that can be found in the area.

Quema del Diablo

All over the country (but particularly in the highlands) people haul their trash out into the street on December 7 and make huge bonfires while men dressed as devils run and dance amid the smoke.

Whale-Watching Season

From mid-December until the end of May, humpback and sperm whales can be seen migrating along the Pacific coast.

Plan Your Trip
Itineraries

Hit the Highlights

On a short break and you want to see it all? Well, that's not going to happen, but with a week up your sleeve you can at least see Guatemala's Big Three.

Flying into Guatemala City, get a shuttle bus directly to **Antigua**. If you don't arrive too late, grab a bite to eat at any one of the city's many fabulous restaurants and finish the night off with a nightcap in one of the cozy bars around town.

The next morning, stock up on a big breakfast – you're going to need some energy. Take a walk around town following

our walking tour (p71) – cut corners if you like, but don't miss the Iglesia de la Merced or the Las Capuchinas convent. For a real taste of Antigua, plan a dinner at La Cuevita de los Urquizú.

You'll probably want an early night because the next day you'll be climbing a volcano – check with the locals to see which one is safe/recommended to climb at the moment. Back in town, if you've still got energy, catch dinner and a show at the wonderfully atmospheric La Peña de Sol Latino.

The next day catch another shuttle to **Panajachel** on Lago de Atitlán – Pana's a

Lago de Atitlán (p91)

great place to shop and eat out, but read up on other villages around the lake to decide where you want to stay; they're all different and each has its own appeal. Regardless of where you end up staying, spend a half a day or so exploring your village and the next day exploring the rest of the lake. You can do this on a day tour from Panajachel or you can just as easily use the public boats and make your own way around, from Pana or any of the other villages.

Next day you're off to **Tikal**, so shuttle back to **Guatemala City** and from there (depending on your budget) either fly to **Flores** or catch an overnight luxury bus. Either way, you can arrive in the morning, make your way straight out to the site, spend the day exploring and be back on the bus or plane that night for the return to Guatemala City and your flight home.

10 DAYS **Highland Fling**

Guatemala's most spectacular scenery
and strongest Maya traditions await you
along this well-traveled route. It could take
a few months if you stop off to learn some
Spanish or to take advantage of the great
sightseeing and hiking possibilities along
the way.

From the capital head first to picturesque
Antigua, enjoying the country's finest colonial
architecture, the great restaurants and the
traveler and language-student scene. Several
volcanoes wait to be climbed here including the
fiery Volcán Fuego – but ask around for current
conditions before planning anything. From
Antigua move on to **Panajachel** on volcano-
ringed **Lago de Atitlán**. Hop in a boat to check
out some of the quieter, more traditional Maya
villages around the lake such as **Santiago Atitlán**, where the curious deity Maximón awaits,
or **San Pedro La Laguna**, a party town with
a certain fame countrywide. **San Marcos La
Laguna** is much more laidback and a magnet
for yoga and natural healing types. And **Santa
Cruz La Laguna** is just plain tiny and gorgeous. From the lake, hop a shuttle or chicken
bus north to **Chichicastenango** for its huge
Thursday or Sunday market and, if you're lucky,
a religious ceremony where it's hard to tell
where the Maya-ism ends and the Catholicism
starts.

From Chichicastenango you can follow the
Interamericana Hwy west along the mountain
ridges to **Quetzaltenango**, Guatemala's clean,
orderly second city, with a host of intriguing
villages, markets and natural wonders waiting
within short bus rides away. From Quetzaltenango it's possible to go further into the hills
to **Todos Santos Cuchumatán**, a fascinating
Maya mountain town with great walking
possibilities.

If you have extra time, consider pushing east
to explore **Nebaj** and the Ixil Triangle, where
you'll find great walking and a strong Maya
way of life amid stunning scenery. A rough but
passable road leads further eastward from here,
passing **Uspantan** and providing a back-door
route to Alta Verapaz, where you can check out
Cobán, **Semuc Champey** or head further north
towards **Tikal**.

Top: Iglesia de Santo Tomás (p120), Chichicastenango
Bottom: Hiker ascending a volcano south of Antigua

The Big Loop

3 WEEKS

This 1900km round trip takes you to the best of Guatemala's Maya ruins, into its dense jungles and to some of its spectacular natural marvels, covering the center, east and north of the country. Really pushing, you might do it in two weeks, but if you have four, you'll enjoy it more.

Start out northeastward from **Guatemala City** and detour south into Honduras to see the great Maya site of **Copán**. Don't just make it a flying visit, though – Copán is a great town and there's plenty to do in the surrounding countryside. Return to Guatemala and continue northeastward to another fine Maya site, **Quiriguá**, where you can marvel at the 10m-plus carved stelae and you may just have the place to yourself. From there move on to the curious Garífuna enclave of **Lívingston** on the sweaty Caribbean coast. Soak in the atmosphere in this entirely different corner of Guatemala and get in some beach time on the country's finest beaches. Take a boat up the jungle-lined **Río Dulce**, stopping for a dip in the hot springs along the way before reaching **Río Dulce town**. Head north up Hwy 13 to chill out at **Finca Ixobel** before continuing to **Flores**, a quaint small town on an island in the Lago de Petén Itzá. From Flores, head for **Tikal**, the most majestic of all Maya sites. Spend a night at Tikal itself or nearby **El Remate**. While in the Flores/Tikal area, you should have time to take in further impressive Maya sites such as **Yaxhá** and **Uaxactún**.

From Flores head southwest to the relaxed riverside town of **Sayaxché**, which is at the center of another group of intriguing Maya sites – **Ceibal**, **Aguateca** and **Dos Pilas**. The road south from Sayaxché is now paved all the way to **Chisec** and **Cobán**, jumping-off points for a whole series of pristine natural wonders such as jungle-ringed **Laguna Lachuá**, the **Grutas de Lanquín** and the turquoise lagoons and waterfalls of **Semuc Champey**. Finally, make your way back to Guatemala City for your flight home.

Top: Río Dulce (p211)
Bottom: Templo I, Gran Plaza (p248), Tikal

Guatemala: Off the Beaten Track

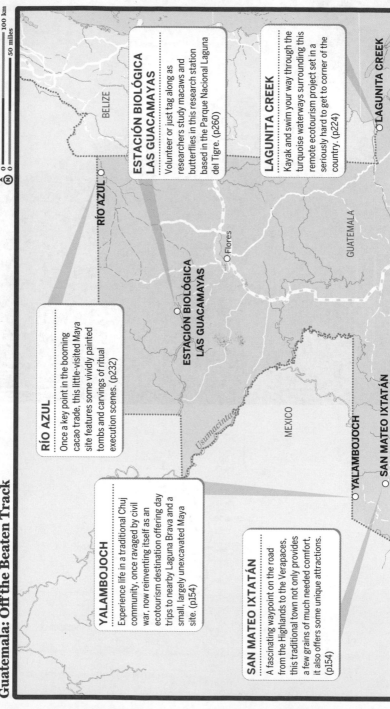

RÍO AZUL

Once a key point in the booming cacao trade, this little-visited Maya site features some vividly painted tombs and carvings of ritual execution scenes. (p232)

ESTACIÓN BIOLÓGICA LAS GUACAMAYAS

Volunteer or just tag along as researchers study macaws and butterflies in this research station based in the Parque Nacional Laguna del Tigre. (p260)

LAGUNITA CREEK

Kayak and swim your way through the turquoise waterways surrounding this remote ecotourism project set in a seriously hard to get to corner of the country. (p224)

YALAMBOJOCH

Experience life in a traditional Chuj community, once ravaged by civil war, now reinventing itself as an ecotourism destination offering day trips to nearby Laguna Brava and a small, largely unexcavated Maya site. (p154)

SAN MATEO IXTATÁN

A fascinating waypoint on the road from the Highlands to the Verapaces, this traditional town not only provides a few grains of much needed comfort, it also offers some unique attractions. (p154)

LAGUNA SALVADOR

Located in the Biotopo Chocón Machacas manatee reserve, this tiny Q'eqchi' village offers sweet accommodation, tours of the wildlife reserve and a chance to experience traditional Q'eqchi' life. (p224)

CHAPÍN ABAJO

Set in a charming tiny village on the little-visited southern shore of Lago de Izabal, the community tourism project here offers boat tours to the nearby Bocas del Polochic wildlife reserve. (p216)

SANTA LUCÍA COTZUMALGUAPA

On the sweltering Pacific coast, but not on the beach, there would be no reason to come here if not for the multitude of fascinating sculptures left behind by the mysterious Pipil culture. (p165)

LAGUNA MAGDALENA

High up in the Cuchumatanes mountains near the Mexican border, this tourquoise lagoon is best reached on horseback. Surrounded by gnarled trees and surreally shaped boulders, this place really is a photographer's delight. (p151)

TILAPITA

Arguably the Pacific coast's most laid-back beach town, this is a one-hotel, all-sand-roads affair. Don't come seeking luxury, but any time outside of Christmas and Easter this place is the epitome of *tranquilo*. (p157)

Plan Your Trip

Guatemala's Ancient Ruins

Stretching at its peak from northern El Salvador to the Gulf of Mexico, the Maya empire during its Classic period was arguably pre-Hispanic America's most brilliant civilization. The great ceremonial and cultural centers in Guatemala included Quiriguá, Kaminaljuyú, Tikal, Uaxactún, Río Azul, El Perú, Yaxhá, Dos Pilas and Piedras Negras. Copán in Honduras also gained and lost importance as the empire and its individual kingdoms ebbed and waned.

Need to Know

Where

The majority of Maya sites are in El Petén region, in the country's north. The other major grouping is in the southwest, roughly centered around Lake Atitlán.

When

The ideal months to visit archaeological sites are outside of the rainy season. In El Petén you want to avoid the heat, while in the highlands seriously cold nighttime temperatures can make travel uncomfortable. Roughly speaking, the better times to visit El Petén are from November to April, while the highlands are best from February to May.

Opening Hours

Most sites are open from 8am to 4pm daily, but check times ahead of your visit. For the more popular sites, the best time to go is soon after opening time, thereby beating the tour bus crowds and the midday sun.

Visiting the Ruins

Maya achievement during this period rivaled anything that was going on in Europe at the time, boasting an advanced writing system, awe-inspiring engineering feats, advanced mathematics and astrology, and stone-working skills that remain impressive to this day.

Many legacies of the Maya have disappeared over time. Archaeological pieces have been carried off either by tomb raiders or foreign governments and much cultural heritage has been lost over the centuries due to government and church campaigns to assimilate the Maya into mainstream Hispanic culture. Outside of Guatemala City's fantastic selection of museums, the best way to get a feel for the amazing achievements of this unique culture is to visit archaeological sites.

Visiting a Maya ruin can be a powerful experience, a true step back in time. While some sites are little more than a pile of rubble or some grassy mounds, others (such as Tikal and Copán) have been extensively restored, and the temples, plazas and ballcourts give an excellent insight into what life must have been like in these places.

Exploring Maya Ruins

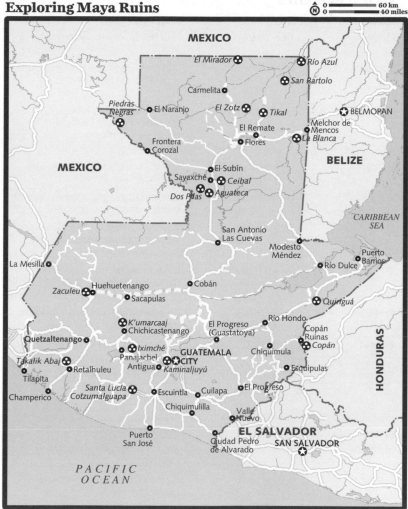

The most famous sites are generally thronged with visitors. Others are hidden away in thick jungle, reachable only by multiday treks or helicopter – for those with a sense of adventure, these can be the most exciting and rewarding to visit.

Site Practicalities

➡ Admission to sites costs between nothing (rare) and Q150 (also rare and generally reserved for top sites such as Tikal and Copán). Most sites charge around Q80.

➡ Protect yourself against the sun and, at jungle sites, mosquitoes.

➡ Sites like Tikal and Copán have restaurants, bookstores, toilets and authorized guides.

➡ Little-visited sites may have no food or water available.

➡ Guided tours to many sites are usually available from nearby towns, but many (but not all) are accessible independently.

ANCIENT MAYA SITES

REGION	SITE	DESCRIPTION
El Petén	Tikal (p246)	Most famous of all Guatemalan Maya sites
El Petén	El Mirador (p260)	Late Preclassic site with largest cluster of buildings in Maya world
El Petén	San Bartolo (p232)	Over 100 structures in 1 sq km 'discovered' in 2003 after looters began sacking the site
El Petén	Piedras Negras (p232)	One of Guatemala's most extensive, least-accessible sites
El Petén	La Blanca (p232)	Late Classic Period trading center with impressively preserved walls
El Petén	El Zotz (p232)	A sprawling, largely unexcavated site occupying its own *biotopo* abutting Parque Nacional Tikal
El Petén	Río Azul (p232)	Key trading post for cacao from the Caribbean in the early Classic Period
El Petén	Ceibal (p229)	Ceremonial site featuring impressive stelae
El Petén	Aguateca (p231)	Easily accessible lakeside walled city
El Petén	Dos Pilas (p231)	Breakaway city from the Tikal group
Guatemala City	Kaminaljuyú (p45)	Important Preclassic site a few kilometers from downtown area
Highlands	Iximché (p93)	Naturally fortified ex-Kaqchiquel capital
Highlands	K'umarcaaj (p124)	Former K'iche' capital surrounded by ravines
Highlands	Zaculeu (p148)	Postclassic Mam religious center
Pacific Slope	Takalik Abaj (p163)	Important late Preclassic trading center
Pacific Slope	Santa Lucía Cotzumalguapa (p165)	Various small sites centered on a small town
Eastern Guatemala	Quiriguá (p198)	Important ceremonial center with strong links to nearby Copán
Honduras	Copán (p199)	Religious and political capital rivaling Tikal for importance

HIGHLIGHTS	LOCATION	TRANSPORTATION
Towering temples, including the 65m-high Templo IV	60km northeast of Flores	public transport or tour
La Danta, the largest Maya pyramid yet discovered	7km south of Mexican border	82km by bus plus two days walking (or direct helicopter)
Features one of the best-preserved Maya murals with a depiction of the creation myth from the Popol Vuh	Approximately 40km northeast of Uaxactún	Tours from Uaxactún or Flores
Impressive carvings and a sizable acropolis complex	40km downstream from Yaxhilán	Tours from Flores or Bethel
On the Río Mopan near the Belize border	Tours from Flores or Melchor de Mencos.	
Climb the Pirámide del Diablo for views all the way to Tikal	25km west of Uaxactún	Tours from Uaxactún or Flores.
Tombs featuring vibrant painted glyphs	Near the corner where the Belize, Guatemala and Mexico borders meet	Tours from Uaxactún
Intricate carvings, atmospheric riverboat ride to get there	17km from Sayaxché	Boat tour or bus from Sayaxché
Maya world's only bridge, intricate carvings	Southern tip of Laguna Petexbatún	Boat tour from Sayaxché
Heiroglyphic stairway, impressive carvings	16km from Sayaxché	Boat tour from Sayaxché plus 4hr jungle trek
Ongoing excavations open to public	Guatemala City suburbs	Bus or taxi
Important ceremonial site for modern Maya	1km from Tecpán	Walk or bus
Sacred tunnel still used for Maya ceremonies	3km west of Quiché	Minibus
Spectacular setting, park-like grounds	4km west of Huehuetenango	Bus or taxi
Sculptures, ceremonial baths and broad stone causeway	19km north of Retalhueu	Bus, taxi and pickup
Stone sculptures, links with Mexican Olmec culture	29 km west of Escuintla	Frequent buses
10m-plus stelae	220km west of Guatemala City	Frequent buses
Excellent sculpture museum, hieroglyphic staircase with longest-known Maya hieroglyphic carving	216km west of Guatemala City	Bus, tours from Antigua

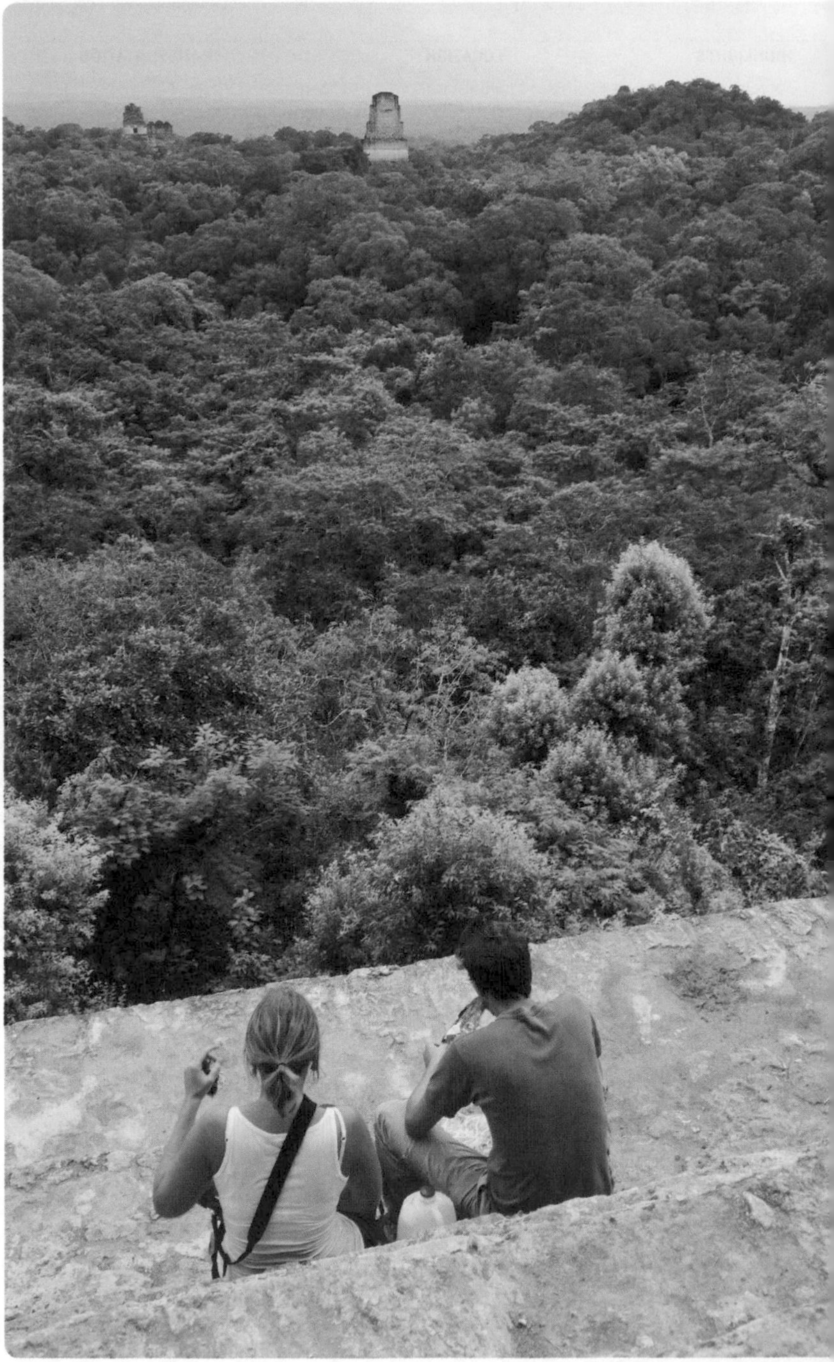

Parque Nacional Tikal (p246)

➡ Explanatory signs may be in Spanish only, Spanish and English, Spanish, English and the local Maya dialect or completely nonexistent.

Resources

➡ Mesoweb (www.mesoweb.com) is a great, diverse resource on ancient Mesoamerican cultures, especially the Maya.

➡ *Archaeology of Ancient Mexico and Central America: An Encyclopedia*, a reference book by Susan Toby Evans and David L Webster, incorporates recent discoveries and scholarship.

➡ *Maya Art and Architecture*, by Mary Ellen Miller, is gorgeously illustrated and paints the full picture, from gigantic temples to intricately painted ceramics.

➡ Mostly Maya (www.mostlymaya.com) is a hobby site devoted to exploring the Maya world, with practical info on how to get to some remote sites.

Top Museums

Some sites have their own museums – the ones at Tikal and Copán are well worth the extra admission fee – but there are also important city and regional museums which hold many of the most valuable and impressive pre-Hispanic artifacts.

➡ Museo Nacional de Arqueología y Etnología, Guatemala City (p49) By far the most impressive collection of ancient Maya artifacts, with pieces from all the important ceremonial areas, including an impressive throne from the Piedras Negras site.

➡ Museo Popol Vuh, Guatemala City (p48) A wealth of smaller pieces, including figurines, wooden masks, textiles and a faithful copy of the Dresden Codex.

➡ Museo El Baúl, Santa Lucía Cotzumalguapa (p165) An open-air museum situated on the grounds of the sugar cane farm where dozens of human-sized stone sculptures have been found.

➡ Museo Santa Bárbara, Flores (p234) Over 9000 archaeological pieces originating from El Petén sites, all crammed into one room.

Don't Miss Sites

➡ Tikal – Guatemala's most famous Maya ruins.

➡ Copán – Across the border in Honduras, one of the most outstanding achievements of the Maya.

➡ El Mirador – Late-Preclassic metropolis buried in the deepest jungle.

➡ Ceibal – Memorable river journey to low, ruined temples.

➡ Santa Lucía Cotzumalguapa – Great stone heads carved with grotesque faces and fine relief scenes.

Regions at a Glance

The six regions that make up this book could just as easily be six separate countries. Travel a hundred kilometers or so and everything changes – the food, the clothes, the way people talk and, of course, the scenery. The capital is all big-city buzz, while it's hard to imagine things getting any more laid-back than they do in the little beach towns down on the coast. Antigua is the epitome of stately colonial charm whereas the temple-laden jungles and small towns of El Petén have a very rough-and-ready frontier atmosphere. The highlands of the center and west are probably the most similar, but where the volcano-studded west gets chilly and sometimes bleak, the cloud forest–covered center is much milder and more lush.

Guatemala City

Art & Archaeology
Nightlife
Buzz

Museums & Galleries

You might be tempted to dodge the capital, but if you're at all interested in art and archaeology, you need to spend some time here. All the best pieces end up here, often in world-class, superbly curated spaces.

The Big Night Out

The capital's massive population of students, rock-steady live music scene and burgeoning nightlife district just off the Central Park make it the best place to go out in the country, hands down.

That Feeling...

For all its craziness and stress, you're not going to get that big-city kick anywhere else in the country. Just walking down the street can be an adventure – keep your wits about you and you'll soon learn to love (or at least tolerate) it.

p42

Antigua

Colonial Architecture
Spanish
Food

Colonial Charms
Though much of the Spanish legacy in the former capital lies in ruins, even the remaining fragments add allure to the streetscapes, offering picture postcard views at every corner and a chance to scramble through history.

Back to School
Despite some tough competition, Antigua remains the capital of Spanish-language study in Latin America. Dozens of small, affably run institutes offer personalized instruction in colonial/tropical surrounds at bargain prices.

Gourmet Traveling
Owing to its globally varied visitor profile, Antigua rivals much loftier destinations as a cuisine capital. Here you can enjoy everything from *l'escargot Bourguignon* to Argentine *empanadas* at restaurants run by transplants from their culinary places of origin.

p62

The Highlands

Indigenous Dress
Volcanoes
Festivals

Fancy Dress
From the pom-pommed headdresses of women in Chajul to the flamboyant red-and-white striped trousers of men in Todos Santos Cuchumatán, traditional Maya clothing is a dazzling display of identity throughout the highlands.

Peaking Out
With a chain of 33 volcanoes, four of them active, climbers, geology buffs and landscape painters find plenty to inspire them here. An early morning hike up the Santa María volcano leads to a mesmerizing view of the periodically erupting Santiaguito.

Party Time
Every highlands town likes to let its hair down at an annual fest and outsiders are always welcome. Good bets include Quetzaltenango's late September toast to its Virgen del Rosario and Todos Santos Cuchumatán's patron saint's day with madcap horse racing and drunken marimba dancing.

p89

The Pacific Slope

Beaches
Food
Wildlife

Sun, Sand & Surf
If you've been up in the hills or traveling hard, the whole Pacific coast is dotted with little beach towns where you can crank it back a notch or two and get in some quality do-nothing time.

This Fish is Delish!
With so much coastline it's no surprise that the seafood here is excellent – fried fish and shrimp are staples, but don't miss out on the *caldo de mariscos* (seafood stew) if you see it on a menu.

Animal Frenzy
With whales and turtles in the waters off the beaches and the mangroves buzzing with birdlife, this region is a wildlife-watcher's paradise. If you don't get your fill there, stop by the drive-through Autosafari Chapin wildlife reserve.

p156

Central & Eastern Guatemala

Nature
Culture
Caves

Natural Paradise

From the lush cloudforests of the Verapaz to the verdant landscapes of Lago de Izabal and the Río Dulce, the rivers, lakes, canyons, waterfalls and jungles of this region showcase Guatemala at its natural best.

A Cultural Mosaic

Ethnically diverse and at times intensely traditional, the center and east of the country are home to Achi', Poqomchi', Ch'ortí and Q'eqchi' Maya, many of whom maintain traditional customs and practice centuries-old rituals. Over on the Caribbean, the culturally distinct Garífuna represent one more ingredient in Guatemala's ethnic stew.

Going Underground

The limestone crags, particularly north of Cobán, play host to a network of caves and caverns, making for great photo opportunities and fascinating forays for casual strollers and serious spelunkers alike.

p176

El Petén

Classic Maya Sites
Wildlife
Trekking

Site Seeing

With literally hundreds of sites sprinkled across the jungle lowlands, you may delve as deeply as you choose into the mysteries of Classic Maya civilization, from the oft-scaled temples of Tikal to the seldom-seen astronomical observatory of Uaxactún.

Animal Planet

Rare and endangered creatures still roam the protected expanses of the Maya Biosphere Reserve, and guides from *petenera* communities can help you track them down, whether it's nocturnal crocodile cruising at the Estación Biológica Las Guacamayas or awakening to howler monkeys at Biotopo Cerro Cahuí.

Going Bush

Seasoned guides at places like Ni'tun Ecolodge on Lago de Petén Itzá or Aldana's Lodge in Uaxactún accompany you on multiday odysseys through the mud and mosquitoes to such remote Maya sites as El Zotz and El Mirador.

p225

On the Road

Guatemala City

POP 4.1 MILLION / ELEV 1500M

Best Places to Eat

➡ Kakao (p55)
➡ Café-Restaurante Hamburgo (p54)
➡ La Maison de France (p55)
➡ Café de Imeri (p54)

Best Places to Stay

➡ Otelito (p53)
➡ Quetzalroo (p53)
➡ Hotel Colonial (p52)
➡ Hotel Ajau (p49)
➡ Hostal Los Lagos (p53)

Why Go?

Depending on who you talk to, Guatemala City (or Guate as it's known) is either big, dirty, dangerous and utterly forgettable or big, dirty, dangerous and fascinating. Either way, there's no doubt that there's an energy here unlike that found in the rest of Guatemala. It's a place where dilapidated buses belch fumes next to Beamers and Hummers, and skyscrapers drop shadows on shantytowns.

Guate is busy reinventing itself as a people-friendly city. Downtown Zona 1, for years a no-go zone of abandoned buildings and crime hot spots, is leading the way with the pedestrianized 6a Calle attracting bars, cafes and restaurants.

Many travelers skip the city altogether, preferring to make Antigua their base. Still, you may want, or need, to get acquainted with the capital because this is the hub of the country, home to the best museums and galleries, transport hubs and other traveler's services.

When to Go

Guatemala City's weather patterns follow the rest of the country – particularly noteworthy are the rainy afternoons during the wet season (May to October). As with most urban environments, Guate feels muggier during humid months and colder during cooler times. Surprisingly, the lead-up to Easter is a good time to be in town. You can use the city as a base to visit overcrowded Antigua on day trips, and the capital (particularly Zona 1) also hosts its own religious processions, which may not be as atmospheric as Antigua's but tend to be more grandiose.

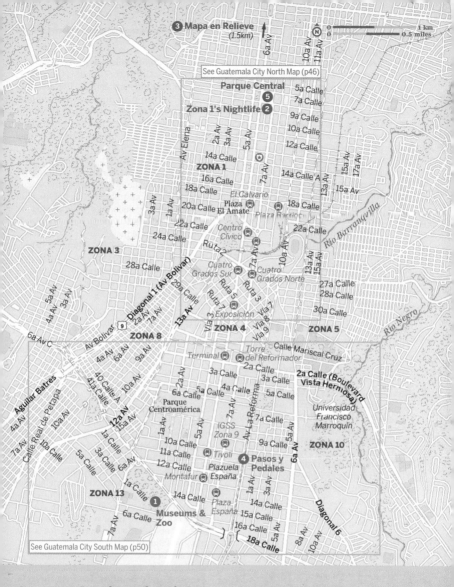

Guatemala City Highlights

① Visit the country's best **museums** and **zoo** (p48)

② Check out Zona 1's bustling **nightlife** (p55)

③ Gaze at Guatemala from above at the **Mapa en Relieve** (p45)

④ Take a stroll along Zona 10's **Pasos y Pedales** (p48)

⑤ Catch a free concert or feed the pigeons in **Parque Central** (p44)

History

Kaminaljuyú (kah-mih-nahl-huh-yuh), one of the first important cities in the Maya region, flourished two millennia ago in what's now the western part of Guatemala City. By the time Spanish conquistadors arrived in the 16th century, only overgrown mounds were left. The site remained insignificant until the earthquake of July 29, 1773 razed much of the then Spanish colonial capital, Antigua. The authorities decided to move their headquarters to La Ermita valley, hoping to escape further destruction, and on September 27, 1775, King Carlos III of Spain signed a royal charter for the founding of La Nueva Guatemala de la Asunción. Guatemala City was officially born.

The colonial powers didn't quite move the capital far enough, for earthquakes in 1917, 1918 and 1976 rocked the capital, reducing buildings to rubble. The 1976 quake killed nearly 23,000, injured another 75,000 and left an estimated one million homeless.

◉ Sights & Activities

The major sights are in Zona 1 (the historic center) and Zonas 10 and 13, where the museums are grouped. If you're in town on a Sunday, consider taking the TransMetro's **SubiBaja** (free; ⊗ 9am-2pm) hop-on, hop-off self-guided tour. Modern, air-conditioned TransMetro buses run a circuit passing every 20 minutes, with 10 stops including Parque Central, Centro Cívico, the zoo (and museums), Zona Viva, Pasos y Pedales, Cuatro Grados Norte and Mapa en Relieve. Volunteer guides give an on-board commentary and each bus is staffed by a member of the Transit Police. It's an excellent way to see many of these sights without worrying about public transport or taxis.

BONJOUR, AMIGO

It's been a long time since anybody called Guatemala City the Paris of anywhere, which makes it all the more remarkable to find a replica of the Eiffel Tower straddling a busy downtown intersection. The **Torre del Reformador** (Map p50; cnr 7a Av & 2a Calle, Zona 9), originally named the 'Torre Conmemorativa del 19 del Julio,' was completed in 1935 to celebrate the 100th anniversary of the birth of former president and reformer Justo Rufino Barrios.

◉ Zona 1

The main sights here are grouped around the **Parque Central** (Plaza de la Constitución; Map p46; Parque Central, Zona 1). The standard colonial urban-planning scheme required every town in the New World to have a large plaza for military exercises and ceremonies. On the north side of the plaza was usually the *palacio de gobierno* (colonial government headquarters). On another side, preferably the east, would be a church (or cathedral). On the other sides of the square there could be additional civic buildings or the imposing mansions of wealthy citizens. Guatemala City's Parque Central is a classic example of the plan.

The Parque Central and adjoining Parque Centenario are never empty during daylight hours, with shoeshine boys, ice-cream vendors and sometimes open-air political meetings and concerts adding to the general bustle.

**Palacio Nacional
de la Cultura**   HISTORIC BUILDING
(Map p46; ☎ 2253-0748; cnr 6a Av & 6a Calle, Zona 1; admission Q30; ⊗ 9-11:45am & 2-4:45pm Mon-Sat) On the north side of the Parque Central is this imposing presidential palace, built between 1936 and 1943 during the dictatorial rule of General Jorge Ubico at enormous cost to the lives of the prisoners who were forced to labor here. It's the third palace to stand on the site.

Despite its tragic background, architecturally the palace is one of the country's most interesting constructions, a mélange of multiple earlier styles from Spanish Renaissance to neoclassical. Today, most government offices have been removed from here and it's open as a museum and for a few ceremonial events.

Visits are by guided tour (available in English). You pass through a labyrinth of gleaming brass, polished wood, carved stone and frescoed arches. Features include an optimistic mural of Guatemalan history by Alberto Gálvez Suárez above the main stairway, and a two-ton gold, bronze and Bohemian-crystal chandelier in the reception hall. The banqueting hall sports stained-glass panels depicting – with delicious irony – the virtues of good government. From here your guide will probably take you out onto the presidential balcony, where you can imagine yourself a banana-republic dictator reviewing your troops. In the western courtyard, the Patio de la Paz, a monument depicting two hands, stands where Guatemala's Peace Accords were signed in 1996; each day at 11am the rose held by the hands is changed by a military guard and the one from the previous day is tossed to a woman among the spectators.

Centro Cultural Metropolitano
CULTURAL CENTER

(Map p46; 7a Av 11-67, Zona 1; ⊙ 9am-5pm Mon-Fri) To the rear of the ground floor of the *palacio de correos* (post office) you'll find a surprisingly avant-garde cultural center, hosting art exhibitions, book launches, handicraft workshops and film nights.

Casa MIMA
CULTURAL CENTER

(Map p46; 8a Av 14-12, Zona 1; ⊙ 10am-5pm Mon-Sat) A wonderfully presented museum and cultural center set in a house dating from the late 1800s. The owners of the house were collectors with eclectic tastes ranging from French neo-rococo, Chinese, and art deco to indigenous artifacts. The place is set up like a functioning house, filled with curios and furniture spanning the centuries.

Railway Museum
MUSEUM

(Museo de Ferrocarril; Map p46; 9a Av 18-03, Zona 1; ⊙ 9am-5pm Tue-Fri, 10am-5pm Sat & Sun) This is one of the city's more intriguing museums. Documented here are the glory days of the troubled Guatemalan rail system, along with some quirky artifacts, such as hand-drawn diagrams of derailments and a kitchen set up with items used in dining cars. You can go climbing around the passenger carriages, but not the locomotives.

Catedral Metropolitana
CATHEDRAL

(Map p46; 7a Av, Zona 1; ⊙ 6am-noon & 2-7pm) Facing Parque Central, this was constructed between 1782 and 1815 (the towers were finished in 1867). It has survived earthquake and fire well, though the earthquakes of 1917 and 1976 did substantial damage. Its heavy proportions and sparse ornamentation don't make for a particularly beautiful building, but it has a certain stateliness, and the altars are worth a look.

Mercado Central
MARKET

(Map p46; cnr 8a Av & 8a Calle, Zona 1; ⊙ 8am-6pm) Located behind the cathedral, this was one of the city's major markets for food and other daily necessities until the building was destroyed by the 1976 earthquake. Reconstructed in the late 1970s, it now special-

izes in tourist-oriented handicrafts. The food market thrives on the lowest floor.

⊙ Zona 2

Mapa en Relieve
MONUMENT

(Relief Map; www.mapaenrelieve.org; Av Simeón Cañas Final; admission Q30; ⊙ 9am-5pm) North of Zona 1, Zona 2 is mostly a middle-class residential district, but it's worth venturing along to Parque Minerva to see this huge open-air map of Guatemala showing the country at a scale of 1:10,000. The vertical scale is exaggerated to 1:2000 to make the volcanoes and mountains appear dramatically higher and steeper than they really are.

Constructed in 1905 under the direction of Francisco Vela, it was fully restored and repainted in 1999. Viewing towers afford a panoramic view. This is an odd but fun place, and it's curious to observe that Belize is still represented as part of Guatemala. It's an easy walk (or short cab ride) from the Parque Central.

⊙ Zona 4 & Around

Pride of Zona 4 (actually straddling its borders with Zonas 1 and 5) is the **Centro Cívico** (Map p46; Centro Cívico, Zona 4), a set of large government and institutional buildings constructed during the 1950s and '60s. One is the headquarters of **Inguat** (Guatemalan Tourist Institute), housing the city's main tourist office (p58). Nearby are the **Palacio de Justicia** (High Court; Map p46; cnr 7a Av & 21a Calle, Zona 1), the **Banco de Guatemala** (Map p46; 7a Av, Zona 1; ⊙ 9am-5pm Mon-Fri) and the **Municipalidad de Guatemala** (City Hall; Map p46; 22a Calle, Zona 1) The bank building bears relief sculptures by Dagoberto Vásquez depicting his country's history; the city hall contains a huge mosaic by Carlos Mérida, completed in 1959.

Behind Inguat is the national stadium, **Estadio Nacional Mateo Flores** (Map p46; 10a Av, Zona 5).

⊙ Zona 7

Parque Arqueológico Kaminaljuyú
ARCHAEOLOGICAL SITE

(cnr 11a Calle & 24a Av, Zona 7; admission Q30; ⊙ 8am-4:30pm) With remnants of one of the first important cities in the Maya region, this park is just west of 23a Av and

Guatemala City North

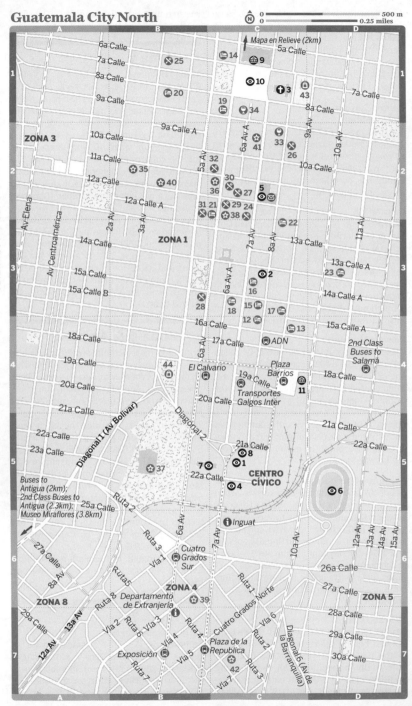

Guatemala City North

is some 4km west of the city center. At its peak, from about 400 BC to AD 100, ancient Kaminaljuyú had thousands of inhabitants and scores of temples, and probably dominated much of highland Guatemala.

Large-scale carvings found here were the forerunners of Classic Maya carving, and Kaminaljuyú had a literate elite before anywhere else in the Maya world. The city fell into ruin before being reoccupied around AD 400 by invaders from Teotihuacán in central Mexico, who rebuilt it in Teotihuacán's talud-tablero style, with buildings stepped in alternating vertical (*tablero*) and sloping (*talud*) sections. Unfortunately, most of Kaminaljuyú has been covered by urban sprawl: the archaeological park is but a small portion of the ancient city and even here the remnants consist chiefly of grassy mounds. To the left from the entrance is La Acrópolis, where you can inspect excavations of a ball court and talud-tablero buildings from AD 450 to 550.

A couple of hundred meters south of the entrance and across the road are two burial statues from the late Preclassic period.

They're badly deteriorated, but are the only examples of carving left at the site – the best examples have been moved to the new Museo Nacional de Arqueología y Etnología (p49).

You can get here by bus No 35 from 4a Av, Zona 1, but check that the bus is going to the ruinas de Kaminaljuyú – not all do (and city buses are not really recommended). A taxi from Zona 1 costs around Q50.

◎ Zona 10

Two of the country's best museums are housed in large, modern buildings at the Universidad Francisco Marroquín, 1km east of Av La Reforma.

Museo Ixchel   MUSEUM
(Map p50; ☑ 2361-8081; www.museoixchel.org; 6a Calle Final, Zona 10; admission Q35; ⊙9am-5pm Mon-Fri, 9am-1pm Sat) This museum is named for the Maya goddess of the moon, women, reproduction and, of course, textiles. Photographs and exhibits of indigenous costumes and other crafts show the incredible richness of traditional arts in Guatemala's highland towns.

GUATEMALA CITY FOR CHILDREN

Guatemala City has enough children's attractions to make it worth considering as an outing from Antigua if you have kids to please. The Museo de los Niños and La Aurora Zoo, conveniently over the road from each other in Zona 13, top the list. Kids might also relish the dead animals in various states of preservation at the nearby Museo Nacional de Historia Natural Jorge Ibarra. It shouldn't be too hard to find some food that the littl'uns are willing to eat at the food courts in the Centro Comercial Los Próceres (p57) or Oakland Mall (p57), where everyone can also enjoy a little air-con and shopping (window or otherwise). At Oakland Mall you'll also find the restaurant **Nais** (Map p50; Oakland Mall, Diagonal 6 13-01, Zona 10; mains Q40-120; 🕓 6am-10pm), which is a winner with the kids for the huge aquarium (a scuba diver swims through periodically, cleaning the tank and feeding the fish) filled with tropical fish.

On Sundays, kids and adults will enjoy the relaxed atmosphere and abundant free entertainment on offer at Pasos y Pedales.

The Mapa en Relieve (p45), too, amuses most ages, and there are a few swings and climbing frames in the adjacent park.

If you enjoy Guatemalan textiles at all, you must visit this museum. It has access for travelers with disabilities, a section for children, a cafe, a shop and a library, and guided tours are available in English (with prior reservation) or Spanish.

Museo Popol Vuh   MUSEUM
(Map p50; ☎ 2338-7896; www.popolvuh.ufm.edu; 6a Calle Final, Zona 10; adult/child Q35/10; 🕓 9am-5pm Mon-Fri, 9am-1pm Sat) Behind Museo Ixchel, here you'll find well-displayed pre-Hispanic figurines, incense burners and burial urns, plus carved wooden masks and traditional textiles, filling several rooms. Other rooms hold colonial paintings and gilded wood and silver artifacts. A faithful copy of the *Dresden Codex*, one of the precious 'painted books' of the Maya, is among the most interesting pieces.

Also here is a colorful display of animals in Maya art.

Pasos y Pedales   WALKING
(Map p50; www.pasosypedales.com; 🕓 10am-2pm Sun) If you're here on a Sunday, check out a wonderful municipal initiative that sees the Av de las Americas (Zona 10) and its continuation, Av la Reforma in Zona 13, blocked off to traffic for 3km and taken over by jugglers, clowns, in-line skaters, dogwalkers, food vendors, t'ai chi classes, skate parks and playgrounds for kids.

It's a great place to go for a walk (or you can hire bikes or in-line skates on the street) and check out a very relaxed, sociable side of the city that is rarely otherwise seen.

🔘 Zona 11

Museo Miraflores   MUSEUM
(☎ 2470-3415; www.museomiraflores.org; 7a Calle 21-55, Zona 11; admission Q40; 🕓 9am-7pm Tue-Sun) This is an excellent modern museum inauspiciously jammed between two shopping malls a few kilometers out of town. Downstairs focuses on objects found at Kaminaljuyú, with fascinating trade route maps showing the site's importance.

Upstairs there are displays on textiles and indigenous clothing, separated by region, from around the country. Signs are in Spanish and (for the most part) English. Out back is a pleasant grassy area with paths and seating – a good place to take a breather. To get there, catch any bus from the center going to Centro Comercial Tikal Futura and get off there. The museum is 250m down the road between it and the Miraflores shopping center.

🔘 Zona 13

The attractions here in the city's southern reaches are all ranged along 5a Calle in the Finca Aurora area, northwest of the airport. While here you can also drop into the **Mercado de Artesanías** (Crafts Market; Map p50; ☎ 2475-5915; cnr 5a Calle & 11a Av, Zona 13; 🕓 9:30am-6pm).

La Aurora Zoo   ZOO
(Map p50; ☎ 2472-0507; www.aurorazoo.org.gt; 5a Calle; adult/child Q25/10; 🕓 9am-5pm Tue-Sun) This is not badly kept as zoos in this part of the world go, and the lovely, parklike grounds alone are worth the admission fee.

Museo de los Niños
MUSEUM
(Children's Museum; Map p50; ☑2475-5076; www.museodelosninos.com.gt; 5a Calle 10-00; admission Q35; ☺8am-noon & 1-4:30pm Tue-Fri, 9:30am-1:30pm & 2:30-6pm Sat & Sun) Almost opposite the zoo entrance is this hands-on affair that is a sure success if you have kids to keep happy. The fun ranges from a giant jigsaw-map of Guatemala to an earthquake simulator and, most popular of all, a room of original and entertaining ball games.

Museo Nacional de Arqueología y Etnología
MUSEUM
(Map p50; ☑2475-4399; www.munae.gob.gt; Sala 5, Finca La Aurora; admission Q60; ☺9am-4pm Tue-Fri, 9am-noon & 1:30-4pm Sat & Sun) This museum has the country's biggest collection of ancient Maya artifacts, but explanatory information is very sparse. There's a great wealth of monumental stone sculpture, including Classic-period stelae from Tikal, Uaxactún and Piedras Negras; a superb throne from Piedras Negras; and animal representations from Preclassic Kaminaljuyú.

Also here are rare wooden lintels from temples at Tikal and El Zotz, and a room with beautiful jade necklaces and masks. Don't miss the large-scale model of Tikal. The ethnology section has displays on the languages, costumes, dances, masks and homes of Guatemala's indigenous peoples.

Museo Nacional de Arte Moderno
GALLERY
(Map p50; ☑2472-0467; Sala 6, Finca La Aurora; admission Q30; ☺9am-4pm Tue-Fri, 9am-12:30pm & 2-4pm Sat & Sun) Here you'll find a collection of 20th-century Guatemalan art including works by well-known Guatemalan artists such as Carlos Mérida, Carlos Valente and Humberto Gavarito.

Museo Nacional de Historia Natural Jorge Ibarra
MUSEUM
(Map p50; ☑2472-0468; 6a Calle 7-30; admission Q50; ☺9am-4pm Tue-Sun) Behind the archaeology museum is this natural history museum, whose claim to fame is its large collection of dissected animals.

X-Park
ADVENTURE SPORTS
(☑2380-2080; www.xpark.net; Av Hincapié, Km 11.5; admission Q15; ☺10am-7pm Mon-Fri, 10am-9pm Sat, 10am-7pm Sun) About 10 minutes' drive south of the airport is this very well-constructed 'adventure sports' park. Attractions (they prefer to call them 'challenges') cost between Q10 each and include bouldering and climb-

ing walls, reverse bungees, mechanical bulls, a rope course, zip lines and a playground for kids. A fairly limited range of fast food is available at the cafeteria.

A taxi here from Zona 10 should cost you around Q35.

Tours

Clark Tours
TOUR
(Map p50; ☑2412-4700; www.clarktours.com.gt; 7a Av 14-76, Zona 9; morning tour per person Q237, private day tour per person from Q754) Guatemala's longest-established tour operator offers morning and full-day city tours. The morning tour (available Saturday to Wednesday) visits the Palacio Nacional de la Cultura, cathedral and Centro Cívico. The day tour adds the Ixchel and Popul Vuh museums. Clark Tours also has branches in **Zona 10** (Map p50; ☑2363-3920; cnr 14a Calle & Av La Reforma) in the Westin Camino Real, and in **Zona 9** (Map p50; ☑2362-9716; 7a Av 15-45) in the Hotel Barceló Guatemala.

Maya Expeditions
ADVENTURE TOUR
(Map p50; ☑2366-9950; www.mayaexpeditions.com; 13 Av 14-70, Zona 10) Guatemala's most respected adventure-tourism company specializes in white-water rafting and trekking, but also offers archaeological trips, wildlife-watching expeditions and a whole lot more, mostly in the Alta Verapaz and Petén regions.

Sleeping

For budget and many midrange hotels, make a beeline for Zona 1. If you have just flown in or are about to fly out, a few guesthouses near the airport are as convenient as you could get. Top-end hotels are mostly around Zona 10.

Zona 1

Many of the city's cheaper lodgings are clustered in the area between 6a and 9a Avs and 14a and 17a Calles, 10 to 15 minutes' walk south from the Parque Central. Keep street noise in mind as you look for a room.

Hotel Ajau
HOTEL $
(Map p46; ☑2232-0488; hotelajau@hotmail.com; 8a Av 15-62, Zona 1; s/d Q160/205, without bathroom Q85/120; P@🕏) One of the few budget hotels in Guate with any tangible sense of style, the Ajau is a pretty good deal, with lovely polished floor tiles and cool, clean rooms. Room sizes vary and those at the front can get very noisy.

Guatemala City South

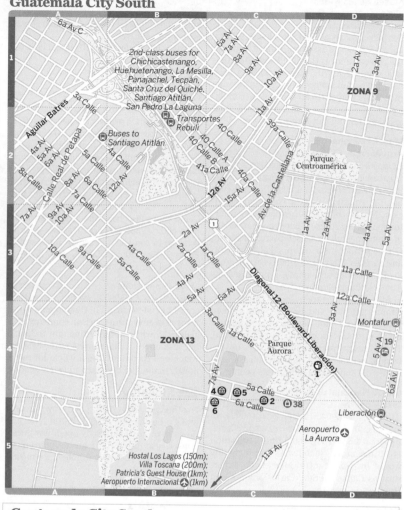

Guatemala City South

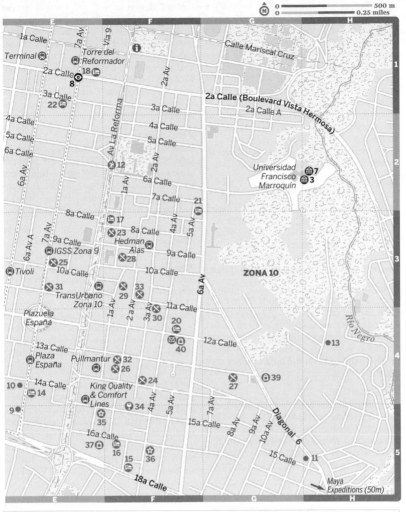

Hotel Spring
HOTEL $

(Map p46; ☑2230-2858; www.hotelspring.com; 8a Av 12-65, Zona 1; s/d from Q160/200, without bathroom Q110/140; P@⊛) With a beautiful courtyard setting, the Spring has a lot more style than other Zona 1 joints. It has central but quiet sunny patios. The 43 rooms vary greatly, but most are spacious and clean with high ceilings. Have a look around if you can. All rooms have cable TV; some of the more expensive ones are wheelchair accessible.

It's worth booking ahead. A *cafetería* serves meals from 6:30am to 1:30pm.

Hotel Fenix
HOTEL $

(Map p46; ☑2232-2839; 15a Calle 6-56, Zona 1; s/d Q100/160) Zona 1's classic budget hotel moved a few years ago, just around the corner from where it used to be. The building's actually more atmospheric than the last and the reasonably spacious, straightforward budget rooms here are still a very good deal.

Hotel Clariss
HOTEL $

(Map p46; ☑2232-1113; 8a Av 15-14, Zona 1; s/d Q170/220, without bathroom Q130/175; P@) This friendly place is set in a modern building with some good-sized rooms (and other, smaller ones). Those at the front get more air and light, but also the bulk of the street noise.

Hotel Capri
HOTEL $

(Map p46; ☑2232-8191; 9a Av 15-63, Zona 1; s/d Q150/195, without bathroom Q95/140; P) This modern four-story number is in a decent location and rooms are set back from the street, so they're quiet. Big windows looking onto patios and light wells keep the place sunny and airy.

Hotel Excel
HOTEL $$

(Map p46; ☑2253-2709; hotelexcel@hotmail.com; 9a Av 15-12, Zona 1; s/d Q175/225; P@) The Excel's bright, modern motel style may be a bit bland for some, but the rooms are spotless and the showers blast hot water.

Posada Belen
B&B $$

(Map p46; ☑2232-9226; www.posadabelen.com; 13a Calle A 10-20, Zona 1; s/d Q360/420; @⊛) One of Zona 1's most stylish options, this boutique hotel has just 10 rooms, arranged around a couple of lush patios. Rooms are well decorated with *típico* (traditional) furnishings and there's a good restaurant onsite.

Hotel Colonial
HOTEL $$

(Map p46; ☑2232-6722; www.hotelcolonial.net; 7a Av 14-19, Zona 1; s/d Q170/250, without bathroom Q130/190; P@⊛) This converted large old house has spacious communal areas and heavy, dark, colonial decor. It's a very well-run establishment whose 42 rooms are clean, good-sized and adequately furnished. Nearly all have a private bathroom and TV.

Hotel Quality Service
HOTEL $$

(Map p46; ☑2251-8005; www.qualityguate.com; 8a Calle 3-18, Zona 1; s/d Q180/240; P@⊛) There's a pleasing, old-timey feel about this place, which is balanced perfectly by the modern-but-not-overly-so rooms. Prices include breakfast. The best pick near the park.

Hotel Pan American
HOTEL $$

(Map p46; ☑2232-6807; www.hotelpanamerican .com.gt; 9a Calle 5-63, Zona 1; s/d Q385/405; P@⊛) Guatemala City's luxury hotel before WWII, the Pan American is one of the few hotels in the city with any air of history. There's a fine, art-deco lobby that's filled with plants and a not-too-shabby restaurant (p54). Rooms are spacious and simple, often with three or more beds. The bathrooms are stylish and modern, with good-sized tubs. Avoid rooms facing the noisy street.

Hotel Centenario
HOTEL $$

(Map p46; ☑2338-0381; www.hotelcentenario. wordpress.com; 6a Calle 5-33, Zona 1; s/d Q185/235; P⊛) Although it's looking a bit worn around the edges (and not that flash in the middle, either), the Centenario offers a pretty good deal, right on the park. Rooms are basic and unrenovated, with TV and hot showers.

Hotel Royal Palace
HOTEL $$$

(Map p46; ☑2416-4400; www.hotelroyalpalace. com; 6a Av 12-66, Zona 1; s/d Q495/580; P✳⊛) A little island of glamor amid the rough and tumble of 6a Av, this place offers most comforts. The style is modern-reconstruction, with plenty of dark woods and fancy tiling around the place. Rooms are large, sparkling clean and wheelchair-accessible. Those at the front have balconies overlooking the street – a fascinating, if noisy, spectacle.

Facilities include a restaurant, bar, gym, sauna and free airport transfers.

🛏 Zona 9

Hotel Villa Española HOTEL $$
(Map p50; ☑ 2205-0200; www.hotelvillaespanola.
com; 2a Calle 7-51, Zona 9; s/d Q370/410; P ❄ 🛜)
One of the very few options with colonial
stylings in this part of town, the Villa Es-
pañola has some beautiful touches. It's on a
busy road, but rooms are set well back, so
there's little noise. There's a good restaurant
on the premises.

Mi Casa HOTEL $$$
(Map p50; ☑ 2332-1364; www.hotelmicasa.com; 5a
Av A 13-51, Zona 9; s/d Q440/520; P @ 🛜) Set in
a family house on a quiet street, rooms here
are big and sunny, with private bathrooms,
lino floors, standard acrylic paintings, fans
and reading lamps. Price includes breakfast,
which is served in a leafy little patio out
back. You can call ahead for airport pickup.

Residencia del Sol HOTEL $$$
(Map p50; ☑ 2360 4823; www.residenciadelsol
.com; 3a Calle 6-42, Zona 9; s/d Q500/580;
P ❄ @) The spacious, good-looking rooms
here make up for the slightly out-of-the-
way location. There's no wi-fi, but you can
hook your computer up via network cables
in your room. Pay an extra Q80 for wooden
floorboards and a balcony.

Barceló Guatemala BUSINESS HOTEL $$$
(Map p50; ☑ 1-800-423-0100; www.barcelo
guatemalacity.com; 7a Av 15-45, Zona 9; s/d
from Q700/770; P ❄ @ 🛜 ▦) For that big,
corporate, I'd-rather-not-be-here hotel experience, it's hard to go past the local outlet of
the Spanish Barceló hotel chain.

🛏 Zona 10

Quetzalroo HOSTEL $
(Map p50; ☑ 5746-0830; www.quetzalroo.com;
6a Av 7-84, Zona 10; dm/s/d without bathroom
Q140/200/280; P @ 🛜) Guatemala City's
best downtown hostel has reasonable rooms
and dorms, a cramped kitchen area and a
great rooftop terrace. The location's handy
for the Zona Viva eating and nightlife scene.
Call for free pickup from the airport or bus
terminal.

Eco Hotel los Próceres HOTEL $$
(Map p50; ☑ 2337-3250; www.posadadelosproceres
.com; 18a Calle 3-03, Zona 10; s/d Q320/400;
P ❄ 🛜) The spotless, brightly painted rooms

here are a pretty good deal. They're a bit
cramped, but tasteful decoration and mod-
ern bathrooms (with tub!) make up for that.
Price includes free airport pickup.

Hotel Posada de los Próceres HOTEL $$
(Map p50; ☑ 2385-4302; www.posadadelosproceres
.com; 16a Calle 2-40, Zona 10; s/d Q320/400;
P ❄ @ 🛜) Twenty brightly decorated, if
slightly tatty, rooms right on the edge of
Zona Viva. They're surprisingly large, with
attractive tiled bathrooms, phone, clock, cable
TV, wooden furniture, and minifridge. Price
includes free airport pickup.

Hotel San Carlos HOTEL $$$
(Map p50; ☑ 2332-6055; www.hsancarlos.com; Av
La Reforma 7-89, Zona 10; s/d Q660/750, apt from
Q1250; P @ 🛜 ▦) OK, so it goes a little heavy
on the baroque furnishings, but this place
is still a good deal. Set well back from the
busy street, it's quiet and the well-appointed
rooms and apartments are spacious and
comfortable. Rates include breakfast and
airport pickup.

Otelito BOUTIQUE HOTEL $$$
(Map p50; ☑ 2339-1811; www.otelito.com; 12a Calle
4-51, Zona 10; s/d/ste Q572/680/800; P ❄ @ 🛜)
Imbued with Zen tranquillity, this place features bamboo, mood lighting and polished
steel. Rooms are spacious and minimalist
and bathrooms modern, with big glassed-in
shower stalls. There's a garden restaurant/
cafe out the front and rates include breakfast and airport pickup. Book ahead.

🛏 Zona 13

The middle-class residential area in Zona 13
around the airport is filling up with guesthouses catering to arriving and departing
travelers. All their room rates include breakfast and airport transfers (call from the airport on arrival). There are no restaurants
out here, but hotel workers have the complete lowdown on fast-food home delivery
options.

Patricia's Guest House GUESTHOUSE $
(☑ 2261-4251; www.patriciashotel.com; 19 Calle 10-
65, Aurora II; r per person without bathroom Q115;
P @ 🛜) The most relaxed and comfortable
option is in this family house with a sweet
little backyard where guests can hang out. It
also offers private transport around the city
and shuttles to bus stations.

Hostal Los Lagos
HOSTEL $

(2261-2809; www.loslagoshostal.com; 8a Av 15-85, Aurora I; dm Q120, s/d Q200/320; P@🖀) This is the most hostel-like of the near-the-airport options. Rooms are mostly set aside for dorms, which are airy and spacious, but there are a couple of reasonable-value private rooms. The whole place is extremely comfortable, with big indoor and outdoor sitting areas.

Villa Toscana
HOTEL $$

(☑2261-2854; www.hostalvillatoscana.com; 16a Calle 8-20, Aurora I; s/tw/d/ste Q310/400/460/570; P@🖀) One of the 'new breed' of airport hotels, this one features big, comfortable rooms, a tranquil atmosphere, a kitchen for guest use and a lovely backyard. Airport transfers are only available from 5.30am to 9.30pm – outside those hours, you pay the taxi.

✕ Eating

✕ Zona 1

Cheap eats are easy to find in Zona 1 – dozens of restaurants and fast-food shops are strung along, and just off, 6a Av between 8a and 15a Calles. American fast-food chains such as McDonald's and Burger King are sprinkled liberally throughout Zona 1 and the rest of the city. Pollo Campero is Guatemala's KFC clone.

Coffee culture is just beginning to hit Zona 1, and there are a number of cool little cafes springing up where you can enjoy good coffee, sandwiches and snacks.

Bar Céntrico
CAFE $

(Map p46; 7a Av 12-32, Zona 1; snacks from Q20; ⊘9am-6pm Mon-Sat) A hip little bar/cafe with comfy sofas out on the passageway and local artworks on the walls.

Café de Imeri
CAFE $

(Map p46; 6a Calle 3-34, Zona 1; mains Q30-50; ⊘8am-7pm Mon-Sat; 🖀) Interesting breakfasts, soups and pastas. The list of sandwiches is impressive and there's a beautiful little courtyard area out the back.

Restaurante Rey Sol
VEGETARIAN $

(Map p46; 11a Calle 5-51, Zona 1; mains Q20-30; ⊘7am-7pm Mon-Sat, 7am-4pm Sun; ☑) Good, fresh ingredients and some innovative cooking keep this strictly vegetarian restaurant busy at lunchtime.

Café-Restaurante Hamburgo
GUATEMALAN $

(Map p46; 15a Calle 5-34, Zona 1; set meal Q30-50; ⊘7am-9:30pm) This bustling spot facing the south side of Parque Concordia serves good Guatemalan food, with chefs at work along one side and orange-aproned waitresses scurrying about. At weekends a marimba band adds atmosphere.

Fu Lu Sho
CHINESE $

(Map p46; 6a Av 12-05, Zona 1; mains Q30-60; ⊘8am-11pm daily) This classic Zona 1 Chinese joint has been going for years and is a reliable if somewhat unexciting choice. It's straight up Chinese with a few Guatemalan staples thrown in, but for late-night cheap eats, it's hard to beat.

Café Leon
CAFE $$

(Map p46; 8a Av 9-15, Zona 1; breakfast from Q40; ⊘7am-6pm Mon-Thu, 7am-7:30pm Fri, 8:30am-5pm Sat; 🖀) Hugely popular and atmospheric, with some great old photos of the city on the walls. Some good breakfasts and sandwiches are on offer, but the coffee is the drawcard. There's another branch (Map p46; 12a Calle 6-23) a few blocks south.

Picadilly
INTERNATIONAL $$

(Map p46; cnr 6 Av & 11a Calle, Zona 1; mains Q45-90; ⊘11am-9:30pm) Right in the thick of the 6a Av action, this bustling restaurant does OK pizzas and pastas and good steak dishes. The place is clean and street views out of the big front windows are mesmerizing.

Hotel Pan American
INTERNATIONAL $$

(Map p46; ☑2232-6807; 9a Calle 5-63, Zona 1; breakfast Q50-90, mains Q70-130; ⊘7am-9pm; 🖀) The restaurant at this venerable hotel is high on ambiance. It has highly experienced and polished waiters sporting traditional Maya regalia. The food (Guatemalan, Italian and American) is fine, although it is a little on the expensive side.

Restaurante Altuna
GUATEMALAN $$

(Map p46; ☑2232-0669; 5a Av 12-31, Zona 1; mains Q80-150; ⊘12-10pm Tue-Sat, 12-4pm Sun) This large and classy restaurant has the atmosphere of a private club. It has tables in several rooms that are off a skylit patio. The specialties are seafood and Spanish dishes; service is both professional and welcoming.

✕ Zona 9

Celeste Imperio
CHINESE $$

(Map p50; cnr 7a Av & 10a Calle, Zona 9; mains Q70-120; ⊘11am-11pm Mon-Sat, 11am-10pm Sun) One

---

ZONA 10 CHEAP EATS

A cheap lunch in GC's hoity-toity Zona 10? These places are nothing fancy, but are popular with local office workers.

Paco's Café (Map p50; 1a Av 10-50; mains Q20-40; ⊗7am-4pm Mon-Sat) Down-home Guatemalan food served in the eatery at the side of a *kiosko* (small store).

Cafetería Solé (Map p50; 14a Calle, btwn 3a & 4a Avs; set lunch Q30; ⊗noon-4pm) Good value set meals.

Cafetería Patsy (Map p50; Av La Reforma 8-01; set lunch from Q35; ⊗7:30am-8pm) A bright, cheerful place popular with local office workers, offering subs, sandwiches and good-value set lunches.

---

of the city's many Chinese restaurants, this one gets the thumbs up from locals. All your favorites are here, plus some unusual options such as baked pigeon (Q85).

Puerto Barrios SEAFOOD $$
(Map p50; ☑2334-1302; 7a Av 10-65, Zona 9; mains Q90-170; ⊗12-3:30pm & 6-11pm) Puerto Barrios specializes in tasty prawn and fish dishes and is awash in nautical themes – paintings of buccaneers, portholes for windows, a big compass by the door. If you're having trouble finding it, just look for the big pirate ship in which it's housed.

✖ Zona 10

Zona 10's upmarket ambience is matched with its range of restaurant choices – prices are higher here, but you're bound to find more variety on the menus and more comfortable surroundings.

San Martín & Company CAFE, BAKERY $
(Map p50; 13a Calle 1-62, Zona 10; light meals Q30-50; ⊗6am-8pm; ☎) Cool and clean, with ceiling fans inside and a small terrace outside, this Zona Viva cafe and bakery is great at any time of day. For breakfast try a scrumptious omelet and croissant (the former arrives inside the latter). Later there are tempting and original sandwiches, soups and salads.

Los Alpes CAFE, BAKERY $$
(Map p50; 10a Calle 1-09, Zona 10; breakfast Q40-60; ⊗7am-9pm) A relaxing garden restaurant/bakery. It's set well back from the

road, behind a wall of vegetation, giving it a feeling of deep seclusion. The freshly made sandwiches and cakes really hit the spot.

La Maison de France FRENCH $$
(Map p50; 13a Calle 7-98, Zona 10; mains Q80-170; ⊗noon-10:30pm Mon-Sat) French/Guatemalan probably isn't a combination you were expecting, but this little place does it well, with some good French dishes (including garlic snails, Q60), imported wines and live music on Fridays.

Kakao GUATEMALAN $$$
(Map p50; 2a Av 13-44, Zona 10; mains Q70-120; ⊗noon-3pm & 7-11pm Mon-Sat, noon-4pm Sun) Set under a thatched *palapa* roof with a soft marimba soundtrack, this is Zona 10's best *comida típica* (regional food) restaurant. The atmosphere and food are both outstanding.

Pecorino ITALIAN $$$
(Map p50; ☑2360-3035; 11a Calle 3-36, Zona 10; mains Q100-200; ⊗12pm-1am Mon-Sat, noon-6pm Sun; ☎) With a beautiful courtyard setting, this is widely regarded as the city's best Italian restaurant. The menu features a huge selection of antipasto, pizza, pasta, meat and seafood dishes.

Tamarindos FUSION $$$
(Map p50; ☑2360-2815; 11a Calle 2-19, Zona 10; mains Q110-180; ⊗12:30-2pm & 7.30-10.30pm Mon-Sat; ☎) A chic and delicious Asian/Italian restaurant with a Guatemalan twist. There's an inspiring range of salads on offer and some very good Japanese and Thai-inspired dishes. The decor is stylish and service prompt but friendly.

Drinking & Nightlife

Zona 1

Staggering from bar to bar about the darkened streets of Zona 1 is not recommended, but fortunately there's a clutch of good drinking places all within half a block of each other just south of the Parque Central.

Las Cien Puertas BAR
(Map p46; 9a Calle 6-45, Pasaje Aycinena 8-44; ⊗12pm-1am) This superhip (but not studiously so) little watering hole is set in a shabby colonial arcade that's said to have a hundred doors (hence the name) and is sometimes closed off for live bands. Little

KNOWING EXACTLY WHERE YOU ARE

Guatemala City, like (almost) all Guatemalan towns, is laid out on a logical street grid. Avenidas run north–south; calles run east–west. Each avenida and calle has a number, with the numbers usually rising as you move from west to east and north to south. Addresses enable you to pinpoint exactly which block a building is in, and which side of the street it's on. The address 9a Av 15-24 means building No 24 on 9a Av in the block after 15a Calle; 9a Av 16-19 refers to building No 19 on 9a Av in the block after 16a Calle; 4a Calle 7-3 is building No 3 on 4a Calle in the block after 7a Av. Odd-numbered buildings are on the left-hand side as you move in the rising-numbers direction; even numbers are on the right.

In addition, most cities and towns are divided into a number of zonas – 25 in Guatemala City, fewer in other places. You need to know the zona as well as the street address, for in some places the numbers of avenidas and calles are repeated in more than one zona. Beware, too, of a couple of other minor wrinkles in the system. Short streets may be suffixed 'A,' as in 14a Calle A, which will be found between 14a Calle and 15a Calle. In some smaller towns and villages no one uses street names, even when they're posted on signs.

bars spring up in this area all the time – it's one of the few places in Zona 1 you can really go bar-hopping.

El Gran Hotel PUB
(Map p46; 9a Calle 7-64, Zona 1; ⊙6pm-1am Tue-Sun) You can't actually stay here, but the down-market renovated lobby of this classic hotel is one of downtown's better-looking bars. It also hosts one of the area's more reliable dancefloors, alternating between Latin and electronic music.

🍷 Zona 10

Zona 10 has a bunch of clubs attracting 20-something local crowds along 13a Calle and adjacent streets such as 1a Av. Check flyers around town for special nights.

Bajo Fondo BAR
(Map p50; 15a Calle 2-55; ⊙7pm-1am Wed-Sat) One of the more atmospheric little bars in the area, this place has good music and the occasional spontaneous jam session.

☆ Entertainment

Cinema

Various multiscreen cinema complexes show Hollywood blockbuster movies, often in English with Spanish subtitles (unless they're kids' movies, in which case they'll most likely be dubbed into Spanish). Most convenient are **Cine Capitol Royal** (Centro Comercial Capitol; Map p46; ☑2251-8733; 6a Av 12-51, Zona 1) or **Cinépolis Oakland Mall** (Oakland Mall; Map p50; ☑2269-6990; www.cinepolis.

com.gt; Diagonal 6 13-01, Zona 10). Tickets cost around Q35. Movie listings can be found in the *Prensa Libre* newspaper.

Theater

The English-language magazine *Revue* (www.revuemag.com) has events details, although it focuses more on Antigua. Your hotel should have a copy, or know where to get one. Free events mags in Spanish come and go. At the time of writing, *El Azar* (www.elazarcultural.blogspot.com) had the best info. Pick up a copy at the cultural centers listed below.

Centro Cultural de España PERFORMING ARTS
(Map p46; ☑4752-7226; www.centroculturalespana.com.gt; 6a Av 11-02, Zona 1; ⊙9:30am-1pm & 2-5pm Mon-Fri, 10am-2pm Sat) The Spanish Cultural Center hosts an excellent range of events, including live music, film nights and art exhibitions, mostly with free admission.

Centro Cultural Miguel Ángel Asturias PERFORMING ARTS
(Map p46; ☑2332-4041; www.teatronacional.com.gt; 24a Calle 3-81, Zona 1) Cultural events are held here.

Live Music & Clubs

La Bodeguita del Centro LIVE MUSIC
(Map p46; 12a Calle 3-55, Zona 1; ⊙9pm-1am Tue-Sat) There's a hopping, creative local scene in Guatemala City, and this large, bohemian hangout is one of the best places to connect with it. Posters featuring the likes of Che, Marley, Lennon, Victor Jara, Van Gogh and Pablo Neruda cover the walls from floor to ceiling.

There's live music of some kind almost every night from Tuesday to Saturday, usually starting at 9pm, plus occasional poetry readings, films or forums. Entry is usually free Tuesday to Thursday, with a charge of Q25 to Q60 on Friday and Saturday nights. Food and drinks are served. Pick up a monthly schedule of events.

Rattle & Hum
LIVE MUSIC

(Map p50; cnr 4a Av & 16 Calle, Zona 10; ⊗12pm-1am) One of the last places in Zona 10 to still be hosting live music (Tuesdays), this Australian-owned place has a warm and friendly atmosphere and nightly drink specials.

TrovaJazz
LIVE MUSIC

(Map p46; www.trovajazz.com; Vía 6 No 3-55, Zona 4) Jazz, blues and folk fans should look into what's happening here.

Los Lirios
LIVE MUSIC

(Map p46; 7a Av 9-20, Zona 1; ⊗ Wed-Sat 7pm-1am) With live Latin music and dancing most nights, this is a popular choice for the 25+ crowd.

Kahlua
CLUB

(Map p50; 15a Calle & 1a Av, Zona 10; admission from Q30; ⊗7pm-1am Thu-Sat) For electronica and bright young things.

Gay Venues

Don't get too excited about this heading: there are only a couple of places worthy of mention for men, and nothing much for women.

Genetic
GAY

(Map p46; Ruta 3 3-08, Zona 4; admission from Q30; ⊗9pm-1am Wed-Sat) This used to be called Pandora's Box, and has been hosting Guatemala's gay crowd since the '70s, although these days it gets a mixed crowd and is one of the best places in town to go for trance/dance music. It has two dance floors, a rooftop patio and a relaxed atmosphere. Friday is 'all you can drink.'

Black & White Lounge
GAY

(Map p46; www.blackandwhitebar.com; 11a Calle 2-54, Zona 1; ⊗7pm-1am Wed-Sat) This well-established gay disco-bar is in a former private house near the city center.

🛍 Shopping

For fashion boutiques, electronic goods and other first-world paraphernalia, head for the large shopping malls such as **Centro Comercial Los Próceres** (Map p50; www.proceres.com;

16a Calle, Zona 10; ⊗8am-8pm) or **Oakland Mall** (Map p50; www.oaklandmall.com.gt; Diagonal 6 13-01, Zona 10; ⊗8am-8pm). For a more everyday Guatemalan experience, check out the stalls at **Plaza El Amate** (Map p46; cnr 18a Calle & 4a Av, Zona 1; ⊗8am-6pm), where you can find CDs, shoes, underwear, overalls and pretty much everything else under the sun.

Mercado Central
MARKET

(Map p46; 9a Av, btwn 6a & 8a Calles; ⊗9am-6pm Mon-Sat, 9am-noon Sun) Until the quake of 1976, Mercado Central, behind the cathedral, was where locals shopped for food and other necessities. Reconstructed after the earthquake, it now deals in colorful Guatemalan handicrafts such as textiles, carved wood, metalwork, pottery, leather goods and basketry, and is a pretty good place to shop for these kinds of things, with reasonable prices.

Sophos
BOOKS

(Map p50; ☎ 2419-7070; www.sophosenlinea.com; 4a Av 12-59, Plaza Fontabella, Zona 10; ⊗9am-9pm Mon-Sat, 10am-7pm Sun) A relaxed place to read while in the Zona Viva, with a good selection of books in English on Guatemala and the Maya, including maps and Lonely Planet guides.

ℹ Orientation

Guatemala City is quite spread out, with the airport to the south, the two major bus terminals to the southwest and northeast, the majority of interesting sights in downtown Zona 1 and museums and higher-end accommodation clustered around Zona 10. None of these are really within walking distance from each other (except maybe the airport and Zona 10), but taxis are plentiful and cheap and two new, relatively safe bus networks connect various parts of the city.

MAPS

Intelimapas' *Mapa Turístico Guatemala,* Inguat's *Mapa Vial Turístico* and International Travel Maps' *Guatemala* all contain useful maps of Guatemala City. Sophos (p57) is one of the most reliable places to get maps. The **Instituto Geográfico Nacional** (IGN; ☎ 2248-8100; www.ign.gob.gt; Av Las Américas 5-76, Zona 13; ⊗ 9am-5pm Mon-Fri) sells 1:50,000 and 1:250,000 topographical sheets of all parts of Guatemala, costing Q140 each.

ℹ Information

DANGERS & ANNOYANCES

Street crime, including armed robbery, has increased in recent years. Use normal urban caution (behaving as you would in, say, Manhattan or Rome): don't walk down the street with your wallet bulging out of your back pocket, and avoid walking alone downtown late at night. Work out your route before you start so that you're not standing on corners looking lost or peering at a map. It's safe to walk downtown in the early evening, as long as you stick to streets with plenty of lighting and people. Stay alert and leave your valuables in your hotel. Don't flaunt anything of value, and be aware that women and children swell the ranks of thieves here. The incidence of robbery increases around the 15th and the end of each month, when workers get paid.

Pretty much anywhere in Zona 1 off the 6a Av pedestrian strip is troublesome at night – a taxi is a worthwhile investment after a night on the town.

The more affluent sections of the city – Zonas 9, 10 and 14, for example – are safer but crimes against tourists and street crime in general is on the rise in these areas, too. The Zona Viva, in Zona 10, has police patrols at night. But even here, going in pairs is better than going alone. Never try to resist if you are confronted by a robber.

MEDICAL SERVICES

Guatemala City has many private hospitals and clinics. Public hospitals and clinics provide free consultations but can be busy; to reduce waiting time, get there before 7am.

Hospital Centro Médico (☑ 2361-1650, 2361-1649; 6a Av 3-47, Zona 10) Recommended. This private hospital has some English-speaking doctors.

Hospital General San Juan de Dios (☑ 2256-1486; 1a Av 10-50, Zona 1) One of the city's best public hospitals.

MONEY

Card skimming is rife in Guatemala City – try to use ATMs that are under some sort of watch at all times, such as those inside stores or shopping malls.

American Express (☑ 2331-7422; 12a Calle 0-93, Centro Comercial Montufar, Zona 9; ☺8am-5pm Mon-Fri, 8am-noon Sat) In an office of Clark Tours.

Banco Agromercantil (7a Av 9-11, Zona 1; ☺9am-7pm Mon-Fri, 9am-1pm Sat) Changes US dollars (cash, not traveler's checks).

Banco de la República (Aeropuerto Internacional La Aurora; ☺6am-8pm Mon-Fri, 6am-6pm Sat & Sun) Currency-exchange services; on the airport departures level.

Visa/Mastercard ATM, Zona 1 (18 Calle 6-85, Zona 1) Inside the Paiz Supermarket.

Visa/Mastercard ATMs, Zona 10 (16a Calle, Zona 10) Inside Los Proceres mall.

POST

DHL (☑ 2379-1111; www.dhl.com; 12a Calle 5-12, Zona 10) Courier service.

Main Post Office (Palacio de Correos; 7a Av 11-67, Zona 1; ☺8:30am-5pm Mon-Fri, 8:30am-1pm Sat) In a huge yellow building at the Palacio de Correos. There's also a small post office at the airport.

TOURIST INFORMATION

Guatemala's tourist police are called **Disetur** (Tourist Police; ☑ 2232 0202; 11 Calle 12-06). Travelers are advised to contact their liaison, **Proatur** (☑ toll free, in English 1500; ☺24hr).

Located in the lobby of the Inguat (Guatemalan Tourism Institute) headquarters in the Centro Cívico, the **main tourist office** (☑ 2421-2854; www.visitguatemala.com; 7a Av 1-17; ☺8am-4pm Mon-Fri) has limited handout material, but staff are extremely helpful. There's also a branch at the **Aeropuerto La Aurora** (☑ 2322-5055; in the arrivals hall; ☺6am-9pm).

TRAVEL AGENCIES

Viajes Tivoli (☑ 2285-1050; www.viajestivoli.com; 12a Calle 4-55, Edificio Herrera, Zona 1) Housed in a building with several other travel agencies; take your pick.

❶ Getting There & Away

AIR

Guatemala City's **Aeropuerto La Aurora** (www.dgacguate.com) is the country's major airport. All international flights to Guatemala City land and take off here. The arrivals hall boasts a sometimes-working ATM, sometimes-attended tourist information booth and currency-exchange desks. Various travelers have complained about the rates given at the exchange booth inside arrivals and instead recommend the Banrural bank in the departures hall. There is also a more reliable ATM in the departures hall.

At the time of writing, the country's only *scheduled* domestic flights were between Guatemala City and Flores with **Grupo Taca** (☑ 2470-8222; www.taca.com; Avenida Hincapié 12-22, Zona 13), leaving Guatemala City at 6:30am and 6:20pm, and **TAG** (☑ 2380-9494; www.tag.com.gt; cnr Av Hincapié & 18 Calle, Zona 13), which departs at 6:30am. Domestic flights *may* leave from the domestic terminal, a 15-minute cab ride from the international terminal.

Tickets to Flores cost around Q1330/2300 one-way/round-trip with Grupo Taca and Q1250/2100 with TAG, but some travel agents, especially in Antigua, offer large discounts on these prices.

Sixteen international airlines also serve Guatemala, flying direct from North, Central and South America, Europe, Israel and Japan.

GETTING TO ANTIGUA

The classic exit strategy on arrival at Guatemala City airport is to make a beeline for elsewhere, usually Antigua. Door-to-door minibuses run to any address in Antigua (usually Q80 per person, one hour). Look for signs in the airport exit hall or people holding up 'Antigua Shuttle' signs. The first shuttle leaves for Antigua at about 7am and the last around 8pm or 9pm, although there's often one hanging around to meet the last flight (around midnight). For groups, the other option is a taxi (around Q250), but if there are only one or two of you, shuttle minibuses are more economical (if a bit slower and less comfortable).

See p305 for more information on international flights.

BUS

Buses from here run all over Guatemala and into Mexico, Belize, Honduras, El Salvador and beyond. Many bus companies have their own terminals, some of which are in Zona 1. The city council has been on a campaign to get long-distance bus companies out of the city center, so it may be wise to double check with Inguat or staff at your hotel about the office location before heading out there. Buses for the Pacific Coast mostly leave from the CentraSur terminal. Departures for Central and Eastern Guatemala and the Petén mostly leave from CentraNorte. Second-class buses for the Western Highlands leave from a series of roadside *paradas* (bus stops) on 41a Calle between 6a and 7a Avs in Zona 8.

International Bus Services

The following companies offer first-class bus services to international destinations. Hedman Alas also serves multiple destinations in Honduras.

King Quality & Comfort Lines (2337-2991; www.king-qualityca.com; 15 Calle 0-31, Zona 10, inside Biltmore Hotel) Serves most Central American capitals.

Línea Dorada (2415-8900; www.lineado rada.com.gt; cnr 10a Av & 16a Calle, Zona 1) Has a service to Tapachula, Mexico.

Pullmantur (2495-7000; www.pullmantur. com; 1a Av 13-22, Holiday Inn, Zona 10) Covers El Salvador and Honduras.

Tica Bus (2473-3737; www.ticabus.com; Calzada Aguilar Batres 22-55, Zona 12) Covers all of Central America and Mexico.

Transportes Galgos Inter (2232-3661; www. transgalgosinter.com.gt; 7a Av 19-44, Zona 1) Can book connections as far north as the US, including Tapachula, Mexico. Also goes to El Salvador.

International Bus Departures from Guatemala City

Copán, Honduras (Q520, five hours, two daily) Hedman Alas.

La Ceiba, Honduras (Q700, 12 hours, two daily) Hedman Alas.

Managua, Nicaragua (Q450 to Q1500, 16 to 35 hours, three daily) King Quality & Comfort Lines, Tica Bus.

Panama City, Panama (Q1220, 76 hours, two daily) Tica Bus.

San José, Costa Rica (Q640 to Q1200, 40 to 63 hours, three daily) King Quality & Comfort Lines, Tica Bus.

San Pedro Sula, Honduras (Q520 to Q860, eight hours, three daily) Hedman Alas, King Quality & Comfort Lines.

San Salvador, El Salvador (Q120 to Q720, five hours, seven daily) King Quality & Comfort Lines, Tica Bus, Pullmantur, Transportes Galgos Inter.

Tapachula, Mexico (Q170 to Q293, five to seven hours, four daily) Tica Bus, Línea Dorada, Transportes Galgos Inter.

Tegucigalpa, Honduras (Q27 to Q1370, 10 to 35 hours, six daily) Hedman Alas, King Quality & Comfort Lines, Tica Bus, Pullmantur.

National Pullman Bus Services

The following bus companies have Pullman services to Guatemalan destinations.

ADN (2251-0610; www.adnautobuses delnorte.com; 8a Av 16-41, Zona 1) Flores and Quetzaltenango.

Fortaleza del Sur (2230-3390; CentraSur, Zona 12) Covers the Pacific coast.

Fuente del Norte (2238-3894; www.auto busesfuentedelnorte.com; 17a Calle 8-46, Zona 1) Covers the whole country.

Hedman Alas (2362-5072; www. hedmanalas.com; 2a Av 8-73, Zona 10) Daily departures between Guatemala City and Antigua.

Línea Dorada (2415-8900; www.line adorada.info; cnr 10a Av & 16a Calle, Zona 1) Luxury buses to El Petén, Quetzaltenango, Huehuetenango, Río Dulce etc.

Litegua (2220-8840; www.litegua.com; 15a Calle 10-40, Zona 1) Covers the east and Antigua.

Los Halcones (2433-9180; Calzada Roosevelt 37-47, Zona 11) For Huehuetenango.

Monja Blanca (CentraNorte, Zona 18) For Cobán and points in between.

Rapidos del Sur (2232-7025; CentraSur, Zona 12) For the Pacific coast.

Rutas Orientales (☎5481-2946; CentraNorte, Zona 18) Covers the east.

Transportes Álamo (☎2471-8646; 12a Av A 0-65, Zona 7) For Quetzaltenango.

Transportes Galgos (☎2253-4868; 7a Av 19-44, Zona 1) For Quetzaltenango and Retalhuleu.

Transportes Rebuli (☎2230-2748; 41 Calle btwn 6a & 7a Av, Zona 8) For Panajachel.

National Pullman Bus Departures from Guatemala City

Antigua (Q64 to Q70, one hour, four daily) Litegua, Hedman Alas.

Chiquimula (Q50 to Q60, three hours, half hourly 4:30am to 6pm) Rutas Orientales.

Cobán (Q50 to Q60, 4½ hours, hourly from 4am to 5pm) Monja Blanca.

El Carmen (Q80, seven hours, half hourly from 12:15am to 6:30pm) Fortaleza del Sur.

Esquipulas (Q50 to Q60, 4½ hours, half hourly from 4:30am to 6pm) Rutas Orientales.

Flores & Santa Elena (Q100 to Q220, eight to 10 hours, 26 daily) Fuente del Norte, Línea Dorada, ADN.

Huehuetenango (Q60 to Q110, five hours, four daily) Los Halcones, Línea Dorada.

La Mesilla (Q170, seven hours, three daily) Línea Dorada.

Panajachel (Q50, three hours, 5:15am) Transportes Rebuli.

Poptún (Q150 to Q190, eight hours, three daily) Línea Dorada.

Puerto Barrios (Q60 to Q100, five hours, half hourly from 3:45am to 7pm) Litegua.

Quetzaltenango (Q65 to Q70, four hours, 11 daily) Transportes Galgos, Alamo, Línea Dorada, ADN.

Retalhuleu (Q80, three hours, five daily 9:30am to 7:30pm) Fuente del Norte.

Río Dulce (Q65, five hours, half hourly from 6am to 4:30pm) Litegua.

Sayaxché (Q135, 11 hours, two daily) Fuente del Norte.

Tecún Umán (Q65, six hours, four daily) Fortaleza del Sur.

Second-Class Bus Services

The services listed below are all 2nd-class bus ('chicken bus') services.

Amatitlán (Q5, 30 minutes, every five minutes from 7am to 8:45pm) CentraSur.

Antigua (Q9, one hour, every five minutes from 7am to 8pm) Calz Roosevelt btwn 4a Av & 5a Av, Zona 7.

Chichicastenango (Q25, three hours, hourly from 5am to 6pm) Parada, Zona 8.

Ciudad Pedro de Alvarado (Q45, 2½ hours, half hourly from 5am to 4pm) CentraSur.

Escuintla (Q20, one hour, half hourly from 6am to 4:30pm) CentraSur.

Huehuetenango (Q60, five hours, half hourly from 7am to 5pm) Parada, Zona 8.

La Democracia (Q20, two hours, half hourly from 6am to 4:30pm) CentraSur.

La Mesilla (Q90, eight hours, hourly from 8am to 4pm) Parada, Zona 8.

Monterrico (Q40, three hours, three daily) CentraSur.

Panajachel (Q30, three hours, half hourly from 7am to 5pm) Parada, Zona 8.

Puerto San José (Q20, one hour, every 15 minutes from 4:30am to 4:45pm) CentraSur.

Salamá (Q45, three hours, half hourly from 5am to 5pm) 17a Calle 11-32, Zona 1.

San Pedro La Laguna (Q40, four hours, hourly from 2am to 2pm) Parada, Zona 8.

Santa Cruz del Quiché (Q40, 3½ hours, hourly from 5am to 5pm) Parada, Zona 8.

Santiago Atitlán (Q35, four hours, half hourly from 4am to 5pm) Parada, Zona 8.

Tecpán (Q15, two hours, every 15 minutes from 5:30am to 7pm) Parada, Zona 8.

CAR

Most major rental companies have offices both at La Aurora airport (in the arrivals area) and in Zona 9 or 10. Companies include the following:

Avis (www.avis.com) Aeropuerto Internacional La Aurora (☎2324-9000); Zona 9 (☎2324-9000; 6a Calle 7-64)

Guatemala Rent a Car (www.guatemalarentacar.com) Aeropuerto Internacional La Aurora (☎2329-9012); Zona 9 (☎2329-9020; Oficina 15, 12a Calle 5-54)

Tabarini (www.tabarini.com) Aeropuerto Internacional La Aurora (☎2331-4755); Zona 10 (☎2444-4200; 2a Calle A 7-30)

Tally Renta Autos (www.tallyrentaautos.com) Aeropuerto Internacional La Aurora (☎2261-2526); Zona 1 (☎2230-3780; 7a Av 14-60)

SHUTTLE MINIBUS

Shuttle services from Guatemala City to popular destinations such as Panajachel and Chichicastenango (via Antigua – both around Q230) are offered by travel agencies in Antigua. Quetzaltenango-based travel agents also have shuttles to and from Guatemala City.

❶ Getting Around

TO/FROM THE AIRPORT

Aeropuerto La Aurora is in Zona 13, in the southern part of the city, 10 to 15 minutes from Zona 1 by taxi, or 30 minutes by bus.

Taxis wait outside the airport's arrivals exit. 'Official' fares are Q60 to Zona 9 or 10, Q85 to Zona 1, but in reality you may have to pay a bit more. Be sure to establish the destination and price before getting in. Prices for taxis to the

TRANSMETRO

In early 2007, in answer to growing concerns about traffic congestion and insecurity on urban buses, Guatemala City inaugurated the **TransMetro** (http://transmetro.muniguate. com) system. TransMetro buses differ from regular old, red urban buses because they are prepaid (the driver carries no money, thus reducing the risk of robberies), travel in their own lanes (not getting caught in traffic jams), only stop at designated stops and are new, comfortable and bright green.

There are currently two routes in operation – one connects Zona 1's Plaza Barrios with the CentraSur bus terminal where the majority of buses for the Pacific coast now depart. The other runs south from Plaza Barrios through Zonas 9 and 10. This route and its stops are marked on the Guatemala City map.

Crime has got so bad on Guate's regular red buses that travelers are advised not to use them, but TransMetro buses are safe, fast and comfortable. All rides cost Q1, payable with a Q1 coin at the bus stop before boarding.

airport, hailed on the street, are likely to be lower – around Q60 from Zona 1.

BUS & MINIBUS

Due to an alarming increase in (often violent) crime on Guatemala City's red city buses, it is pretty much universally accepted that tourists should only use them in case of dire emergency. The major exceptions are the TransMetro and TransUrbano buses which are most useful for getting to the CentraSur and CentraNorte bus terminals, respectively.

For the thrillseekers out there, listed below are the most useful red bus routes. Buses will stop anywhere they see a passenger, but street corners and traffic lights are your best bet for hailing them – just hold out your hand. Buses should cost Q1 per ride in the daytime (but this can as much as quadruple on public holidays or the driver's whim). You pay the driver or his helper as you get on. Don't catch them at night.

Zona 1 to Zona 10 (Bus No 82 or 101) Travels via 10a Av, Zona 1, then 6a Av and Ruta 6 in Zona 4 and Av La Reforma.

Zona 10 to Zona 1 (Bus No 82 or 101) Travels via Av La Reforma then 7a Av in Zona 4 and 9a Av, Zona 1.

Airport to Zona 1 (Bus No 82) Travels via Zonas 9 and 4.

Zona 1 to Airport (Bus No 82) Travels via 10a Av in Zona 1 then down 6a Av in Zonas 4 and 9.

TransUrbano

A more recent improvement to Guatemala City's bus scene is **TransUrbano** (www.transurbano. com.gt), a much wider network of buses that aren't quite as slick as TransMetro but are still safe, reliable and comfortable. They're slower because they don't have a dedicated lane, but safer than the old red buses because to board you need a magnetic rechargeable card (card and first ride free) which can only be obtained by showing your passport or Guatemalan ID card. The rechargeable cards are available from special booths, the most useful for travelers being in Zona 1's Plaza Barrios, the CentroNorte bus terminal and the Zona 10 office on Avenida Reforma.

TAXI

Plenty of taxis cruise most parts of the city. Fares are negotiable; always establish your destination and fare before getting in. Zona 1 to Zona 10, or vice-versa, costs around Q40 to Q60. If you want to phone for a taxi, **Taxi Amarillo Express** (☎1766) has metered cabs (figure on Q5 per km) that often work out cheaper than others, although true *capitaleños* (capital city residents) will tell you that taxi meters are all rigged and you get a better deal bargaining.

GUATEMALA CITY GETTING AROUND

Antigua

POP 68,637 / ELEV 1530M

Best Places to Eat

➡ La Fonda de la Calle Real (p80)

➡ Bistrot Cinq (p81)

➡ Caffé Mediterráneo (p80)

➡ 39 Azul (p81)

Best Places to Stay

➡ Casa Jacaranda (p76)

➡ Earth Lodge (p85)

➡ Posada San Sebastián (p78)

➡ Hotel Quinta de las Flores (p78)

Why Go?

A place of rare beauty, major historical significance and vibrant culture, Antigua remains Guatemala's must-visit destination.

A former capital, the city boasts an impressive catalogue of colonial relics in a magnificent setting. Streetscapes of pastel facades unfold beneath three volcanoes. Many old ecclesiastical and civic structures are beautifully renovated, while others retain tumbledown charm, with fragments strewn about park-like grounds.

Thanks to the dozens of Spanish language schools that operate here, Antigua is a global hot spot. Yet it remains a vibrant Guatemalan town, its churches, plazas and markets throbbing with activity. Outside the city, indigenous communities, coffee plantations and volcanoes offer ample opportunities for exploration.

Perhaps the real miracle of Antigua is its resilience. Despite earthquakes, volcanic eruptions and floods, followed by virtual abandonment, it has re-emerged with a vengeance, buoyed by the pride of its inhabitants.

When to Go

Blessed with a spring-like climate year round, Antigua is a great destination at any time. Ample sunshine prevails most days with slightly cooler temperatures from mid-May to October when afternoon downpours are the norm. Antigua's biggest deal is Holy Week, when religious processions enliven the streets, Passion Plays are performed and hotels are fully booked. Other particularly lively times include Corpus Christi and All Saints' Day (Nov 1) with obligatory feasts of *fiambre* (chilled mixed salad) and festive visits to the graveyard.

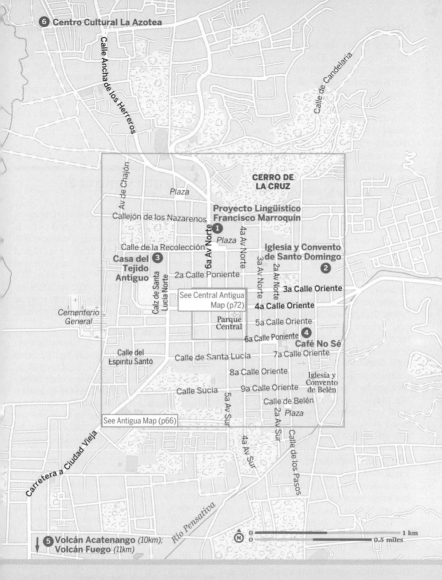

Antigua Highlights

1 Resurrect your high-school Spanish at such highly regarded language schools as **Proyecto Lingüístico Francisco Marroquín** (p74)

2 Get historical in Antigua's myriad museums, monasteries and convents, starting with the spectacular **Iglesia y Convento de Santo Domingo** (p69)

3 Admire and acquire traditional Maya wear at **Casa del Tejido Antiguo** (p68), with a seminal collection of *huipiles* (long, embroidered tunics) and *cortes* (wraparound skirts)

4 Sample a clandestine mezcal at **Café No Sé** (p82), the low-lit lair of choice for Antigua's expat scene

5 Scale **Acatenango** (p70) for jaw-dropping views of its sister volcanoes, including fire-spewing **Fuego** (p70)

6 Savor volcanic coffee beans at the **Centro Cultural La Azotea** (p85)

History

Antigua wasn't the Spaniards' first choice for a capital city. That honor goes to Iximché, settled in 1524 to keep an eye on the Kaqchiquel, with whom they had an uneasy truce. Things got uneasier when the Kaqchiquel rebelled, so the city was moved in 1527 to present-day Ciudad Vieja on the flanks of Volcán Agua. That didn't work out, either – the town practically disappeared under a mudslide in 1541. And so it was that on March 10, 1543, La muy Noble y muy Leal Ciudad de Santiago de los Caballeros de Goathemala, the Spanish colonial capital of Guatemala, was founded. The long-winded title attests to the founders' reverence for Saint James, to whom their early military victories were attributed.

Antigua was once the epicenter of power throughout Central America, and during the 17th and 18th centuries little expense was spared on the city's architecture, despite the regular ominous rumbles from the ground below. Indigenous labor was marshaled to erect schools, hospitals, churches and monasteries, their grandeur only rivaled by the houses of the upper clergy and the politically connected.

At its peak Antigua had no fewer than 38 churches, as well as a university, printing presses, a newspaper and a lively cultural and political scene. Those rumblings never stopped, though, and for a year the city was shaken by earthquakes and tremors until the devastating earthquake of July 29, 1773. A year later, the capital was transferred again, this time to Guatemala City. Antigua was evacuated and plundered for building materials but, despite official mandates that its inhabitants relocate and that the city be systematically dismantled, it was never completely abandoned. Fueled by a coffee boom early in the next century, the town, by then known as La Antigua Guatemala (Old Guatemala), began to grow again. Ongoing renovation of battered buildings helped maintain the city's colonial character despite an official lack of interest. During the 20th century, modernization dealt further blows but lobbying by Antigua's citizens led to President Ubico's declaration of the city as a national monument, and restoration ensued in earnest. But just as serious efforts were being made to return the city to its former splendor, disaster struck again with another major quake in February 1976, leaving thousands dead and undoing much of the restoration work.

Unesco's designation of Antigua as a World Heritage Site in 1979 added new impetus to the restoration campaign. Within this new climate, Spanish-language schools began popping up, pulling in droves of foreign students and leading to a genuine cultural renaissance.

◉ Sights

◉ Parque Central & Around

Surrounded by superb colonial structures, the broad, verdant Parque Central plaza is the gathering place for *antigüeños* and visitors alike – a fine place to sit or stroll and observe the goings-on, from hawkers and shoeshines to school kids and tourists. The buxom mermaids in the fountain are a reconstruction of the original 1738 version, which was trashed early in the 20th century.

Palacio de los Capitanes Generales   HISTORIC BUILDING
(Palace of the Captains General) Dating from 1558, the palace was the governmental center of all Central America, from Chiapas to Costa Rica, until 1773. The stately double-arcaded facade that anchors the south side of the plaza is all that remains of the old palace, recently under renovation. When the upgrade is complete, it is due to reopen as a cultural center.

Catedral de Santiago   CATHEDRAL
(Map p66; ruins admission Q3; ⊙ruins 9am-5pm) Antigua's cathedral was begun in 1545, wrecked by the quake of 1773, and only partially rebuilt over the next century. The present sliver of a church – the parish of San José – occupies only the entrance hall of the original edifice. Behind this structure are the roofless **ruins** of the main part of the cathedral, which is entered from 5a Calle Oriente.

It's a haunting place, with massive chunks of pillars strewn beneath sweeping brick archways and vegetation sprouting from wall cracks. Reproductions of the intricate plasterwork figures and moldings between the arches seem all that more impressive against the ruined backdrop. Behind the main altar, steps lead down to a former crypt now serving as a chapel, with a smoke-blackened Christ.

Palacio del Ayuntamiento   HISTORIC BUILDING

(City Hall Palace; ⊙ 9am-4pm Mon-Fri, 9am-noon & 2-4pm Sat & Sun) This double-arcaded structure on the north side of the park dates from the 18th century. Besides town offices, it houses the **Museo del Libro Antiguo** (Old Book Museum; ☑ 7832-5511; admission Q30; ⊙ 9am-4pm Tue-Fri, 9am-noon & 2-4pm Sat & Sun), showcasing the early days of Guatemalan printing, with a replica of Guatemala's first printing press. One of its earliest products is prominently displayed: a first edition of *Don Quixote de la Mancha* (Part II).

Museo de Arte Colonial   MUSEUM

(Map p66; admission Q50) The former Universidad de San Carlos (now in Guatemala City) is the setting for the Museum of Colonial Art. On display are paintings by leading Mexican artists of the colonial era, most notably *The Life of Saint Francis of Assisi* by Cristóbal del Villalpando, plus assorted sacred statuary.

Antiguo Colegio de la Compañía de Jesús   ARTS CENTRE

(6a Av Norte) Established in 1626, the Jesuit monastery and college was a vital component of Antigua life until the order was expelled by the Spanish crown in 1767; just six years later, the great earthquake left it in ruins. Rescued from the rubble by the Spanish government, the enormous complex has been reborn as a cultural center, the **Centro de Formación de la Cooperación Española** (☑ 7932-3838; www.aecid-cf.org.gt; 6a Av Norte; admission free; ⊙ 9am-6pm).

The former offices, classrooms and refectories now contain lecture halls, exhibit spaces and an excellent library. The three cloisters have been made over with fine wood columns and balconies, a brilliant setting for photo exhibits, films and workshops. One component remains respectfully unrestored, though: the Compañía de Jesús church, whose grand facade stands to the left of the main entrance of the complex.

⊙ West of Parque Central

Once glorious in their gilded baroque finery, Antigua's churches have suffered indignities from both nature and humankind. Rebuilding after earthquakes gave the churches thicker walls, lower towers and belfries, and unembellished interiors. Furthermore, moving the capital to Guatemala City deprived Antigua of the population needed to maintain the churches in their traditional richness, though they remain impressive. You'll find many churches and monasteries scattered around town in various states of decay.

Iglesia y Convento de Nuestra Señora de la Merced   CHURCH, MONASTERY

(Map p66; monastery ruins admission Q5; ⊙ monastery ruins 8:30am-5:30pm) At the northern end of 5a Av is La Merced – a striking yellow building trimmed with plaster filigree. The squat, thick-walled structure was built to withstand earthquakes, and over three centuries after its construction it remains in pretty good shape. Only the church is still in use; a candlelit procession, accompanied by bell ringing and firecrackers, starts and

O BROTHER THOU ART HERE

The spirit of Hermano Pedro, Antigua's most venerated Christian, looms large more than three centuries after his death. The saint's tomb, inside the Iglesia de San Francisco (p70), overflows with devotional plaques, amulets and tokens from the faithful offering gratitude for his miraculous healing powers. Antigua's only public hospital, southeast of the Parque Central, was dubbed in his honor and carries on his mission of providing health services to those unable to afford them.

Born on Tenerife in the Canary Islands in 1627, Pedro de Bethancourt labored as a shepherd until he hung up his staff at the age of 24 and made for Guatemala to help the poor, though the arduous journey left Pedro himself impoverished. Further hardship awaited when he flunked his studies at the Franciscan seminary in Antigua. Undaunted, he took to picking up dying Maya off the street and treating them during the plagues of the 1600s. He had found his true calling, and a few years later built a hospital devoted to healing the indigent, then built homeless shelters and schools for poor students. His efforts gave rise to a new religious order, the Bethlehemites, which took on his mantle after his death in 1667. To this day, flocks of devotees visit his tomb, a phenomenon the Vatican recognized when Pope John Paul II canonized the good brother in 2002, making him Guatemala's only officially authorized saint.

ANTIGUA

Antigua

0 200 m
0 0.1 miles

El Hato
(5km)

Calle de la Candelaria

Calle de los Duelos

Iglesia de la
Candelaria

San Lucas Sacatepéquez (17km);
Santiago Sacatepéquez (21km);
Sumpango (26km);
Guatemala City (46km)

11

16

15

1a Av Norte

CERRO DE
LA CRUZ

Calle de las Ánimas

Alameda de Santa Rosa

2a Av Norte

2a Calle Oriente

6

3a Av Norte

64

59

88

Iglesia
El Carmen

Convento
de Santa
Teresa

58

4a Av Norte

67

San Filipe (1km);
Hospital Nacional Pedro
de Bethancourt (1km)

61

66

5a Av Norte

Arco de
Santa
Catalina

79

33

83

9

Plaza

29

25

13

62 77

6a Av Norte

20

70

71

65

43

42

Calle Ancha de los Herreros

63

60 27

37

17

38

36

48

1a Calle Poniente

7a Av Norte

Callejón Camposeco

52 23

Jocotenango (500m);
San Lorenzo El Tejar (2km);
Pastores (5km);
Chimaltenango (18km);
San Andrés Itzapa (25km)

Av del Desengaño

Plaza

28

2a Calle
Poniente

Caiz de Santa Lucía Norte

Callejón de los Nazarenos

5

Calle Cruz de Piedra

Av de Chajón

1

Calle de la Recolección

8

Av de la Recolección

ANTIGUA

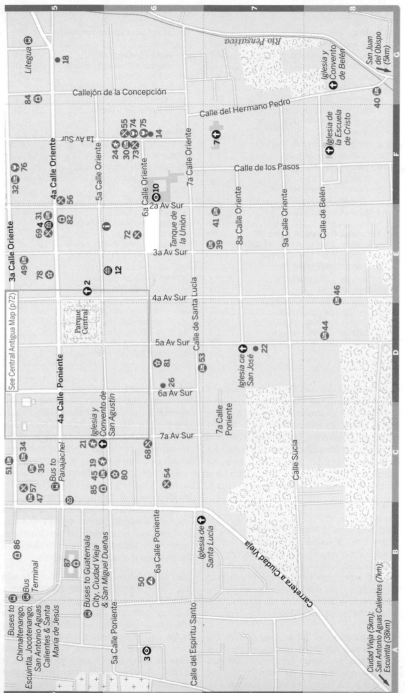

Litegua

● 18

● 84

Callejón de la Concepción

Calle del Hermano Pedro

Iglesia y
Convento
de Belén

San Juan
del Obispo
(5km)

● 40

55
74
75
14

24
30
73

Iglesia de
la Escuela
de Cristo

● 7

32
76

1a Av Sur

4a Calle Oriente

Calle Oriente

5a Calle Oriente

6a Calle Oriente

Calle de los Pasos

● 56

Río Pensativo

69 4 31

82

10

7a Calle Oriente

Calle de Belén

3a Calle Oriente

49
78

72

2a Av Sur

8a Calle Oriente

41
39

9a Calle Oriente

● 46

● 2

Tanque de
la Unión

3a Av Sur

12

See Central Antigua Map (p72)

Parque
Central

4a Av Sur

● 44

4a Calle Poniente

Calle de Santa Lucía

5a Av Sur

53

51

34
35

81

26

Iglesia de
San José

22

Bus to Panajachel

85 45 19
80

6a Av Sur

57
47

21

Iglesia y
Convento de
San Agustín

68

7a Av Sur

54

7a Calle
Poniente

Calle Sucia

86

Bus
Terminal

Buses to Guatemala
City, Ciudad Vieja
& San Miguel Dueñas

87

50

6a Calle Poniente

Iglesia de
Santa Lucía

Carretera a Ciudad Vieja

Buses to
Chimaltenango,
Escuintla, Jocotenango,
San Antonio Aguas
Calientes & Santa
María de Jesús

● 3

5a Calle Poniente

Calle del Espíritu Santo

Ciudad Vieja (5km);
San Antonio Aguas Calientes (7km);
Escuintla (38km)

Antigua

ends there on the last Thursday evening of each month.

Inside the monastery ruins is a fountain 27m in diameter, said to be the largest in Hispanic America. It's in the shape of a water lily (traditionally a symbol of power for Maya lords), and lily motifs also appear on the church's entrance arch. Go upstairs for a bird's-eye view of the fountain and the town.

Iglesia y Convento de la Recolección RUIN

(Map p66; Av de la Recolección; admission Q40; ⊙9am-5pm) A serene air pervades the remains of the monastery of La Recolección, which stands well west of the center. It was erected in the early 1700s by the Récollets (a French branch of the Franciscan order). The earthquake of 1773 toppled the structure, of which the great arched doorway remains intact.

Despite its short life as a monastery, the complex was left alone, serving variously as a squatters' residence, fairground and art-restoration workshop. Clamber up to the 2nd floor for better views, but watch your step.

Colegio de San Jerónimo RUIN

(Real Aduana; Map p66; cnr Calz de Santa Lucía & Calle de la Recolección; adult/student Q30; ⊙9am-5pm) Built in 1757, the Colegio de San Jerónimo was used as a school by friars of the Merced order, but because it did not have royal authorization, it was taken over by Spain's Carlos III and, in 1765, designated for use as the Real Aduana (Royal Customs House). Today it's a tranquil, mostly open-air site.

The handsome cloister centers around an octagonal fountain – it's an evocative setting for dance and other cultural performances. Upstairs you'll find excellent photo angles of Volcán Agua through stone archways.

Casa del Tejido Antiguo MUSEUM

(Map p66; ☑7832-3169; Calle de la Recolección 51; admission Q15; ⊙9am-5pm Mon-Sat) This space is like a museum, market and workshop rolled into one, with exhibits on regional outfits and daily demonstrations of backstrap weaving techniques. Founder Alicia Pérez, an indigenous Kaqchiquel woman, is an expert on the significance of designs that appear on the *tocoyales* (head coverings), *tzutes* (shawls) and *huipiles* displayed here. English tours are available.

Cementerio General CEMETERY
(Map p66; ⊙7am-noon & 2-6pm) Antigua's municipal cemetery, southwest of the market and bus terminal, is a conglomeration of tombs and mausoleums decked with wreaths, exotic flowers and other signs of mourning. Proatur (p83) offers an escort to this out-of-the-way site on request.

⊙ East of Parque Central

Iglesia y Convento de Santo Domingo MONASTERY
(Map p66; ☑7820-1220; 3a Calle Oriente 28; admission Q40; ⊙9am-6pm Mon-Sat, 11am-6pm Sun) Founded by Dominican friars in 1542, Santo Domingo became the biggest and richest monastery in Antigua. Following three 18th-century earthquakes, the buildings were pillaged for construction material. The site was acquired as a private residence in 1970 by an American archaeologist, who performed extensive excavations before it was taken over by the Casa Santo Domingo Hotel (p78).

The archaeological zone has been innovatively restored as a 'cultural route.' It includes the picturesque ruined monastery church, the adjacent cloister with a replica of the original fountain, workshops for candle and pottery makers and two underground crypts that were discovered during the church excavations. One of these, the Calvary Crypt, contains a well-preserved mural of the Crucifixion dating from 1683.

Also part of the archaeological zone are six museums, which can all be visited with one admission ticket. This museum route may be entered either through the hotel or the Universidad de San Carlos extension on 1a Av. Starting from the hotel side, they include the following:

The **Museo de la Platería** has silverwork masterpieces including incense burners, candelabras and crowns. **Museo Colonial** shows canvases and wood sculpture on religious themes from the 16th to 18th centuries, while **Museo Arqueológico** has ceramic and stone objects from the Maya Classic period.

Museo de Arte Precolombino y Vidrio Moderno has glass works by modern artists and the pre-Hispanic ceramic pieces that inspired them. **Museo de Artes y Artesanías Populares de Sacatepéquez** shows exhibits on traditional handicrafts from the Antigua region, while **Museo de la Farmacia** has a restored version of a 19th-century apothecary's shop from Guatemala City.

Iglesia de San Francisco CHURCH, MONASTERY
(Map p66; cnr 8a Calle Oriente & Calle do los Pasos; museum/monastery joint admission adult/child Q5/2; ⊙9am-4:30pm) The church is imbued with the spirit of Santo Hermano Pedro de San José de Bethancourt, a Franciscan monk who founded a hospital for the poor in Antigua and earned the gratitude of generations (also see the boxed text, p65). On the south side are the ruins of the adjoining monastery, with some vivid frescoes still visible amidst the rubble.

Hermano Pedro's intercession is still sought by the ill, who pray fervently by his tomb, housed in an elaborate pavilion north of the church since his canonization in 2002. Devotees may enter via a garden north of the church. A museum houses relics from the church and Santo Hermano's well-preserved personal belongings.

Convento de Capuchinas CONVENT
(Iglesia y Convento de Nuestra Señora del Pilar de Zaragoza; Map p66; cnr 2a Av Norte & 2a Calle Oriente; adult/student Q30/15; ⊙9am-5pm) Inaugurated in 1736 by nuns from Madrid, the convent of Las Capuchinas was seriously damaged by the 1773 earthquake and thereafter abandoned. But thanks to meticulous renovations in recent decades, it's possible to get a sense of the life experienced by those nuns, who ran an orphanage and women's hospital.

Wander round to admire the fine cloister with its stout columns and high arched passageways, remarkably restored wash basins and well-tended gardens. At the rear you'll find the convent's most unique feature, a towerlike structure of 18 nuns' cells built around a circular patio.

Iglesia y Convento de Santa Clara MONASTERY
(Map p66; 2a Av, btwn 6a & 7a Calles Oriente; admission Q40; ⊙9am-5pm) Established by sisters from Puebla, Mexico, Santa Clara was inaugurated in 1734, destroyed four decades later by the great quake and abandoned. Fortunately some elements of the original structure remain intact, such as the church's stonework facade, the arched niches along

the nave that served as confessionals, and an underground chamber where provisions were stored.

Most captivating of all is the cloister, centering on a fountain bordered by gardens, though only one side of the upper-level arcade is still in place.

Choco Museo MUSEUM
(Map p66; www.chocomuseo.com; 4a Calle Oriente 14; ⊙10:30am-6:30pm Mon-Sat, 9:30am-6:30pm Sun; ⊞) It was the Maya who discovered the culinary uses of the cacao bean, which later became a form of currency for the Aztec empire. These are a few of the things you'll learn at this kid-friendly expo, the Antigua branch of a hemisphere-wide project. The chocolate-making process is explained, and visits to a cacao plantation are offered (Q120 per person).

🕴 Activities

The following are professional, established outfits offering a range of activities. Drop by any to chat about possibilities.

Old Town Outfitters ADVENTURE SPORTS
(☑5399-0440; www.adventureguatemala.com; 5a Av Sur 12C) 🏃 Mountain biking, rock climbing, kayaking and trekking are among the high-energy activities offered by this highly responsible operator, which works with guides from local communities.

Guatemala Ventures MOUNTAIN BIKING
(Map p66; fax 7832-3383; 1a Av Sur 15) Offers hike-and-bike tours to Pacaya volcano along with some interesting cloud-forest, bird-watching and ridge-hiking options. You can rent Giant and Marin all-terrain bikes here too (per hour/day Q30/200).

Ox Expeditions ADVENTURE SPORTS
(Map p66; ☑7832-0074; www.guatemalavolcano. com; 1 Av Sur 4B) Offers rigorous climbing opportunities in the area. Part of their profits go to local environmental projects.

Volcano Ascents
All three volcanoes overlooking Antigua – Agua, Acatenango and Fuego – are tempting challenges. How close you can get to Fuego depends on recent levels of activity. In many ways the twin-peaked Acatenango (3975m), overlooking Fuego, is the most exhilarating summit. For an active-volcano experience many people take tours to Pacaya (2552m), 25km southeast of Antigua (a 1½-hour drive).

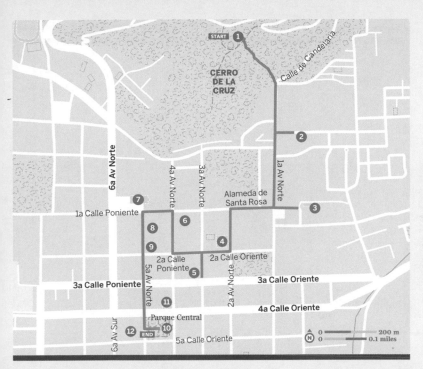

City Walk
Splendor in the Ruins

START CERRO DE LA CRUZ
END PARQUE CENTRAL
LENGTH 2.3KM; 2½ HOURS

For the big picture, take a taxi up **1 Cerro de La Cruz**, north of town. Beyond the stone cross that gives the hill its name, Antigua spreads out, with the majestic Volcán Agua as a backdrop. Descend the wooded slopes via the path to the left. At the bottom, turn right, down a cobblestoned street. You'll come to a basketball court backed by the ruins of **2 Iglesia de la Candelaria**. Examine it closely – there's a lot going on between the swirly columns. Proceed one block south to a small plaza with a fountain. Go left alongside a high yellow wall to glimpse the **3 Templo de Santa Rosa de Lima**, a small church with an elaborate facade that stands on a private estate. Turn around and head west along jacaranda-lined Alameda de Santa Rosa. Take the first left, onto 2a Av, past an ironworks shop. At the next corner on the right are the ruins of the convent of **4 Las Capuchinas**, with its unique tower.

Go right on 2a Calle two blocks. Passing 3a Av, look down to your left to see the multicolumned facade of **5 Iglesia El Carmen** and the adjacent handicrafts market. Continue another block west and turn right on 4a Av. Near the next corner on the right is the old **6 Convento de Santa Teresa**, which until recently served as the men's prison. Go left on 1a Calle. You'll see the yellow bell tower of the **7 Iglesia de Nuestra Señora de la Merced**. Turn left down 5a Av, jam-packed with tourist-friendly locales, including the handicrafts center, **8 Nim Po't**. Proceed beneath the **9 Arco de Santa Catalina**. A remnant of the 17th-century convent that stood here (now occupied by a luxury hotel and B&B), the tunnel-like arch enabled nuns to cross the street unseen. Continue down 5a Av to **10 Parque Central**. Ascend to the balcony of the **11 Palacio del Ayuntamiento** for photo ops of the square and nearby **12 Catedral de Santiago**. Finally, stop into the **13 Café Condesa**, on the square's west side, for a well-deserved wedge of pie and cappuccino.

Central Antigua

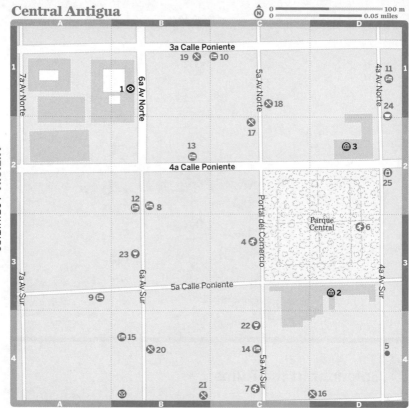

ANTIGUA ACTIVITIES

Old Town Outfitters (p70) leads strenuous hikes up Volcán Acatenango, traversing four ecosystems to reach the summit (Q980, including lunch and transport to the trailhead in the village of La Soledad). The expedition departs at 5am.

Most agencies run seven-hour Pacaya trips daily for Q80 (leaving Antigua at 6am and 2pm); food and drinks are not included, nor is the Q50 admission to the Pacaya protected area. It takes about 1½ hours to make the steep ascent to the simmering cleft black cone. (If you're out of breath, kids will rent you horses on the way up.) From the summit there are stupendous views west to Agua and northeast to Lago de Amatitlán. The descent is quicker as you slide down the powdery slope.

To climb Volcán de Agua, travel to the village of Santa María de Jesús on the volcano's northeast slopes (Q3.50 from bus cano's northeast slopes (Q3.50 from bus terminal). From the tourist office on the Parque Central of Santa María, you can hire Inguat-authorized guides (Q175 to 250 per person, plus park entry fee of Q40).

Other Hikes

Old Town Outfitters (p70) can take you on a three-day trek through the Western Highlands, following the Maya trade routes that linked Lake Atitlán to Quetzaltenango. Guatemala Ventures (p70) offers a range of hikes including some interesting cloud-forest, bird-watching and ridge-hiking options.

Cycling

Old Town Outfitters (p70) has a popular range of guided half-day mountain bike rides (Q380 per person) in the hills around Antigua, at varying levels of difficulty. Their two-day Pedal & Paddle Tour (Q1960 to Q2270) includes kayaking and hiking at Lago de Atitlán.

Central Antigua

Guatemala Ventures (p70) also offers bike tours, from half-day rides through the Antigua valley (Q235) to week-long jaunts encompassing volcanic slopes, highland forest and Pacific mangroves, as well as Lago de Atitlán. Another, lazier, option is their trip up Cerro Alto in a minibus with a coast back down on mountain bike (Q275).

For something different, **Don Quijote Cruisers** (Map p66; ☑ 7832-9427; www.donquijote cruisers.com; 7 Av Norte 2) offers Antigua tours and organic farm tours (Q200 each) on old-fashioned Schwinn Flyers with fat tires (good for those cobblestone streets). They rent the same retro bikes by the hour (Q40) or full day (Q200).

Horseback Riding
Ravenscroft Riding Stables　　　HORSEBACK RIDING
(☑ 7830-6669; 2a Av Sur 3, San Juan del Obispo) This outfit, 3km south of Antigua on the road to Santa María de Jesús, offers English-style riding, with scenic rides of three, four or five hours in the valleys and hills around Antigua, at Q195 per hour per person for experienced riders, Q235 for beginners.

Volunteer Work
Many of Antigua's language schools, such as Cambio Spanish School (p74), can help you find volunteer work.

As Green As It Gets　　　VOLUNTEERING
(☑ 5663-9764; www.asgreenasitgets.org) This NGO, based in San Miguel Escobar, works toward improving the lot of area coffee growers and artisans through sustainable economic development and direct trade. Volunteers are needed for construction projects and coffee harvesting.

🍴 Courses
Language Courses
Antigua's Spanish-language schools attract students from around the world. There are dozens of schools to choose from. Price, teaching quality and student satisfaction vary greatly. Often the quality of instruction depends upon the particular teacher, and thus may vary even within a single school. Visit a few schools before you choose and, if possible, talk to people who have studied recently at schools you like the look of – you're bound to run into a few. The Inguat tourist office (p84) has a list of authorized schools.

Classes start every Monday at most schools, though you can usually be placed with a teacher any day of the week. Most schools cater for all levels and allow you to stay as long as you like. Three or four weeks is typical, though it's perfectly OK to do just one week. The busiest seasons are during January and from April to August, and some schools request advance reservations for these times.

Instruction is nearly always one-on-one and costs Q750 to Q1515 per week for four hours of classes daily, five days a week. You can enroll for up to 10 hours a day of instruction, although most people find that four to five hours is plenty. Most schools offer to arrange room and board (three meals daily, except Sunday) with local families, usually with your own room, for around Q700 per week, a bit more with private bathroom. Some schools may offer accommodations in guesthouses or their own hostels.

Homestays are meant to promote the total immersion concept of language learning, but this becomes less viable where there are several foreigners staying with one family, or where there are separate mealtimes for students and the family. Indeed, there are so many foreigners about Antigua, it takes some real discipline to converse in Spanish rather than your native tongue. Many enjoy this social scene, but if you think it may deter you, consider studying in Quetzaltenango, El Petén or elsewhere, where there are fewer foreign students.

Cambio Spanish School LANGUAGE COURSE
(Map p66; www.cambiospanishschool.com; 4a Calle Oriente 41) Supports Niños de Guatemala, an educational program for underprivileged kids.

**Academia de Español
Probigua** LANGUAGE COURSE
(Map p66; ☑ 7832-2998; www.probigua.org; 6a Av Norte 41B) Well-regarded, nonprofit school that donates profits to establish and maintain libraries in rural villages.

**Academia de Español
Sevilla** LANGUAGE COURSE
(Map p66; ☑ 7832-5101; www.sevillantigua.com; 1a Av Sur 17C) Well managed, with a good program of free activities; can arrange volunteer work in local community projects. Beautiful installations with study carrels amid remnants of a colonial monastery. Offers shared student house as an accommodation option.

**Academia de Profesores
Privados de Español** LANGUAGE COURSE
(Map p66; ☑7882-4284; www.appeschool.com; Alameda de Santa Rosa 15) Founded and run by ex–Peace Corps volunteers. Besides standard Spanish instruction, it offers courses for tourism, educational and healthcare

personnel, and an opportunity to study in the outlying village of San Juan del Obispo.

Centro Lingüístico Maya LANGUAGE COURSE
(Map p66; ☑7832-0656; www.clmaya.com; 5a Calle Poniente 20) Large, professionally managed, pricier institute with 30 years' experience training diplomatic personnel and journalists.

**Escuela de Español
San José el Viejo** LANGUAGE COURSE
(Map p66; ☑ 7832-3028; www.sanjoseelviejo.com; 5a Av Sur 34) Long-standing school with park-like study environment, featuring tennis court and pool and its own tasteful accommodations. Students may switch teachers each week. Accredited by Guatemalan Ministry of Education.

**Antigüeña Spanish
Academy** LANGUAGE COURSE
(Map p66; ☑5375-4638; www.spanishacademyantiguena.com; 1a Calle Poniente 10) Oft-recommended school, authorized by Ministry of Education. They can arrange volunteer work at Hermano Pedro hospital for social workers on request.

**Proyecto Lingüístico
Francisco Marroquín** LANGUAGE COURSE
(Map p66; ☑ 7832-1422; www.spanishschoolplfm.com; 6a Av Norte 43) Antigua's oldest Spanish school, founded in 1969; run by a nonprofit foundation to preserve indigenous languages and culture, with capacity to teach K'iche' and Kaqchiquel, among other Maya tongues.

Christian Spanish Academy LANGUAGE COURSE
(Map p66; ☑7832-3922; www.learncsa.com; 6a Av Norte 15) Professional outfit where students report on the teachers weekly.

Cooking Courses

El Frijol Feliz COOKING COURSE
(☑7832-5274; www.frijolfeliz.com; 4a Av Sur 1; 3hr class Q360) Hands-on instruction preparing Guatemalan meals; students may choose their own menu.

☞ Tours

Inguat-authorized guides around the Parque Central offer city walking tours, with visits to convents, ruins and museums, for Q100 to Q200. Similar guided walks are offered daily by Antigua travel agencies such as Adventure Travel Center (p84) and Atitrans (p84). Also on offer are trips to the surrounding villages and coffee plantations for around Q200.

Elizabeth Bell, a local scholar of Antigua history, or her knowledgeable associates lead three-hour cultural walking tours of the town (in English and/or Spanish) on Tuesday, Wednesday, Friday and Saturday at 9:30am, and on Monday and Thursday at 2pm. The cost is Q160. Reservations can be made through **Antigua Tours** (Map p66; ☑ 7832-5821; www.antiguatours.net; 5a Av Norte 6), inside the **Casa del Conde bookstore** (5a Av Norte 4) off the Parque Central; groups congregate at the park's fountain at the appointed hour. Bell's book, *Antigua Guatemala: The City and its Heritage,* is well worth picking up: it has extensive descriptions of all the monuments and neatly encapsulates the history and fiestas. Bell and company also do tours to the nearby villages of San Antonio Aguas Calientes and San Andrés Itzapa to investigate weaving workshops and Maya shrines, respectively.

La Antigua City Tour (☑ 2268-2712; www.antiguacitytour.com; adult/child under 13yr Q80/55; ☺ 9am-6pm) runs a pseudo streetcar around town, hitting all the key sites from Cerro de la Cruz to Parque Central.

As Green As It Gets (p72) offers tours of coffee plantations around San Miguel Escobar, a suburb of Ciudad Vieja, with local growers demonstrating cultivation, harvesting and processing techniques. Tours (Q200 per person) depart daily at 9am and 2pm from the central plaza of San Miguel Escobar.

Agencies also offer tours to more distant places, including Tikal, the Cobán area, Monterrico, Chichicastenango and Lago de Atitlán. Two-day trips to Tikal, flying from Guatemala City to Flores and back, start at Q3000 per person. Two-day land tours to Copán (some including Quiriguá and Río Dulce) run around Q1140 per person. CATours (p85) offers two-day motorbike tours to Lago de Atitlán or Monterrico from Q1175.

★☆ Festivals & Events

The most exciting time to be in Antigua is **Semana Santa** (Easter), when hundreds of devotees garbed in deep purple robes bear revered icons from their churches in daily street processions in remembrance of Christ's crucifixion and the events surrounding it. Dense clouds of incense envelop the parades and the streets are covered in elaborate *alfombras* (carpets) of colored sawdust and flower petals. These fragile works of art are destroyed as the processions shuffle over them but are re-created each morning for another day of parades.

The fervor and the crowds peak on Good Friday, when an early-morning procession departs from La Merced (p65) and a late afternoon one leaves from the Escuela de Cristo. There may also be an enactment of the crucifixion in Parque Central. Have ironclad Antigua room reservations well in advance of Semana Santa, or plan to stay in Guatemala City or elsewhere and commute to the festivities.

Processions, *velaciones* (vigils) and other events actually go on every weekend through Lent, the 40-day period prior to Semana Santa. Antigua's tourist office has schedules of everything, and the booklet *Lent and Holy Week in Antigua* by Elizabeth Bell gives explanations.

🛏 Sleeping

With 140 hotels, *posadas* (guesthouses) and hostels, by Inguat's estimate, Antigua has a wide range of accommodations to suit any traveler's style or budget. Some of Antigua's midrange hotels allow you to wallow in colonial charm for a moderate outlay of cash. Finding a room is generally a simple task, with the major exception of Semana Santa, for which you should book as far ahead as possible and be prepared to pay double normal rates.

El Hostal HOSTEL $
(Map p66; ☑ 7832-0442; www.elhostal-antigua.com; 1a Av Sur 8; dm Q80, s/d without bathroom Q130/260; 🛜) Within stumbling distance of the popular Café No Sé, El Hostal is an efficiently run budget option with a bit of colonial style. Set around a cheery little patio-cafe are half a dozen neatly kept private rooms and dorms with sturdy single beds or well-spaced bunks, a few sticks of furniture and freshly painted walls with patches of exposed brick.

Posada Juma Ocag HOTEL $
(Map p66; ☑ 7832-3109; Calz de Santa Lucía Norte 13; s/d Q120/160) The seven spotless, comfortable rooms here have quality mattresses and traditional appointments including wrought-iron bedsteads, decorative ceramic masks and mirrors crafted in-house. Despite the hectic location opposite the market, it remains peaceful – especially the upstairs

rooms – with a rooftop patio and well-tended little garden. Reservations are accepted in person only.

Zoola Antigua
HOSTEL $

(Map p66; ☑7832-0364; www.zoola-antigua. com; Calle de Santa Lucía 15; dm/r incl breakfast Q75/200; �) Such was the success of its flag-ship hostel on Lake Atitlán that the Israeli-run Zoola opened an Antigua branch in 2012. The concept successfully translates to the new colonial setting: sparely furnished dorms surround an open courtyard where global travelers chill and nosh on healthy Middle-Eastern snacks beneath a rainbow canopy.

Yellow House
HOSTEL $

(Map p66; ☑7832-6646; yellowhouseantigua@ hotmail.com; 1a Calle Poniente 24; dm/d without bathroom incl breakfast Q80/190; ☺) Thought-fully designed, ecologically conscious and damn friendly, this makes a fine budget choice. Rooms vary in style and size but comfy beds, recessed lighting, and screened windows are the norm. It can get crowded with just three bathrooms downstairs, but they're kept clean and use solar-heated water. The plant-filled terrace is perfect for enjoy-ing the huge, healthy breakfast served each morning.

Hotel la Casa de Don Ismael
HOTEL $

(Map p66; ☑7832-1932; www.casadonismael.com; 3a Calle Poniente 6, Lotificación Cofiño 2a Callejón; s/d Q120/175, incl breakfast Q160/225; �) Expect to share the premises with the family at this homey, humble guesthouse, hidden down a side street and overseen by its kind, cordial namesake. Seven rustic rooms share three hot-water bathrooms, and there's a pleasant roof terrace.

Hotel Dionisio
HOSTEL $

(Map p66; ☑7832-6078; hoteldionisioantigua.net; 3a Calle Poniente Callejón 19A; dm 50, r with/without bathroom Q200/150; ☺ ☐) This is the most re-laxed of four guesthouses along a cul-de-sac between 7a Av and Calz Santa Lucía. Quirk-ily decorated rooms line up along a sunny terrace. Downstairs, there's a well-supplied kitchen and a cozy recreational nook where guests settle down to check their laptops or watch Bob Marley videos.

Black Cat Hostel
HOSTEL $

(☑7832-1229; www.blackcathostels.net; 6 Av Norte 1A; dm/d/tr Q65/160/240) Though the dorms are cramped and you can't use the kitchen, this place is always hopping, both as a hostel and at the bar out the front for the nightly happy hour. Plenty of tours are on offer, plus free movies, good local advice and a huge breakfast, included in the price.

Jungle Party Hostal
HOSTEL $

(Map p66; ☑7832-0463; www.junglepartyhostal. com; 6a Av Norte 20; dm Q60; ☐) With bar ser-vice, hammock hangouts and the famous all-you-can-eat Saturday barbecue, the Jun-gle Party has a great atmosphere, and the smiling staff know exactly what's needed by travelers.

The Terrace Hostel
HOTEL $

(Map p66; ☑7832-3463; www.terracehostel.com; 3a Calle Poniente 24; incl breakfast dm Q65, r with/ without bath Q275/200) The key feature at this fun-filled establishment is the rooftop terrace, a fabulous perch for both volcano views and Q10 Brahvas (Happy Hour starts at noon). Below deck, rooms are fairly bare but kept tidy. Don't miss the Monday pub crawl, taking off from here at 3pm.

Casa Santa Lucía No 1
HOTEL $

(Map p66; ☑7832-1386; 6a Av Norte 43; r Q183) Step back in time, down arched hallways with heavy exposed beams, to reach the well-maintained paint-dappled rooms equipped with blasting hot showers. Though the staff could be a tad more communicative, the price is right and the location is convenient, just north of La Merced.

Hotel Burkhard
HOTEL $

(Map p66; ☑7832-4316; hotelburkhard@hotmail. com; 3a Calle Oriente 19A; r Q110; ☐) Usefully located next to the excellent bar El Muro (p82), this tiny establishment has a dozen compact, fancifully decorated rooms over two levels.

Proatur
CAMPGROUND

(Map p66; ☑5978-3586; 6a Calle Poniente Final; ☐☐) ☑☑☑☑ You can park an RV or pitch a tent on the grounds of Proatur, the tourism police. There's no charge, but it's appreciated if campers contribute items such as tools or bug spray.

★ Casa Jacaranda
HOSTEL $$

(Map p66; ☑7832-7589; www.hosteljacaranda. com; 1a Calle Poniente 37; incl breakfast dm Q95, s/d without bathroom Q120/240; ☺☐) At this origi-nal hostel (not a party center), the rooms are simple but display a bit of flair. So does the airy front lounge, with plush armchairs and a mural after Klimt (except the female figure is garbed in a *huipil*). At the rear is a grassy patio under a jacaranda tree – a surprisingly tranquil retreat considering the hostel's busy location.

Casa Cristina   BOUTIQUE HOTEL $$
(Map p66; ☑7832-0623; www.casa-cristina.com; Callejón Camposeco 3A; s/d downstairs Q200/240, upstairs Q320/360; ☎) There are just a dozen rooms at this three-level hotel on a pretty backstreet near La Merced. Though rather compact, all are quaintly appointed with *típica* (traditional) bedspreads, brushed-on pastels and wood-stained furniture, and the plant-laden roof terrace makes a nice retreat. *Muy tranquilo.*

Hotel Posada La Merced   HOTEL $$
(Map p66; ☑7832-3197; www.posadalamerced antigua.com; 7a Av Norte 43A; s/d from Q265/340; ☎) Behind the big wooden doors, La Merced sports a modern interior. Rooms in the rear section have a bit more pizzazz, with *típico* weavings and colonial furniture. Bonuses include a rooftop terrace, well-appointed guest kitchen, morning coffee and gracious staff.

Hotel Casa Rústica   HOTEL $$
(☑7832-3709; www.casarusticagt.com; 6a Av Norte 8; s/d Q357/440, without bathroom Q274/323; @☎) Everything about the 'rustic house' feels right, from the lily-shaped fountain in the cobblestoned patio to the tiled tables on the sun-splashed top deck. Designed by the Tennessee-bred owner, it's also one of the few hotels in this price range to offer guests full kitchen access, not to mention a pool table and entertainment lounge. Attractively done up with regional textiles, the 14 rooms occupy two buildings on the upper level.

Under the same scrupulous ownership and similar in style, though a tad more luxurious, are the **Casa Antigua** (☑7832-9090; www.hotelcasa-antigua.com; 3a Calle Poniente 5; s/d/tr Q390/517/612; ☑@☎⛱), **Casa del Parque** (☑7832-0961; www.hotelcasadelparque. com; 4a Av Norte 5; s/d Q745/900; ☑☎⛱) and **Euro Maya** (☑7832-6298; www.hoteleuromaya. com; 4a Calle Poniente 22A; s/d incl breakfast Q590/705).

Posada Los Búcaros   BOUTIQUE HOTEL $$
(Map p66; www.hotelbucaros.com; 7a Av Norte 94; s/d Q278/358; ☑☎) West of La Merced, this converted 150-year-old residence strikes a nice balance between colonial splendor and contemporary comfort. Rooms with pastel walls and high wood-beam ceilings open on

to three lushly planted courtyards graced with *los búcaros* – semi-circular fountains that are set into the walls.

Hotel Posada San Vicente   HOTEL $$
(☑7832-3311; www.posadasanvicente.com; 6a Av Sur 6; s/d Q280/360; ☑☎) One of eight Antigua lodgings under the stewardship of a Tennessee native, this long-standing lodging a block west of the Parque Central was recently made over in contemporary colonial style. Sporting *típica* bedspreads and plenty of exposed brick and stone, the 23 rooms wrap around a lovely lily-shaped fountain; above it all, there's an inviting roof terrace.

Hotel Palacio Chico
(Casa 1940)   BOUTIQUE HOTEL $$
(Map p66; ☑7832-3895; www.hotelpalaciochico. com; 7a Av Norte 15; s/d/tr incl breakfast Q302/413/493; ☎) Though on the small side, rooms at this stylish, well-managed place are nicely decked out, with classic tile work, crafted iron bed frames and sponged on paint. Get a pedicure at the ground-level spa or catch some rays on the top deck terrace.

Las Golondrinas   APARTMENT $$
(Map p66; ☑7832-3343; lasgolondrinasapts.info; 6a Av Norte 34; s/d Q150/250; ☎) The apartment-like rooms at this tranquil complex are an excellent option for serious self-caterers. Units are set around a tree-studded garden, and all feature front terraces with tables suitable for al fresco dining. The place is run by an inveterate traveler who's climbed hundreds of volcanoes, and good weekly and monthly discounts are available.

Hotel Posada San Pedro   HOTEL $$
(Map p66; ☑7832-0718; www.posadasanpedro. net; 7a Av Norte 29; s/d/tr Q240/360/400) Somebody's restored this place with a whole lot of love and attention to detail. Rooms are spacious and well furnished and look out onto two lush patios surrounded by hanging plants.

Hotel Posada
San Pedro (3a Av)   HOTEL $$
(Map p66; ☑7832-3594; www.posadasanpedro. net; 3a Av Sur 15; s/d/tr Q240/320/360) The 10 rooms at the second San Pedro are extremely neat and inviting, with swabbed-on mustard or chocolate tones, azulejo-tiled bathrooms and cable TV. A guest kitchen, several spacious sitting rooms and two terraces with great views add to the comfortable, friendly atmosphere.

Posada de Don Valentino
HOTEL **$$**

(Map p66; ☑ 7832-0384; www.posadadonvalentino. com; 5a Calle Poniente 28; s/d/tr Q307/390/457; @ 🛜) Beyond the busy cybercafe in the entry hall is a friendly little guesthouse with spacious, cheerfully decorated rooms of varying brightness. Best of all are the three suites around the upper-level terrace.

Hotel Santa Clara
HOTEL **$$**

(Map p66; ☑ 7832-4291; www.hotelsantaclaraantigua.com; 2a Av Sur 2; s/d/tr Q291/398/477) In a quiet area south of the center, the Santa Clara boasts brilliantly restored antique chambers alongside a small courtyard, with carved-wood bedsteads and skylights set into the roof beams. Toward the rear are two levels of newer, mostly brighter rooms, with glimpses of the Iglesia de San Francisco from the upper level.

Black Cat Inn
HOSTEL **$$**

(☑ 7832-4698; blackcathostels.net; 5a Calle Poniente 11A; incl breakfast dm/s/d Q65/220/350; 🛜) This upscale version of its nearby sister hostel (p76) shares a maroon color scheme, hip global staff, laundry service and free breakfast. Rooms are larger, though (if just as haphazardly furnished), and set along a colonial corridor that opens onto a neat patio. A dozen people squeeze into the dorm.

Hotel La Sin Ventura
HOTEL **$$**

(☑ 7832-0581; www.lasinventura.com; 5a Av Sur 8; s/d/tr Q144/288/432; 🅿) Just half a block south of the Parque Central, this faux colonial palace is above an entertainment center that includes a disco and the ever-popular **Monoloco** (5a Av Sur 6, Pasaje El Corregidor) bar. The 35 pastel-tinted rooms line up along attractively tiled corridors on three levels.

Casa Santo Domingo Hotel
LUXURY HOTEL **$$$**

(Map p66; ☑ 7820-1222; www.casasantodomingo .com.gt; 3a Calle Oriente 28A; r from Q1619; 🅿 @ 🛜 🏊) 🡒 Innovatively resurrected from the remains of the sprawling Santo Domingo monastery, this is Antigua's premier lodging. The 128 rooms and suites are of an international five-star standard, while the grounds retain their colonial splendor, dotted with archaeological relics and featuring a large swimming pool, several fine restaurants, shops and five museums. The Dominican friars never had it so good. Prices go down from September to November and up during weekends.

Posada del Ángel
BOUTIQUE HOTEL **$$$**

(Map p66; ☑ 7832-5244; www.posadadelangel.com; 4a Av Sur 24A; r Q1670; 🅿 🏊) The Posada became Antigua's most celebrated B&B when Bill Clinton bedded down here in 1999. It doesn't look like much from the outside, but behind the garage door the luxury just keeps unfolding. If you didn't think it was possible to fit a swimming pool into an Antigua patio, stop by. The five rooms and two suites all have fireplaces, fresh lilies, four-poster beds and highly polished tile floors.

Mesón Panza Verde
BOUTIQUE HOTEL **$$$**

(Map p66; ☑ 7832-2925; www.panzaverde.com; 5a Av Sur 19; r/ste Q830/1370; 🅿 @ 🛜 🏊) 🡒 Possibly the ultimate in Antigua luxury, the Panza Verde is cloistered in a serene compound south of the center. The three doubles and nine lavishly appointed suites open on to private terraces amidst gardens overflowing with orchids, ferns and bamboo. Aside from its renowned restaurant (p81), the hotel features its own art gallery.

Hotel Quinta de las Flores
HOTEL **$$$**

(Map p66; ☑ 7832-3721; www.quintadelasflores. com; Calle del Hermano Pedro 6; s/d from Q520/600, bungalow Q1115; 🅿 @ 🏊) More a village than a hotel, this property on the southeastern edge of town is bursting with charms. Pebbly paths weave by stands of bird-of-paradise and African tulip trees, cobblestoned plazas with weathered colonial fountains, a good-sized swimming pool amid tropical foliage, and an open-air restaurant. There are eight large, luxurious rooms in the main building, most with a fireplace, and five more secluded 'garden rooms' with private terraces, plus five two-story *casitas,* each with two bedrooms, a kitchen and living room. Considerable discounts are offered for stays by the week.

Posada San Sebastián
GUESTHOUSE **$$$**

(Map p66; ☑ 7832-2621; snsebast@hotmail.com; 3a Av Norte 4; s/d/tr Q437/517/597; 🛜) As carpenter, antique restorer and occasional xylophone player, Luis Méndez Rodríguez is the auteur of this converted mansion. Each of the nine uniquely appointed rooms display his knack for finding and refurbishing art and furniture. Big bathrooms with tub are a bonus, as are the roof terrace, the pretty little courtyard garden, and use of a kitchen.

Hotel Convento Santa Catalina
LUXURY HOTEL $$$

(Map p66; ☑ 7832-3080; www.hotelconventosanta catalina.com; 5a Av Norte 28; s/d/tr Q664/763/863; ⓟ ⓐ) Of all the dressed-up renovations in town, this is among the most impressive. Antigua's signature arch, right outside the front door, was built for the nuns of the convent the hotel now occupies. Both the front colonial section and the rear 'modern' part are beautiful, though the latter is quieter, with picture windows facing the old convent walls across a lawn; these have good kitchenettes.

Hotel Aurora
HOTEL $$$

(Map p66; ☑ 7956-1000; www.hotelauroraantigua. com; 4a Calle Oriente 16; s/d/tr incl breakfast Q573/604/668; ⓟ ⓐ ⓢ) Dating from 1926, the Aurora has a good, old-timey feel to it. The 17 large rooms wrap around a manicured garden brimming with bougainvillea, with wicker rockers along the corridors. Breakfast (included in the price) is served in the genteelly appointed dining room.

✖ Eating

For global gourmands, Antigua is a banquet. Within 10 minutes' walk of Parque Central you can dine well and inexpensively on Italian, Belgian, French, Thai, Indian, Irish, Israeli, German, Danish, Chinese, Mexican and Salvadoran cuisines.

Saturday and Sunday evenings, tables are set up in front of Convento La Merced (p65), serving, among other snacks, chicken salad sandwiches, *rellenitos*, *enchiladas*, tamales and *chuchitos* laced with hot sauce and pickled cabbage, along with bowls of *atol blanco* (corn-based hot beverage). Talk about comfort food!

Note that most formal restaurants in Antigua whack on a 10% tip before presenting the bill. It should be itemized, but if in doubt, ask.

★ Tienda La Canche
GUATEMALAN $

(Map p66; 6a Av Norte 42; set lunch Q20) A hole in the wall if there ever was one, the restaurant, behind a 'mom and pop' store, consists of two tables with floral tablecloths. It prepares a couple of traditional options daily, such as *pepián de pollo,* a hearty chicken stew containing chunks of potato and *huizquil,* a yucca-like tuber, accompanied by a tray of thick tortillas. *Frescos,* home-squeezed fruit beverages, are served alongside.

Restaurante Doña Luisa Xicotencatl
CAFE $

(Map p66; ☑ 7832-2578; 4a Calle Oriente 12; sandwiches & breakfast dishes Q30-40; ⓢ 7am-9:30pm) Probably Antigua's best-known restaurant, this is a place to enjoy the colonial patio ambience over breakfast or a light meal. The attached bakery sells all kinds of bread and rolls; banana bread comes hot from the oven around 2pm daily.

Café Condesa
CAFE $

(☑ 7832-0038; Portal del Comercio 4; cakes & pastries Q18-26; ⓢ 7am-8pm Sun-Thu, 7am-9pm Fri & Sat) Go through the bookstore to reach this restaurant, set around the patio of a 16th-century mansion. Baked goods are the strong suit – pies, cakes, quiches, scones and housebaked whole-wheat sandwich bread. The Sunday buffet, from 9am to 1pm, a lavish spread for Q78, is an Antigua institution.

Sabe Rico
DELI $

(☑ 7832-0648; 6a Av Sur 7; sandwiches & salads Q40; ⓢ 8am-7pm Mon & Wed, 11am-3pm Tue, 8am-8pm Thu-Sat, 9am-4pm Sun) This little deli whips up tasty salads and sandwiches, using ingredients from its herb garden, as well as offering fresh-baked breads and brownies. It also sells fine wines and imported foods. Eat in one of the various salons or have a picnic.

Fernando's Kaffe
CAFE $

(Map p66; cnr 7a Av Norte & Callejón Camposeco; ⓢ 7am-7pm; ⓢ) Long a draw for coffee and chocolate mavens, this friendly corner cafe also bakes an array of fine pastries including some delightfully gooey cinnamon rolls. Beyond the counter is an inviting patio that's ideal for a low-key breakfast and linger.

Zoola Antigua
ISRAELI $

(Map p66; www.zoola-antigua.com; Calle de Santa Lucia 15; ⓢ 8am-10pm; ⓐ) The restaurant component of Zoola hostel (p76) whips up highly authentic Israeli fare. Nosh on felafel, kebabs or a *sabich* sandwich, stuffed with hummus, eggplant and salad. Seating is at low coffee tables surrounded by pillows. Friday evenings Zoola offers a buffet-style spread of salads.

Luna de Miel
CREPERIE $

(Map p66; www.lunademielantigua.com; 6a Av Norte 40; ⓢ 10am-10pm; ⓢ) Loungey Luna de Miel does dozens of variations on the classic crêpe – the *chapín* version is stuffed with avocado, cheese and fried tomatoes –

plus tropical smoothies. As if that weren't enough, the graffitied roof deck makes a remarkably relaxing place to enjoy them, then kick back with a hookah.

Y Tu Piña También
SANDWICHES **$**

(Map p66; 1a Av Sur 10B; sandwiches & salads Q30-35; ⊗ 7am-8pm Mon-Fri, 8am-9pm Sat & Sun; ⊛ ⊛ ⊛) This natural-foods cafe does healthy, sophisticated fare for foreign students on the go. There's a tempting array of sandwiches (served on whole wheat, pita or bagel), salads and crêpes. It opens early and makes for a good breakfast stop, with omelets, waffles and abundant fruit salads, plus excellent coffee.

Casa de las Mixtas
GUATEMALAN **$**

(Map p66; 3a Callejón; mains Q20-30; ⊗ breakfast, lunch & dinner Mon-Sat) For down-home Guatemalan fare with a bit of style, try this family-run operation on a quiet backstreet across from the market. Aside from its namesake snack (*mixtas* are Guatemalan-style hot dogs, wrapped in tortillas) it also serves a range of set breakfasts. Regulars make for the little terrace upstairs.

Travel Menu
INTERNATIONAL **$**

(6a Calle Poniente 14; mains Q28-32; ⊗noon-7:30pm; ⊛) Not nearly as unimaginative as the name would imply, this little bar-restaurant serves up food that you may have been craving (chow mein, curry etc) in an intimate candlelit environment. Its motto: 'small place, big portions'.

★ Caffé Mediterráneo
ITALIAN **$$**

(⊛ 7882-7180; 6a Calle Poniente 6A; mains Q90-130; ⊗lunch & dinner Wed-Mon) Here you'll find the finest, most authentic Italian food in Antigua – if not all Latin America – in a lovely candlelit setting with superb service. Hailing from Calabria, chef Francesco does a tantalizing array of salads and pasta, using seasonally available ingredients.

La Fonda de la Calle Real
GUATEMALAN **$$**

(5a Av Norte 5; mains Q70-80; ⊗ noon-10pm Tue-Sun) This restaurant, with three branches, all in appealing colonial style, has a good menu ranging from generous salads and sandwiches (Q40) to grilled meats (up to Q99). The specialty is *caldo real,* a hearty chicken soup that makes a good meal. The branch at **3a Calle Poniente 7** (⊛ 7832-0507; mains Q70-80; ⊗noon-10pm Tue-Sun) is the most attractive, with several rooms and patios.

There's another branch at **5a Av Norte 12** (mains Q70-80; ⊗ 8am-10pm).

Hector's Bistro
FRENCH **$$**

(Map p66; ⊛7832-9867; 1a Calle Poniente 9A; mains Q85-110) A hit with the expat community, this tiny salon across the way from La Merced has just a few tables, with the kitchen behind the bar. Guatemala City native Hector has garnered acclaim for his versions of beef bourguignon, grilled duck breast and so on. There's no proper sign: check the chalkboard for daily specials and the quiche of the week.

Angie Angie
ARGENTINE **$$**

(Map p66; 1a Av Sur 11A; pastas Q65-80) Equal parts Southern Cone eatery, art gallery and social club, Angie's place is always worth stopping into, if only to lounge around the tropically abundant back garden. Besides the *empanadas*, mixed grills and homemade pastas, there's a good-value set lunch. There are bonfires nightly plus live blues and jazz on weekends.

Epicure
DELI **$$**

(Map p66; 3 Av Norte 11B; sandwiches Q50-58, mains Q65-100) A good place to stock up on sandwiches for the volcano climb is this Euro-standard deli, with all kinds of gourmet items. Offers elegant open-air dining under the rear arbor.

Quesos y Vino
ITALIAN **$$**

(Map p66; ⊛7832-7785; www.quesosyvino.com; 5a Av Norte 32A, enter 1a Calle Poniente 1; pizzas Q50-120; ⊗ noon-4pm & 6-10pm Wed-Mon) This Italian-owned establishment is comprised of three rustic buildings, with a lovely outdoor patio and adjoining deli. Like the 'cheese and wine' of the restaurant's name, the food is basic and satisfying: hearty soups, well-stuffed sandwiches on homemade bread, salads and wood-fired pizzas.

Sunshine Grill
PIZZERIA **$$**

(Map p66; ⊛7832-4702; 6a Av Norte 68; pizza Q60-140; ⊗11am-11pm Wed-Mon) A friendly neighborhood joint with scribbling on the walls, a karaoke jukebox and a big screen for the game, the Grill makes amazing pizzas, just like the kind owner Edgar learned to make in New Jersey pizzerias. It also does some fine French fries.

Rainbow Café
INTERNATIONAL **$$**

(Map p66; ⊛7832-1919; 7a Av Sur 8; mains Q50-60; ⊗8am-midnight Mon-Sat, 7am-11pm Sun; ⊛) Fill up from an eclectic range of all-day breakfasts, curries, stir-fries, Cajun chicken, guacamole and more, and enjoy the relaxed patio atmosphere. Between meals, check out the bookstore, bulletin board and live music.

Jardín Bavaria
EUROPEAN $$

(Map p66; ☑7832-5904; 7a Av Norte 49; breakfast Q32, sausages Q64; ☺8am-4pm Mon & Tue, 8am-8pm Wed-Sun) This bar-restaurant has a verdant patio and spacious roof terrace, and offers a mixed Guatemalan-German menu including suckling pig and various *wursts*. Among the extensive range of brews on offer are Bavarian lagers and *hefeweizens*.

El Papaturro
SALVADORAN $$

(Map p66; ☑7832-0445; 2a Calle Oriente 4; pupusas Q28, mains Q60-95; ☺lunch & dinner) For *pupusas* (filled corn tortilla), *rellenitos* (deep-fried mashed plantains) and other Salvadoran staples, this homey spot run by natives of Guatemala's southern neighbor serves authentic dishes and good steak plates in a relaxed courtyard.

La Cuevita de Los Urquizú
GUATEMALAN $$

(Map p66; ☑4593-5619; 2a Calle Oriente 9D; lunch combo Q80; ☺lunch & dinner) Sumptuous *típico* food is the draw here, all kept warm in earthenware pots out front. Choose from *pepián* (chicken and vegetables in a piquant sesame and pumpkin seed sauce), *kaq'ik* (spicy turkey stew), *jocón* (green stew of chicken or pork with green vegetables and herbs) or other such Guatemalan favorites, and you'll get two accompaniments.

Fridas
MEXICAN $$

(Map p66; ☑7832-1296; 5a Av Norte 29; mains Q70-90; ☺lunch & dinner) Dedicated to Ms Kahlo, this bright bar-restaurant serves tasty Mexican fare and is always busy.

Bistrot Cinq
FRENCH $$$

(Map p66; ☑7832-5510; www.bistrotcinq.com; 4a Calle Oriente 7; mains Q100-150; ☺6-11pm Mon-Thu, noon-11pm Fri-Sun) Popular among the mature expat crowd, the Cinq is a faithful replica of its Parisian counterparts, offering zesty salads and classic entrees such as trout *amandine* and filet mignon. Check the blackboard for exciting nightly specials. Be sure to make it down for Sunday brunch (served from noon to 5pm). Now serving absinthe.

39 Azul
EUROPEAN $$$

(Map p66; www.39azul.com; 6a Calle Poniente 39; ☺12:30pm-3pm & 7-11pm Thu-Tue) At his elegant yet homey space, longtime Antigua restauranteur Nils Rykken combines the abundance of the tropics with European haute cuisine, resulting in such incredible creations as suckling pig confit in guava sauce and coffee-marinated lamb chops. For lunch, there's a tempting array of open-faced Danish sandwiches.

Posada de Don Rodrigo
GUATEMALAN $$$

(Map p66; ☑7832-0387; 5a Av Norte 17; mains Q135-150; ☺breakfast, lunch & dinner) The seafood crêpes, steaks and sausages have a subtle Guatemalan accent here. The real draw, though, is the setting, a gorgeous courtyard with plenty of wrought iron, blossoming flowers and tinkling fountains.

Mesón Panza Verde
FUSION $$$

(Map p66; ☑7832-2925; 5a Av Sur 19; mains Q100-165; ☺lunch & dinner Tue-Sat, dinner Mon, brunch Sun) The restaurant of the exclusive B&B (p78) dishes up divine continental cuisine in an appealing Antiguan atmosphere. There are just 10 items on the menu; the French-trained chef puts an emphasis on fresh seafood and local ingredients. Live jazz or Cuban combos perform several nights a week.

🍷 Drinking

The bar scene jumps, especially on Friday and Saturday evenings when the hordes roll in from Guatemala City for some Antigua-style revelry. While the nationwide mandate that all bars close at 1am puts a damper on things, keep your eye out for flyers advertising 'after parties', unauthorized events in people's homes. Besides the watering holes, the restaurants Fridas and Bistrot Cinq are at least as popular for the cocktails as the cuisine. Start drinking early and save: *cuba libres* and mojitos are half price between 5pm and 8pm at many bars.

To get an overview of Antigua's watering holes, join the pub crawl that embarks every Monday at 3pm from the Terrace Hostel (p76).

You can learn to move at several places around town. Both **New Sensation Salsa Studio** (Map p66; ☑4374-1391; 1a Calle Poniente 22B) and **Salsa Pasión y Ritmo** (Map p66; ☑5253-0023; salsaestaenmicorazon@hotmail.com; 6a Av Sur 11D) offer one-on-one instruction in salsa, merengue, bachata and cha-cha.

Tretto Caffé
CAFE $

(Map p66; 6a Calle Oriente 10; ☺7am-8pm) Run by a young connoisseur, this hole-in-the-wall near Santa Clara convent is the best place to savor the region's wondrous coffee, with

ANTIGUA DRINKING

beans from the acclaimed Finca Filadelfia. The cakes and pies are dandy, too.

Reilly's
PUB

(6a Av Norte 2) Antigua's Irish pub packs them in from afternoon onwards during its extended happy hour (noon to 7pm). The music is loud, the pub grub tasty and the Guinness pricey, at Q66. The Monday evening trivia quiz (7pm) is a pretty big deal.

El Muro
BAR

(Map p66; 3a Calle Oriente 19D; ⊙7-11pm Mon-Sat) In its current incarnation, this long-standing pillar of Antigua nightlife draws a mostly Guatemalan crowd with a smattering of foreign volunteers, and the vibe can turn raucous, especially on all-u-can-drink Thursdays. Resident DJs favor pulsating beats.

Café No Sé
BAR

(Map p66; cafenose.com; 1a Av Sur 11C) This downbeat little bar is a point of reference for Antigua's budding young Burroughses and Kerouacs. It's also the core of a lively music scene, with players wailing from a corner of the room most evenings. A semi-clandestine attached salon serves its own brand of mescal, 'smuggled' over from Oaxaca. After hours, just bang on the door.

Monoloco
PUB

(5a Av Sur 6) A long-time tourist hangout, the 'wacky monkey' serves up a good blend of comfort foods and local dishes, as well as ice-cold beers, in a relaxed environment.

Café Sky
BAR

(Map p66; ☑7832-7300; 1a Av Sur 15) The rooftop is deservedly popular for sunset drinks and snacks, weather permitting. Below deck, there's a candlelit tiki bar with freaky warrior outfits covering the walls.

Ocelot Bar
BAR

(4a Av Norte 3; ⊙noon-midnight) Just off the Parque Central, the Ocelot feels like a large living room, with wall-length sofas, rock posters and board games, not to mention the best-stocked bar in town. It's highly popular with the mature expat crowd; the Sunday evening pub quiz really packs them in.

Whisky Den & Coffee Bar
CAFE

(4a Av Norte 3) This little lounge highlights two great pick-me-ups. There's an all-star lineup of world whiskies and coffee produced by a local cooperative whose members take turns setting up espressos and lattes.

El Chamán
BAR

(Map p66; 7a Av Norte 2; ⊙Thu-Mon) Done up in Guatemalan pop iconography, this is one of the smarter watering holes in town, with a shrine to Maximón beside the staircase. The roof terrace venue is attached to the ruins of the Convento de San Agustín, a suitably magical backdrop for Antigua's most interesting cocktail selection, long on local spirits like Quetzalteca and *cusha*.

★ Nightlife & Entertainment

The Centro de Formación de la Cooperación Española (p65) runs thematic series of documentaries or foreign art-house films on Wednesday night.

For North American and European sports on TV, check the programs at **Reds** (Map p66; 1a Calle Poniente 3) or Monoloco.

Café No Sé, Angie Angie, the Rainbow Café and Mesón Panza Verde host folk, rock and jazz performances.

La Casbah
CLUB

(Map p66; ☑7832-2640; 5a Av Norte 30; admission Q30; ⊙8:30pm-1am Tue-Sat) This two-level disco near the Santa Catalina arch has a warm atmosphere, is reportedly gay-friendly and quite a party most nights.

La Sin Ventura
CLUB

(5a Av Sur 8; ⊙Tue-Sat) The liveliest dance floor in town is packed with Guatemalan youth toward the weekend. There's live salsa and merengue on Thursday night.

La Sala
LIVE MUSIC

(Map p66; 6a Calle Poniente 9; ⊙Tue-Sun) Crowds pour into this boisterous hall for live rock, blues or reggae – or maybe it's the cheap liquor. Bands hit the stage nightly at around 9pm.

La Peña de Sol Latino
LIVE MUSIC

(Map p66; ☑7882-4468; www.lapenaantigua.com; 5a Calle Poniente 15C) This supper club is named after its headlining band, who play their distinctive brand of Andean progressive music Wednesday to Sunday night from 7pm.

Circus Bar
LIVE MUSIC

(Map p66; www.circusbar.com.gt; 4a Calle Oriente 10; ⊙noon-midnight) On the upper level of the Casa Antigua El Jaulón shopping center, the balconied nightspot hosts flamenco sets Friday and Saturday evenings.

🛍 Shopping

Antigua's **market** (Map p66; Calz de Santa Lucía Sur) – chaotic, colorful and always busy – sprawls north of 4a Calle. The best days are the official market days – Monday, Thursday and Friday – when villagers from the vicinity roll in and spread their wares north and west of the main market building. Immediately south, the **Mercado de Artesanías** (Map p66; 4a Calle Poniente; ⊗ 8am-7pm) displays masses of Guatemalan handicrafts. While they're not at the top end of quality, you'll find colorful masks, blankets, jewelry, purses and more. Don't be afraid to bargain. The **Mercado del Carmen** (Map p66), next to the ruins of the Iglesia del Carmen, is a good place to browse for textiles, pottery and jade, particularly on weekends, when activity spills out onto 3a Av.

Several Antigua shops specialize in jade, including **La Casa del Jade** (Map p66; www.lacasadeljade.com; 4a Calle Oriente 10), **Jade Maya** (www.jademaya.com; 4a Calle Oriente 1) and **El Reino del Jade** (Map p66; 5a Av Norte 28). At La Casa del Jade and Jade Maya's **4a Calle Oriente 34 branch** (Map p66), you can visit the workshops behind the showrooms. Ask about prices at a few places before making any purchases.

Nim Po't　　　　　　　　　HANDICRAFTS
(Map p66; ☑7832-2681; www.nimpot.com; 5a Av Norte 29) This sprawling hall boasts a huge collection of Maya clothing, as well as hundreds of masks and wood carvings. The *huipiles, cortes, fajas* (waist sashes) and other garments are arranged by region, so it makes for a fascinating visit whether you're buying or not.

Centro de Arte Popular　　　　　　ART
(Map p66; 4a Calle Oriente 10; ⊗9:30am-6:30pm) Inside the Casa Antigua El Jaulón, a courtyard shopping arcade, this shop/museum displays Tz'utujil oil paintings, cedar figurines, masks and other crafts in four galleries.

**Doña María Gordillo
Dulces Típicos**　　　　　　　　FOOD
(Map p66; 4a Calle Oriente 11) This shop opposite Hotel Aurora is filled with traditional Guatemalan sweets, and there's often a crowd of *antigüeños* lined up to buy them.

Librería La Casa del Conde　　　　BOOKS
(Portal del Comercio 4) Excellent selection of Central American history and politics and nature guides in English, literature in Spanish, and Lonely Planet guides.

ℹ Orientation

Antigua's focal point is the broad Parque Central; few places in town are more than 15 minutes' walk from here. Compass points are added to the numbered Calles and Avs, indicating whether an address is *norte* (north), *sur* (south), *poniente* (west) or *oriente* (east) of the Parque Central, though signage is frustratingly sparse.

Three volcanoes provide easy reference points: Volcán Agua is south of the city and visible from most points within it; Volcán Fuego and Volcán Acatenango rise to the southwest (Acatenango is the more northerly of the two).

Another useful Antigua landmark is the **Arco de Santa Catalina** (5a Av Norte), an arch spanning 5a Av Norte, 2½ blocks north of the Parque Central, on the way to La Merced church.

ℹ Information

DANGERS & ANNOYANCES

Antigua generally feels safe to walk around but muggings do occur, so don't let your guard down completely. This holds doubly true after the bars close at 1am, when muggers are on the lookout for inebriated visitors. After 10pm, consider taking a taxi back to your lodging, especially if you're female.

Pickpockets work the busy market, doing overtime on paydays at the middle and end of the month. December (bonus time) brings a renewed wave of robberies.

Some of the more remote hiking trails have been the scene of muggings, though stepped-up police patrols have reduced the likelihood of such incidents in recent years. If you're planning on hiking independently to any of the volcanoes, check with Proatur about the current situation.

EMERGENCY

Proatur (☑5578-9835; operacionesproatur@inguat.gob.gt; 6a Calle Poniente Final; ⊗24hr) The helpful tourism assistance agency has its headquarters on the west side of town, three blocks south of the market. If you're the victim of a crime, they'll accompany you to the national police and assist with the formalities, including any translating that's needed. Given advance notice, they can provide an escort for drivers heading out on potentially risky roads.

INTERNET ACCESS

Aside from an abundance of affordable cybercafes, wi-fi is available in restaurants, cafes and elsewhere.

Funky Monkey (5a Av Sur 6, Pasaje El Corregidor; per hr Q10; ⊗8am-12:30am) Inside Monoloco; open the latest of Antigua's cybercafes.

Roy.com (1a Av Sur 21; per hr Q8)

MEDIA

The Antigua-based **Revue Magazine** (www. revuemag.com) runs about 90% ads, but has reasonable information about cultural events. It's available everywhere.

La Cuadra (www.lacuadraonline.com), published by Café No Sé (p82), presents the gringo-bohemian perspective, mixing politics with irreverent commentary. Pick up a copy at the cafe.

MEDICAL SERVICES

Centro Médico Santiago Apóstol (☑7832-0884; Calle del Manchén 7)

Farmacia Ivori Select (☑7832-1559; 6a Av Norte 19; ☺24hr) Pharmacy.

Hospital Nacional Pedro de Bethancourt (☑7831-1319) A public hospital in San Felipe, 2km north of the center, with emergency service.

Hospital Privado Hermano Pedro (☑7832-1190; Av de la Recolección 4) Private hospital that offers 24-hour emergency service and accepts foreign insurance.

MONEY

Banco Agromercantil (4a Calle Poniente 8; ☺9am-7pm Mon-Fri, 9am-5pm Sat & Sun) Changes US dollars and euros (cash or traveler's checks). It also houses a branch of Western Union.

Banco Industrial (BI; 5a Av Sur 4; ☺9am-7pm Mon-Fri, 9am-1pm Sat) Has a reliable ATM and changes US dollars. Another useful BI ATM is inside Café Barista, on the northwest corner of Parque Central.

Citibank (cnr 4a Calle Oriente & 4a Av Norte; ☺9am-4:30pm Mon-Fri, 9:30am-1pm Sat) Changes US dollars and euros.

Visa & MasterCard ATM (Portal del Comercio) Facing Parque Central.

POST

DHL (☑7832-3718; 6a Calle Poniente 16) Offers door-to-door service.

Post Office (cnr 4a Calle Poniente & Calz de Santa Lucía) Opposite the market.

TELEPHONE & FAX

Most internet cafes offer cut-rate international calls, though Skype calls may be even cheaper. If you plan to be around a while, consider purchasing a local cell phone; you can pick one up at **La Bodegona** (Map p66; 5a Calle Poniente 32; ☺7am-8pm).

Conher (☑5521-2823; 4a Calle Poniente 4; per hr Q10) All-purpose communications center, offering printing, scanning and CD burning.

TOURIST INFORMATION

Inguat (☑7832-0787; info-antigua@inguat. gob.gt; 5a Calle Oriente 11; ☺8am-5pm Mon-Fri, 9am-5pm Sat & Sun) The tourist office has free city maps, bus information and helpful, bilingual staff.

TRAVEL AGENCIES

Numerous agencies offer international flights, shuttle minibuses, tours to interesting sites around Antigua and elsewhere in Guatemala, and more.

Adventure Travel Center (www.adventravel guatemala.com; 5a Av Norte 25B) Offers daily city walking tours, visiting a variety of convents, ruins and museums. Also does interesting tours of assorted villages and coffee or macadamia plantations.

Atitrans (☑7832-3371; www.atitrans.com; 6a Av Sur 8)

LAX Travel (☑7832-2674; laxantigua@intel nett.com; 3a Calle Poniente 12) International flight specialist.

National Travel (☑7832-8383; antigua@ nationalgua.com; 6a Av Sur 1A) Offers one-way flights, including student and teacher fares.

Onvisa Travel Agency (☑5226-3441; onvi-satravel@hotmail.com; 6a Calle Poniente 40) Operates shuttles to Copán and elsewhere.

Rainbow Travel Center (www.rainbowtravel center.com; 7a Av Sur 8) Student and teacher air fares are their specialty.

WEBSITES

Head to www.lonelyplanet.com/guatemala/antigua for planning advice, author recommendations, traveler reviews and insider tips.

❶ Getting There & Around

BUS

Buses from Guatemala City, Ciudad Vieja and San Miguel Dueñas arrive and depart from a street just south of the market, alongside the Mercado de Artesanías. Buses to Chimaltenango, Escuintla, San Antonio Aguas Calientes and Santa María de Jesús go from a lot behind the main market building. If you're heading out to local villages, go early in the morning and return by mid-afternoon, as bus services drop off dramatically as evening approaches.

To reach highland towns such as Chichicastenango, Quetzaltenango, Huehuetenango or Panajachel, take one of the frequent buses to Chimaltenango, on the Interamericana Hwy, then catch an onward bus. Making connections is easy, as many folks will jump to your aid as you alight from one bus looking for another. But stay alert and watch your pack.

Chimaltenango (Q5, 45 minutes, every 10 minutes from 5am to 6:30pm)

Ciudad Vieja (Q3, 20 minutes, every 15 minutes from 3am to 8pm) Take a San Miguel Dueñas bus.

Escuintla (Q7, one hour, every half hour from 5am to 4pm)

Guatemala City (Q9, one hour, every few minutes from 5am to 7:30pm) A Pullman service (Q45, 10am and 4pm) by **Litegua** (☑ 7832-9850; www.litegua.com; 4a Calle Oriente 48) runs from its office at the east end of town.

Panajachel (Q36, 2½ hours) One Pullman bus daily at 7am by Transportes Rebulli, departing from Panadería Colombia on 4a Calle Poniente, half a block east of the market.

San Antonio Aguas Calientes (Q3.50, 30 minutes, every half hour from 6am to 8pm)

SHUTTLE MINIBUS

Numerous travel agencies and tourist minibus operators offer frequent shuttle services to places tourists go, including Guatemala City and its airport, Panajachel and Chichicastenango. They cost more than buses, but they're comfortable and convenient, with door-to-door service at both ends. These are some typical one-way prices:

Chichicastenango Q140
Cobán Q250
Copán (Honduras) Q235
Guatemala City Q80
Monterrico Q100
Panajachel Q120
Quetzaltenango Q210

Pin down shuttle operators about departure times and whether they require a minimum number of passengers.

CAR & MOTORCYCLE

To park in Antigua, you're supposed to have a *marbete* (label) hanging from your rearview mirror, or risk a fine. Purchase these from traffic cops for Q10.

If you're planning to drive out of town on a reportedly hijack-prone road (such as to Panajachel via Patzún), you may request an escort from Proatur (p83) by emailing them at least 72 hours in advance. There's no fee other than the escort's expenses.

CATour (☑ 7832-9638; www.catours.co.uk; 6a Calle Oriente 14) Rents motorcycles from Q10/45 per hour/day and offers motorcycle tours from Q140.

Guatemala Renta Autos (☑ 2329-9030; www.guatemalarentacar.com; 4a Av Norte 6)

Tabarini (☑ 7832-8107; www.tabarini.com; 6a Av Sur 22)

TAXI

Taxis and *tuk-tuks* wait where the Guatemala City buses stop and on the east side of Parque Central. An in-town taxi ride costs around Q25; *tuk-tuks* are Q10. Note that *tuk-tuks* are not allowed in the center of town; you'll have to hike a few blocks out to find one.

AROUND ANTIGUA

Jocotenango

This village just northwest of Antigua provides a window on to a less self-conscious, less Unesco-authorized version of Guatemalan life than does central Antigua. Though Jocotenango is now plagued by traffic, the church stands proudly at the center as it has for centuries, with its peach facade graced by baroque columns and elaborate stuccowork, facing a garden aflame with African tulip trees. The town is known for its processions during Lent – or perhaps more so as the birthplace of Latin American pop star Ricardo Arjona.

A sprawling coffee plantation outside Jocotenango, **Centro Cultural La Azotea** (☑ 7831-1120; info@centroazotea.com; Calle del Cementerio Final; adult/child Q50/25; ☺ 8:30am-5pm Mon-Fri, 8:30am-3pm Sat) features a complex of three museums. The **Museo del Café** covers the history and process of coffee cultivation; the **Casa K'ojom** holds a superb collection of traditional Maya musical instruments, masks, paintings and other artifacts; and the **Rincón de Sacatepéquez** displays the multicolored outfits and crafts of the Antigua valley.

You can roam the coffee plantation itself, which is crisscrossed by nature trails. A shop sells quality coffee, local crafts and Maya instruments, and a restaurant offers good, moderately priced Guatemalan food. There is also the **Establo La Ronda**, where you can take a one-hour morning horse ride around the grounds (minimum two persons; ring the museum two days ahead).

Free minibuses to La Azotea leave from Antigua's Parque Central hourly from 9am to 3pm, with the last one returning at 4:40pm.

El Hato

High in the hills above Jocotenango is **Earth Lodge** (☑ 5664-0713; www.earthlodgeguatemala.com; dm Q50, s/d/tr cabin Q100/170/195) 🍃. The 40-acre spread set on a working avocado farm has views of the Panchoy valley and volcanoes that are truly mesmerizing. Developed and overseen by an affable Canadian-American couple, the eco-friendly retre

EXPLORE MORE OF ANTIGUA

While Antigua itself is pretty much well-trodden territory from end to end, there are plenty of little villages just outside of town just begging to be explored:

Santa María de Jesús At the foot of Volcán Agua, holds a major market on Sundays.

San Juan del Obispo Has a wonderful colonial church and panoramic views of Antigua.

San Felipe An artisans' village with some of the finest jade, silver and ceramic work in the area.

San Lorenzo El Tejar Worth the 25-minute ride northwest to soak in its popular hot springs.

Pastores Ground zero for leatherwork. This is the place to come for handmade cowboy boots and stock whips.

Cerro Alux (www.cerroalux.com) Near the village of San Lucas Sacatepéquez, is a hilltop ecopark with interpretive trails and good bird-watching opportunities.

offers plenty to do: hiking, bird-watching, Spanish lessons, a *chuj* (Maya sauna) or just hanging in a hammock.

Accommodation is in comfortable A-frame cabins, an eight-bed dorm and a couple of fabulous tree houses. Lip-smacking, nutritious vegetarian food is served with a slew of avocado-based fare at harvest time (January and July). A portion of the profits buys supplies for the village school.

To get there, your best bet is to call at least a day in advance to see if the lodge can pick you up from Antigua (Q30 per person with two passengers). Otherwise, a bus leaves infrequently from in front of the Iglesia de la Candelaria on 1a Av Norte in Antigua for Aldea El Hato. From there it's a 25-minute walk – any villager can give you directions – just ask for 'los gringos'.

Ciudad Vieja & Around

ⓘ Getting There & Around

A good way to tour this area is by bicycle. Head out of Antigua along the Ciudad Vieja road south of the market. It's a 4km ride along a moderately busy road to Ciudad Vieja. Take 4a

Calle west through the restored colonial part of town. Back at the main road, turn left. When you reach the cemetery, go right, following signs for San Miguel Dueñas. From there, it's about a 10-minute ride downhill to the Valhalla Experimental Station, on the left side. The road goes on to San Miguel Dueñas. Coming into that town, you'll go over a small bridge. Bear right, then turn right at the sign for San Antonio Aguas Calientes. This road, unpaved for much of the way, winds for the next 5km through coffee *fincas* (plantations), hamlets and vegetable fields. Arriving in San Antonio, turn right at the communal wash basins to reach the main plaza.

Leaving town, go around the left side of the church, then head left up 2a Calle. From there, it's a steep climb but you're rewarded with breathtaking views of the village. Beyond the Finca Los Nietos coffee plantation, you'll reach the RN-14 Hwy. Turn left there and go 2km, taking the second right onto a dirt road. This will take you back to the Ciudad Vieja–Antigua road, where a left turn leads you back into town.

Ciudad Vieja

Seven kilometers southwest of Antigua along the Escuintla road is Ciudad Vieja (Old City), near the site of the first capital of the Captaincy General of Guatemala. Founded in 1527, it met its demise 14 years later when Volcán Agua let loose a flood of water that had been penned up in its crater. The water deluged the town with tons of rock and mud, leaving only the ruins of La Concepción church.

The actual site of the former capital is a bit to the east at **San Miguel Escobar**; Ciudad Vieja was populated by survivors of the flood. The pretty church on the main square has an impressive stucco-work facade, though it's about two centuries newer than the plaque by the door boasts it to be.

The NGO Niños de Guatemala, which runs a school for low-income kids above the town, leads alternative **tours** (adult/child Q200/100; ⊙ Tue, Thu & Fri) of Ciudad Vieja that really get beneath the surface of the community. A half-day tour takes you through the poorer section of town, then focuses on two of the town's principal industries: 'chicken bus' rebuilding and coffin-making. At the end of the tour, local chefs prepare you a traditional meal.

Your best bet for accommodation in Ciudad Vieja is **Hotel Santa Valentina** (☏7831-5044; 2a Av 0-01, Zona 3; s/d Q150/250; ℗), offerring rooms with private bathroom and TV.

Valhalla Experimental Station

Between San Antonio and Ciudad Vieja, near the village of San Miguel Dueñas, is this **macadamia farm** (⌨ 7831-5799; www.exvalhalla.net; ☺ 8am-4:30pm) 🍃 raising 300 species of the remarkable nut. You can tour this organic, sustainable agriculture project and sample nuts, oils and cosmetics made from the harvest. Be sure to sample the macadamia-nut pancakes, served amid lush tropical foliage.

Finca los Nietos

Java junkies in this neck of the woods should investigate this **coffee plantation** (⌨ 7831-5438; www.fincalosnietos.com; ☺ 8-11am Mon-Fri) for a tour and a taste. The hour-long tour (Q50 per person, minimum two people) answers all your nitty-gritty coffee questions, from how seedlings are propagated to how beans are roasted.

Phone for an appointment and mention if you want to roast your own beans (minimum 2.5kg or 5lb). The *finca* is 7km from Antigua, just off the bus route to San Antonio Aguas Calientes: you go through Ciudad Vieja and San Lorenzo El Cubo, then get off at the crossroads known as 'El Guarda,' just before the road goes downhill to San Antonio. Walk two blocks to the right (toward Volcán Agua) until you come to a wall with a mosaic sign; ring the bell to enter.

San Antonio Aguas Calientes

This tranquil village surrounded by farmed volcanic slopes is noted for its textiles, and the Mercado de Artesanías (handicrafts market) stands prominently beside the town hall. Inside, women work on hip-strap looms and on the upper level there's an exhibit of traditional outfits, with examples from all over Guatemala. Ceremonial *huipiles*, embroidered on both sides, can go for as much as Q2800 here.

San Juan Comalapa

Set on the side of a deep ravine, this artisans' village 16km north of Chimaltenango is best known for its tradition of primitive folk painting. It's a relatively modern town, founded by the Spanish when they amalgamated several Kaqchiquel communities.

Comalapa gained its reputation during the 1950s when native son Andrés Curruchich (1891–1969) rose to fame for his primitive paintings of village life and his works ended up on display as far away as San Francisco, Dallas and Detroit. Considered the father of Guatemalan primitivist painting, he was awarded the prestigious Order of the Quetzal in the 1960s. Several pieces are displayed at the Museo Ixchel (p47) in Guatemala City – though sadly, the artist remains more seriously collected abroad than in his native land.

In Comalapa, you can visit the house Curruchich was born in, on the main street. His daughter and granddaughter will show you around and there is some information about the artist. His legacy lives on as some of his offspring and other villagers took up the brush and started working in a similar primitive style. Scenes of traditional festivals and ritual dances predominate in the paintings of Comalapa, though you'll also see some highland landscapes. Several galleries around the plaza show and sell their work.

Several *comedores* (cheap eateries) line the plaza, dishing out decent grub. If you want to stay the night, your best bet is **Hotel Pixcayá** (⌨ 7849-8260; 0 Av 1-82; s/d Q70/140, without bathroom Q40/80; 🅿).

Buses (Q13, 45 minutes, every half hour) run from Chimaltenango; minibuses and pickups leave when full.

Santiago Sacatepéquez & Sumpango

All Saints' Day (November 1) is best known in Guatemala as the time when families visit cemeteries to spruce up the tombstones of loved ones with poignant floral designs, but locals add another quirk to this seasonal ritual. It's also the time of the **Feria del Barrilete Gigante** (Festival of the Giant Kite). The biggest parties happen in Santiago Sacatepéquez and Sumpango, about 20km and 25km north of Antigua respectively. Fabricated weeks ahead of the event, these kites are giants. Made from tissue paper with wood or bamboo braces, and with guide ropes as thick as a human arm, most are more than 13m wide, with intricate, colorful designs that combine Maya cosmology and popular iconography. In Santiago they're flown over the cemetery, some say to communicate with the souls of the dead. Kids fly their own small kites right in the cemetery, running around the gravestones. Food and knickknack vendors sell their wares next to the graveyard. In Sumpango it's a somewhat more formal affair (and the crowds are more manageable), with the kites lined up at one end of a football field and bleachers set up at the other. Judges rank the big flyers according to size, design, color, originality and elevation. Part of the fun is watching the crowd flee when a giant kite takes a nose dive!

Various travel agencies run day trips from Antigua to Santiago Sacatepéquez on November 1 (charging around Q200 per person including lunch and an English-speaking guide), though you can easily get there on your own by taking any Guatemala City-bound bus and getting off with the throngs at the junction for Santiago. From here, take one of the scores of buses covering the last few kilometers. The fastest way to Sumpango is to take a bus to Chimaltenango and backtrack to Sumpango; this will bypass all of the Santiago-bound traffic, which is bumper to bumper on fair day.

The Highlands

Best Places to Hike

➡ Nebaj & the Ixil Triangle (p127)

➡ Todos Santos Cuchumatán (p152)

➡ Banks of Lago de Atitlán (p97)

➡ Laj Chimel (p125)

➡ Volcán Santa María (p131)

Best Markets

➡ Chichicastenango (p118)

➡ Almolonga (p143)

➡ San Francisco El Alto (p146)

➡ Santa Cruz del Quiché (p123)

➡ Panajachel (p102)

Why Go?

Guatemala's most dramatic region – Los Altos – stretches from Antigua to the Mexican border. Traditional values and customs are strongest here. Maya dialects are spoken far more widely than Spanish, and over a dozen distinct groups dwell within the region, each with its own language and clothing, perhaps most vividly displayed in the weekly markets of Chichicastenango and San Francisco El Alto. This is where indigenous tradition blends most tantalizingly with Spanish, and it is common to see Maya rituals taking place in front of and inside colonial churches.

Most travelers spend a spell at volcano-ringed Lago de Atitlán. West of the lake stands Guatemala's second city, Quetzaltenango. Northward spread the Cuchumatanes mountains, where indigenous life follows its own rhythms amidst fantastic mountain landscapes. For hikers, this is the promised land.

When to Go

Though pleasant weather can be enjoyed year-round up in the highlands, between May and October abundant rains fall so be prepared for some chilly, damp conditions then. If you're up for trekking the Ixil Triangle or scaling Volcán Santa María, trails tend to be less muddy and volcano visibility best from November to April. Key events to plan a trip around include Quetzaltenango's annual blast (late September or early October); devil-burning ceremonies in Chichicastenango (early December); and folk saint Maximón's spring move in Santiago Atitlán (Holy Week). Try to be in Todos Santos Cuchumatán on November 1, when the normally sedate town hosts a no-holds-barred celebration with rowdy horse races and all-male marimba dancing.

The Highlands Highlights

1 Soar over, dive under or relax by sublime **Lago de Atitlán** (p91)

2 Hunt for *huipiles* (embroidered tunics) and other Maya weavings at vibrant indigenous markets in **Chichicastenango** (p118) and **San Francisco El Alto** (p146)

3 Polish your Spanish and hike volcanoes in and around **Quetzaltenango** (p130)

4 Take in the stunning Cuchumatanes scenery and village life of the Ixil Triangle around **Nebaj** (p126)

5 Mingle with the Maya in **Todos Santos Cuchumatán** (p151), **San Mateo Ixtatán** (p154) and other remote villages

ℹ️ Getting Around

Public transport connections between towns and villages are easy and cheap, accommodation is plentiful, and people are generally welcoming and helpful, making it a cinch to get around.

The meandering Interamericana (Hwy 1), running 345km along the mountain ridges between Guatemala City and the Mexican border at La Mesilla, passes close to all of the region's most important places, and countless buses roar up and down it all day, every day. Two key intersections act as major bus interchanges: Los Encuentros for Panajachel and Chichicastenango, and Cuatro Caminos for Quetzaltenango. If you can't find a bus going to your destination, simply get one to either of those points. Transfers are usually seamless, with not-too-frustrating waiting times and locals who are ready to help travelers find the right bus.

Travel is easiest in the morning and, for smaller places, on market days. By mid- or late afternoon, buses may be difficult to find. Further off the beaten track you may be relying more on pickups than buses for transportation.

Microbuses – large vans that depart as soon as they fill with passengers – are becoming the dominant mode of transport along highland routes such as Santa Cruz del Quiché–Nebaj and Chichicastenango–Los Encuentros. They're preferred by many locals for their convenience and are only slightly more expensive than buses.

Otherwise, vans run by tour operators shuttle tourists between the major destinations of the region and beyond. They travel faster, more comfortably and more expensively than buses.

LAGO DE ATITLÁN

Nineteenth-century traveler/chronicler John L Stephens, writing in *Incidents of Travel in Central America,* called Lago de Atitlán 'the most magnificent spectacle we ever saw,' and he had been around a bit. Today even seasoned travelers marvel at this spectacular environment. Fishermen in rustic crafts ply the lake's aquamarine surface, while indigenous women in multicolored outfits do their washing by the banks where trees burst into bloom. Fertile hills dot the landscape, and over everything loom the volcanoes, permeating the entire area with a mysterious beauty. It never looks the same twice. No wonder many outsiders have fallen in love with the place and made their homes here.

Though volcanic explosions have been going on here for millions of years, today's landscape has its origins in the massive eruption of 85,000 years ago, termed Los

WANT MORE?
....

Head to **Lonely Planet** (www.lonely planet.com/guatemala/the-highlands-lago -de-atitlan) for planning advice, author recommendations, traveler reviews and insider tips.

Chocoyos, which blew volcanic ash as far as Florida and Panama. The quantity of magma expelled from below the earth's crust caused the surface terrain to collapse, forming a huge, roughly circular hollow that soon filled with water – the Lago de Atitlán. Smaller volcanoes rose out of the lake's southern waters thousands of years later: Volcán San Pedro (today 3020m above sea level) about 60,000 years ago, followed by Volcán Atitlán (3537m) and Volcán Tolimán (3158m). The lake today is 8km across from north to south, 18km from east to west, and averages around 300m deep, though the water level has been on the rise since 2009.

Around AD 900, when the Maya highland civilization was in decline, the region was settled by two groups that had migrated from the Toltec capital of Tula in Mexico, the Kaqchiquel and Tz'utujil. The latter group settled at Chuitinamit, across the way from the present-day village of Santiago Atitlán, while the former occupied the lake's northern shores; this demographic composition persists to this day. By the time the Spanish showed up in 1524, the Tz'utujil had expanded their domain to occupy most of the lakeshore. Pedro de Alvarado exploited the situation by allying with the Kaqchiquels against their Tz'utujil rivals, whom they defeated in a bloody battle at Tzanajuyú. The Kaqchiquels subsequently rebelled against the Spanish and were themselves subjugated by 1531.

Today, the main lakeside town is Panajachel, or 'Gringotenango' as it is sometimes unkindly called, and most people initially head here to launch their Atitlán explorations. Santiago Atitlán, along the lake's southern spur, has the strongest indigenous identity of any of the major lake towns. Up the western shore, the town of San Pedro La Laguna has a reputation as a countercultural party center. On the north side, San Marcos La Laguna is a haven for contemporary new-agers, while Santa Cruz La Laguna and Jaibalito, nearer to Panajachel, are among the lake's most idyllic, picturesque locales.

Lago de Atitlán

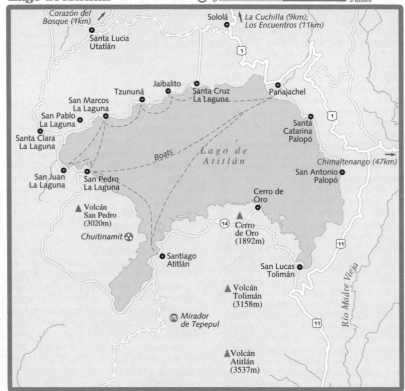

The lake is a three-hour bus ride west from Guatemala City or Antigua. There is an ersatz town at the highway junction of Los Encuentros, based on throngs of people changing buses here. From La Cuchilla junction, 2km further west along the Interamericana, a road descends 12km southward to Sololá, and then there's a sinuous 8km descent to Panajachel. Sit on the right-hand side of the bus for views of the lake and its surrounding volcanoes.

The lake faces daunting environmental challenges. In late 2009, during an unusually warm spell, a massive bloom of cyanobacteria covered the turquoise waters of Lago de Atitlán with malodorous sheets of brownish sludge.

❶ Dangers & Annoyances

Although most visitors never experience any trouble, robberies have occurred along the paths that run around Lago de Atitlán. The security situation is forever changing – some months it's OK to walk between certain villages, then that route suddenly becomes dangerous. It's best to check with Proatur (p102) about the current situation.

Sololá

POP 43,412 / ELEV 1978M

There was a Kaqchiquel town (called Tzoloyá) here long before the Spanish showed up. Sololá's importance comes from its location on trade routes between the *tierra caliente* (hot lands of the Pacific Slope) and *tierra fría* (the chilly highlands). All the traders meet here, and Sololá's **market** (⊙ Tue, Fri & Sun) is one of the most vivid in the highlands. On market mornings the plaza next to the cathedral is ablaze with the colorful costumes of people from surrounding villages and towns. Displays of meat, vegetables, fruit, homewares and clothing are neatly arranged in every available space, with tides of buyers ebbing and flowing around the vendors. Elaborate stands are stocked with brightly colored yarn for making the traditional costumes you see around you. Friday sees the most activity.

On Sunday mornings the officers of the traditional *cofradías* (religious brotherhoods) parade ceremoniously to the cathedral.

All buses between Panajachel and Los Encuentros stop at Sololá. It's Q3 and 15 minutes to either place from Sololá.

Panajachel

POP 23,534 / ELEV 1595M

The busiest and most built-up lakeside settlement, Panajachel ('Pana' to pretty much the entire country) has developed haphazardly and, some say, in a less than beautiful way. Strolling the main street, Calle Santander, crammed with cybercafes, travel agencies, handicraft hawkers and rowdy bars, dodging noisome *tuk-tuks* all the way, you may be forgiven for supposing this paradise lost.

A hike down to the lakeshore, though, will give you a better idea why Pana attracts so many visitors. Aside from the astounding volcano panorama, the town's excellent transportation connections, copious accommodations, varied restaurants and thumping nightlife make it a favorite destination for weekending Guatemalans.

Several different cultures mingle on Panajachel's dusty streets. *Ladinos* (people of mixed indigenous and European heritage) and gringos control the tourist industry. The Kaqchiquel and Tz'utujil Maya from surrounding villages come to sell their handicrafts to tourists. Tour groups arrive by bus. This mix makes Pana a curiously cosmopolitan crossroads in an otherwise remote, rural vicinity. All of this makes for a convenient transition into the Atitlán universe – but to truly experience the beauty of the lake, most travelers venture onward soon after arrival.

◎ Sights

Museo Lacustre Atitlán MUSEUM
(Calle Santander; admission Q35; ☉ 8am-6pm) Inside the Hotel Posada de Don Rodrigo, this museum has displays on the history of the Atitlán region and the volcanic eruptions that created its landscape, plus a collection of ancient artifacts recovered from the lake. A new section of the museum covers Samabaj, an ancient ceremonial center discovered at the bottom of the lake near Cerro de Oro.

WORTH A TRIP

IXIMCHÉ

The remnants of the Kaqchiquels' 15th-century capital stand some 15km due east of Lago de Atitlán. The 'palaces' and temples uncovered here are modest in scale but ensconced in a serene, park-like setting. Iximché remains an important ceremonial site for indigenous pilgrims, who visit the area to perform magic rituals, burning liquor, paraffin or sticks of wood in front of the pyramids to ward off illness or bring down enemies.

K'icab the Great, leader of the Kaqchiquels, relocated his capital here in 1463 from its previous location near the K'iche' Maya stronghold of K'umarcaaj. At that time, the Kaqchiquel were at war with the K'iche', and the natural defences of the new location, a flat promontory surrounded by ravines, served them well. The Spanish, who arrived in 1524, set up their first Guatemalan headquarters here, forming an alliance with the resident Kaqchiquels against their K'iche' enemies. However, the Europeans' demands for gold and other loot soon put an end to their alliance with the Kaqchiquel, who were defeated in an ensuing guerrilla war.

Entering the archaeological site, visit the small **museum** (closed Monday) on the right, then continue to the four ceremonial plazas, which are surrounded by temple structures up to 10m high, and ball courts. Some structures have been uncovered; on a few the original plaster coating is still in place.

The ruins are reached from the town of Tecpán, off the Interamericana. Buses traveling east from La Cuchilla junction can drop you at the turnoff; from there it's about a 1km walk (or, if you're lucky, a short ride on an urban bus) to the center of town. 'Ruinas' microbuses to the site (Q5, 10 minutes) leave from near Tecpán's main plaza every 15 minutes till 4pm. The last bus back leaves the site no later than 4:30pm.

Reserva
Natural Atitlán
(200m)
13

Sololá (7km);
Los Encuentros (19km)

San Lucas
Tolimán (24km)

Market
37

Town Hall

Calle del Campanario

Callejón Don Tino

Calle de la Navidad

35

Calle El Amate

16
29
3

40

Av Los Árboles

Calle Rancho Grande (Calle del Balneario)

Calle Frutales

See Enlargement

6

i

21

46

48

36
34

6

Calle Santander

26

Calle Principal (Calle Real)

Calle del Chalí

Calle del Embarcadero

43
45
32
44

41

Av Los Árboles

38

30

Calle Principal (Calle Real)

f

47

Calle Santander

Main Bus
Stop

100 m
0

200 m
0.1 miles
0
0

N

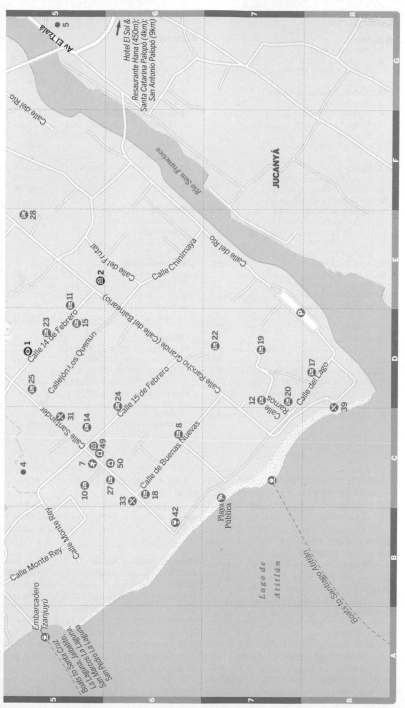

Hotel El Sol &
Resaurante Hana (450m);
Santa Catarina Palopó (4km);
San Antonio Palopó (9km)

AV EL Tzalá
● 5

Calle del Rio

Río San Francisco

JUCANYÁ

Calle del Rio

Calle Chinimaya

Calle del Frutal

🏛 28

🏛 2

11
15

23
🏛 14 de Febrero

◎ 1
Calle 14 de Febrero

Callejón Los Quenun

Calle Rancho Grande (Calle del Balneario)

Calle 15 de Febrero

🏛 22

🏛 19

🏛 25

🏛 24

Calle Santander

31
14

49
50

7

🏛 10

27
33 ✕

18

42

8

Calle de Buenas Nuevas

12
Calle Ramos

🏛 20

Calle del Lago

17

39 ✕

Playa Pública

● 4

Calle Monte Rey

Calle Monte Rey

Embarcadero
Tzanjuyú

Boats to Santa Cruz
La Laguna, Jaibalito,
La Laguna, San Marcos La Laguna,
San Pedro La Laguna

Lago de
Atitlán

Boats to Santiago Atitlán

Panajachel

◉ Sights

⊕ Activities, Courses & Tours

⊜ Sleeping

⊗ Eating

⊙ Drinking & Nightlife

⊛ Entertainment

⊜ Shopping

La Galería   GALLERY
(☑ 7762-2432; panagaleria@hotmail.com; Calle Rancho Grande; ⊙ 9am-noon & 2-6pm Wed-Mon) FREE Overflowing with art by Guatemalan painters and sculptors, this gallery functions as both an exhibit space and cultural center, hosting lectures, films and occasional concerts. Started in 1971 by Nan Cuz, an indigenous Guatemalan painter who grew up in Germany, the gallery has canvases by some 500 painters. Among them are a number of the hallucinatory landscapes that garnered Cuz recognition in the European art world.

Casa Cakchiquel   ARTS CENTER
(Calle 14 de Febrero; ⊙ 7:30am-7pm; ☎) Pana's new cultural center started life as one of the first hotels on the lake, built by a Swedish countess in 1948. Now it holds a radio station, cafe, indigenous crafts shop, cinema and a gallery of photos and postcards of Atitlán in simpler times, when steamboats plied the lake.

During its 1950s heyday such illustrious guests as Ingrid Bergman, Aldous Huxley and Ernesto 'Che' Guevara chatted around the fireplace.

Reserva Natural Atitlán   PARK
(☑ 7762-2565; www.atitlanreserva.com; adult/child Q45/25; ⊙ 8am-5pm) A former coffee plantation being retaken by natural vegetation, this reserve is 200m past the Hotel Atitlán on the northern outskirts of town. It makes a good outing on foot or bicycle. You can leisurely walk the main trail in an hour: it leads up over swing bridges to a waterfall, then down to a platform for viewing local spider monkeys. You may see *pisotes* (coatis), relatives of the raccoon with long snouts and long, furry tails.

The reserve includes a butterfly enclosure and herb garden, an interpretive center, zip lines, a small shade coffee plantation and an aviary. For longer stays, there are some excellent rooms with private decks, and a campground.

Activities

Cycling, Hiking & Kayaking

Lago de Atitlán is a cycling and hiking wonderland, spreading across hill and dale. But before setting out for any hike or ride, make enquiries about safety with Proatur (p102) and keep asking as you go. Volcán San Pedro climbs with numerous operators in town cost around Q350, including boat transport, taxi to the trailhead, entry fees and guide. Kayaks are available for rent (Q25 per hour) from the pier at the foot of Calle del Rancho Grande.

Roger's Tours   CYCLING
(☑ 7762-6060; www.rogerstours.com; Calle Santander) This outfit rents quality mountain bikes for Q30/120 per hour/day and leads a variety of cycling tours (Q440 per person including helmet, guide and lunch). One tour travels by boat from Panajachel to the village of Tzununá, then proceeds by bike west via dirt trail to San Marcos La Laguna and paved road to San Pedro La Laguna, finally returning to Pana by boat. Another tour hits the villages on the lake's east side.

Paragliding

'Too much of a good thing' is how Aldous Huxley described Lago de Atitlán in his 1934 travel work *Beyond the Mexique Bay*. That applies well to the experience of soaring over the Lago de Atitlán with parachute-like wings, enjoying a falcon's view of the lake's rippling expanse and the villages that tumble down from green hills to its shores. The lake has become a center for paragliding enthusiasts and several operators provide tandem flights, with passengers seated in a canvas chair attached to the flyer's harness so they're free to take photos or simply gaze in amazement at the panorama below.

Realworld Paragliding   GLIDING
(☑ 5634-5699; realworldparagliding.jimdo.com; Calle Santander, Centro Comercial San Rafael) This is the most reliable outfit around. Christian is a patient, personable English-speaking guide who's made more than 500 tandem flights. If wind conditions are right, you'll take off from above Santa Catarina Palopó and land at Panajachel. The charge is Q700

for the flight, which takes 20 minutes to an hour, depending on the wind and passenger preferences.

In optimal conditions, you can fly as high as 700m above the lake (2300m above sea level). You might also do a few acrobatics, approaching the cliffs to pick up dynamic winds that lift you up like a wave.

Courses

Panajachel has a niche in the language-school scene. Two well-organized schools are **Jardín de América** (☑ 7762-2637; www.jardindeamerica.com; Calle del Chalí) and **Jabel Tinamit** (☑ 7762-6056; www.jabeltinamit.com; cnr Av de Los Árboles & Callejón Las Armonías). The former is set amidst ample gardens while the latter is in the center of town. Four hours of one-on-one study five days per week, including a homestay with a local family, will cost around Q1500 per week. Jabel Tinamit also offers courses in Kaqchiquel and Maya weaving.

Tours

If you're pressed for time, a boat tour of the lake, stopping at a few villages, is a fine idea. Boats leave the Playa Pública quay daily at 8:30am and 9am for tours to San Pedro La Laguna (where you stop for about 1½ hours) and Santiago Atitlán, returning at 3pm and 3:30pm respectively. The earlier tour also takes in San Antonio Palopó, the later one San Marcos La Laguna; they cost Q100 and Q150 respectively. Travel agencies offer more expensive tours (around Q540 per person), which may include weaving demonstrations, visits to the shrine of Maximón in Santiago, and so on.

The women's empowerment organization Oxlajul B'atz' (p102) offers day tours (Q240) of Panajachel and other lakeside villages with visits to its member weaving cooperatives.

Posada Los Encuentros   TOUR
(☑ 7762-2093; www.losencuentros.com; Callejón Chotzar 0-41) Offers educational tours to lakeside villages, focusing on such topics as Maya medicine, Tz'utujil oil painting and organic coffee cultivation. A half-day tour is Q320 to Q475 per person with minimum four participants, less with a larger group. The guide, Richard Morgan, is a scholar of Maya history and culture and longtime lake resident. Hiking tours and volcano climbs are also offered.

✮ Festivals & Events

The **festival of San Francisco de Asís**, October 4, is celebrated with massive drinking and fireworks in Panajachel. On September 14, the day before **Independence Day**, torch-bearing athletes run in marathons throughout the country, but the tradition is celebrated with special fervor in Panajachel, where it all started in 1957. Early that morning schoolchildren from different villages arrive in buses to visit the lake; around noon, each group of kids gets a torch and runs back home. The main event, though, is the marathon from Guatemala City to Panajachel. The runners arrive in Pana's main square around midnight, heralded by cheering crowds, marimbas and fireworks displays.

🛏 Sleeping

Budget travelers will rejoice at the profusion of family-run *hospedajes* (guesthouses). They're simple – perhaps two rough beds, a small table and a light bulb in a bare room – but cheap. The pricier ones offer generous discounts for longer stays.

Midrange lodgings are busiest on weekends. From Sunday to Thursday you may get a discount, likewise if you're planning on staying for longer than four days. Many establishments raise rates during July, August, Semana Santa and the Christmas–New Year holidays.

★ Hotel Larry's Place   HOTEL $
(☑7762-0767; Calle 14 de Febrero; s/d Q100/150; 🅿) Set back from the road behind a wall of vegetation, Larry's Place offers good-sized, cool rooms in a sylvan setting. Furnishings are tasteful, ceilings high and the balconies welcome. No TV or internet, but who needs 'em anyway?

Mario's Rooms   HOTEL $
(☑7762-2370; www.mariosrooms.com.gt; Calle Santander; s/d incl breakfast Q100/160, without bathroom Q60/120; @) Among the best in the budget category, Mario's scrupulously maintained rooms are arranged on two floors facing a plant-filled courtyard. It's in the middle of everything but somehow remains low-key, with helpful staff.

Hospedaje Casa Linda   HOTEL $
(☑7762-0386; Callejón El Capulin; r Q100, s/d without bathroom Q49/85) Spotless little rooms surround a lush garden at this tranquil family-run establishment down a lane off Calle Santander. Upstairs units get a nice breeze and the balconies are good for afternoon siestas.

Villa Lupita   HOTEL $
(☑5054-2447; Callejón Don Tino; s/d Q50/100, without bathroom Q40/75) Family-run Lupita is great value for staying in the town center. Facing a plaza below the church, it's removed from the tourist drag. Accommodations are basic but spiffy, and a flower-filled patio with broken-tile mosaic softens the environment.

Hospedaje El Viajero   HOTEL $
(☑7762-0128; www.hospedajeelviajero.com; s/d/tr Q80/150/220; 🛜) El Viajero is at the end of a short lane off lower Calle Santander, making it quiet and peaceful yet near everything. Nothing fancy here but the rooms are spacious and bright and there's plenty of balcony seating. You can use the kitchen, and there's free drinking water.

Hospedaje García   HOTEL $
(☑7762-2187; Calle 14 de Febrero; s/d Q80/160, without bathroom Q60/110) Located on a side street off Santander, this is a sprawling, airy place with an affable manager and numerous rooms of varying shape and size. Some of the upper-level units are very good with huge bathrooms and balconies looking out onto the patio.

Mini Hotel Riva Bella   BUNGALOW $
(☑7762-1348; Calle Principal 2-21; s/d Q130/180; 🅿) These neat two-room bungalows are attractively spread amid park-like grounds studded with coffee plants, right off the smog-choked main drag. Clean and modern units sport huge bathrooms.

Hotel Posada Viñas del Lago   HOTEL $
(☑7762-0389; Playa Pública; s/d/tr Q75/125/175; 🅿🛜) Steps from the lakefront, this garishly painted lodging is managed by a Kaqchiquel extended family whose activities are on full view. Mattresses sag and water outages are common but the lake views make up for it, particularly from units 21 to 23.

Hotel Tzutujil   HOTEL $
(☑7762-0102; www.panajachel.com/tzutujil.htm; Calle Rancho Grande; s/d 75/125) Almost hidden down a narrow alley through cornfields is this solitary structure with balconies, arched windows and a spiral staircase to a roof terrace. Though it could use an upgrade – or

just a fresh coat of paint – it still makes a nifty budget retreat.

★Posada Los Encuentros   LODGE $$

(☑7762-1603; www.losencuentros.com; Callejón Chotzar 0-41; s/d Q240/320, with kitchen Q400/475; @🛜) Just across the river is this 'ecocultural B&B,' featuring seven cozy rooms in a relaxed home, plus a volcanically heated pool, medicinal plant garden, sunning terrace and fitness center. Owner Richard Morgan is happy to share his encyclopedic knowledge of the lake and offers cultural tours of the area.

Hotel Primavera   HOTEL $$

(☑7762-2052; www.primaveratitlan.com; Calle Santander; s/d/tr Q240/320/400; 🛜) This stylish, German-owned hotel near Pana's main intersection just feels right. Ten large rooms with plant-filled window boxes, soft lighting and handsome fabrics face a wood-decked patio, making for a relaxing atmosphere.

Hotel Posada K'amol B'ey   HOTEL $$

(☑7762-0215; www.kamolbey.com; Final Calle Ramos; s/d Q150/250, bungalow Q550 for five persons; P🛜) At the end of the row of hotels leading up from the Playa Pública, the 'king of the road' is about the tidiest and quietest option, and everything works. Two levels of spacious units with quality beds face a clipped suburban lawn where hummingbirds flit around. At the rear are three bungalows, each with two rooms and kitchens.

Hotel El Sol   HOTEL $$

(☑7762-6090; www.hotelelsolpanajachel.com; Carretera a Santa Catarina Palopó; dm/s/d/tr Q50/150/200/250; P🛜) Along the road to Santa Catarina, about a 15-minute walk or lightning *tuk-tuk* ride outside Pana, this modern hostel is a slice of Japan. Hailing from Hiroshima, owner Kazuomi and family prepare sushi (p101) and offer a Japanese tub fed by natural hot springs. Accommodations include an eight-bed dorm and five private rooms.

Hotel Utz-Jay   HOTEL $$

(☑7762-0217; www.hotelutzjay.com; Calle 15 de Febrero 2-50; s/d/tr incl breakfast Q225/310/395; P@🛜) These eight adobe cottages stand amidst lovely gardens bursting with heliconia, orange trumpet and ferns. Rooms are decorated with traditional fabrics and have cozy porches out front. Good breakfasts are available and there's a *chuj* (traditional Maya sauna).

Posada de los Volcanes   HOTEL $$

(☑7762-0244; www.posadadelosvolcanes.com; Calle Santander 5-51; s/d Q300/360) Sharing the property with its own travel agency, this chalet-style lodging has lovely wood-paneled rooms redolent of pine. On the 4th floor, you'll be rewarded with your own private terrace, suitable for kicking back with cocktails and surveying the lakescape.

Hotel Montana   HOTEL $$

(☑7762-0326; Callejón Don Tino; s/d Q150/250; P) Down a narrow street near the church, the Montana is an old-fashioned establishment with wonderful plant-laden balconies. Choose a room on the upper level for brilliant views of the mountainside through large windows.

Hospedaje Sueño Real   HOTEL $$

(☑7762-0608; suenorealhotel@hotmail.com; Calle Ramos; s/d Q150/225; P@🛜) Better than most of the budget options along this lane, the Sueño Real has cheerfully decorated, if cramped, rooms with TV and fan. The best are the upstairs triples, opening on a plant-festooned, lakeview terrace.

Hotel Utz Rajil   HOTEL $$

(☑7762-0303; gguated@yahoo.com; Calle 14 de Febrero; s/d/tr Q125/200/275) A modern, three-story hotel with large, well-maintained rooms and quality furniture, the Utz Rajil (Kaqchiquel for 'good deal') features cool balconies for photo ops of the street activity below. (Don't expect to get any sleep past 6am, though.)

Hotel Playa Linda   HOTEL $$

(☑7762-0097; www.hotelplayalinda.com; Calle del Lago, Playa Pública; s/d/tr Q200/350/400; P⛱) The rambling Playa Linda has 17 good-sized rooms with fireplaces, and welcoming owners and staff. Rooms 1 to 5 have the best lake views, with large balconies from which to enjoy them. The gardens out front are a fecund fantasy of blooming roses and squawking parrots.

Bungalows El Aguacatal   BUNGALOW $$

(☑7762-1482; www.atitlandonmoises.com; Calle las Buenas Nuevas; 4-person bungalow with/without kitchen Q550/450; P) The decor may seem drab, but these concrete bungalows, each equipped with two bedrooms (two beds each) and salon, are a good deal for groups. They're kept tidy and stand in a peaceful spot quite near the lake.

Hotel Atitlán
LUXURY HOTEL **$$$**

(☑ 7762-1441; www.hotelatitlan.com; Finca San Buenaventura; r incl breakfast Q1400; [P] [@] [🛜] [☒]) A coffee plantation for much of the 20th century, this estate was remade as Pana's loveliest hotel in the 1970s. Located on the lake shore 1.5km northwest of the town center, it's a rambling, semi-colonial affair surrounded by manicured tropical gardens.

The 65 rooms all have lake-facing balconies; decorations go heavy on religious imagery, wood carvings and wrought iron. A restaurant, bar and lakefront pool with killer volcano views ensure you'll never want to leave the premises.

Hotel Posada de Don Rodrigo
HOTEL **$$$**

(☑ 7832-9858; www.posadadedonrodrigo.com; Calle Santander; s/d Q870/964, with lake view 964/1060; [P] [☒]) Down by the lakeside, the landscaped grounds here hold many delights – squash courts, a swimming pool with water slide, a couple of saunas and a fine museum. Large rooms are decorated in colonial style and open onto the lawn. Breakfast is served on the fabulous lakeview terrace.

Hotel Dos Mundos
HOTEL **$$$**

(☑ 7762-2078; www.hoteldosmundos.com; Calle Santander 4-72; s/d/tr incl breakfast Q400/560/720; [P] [☒]) Italian-owned Dos Mundos stands toward the lake end of busy Calle Santander but its installations are set well away from the street. The 22 cottage-style rooms are set around tropical gardens with a palm-fringed pool, all decked out with attractive woven bedspreads.

Rancho Grande Inn
HOTEL **$$$**

(☑ 7762-2255; www.ranchograndeinn.com; Calle Rancho Grande; s/d incl breakfast from Q360/545; [P] [🛜] [☒]) Founded in the 1940s, the Rancho Grande has a dozen rooms, suites and *cabañas* in German country-style villas amid manicured lawns dotted with fruit trees. Rates include a filling breakfast featuring original pancakes and homegrown honey and coffee. Best of all, there's bar service in the swimming pool until 9pm.

✖ Eating

Near the south end of Calle del Lago, an agglomeration of thatched-roof restaurants crowds the lakefront. All serve lake *mojarra* (bream, Q75) and black bass (Q100), with skinny, bow-tied youths taking your order. **Restaurante El Atitlán** (Calle del Lago; black

bass Q100; ☺ 8am-9pm), the last one on the left, offers the best quality and variety.

Another obvious choice for cheap meals are the myriad taco and fried chicken stalls that proliferate along Calle Santander every afternoon and evening. You might try the appropriately named Humo en Tus Ojos, last spotted near the intersection of Calles Principal and Santander; this is where the cops eat.

For food shopping, there's the **Despensa Familiar** (Calle El Amate), at the north end of Calle El Amate.

Deli Jasmín
ORGANIC **$**

(☑ 7762-2585; Calle Santander; items Q25-45; ☺ 7am-6pm Wed-Mon) This tranquil garden restaurant serves a range of healthy foods and drinks to the strains of soft classical music. Breakfast is served all day, and you can buy whole-wheat or pita bread, hummus or mango chutney to take away.

Chero's Bar
SALVADORAN **$**

(Av Los Árboles; pupusas Q9; ☺ 12:30pm-1am Tue-Sat) Usefully located amidst the Zona Viva, Chero's can get pretty lively, with beer-drinking patrons gathering around simple shiny wood tables as *tuk-tuks* zip by. Behind the bar Carmen slaps out irresistible cheese tortillas known as *pupusas*, filled with beans or the exotic spinach-like herb *chipilín*, and served with the customary pickled cabbage and salsa.

Deli Llama de Fuego
ORGANIC **$**

(☑ 7762-2586; Calle Santander; items Q25-45; ☺ 7am-10pm Thu-Tue) Offering a variety of healthy food and drink, this natural-foods haven revolves around a *llama de fuego* tree (African tulip).

Fuentes de Vida
GUATEMALAN **$**

(lunch Q15) This is the largest of a group of cook stalls at the rear of the market building, near the pork vendors in a bright courtyard surrounded by tall trees. They offer half a dozen menu options daily, all of which come with beans, tortillas and a fiery salsa made from dried red chilies.

Las Chinitas
ASIAN **$**

(Calle Santander, Plaza Los Patios; ☺ lunch & dinner; [☑]) Indonesian-run Las Chinitas has a pan-Asian menu – miso, Singapore salad, stir frys and pot stickers, as well as changing *menú del día* choices with tofu and shiitake mushrooms. Dining is under the open-air dome of the Centro Comercial El Patio.

Ristorante La Lanterna   ITALIAN $$
(Calle Santander 4-72; mains Q80; ⊙7am-3pm & 6-10pm) Part of the Hotel Dos Mundos, this Italian restaurant makes its own pasta and stocks an impressive range of wines from the motherland. The adjacent cafe makes a mean espresso from Guatemala's prized beans. Bonus: you're welcome to use the hotel swimming pool if you eat here.

Guajimbo's   STEAKHOUSE $$
(Calle Santander; mains Q50-90; ⊙7:30am-11pm) This Uruguayan grill serves up generous helpings of steak, sausage and chicken dishes with vegetables, salad, garlic bread and rice or boiled potatoes. Vegetarians can enjoy tofu kebabs. You won't leave hungry.

El Patio   GUATEMALAN $$
(☑7762-2041; Plaza Los Patios, Calle Santander; mains Q35-65; ⊙7am-10:30pm) This is a locally popular joint for lunch; the front terrace makes an obvious meeting place. Try to make it for Monday lunch when everyone chows down on *caldo de res* (chunky broth), served with all the trimmings.

Resaurante Hana   JAPANESE $$
(Carretera a Santa Catarina Palopó, Barrio Jucanyá; mains Q60) The restaurant of Hotel El Sol caters to the hotel's largely Japanese clientele with raw tuna dipped in ginger soy sauce (Q60), various sushi dishes (Q60) and tempura shrimp roll

Café Bombay   VEGETARIAN $$
(☑7762-0611; Calle Santander; mains Q45; ⊙11am-10pm Wed-Mon; ☑) This cozy joint plays up the international angle, with creative vegetarian dishes from 14 countries: everything from spinach lasagne to miso to curries, and there's even a veggie version of that Guatemalan classic *pepián* (hearty chicken stew with a piquant sesame-and-pumpkin-seed sauce) served with veggies, rice and *chuchito* (a small tamal).

Restaurante Casablanca   EUROPEAN $$
(☑7762-1015; Calle Principal; mains Q55-96; ⊙11am-11pm) Easily spotted at the top end of Calle Santander by its magical mystery mural, this restaurant run by the German honorary consul features fondues, steaks and pastas of a Euro standard. There are airy dining rooms both upstairs and down, plus an excellent bar.

Atlantis   SANDWICHES $$
(Calle Principal; mains Q40-60; ⊙7:30am-midnight; ☎) This cafe-bar serves up excellent submarines (Q35) alongside pizzas, pastas and tofu burritos. The back garden is the place to be on a balmy night.

Chez Alex   EUROPEAN $$$
(☑7762-2052; www.primaveraatitlan.com; Calle Santander, Hotel Primavera; mains Q100-200; ⊙lunch & dinner) Some of Pana's finest cuisine is served here, with plenty of European influence. After a meal of mussels in white wine sauce or rack of lamb, kick back with a Habana cigar.

⏻ Drinking & Entertainment

Panajachel's miniature Zona Viva (party zone) focuses on Av Los Árboles.

Apart from the following venues, check out what's going on at **La Palapa** (Calle Principal).

Crossroads Café   CAFE
(☑5292-8439; www.crossroadscafepana.com; Calle del Campanario 0-27; ⊙9am-1pm & 2:30am-6pm Tue-Sat) Bay area native Mike Roberts has made Panajachel a major crossroads for coffee aficionados. When he's not roasting beans or working the Cimbali at his hole-in-the-wall cafe near the center of town, Mike spends his time combing the highlands for small estate coffees to add to his roster, now starring the flavorful San Pedro volcanic.

Sunset Café   BAR
(cnr Calles Santander & del Lago) This open-air lounge at the end of Calle Santander is the place to enjoy those phantasmagoric volcano sundowns. In high season, there's live music nightly.

Chapiteau   CLUB
(Av Los Árboles; minimum Q20) This strobe-lit disco-bar is the anchor of Pana's little Zona Viva. Check out the phantasmagoric marquee before you cross the threshold.

El Aleph   DJS
(Av Los Árboles) DJs keep the multitudes moving here with a spirited mix of reggaetón, merengue, electronica and salsa.

Pana Rock Café   LIVE MUSIC
(☑7762-2194; panarockcafe.com; Calle Santander) Like a Hard Rock by the lake, this lively little pub hosts plugged-in bands nightly from 9pm. It's big with Guatemala City youth, who settle in for the evening with a *cubetazo* (bucket of beer) or two.

Circus Bar
LIVE MUSIC

(☎7762-2056; Av Los Árboles; ⏰noon-midnight) Behind the cowboy swinging doors, Circus Bar has a cabaret atmosphere, with live music nightly from 8:30pm to 11pm. Flamenco, folk or marimbas nicely complement the cozy atmosphere, as do the substantial list of imported liquors, Q10 cocktails and good pizza.

Salomon's Porch
CLUB

(☎7762-6032; www.porchdesalomon.org; Calle Principal, Centro Comercial El Dorado; ⏰noon-10pm Tue-Sat; ☎) A coffee house inside a shopping center, Salomon's Porch hosts a variety of activities, from billiards to movies to live music, often by foreign visiting artists. And for something completely different, there's a 'worship gathering' every Sunday at 4pm (with free coffee).

🛍 Shopping

Some travelers prefer the Pana shopping scene to the well-known market at Chichicastenango (p118) because the atmosphere is lower key. Calle Santander is lined with booths, stores and complexes that sell (among other things) traditional Maya clothing, jade, Rasta berets with built-in dreadlocks, colorful blankets, leather goods and wood carvings. Otherwise, head for the traditional market building in the town center, busiest on Sundays when every square meter of ground alongside is occupied by vendors in indigenous garb.

Comerciales de Artesanías Típicas Tinamit Maya
HANDICRAFTS

(⏰7am-7pm) Be sure to browse the many stalls of this extensive handicrafts market, which has an impressive variety. Booths also adorn the beach end of Calle Santander.

Oxlajuj B'atz'
HANDICRAFTS

(Thirteen Threads; www.thirteenthreads.org; Calle 14 de Febrero) Supporting an NGO for the empowerment of indigenous women, this fair-trade shop features naturally dyed rugs, handbags, hand-woven goods and beaded jewelry.

La Señora de Cancuén
CLOTHING

(☎7762-2602; Calle Santander) Displays the innovative clothing of Guatemalan designer Ana Kayax, produced by a cooperative of indigenous weavers.

Libros del Lago
BOOKS

(Calle Santander) Excellent stock of books in English and other languages on Guatemala, the Maya and Mesoamerica, plus maps and Latin American literature in English.

The Book Store
BOOKS

(Calle Santander, Centro Comercial El Patio) Eclectic selection of fiction and non-fiction run by a well-read gringo; also features a lending library.

ℹ Orientation

Most buses stop at the intersection of Calle Principal and Calle Santander, the main road to the lake with a plethora of lodgings and other tourist-oriented businesses. Calle Principal continues 400m to 500m northeast to the town center, where you'll find the daily market (busiest on Sunday and Thursday), church, town hall and a further smattering of places to sleep and eat.

ℹ Information

EMERGENCY

Proatur (Programa Asistencia al Turista; ☎5874-9450; proatur.solola@gmail.com; Calle Rancho Grande; ⏰9am-5pm) Tourist police.

INTERNET ACCESS

MayaNet (Calle Santander, Centro Comercial El Patio)

MEDICAL SERVICES

The nearest hospital is at Sololá.

Pana Medic (☎4892-3499; drzulmashalom@hotmail.com; Calle Principal 0-72) Clinic run by an English-speaking doctor.

MONEY

Banco de América Central (Calle Santander, Centro Comercial San Rafael; ⏰9am-5pm Mon-Fri, 9am-1pm Sat) ATM; Visa, American Express and MasterCard cash advances; US dollars exchanged.

Banco Industrial (Calle Santander, Comercial Los Pinos; ⏰9am-4pm Mon-Fri, 9am-1pm Sat) Visa/MasterCard ATM

POST

DHL (Calle Santander, Edificio Rincón Sai) Courier service.

Get Guated Out (☎tel/fax 7762-0595; gguated@yahoo.com; Av Los Árboles, Comercial El Pueblito) English-speaking outfit that can ship your important letters and parcels by air freight or international courier.

Post Office (cnr Calles Santander & 15 de Febrero)

TOURIST INFORMATION

Inguat (☎2421-2953; info-pana@inguat.gob.gt; Calle Principal 0-87; ⏰9am-1pm & 2-7pm Tue-Sat) This tourist office is over the traffic-jammed intersection of Calle Principal and Av Los Árboles. The English-speaking director provides a wealth of information.

TRAVEL AGENCIES

Many of Panajachel's full-service travel agencies are scattered along Calle Santander. These establishments offer trips, tours and shuttle services to other destinations around Guatemala.

Atitrans (☑7762-0146; www.atitranspanajachel.com; Calle Santander; ⊗8am-8pm) Trips, tours and shuttle services.

Eternal Spring (☑7762-6043; eternalspring_conexiones@hotmail.com; Calle Santander) Shuttles to San Cristóbal de Las Casas, Mexico.

Servicios Turísticos Los Volcanes (☑7762-0244; www.posadadelosvolcanes.com; Calle Santander 5-51) Inside Posada Los Volcanes.

ℹ Getting There & Away

BOAT

Passenger boats for Santiago Atitlán (35 minutes) depart from the Playa Pública (public beach) at the foot of Calle Rancho Grande. All other departures leave from the **Embarcadero Tzanjuyú**, at the foot of Calle del Embarcadero. Frequent canopied *lanchas* (small motorboats) go counterclockwise around the lake, with direct and local service to San Pedro La Laguna. The local services stop in Santa Cruz La Laguna (15 minutes), Jaibalito, Tzununá, San Marcos La Laguna (30 minutes), San Juan La Laguna and San Pedro La laguna (45 minutes). The last boat departs around 7:30pm. To San Lucas Tolimán, there are five boats daily between 8:30am and 5:30pm.

One-way passage to San Pedro, Santiago or San Lucas costs Q25 (though local inhabitants are charged less). *Lanchas* are also available for private hire from the Playa Pública or Embarcadero Tzanjuyú: expect to pay around Q400 to San Pedro La Laguna.

BUS

Panajachel's **main bus stop** is at the junction of Calles Santander and Principal, immediately west of the Centro Comercial El Dorado. **Café La Parada** (Centro Comercial El Dorado; ⊗6am-7pm; 🕾), inside the little shopping center, can give you the general picture on bus schedules. Departures – approximately and subject to change – are as follows:

Antigua A direct Pullman bus (Q45, 2½ hours, 146km) by Transportes Rébuli departs at 11am Monday to Saturday. Or take a Guatemala City bus and change at Chimaltenango.

Chichicastenango Six buses (Q20, 1½ hours, 37km) depart between 6:30am and 6pm daily. Or take any bus heading to Los Encuentros and change buses there.

MOVING ON?

For tips, recommendations and reviews, head to shop.lonelyplanet.com to purchase a downloadable PDF of the Chiapas chapter from Lonely Planet's *Mexico* guide.

Ciudad Tecún Umán (Mexican border) By the Pacific route (220km), take a bus to Cocales and change there; by the highland route (204km), transfer at Quetzaltenango.

Cocales (Carretera al Pacífico) Buses en route from Chichicastenango to Nueva Concepción stop at Cocales (Q15, 2½ hours, 65km), passing through Pana five times daily between 5:45am and 3pm.

Guatemala City Eight departures daily (3½ hours, 150km) from 4:30am to 4:45pm. The 11am departure is a Pullman (Q45), the rest are chicken buses (Q35). Or take a bus to Los Encuentros and change there.

Huehuetenango (3½ hours, 140km) Take a bus to Los Encuentros then wait for a Huehue- or La Mesilla–bound bus. Or catch one heading to Quetzaltenango, alight at Cuatro Caminos and change buses there. There are buses at least hourly from these junctions.

Los Encuentros Take any bus heading towards Guatemala City, Chichicastenango, Quetzaltenango or the Interamericana (Q6, 35 minutes, 20km).

Quetzaltenango Six buses daily (Q25, 2½ hours, 90km), starting at 5:30am, the last leaving at 1pm (3pm on Sunday). Or take a bus to Los Encuentros and change there.

Sololá Frequent direct local buses (Q3, 15 minutes, 8km). Or take any bus heading to Guatemala City, Chichicastenango, Quetzaltenango or Los Encuentros.

SHUTTLE MINIBUS

Tourist shuttle buses take half the time of buses, for several times the price. You can book at a number of travel agencies on Calle Santander. The **Microbuses y Taxis San Francisco booth** (☑7762-0556; Calle Principal) at the main bus station also sells shuttle-bus seats. Typical one-way fares: Antigua Q120; Chichicastenango Q55; Guatemala City Q200; San Cristóbal de Las Casas, Mexico Q275, Quetzaltenango Q200.

Around Panajachel

Southeast of Pana, 5km and 10km respectively along a winding road, lie the lakeside hamlets of Santa Catarina Palopó and San Antonio Palopó. (The name 'Palopó is a

Spanish-Kaqchiquel amalgam referring to a type of fig tree that grows here.) Compared with nearby Pana, the Palopós feel sublimely remote, with narrow streets paved in stone blocks and adobe houses with roofs of thatch or tin. Many villagers, both men and women, go about their daily activities clad in traditional outfits, and these are good places to look for the luminescent indigo weavings you see all around Lago de Atitlán. Also out here is a surprising little clutch of midrange and top-end places to stay.

Pickups to both Santa Catarina and San Antonio leave about every half-hour from Calle El Amate in Panajachel, near its intersection with Calle Principal. It takes 20 minutes to Santa Catarina (Q3) and 30 minutes to San Antonio (Q5). The last pickup back to Pana leaves San Antonio about 6pm.

Santa Catarina Palopó

POP 4976 / ELEV 1663M

On weekends and holidays young textile vendors line the path to the lakeside at Santa Catarina Palopó with their wares, and on any day you can step into wooden storefronts hung thick with bright cloth.

In stark contrast to its humble surroundings stands **Villa Santa Catarina** (✆7762-1291; www.villasdeguatemala.com; r/ste Q975/1430; P☀), a luxury spread with an elegant restaurant, pool fringed by palm trees and sumptuous gardens. The 38 spacious and simply furnished rooms sport tasteful weavings and cool adobe walls. The two suites (and rooms 23 to 27, partly) face across the lake to Volcán San Pedro.

San Antonio Palopó

POP 4035 / ELEV 1773M

San Antonio Palopó is a remote and captivating hillside village where entire families tend their terraced fields in traditional garb – women in indigo-striped *huipiles* (embroidered tunics), dark blue *cortes* (long skirts) and sparkly headbands, men in traditional wool skirts. At the top, a gleaming white church forms the center of activity. About 150m down the path to the right, the **Tienda Candelaria** houses a weaving cooperative where women produce shawls, *huipiles* and *tocoyales* (headdresses) on backstrap looms and get a fair price for them.

At **Hotel Terrazas del Lago** (✆7762-0157; www.hotelterrazasdellago.com; s/d/tr Q180/240/310; P☎), a magical and affordable retreat, 15 attractive stone-walled rooms climb the hillside, with small terraces and hammocks. Good inexpensive meals (Q45 to Q75) are served on the lakefront deck with views straight across to Volcán Tolimán.

San Lucas Tolimán

POP 21,109 / ELEV 1962M

Further around the lake from San Antonio Palopó, but reached by a different, higher-level road, San Lucas Tolimán is busier and more commercial than most lakeside villages. Set at the foot of the dramatic Volcán Tolimán, it's a coffee-growing town and a transportation point on a route between the Interamericana and the Carretera al Pacífico (Hwy 2). Market days are Sunday, Tuesday and Friday. Atypically not standing on the town's plaza but along the street to the lakefront is the 16th-century **Parroquia de San Lucas** parish church. The parish, aided by Catholic missionaries from Minnesota and volunteers from North America and Europe, has been active in redistributing coffee-plantation land, setting up a fair-trade coffee cooperative and founding a women's center, a clinic and a reforestation program. For visits to the cooperative and information on volunteering, contact the **parish office** (✆7722-0112; www.sanlucasmission.org).

Down by the waterfront, **Hotel Don Pedro** (✆7722-0028; Final de Calle Principal; s/d/tr Q70/130/190; P) is made entirely of stone and rough-hewn timber beams. The unfinished construction feels like a medieval inn, and the relaxed restaurant/bar (meals Q40 to Q60) sports the same motif.

Hotel Tolimán (✆7722-0033; www.hoteltoliman.com; Calle Principal Final; s/d Q324/566; P☎☀) is a low-key resort on the site of a former coffee-processing plant, with 20 colonial-style rooms and suites in cottages around an *amate* tree. A restaurant overlooks a fountain-fed pool amid landscaped grounds leading down to the lakeshore.

Santiago Atitlán

POP 50,583 / ELEV 1606M

Across the lake from Panajachel, on an inlet between the volcanoes of Tolimán and San Pedro, lies Santiago Atitlán, the largest of the lake communities, with a strong indigenous identity. Many *atitecos* (as its people are known) cling to a traditional Tz'utujil Maya lifestyle. Women wear purple-striped skirts and *huipiles* embroidered with colored birds and flowers, while a few older men still wear white-striped embroidered pants. The town's *cofradías* maintain the syncretic traditions and rituals of Maya Catholicism. There's a large art and crafts scene here, too. Boat-building is a local industry, and rows of rough-hewn *cayucos* are lined up along the shore. The best days to visit are Friday and Sunday, the main market days, but any day will do.

It's the most workaday of the lake villages, home to Maximón (mah-shee-*mohn*), who is ceremonially moved to a new home on May 8 (after Semana Santa). The rest of the year, Maximón resides with a caretaker, receiving offerings. He changes house every year, but he's easy enough to find by asking around.

The Tz'utujil had been in this area for generations when the Spanish arrived, with their ceremonial capital at Chuitinamit, across the inlet. Santiago was established by Franciscan friars in 1547, as part of the colonial strategy to consolidate the indigenous population. In the 1980s, left-wing guerrillas had a strong presence in the area, prompting the Guatemalan army to kill or disappear hundreds of villagers.

⊙ Sights

Iglesia Parroquial
Santiago Apóstol   CHURCH
The formidable parish church was built by the Franciscans in the mid-16th century. A memorial plaque just inside the entrance on your right commemorates Father Stanley Francis Rother, a missionary priest from Oklahoma. At the far end of the church stand three colonial altarpieces that were renovated between 1976 and 1981 by brothers Diego Chávez Petzey and Nicolás Chávez Sojuel.

Beloved by the local people, Father Rother was murdered by ultrarightists in the parish rectory next door in 1981; the bedroom where he slept remains open to visitors. Along the walls of the church are wooden statues of the saints, each of whom has new clothes made by local women every year. The altarpieces symbolize the three volcanoes around Santiago, which are believed to protect the town. The central one was subtly changed from a traditional European vision of heaven to a more Maya representation of a sacred mountain with two *cofradia* members climbing towards a sacred cave.

Parque Central   PLAZA
Here you'll find a stone monument that commemorates Concepción Ramírez, the woman on the back of the 25-centavo coin, and a basin that contains a relief version of the lake.

Parque de Paz   MEMORIAL
(Peace Park) During the civil war Santiago became the first village in the country to succeed in expelling the army, following a notorious massacre of 13 villagers on December 2, 1990. The site of this massacre, where troops were encamped, is now the Parque de Paz, about 500m beyond the Posada de Santiago.

Cojolya Association of
Maya Women Weavers   MUSEUM
(☏7721-7268; www.cojolya.org; Calle Real, Comercial Las Máscaras, 2nd floor; donation requested; ⊙9am-5pm Mon-Fri, 9am-1pm Sat) This small museum is devoted to the art of backstrap loom weaving. The well-designed exhibit shows the history of the craft and the process from spinning the cotton fibers to the finished textile. There are also daily demonstrations of backstrap loom techniques, and a small shop.

THAT'S ONE SMOKIN' GOD

The Spanish called him San Simón, the *ladinos* (persons of mixed indigenous and European race) named him Maximón, and the Maya know him as Rilaj Maam (ree-lah-*mahm*). By any name, he's a deity revered throughout the Guatemalan highlands. Assumed to be a combination of Maya gods, Pedro de Alvarado (the Spanish conquistador of Guatemala) and the biblical Judas, San Simón is an effigy to which Guatemalans of every stripe go to make offerings and ask for blessings. The effigy is usually housed by a member of a *cofradía* (Maya Catholic brotherhood), moving from one place to another from year to year, a custom anthropologists believe was established to maintain the local balance of power. The name, shape and ceremonies associated with this deity vary from town to town, but a visit will be memorable no matter where you encounter him. For a small fee, photography is usually permitted, and offerings of cigarettes, liquor or candles are always appreciated.

TZ'UTUJIL OIL PAINTING

Emanating primarily from the Lago de Atitlán towns of Santiago Atitlán, San Pedro La Laguna and San Juan La Laguna, Tz'utujil oil painting has a distinctive primitivist style, with depictions of rural life, local traditions and landscapes in vibrant colors.

This distinctly Maya mode is generally handed down through generations of the same family, and the leading artists share surnames. In San Pedro La Laguna the name of note is González. Legend has it that Tz'utujil art began when Rafael González y González noticed some dye that had dripped and mixed with the sap of a tree; he made a paint-brush from his hair and began creating the type of canvases still popular today. His grandson Pedro Rafael González Chavajay and Pedro's cousin Mariano González Chavajay are leading contemporary exponents of the Tz'utujil style. The artist Emilio González Morales pioneered the motif of depicting rural scenes from above – the *vista del pájaro*, or bird's-eye view – as well as from below, an ant's-eye view.

The granddaddy of Santiago painting was Juan Sisay; success at an international art exhibition in 1969 sparked an explosion of painters working in his style. Their work is exhibited at the **Galería Juan Sisay**, 200m up from Santiago's main dock, and at a number of galleries along the main street. You can even learn to paint in this style at several studios around town. Among the leading figures in San Juan are husband and wife Antonio Coché Mendoza and Angelina Quic, whose paintings are exhibited at the **Galería Xocomil** on the way up from the main dock. Artists in all three communities are experimenting with new forms while continuing to explore Maya cultural themes.

If you've got more than a passing interest, consider taking the 'Maya Artists & Artisans' tour offered by Posada Los Encuentros (p99) in Panajachel or visit the website **Arte Maya Tz'utuhil** (www.artemaya.com).

Activities

There are several rewarding **day hikes** around Santiago. Most enticing of all are the three volcanoes in the vicinity: Tolimán, Atitlán and San Pedro. Before attempting a climb, enquire about the current security situation. It's best to go with a guide; the Posada de Santiago (p107) can set up a reliable one. Guided volcano climbs run about Q400 for two to five persons.

Less daunting a challenge than the massive volcanoes in the vicinity, **Cerro de Oro** (1892m) still yields great views and features several Maya ceremonial sites. It's some 8km northeast, about halfway between Santiago and San Lucas Tolimán.

Asotur (Asociación guías de Turismo 'Aj tz'ikin jaay'; ☑ 5160-9805; asotur@hotmail.es; Playa Pública; ☉ 8am-5pm Mon-Sat), an association of local Inguat-authorized guides, leads a variety of fascinating tours in and around Santiago Atitlán. You can visit the Tz'utujil community of Chuk Muk on the slopes of Volcán Tolimán, with an unexcavated archaelogical site (Q120 per person); participate in workshops by local weavers, painters, sculptors and chefs, with a visit to the market for ingredients; or take a lake trip by *coyuco* (wooden rowboat) to accompany reed cutters who'll demonstrate how they use reeds to weave mats (Q170). Their office is in an orange storefront on the left as you're coming from the dock.

Another worthy destination is the **Mirador de Tepepul**, about 4km south of Santiago (four to five hours round trip, Q150 per person). The hike goes through cloud forest populated with many birds, including parakeets, currassows, swifts, boat-tailed grackles and tucanets, and on to a lookout point with views all the way to the coast.

The pre-Hispanic Tz'utujil capital of **Chuitinamit** is across the inlet from Santiago. The hilltop archaeological site features some carved petroglyphs as well as some fanciful painted carvings of more recent vintage. From the dock, it's a 20-minute hike to the top, where there are good views of Santiago. Asotur's guides can take you across the inlet by *coyuco* and accompany you up the tenuous trail to the site.

☞ Tours

Dolores Ratzan Pablo CULTURAL TOUR
(☑ 5730-4570; dolores_ratzan@yahoo.com) This English-speaking Tz'utujil woman can introduce you to the wonders of Maya birthing and healing, point out examples of Maya-Catholic syncretism at the church and *cofradías*, and describe the incidents that

led to the massacre at Peace Park in 1990. Tours typically last two hours and cost Q235 per person

Cojolya Association of Maya Women Weavers
CULTURAL TOUR

(📞7721-7268; www.cojolya.org) Here you can join 'Meet the Weavers' tours (Q50, in Spanish). You'll visit three traditional homes where women demonstrate how to set up a backstrap loom, warp the threads and perform the *jaspe* technique, a form of Japanese tie-dye that reached Guatemala through indirect contact with Spain's Pacific trade routes.

🛏 Sleeping

Hotel Ratzán
HOTEL $

(📞7721-7840; www.hotelyposadaratzan.blogspot.nl; Calle a la Playa Pública; s/d 100/150) Santiago's best budget option, near the center of town, is a newish establishment with nice woodbeam ceilings and large, modern bathrooms. Only rooms 4 and 5 have exterior windows but considering it's just down the street from the giant new Evangelical church, with raucous services nightly, maybe that's a good thing.

Posada de Santiago
LODGE $$

(📞7721-7366; www.posadadesantiago.com; s/d Q235/400, cottages s/d/tr Q475/600/675, ste from Q755; 🅿@🛜🏊) Striking a balance between rustic charm and luxury, the American-owned *posada* makes a great retreat. Seven cottages and three suites, all with stone walls, fireplaces, porches, hammocks and folk art, are set around gardens stretching up from the lake.

The restaurant serves delicious, natural fare, as well as homegrown roasted coffee. Hikes and cycling trips can be set up here. It's 1.5km from the dock. Catch a *tuk-tuk* (Q10) or hire a *lancha* over to the hotel dock (Q70).

Hotel La Estrella
HOTEL $$

(📞7721-7814; www.hotel-laestrella.blogspot.com; Calle Campo; s/d Q150/250; 🅿🛜) A short hike north of the ferry dock along the road to San Lucas is this newcomer, featuring modern, comfortable units with handsome wood ceilings and locally woven bedspreads. Room 13, adjacent to the top terrace, takes best advantage of the hotel's lakeside position looking straight across the inlet at San Pedro volcano.

Hotel Bambú
LODGE $$$

(📞7721-7332; www.ecobambu.com; Carretera San Lucas Tolimán, Km 16; s/d incl breakfast Q435/515; 🅿🛏) 🏊 Run by an amiable Spaniard, the Bambú is an ecologically harmonious hotel. Scattered around wild yet manicured grounds, the 10 spacious rooms are in grass- or bamboo-roofed buildings, with cypress fittings and earthy tile floors. A pebbly path leads to a swimming pool in a serene, jungly setting. It's 600m from the dock; if you're arriving by boat, ask to be dropped off at the hotel dock.

🍴 Eating & Drinking

Restaurant El Gran Sol
GUATEMALAN $

(📞7721-7157; mains Q55; ⏰7:30am-7:30pm) One block up from the dock on the left, this family-run establishment is a good bet for breakfast, lunch or snacks, with a spiffy kitchen and thatched-roof deck over a cacophonous junction. Thelma and clan love to cook; ask for one of her specials.

Comedor Santa Rita
GUATEMALAN $

(lunch Q20; ⏰noon-7pm Mon-Fri) The latest incarnation of a generations-old dining hall, Santa Rita is a good place to try such Maya specialties as *pulique* (a veggie-rich stew) and *patin* (spicy tomato and minnow dish), served with a stack of tortillas and *refresco*. It's located half a block east of the market.

Café Quila's
PUB

(burgers Q20-30; ⏰5-10pm Wed-Sun) Quila's is a casual gathering place where expats and lake-dwellers can bond over sports TV or ping pong. Some of the best burgers on the lake are served in the front lounge or wonderful rear patio, which has a mural of Santiago. Coming up from the dock take the first right.

🔒 Shopping

Colorful textiles, wooden animals, beadwork jewelry, leather belts and paintings are produced and sold at workshops along the street leading up from the dock. For contemporary bags, clothing and accessories with Tz'utujil elements, check out the Cojolya Association of Maya Women Weavers (p105), whose shop displays woven items designed by the association's American founder, Candis E Krummel.

❶ Orientation

From the dock, a path leads up to the main shopping street, Calle Principal. About 500m up from the dock, turn left past the Restaurant El Pescador to arrive at the central plaza and, behind it, the Catholic church.

❶ Information

You'll find a lot of fascinating information about Santiago, in English, at www.santiagoatitlan.com.

Asotur (p106), just up from the dock on the left side, can provide information about accommodations, tours, transport, etc.

There's a Cajero 5B ATM at **Banrural** (⊘8:30am-5pm Mon-Fri, 9am-1pm Sat), a block south of the plaza.

The **Nuevo Hospitalito Atitlán** (📋7721-7683; www.hospitalitoatitlan.org; Canton Ch'utch'aj), on the way out of town toward San Lucas Tolimán, is a modern hospital staffed by English-speaking doctors and American volunteers.

DANGERS & ANNOYANCES

The road between Santiago and San Pedro La Laguna has a certain notoriety for bandits, carjackers, kidnappers etc. Proatur, the security branch of the tourist board, recommends taking a ferry between the towns instead.

❶ Getting There & Away

Boats leave hourly for San Pedro La Laguna (Q20, 30 minutes). Pickups to Cerro de Oro and San Lucas Tolimán depart from in front of the market. Buses to Guatemala City (Q40, 3½ hours) leave every half hour from 3am to 6am, then hourly until 3pm, from the main plaza.

San Pedro La Laguna

POP 11,545 / ELEV 1610M

Spreading onto a peninsula at the base of the volcano of the same name, San Pedro remains among the most visited of the lakeside villages – due as much to its reasonably priced accommodations and global social scene as its spectacular setting. Travelers tend to dig in here for a spell, in pursuit of (in no particular order) drinking, firetwirling, African drumming, Spanish classes, painting classes, volcano hiking, hot-tub soaking and hammock swinging.

While this scene unfolds at the lakefront, up the hill San Pedro follows more traditional rhythms. Clad in indigenous outfits, the predominantly indigenous *pedranos* (as the locals are called) congregate around the market zone. You'll see coffee being picked on the volcano's slopes and spread out to dry on wide platforms at the beginning of the dry season.

⊙ Sights

Two museums focusing on local Maya culture operate in San Pedro, both on the path between the docks.

Museo Maya Tz'utujil   MUSEUM
(admission Q10; ⊘8am-noon Mon-Fri) This humble museum displays the various *trajes* (traditional costumes) worn by San Pedro's predominately Tz'utujil inhabitants and those of other lake communities, plus some great old photographs. Once a month or so, a Maya priest performs ceremonies here.

Museo Tz'unun 'Ya   MUSEUM
(7a Av; admission Q35; ⊘9am-5pm Mon-Fri, 8:30am-10:30am Sat & Sun) This museum focuses on the history of the Tz'utujil people and geology of the region, with a film on the formation of the lake. For an optional fee, they'll identify and interpret your *nahual* (animal counterpart), based on your birth date.

ⳡ Activities

Ascending Volcán San Pedro

Looming above the village, Volcán San Pedro almost asks to be climbed by anyone with an adventurous spirit. It is the most accessible of the three volcanoes in the zone and, as it's classified as a municipal ecological park, it's regularly patrolled by tourism police.

Excursion Big Foot   GUIDED HIKE
(📋7721-8203; 7a Av, Zona 2) At the first crossroads up from the Panajachel dock, this group has a track record of responsibility. Departures are at 6am with at least six participants (Q100 each, including entry fees). The ascent is through fields of maize, beans and squash, followed by primary cloud forest. It's a three-hour climb; take water, snacks, a hat and sunblock.

Other Activities

Another popular hike goes up the hill to the west of the village that is referred to as **Indian Nose** – its skyline resembles the profile of an ancient Maya dignitary. **Asoantur** (📋4379-4545; asoantur21@gmail.com; ⊘7am-7pm), an association made up of 25 Tz'utujil guides from the local community, leads expeditions to the peak for Q100 per person. They also offer cultural tours of San Pedro and nearby coffee plantations, horseback riding tours, and kayak, bicycle and motorbike rentals. They operate from a hut on the lane up from the Pana dock.

Kayaks are available for hire (per hour Q15), turning right from the Pana dock. Ask for Nicolás at Natalí hairdressers.

Solar Pools   SPA
(7a Av 2-22) After all that activity, it's time for a good soak in one of the Solar Pools (from Q50 per person), next to the Buddha bar (p111). Book ahead so that your pool is already hot when you arrive.

La Piscina   SWIMMING
(adult/child Q20/10; ☺ 11am-dusk Tue-Sun; 🐦) If the lake hasn't swallowed it up by the time your read this, have a swim at La Piscina, by the Santiago dock, a global gathering place that revolves around a pool. Sundays are busiest with barbecues and boccie ball.

Hatha Yoga Sessions   YOGA
(Q30) Sessions are held Monday to Saturday at 9am in a circular garden along the path below the Buddha bar.

🍃 Courses
San Pedro is making a name for itself in the language game with ultra-economical rates at its various Spanish institutes. The standard price for four hours of one-on-one classes, five days a week, is Q800. Accommodation with a local family, with three meals daily (except Sunday) typically costs Q600. Volcano hikes, Maya culture seminars and dance classes are among the extracurricular activities offered.

Casa Rosario   LANGUAGE COURSE
(☑ 5613-6401; www.casarosario.com) Classes are held in little huts amid gardens near the lake. Weaving classes and *huipil* appreciation (from the owner's voluminous collection) are among the extracurricular activities. In addition to homestays, accommodation is offered at the school. The office is along the first street to the right as you walk up from Santiago dock.

Cooperativa
Spanish School   LANGUAGE COURSE
(☑ 5398-6448; www.cooperativeschoolsanpedro. com) Run as a cooperative, a percentage of profits goes to needy families around the lake. After-school activities include conferences, salsa classes, kayaking and zip-lining. Access is via a path off the street that ascends from the Santiago dock.

Corazón Maya   LANGUAGE COURSE
(☑ 7721-8160; www.corazonmaya.com) Well-established, family-run school with gorgeous lakeside setting, offering activities such as canoe trips, visits to local artists, and conferences on Guatemalan history and economics. Accommodation in on-site bungalows. Take the first left up from Santiago dock.

San Pedro Spanish
School   LANGUAGE COURSE
(☑ 5715-4604; www.sanpedrospanishschool.org; 7a Av 2-20) Well-organized school on the street between the two docks, with consistently good reviews. Classes are held under thatched-roof huts amidst an attractive garden setting. The school supports Niños del Lago, an organization that provides education, health care and nutrition for local Tz'utujil children.

🛏 Sleeping
In many places in San Pedro it is possible to negotiate deals during the low season and for longer stays. It's also possible to rent a room or an entire house in town – ask around.

🛏 Near the Pana Dock

★ Hotel Gran Sueño   HOTEL $
(☑ 7721-8110; 8a Calle 4-40, Zona 2; s/d Q75/125; 🐦) Beyond a plant-draped entryway and up a spiral staircase are bright rooms with colorful abstract designs, comfortable beds and thoughtfully designed bathrooms. Rooms 9 and 11 are fantastic lake-view perches. From the Pana dock, it's a few doors left of the first crossing.

Hotel Mansión del Lago   HOTEL $
(☑ 7721-8124; www.hotelmansiondellago.com; 3a Vía & 4a Av, Zona 2; s/d/tr Q100/150/225) If you'd just like to drop your bags, this massive L-shaped accommodation is just above the Pana dock. Sparkling clean rooms are done up in cloud or dove motifs, with rockers on wide balconies looking right at the Indian's Nose.

Hotel Nahual Maya   HOTEL $
(☑ 7721-8158; 6 Av 8C-12; s/d Q75/100; P 🐦) The forest of rooftop reinforcing bar somewhat mars the Mediterranean villa motif, but the rooms are sparkling clean and homey and have little balconies with hammocks out front. Former teacher/owner Guillermo and family do their utmost to please.

Hotel San Antonio   HOTEL $
(☑ 5953-1917; s/d Q80/140; 🐦) Orange trumpet flowers cascade over the balconies of the San

Antonio, last of the myriad lodgings east of the Pana dock. The cosy three-level structure has plenty of hammocks strung along the tiled corridors and a handy guest kitchen.

🛏 Between the Docks

Zoola HOSTEL $
(☎5847-4857; dm Q35, s/d Q100/125, without bathroom Q50/100) 'Laid-back' best describes this Israeli-run establishment, a place to crash after a Mideast feast at the adjoining restaurant (p111). It's reached down a long, jungly boardwalk opposite the Museo Tz'unun Ya'. Behind the cafe/chillout lounge, low adobe blocks of dorms extend to the lake, where a new canopied swimming pool is the focus of nightly parties. Two-night minimum stay.

★Hotel Sak'cari El Amanecer HOTEL $$
(☎7721-8096; www.hotel-sakcari.com; 7a Av 2-12, Zona 2; s/d from Q125/225; P🛜) ⚐ On the left just after San Pedro Spanish School, the eco-friendly Sak'cari has clean, tangerine-colored rooms with lots of shelves and wood paneling. Rooms at the rear are best (and priciest), with big balconies overlooking a vast landscaped lawn.

Hotel Mikaso HOTEL $$
(☎7721-8232; www.mikasohotel.com; 4a Callejon A-88; dm/d/quad Q75/195/340; 🛜) Despite encroaching lake waters, the Mikaso still stands proudly at Atitlán's shores. Big, colonially furnished rooms cooled by ceiling fans ring a garden bursting with birds-of-paradise. The rooftop bar/Spanish restaurant boasts fantastic lake views and the deck/lounge features a Jacuzzi and pool table.

🛏 Near the Santiago Dock

Hotel Peneleu HOTEL $
(☎7721-8182; 5a Av 2-20, Zona 2; s/d Q30/60, without bathroom Q20/40; 🛜) The best of four budget options along a side street, this concrete tower offers well-maintained if modestly furnished rooms. It's all about the views; fly a kite from the amazing top terrace. Genial proprietor Don Alberto will gladly negotiate rates for longer stays. To find it, walk 500m up from the dock and turn left; or take a *tuk-tuk* up the steep approach.

Hotel Villa Cuba HOTEL $
(☎7959-5044; www.hotelvillacuba.com; Camino a la Finca, Zona 4; s/d Q60/120) Peacefully poised

on grounds that sweep down to the lake, this former private residence sits amid cornfields on the road to Santiago. It's a good deal for getting away from it all: swimming is good here, and it's only a *tuk-tuk* away from town. Take the first road to the left up from the dock and continue for 2km.

🍴 Eating

★Ventana Blue FUSION $
(mains Q30-46; ☺6-9:30pm Wed-Sun; 🖉) There are just four tables at this cozy bistro at a bend in the path between the docks. Created by lake native Santos Canel, the brief but exciting menu features an array of Asian and Guatemalan dishes, from Thai curries to *kaq-ik* (chicken and vegetables in a fiery salsa). The Diosa Blue headlines the highly original cocktail selection.

Café La Puerta CAFE $
(☎4050-0500; 7a Av 2-20; breakfast Q25; ☺7am-5pm Mon-Sat; 🖉) Relocated to San Pedro Spanish School after being submerged under rising lake waters, the cafe remains a deeply appealing spot for abundant natural fare. Breakfast on homemade granola, grainy bread, delicious raspberry jam and avocado milkshakes, all served on beautiful mosaic tile tables by the sweetest waitresses ever to wear a *huipil*. Burritos, tacos and quesadillas highlight the lunch menu.

D'Noz INTERNATIONAL $
(☎7721-8078; 4a Av 8-18; mains Q36-45; ☺9am-10pm Mon-Sat; 🖉) Right up from the Pana dock, Dino's place sports a terrific deck for lake-view dining. The menu spans the globe from tempeh fajitas to Chinese tacos to Tecpán sausage. Offering movies, a lending library and a popular bar, it's San Pedro's closest thing to a cultural center.

Hummus-Ya ISRAELI $
(felafel Q25; ☺7:30am-9pm) *Sabich*, an Israeli sandwich lovingly stuffed with hard-boiled eggs, hummus, and fried eggplant, is just one highlight on the menu at this cheerful open-air eatery on the Pana dock side, near the connecting path. Saturday mornings there's *jachnun*, Yemeni bread rolls that sit in the oven overnight.

Shanti Shanti ISRAELI $
(8a Calle 3-93; mains Q20-25; ☺7am-8pm; 🖉) With terraced seating cascading down to the lakeside, this makes a pleasant perch

for hippie staples like falafel, curried veggies and hearty soups.

Drinking & Nightlife

While many *pedranos* spend their evenings shouting the lord's praises at evangelical congregations, visitors tend to prowl San Pedro's hard-partying bar scene.

Café Las Cristalinas   CAFE
(⊙7am-9pm; 🛜) To savor a shot of the coffee grown on the surrounding slopes (and roasted here), head for this thatched-roof structure on the way up from the Pana dock to the center of town.

El Barrio   PUB
(7a Av 2-07, Zona 2; ⊙5pm-1am) This boisterous pub on the path between the two docks has one of the most happening happy hours in town. Every night has a different theme but come Friday evenings, the fun reaches a crescendo.

Alegre Pub   PUB
(8a Calle 4-10) Near the Pana dock, the Alegre is a bit worse for wear but still a cheerful watering hole for San Pedro's cast of characters. Shoot pool with the locals (Tz'tujil rules) in the way-laid-back rooftop garden.

The Buddha   PUB
(🖉4178-7979; 2a Av 2-24; ⊙noon-1am) The Buddha can be enjoyed on various levels – downstairs there's a boisterous bar with darts and rock concert videos, upstairs a restaurant doing convincing versions of Thai, Indian and Mideast fare, and up top a thatched roof lounge for smoking, conversation and original cocktails.

Zoola   ISRAELI
(⊙11am-midnight; 🛜) Zoola remains San Pedro's premier global chillage venue. Travelers kick back on cushions around low tables, munching scrumptious Mideast fare, grooving on Manu, playing board games and generally unwinding. For serious DJ sessions, follow the cobblestone path to the sensational new lakefront lounge with swimming pool.

Shopping

Grupo Ecológico Teixchel (🖉5932-0000; berta_nc@yahoo.com; ⊙8:30am-noon & 2-6pm) is a Tz'utujil women's collective that sells fair-trade woven goods and offers weaving classes for Q25 per hour (not including ma-

terials). It's about 150m uphill from the Pana dock toward the center of town. Yabalám, downstairs from D'Noz (p110), is a good place to look for contemporary indigenous handicrafts, including jewelry, textiles and paper hot-air balloons.

ⓘ Orientation

San Pedro has two docks, about 1km apart. The one on the southeast side of town serves boats going to and from Santiago Atitlán; the other, on the northwest side, serves Panajachel. From each dock, streets run ahead to meet outside the market in the town center, a few hundred meters uphill. Most of the tourism activity is in the lower part of town, between and on either side of the two docks. To work your way across this lower area from the Panajachel dock, turn left at the first intersection. Follow this path about 200m until you reach a store called La Estrellita, then take the trail on the right. Soon afterward, the path angles left and passes the Museo Tz'unun'Ya, then takes a sharp left into a busy bar and restaurant zone. From the Santiago dock, turn right immediately before the Hotel Villasol.

ⓘ Information

There's a Cajero 5B ATM just up from the Panajachel dock on the left. You can change traveler's checks at **Banrural** (⊙8:30am-5pm Mon-Fri, 9am-1pm Sat) in the town center, 1½ blocks south of the market.

Zuyuva (⊙11am-3pm Tue-Sat) is a second-hand bookstore with a decent selection of fiction and Guatemala titles. It's opposite Hotel San Francisco, 500m up from the Santiago dock on the left.

Clínica Los Volcanes (🖉7823-7656; www. clinicalosvolcanes.com) is a private clinic providing medical and dental services, with English-speaking staff.

ⓘ Getting There & Away

Passenger boats arrive and depart for Panajachel and Santiago Atitlán. Boats from San Pedro to Santiago (Q20, 30 minutes) run hourly from 6am to 4pm. Boats from San Pedro to Panajachel (Q25) run every half hour or so from 6am to 5pm. Some go direct; others make stops at San Juan, San Marcos (Q10) and Jaibalito/Santa Cruz (Q20) en route.

San Pedro is connected by paved roads to Santiago Atitlán (although this stretch is plagued by bandits) and to the Interamericana at Km 148 (about 20km west of Los Encuentros), the latter a hair-raising journey with spectacular lake vistas on the way up. A paved branch of the San Pedro–Interamericana road runs along the northwest side of the lake from Santa Clara to San Marcos La Laguna. Buses leave for Quetzaltenango (Q35, three hours) from San Pedro's Catholic church, up in the town center, roughly hourly from 5am to 10:30am.

San Juan La Laguna

POP 5868 / ELEV 1567M

Just 2km east of San Pedro, on a rise above a spectacular bay, this mellow village has escaped many of the excesses of its neighbors, and some travelers find it a more tranquil setting in which to study Spanish or experience indigenous life. San Juan is special: the Tz'utujil inhabitants take pride in their craft traditions – particularly painting and weaving – and have developed their own tourism infrastructure to highlight these traditions to outsiders.

As you wander round the village, you'll notice various murals depicting aspects of San Juan life and legend.

Tours

Asociación de Guías de Ecoturismo Rupalaj K'istalin TOUR
(☏ 4772-2527; www.sanjuanlalaguna.org; ⊙ 8am-noon & 2-5pm) The association offers a worthwhile tour of San Juan La Laguna's points of interest, led by indigenous guides (Q110 per person), in Spanish. You'll visit two weaving cooperatives, both of which use dyes from native plants, and an art studio/gallery featuring the Tz'utujil primitivist painting style (see the boxed text, p106). The office is 300m up the hill from the dock.

Other tours offered include trips with local fisherman in rustic *cayucos* to learn about traditional lake fishing techniques and a demonstration of the harvesting of the lakeshore reeds, which are used as material for *petates*, the woven mats the town is known for.

The association can also set up guides for one-way walks to San Marcos La Laguna (Q125 per person), returning by *lancha*; and hikes up Rupalaj K'istalin (Q130 per person), the mountain that towers above San Juan and is the site of Maya religious rituals.

Tza'an Ab'aaj TOUR
To see how organic agriculture is practiced on the lake, visit this innovatively managed garden 50m left of the dock (when facing the lake). Tours (Q30) focus on medicinal plants and sustainable growing methods and crops, including the super-food *tzan*, now being used to treat child malnutrition naturally.

Many of these organic ingredients show up in salads, desserts and teas at the adjacent cafe.

Courses

Eco Spanish School LANGUAGE COURSE
(☏ 4727-6481; www.ecolanguages.net) Along a path that's 500m up from the dock on the right.

ATITLÁN RISING

At San Juan La Laguna an art gallery is half submerged, its upper floor abandoned. At Tzunaná, only the roof is visible of what used to be a shelter for waiting boat passengers. And in Panajachel the public beach has been washed off the map. Makeshift docks have been erected in all the lakeside villages and in Santa Cruz, a rickety plank walk has replaced the lakeside trail, now underwater. It may appear that a tsunami or some similar disaster has struck. But what's actually happening is that the lake level is rising, inexorably – around 5m since 2009. In the process, it keeps swallowing dwellings and businesses, most of them owned by outsiders. Foreign residents are learning the hard way why it is that almost all local towns are built well above the lake shore. The lake's capricious behavior is well-lodged in the community's collective memory. The elders of Atitlán know of its cyclical rise and fall, a phenomenon noted as far back as the 16th century by the Spanish conquistadors. The water level has been considerably higher in the past and it will no doubt drop again. In the meantime, the rising trend is the talk of the lake, with various theories proposed. Some attribute it to the deforestation of the lakeside slopes which causes soil erosion. When Tropical Storm Agatha hit in 2010, it might have washed a great deal of this sediment into the lake, clogging the crevices in its basin that provide natural drainage. A more authoritative theory attributes the phenomenon to the lake's volcanic origins. According to this view, seismic activity heats the ground beneath the lake bed and forms a sort of subterranean 'bladder' that keeps expanding until exit vents appear. This periodic expansion causes the lake level to rise.

San Juan Spanish School LANGUAGE COURSE

(☑4257-7899) The school operates from the Hotel Pa Muelle.

🛏 Sleeping & Eating

Hotel Pa Muelle HOTEL $

(☑4141-0820; hotelpamuelle@turbonett.com; Camino al Muelle; s/d Q100/150) The small hotel has a delightful setting, with blue rooms along a patch of lawn high above the lake. It's near the top of the hill coming up from the dock.

Hotel Chi-Yá BUNGALOW $$

(☑5293-2417; www.hotelchi-ya.com; s/d Q125/190) Organically developed upon the promontory between San Juan and San Pedro, Hotel Chi-Yá consists of secluded, handsomely constructed cedar cabins, all with lake-view terraces and picture windows. Stone steps lead to a private dock.

Uxlabil Eco Hotel HOTEL $$

(☑2366-9555; www.uxlabil.com; s/d/tr Q360/437/560) The Uxlabil stands on a small coffee plantation on the southern edge of San Juan's bay. Featuring hand-carved stone trimmings by local craftsmen, all the rooms face the lake.

Café El Artesano EUROPEAN $$

(☑4555-4773; cheese platter Q70; ☺11:30am-6pm Mon-Fri) Bring a group of friends and make an afternoon of this unique restaurant. Fine cheeses (25 varieties, all produced locally and aged in-house), smoked meats and spreads are served under a delightful arbor, with wines personally selected by the manager, a young man of Swiss heritage. Reservations are recommended.

Comedor Elenita GUATEMALAN $

(Calle al Estadio Municipal; lunch Q20; ☺7am-9pm) Locals crowd in for the daily specials at this excellent little dining hall in the center of town, where a brimming bowl of *caldo de res*, served with rice, avocado and tortillas, is well within anyone's budget.

ⓘ Getting There & Away

To get to San Juan, ask any boat coming from Pana to drop you off at the dock. Otherwise it's a 15-minute pickup or *tuk-tuk* ride (Q10) from San Pedro.

San Marcos La Laguna

POP 4410 / ELEV 1562M

Without doubt the prettiest of the lakeside villages, San Marcos La Laguna lives a double life. The mostly Maya community occupies the higher ground, while expats and visitors cover a flat jungly patch toward the shoreline with paths snaking through banana, coffee and avocado trees. The two converge under the spreading *matapalo* (strangler fig) tree of the delightful central plaza.

San Marcos has become a magnet for global seekers, who believe the place has a spiritual energy that's conducive to learning and practicing meditation, holistic therapies, massage, reiki and other spiritually oriented activities. Whatever you're into, it's a great spot to kick back and distance the everyday world for a spell. Lago de Atitlán is beautiful and clean here, and you can swim off the rocks. Boats put in at a central dock below Posada Schumann. The path leading from there to the village center, and a parallel one about 100m west, are the main axes for most visitors.

There's a community information board in front of the San Marcos Holistic Center with postings on events and housing options. Get online at **Prolink** (per hr Q12; ☺9am-7pm Mon-Sat, 10am-5pm Sun), across from the Paco Real hotel.

Tikonem (main path from dock), an initiative to support the local Escuela Los Caracoles, has a few shelves of fiction in English, Spanish and other languages, plus muffins and cookies.

◎ Sights & Activities

Las Pirámides Meditation
Center MEDITATION

(☑5205-7302; www.laspiramidesdelka.com) San Marcos La Laguna's claim to fame has been providing spiritual guidance for more than two decades. Most structures on the lakeshore retreat are pyramidal in shape and oriented to the four cardinal points, including the two temples where sessions are held. A one-month personal development course begins every full moon, with three sessions daily.

There's also a three-month solar course running from each equinox to the following solstice (the moon course is a prerequisite). Nonguests can come for the meditation (Q50) or Hatha yoga (Q40, 7am to 8am) sessions. Accommodations are available, to course participants only, in pyramid-shaped houses for Q175 per day, slightly less by the week or month. This price includes the course, use of the sauna, and access to a fascinating library. It also has a vegetarian restaurant, and room to wander about in the medicinal herb garden.

San Marcos Holistic Centre
MEDITATION

(www.sanmholisticcentre.com; ⊙10am-5pm Mon-Sat) Run by various resident and visiting practitioners, the center provides a range of massages, holistic therapies and training courses in kinesiology, EFT, reiki, shiatsu, massage and reflexology. The approach is relaxed and you're welcome to discuss possibilities before committing to anything. Most massages and therapies cost around Q250 per 90-minute session.

Cerro Tzankujil
PARK

(admission Q15; ⊙8am-6pm) Completed in 2011, this nature reserve is on a sacred hill west of San Marcos village. Well-maintained pebbly trails lead to swimming areas with shelters by the bank and a diving platform. The water is crystal clear here. A branch off the main trail ascends to a Maya altar on the summit, while a lower spur reaches a volcano lookout.

Jovenes Maya Kaqchikeles
HIKING

(☎5787-7728; atitlanresource.com/jovenesmayas_eng.htm; ⊙9am-5pm Mon-Sat) This group of bright, ecologically minded locals, some of whom speak English, offer guided hikes to San Pedro La Laguna (2½ hours) and Santa Cruz La Laguna (four hours), each at Q100 per person, including the *lancha* back. Stop by their clubhouse, just above the Posada del Bosque Encantado, to discuss the possibilities.

The Jovenes can also take you to Tzununá via the Palitz waterfalls; to Santa Lucía Utatlán along the old Maya trail; around the barrios of San Marcos to visit families who weave bags with maguey fibers; and to a garden where you'll learn the names and uses of medicinal herbs and talk to elderly healers who administer them.

🛏 Sleeping

There aren't any street signs but most lodgings have posted their own fanciful painted versions to point you in the right direction.

Hotel La Paz
HOSTEL **$**

(☎5061-5316; www.lakeatitlanlapaz.com; dm/r/bungalow Q50/150/250) ◈ Along the upper trail that links the two main paths, the holistically-minded La Paz has rambling gardens holding bungalows of traditional *bajareque* (a stone, bamboo and mud material) with thatch roofs. A vegetarian restaurant, traditional Maya sauna, Spanish

---

TRADITIONAL MAYA CLOTHING

Anyone visiting the highlands can delight in the beautiful *traje indígena* (traditional Maya clothing). The styles, patterns and colors used by each village – originally devised by the Spanish colonists to distinguish one village from another – are unique, and each garment is the creation of its weaver, with subtle individual differences.

The basic elements of the traditional wardrobe are the *tocoyal* (head covering), *huipil* (blouse), *corte* or *refago* (skirt), *calzones* (trousers), *tzut* or *kaperraj* (cloth), *paz* (belt) or *faja* (sash) and *caítes* or *xajáp* (sandals).

Women's head coverings are beautiful and elaborate bands of cloth up to several meters long, wound about the head and often decorated with tassels, pompoms and silver ornaments.

Women proudly wear *huipiles* every day. Though some machine-made fabrics are now being used, many *huipiles* are still made completely by hand. The white blouse is woven on a backstrap loom, then decorated with appliqué and embroidery designs and motifs common to the weaver's village. Many of the motifs are traditional symbols. No doubt all motifs originally had religious or historical significance, but today that meaning is often lost to memory.

Cortes (refagos) are pieces of cloth 7m to 10m long that are wrapped around the body. Traditionally, girls wear theirs above the knee, married women at the knee and old women below the knee, though the style can differ markedly from region to region.

Both men and women wear *fajas*, long strips of backstrap-loom-woven cloth wrapped around the midriff as belts. When they're wrapped with folds upward like a cummerbund, the folds serve as pockets.

Tzutes (for men) or *kaperraj* (for women) are the all-purpose cloths carried by local people and used as head coverings, baby slings, produce sacks, basket covers and shawls. There are also shawls for women called *perraj*.

lessons and morning yoga sessions (Q40) are additional attractions.

Hotel Paco Real
HOTEL $

(☑4084-5974; info@hotelpacoreal.com; dm Q50, s/d from Q70/140; 🛜) A two-minute walk down the path off San Marcos' central plaza, the Paco Real has simple but stylish rooms in thatched cottages, each uniquely designed. The little shelters that dot the grounds make great hangout areas.

Posada Schumann
HOTEL $

(☑5202-2216; r with/without bathroom Q145/115) Set in gardens that stretch right to the shores of Lago de Atitlán, Posada Schumann has neat rooms in stone or wooden cottages, some with kitchen, most with bathroom. A cafe deck has been salvaged from the lakefront accommodations submerged by encroaching waters. Don't miss the igloo-shaped sauna. San Marcos' main boat dock is right outside the gate.

Hospedaje Panabaj
HOTEL $

(☑5678-0181; s/d Q35/70) The only accommodation in San Marco's center, the basic Panabaj stands behind the school that's immediately above the main plaza. Elevated rooms get plenty of light through stained-glass windows, and though the wooden beds are somewhat droopy, it's pretty quiet aside from the fluttering of butterfly wings in the garden. Clean toilets and showers are down the hall.

★Aaculaax
HOTEL $$

(☑5287-0521; www.aaculaax.com; r Q100-515, ste from Q800; 🛜) 🖉 The eco-chic Aaculaax seems to sprout organically from the living rock of the hillside, with recycled glass, plastic and other flotsam ingeniously incorporated as construction materials. Each of the 11 rooms is unique, with handcrafted furnishings, picture windows and lake-view balconies; some have kitchens. An abundant buffet breakfast (Q50), with homemade bread and granola, is served on the main terrace.

From the dock, it's a six-minute walk to the left (west) along the lakeside path.

Hostel San Marcos
HOSTEL $

(☑3009-5537; www.hostelsanmarcos.com; incl breakfast r Q75, without bathroom Q60) This newcomer features seven rustic bungalows (three log, four stone) in two separate banks with large front windows (which unfortunately cannot be opened). The on-site restaurant/bar does wood-fired pizzas. From the dock, take the first left.

Posada del Bosque Encantado
HOTEL $$

(☑5208-5334; www.hotelposadaencantado.com; s/d Q125/180) Set in jungly grounds that could well be an enchanted forest, the *posada* is a naturally cool adobe brick structure. Each of the three rustic-style rooms features three beds, one in an overhead loft. American owner Terry annually hosts ceremonies to observe the five-day Wayeb' period, an addendum to the Maya calendar.

✖ Eating

Blind Lemon's
BURGERS $

(www.blindlemons.com; mains Q35; ⏰noon-10pm; 🛜) Named after one of owner Carlos' blues heroes, this hangout brings the Mississippi Delta to Atitlán, with weekly blues jams by Carlos and special guests in a colonial-style mansion. The menu features chicken platters, Cajun-blackened fish, pizza, burgers and other gringo comfort food. It's at the top of the western path.

Allala
JAPANESE $

(mains Q35-45; 🖉) This groovy little shack can be found by the creek east of the village. Japanese owner Seiko makes a mean miso soup, plus vegetarian sushi and tempura platters, and the plum wine is divine. All this, and complimentary cheesecake for dessert! Service can be slow, but the funky decor gives you something to look at.

Moonfish
ORGANIC $

(sandwiches, burritos Q30; ⏰7am-6pm Wed-Mon; 🖉) Along the main thoroughfare west of the square, Moonfish whips up hippie-friendly fare including tempeh sandwiches, tofu scrambles, and salads with ingredients fresh from the garden.

Comedor Susy
GUATEMALAN $

(Comedor Mi Marquensita; Parque Central; set lunch Q30; ⏰7am-8pm) This 'mom and pop' store on the central plaza is where many expats go for a cheap, home-cooked meal, which might explain why tofu dishes pop up among the chicken and pork chops.

El Tul y Sol
FRENCH $$

(mains Q100) When he's not out paragliding over the lake, long-time San Marcos dweller Guy turns his attention to the kitchen, whipping up a locally renowned pepper steak or Provence-style fish. Dinner is served on the lakefront deck.

❶ Getting There & Away

The last dependable boat to Jaibalito, Santa Cruz La Laguna and Panajachel departs about 5pm.

A paved road runs east from San Marcos to Tzununá and west to San Pablo and Santa Clara, where it meets the road running from the Interamericana to San Pedro. You can travel between San Marcos and San Pedro by pickup, with a transfer at San Pablo.

Jaibalito

POP 600 / ELEV 1562M

This Kaqchiquel hamlet is only accessible by boat (a 20-minutes *lancha* ride from Panajachel or San Pedro, Q20), or on foot via a ridgeline trail from Santa Cruz La Laguna, 4km to the east (45 minutes). The equally picturesque hike west, to San Marcos (6km), is best undertaken with local guides, such as Jovenes Maya Kaqchikeles (p114). There are several marvelous places to stay.

🛏 Sleeping & Eating

Posada Jaibilito   HOSTEL **$**
(✆5192-4334; www.posadajaibalito.com; dm/s/d Q35/70/95; ☎) Jaibalito's budget choice is just up from the dock on the left. The Germanowned operation is remarkable value, with dorm and a few private rooms occupying a garden flanked by coffee plants. Some little houses are available for longer-term renters. Authentic bratwurst and goulash (Q24) are served at the cafe, along with shots of Zacapa rum (Q15).

Vulcano Lodge   HOTEL **$$**
(✆5744-0620; www.vulcanolodge.com; r from Q315) This Norwegian designed and operated retreat contains eight trim and spotless rooms scattered amidst srawling gardens dotted with cactus, agave and heliconia. There's also a restaurant serving a lavish five-course dinner with fresh, local ingredients. Owners Terje and Monica are well versed in local walking routes. Coming up from the dock, take a right though the village and over a bridge.

★La Casa del Mundo
Hotel & Café   HOTEL **$$$**
(✆5218-5332; www.lacasadelmundo.com; r with/without bathroom Q550/275) On a secluded cliff facing the volcanoes is one of Guatemala's most spectacular hotels. It features sumptuous gardens, lake swimming from Mediterranean-style terraces, and a wood-fired hot tub overhanging the lake (Q275 for up to 10 bathers). The best rooms seem to float above the water, with no land visible beneath.

Every room is outfitted with comfortable beds, Guatemalan fabrics and fresh flowers. The restaurant serves a toothsome four-course dinner (Q100). You can rent kayaks (Q50 per hour) for exploring the lake. Reservations are advisable.

Club Ven Acá   FUSION **$$**
(✆5051-4520; sandwiches Q55-75, mains Q80-100) Right at the dock is this trendy restaurant with a seasonally varying menu and a popular happy hour highlighted by purplebasil mojitos. Sunday brunch is a big deal with to-die-for eggs Benedict. Guests tend to unwind in the hot tub or infinity pool.

Santa Cruz La Laguna

POP 1739 / ELEV 1833M

With the typically dual nature of the Atitlán villages, Santa Cruz comprises both a waterfront resort – home of the lake's scubadiving outfit – and an indigenous Kaqchiquel village, about 600m uphill from the dock. The cobblestoned road up is a route villagers customarily take lugging sacks of avocados or firewood. The inaccessibility of the spot – it can only be reached by boat or on foot – may impede its development but also enhances its rugged beauty.

🏃 Activities

ATI Divers   DIVING
(✆5706-4117; www.atidivers.com) Lago de Atitlán is one of the rare places in the world where you can dive at altitude without using a dry suit. This group leads dive trips from Santa Cruz. They offer a four-day PADI open-water diving certification course (Q1725), as well as a PADI high-altitude course and fun dives. It's based at La Iguana Perdida hotel.

The lake fills a collapsed volcanic cone with bizarre geological formations and aquatic life like cichlids, which spawn near an active fault line where hot water vents into the lake. Diving at altitude brings its own challenges – you need better control over your buoyancy, and visibility is reduced. During the rainy season the water clouds up, so the best time to dive is between October and May.

LOOK, UP IN THE SKY

Surely one of the most spectacular pre-Hispanic rituals alive today is that of the *palo volador* (flying pole). Dating from the Postclassic era, the ritual involves the installation of a tree trunk measuring up to 30m in the town square. One man sits atop the pole, playing the flute and directing the ceremony. Four flyers, or angels (the number four symbolizing the cardinal points of the compass) then leap off the top of the trunk, attached by ropes, and spin back to earth.

If all goes according to plan, the four flyers will circle the pole 13 times – thus making the number 52, which corresponds to the number of years in a Maya Calendar Round. In some places there are only two flyers, symbolizing Hun-Hunahpú and Vucub-Hunahpú, the wizard twins from the Popul Vuh, who descended to the underworld to battle the lords of darkness.

The tradition has changed somewhat since the time of its origins – the tree trunk is no longer carried by hand to town for one, and the flyers' costumes have become increasingly gaudy over the years, incorporating such nontraditional items as mirrors sewn into the fabric. The *palo volador* is widely practiced in Mexico, most notably in Puebla and Veracruz, but is becoming less common in Guatemala. Your best chance of seeing it is during the fiestas of Chichicastenango (December 21), Cubulco (July 25) and nearby Joyabaj (August 15) in the department of Quiché.

Los Elementos Adventure Center KAYAKING
(☑ 5359-8328; www.kayakguatemala.com) Kayak rentals and multiday excursions around the lake are offered by this outfit. Its two-day paddle-and-hike tour includes a visit to Santa Catarina Palopó, followed by kayaking along the lake's northern shore and hiking along the old Maya trail through Tzununá and Jaibalito. The cost of Q1250 per person (minimum four participants) includes meals and a night's lodging.

Its base is a 10-minute walk west of La Iguana Perdida along the lakeside trail.

🛏 Sleeping & Eating

La Iguana Perdida LODGE $$
(☑ 5706-4117; www.laiguanaperdida.com; dm Q45, r from Q235, s/d without bathroom Q95/125; @) The first place you see as you step off the dock, La Iguana Perdida makes a great hangout to enjoy the lake views and meet other travelers, go scuba diving or kayaking, learn Spanish or sweat it out in the sauna. Don't miss the Saturday night cross-dressing, fire and music barbecues!

Managed mainly by alternative-minded gringos (volunteers often needed), it features a range of rooms, from primitive (electricity-free dorm in an A-frame cabin) to luxurious (an adobe structure with stylish furnishings and private balconies). Meals are served family-style; a three-course dinner is Q60.

★ **Hotel Isla Verde** BUNGALOW $$
(☑ 5760-2648; www.islaverdeatitlan.com; s/d Q315/355, without bathroom Q235/275; ☎) ⚲ Designed by an artist from Bilbao, Spain, this stylish, environmentally friendly lodging makes the most of its spectacular setting. A mosaic stone path winds through exuberant vegetation to the nine hillside cabins (six with private bathroom); the higher you go, the more jaw-dropping the picture-window views.

Simple rooms are tastefully decorated with the owner's paintings and recycled elements. Bathrooms are jungle-chic affairs, and water and electricity are solar powered. A terrace restaurant serves slow-food cuisine, and there's a glass pavilion for meditation and dance. It's a 10-minute walk west of the dock along the lakefront trail.

La Fortuna BUNGALOW $$$
(☑ 5203-1033; www.lafortunaatitlan.com; bungalow from Q520) ⚲ These four thatch-roof cabins are at Patzisotz, a secluded bay just east of Santa Cruz around a rocky cliff. Constructed of locally forested guanacaste, they're elegantly designed with Asian influences. Each features a porch and upper deck overlooking the lake, mosquito-netted beds and an open-air tub at the rear.

The former coffee plantation has been ecologically outfitted by American owner Steve, a former guide and chef who prepares delectable meals from his own garden.

Lanchas will drop you at the dock (Q10 from Santa Cruz).

Café Sabor Cruceño GUATEMALAN $
(mains Q30-40; ⊙11am-3pm Mon-Fri) This innovative *comedor* is run by local students who are learning to make traditional Guatemalan dishes up to global tourism standards. Kaqchiquel fare such as *subanik* (a tomato sauce of ground seeds and chilis accompanied by *tamalitos*) is prepared with locally grown herbs and veggies and served in the bay-view dining hall.

It's inside the CECAP training center, at the lower end of the central plaza.

QUICHÉ

The road into Quiché department leaves the Interamericana at Los Encuentros, winding northward through pine forests and cornfields. Quiché is the homeland of the K'iche' people, though other groups form the fabric of this culturally diverse region, most notably the Ixil of the eastern Cuchumatanes mountains. Most visitors who come to this largely forgotten pocket of the country are on a jaunt to the famous market at Chichicastenango, though similarly captivating commerce is conducted in Santa Cruz del Quiché, the departmental capital to the north, and it's less trammeled territory. On its outskirts lie the mysterious ruins of K'umarcaaj, the last capital city of the K'iche'. Adventurous souls push further north for Nebaj, heart of the culturally vibrant Ixil Triangle, with myriad hiking opportunities.

Chichicastenango

POP 71,995 / ELEV 2172M

Surrounded by valleys, with mountains serrating the horizons, Chichicastenango can seem isolated in time and space from the rest of Guatemala. When its narrow cobbled streets and red-tiled roofs are enveloped in mist, it's downright magical. The crowds of crafts vendors and tour groups who flock in for the huge Thursday and Sunday markets lend it a much worldlier, more commercial atmosphere, but Chichi retains its mystery. *Masheños* (citizens of Chichicastenango) are famous for their adherence to pre-Christian beliefs and ceremonies. *Cofradías* hold processions in and around the church of Santo Tomás on Sunday.

Once called Chaviar, Chichi was an important Kaqchiquel trading town long before the Spanish conquest. In the 15th century the group clashed with the K'iche' (based at K'umarcaaj, 20km north) and were forced to move their headquarters to the more defensible Iximché. When the Spanish conquered K'umarcaaj in 1524, many of its residents fled to Chaviar, which they renamed Chugüilá (Above the Nettles) and Tziguan Tinamit (Surrounded by Canyons). These are the names still used by the K'iche' Maya, although everyone else calls the place Chichicastenango, a name given by the Spaniards' Mexican allies.

Today, Chichi has two religious and governmental establishments. On the one hand, the Catholic Church and the Republic of Guatemala appoint priests and town officials; on the other, the indigenous people elect their own religious and civil officers to manage local matters, with a separate council and mayor, and a court that decides cases involving only local indigenous people.

Due to a long-running land dispute between the indigenous community and Telgua, Chichicastenango has been without land lines for the past two years and no resolution is foreseen anytime soon. Thus, all numbers listed here are for cell phones and may be temporary.

◉ Sights

Take a close look at the mural running alongside the wall of the town hall on the east side of the plaza. It's dedicated to the victims of the civil war and tells the story using symbology from the Popol Vuh.

Inguat-authorized guides in beige vests offer cultural walks of Chichi and up to Pascual Abaj.

Market MARKET
Some villagers still walk for hours carrying their wares to reach Chichi's market, one of Guatemala's largest. At dawn on Thursday and Sunday they spread out their vegetables, chunks of chalk (ground to a powder, mixed with water and used to soften dried maize), handmade harnesses and other merchandise and wait for customers.

Tourist-oriented handicraft stalls selling masks, textiles, pottery and so on now occupy much of the plaza and the streets to the north. Things villagers need – food, soap, clothing, sewing notions, toys – cluster at the north end of the square and in the Centro Comercial Santo Tomás off the north

Chichicastenango

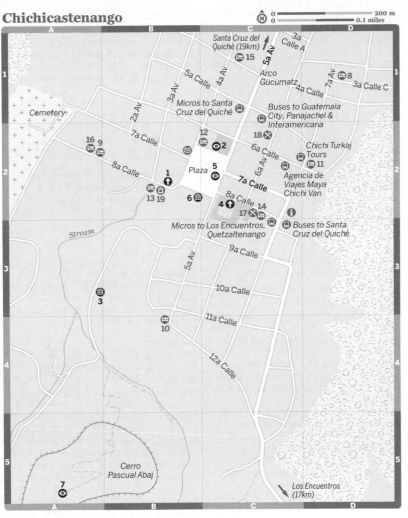

THE HIGHLANDS CHICHICASTENANGO

Chichicastenango

◉ Sights

1 Capilla del Calvario	B2
2 Centro Comercial Santo Tomás	C2
3 Galería Pop-Wuj	A3
4 Iglesia de Santo Tomás	C2
5 Market	C2
6 Museo Arqueológico Regional	B2
7 Pascual Abaj	A5

◉ Sleeping

8 Chalet House	D1
9 Hotel Mashito	A2
10 Hotel San Jerónimo	B4
11 Hotel Santo Tomás	D2
12 Maya Lodge	C2
13 Mayan Inn	B2
14 Posada Conchita	C2
15 Posada El Arco	C1
16 Posada El Teléfono	A2

◉ Eating

17 Casa de San Juan	C2
Mayan Inn	(see 13)
18 Tziguan Tinamit	C2

◉ Shopping

19 Ut'z Bat'z	B2

COFRADÍAS

Chichicastenango's religious life is centered on traditional brotherhoods known as *cofradías*. Membership is an honorable civic duty, and election as leader is the greatest honor. Leaders must provide banquets and pay for festivities for the *cofradía* throughout their term. Though it is expensive, a *cofrade* (brotherhood member) happily accepts the burden, even going into debt if necessary.

Each of Chichi's 14 *cofradías* has a patron saint. Most notable is the *cofradía* of Santo Tomás, the town's patron saint. *Cofradías* march in procession to church every Sunday morning and during religious festivals, with the officers dressed in costumes showing their rank. Before them is carried a ceremonial staff topped by a silver crucifix or sun-badge that signifies the *cofradía's* patron saint. A drum, flute and perhaps a trumpet may accompany the procession, as do fireworks.

During major church festivals, effigies of the saints are carried in grand processions, and richly costumed dancers wearing wooden masks act out legends of the ancient Maya and of the Spanish conquest. For the rest of the year, these items are kept in storehouses-cum-workshops called *morerías;* two prominent ones are at the start of the trail leading up to the Maya shrine of Pascual Abaj.

side, whose upper deck offers irresistible photo opportunities of the business conducted below.

Iglesia de Santo Tomás CHURCH
The church on the plaza's east side dates from 1540 and is often the scene of rituals that are more distinctly Maya than Catholic. Inside, the floor of the church may be dotted with offerings of maize, flowers and bottles of liquor wrapped in corn husks; candles are arranged in specific patterns along low stone platforms.

The front steps serve much the same purpose as did the great flights of stairs leading up to Maya pyramids. For much of the day (especially Sunday), they smolder with incense of copal resin, while indigenous prayer leaders called *chuchkajaues* (mother-fathers) swing censers (usually tin cans poked with holes) and chant magic words marking the days of the ancient Maya calendar and honoring ancestors. The candles and offerings inside recall those ancestors, many of whom are buried beneath the floor just as Maya kings were buried beneath pyramids. Note that photography is not permitted in this church.

On the west side of the plaza is another whitewashed church, the **Capilla del Calvario**, similar in form and function to Santo Tomás, but smaller.

Museo Arqueológico Regional MUSEUM
(5a Av 4-47; admission Q5; ☺8am-12:30pm & 2-4:30pm Tue-Sat, 8am-2pm Sun) Chichi's archaeology museum holds the collection of Hugo Rossbach, a German who served as Chichi's Catholic priest until his death in 1944. It includes some beautiful jade necklaces and figurines, along with ceremonial masks, obsidian spearheads, incense burners, figurines and *metates* (grindstones for maize).

Pascual Abaj SHRINE
On a hilltop south of town, Pascual Abaj (Sacrifice Stone) is a shrine to the Maya earth god Huyup Tak'ah (Mountain Plain). A stone-faced idol stands amid a circle of squat stone crosses in a clearing. Said to be hundreds – perhaps thousands – of years old, it has suffered numerous indignities at the hands of outsiders, but local people still revere it.

Chuchkajaues come regularly to offer incense, food, cigarettes, flowers, liquor, and perhaps even a sacrificial chicken, in thanks and hope for the earth's continuing fertility. The area is littered with past offerings. The worshippers won't mind if you watch the goings on, but be sure to request permission before taking any photos. You may be asked if you want to make an offering yourself.

Even if there are no ceremonies going on, you can still see the idol and enjoy the walk up the pine-clad hill. To get there from the plaza, walk down 5a Av, turn right into 9a Calle and proceed downhill. At the bottom, bear left along a path and head up through either of the *morerías* (ceremonial mask workshops) that are signposted here; the one on the right houses a museum of local culture. Exiting at the rear, follow the path uphill through the trees to the top of the hill.

On the way back to town, you might stop into the Galería Pop-Wuj (☑7756-1324). Developed as an art institute for local children with the backing of Project Guggenheim, it holds a small but *sui generis* collection of oil paintings by the artist brothers Cortéz and their pupils.

✷ Festivals & Events

December 7 sees the Quema del Diablo (Burning of the Devil), when residents burn their garbage in the streets and usher a statue of the Virgin Mary to the steps of the Iglesia de Santo Tomás. There are lots of incense and candles, a marimba band and a fireworks display that has observers running for cover. The following day is the Feast of the Immaculate Conception; don't miss the early-morning dance of the giant, drunken cartoon characters in the plaza.

The fiesta of Santo Tomás starts on December 13 and culminates on December 21 when pairs of brave (some would say mad) men fly about at high speeds suspended from a tall, vertical pole. Traditional dances and parades also feature.

🛏 Sleeping

If you want to secure a room the night before the Thursday or Sunday market, it's a good idea to call or arrive early the day before.

★Posada Conchita   GUESTHOUSE $
(☑5110-0866; posadaconchita@gua.net; 8a Calle 6-14; s/d Q100/150) Right beside Santo Tomás church stands this yellow colonial structure. Run by a friendly family, it has just four rooms, all done up in homey style with wood-beams overhead, fireplaces and paintings of the family's elders.

Hotel Mashito   HOTEL $
(☑5168-7178; 8a Calle 1-72; s/d Q50/100, without bathroom Q40/80) On the road to the cemetery, the homey Mashito is built around a plant-filled patio where local characters exchange views. Maintained by the kind matriarch of the establishment, the rooms have multicolored patchwork bedspreads. The shared-bath units get more light.

Hotel San Jerónimo   HOTEL $
(☑4929-1138; Final de 5a Av; r Q75/150, without bathroom Q50/100) The neat brick colonial structure stands at the top end of 5a Av, pleasantly above the fray of the market. Decorative touches are few but rooms sparkle,

with neatly made, firm beds, and the upper levels feature fantastic balconies.

Posada El Teléfono   HOTEL $
(☑4624-5052; 8a Calle 1-64; r Q30/60) The former phone call center (if you were wondering) has vertically stacked rooms, some sporting terraces, all sharing clean toilets and showers. Stay on the tippy top for views of the town's technicolor cemetery.

Chalet House   GUESTHOUSE $$
(☑3084-5691; www.chalethotelguatemala.com; 3a Calle C 7-44; s/d incl breakfast Q265/290) In a quieter residential zone north of the center, this feels like an apartment building, though the rooftop terrace is an exotic extra. Simply furnished rooms have thick *típica* blankets, real solar-powered showers, and there's a guest kitchen. Gregarious owner Manuel has plenty to tell you about his town.

Posada El Arco   GUESTHOUSE $$
(☑5883-3677; 4a Calle 4-36; s/d Q225/240) Near the Arco Gucumatz, this homey spread is one of Chichi's more original accommodations. All nine rooms are idiosyncratically appointed, with Maya weavings, colonial bedsteads and fireplaces. Rooms 6, 7 and 8 have views over the tranquil rear garden and northward to the mountains. Reservations are a good idea.

Maya Lodge   HOTEL $$
(☑4258-8882; 6a Calle A 4-08; s/d Q200/245; P) Right on the plaza, Maya Lodge has a colonial atmosphere. Adorned with woven rugs and Maya-style bedspreads, the 10 huge rooms are set alongside a patio dotted with rosebushes. Though it's a bit frayed at the edges, the welcoming attitude smooths things considerably.

Mayan Inn   HOTEL $$$
(☑5966-9127; www.mayaninn.com.gt; 8a Calle A 1-91; ☉s/d/tr Q865/1055/1150) Founded in 1932, the Inn today encompasses several restored colonial houses on either side of 8a Calle, their courtyards planted with tropical flora, their walls draped in indigenous textiles. Each of the 16 rooms is uniquely appointed, with carved armoires and fireplaces. Those on the south side have the best views.

Hotel Santo Tomás   HOTEL $$$
(☑7756-1061; www.hotelsantotomas.com.gt; 7a Av 5-32; s/d/tr Q745/865/1100; P☒) Popular with package holiday groups, this sprawling hotel is big on plant-filled patios, tinkling fountains and religious relics, and each of

WEAVING COOPERATIVES

Any traveler who's spent time in Chichicastenango, Antigua or Panajachel is familiar with the scene: an indigenous woman, weighed down by scarves, bags and blankets, approaches a group of tourists with a 'good price'. But the price isn't good enough for the tourists, who insist on bargaining it down to Wal-Mart levels. Never mind that the garment in question represents generations of accumulated artistic knowledge and takes weeks of painstaking labor plus a considerable investment in materials and dyes. In need of a quick sale, the vendor takes whatever price she can get.

Weaving cooperatives provide a viable alternative for Guatemalan women to carry on the traditional craft of backstrap loom weaving. Not only do the following associations of craftswomen pool the cost of materials, provide the artisans with a place to work and seek markets for their products, they also instill a sense of value among the weavers and help them get a fair price for their work. Most also give visitors a chance to observe the weaving process and a few offer instruction in the craft.

➜ Antigua: Casa del Tejido Antiguo (p68)

➜ Chichicastenango: Ut'z Bat'z

➜ Quetzaltenango: Manos Creativas (p135)

➜ San Antonio Palopó: Tienda Candelaria (p104)

➜ San Juan La Laguna: **Lema** (☑5866-8446; www.asociacionlema.org; 2a Calle)

➜ San Pedro La Laguna: Grupo Ecológico Teixchel (p111)

➜ Santiago Atitlán: Cojolya Association of Maya Women Weavers (p107)

➜ Zunil: Cooperativa Santa Ana (p144)

the 70 rooms features a tub and fireplace. There's a good bar and sumptuous dining room where marimba groups perform on market days.

Eating

As may be expected, most restaurants here remain empty when not occupied by tour groups, with meek underage waiters hovering in the background. The real action is in the central plaza, where attentive *abuelitas* (grandmas) ladle chicken soup, beef stew, tamales and *chiles rellenos* from huge pots as their daughters and granddaughters minister to the throngs of country folk sitting at long tables covered with oilcloth. At least four vendors line up by the central fountain, where a *chuchito* – small tamal wrapped in a corn husk – and chocolate will get you change from Q10. What are called *tamales* here are made of rice and laced with sauce. Sliced watermelon and papaya can be had at other stalls. On non-market evenings you'll find awesome enchiladas and *pupusas* in front of the town hall, served with *atole de plátano,* a warm plantain beverage spiked with cinnamon.

Tziguan Tinamit GUATEMALAN $
(6 Av, Centro Comercial Chagüila; Sandwiches Q30-45; ⊘6am-10pm) Popular with Guatemalan tourists, this makes a decent neutral choice – a clean, modern establishment with decorative nods to local culture and filling *típica* breakfasts. Service is on the clueless side.

Casa de San Juan GUATEMALAN $$
(☑7756-2086; 6a Av 7-28; mains Q60; ⊘9:30am-9:30pm Tue-Sun) One of the more stylish eateries, the San Juan occupies a beautiful colonial structure beside Santo Tomás with seating in various salons. Offerings range from burgers and sandwiches to more traditional fare, including good *chiles rellenos* laced with zesty salsa.

Mayan Inn GUATEMALAN $$
(☑5966 9127; 8a Calle A 1-91; mains Q70-90; ⊘7am-10pm) The three dining rooms at Chichi's classiest hotel feature colonial-style furnishings and canvases by Guatemala's most renowned painter, Humberto Garabito. Waiters wear costumes evolved from the dress of Spanish colonial farmers. The food is less traditional – steak platters, roast chicken, mixed grills – though lavishly presented and abundantly served.

🛍 Shopping

Ut'z Bat'z HANDICRAFTS
(8a Calle 3-14) This 'fair-trade' shop by the plaza's southwest corner displays the work of a local women's cooperative of 30 weavers, and sells scarves, shawls, table runners, bags and pillows.

ℹ Information

DANGERS & ANNOYANCES

Hola, amigo! is the refrain you'll hear from the myriad vendors and touts who depend on tourism for their livelihood; it can wear you down, but try to be polite. Ignore touts offering assistance in finding a hotel; in fact, you'll have no difficulty finding lodgings on your own.

Chichi is plagued by traffic and exhaust fumes. Keep an eye out for buses tearing around corners.

MEDICAL SERVICES

Hospital El Buen Samaritano (☑ 7756-1163; 6a Calle 3-60) Maintains a 24-hour emergency clinic.

MONEY

Chichi's many banks all stay open on Sunday.
Banco Industrial (6a Calle 6-05) Visa/MasterCard ATM.
Visa/MasterCard ATM (cnr 5a Av & 6a Calle)

POST

Post Office (4a Av 6-58) Northwest of the main plaza.

TOURIST INFORMATION

Inguat (☑ 5966-1162; info-quiche@inguat.gob.gt; 7a Av 7-14; ⊙ 8am-4pm Sun-Thu, 8am-noon Fri) Authorized guides can be hired here for cultural tours of the town and up to Pascual Abaj.

WEBSITES

Head to **Lonely Planet** (www.lonelyplanet.com/guatemala/the-highlands-quiche/chichicastenango) for planning advice, author recommendations, traveler reviews and insider tips.

ℹ Getting There & Away

Buses heading south to Panajachel, Quetzaltenango and all other points reached from the Interamericana arrive and depart from 5a Calle near the corner of 5a Av, one block uphill from the Arco Gucumatz. Buses approaching from the south go up 7a Av, dropping off passengers two blocks east of the central plaza.
Antigua (3½ hours) Take any bus heading for Guatemala City and change at Chimaltenango.
Guatemala City (Q30, 2½ hours) Every 30 minutes from 3am to 5pm.

Los Encuentros (Q6, 30 minutes) Frequent microbuses leave from in front of the Telgua building on 7a Av.
Panajachel (Q15, two hours) Buses at 6am, 9am, noon & 1pm, or take any southbound bus and change at Los Encuentros.
Quetzaltenango (Q20, two hours) Five buses between 7am and 3pm, or take any southbound bus and change at Los Encuentros.
Santa Cruz del Quiché (Q6, 35 minutes) Microbuses from 5a Calle on the west side of 5a Av between 6am and 11pm.

Chichi Turkaj Tours (☑ 5372-1349; 7a Av 5-41) offers shuttles to Guatemala City (Q200), Antigua (Q95), Panajachel (Q55) and Quetzaltenango (Q140) on Monday and Friday at 9am and Sunday and Thursday at 5pm. **Agencia de Viajes Maya Chichi Van** (☑ 5007-2051; 6a Calle 6-45) goes to the same destinations on Sunday and Thursday, at similar fares. In most cases they need at least five passengers. These agencies also run tours to K'umarcaaj near Santa Cruz del Quiché, Nebaj and elsewhere.

Santa Cruz del Quiché

POP 32,256 / ELEV 1979M

Without Chichicastenango's big market and attendant tourism, Santa Cruz – or just El Quiché – presents a less self-conscious slice of regional life and is refreshingly free of competition for tourist lucre. Just 19km north of Chichi, it's the capital of Quiché department, drawing a diverse populace on business and administrative affairs. The main market days are Thursday and Sunday, boosting the bustle considerably. Travelers who come here usually do so to visit K'umarcaaj, the ruins of the old K'iche' Maya capital, or to change buses en route further north.

The most exciting time to be here is mid-August during the **Fiestas Elenas** (www.fiestaselenas.com), a week of festivities and a proud display of indigenous traditions. It all leads up to the *convite feminino*, when El Quiché's women don masks and dance up a storm to marimba accompaniment.

◉ Sights

Most points of interest are within a few short blocks of the tripartite plaza, usually a hive of activity. The top square is flanked on its east side by Gobernación (the departmental government palace), the middle one by the cathedral and *municipalidad* (town hall), and the bottom one by the big domed events hall, in front of which stands a statue of K'iche' warrior Tecún Umán in a fierce posture, as if poised for battle against conquistador Pedro Alvarado. The main market occupies a series of buildings east of the plaza.

K'umarcaaj   ARCHAEOLOGICAL SITE

(Gumarkaaj | Utatlán; admission Q30; ☺8am-4:30pm) The ruins of the ancient K'iche' Maya capital of K'umarcaaj remain a sacred site for the Maya, and contemporary rituals are customarily enacted there. Archaeologists have identified 100 or so large structures here, but only limited restoration has been done. The ruins have a fine setting, shaded by tall trees and surrounded by ravines. Bring a flashlight.

The kingdom of K'iche' was established in late Postclassic times (about the 14th century) by a mixture of indigenous people and invaders from the Tabasco-Campeche border area in Mexico. Around 1400, King Ku'ucumatz founded K'umarcaaj and conquered many neighboring settlements. During the long reign of his successor Q'uik'ab (1425–75), the K'iche' kingdom extended its borders to Huehuetenango, Nebaj, Rabinal and the Pacific Slope. At the same time the Kaqchiquel, a vassal people who once fought alongside the K'iche', rebelled, establishing an independent capital at Iximché.

When Pedro de Alvarado and his Spanish conquistadors hit Guatemala in 1524, it was the K'iche', under their king Tecún Umán, who led the resistance against them. In the decisive battle fought near Quetzaltenango on February 12, 1524, Alvarado and Tecún locked in mortal combat. Alvarado prevailed. The defeated K'iche' invited him to visit K'umarcaaj. Smelling a rat, Alvarado enlisted the aid of his Mexican auxiliaries and the anti-K'iche' Kaqchiquel, and together they captured the K'iche' leaders, burnt them alive in K'umarcaaj's main plaza and then destroyed the city.

The museum at the entrance will help orientate you. The tallest of the structures round the central plaza, the Templo de Tohil (a sky god), is blackened by smoke and has a niche where contemporary prayer-men regularly make offerings to Maya gods.

Down the hillside to the right of the plaza is the entrance to a long tunnel known as the *cueva*. Legend has it that the K'iche' dug the tunnel as a refuge for their women and children in preparation for Alvarado's coming, and that a K'iche' princess was later buried in a deep shaft off this tunnel. Revered as the place where the K'iche' kingdom died, the *cueva* is sacred to highland Maya and is an important location for prayers, candle burning, offerings and chicken sacrifices.

If there's anyone around the entrance, ask permission before entering. Inside, the long tunnel (perhaps 100m long) is blackened with smoke and incense and littered with candles and flower petals. Use your flashlight and watch your footing: there are several side tunnels and at least one of them, on the right near the end, contains a deep, black shaft.

The ruins of K'umarcaaj are 3km west of El Quiché. Gray 'Ruinas' microbuses depart from in front of the cathedral in Santa Cruz every 20 minutes (Q1). The last one back is at 6:50pm.

🛏 Sleeping

The main hotel district is along 1a Av (Zona 5) north of the bus terminal, with at least five hotels within two blocks, and two more on either side along 9a Calle.

Hotel Rey K'iche   HOTEL $

(☏7755-0827; 8a Calle 0-39, Zona 5; s/d Q100/180; @) Between the bus station and plaza, the Rey K'iche is excellent value with well-maintained, brick-walled rooms around a quiet interior and has affable staff. There's free drinking water and a decent cafe upstairs serving breakfast and dinner.

Posada Santa Cecilia   HOTEL $$

(☏5332-8811; cnr 1a Av & 6a Calle; s/d Q125/200) Conveniently placed above an espresso vendor just south of the main plaza, this modern establishment offers a handful of bright, spiffy units with large firm beds and pretty quilts.

El Sitio Hotel   HOTEL $$

(☏7755-3656; elsitiohotel@gmail.com; 9a Calle 0-41, Zona 5; s/d/tr Q200/300/400; P✶) *Muy nice*, this efficiently-run hotel two blocks north of the bus terminal resembles a modern Evangelical church. The business-class accommodations have a bit of *típica* decor. Breakfast is served in the stylish cafe.

🍴 Eating

For budget grub, there's plenty of grilling action going on around and within the market.

Café San Miguel   BAKERY $

(☏7755-1488; 2 Av 4-42; sandwiches Q12; ☺8am-8pm) Opposite the cathedral, this little bakery-cafe is a popular gathering place, with good coffee and fresh baked goods on offer. Muffins are called *cubos* here; *pan dormido* is bread that's been allowed to lie around for a few days.

Restaurant El Chalet   STEAKHOUSE $$
(☑7755-0618; 1a Av 2-02, Zona 5; mains Q55-70; ☺7am-9pm) The specialty here is grilled meats, served with homemade salsas. You could make a light meal of the tortilla-sized portions. Dining is in pleasant gardens beneath an arbor. It's a few blocks east of the big clock tower.

ℹ Information

Quiché's **tourist office** (☑7755-1106; turismo enquiche@gmail.com; ☺8am-4:30pm Mon-Fri), inside the town hall, has all the answers and they'll give you a baroquely detailed map. Banco Agromercantil, at the plaza's north end, has a Cajero 5B ATM. Get online at **Bear Net** (7a Calle 0-15B; ☺8:30am-9pm), a block south of the plaza.

Note that each *zona* has its own street-avenue grid, so numbered *calles* and *avenidas* repeat themselves.

ℹ Getting There & Away

El Quiché is the jumping-off point for the remote reaches of northern Quiché, which extend all the way to the Mexican border. The main bus terminal, a dusty lot in Zona 5, is located four blocks south and two blocks east of the plaza.

Chichicastenango (Q6, 35 minutes) Frequent microbuses depart from a parking lot off the southwest corner of the main plaza.

Guatemala City (Q35, three hours) Every 15 minutes, 3am to 5pm.

Huehuetenango (Q25, two hours) Every half hour from 5am to 5:30pm.

Nebaj (Q20, two hours) Five buses via Sacapulas 9am to 4:30pm.

Sacapulas (Q12, one hour) Microbuses depart from 1a Av off the northeast corner of main plaza every half hour till 6:30pm.

Uspantán (Q25, two hours) Microbuses every 20 minutes from 5:30am to 8:30pm.

Uspantán

POP 6792

About halfway between Huehuetenango and Cobán along the 7W road, Uspantán is a benevolent town, offering a few attractions of its own, though the sky-high journey through the Cuchumatanes is reason enough to travel there.

COMMUNITY TOURISM IN LAJ CHIMEL

Renowned as the place that spawned Nobel Peace Prize winner Rigoberta Menchú (see the boxed text, p272), Laj Chimel offers homegrown tours of the community and surroundings. Local K'iche' guides lead relaxed walks along a well-conditioned trail through the cloud forest, pointing out birds and wildlife and stopping at a lookout point for impressive views over the Cuchumatanes range. Along the way, you'll learn about medicinal plants, *milpa* cultivation and the civil war atrocities that occurred here. The cost of the tour, including lunch at a community home, is Q240 per person with a minimum of two persons. Transport from Uspantán (9km, Q400) can be arranged, or a local bus departing at 6am can get you as far as the community of La Danta, by a secluded lake one hour's walk from Laj Chimel. For more info about the program, see lajchimelecoturismo.com.

The setting of the town is stunning in a fertile valley at the base of green forested mountains, over which a bank of clouds roll in each afternoon. Women wear lacy, loose-fitting *huipiles* in bright orange or pink.

Founded by the Uspanteko Maya around the 6th century AD, it was originally dubbed Tz'unun Kaab' – place of hummingbirds. The severe repression it experienced during the armed conflict of the 1980s forged indigenous leader Rigoberta Menchú, who grew up a five-hour walk through the mountains in the village of Laj Chimel – though some locals wonder why she hasn't returned to her hometown. Cardamom is grown, pigs and sheep are raised on the surrounding slopes and gravel mining is a key industry.

The helpful **tourist office** (☑5204-9145; vivian_aj89@hotmail.com; ☺8am-5pm Mon-Fri), on the central plaza, provides info on a range of interesting trips, including community-led tours of the cloud forest around Laj Chimel. Another tour visits the Maya ceremonial center at Cerro Xoqoneb' (Q50 per person), a half-hour hike from the center of town.

There's a 5B ATM at Banrural, a block east of the church.

🛏 Sleeping & Eating

Hotel Don Gabriel
HOTEL $

(📞7951-8540; hoteldongabriel@yahoo.es; 7a Av 6-22; s/d/tr Q75/150/210) Rooms at this excellent value lodging, just around the corner from the Parque Central, have plenty of thick blankets for the evening chill. If possible, choose a room on the top level opening onto a Gaudiesque terrace with various plant-laden gazebos and fabulous views of the mountains. Downstairs is a neat and clean little restaurant serving breakfast from 7am.

Hotel Posada Doña Leonor
HOTEL $

(📞7951-8041; caluti54@hotmail.com; 6a Calle 4-25, Zona 1; s/d/tr Q80/140/180; P 🛜) This well-maintained option a couple of blocks east of the plaza features 21 rooms around a courtyard with a cook shack in the middle for breakfast and supper. You'll find firm beds, fresh paint, and huge spotless bathrooms with blasting-hot showers.

Restaurant Al Ast'
SPANISH $

(6a Av 7-50, Zona 3; mains Q30-45; ⊙ 7:30am-9pm) Catalonian cuisine in Uspantán? Hailing from that Iberian region, the owner of this unpretentious eatery whips up dishes like *fidevada* (a paella variation) and *fricandó* (a beef-mushroom stew). It's two blocks west of the bandshell on the central plaza.

❶ Getting There & Away

Microbuses for Quiché (Q30, 2½ hours), via Sacapulas, leave whenever full from Uspantán's bus terminal on 6a Calle, three blocks west of the Parque Central, until 7pm. For Cobán (Q40, three hours), microbuses go hourly from 4am to 4pm. For Nebaj, there are a couple of direct microbuses (coming from Cobán), or get a Sacapulas microbus and change at the *entronque de Nebaj* (Nebaj turnoff), about 8km before Sacapulas.

Nebaj

POP 42,382 / ELEV 2000M

Hidden in a remote fold of the Cuchumatanes mountains north of Sacapulas is the Triángulo Ixil (Ixil Triangle), a 2300-sq-km zone comprising the towns of Santa María Nebaj, San Juan Cotzal and San Gaspar Chajul, as well as dozens of outlying villages and hamlets. The local Ixil Maya people, though they suffered perhaps more than anybody in Guatemala's civil war, cling proudly to their traditions and speak the Ixil language. Nebaj women are celebrated for their beautiful purple, green and yellow pom-pommed hair braids, scarlet *cortes*, and their *huipiles* and *rebozos* (shawls), with many bird and animal motifs.

Living in this beautiful mountain vastness has long been both a blessing and a curse. The invading Spaniards found it difficult to conquer, and they laid waste to the inhabitants when they did. During the civil war years, massacres and disappearances were rife, with more than two dozen villages destroyed. According to estimates by church groups and human-rights organizations, some 25,000 Ixil inhabitants (of a population of 85,000) were either killed or displaced by the army between 1978 and 1983 as part of the campaign to expunge guerrilla activity. You may hear some appalling personal experiences from locals while you're here.

The people of the Ixil Triangle are making a heroic effort to build a new future with the help of development organizations and NGOs, whose workers you're likely to encounter during your visit.

◎ Sights

A block east of the Parque Principal is the market (busiest on Sunday). Calz 15 de Septiembre runs northeast from the Parque to become the road to Cotzal and Chajul.

Iglesia de Nebaj
CHURCH

This formidable church dominates the south side of Parque Principal. Inside, to the left of the entrance is a memorial to Juan José Gerardi, the socially progressive priest who as bishop of Quiché witnessed widespread human rights abuses here. Soon after he released a report about these atrocities, Gerardi himself was assassinated. Several hundred crosses around the monument memorialize the Nebaj inhabitants who were murdered during a massacre in the early 1980s.

Centro Cultural Kumool
MUSEUM

(5a Av 1-32; admission Q10; ⊙ 9am-noon & 1-6pm Mon-Fri, 8am-1pm Sat) Housed in the Radio Ixil building, this recently opened museum displays a collection of mostly ceramic objects excavated in the Ixil region, all arranged by historical period. Among the more interesting pieces are a ceremonial ax with a skull handle and a giant funerary urn with a jaguar face, plus some well-preserved polychrome vases.

Nebaj

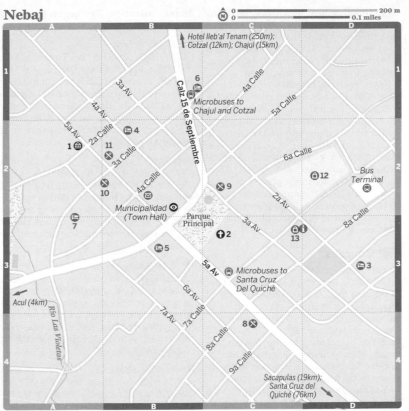

Nebaj

⊙ Sights
1 Centro Cultural Kumool A2
2 Iglesia de Nebaj C3

⊕ Activities, Courses & Tours
El Descanso .... (see 10)
Nebaj Language School .... (see 10)

⊜ Sleeping
3 Hotel Ixil D3
4 Hotel Santa María B2
5 Hotel Turansa B3

6 Hotel Villa Nebaj B1
7 Media Luna Medio Sol A3

⊗ Eating
8 Asados El Pasabien C4
9 Comedor El Si'm C2
10 El Descanso B2
11 Popi's Restaurant B2

⌂ Shopping
12 Market D2
13 Mercado de Artesanías C3

🏃 Activities

Hiking

Started as a Peace Corps project, **El Descan-so** (☎ 7756-0207; www.nebaj.com; 3a Calle, Zona 1) offers a range of hikes, courses, projects and other activities. The hiking component of the organization, **Guías Ixiles** (☎ 5847-4747; www.nebaj.com; 3a Calle, El Descanso Bldg, Zona 1; ⊙ 8am-12:30pm & 2-5pm), offers half-day walks to Las Cataratas (Q55 for one person plus Q25 for each extra person), a series of waterfalls north of town, or town walks with visits to the sacred sites of the *costumbristas* (people who practice non-Christian Maya rites). Another hike leads 4km east along the peaceful Nebaj River valley to Cocop, a mountain-top village that was particularly hard hit during the civil war. Guías Ixiles also lead three-day treks over the Cuchumatanes to Todos Santos Cuchumatán.

If you prefer to hike on your own, take a copy of the *Guía de Senderismo Región Ixil* (Q50), with detailed descriptions and maps (in Spanish) for 20 treks in the Ixil region, and organize lodging and food on arrival in villages at *posadas comunitarias* (which are community-run lodges with wooden-board beds, drinking water and toilets). There humble accommodations operate at Xexocom, Chortiz and Parramos Grande, west of Nebaj, on a possible four-day hike route. The guidebook is sold at the tourist office in the Mercado de Artesanías.

Courses

Nebaj Language School

(📞 7756-0207; www.nebaj.com/nls.html; 3a Calle, El Descanso Bldg, Zona 1) Affiliated with El Descanso, this institute offers instruction in Spanish (Q600 for 20 hours per week). Combined with accommodation with a local family, including two meals a day, two guided hikes to nearby villages and internet use, the fee is Q1300. Instruction in the indigenous Ixil language is another option.

You can also learn how to make regional dishes like *boxboles* (corn dough wrapped in squash leaves, served with a spicy peanut sauce) for Q50 per hour.

Festivals & Events

Nebaj's annual **festival**, coinciding with the Assumption of the Virgin Mary, runs for 10 days in mid-August.

Sleeping

Media Luna Medio Sol   HOSTEL $

(📞 5749-7450; www.nebaj.com/medialuna.html; 3a Calle 6-25; dm Q35, r per person Q45; 🛜) Nebaj's spiffiest hostel is around the corner from its parent organization, El Descanso, where you can check in. Two six-bed dorms and a few private rooms share clean toilets and showers. There's a sauna, TV lounge and kitchen facilities to keep you busy.

Hotel Turansa   HOTEL $

(📞 4144-7709; cnr 5a Calle & 6a Av; s/d from Q80/135; 🅿) This friendly, central establishment has decent-sized rooms along plant-draped balconies. Top-floor triples open onto a sunny terrace.

Hotel Ileb'al Tenam   HOTEL $

(📞 7755-8039; Calz 15 de Septiembre; s/d Q60/105, without bathroom Q35/65; 🅿) This cordially managed lodging at the north edge of town (only 500m from the park) features two sections: a long wooden house with simple rooms along a plank veranda; and at the rear, an 'annex' with more modern units around a tranquil patio.

Hotel Ixil   HOTEL $

(📞 7756-0036; cnr 2a Av & 9a Calle; s/d/tr Q75/122/170; 🅿) Rooms here are set around a leafy courtyard. The ones on the top level are more spacious, with wood-beamed ceilings. Warning: services at the Evangelical church round the corner can reach thunderous volumes.

★Hotel Santa María   HOTEL $$

(📞 4212-7927; www.hotelsantamarianebaj.com; cnr 4a Av & 2a Calle; s/d Q125/200; 🅿🛜) Scarlet woven bedspreads, carved wood headboards and other Ixil handicrafts decorate the bright, spotless rooms at this well-maintained property three blocks northwest of the main plaza.

Hotel Villa Nebaj   HOTEL $$

(📞 7756-0005; Calz 15 de Septiembre 2-37; s/d Q150/225, without bathroom Q75/125; 🅿🛜) Behind the elaborate facade is a neat, modern hotel with fountains in the courtyard and elaborate paintings of *nebajenses* in fiesta wear. Rooms on three levels have a dash of style, with *típica* bedspreads, carved headboards and piping hot showers.

Eating

Comedor El Si'm   GUATEMALAN $

(3a Av; breakfast Q15; ⏰ 7am-9pm) This below-street-level place off the main plaza is great for a classic *desayuno* (breakfast), served with a bonus bowl of *mosh* (granola and bananas) and freshly baked cookie, and they refill your coffee cup. It's usually crammed with local characters by 8am.

Popi's Restaurant   CAFE $

(📞 7756-0159; 5a Calle 6-74; mains Q22-40; ⏰ breakfast, lunch & dinner) This low-key cafe/hostel/expat hangout whips up gringo comfort foods. A copious breakfast menu includes three-egg omelets, granola and burritos.

El Descanso CAFE $
(3a Calle, Zona 1; mains Q25-30; ☺ breakfast, lunch & dinner) Sharing a property with the Nebaj Language School, this cozy restaurant features a bar and lounge areas in Nebaj's most alternative ambience. A range of snacks, salads and soups is served.

Asados El Pasabien STEAKHOUSE $
(cnr 5a Av & 9a Calle; mains Q35-45; ☺ noon-9pm) Steaks, chicken and shrimp are skillfully grilled and served up with heaping portions of halved potatoes, salad and nice homemade salsas at this locally popular dining hall.

🛍 Shopping

Mercado de Artesanías HANDICRAFTS
(Handicrafts Market; cnr 7a Calle & 2a Av, Zona 1; ☺ 8am-6pm) You can buy local textiles inside this market. The numerous vendor stalls offer well-made *rebozos, cintas* (the pom-pommed braid woven into Ixil women's hair) and *huipiles*, which can cost anywhere from Q300 to Q5000, depending on quality.

ℹ Information

The **tourist office** (☎ 7755-8182; cnr 7a Calle & 2a Av, Zona 1; ☺ 8am-5pm Mon-Sat, 8am-noon Sun), inside the Mercado de Artesanías, can answer any question as long as it's posed in Spanish.

Banrural (☺ 8:30am-5pm Mon-Fri, 7am-1pm Sat), on the Parque Principal, changes traveler's checks; the Cajero 5B is in the Town Hall building, opposite the park. The **post office** (5a Av 4-37) is one block northwest of the park. La Red, inside El Descanso, offers internet access.

ℹ Getting There & Away

The bus terminal is just below the market. Microbuses bound for Santa Cruz del Quiché, via Sacapulas, go every half hour from 4am until 5pm (Q25, two hours), departing from behind the church at the corner of 5a Av and 7a Calle. To head west to Huehuetenango, change at Sacapulas. To get to Uspantán and Cobán, get off at the Cunén junction (Q15) and hail any eastbound microbus.

Microbuses to Chajul (Q7, 45 minutes) depart every 20 minutes or so until 6pm from in front of the Hotel Villa Nebaj, on Calz 15 de Septiembre.

The main bus terminal, behind the market, mainly serves outlying villages such as Tzalbal, Vicalama and Palop; a midnight bus travels all the way to Guatemala City (Q55, 5½ hours) via Chichicastenango.

Around Nebaj

Chajul

POP 16,523

A good paved road winds northeast through piney slopes to Chajul, an impoverished but intensely traditional village, where age-old customs are still widely practiced. Women stroll arm-in-arm wearing maroon *cortes* (wraparound skirts), earrings made from silver coins, and bright blue or purple *huipiles* woven with geometric patterns. Along the dirt streets, adobe structures with tile roofs propped up by carved wooden pillars are interspersed with patches of maize and squash. Tuesday and Friday are market days.

Located in the community of Xetze, 2km southwest of Chajul, the **Museo Maya Ixil** (admission Q25; ☺ 8am-5pm) displays local artifacts and jewelry, archaeological finds and indigenous outfits, as well as evidence of Chajul's resistance during the armed conflict of the 1980s.

Limitless Horizons Ixil (☎ 5332-6264; www.limitlesshorizonsixil.org) is an NGO based in Chajul working to expand educational opportunities for local children. It offers home visits and meals with indigenous families,

---

CHAJUL'S HIDDEN MURALS

While renovating the kitchen of his ancient dwelling in Chajul, resident Lucas Ariscona made a momentous discovery. Removing several layers of plaster revealed a series of murals that had probably not seen light for centuries. The paintings, which cover several walls of Ariscona's home, depict some kind of procession made up of both Spaniards and Mayas. Though they're seriously faded by sudden exposure to the elements after being concealed for so long, it is still possible to make out a figure in European attire playing a drum for another character in Maya ceremonial costume as well as a caped reveler bearing a human heart in his hand. Though Ariscona has made efforts to preserve the murals, his resources are limited and in the smoke-filled environment of a typical Chajul home, the rare testament to a Euro-Maya encounter faces inevitable deterioration.

guided hikes to sacred Maya sites, classes in weaving and the Ixil language, and lots of other fun and fascinating activities.

Standing in a patch of forest, the **Posada Vetz K'aol** (☑ 5784-8802; eduarim5@yahoo.es; dm/r per person Q66/77) is a former stable, built in the local style with carved wood columns along an arcade. Most of the pine-paneled rooms have four or five bunk beds and there's one double with its own bathroom. A cozy sitting room has a large fireplace and coffee maker. Located a 10-minute stroll from the center of Chajul, down a path off the road from Nebaj, it's owned by a local coffee growers' cooperative that offers half-day tours of the area for Q50 per person. Host Eduardo can meet you in the village and accompany you to the lodge.

Acul

Acul, 4km west of Nebaj, was founded as the first *polo de desarrollo* (pole of development) in 1983. Considered 'strategic hamlets', these settlements were constructed to enable the army to keep inhabitants from having contact with the guerrillas. After the civil war, some people returned to their original homes but others stayed on since they'd received plots of land. Set astride the bucolic Río Acul Valley, it retains a functional appearance, with stores and Evangelical prayer halls along either side of a broad dirt street. These days the main activities are weaving, cattle ranching and loom building.

Just north of Acul is a pair of farms devoted to the making of cheese. They were started by two immigrant brothers, the Azzaris, cheese makers in their native Italian Alps who moved to Guatemala in the 1930s, perhaps choosing the Acul valley because of its alpine appearance. Older brother José gained renown as a prize wrestler before being killed in the ring.

Both farms offer excellent accommodations. The first you come to, the **Hacienda Mil Amores** (☑ 5704-4817; r per person Q183), has four country cabins on a hillside and serves a superb lunch (Q55, by reservation). Just across the way, the humbler **Hacienda San Antonio** (☑ 5702-1907; haciendasanantonio.webs.com; r per person Q160) has half a dozen neat, wood-floored rooms, some with hot-water bathroom, and does meals (Q55). Microbuses ply the paved road between Nebaj and Acul every half hour, or consider hiking over with Guías Ixiles (p128) and taking the bus back.

WESTERN HIGHLANDS

The mountainous departments of Quetzaltenango, Totonicapán and Huehuetenango are generally less frequented by tourists than regions closer to Guatemala City. But with extraordinarily dramatic scenery and vibrant indigenous culture, this part of the country presents an invariably fascinating panorama. Highlights of any visit include Quetzaltenango, Guatemala's second-largest city, with an ever-growing language-school and volunteer-work scene; the pretty nearby town of Zunil, with its volcanically heated springs; ascents of the volcanoes around Quetzaltenango; and the remote mountain enclave of Todos Santos Cuchumatán, north of Huehuetenango, with a strong traditional culture and excellent walking possibilities.

Quetzaltenango

POP 167,200 / ELEV 2367M

Quetzaltenango may well be the perfect Guatemalan town – not too big, not too small, enough foreigners to support a good range of hotels and restaurants, but not so many that it loses its national flavor. The Guatemalan 'layering' effect is at work in the city center – once the Spanish moved out, the Germans moved in and their architecture gives the zone a somber, even Gothic, feel.

Quetzaltenango is big, like its name – which the locals kindly shorten to Xela (*shell*-ah), itself an abbreviation of the original Quiché Maya name, Xelajú – but by Guatemalan standards, it is an orderly, clean and safe city. It tends to attract a more serious type of traveler – people who really want to learn Spanish and then stay around and get involved in the myriad volunteer projects on offer.

Xela also functions as a base for a range of spectacular hikes through the surrounding countryside – the ascent to the summit of Volcán Tajumulco (Central America's highest point) and the three-day trek to Lago de Atitlán, to name a few.

Quetzaltenango came under the sway of the K'iche' Maya of K'umarcaaj when they began their great expansion in the 14th century. Before that it had been a Mam Maya town. It was near here that the K'iche' leader Tecún Umán was defeated and killed by the Spanish conquistador Pedro de Alvarado in 1524.

The town prospered in the late-19th-century coffee boom, with brokers opening warehouses and *finca* (plantation) owners coming to town to buy supplies. This boom busted when the combined earthquake and eruption of Santa María in 1902 wreaked mass destruction. Still, the city's position at the intersection of roads to the Pacific Slope, Mexico and Guatemala City guaranteed it some degree of prosperity. Today it's again busy with commerce, of the indigenous, foreign and *ladino* varieties.

⊙ Sights

Parque Centro América   PLAZA
(Map p136) Most of Xela's sights crowd in and around the broad central plaza, known as the Parque Centro América. The original version, designed by Italian architect Alberto Porta in the 1800s, comprised two separate parks; these were combined in a 1930s update into its current oblong shape. Most notable of the monuments scattered along its expanse is a rotunda of Ionic columns dedicated to the composer Rafael Álvarez Ovalle, locally known as 'The Kiosk'. In the center of the plaza is a **pillar** dedicated to Justo Rufino Barrios, the 19th-century president whose 'reforms' transferred land ownership from Maya peasants to coffee-plantation owners. At the southern end, the Casa de Cultura houses the **Museo de Historia Natural** (Map p136; ☑ 7761-6427; 7a Calle; admission Q6; ☺ 8am-noon & 2-6pm Mon-Fri, 9am-5pm Sat & Sun). The museum holds a hodgepodge of Maya artifacts, vintage photos, dried leaves, old coins, marimbas, sports trophies, stuffed mammals and birds, all displayed in cases reminiscent of elementary school outings.

The ornately carved facade of the **Iglesia del Espíritu Santo** marks the site of the original 1532 construction, pulverized by the quakes of 1853 and 1902. The modern **Metropolitan Cathedral** behind it was finished in the 1990s.

The **municipalidad** (Town Hall; Map p136), at the northeastern end of the park, was rebuilt after the 1902 earthquake in the grandiose neoclassical style. Step inside to see a planted mosaic of the town seal. Another neoclassical structure just north, the **Edificio Rivera** (Map p136), has been handsomely renovated (complete with fast-food franchise).

On the west side of the park between 4a and 5a Calles is the **Pasaje Enríquez** (Map p136; btwn 4a & 5a Calles), an imposing arcade patterned after a structure in Florence, Italy, housing an assortment of travel agencies, language institutes, cafes and one major bar.

Parque Zoológico Minerva   ZOO
(Map p132; ☑ 7763-5637; Av Las Américas 0-50, Zona 3; ☺ 9am-5pm Tue-Sun) About 2km northwest of Parque Centro América, near the Terminal Minerva bus station is this zoo, with monkeys, coyotes and Barbary sheep, plus a few rides for children.

Templo de Minerva   MONUMENT
(Map p132) Outside the zoo on an island in the middle of 4a Calle stands this neoclassical temple built by dictator Estrada Cabrera to honor the Roman goddess of education and to inspire Guatemalans to new heights of learning.

Centro Intercultural de Quetzaltenango   CULTURAL CENTER
(Map p132; 4a Calle & 19 Av, Zona 3) Quetzaltenango's railroad station, 1km east of the Templo de Minerva along 4a Calle, lay dormant for years until the city converted it into this center with schools of art and dance and three fine museums.

The **Museo Ixkik'** (☑ 7761-6472; admission Q25; ☺ 9am-1pm & 2-6pm) is devoted to Maya weaving and traditional outfits, while some 200 paintings by Guatemala's leading modernists are exhibited in the **Museo de Arte** (admission Q6; ☺ 8am-noon & 2-6pm), including works by Efraín Recinos, Juan Antonio Franco and the landscape artist José Luis Álvarez. The **Museo del Ferrocarril de los Altos** (admission Q6; ☺ 8am-noon & 2-6pm) covers the ambitious rail project that connected Quetzaltenango to the Pacific coast but operated for just three years from 1930 to 1933.

🕴 Activities

Volcano Ascents & Treks
There are many exciting walks and climbs to be done from Xela. **Volcán Tajumulco** (4220m), 50km northwest, is the highest point in Central America and is a challenging trip of one long day from the city or two days with a night camping on the mountain. This includes about five hours' walking up from the starting point, Tuhichan (2½ hours by bus from Xela).

With early starts, **Volcán Santa María** (3772m), towering to the south of the city, and the highly active **Santiaguito** (2488m), on Santa María's southwest flank, can both be done in long mornings from Xela, though the tough, slippery trail is recommended only for seasoned hikers. You start walking at the village of **Llanos del Pinal**, 5km south of Xela (Q5 by bus), from which it's four to

Quetzaltenango

N

0   500 m
0   0.25 miles

San Martín Sacatepéquez (20km)

Salcajá (5km);
Cuatro Caminos &
Interamericana (9km);
San Andrés Xecul (11km);
San Francisco El Alto (13km);
Totonicapán (20km);
Momostenango (24km)

Zunil (via Cantel, 14km)

Río Seco

ZONA 2

13a Calle
11a Calle
10a Calle
7a Calle

6a Av
4a Av
3a Av

Monumento a la Marimba

7a Av (Calzada Independencia)

Calle Cirilo Flores

Av El Central

Diagonal 2

2a Av
3a Av
4a Av
5a Av
6a Av

Diagonal 13

5a Calle

Av Jesús Castillo

12a Av
13a Av
14a Av

Transportes Álamo

Línea Dorada

Estadio Mario Camposeco

ZONA 3

8a Calle
7a Calle
6a Calle
5a Calle

15a Av
16a Av
17a Av
18a Av
19a Av
20a Av

Parque Benito Juárez
4a Calle
3a Calle
1a Calle
2a Calle

14a Av
12a Av

ZONA 1

4a Calle

Parque Centro América

See Central Quetzaltenango Map (p136)

Transportes Galgos

21a Av
22a Av
23a Av
24a Av

6a Av

ADN

4a Calle
3a Calle

Calle Rodolfo Robles

1a Calle

Parque El Calvario

Iglesia El Calvario

Cemetery

Diagonal 14

Diagonal 11

Diagonal 8

Diagonal 12
Diagonal 13

Terminal Minerva

Mercado La Terminal

Complejo Deportivo

Microbuses to City Center

San Martín Sacatepéquez (20km)

Quetzaltenango

five hours up to the summit of Santa María. Getting too close to Santiaguito is dangerous, so people usually just look at it from a point about 1½ hours' walk from Llanos del Pinal.

Kaqchikel Tours   HIKING
(Map p136; ☎ 5010-4465; www.kaqchikeltoursxela. com; 7a Calle 15-36, Zona 1) This locally owned outfit specializes in volcano ascents. Two-day Tajumulco trips cost Q375 per person. Kaqchikel also offers full-moon ascents of Santa María (Q150) and challenging two-day Santiaguito trips (Q600), camping on a small hill as close as is safely possible to the crater. Prices (all with a minimum of four participants) include transportation, food, equipment and a guide.

Monte Verde Tours   HIKING
(Map p136; ☎ 5729-6279; www.monte-verdetours. com; 13a Av 8-34, Zona 1) Offers a variety of volcano hikes and tours of villages around Xela.

Quetzaltrekkers   HIKING
(Map p132; ☎ 7765-5895; www.quetzaltrekkers. com; Diagonal 12 8-37, Zona 1) Most of the guides at this unique outfit are foreign volunteers

(and experienced trekkers can join their ranks). Based at the Casa Argentina hotel, they provide both monetary and logistical support for various social projects.

Two-day hikes to Fuentes Georginas and Pico Zunil (Q400 per person), three-day trips to Lago de Atitlán (Q600) and six-day treks to Nebaj (Q1100) run on a weekly basis; check the calendar to see when they go. Also offered are rock-climbing expeditions to La Muela, a pilgrimage site in the Almolonga Valley where rock pillars rise out of an extinct lava field.

Cycling
Biking is a great way to explore the surrounding countryside or commute to Spanish class. Fuentes Georginas, San Andrés Xecul and the steam vents at Los Vahos are all attainable day trips.

The Bike House   CYCLING
(Map p136; 15a Av 5-22) Street bikes (Q40 per day) and mountain bikes (Q80 per day) for rent.

Vrisa Books   CYCLING
(Map p136; 15a Av 3-64, Zona 1) This place rents mountain and town bikes for Q40/100/200 per day/week/month; it also offers cycling tours.

 Courses

Language Courses
Quetzaltenango's many language schools attract students from around the world. Unlike Antigua, it isn't overrun with foreigners, though there is a growing social scene revolving around language students and volunteer workers.

Most schools provide opportunities to get involved in social action programs working with the local K'iche' Maya. The standard weekly price is Q920/1050 for four/five hours of instruction per day, Monday to Friday. Add around Q330 for room and board with a local family. Some places charge up to 20% more for tuition from June to August, and many require nonrefundable registration fees. Extras range from movies and free internet to dancing, cooking classes and lectures on Guatemalan politics and culture.

Celas Maya   LANGUAGE COURSE
(Map p136; ☎ 7761-4342; www.celasmaya.edu.gt; 6a Calle 14-55, Zona 1) Busy, professional outfit with a good library and internet cafe. Official

training and testing center for DELE (test of Spanish as a foreign language).

Inepas
LANGUAGE COURSE

(Instituto de Español y Participación en Ayuda Social; Map p136; ☑ 7765-1308; www.inepas.org; 15a Av 4-59) Students can participate in a variety of worthy projects. Offers a selection of inexpensive accommodations besides home stays.

Proyecto Lingüístico
Quetzalteco de Español
LANGUAGE COURSE

(Map p132; ☑ 7763-1061; www.plqe.org; 5a Calle 2-40, Zona 1) This collectively managed and politically minded institute also runs the Escuela de la Montaña, a limited-enrollment language-learning program in a rural zone nearby the town of Colomba. Courses in K'iche' are also offered.

Centro de Estudios
de Español Pop Wuj
LANGUAGE COURSE

(Map p132; ☑ 7761-8286; www.pop-wuj.org; 1a Calle 17-72, Zona 1) Pop Wuj's profits go to development projects in nearby villages, in which students can participate.

El Portal Spanish School
LANGUAGE COURSE

(Map p136; ☑ 7761-5275; www.spanishschoolelportal.com; 9a Callejón A 11-49, Zona 1) Small outfit with enthusiastic and supportive atmosphere. Earnings provide scholarships for children of single mothers.

Dance Courses
Sangre Latina

(Map p136; ☑ 7768-3270; info@sangrelatinaguatemala.com; 7a Calle 14-27, Zona 1) Centrally located, Sangre Latina is staffed by internationally prominent instructors. If you're just looking to make a night of it, the dance club La Parranda (p141) offers free salsa classes on Wednesday from 9pm.

Weaving Courses
Women's cooperatives **Manos Creativas** (Map p132; ☑ 7761-6408; www.amaguate.org; 5 Av 6-17) and **Trama Textiles** (Map p136; ☑ 7765-8564; trama.textiles@yahoo.com; 3a Calle 10-56, Zona 1) offer backstrap weaving classes and operate fair-trade fabric shops. Both places charge Q325 for 10 hours of instruction, in which learners produce a scarf, Q650 for 20 hours, and the chance to make an

---

VOLUNTEERING IN XELA

The Quetzaltenango area has many nonprofit organizations working on social projects with the local K'iche' Maya people that need volunteers. Volunteer jobs can range from designing websites for indigenous organizations to working in animal shelters. You can volunteer part-time for a week or two while also studying Spanish, or you can live and work in a close-knit indigenous village for a year. Indeed, some schools exist primarily to generate funds for social projects and can help students to participate in their free time. Skills in fields such as medicine, nursing, teaching, youth work and computers are prized, but there are possibilities for anyone with the will to help. Volunteers must normally meet all their own costs and be willing to commit to a project for a specified minimum time. Three months is fairly typical for full-time posts, though the minimum can be as little as a week or as long as a year.

EntreMundos (Map p136; ☑ 7761-2179; www.entremundos.org; 6a Calle 7-31, Zona 1; ⊙ 2-5pm Mon-Thu) is a nonprofit that works with NGOs and community groups, offering capacity building workshops and computer classes to local NGO workers. Its website has details of 100 projects all over Guatemala looking for volunteers, and its free bilingual bimonthly magazine features articles about social development and human rights issues, as well as local volunteer opportunities. EntreMundos asks a donation of Q25 for drop-in visitors wanting to be placed.

Below are a few of the short-term volunteer opportunities provided by EntreMundos.

Amigo Fiel An animal-rights project with a shelter and focus on street-dog rehabilitation.

Chico Méndes Project Reforestation project in rural village just outside of Xela.

Fundabiem A foundation providing social and medical support to individuals with physical and mental disabilities; two-week minimum.

La Red Kuchub'al Fair-trade organization working with over 20 community organizations; two-week minimum.

Trama Women's Weaving co-operative designed for education and production.

embroidered table runner. For a simple demonstration of techniques they charge Q35.

Tours

Adrenalina Tours
GUIDED TOURS

(Map p136; ☑ 7761-4509; www.adrenalinatours. com; Pasaje Enríquez, Zona 1) Provides a range of trips in the Xela area, including to Zunil, Fuentes Georginas and little-visited parts of the department of Huehuetenango.

Altiplano's Tour Operator
CULTURAL TOURS

(Map p136; ☑ 7766-9614; www.altiplanos.com. gt; 12a Av 3-35, Zona 1) This outfit offers some interesting half-day tours to indigenous villages and markets, colonial churches and coffee plantations around Xela.

Tranvía de los Altos
TOUR

(Map p136; ☑ 7765-5342; www.tranviadelosaltos. com) This pseudo-streetcar does various circuits of the city, complete with knowledgeable commentary (in Spanish) and cheesy sound effects. Two-hour tours start at 11am and 3pm (Q50 per person), departing from the *municipalidad* building on the east side of the Parque Central.

Maya Viva
CULTURAL TOUR

(Map p132; ☑ 7761-6408; www.amaguate.org; 5a Av & 6a Calle 6-17, Zona 1) This community tourism program is organized by the **Asociación de Mujeres del Altiplano** (Map p132; ☑ 7761-6408; www.amaguate.org; 5a Av 6-17, Zona 1), a group that seeks to empower Maya women in the countryside. Visitors get to experience life in one of five rural communities near Quetzaltenango and learn about their customs, traditions and daily activities.

Festivals & Events

Xela Music Festival
MUSIC FESTIVAL

Organized by the French Cultural Institute, this event takes place in late March or early April, with local musicians playing on five or six stages around the city center.

Feria de la Virgen del Rosario
CULTURAL FESTIVAL

(Feria Centroamericana de Independencia) Held in late September or early October, this is Xela's big annual party. Residents kick up their heels at a fairground on the city's perimeter and there's plenty of entertainment at selected venues around town, including a battle of the brass bands in the Parque Centro América. An international Spanish-language literary competition, hosted by the city, runs simultaneously.

Sleeping

All of the places listed here are in Zona 1.

★ Casa Renaissance
HOTEL $

(Map p136; ☑ 3121-6315; www.casarenaissance. com; 9a Calle 11-26, Zona 1; r Q150, without bathroom Q110; 🛜) This colonial mansion has been reborn as a casual guesthouse with five huge, beautifully restored rooms along a delightful patio. Managed by friendly, informative Dutch hosts, the place has a relaxed atmosphere: take drinks from the cooler, prepare your own meals in the kitchen or watch videos from their voluminous collection. Rates drop significantly by the week.

Black Cat Hostel
HOSTEL $

(Map p136; ☑ 7756-8951; www.blackcathostels.net; 13a Av 3-33, Zona 1; dm incl breakfast Q60, r Q160; 🛜) A great place to stay if you're looking to meet up with other travelers, this full-service hostel features a sunny courtyard, a bar-restaurant and lounge/TV area. Though sparsely furnished, the rooms are done up in soothing colors with nice wood floors.

Hotel Kiktem-Ja
HOTEL $

(Map p136; ☑ 7761-4304; hotelkiktemja.com; 13a Av 7-18, Zona 1; s/d Q135/160, ℗) Set in a great old colonial building downtown, the Kiktem-Ja is all floorboards at weird angles, stone arches and squiggly wood columns along plant-draped corridors. Rooms are spacious with sturdy bedsteads, fireplaces and pretty tiled bathrooms.

Hostel Nim Sut
HOSTEL $

(Map p136; ☑ 7761-3083; www.hostelnimsut quetzaltenango.weebly.com; 4a Calle 9-42, Zona 1; dm Q62, s/d Q140/170, without bathroom Q95/115) Conveniently placed a block east of the Parque Centro América, this restored colonial relic has plenty of large rooms with basic bedding and clean parquet floors, some considerably brighter than others. The top terrace, with fine views over the town, is a good place to enjoy an espresso from the cafe downstairs.

Guest House El Puente
HOSTEL $

(Map p136; ☑ 7761-4342; celasmaya@gmail.com; 15a Av 6-75, Zona 1; s/d 65/130, without bathroom Q50/100) The four rooms here surround a large garden; three share well-used bath facilities. Connected to the Celas Mayas Spanish school, it's often occupied by language learners who congregate in the kitchen.

THE HIGHLANDS QUETZALTENANGO

Central Quetzaltenango

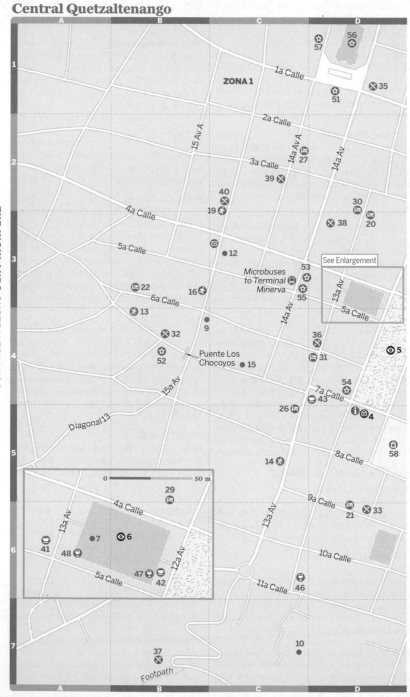

Hotel Casa del Viajero
HOTEL **$**

(Map p136; ☎ 7761-4594; 8a Av 9-17, Zona 1; s/d/tr Q80/160/240; 🛜) This homey hotel stands at a high-traffic intersection, though things are considerably calmer beyond the reception area. A series of flourescent-lit, brick-walled rooms of varying size and shape open onto a quiet interior patio.

Casa Argentina
HOSTEL **$**

(Map p132; ☎ 7763-2320; casargentina.xela@gmail.com; Diagonal 12 8-37, Zona 1; dm/s/d Q25/35/50) This sprawling guesthouse west of the center is a port of call for itinerant quetzalpinchers, but steer clear of the outrageously overcrowded dorms and opt for the marginally pricier private rooms with cinderblock decor. Señora Argentina and daughter Leonor are eager to please.

Hostal Don Diego
HOSTEL **$**

(Map p136; ☎ 7763-1000; www.hostaldondiegoxela.com; 6a Calle 15-12, Zona 1; dm Q45, s/d/tr from Q55/100/150; 🛜) This popular budget traveler's choice has sparely furnished rooms with sagging beds flanking a sunny courtyard. Reduced rates are offered for weekly or monthly stays, including use of a well-equipped kitchen.

Casa San Bartolomé
B&B **$$**

(Map p132; ☎ 7761 9511; www.casasanbartolome.com; 2a Av 7-17, Zona 1; s/d/tr incl breakfast Q205/287/350 ; 🅿🛜) In the family for generations, this atmospheric old residence a 15-minute walk east of the park has been converted into a cozy B&B. All seven rooms have beautiful furniture and modern art, and there's an excellent library. An elaborate breakfast featuring herbal tea grown in the garden is served on the lovely rear terrace.

Hotel Casa Mañen
HOTEL **$$**

(Map p136; ☎ 7765-0786; www.comeseeit.com; 9a Av 4-11, Zona 1; s/d incl breakfast from Q370/455) The town residence of coffee barons through the 19th century, this atmospheric guesthouse was thoughtfully renovated by an American couple in the 1980s, with traditionally outfitted rooms, tranquil gardens and a brilliant roof terrace/bar. Despite the rural ambience, it's quite close to the central square.

Hotel Modelo
HOTEL **$$**

(Map p136; ☎ 7761-2529; www.hotelmodelo1892.com; 14a Av A 2-31, Zona 1; s/d incl breakfast Q350/420; 🅿🛜) A few blocks below the Teatro Municipal, the colonial-style Modelo offers 19 atmospheric rooms with wooden

Central Quetzaltenango

floorboards, firm beds and spacious bathrooms. These are lined up alongside pretty patios with seasonal flower arrangements and volcano paintings. There's an old-fashioned dining room with cupboards of china and a relaxed bar, Perico's. A solid midrange option.

Los Olivos   HOTEL $$
(Map p136; ☑ 7761-0215; hotel.losolivos13@hotmail.com; 13a Av 3-32, Zona 1; s/d/tr Q160/240/330; 🅿) This compact lodging offers freshly painted, comfortable rooms with firm beds and wood slat ceilings, all opening on to plant-filled interior balconies.

Hotel Villa Real Plaza   HOTEL $$
(Map p136; ☑ 7761-4045; 4a Calle 12-22, Zona 1; s/d Q280/380; 🅿🛜) Beyond the frosted glass doorway, this grand old hotel, just off the main square, is the picture of faded

elegance, with stone archways around a lavish courtyard. Spacious rooms have high ceilings and mock fireplaces.

Villa de Don Andrés   B&B $$
(Map p136; ☑ 7761-2014; hotelvilladedonandres.com; 13a Av 6-16, Zona 1; s/d incl breakfast Q225/422, without bathroom Q150/300; 🅿🛜) This B&B in the center of town is a welcoming sort of place. Done up with antique decor and colorful woven bedspreads, the large carpeted rooms are pleasantly arranged along a broad patio where a complimentary breakfast is served.

Hostal 7 Orejas   HOSTEL $$
(Map p132; ☑ 7768-3218; www.7orejas.com; 2a Calle 16-92, Zona 1; dm/s/d/tr Q75/160/265/320; 🅿@) This is a cordially managed and scrupulously maintained hostel on a quiet street northwest of the center. The pseudo-colonial

structure features spacious, fresh-smelling rooms alongside a strip of garden. Each has three queen-size beds with carved-wood chests for storage. Breakfast (Q20) is served on the excellent rooftop terrace.

Hotel Pensión Bonifaz HOTEL $$$

(Map p136; ☑ 7765-1111; www.pensionbonifaz.com. gt; 4a Calle 10-50, Zona 1; s/d/tr Q575/685/795; P@🎤) The oldest and grandest hotel in Xela looms above the Parque Centro América. Rooms are on the top three floors; the 2nd-floor chambers surround a leafy colonial patio where breakfast is served. Though interior decor is not as fabulous as you might expect, the opulent front bar makes up for it.

Eating

Quetzaltenango has a good selection of places to eat in all price ranges. Cheapest are the food stalls on the lower level of the central market, where snacks and main-course plates are sold for Q10 or less. One very popular breakfast spot is Doña Cristy, serving *atol de elote* (a hot maize beverage), *empanadas* and *chuchitos* (small tamales garnished with chopped beets and grated cheese).

Casa Ut'z Hua GUATEMALAN $

(Map p136; ☑ 7768-3469; 12a Av 3-05; mains Q30-40; ⊗7am-8pm) Toothsome authentic Guatemalan and Quetzalteco dishes are the draw at this kitschily decorated country hut.

La Taberna de Don Rodrigo SANDWICHES $

(Map p136; 14a Av C-51, Zona 1; sandwiches Q40; ⊗10am-9:30pm) This lively pub/snack bar is reportedly the first place to serve Xela's signature Cabro beer on tap, poured copiously into pitchers and mugs (three per customer). To go along, they grill up long bologna-and-cheese sandwiches, brought to the table with squeeze bottles of green sauce. Classic!

Artesano BAKERY $

(Map p136; 7a Calle 15-18; sandwiches Q30; ⊗8am-8pm Mon-Sat, noon-6pm Sun) A good place to stock up for that volcano climb, this craft bakery makes whole-wheat sandwiches (tofu, tempeh, eggplant, cheese), excellent cookies and granola.

Maya Café GUATEMALAN $

(Map p136; 13a Av 5-48; mains Q25-30; ⊗7am-6pm) Plenty of *típica* Xela fare on offer at this locally popular dining hall – try the *quichom*, a spicy chicken concoction. Lunch comes with soup and some freshly squeezed beverage.

Café Sagrado Corazón GUATEMALAN $

(Map p136; 9a Calle 11-16; lunch combos Q20-30; ⊗8am-8pm; 🖉) This relic of a dining hall is a good place to savor Quetzalteco home cooking, with daily specials like *jocóm* and *caldo de patas* (cow foot soup) served with a pile of tortillas and little dishes of lemons and tiny chilies. Vegetarian options are available.

★Sabor de la India INDIAN $$

(Map p136; ☑ 7765-2555; 15a Av 3-64; mains Q60-70; ⊗noon-10pm Tue-Sun; 🖉) Authentic south Indian fare is whipped up here by a friendly fellow from Kerala. Servings are huge; the *thalis* – platters of curried veggies, chicken or beef – are highly recommended.

Panorama EUROPEAN $$

(Map p136; ☑ 7765-8580; www.restaurante panorama.com; 13a Av A, D16-44; fondue Q80; ⊗noon-midnight Tue-Sun) A 10-minute hike up the hill at the south end of town with views worthy of its name, Panorama makes a supremely romantic spot for that special night out. Fondues and melted Raclette cheese are the stars of the table at the Swiss-owned establishment.

Royal Paris FRENCH $$

(Map p136; ☑ 7761-1942; 14 Av A 3-06; salads Q50; ⊗noon-10pm Tue-Sun; 🖘) Overseen by the French consul himself, this bistro ought to be authentic, and the escargots, baked Camembert and filet mignon approach Parisian standards. Check the blackboard for nightly specials. The cozy ambience is augmented by a sweet terrace and live folk and jazz Wednesday to Saturday nights.

Restaurante Cardinali ITALIAN $$

(Map p136; ☑ 7761-0924; 14a Av 3-25; pastas Q65-85; ⊗noon-10pm) With checkered tablecloths and hundreds of wine bottles hanging from the rafters, Cardinali feels like it was lifted from the Mediterranean, and indeed owner/chef Benito hails from Parma, Italy. The manicotti and ravioli are made inhouse.

Drinking

Coffee plays an important part in Xela's economy, and there are plenty of places to grab a cup.

Xela's Zona Viva revolves around the Teatro Municipal, with discos and clubs popping up along 1a and 2a Calles and up 14 Av.

★Café La Luna CAFE

(Map p136; ☑ 5174-6769; 8a Av 4-11; ⊗9am-9pm Mon-Sat; 🖘) For chocolate aficionados, this is a shrine. Made from scratch on the premises, the chocolate is velvety smooth and served in a variety of beverages: the chocolate cappuccino, topped with fresh whipped cream, is mind-blowing. Groups of friends gather in the various salons, which are littered with vintage bric-a-brac.

Salón Tecún
PUB

(Map p136; Pasaje Enríquez; ⊙9:30am-12:30am) On the plaza end of the elegant Pasaje Enríquez, alive day and night with a healthy mix of Guatemalans and foreigners quaffing Cabro by the liter, the Tecún claims to be the country's longest-running bar (since 1935). They also serve good bar food. Don't miss it.

Café Baviera
CAFE

(Map p136; ☑7761-5018; 5a Calle 13-14; ⊙7am-8:30pm; 🛜) This cozy cafe has quality espresso, with coffee beans roasted on the premises, and it's a fine place for breakfast or snacks (crêpes, croissants, soups and salads). The wooden walls are hung with countless photos and clippings on Xela and international themes.

Student Bar
PUB

(Map p136; 5a Calle 12-54) The apt name of this split-level corner joint might describe any of the beer-guzzling, sports-viewing establishments along the south side of the Pasaje Enríquez.

Café El Balcón del Enríquez
CAFE

(Map p136; 12 Av 4-40, Pasaje Enríquez; ⊙8am-10pm) With specially designed viewing counters overlooking the Parque Centro América, this lively cafe on the upper level of the Pasaje Enríquez makes a nice perch for morning espresso or evening cocktails.

Café El Cuartito
CAFE

(Map p136; 13a Av 7-09; ⊙9am-11pm; 🛜) This offbeat cafe is a point of reference for travelers and language students, with quirky decor made from found objects. It serves a good range of vegetarian snacks, herbal teas and coffee just about any way you want it, plus some creative cocktails – how about a raspberry mojito? There's live music most nights.

Tilde Boutique
CAFE

(Map p136; tildeboutique.com; 10a Av 5-33) Run by a group of alternatively minded indigenous women, the Boutique is a pocket of boho culture behind the Town Hall. Browsing re-embroidered second-hand duds, sipping mentholated lemonade or munching a tofu wrap are all considered normal behavior here.

Full House Pizza Pub
PUB

(Map p136; 4a Calle 8-08; ⊙Tue-Sat) The simple layout here features a courtyard with a bar and wood-fired oven and a living room for live rock and *cumbia* (Colombian dance tunes) on Wednesday and Saturday, making an attractive haven for global slackers.

Pool & Beer
PUB

(Map p136; 12a Av 10-21; ⊙6pm-1am Tue-Sun) The pool tables are worn and the cues crooked, but this slackers' clubhouse remains a friendly and refreshingly not-trendy spot. While waiting for a table, you can be the DJ, choosing from the PC's 30,000-odd tracks.

☆ Nightlife & Entertainment

It gets chilly when the sun goes down, so you won't want to sit out in the Parque Centro América enjoying the balmy breezes – there aren't any. Nevertheless, it's a pleasant place for an evening stroll.

The music scene is particularly strong in Xela. Many of the town's restaurants, cafes and bars double as performance venues, including the Royal Paris (p139), El Cuartito and Full House Pizza Pub. To see what's on, pick up a copy of *XelaWho* or check www.xelawho.com.

Though there's no proper movie house in the center of town, a number of venues run weekly film series, including Royal Paris and El Orejón, the lounge inside the Hostal 7 Orejas (p139).

Casa No'j
PERFORMING ARTS

(Map p136; ☑7768-3139; www.centroculturalcasanoj.blogspot.com; 7a Calle 12-12, Zona 1; ⊙8am-5pm Mon-Sat) Just off the park's southwest corner, this colonial relic now houses Xela's premier cultural center. Besides photo and art exhibits, it hosts anything from poetry festivals to marimba recitals to archaeology conferences. Check the blog for upcoming events.

Teatro Municipal
THEATER

(Map p136; ☑7761-2218; 14a Av & 1a Calle) Quetzaltenango's grand neoclassical theater north of the center is the main venue for plays, concerts and dance performances. An elaborate two-tiered curved balcony has private boxes for prominent families.

Teatro Roma
THEATER

(Map p136; ☑3010-0100; 14a Av A-34) This palace of culture is a showcase for elaborate theatrical productions and, on occasion, some interesting movies.

Café Leyendas   LIVE MUSIC
(Map p136; 14a Av 4-41) Definitely the mellow alternative to the Pasaje Enríquez scene, this coffee house with loft seating attracts a more contemplative kind of drinker, with live rock and jazz on weekends.

Bari   LIVE MUSIC
(Map p136; 1a Calle 14-31; ☺8pm-1am Wed-Sat) One of several nightspots opposite the Teatro Municipal, Bari regularly hosts live *trova* (socially conscious Latin American folk), rock and pop.

La Parranda   DANCE
(Map p136; 14a Av 4-47, Zona 1; admission Fri & Sat Q30; ☺9pm-12:30am Wed-Sat) This glitzy, strobe-lit disco offers free salsa classes on Wednesday night (basic and intermediate); other evenings have guest DJs and drinks giveaways.

Blue Angel Video Café   CINEMA
(Map p136; 7a Calle 15-79, Zona 1; admission Q10) Shows Hollywood films nightly at 8pm, besides serving a nice range of vegetarian meals, herbal teas and hot chocolate. See the publication *XelaWho* for the schedule.

🛍 Shopping

Xela's central market is three floors of reasonably priced handicrafts and souvenirs. Bargain hard. For a more intense, everyday marketing experience, hit the **Mercado La Democracia** (Map p132; 1a Calle, Zona 3), about 10 blocks north of Parque Centro América in Zona 3, with food, clothing, CDs and other necessities for city dweller and villager alike.

   Manos Creativas (Map p132; ☎7761-6408; cnr 6a Calle & 5 Av 6-17), a shop belonging to the women's empowerment association AMA, sells quality textiles and clothing produced by Maya weavers. Trama Textiles, just uphill from the park, is a similar weaving cooperative, comprised of 400 Maya women.

ℹ Orientation

The heart of Xela is the oblong Parque Centro América, graced with neoclassical monuments and surrounded by the city's important buildings. Most accommodations are within a few blocks of this plaza.

   The main bus station is Terminal Minerva, on the western outskirts and next to one of the principal markets.

ℹ Information

EMERGENCY
Bomberos (☎7761-2002) Firefighters.

Cruz Roja (☎7761-2746) Red Cross.
Policía Municipal (☎7761-5805) Local police force.
Policía Nacional (☎7765-4990) National police force.
Proatur (☎4149-1104) Tourist police.

INTERNET ACCESS
It only costs Q5 to Q6 per hour to get online here. See the publication *XelaWho* for a wi-fi hot-spot finder.
Café El Guru (6a Calle 14-55, Zona 1)

MEDIA
English-language publications are available free in bars, restaurants and cafes around town.
EntreMundos (☎7761-2179; www.entremundos.org) Published every two months by the Xela-based organization of the same name, this newspaper has plenty of information on political developments and volunteer projects in the region.
XelaWho (www.xelawho.com) Billing itself as 'Quetzaltenango's leading Culture & Nightlife Magazine,' this little monthly lists cultural events in the city, with some fairly irreverent takes on life in Guatemala in general.

MEDICAL SERVICES
Hospital Privado Quetzaltenango (☎7774-4700; Calle Rodolfo Robles 23 51) Has 24-hour emergency service. Usually has an English-speaking doctor on staff.

MONEY
Parque Centro América is the place to go for banks. **Banco Industrial** (☺9am-6:30pm Mon-Fri, 9am-1pm Sat) has branches on the north and east sides of the plaza. Both change traveler's checks and give advances on Visa; the latter, in the *municipalidad* building, has an ATM on the Plus network. There's a Cajero 5B ATM in the Edificio Rivera just north of the Muni.

POST
Main Post Office (4a Calle 15-07, Zona 1)

TOURIST INFORMATION
Inguat (☎7761-4931; info-xela@inguat.gob.gt; 7a Calle; ☺9am-5pm Mon-Fri, 9am-1pm Sat), usually staffed by an English speaker, is at the southern end of Parque Centro América.

   There's a plethora of tourist maps circulating; look for them at internet cafes, language schools and hotels. Though they're essentially advertising flyers, the better ones like *Xelamap* include plenty of useful information.

TRAVEL AGENCIES
Altiplano's Tour Operator (☎7766-9614; www.altiplanos.com.gt; 12a Av 3-35, Zona 1) Besides hikes and tours, they offer luggage storage, bike rentals and hotel bookings.

WORTH A TRIP

EXPLORE MORE OF QUETZALTENANGO

The wide-open spaces and mountainous countryside around Xela offer an almost endless array of opportunities for getting out there and doing a bit of solo exploration. Small villages dotted around the valley mean that you shouldn't ever have much trouble getting directions, and the relative safety of the area means that the biggest danger you're likely to face is that of a yapping dog (carry a stick). A few destinations to head towards:

Santiaguito lookout Get a close-up view of volcanic eruptions, going off like clockwork every 20 minutes.

Lava fields Over near Mt Candelaria, these extensive fields are a great place for a picnic and a spot of sunbathing.

San Cristóbal waterfall Halfway between Xela and San Francisco, the falls are most impressive in the wet season.

Las Mojadas The walk to this pretty flower-growing village takes you from Llanos del Pinal and past the Santiago volcano. You can catch a bus back.

Ícaro Tours (✆7761-4342; www.icarotours. com; 6a Calle 14-55, Zona 1)

Turismo de Occidente (✆4505-2470; www. turismodeoccidente.com; 7a Calle 15-41) Reliable private shuttle service.

WEBSITES

Lonely Planet (http://www.lonelyplanet.com/ guatemala/western-highlands/quetzaltenango-xela) Planning advice, author recommendations, traveler reviews and insider tips.

Xela Pages (www.xelapages.com) Packed with information about Xela and nearby attractions, with a useful discussion forum.

❶ Getting There & Away

BUS

All 2nd-class buses depart from **Terminal Minerva** (7a Calle, Zona 3), a dusty, crowded yard in the west of town, unless otherwise noted.

Leaving or entering town, some buses make a stop east of the center at the Rotonda, a traffic circle on Calz Independencia, marked by the Monumento a la Marimba. Getting off here when you're coming into Xela saves the 10 to 15 minutes it will take your bus to cross town to Terminal Minerva.

Almolonga (Q3, 40 minutes, every 15 minutes, 6am to 10pm) Departing from the Shell station at the corner of 9a Av and 10a Calle, southeast of the central market.

Antigua Take any bus bound for Guatemala City via the Interamericana and change at Chimaltenango.

Chichicastenango (Q25, 2½ hours, every half hour from 5am to 4pm) Or take a bus heading to Guatemala City and change at Los Encuentros.

Ciudad Tecún Umán (Mexican border) (Q40, three hours, every 15 minutes until 2pm)

El Carmen/Talismán (Mexican border) Take a bus to San Marcos (Q10, two hours, every 30 minutes), then catch another to Malacatán (Q15, two hours) where you can find a collective taxi (Q5) or microbus to El Carmen (Q4).

Guatemala City (Q40, four hours, every 15 minutes from 6am to 4pm) First-class companies operating between Quetzaltenango and Guatemala City have their own terminals: **Linea Dorada** (✆7767-5198; www.lineadorada.info; 12 Av & 5 Calle) Deluxe buses (Q70) at 3:30am and 4pm; **Transportes Álamo** (✆7767-4582; 14 Av 5-15, Zona 3) Six Pullman buses, from 4:30am to 2:30pm; **Transportes Galgos** (✆7761-2248; Calle Rodolfo Robles 17-43, Zona 1) Pullmans at 4am and 12:30pm. **ADN** (✆6649-2089; www. adnautobusesdelnorte.com; 23a Av 5-06) Deluxe buses (Q60) at 6am and 3pm.

Huehuetenango (Q20, two hours, every 15 minutes from 4am to 6pm) Linea Dorada offers Pullman service at 11:30am (Q40).

La Mesilla (Mexican border) (Q40, four hours, every 30 minutes from 4:30am to 6pm) Or take a bus to Huehuetenango and change there.

Momostenango (Q9, 1½ hours, every 15 minutes from 5:45am to 7pm)

Panajachel (Q25, 2½ hours, hourly from 9am to 5pm) Or take any bus for Guatemala City via the Interamericana and change at Los Encuentros.

Retalhuleu (Q20, 1½ hours, 'Reu' buses every 10 minutes from 4:30am to 7:30pm)

San Andrés Xecul (Q4.50, one hour, every 30 minutes from 6am to 3pm)

San Martín Sacatepéquez/Colomba (Q5, one hour, every half hour till 5:30pm)

San Pedro La Laguna (Q35, three hours, six buses between 11:30am and 5:30pm)

Zunil (Q4.50, one hour, every 10 minutes from 6:30am to 5:30pm) Buses depart from the

Shell station at the corner of 9a Av and 10a Calle, southeast of the central market.

CAR & MOTORCYCLE

Tabarini (☎7763-0418; www.tabarini.com; 9a Calle 9-21, Zona 1) Tabarini rents cars for about Q350 per day.

SHUTTLE MINIBUS

Most Xela travel agencies, including Altiplano's, run shuttle minibuses to such destinations as Antigua (Q240), Chichicastenango (Q180), Panajachel (Q160) and San Cristobal de Las Casas, Mexico (Q235).

ⓘ Getting Around

Terminal Minerva is linked to the city center by microbuses, charging Q1.25 for the 10- to 15-minute ride (Q2 after dark). From the terminal, walk south through the market to the intersection by the Templo de Minerva, where you'll see the vehicles waiting on the south side of 4a Calle. Going from the center to the terminal, catch microbuses on 14a Av north of 5a Calle. Taxis await fares at the north end of Parque Centro América; a ride to the Terminal Minerva costs around Q30.

The Rotonda bus stop on Calz Independencia is served by 'Parque' microbuses running to the center.

Inguat has information on other city bus routes.

Around Quetzaltenango

The beautiful volcanic country around Xela offers up numerous exciting day trips. For many, the volcanoes themselves pose irresistible challenges. You can feast your eyes and soul on the wild church at San Andrés Xecul, hike to the ceremonial shores of Laguna Chicabal, or soak in the idyllic hot springs at Fuentes Georginas. Or simply hop on a bus and explore the myriad small traditional villages that pepper this part of the highlands. Market days are great opportunities to observe locals in action, so Sunday and Wednesday in Momostenango, Monday in Zunil, Tuesday and Saturday in Totonicapán and Friday in San Francisco El Alto are good days to visit.

Almolonga

POP 14,223 / ELEV 2322M

An indigenous town with a population that is more than 90% Evangelical Christian, Almolonga has become relatively wealthy from vegetable growing. The **market** bustles daily, and you'll see piles and piles of cabbages, limes, chilis, *güisquil* (a squash-like vegetable), onions and other gorgeous veggies, handled by hordes of women in embroidered aprons. Don't miss the **Iglesia de San Pedro**, which has a gilded altarpiece with a backdrop of incongruous neon lights, and an inverted galleon ceiling. Almolonga celebrates its annual **fair** on June 27.

At the lower end of the village the road passes through **Los Baños**, an area with natural hot sulfur springs. Several little places down here have bath installations with private tiled tubs available for Q20 an hour. **Baños Termales San Silvestre** has one of the better set-ups, including an 80°F pool with waterfall.

Zunil

POP 14,199 / ELEV 2262M

As you speed downhill toward Zunil from Quetzaltenango, you'll see this pretty market town spreading across a lush valley framed by steep hills and dominated by a towering volcano, its white colonial church gleaming above the red-tiled roofs of the low houses. A road on the left bridges a river and, 1km further, reaches Zunil's plaza.

WORTH A TRIP

FRUIT SOUP & ROMPOPE

The town of Salcajá, 7km northeast of Xela, is best known for its production of two alcoholic beverages that locals consider akin to magical elixirs. *Caldo de frutas* (literally, fruit soup) is like a high-octane sangria, made by combining nances (cherry-like fruits), apples, peaches, and pears and fermenting them for six months or so. You can purchase fifths of it after viewing the production process. *Rompopo* is an entirely different type of potent potable, made from rum, egg yolks, sugar and spices. Little liquor shops all over Salcajá peddle the stuff, but you may like to try the friendly shop of José Daniel Sandoval Santizo, a block east of the main road along 4a Calle.

Founded in 1529, Zunil is a typical Guatemalan highland town, where traditional indigenous agriculture is practiced. The cultivated plots, divided by stone fences, are irrigated by canals; you'll see the farmers scooping up water with a shovel-like instrument and tossing it over their plants. Women wash their clothes near the river bridge in pools of hot water that come out of the rocks.

◉ Sights

Zunil boasts a particularly striking **church**. Its ornate facade, with eight pairs of serpentine columns, is echoed inside by a richly carved gilt altar, with saints garbed in silver-embroidered robes. On Tuesday, Thursday and Saturday, the plaza in front is bright with the purple-striped *huipiles* and richly patterned *cortes* of the local K'iche' Maya women buying and selling.

Half a block downhill from the church plaza, the **Cooperativa Santa Ana** (◎8am-6pm) is a handicrafts cooperative made up of more than 600 local women. Finely woven vests, jackets and traditional *huipiles* (from Q400) are displayed and sold here. Weaving lessons are offered, too.

While you're in Zunil, visit the image of **San Simón**, the name given here to the much-venerated non-Christian deity known elsewhere as Maximón (see the boxed text, p105). His effigy, propped up in a chair, is moved each year to a different house during the **festival of San Simón**, held on October 28. Ask any local where to find him.

🛏 Sleeping & Eating

Hotel Las Cumbres   HOTEL **$$**
(📞5399-0029; www.lascumbres.com.gt; Km 210 Carretera al Pacífico; s/d from Q350/400; 🅿) Located 500m south of Zunil, Las Cumbres seems like a colonial village amid a volcanic landscape where great plumes of steam emanate from the earth. The hotel is built on top of natural steam vents, and each of the 12 cozy rooms comes equipped with its own sauna and/or hot-spring-fed Jacuzzi.

There's a good restaurant (mains Q50 to Q80) serving organic vegetables from the hotel garden, along with a squash court, gymnasium and handicrafts store. Nonguests can use the public sauna (Q30 per hour, open 7am to 7pm), a modern pine-paneled installation, or spa, offering massages and facials. Any bus bound for Retalhuleu or Mazatenango can drop you at the entrance (Q5).

❶ Getting There & Away

Buses depart from the Shell station at the corner of 9a Av and 10a Calle in Quetzaltenango every 10 minutes from 6:30am to 5:30pm. Returning, buses depart from the main road beside the bridge. The Fuentes Georginas shuttle makes a brief (15-minute) stop in Zunil if you'd just like a quick look at the church.

Fuentes Georginas

A superb natural spa in a spectacular setting, **Fuentes Georginas** (📞7763-0596; info@fuentesgeorginas.com; admission Q50; ◎8am-5:30pm) is an 8km drive uphill from Zunil. It's named after the wife of 'benevolent dictator' Jorge Ubico, who customarily commandeered the installations on weekends for his personal use. Four pools of varying temperatures are fed by hot sulfur springs and framed by a steep, high wall of tropical vines, ferns and flowers. Though the setting is intensely tropical, the mountain air currents keep it deliciously cool through the day. There is a little 500m walk starting from beside the pool, worth doing to check out the birds and orchids. Bring a bathing suit; towels are available (Q10 plus deposit). Lockers cost Q5. Hurricane Agatha ripped through the spa in 2010, all but destroying the installations. Fortunately, it's been completely rebuilt and restored, though patches of the road in remain perilously damaged.

Besides the **restaurant/bar** (meals Q60-75; ◎8am-7pm), which serves great grilled steaks, sausage and *papas*, there are three sheltered picnic tables with cooking grills. Big-time soakers will want to spend the night: down the valley a bit are nine rustic but cozy **cottages** (per person Q95), each with a hot tub and cold shower, barbecue and a fireplace to ward off the mountain chill at night (wood and matches provided). Included in the price of the cottages is access to the pools all day and all night, when rules are relaxed.

Trails lead to two nearby volcanoes: **Volcán Zunil** (15km, about three hours one way) and **Volcán Santo Tomás** (25km, about five hours one way). Guides (essential) are available for either trip. Ask at the restaurant.

Fuentes Georginas offers daily shuttles from Xela to the site (Q115 return, including entrance fee), leaving at 9am and 2:30pm from **Xela Café** (Map p136; 6a Calle 9-30). They return to Xela at 1pm and 6pm.

San Andrés Xecul

A few kilometers past Salcajá, the road from Quetzaltenango passes the Morería crossroads, where a branch heads west to San Andrés Xecul. After about 3km on this uphill spur, you'll start seeing rainbow cascades of hand-dyed thread drying on the roofs and you'll know you have arrived in San Andrés Xecul. Boxed in by fertile hills, this small town boasts the most bizarre, stunning **church** imaginable. Technicolored saints, angels, flowers and climbing vines fight for space with angels frolicking on the ledges and a pair of jaguars scratching the top column on a shocking yellow facade. The cones on the bell towers are straight from the circus big top.

Inside, a carpet of candles illuminate bleeding effigies of Christ. Above the altar, 'Fisher of Men' is written in blue neon, a reference to the town's patron saint.

Thursday and Friday are market days. The annual **festival** is November 30, with tightrope walkers.

The community **tourist office** (✆4778-4851; ⊘8am-5pm Mon-Fri), to the left of the church, echoes its playful facade. Here you can set up a guided walk of the town with visits to *huipil* embroiderers, and dyers and candle makers, continuing up to **El Calvario**, the little yellow church at the top of the hill. Maya ceremonies, with plenty of burnt offerings, are still held at the triple-cross altar alongside, and the panoramic view across the valley is phenomenal. The tourist office also offers tours of surrounding villages.

To get here take any northbound bus from Xela, alighting at the Esso station at the Morería crossroads and hailing a pickup or walking the 3km uphill. Buses returning to Xela line up at the edge of the plaza and make the trip until about 5pm.

Totonicapán

POP 56,704 / ELEV 2476M

San Miguel Totonicapán is known for its artisans. Shoemakers, weavers, tinsmiths, potters, leather workers and carpenters all make and sell their goods here. Market days are Tuesday and Saturday; it's a locals' market, not a tourist affair, and it winds down by late morning.

The ride from Cuatro Caminos is along a pine-studded valley. From Totonicapán's bus station it's a 600m walk up 4a Calle to the twin main plazas. The lower plaza has a statue of Atanasio Tzul, leader of an indigenous rebellion that started here in 1820, while the upper one is home to the large **colonial church** and neoclassical **municipal theater**.

🏃 Activities

Aventura Maya K'iche' TOUR
(✆5630-0554; kiche78@hotmail.com; 8a Av 2-17) This project introduces visitors to some of the town's many craftspeople. A one-day program, requiring two weeks' advance booking, includes visits to various craft workshops (including potters, carvers of ceremonial masks and musical instruments, and weavers), a bit of sightseeing, a marimba concert and a traditional lunch in a private home.

Rates are Q475 per person in groups of four, or Q665 including a stay with a local family and two meals.

**Sendero Ecológico
El Aprisco** NATURE RESERVE
(✆5355-0280; admission Q25; ⊘8am-4pm) Encompassing some 13 hectares of old-growth forest northeast of Totonicapán, this makes for some delightful hiking. Well-marked trails traverse the community-run reserve, domain of the endangered *pinabete* tree and 29 endemic bird species such as the amethyst-throated hummingbird, ocellated quail and colorfully plumed *quetzalillo* (mountain trogon). A small museum displays traditional outfits of the region, and there are adobe cabins with fireplaces, bunk beds and straw bedding. El Aprisco is 5km up the Santa Cruz del Quiché road from Toto. Pickup trucks head this way from the east end of 7a Calle. Alternatively, Aventura Maya K'iche' (p145) can organize trips to the reserve at Q175 per person.

🎊 Festivals & Events

The festival of the **Apparition of the Archangel Michael** is on May 8, with fireworks and traditional dances. The **Feria Titular de San Miguel Arcángel** runs from September 24 to 30, peaking on September 29. Totonicapán keeps traditional masked dances very much alive with its **Festival Tradicional de Danza** – dates vary but recently it was over a weekend in late October.

🛏 Sleeping & Eating

Aventura Maya K'iche' can arrange stays with local families, including breakfast and dinner, for Q360/425/500 per person in groups of four/three/two, including dinner and breakfast.

Hospedaje Paco Centro
HOTEL $

(☑7766-2810; 3a Calle 8-18, Zona 2; s/d Q65/130) Practically hidden inside a shopping center a couple of blocks from the lower plaza, this sternly managed place has big, tidy rooms of three to five beds each.

Restaurante Bonanza
RESTAURANT $$

(7a Calle 7-17, Zona 4; meals Q40-60; ☺ 7am-9pm; ☎) Totonicapán's most conventional restaurant is a meat-and-tortillas sort of establishment, where bow-tied waiters deliver heaping helpings of steak, chicken and seafood.

❶ Getting There & Away

'Toto' buses from Quetzaltenango depart every 10 minutes or so (Q6, one hour) throughout the day from the Rotonda on Calz Independencia (passing through Cuatro Caminos). The last direct bus to Quetzaltenango leaves Toto at 6:40pm.

San Francisco El Alto

POP 42,108 / ELEV 2582M

High on a hilltop overlooking Quetzaltenango, some 17km away, stands the town of San Francisco El Alto, whose Friday **market** is regarded as the biggest and most authentic in the country. The large plaza in front of the 18th-century church is covered in goods. Stalls are crowded into neighboring streets, and the press of traffic is so great that a special system of one-way roads is established to avoid colossal traffic jams.

The whole town is Guatemala's garment district: every inch is jammed with vendors selling sweaters, socks, blankets, jeans, scarves and more. Bolts of cloth spill from storefronts packed to the ceiling with miles of material.

Around mid-morning when the clouds roll away, panoramic views can be had from the roof of the **church**. The caretaker will let you go up for a small tip. On the way through, have a look at the six elaborate gilded altarpieces and remains of what must once have been very colorful frescoes.

San Francisco's big party is the **Fiesta de San Francisco de Asís**, celebrated around October 4 with traditional dances.

Hotel Vista Hermosa (☑7738-4010; cnr 2a Calle & 3a Av; s/d Q75/150, without bathroom Q35/70) does indeed have beautiful views out over the valley to the Santa María volcano. Rooms are spacious, with balconies and

(thankfully) hot showers. Thursday nights it's likely to fill up.

Good *chuchitos* (small tamales), *chiles rellenos* and other prepared foods are sold from stacks in the marketplace.

Banco Reformador (2a Calle 3-23; ☺ 9am-4pm Mon-Fri, 9am-1pm Sat) changes traveler's checks and has a Visa ATM.

Buses to San Francisco leave Quetzaltenango's Terminal Minerva (passing through Cuatro Caminos) frequently throughout the day (Q10, one hour). Arriving from Quetzaltenango on market day, get off on 4a Av at the top of the hill and walk towards the church.

Momostenango

POP 51,822 / ELEV 2259M

Beyond San Francisco El Alto, 26km from Quetzaltenango, this town, set in a pretty mountain valley along a road through pine woods, is famous for the making of *chamarras*, or thick woollen blankets, as well as ponchos and other woolen garments. The best days to look for these are Wednesday and Sunday, the main market days.

Momostenango is noted for its adherence to the ancient Maya calendar and observance of traditional rites. The town's five main altars are the scene of ceremonies enacted on important celestial dates such as the summer solstice; the spring equinox; the start of the Maya solar year, known as El Mam, observed in late February; and Wajshakib' B'atz, the start of the 260-day *tzolkin* year. Should you be allowed access to these ceremonies, be sure to treat altars and participants with the utmost respect.

🏃 Activities

Takiliben May Wajshakib Batz
CULTURAL TOUR

(☑7736-5537; www.alunajoy.com/wajshakib-batz.html; 3a Av A 6-85, Zona 3) This is a Maya Mission, dedicated to studying and teaching Maya culture and sacred traditions. Its director, Rigoberto Itzep Chanchavac, is a *chuchkajau* (Maya priest) responsible for advising the community on when special days of the Maya calendars fall. His full- or half-day workshops focus on customs that usually remain hidden from outsiders.

The mission also leads a tour of Momostenango, with visits to the sacred hill of Paclom and the ritual hot springs of Payashú (Q100, including a homestay with a local family).

✦ Festivals & Events

Wajshakib' Batz' (eight thread), marking the start of the ritual *tzolkin* calender, is considered the holiest day in the cycle, when Maya 'daykeepers' are ordained. During the ceremony, usually enacted atop sacred Paclom hill (accessed from the end of 5a Calle), the candidates for priesthood are presented with a 'sacred bundle' of red seeds and crystals, which they'll use for divination readings based on the ritual calendar, then they dance around the ceremonial fire holding their bundle. As it falls at the end of a 260-day cycle, the date varies from year to year. Contact Takiliben May to find out when it falls in the current year.

⏢ Sleeping

Hotel Otoño HOTEL $
(☎ 7736-5078; gruvial.m@gmail.com; 3a Av A 1-48, Zona 2; r per person Q100; ℙ) Momostenango's poshest lodging has 14 modern rooms with glossy tile floors and huge bathrooms. Some feature balconies or picture windows taking in the surrounding hills. The hotel restaurant serves all meals.

ⓘ Information

Banco Reformador (1a Avenida 1-13, Zona 1; ☺ 9am-5pm Mon-Fri, 8am-noon Sat) Changes traveler's checks and has a Cajero 5B ATM.

ⓘ Getting There & Away

You can get buses to Momostenango from Quetzaltenango's Terminal Minerva (Q9, 1½ hours) or from San Francisco El Alto (45 minutes). Buses run about every 15 minutes, with the last one back to Quetzaltenango normally leaving Momostenango at 4:30pm.

Laguna Chicabal

This magical lake is nestled in the crater of Volcán Chicabal (2712m) on the edge of a cloud forest. Considered a cosmic convergence point by the Mam and K'iche' Maya, it is a sacred place and a hotbed of ceremonial activity. There are Maya altars at each of the four cardinal points along its sandy shores, and Maya and worshippers come from far and wide to perform ceremonies and make offerings here. Forty days after Easter Sunday is the observance of 13 Qanil, when faithful farmers flock here to pray for rain. By observing the level of the lagoon and seeing if the roots of surrounding trees are submerged, they can judge whether to

plant. Because the lake and grounds have great ceremonial significance, campers and hikers are asked to treat them with the utmost respect.

Adding to the atmosphere of mystery, a veil of fog dances over the water, alternately revealing and hiding the lake's placid contours. Bird-watchers might spot quetzals, horned guan and pink headed warblers.

Access to Laguna Chicabal is via the community of **Toj Mech**, southwest of the town of San Martín Sacatepéquez (also known as Chile Verde) along the road to Colomba. Microbuses from Xela (Q5) depart every 20 minutes, Monday to Saturday, from 15a Av and 6a Calle in Zona 3. These vehicles drop you at a parking lot in Toj Mech. From here, a cheerful fellow named Juan can take you up the steep, deeply rutted road to the park's **visitor center** (☎ 4349-6870; www.lagunadechicabal.com; admission Q15; ☺ 7am-3pm) in his red pickup truck (Q60, 15 minutes). A trail leads another 3km uphill to the site. About two-thirds of the way up you'll reach a fork, where you can bear right to go directly to the lagoon, or left up to a *mirador* (observation post) and then a whopping 615 steep steps down to the edge of the lake. Start early for best visibility.

There are good accommodations at the visitor center managed by the local Mam community, including a pair of six-sided bungalows with four bunks each (Q40 per person) sharing a cold-water bath house, and a two-level log cabin with private bathrooms (double Q75 per person).

Huehuetenango

POP 155,500 / ELEV 1909M

Often used as a stopoff on the journey to or from Mexico, or as a staging area for forays deeper into the Cuchumatanes mountain range, Huehuetenango offers few charms of its own, though some may appreciate its welcoming if scruffy character. Fortunately, 'Huehue' (*way-way*) packs in plenty of eating and sleeping options along with some striking mountain scenery.

Huehuetenango was a Mam Maya region until the 15th century, when the K'iche', expanding from their capital K'umarcaaj, near present-day Santa Cruz del Quiché, pushed them out. But the weakness of K'iche' rule soon brought about civil war, which engulfed the highlands and provided a chance for Mam independence. The turmoil was still unresolved in 1525 when Gonzalo de Alvarado, the brother of Pedro, arrived to conquer Zaculeu, the Mam capital, for Spain.

◉ Sights & Activities

The lively indigenous market is filled daily with traders who come down from surrounding villages. Actually, it's about the only place you'll see traditional costumes in this town, as most citizens are *ladinos* in modern garb.

Parque Central
PLAZA

Huehuetenango's main square is shaded by cylindrical ficus trees and surrounded by the town's imposing buildings: the **municipalidad** (with a band shell on the upper floor) and the imposing neoclassical **church**. For a bird's-eye view of the situation, check out the little relief map of Huehuetenango department, which lists altitudes, language groups and populations of the various municipal divisions.

Zaculeu
ARCHAEOLOGICAL SITE

(admission Q50; ◎ 8am-4pm) A remnant of the Mam capital, the Zaculeu archaeological zone was restored by the United Fruit Company in the 1940s, leaving its pyramids, ball courts and ceremonial platforms covered by a thick coat of graying plaster. Though hardly authentic, the work goes further than others in simulating the appearance of an active religious center.

With ravines on three sides, the Postclassic religious center Zaculeu ('White Earth' in the Mam language) occupies a strategic defensive location that served its Mam Maya inhabitants well. It finally failed, however, in 1525, when Gonzalo de Alvarado and his conquistadors laid siege to the site for two months. It was starvation that ultimately defeated the Mam.

A small museum at the site holds, among other things, skulls and grave goods found in a tomb beneath Estructura 1, the tallest structure at the site.

Zaculeu is located 4km west of Huehuetenango's main plaza. Buses to the site (Q2.50, 20 minutes) leave about every 30 minutes from 7:30am to 6pm, from in front of the school at the corner of 2a Calle and 7a Av. A taxi from the town center costs Q30 one way. One hour is plenty of time to look around the site and museum.

🛏 Sleeping

Hotel Mary
HOTEL $

(☑ 7764-1618; 2a Calle 3-52; s/d Q80/130; ℗) This echoey older hotel has a cafe on the ground floor and a useful map of the province in the lobby. Though drably furnished, rooms do have comfy beds and large tiled bathrooms. At least one – No 310 – features a balcony.

Hotel Central
HOTEL $

(☑ 7764-1202; 5a Av 1-33; r per person Q30; ℗) This rough-and-ready little number has tidy rooms with wood plank floors and sagging beds; electric showers are downstairs. The pillared wooden interior balcony gives the place a sliver of charm and it sure is central.

Hotel La Sexta
HOTEL $

(☑ 7764-7559; 6a Av 4-29; s/d Q90/150; ℗@🛜) Cubicles flank a barnlike interior here, cheered up a bit by tropical birds and plants, not to mention faux-leather chairs. There's a small, checkered tablecloth cafe near the front. Choose a room as far back as you can – La Sexta, as 6a Av is known, is relentlessly noisy.

★Hotel Zaculeu
HOTEL $$

(☑ 7764-1086; www.hotelzaculeu.com; 5a Av 1-14; s/d/trQ150/275/290; ℗@🛜) The long-standing Zaculeu has loads of character, and despite its advanced age remains quite spiffy. Rooms in the 'new section' (just 20 years old) are a bit pricier but brighter and more stylish. The sprawling patio area, overflowing with plants and chirping birds, is conducive to lounging, as is the excellent brick-walled bar.

Royal Park Hotel
HOTEL $$

(☑ 7762-7774; hotelroyalpark1@gmail.com; 6a Av 2-34; s/d Q135/270; ℗@🛜) This business-class hotel is one of Huehue's poshest, with gold filigree bedspreads, padded headboards and jumbo flatscreen TVs. Rooms ending in -08 have mountain views.

Hotel Casa Blanca
HOTEL $$

(☑ 7769-0775; 7a Av 3-41; s/d Q220/280; ℗🛜) Hanging ferns and sculpted shrubs grace the attractive courtyard here, ringed by spacious, modern rooms with arched pine ceilings and good hot showers. The patio restaurant out back serves up good-value set lunches (Q22) and a Sunday breakfast buffet (Q35).

Hotel San Luis de la Sierra
HOTEL $$

(☑ 7764-9217; hsanluis@gmail.com; 2a Calle 7-00; s/d Q120/185; ℗) The simple, smallish rooms

Huehuetenango

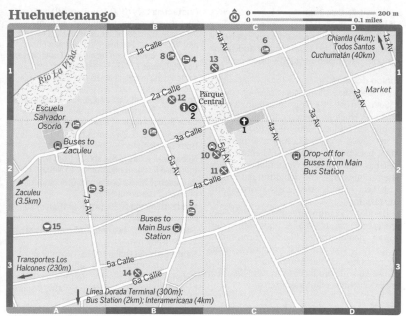

here have pine furniture and homey touches, and there's a decent restaurant on the premises. The real attraction, though, is the rambling rainforest garden out back, with paths for strolling.

🍴 Eating & Drinking

Pastelería Monte Alto   CAFE $
(2a Calle 4-24; cakes & pastries Q8-15; ☺9am-9pm) This old-fashioned establishment just off the plaza has a tempting array of cheesecake, eclairs, plum pie and other tantalizing pastries, plus all the essential espresso variations.

Cafetería Las Palmeras   GUATEMALAN $
(4a Calle 5-10; mains Q25; ☺7am-9pm) Popular Las Palmeras features a breezy upper level with views over the Parque Central. The *caldo de pollo criollo* (Q25) is a must, brimming with chicken, *güisquil* and corn. Saturdays there are tasty tamales.

Cafetería Carilo   GUATEMALAN $
(5a Av 3-54; menú del día Q25; ☺7am-9pm) This humble dining hall on the central plaza fills quickly with families and friends, all digging into abundant portions of home-cooked stews served with avocado wedges and plenty of just-slapped tortillas.

Huehuetenango

◎ Sights
1 Church	C2
2 Municipalidad (Town Hall)	B1

▣ Sleeping
3 Hotel Casa Blanca	A2
4 Hotel Central	B1
5 Hotel La Sexta	B2
6 Hotel Mary	C1
7 Hotel San Luis de la Sierra	A2
8 Hotel Zaculeu	B1
9 Royal Park Hotel	B2

◎ Eating
10 Cafetería Carilo	C2
11 Cafetería Las Palmeras	C2
12 La Fonda de Don Juan	B1
13 Pastelería Monte Alto	C1
14 Restaurante Lekaf	B3

◎ Drinking & Nightlife
15 Museo del Café	A3

Restaurante Lekaf   INTERNATIONAL $$
(☎7764-3202; 6a Calle 6-40; mains Q40-80; ☺10am-11pm) This modern, airy dining hall has a varied menu, including sandwiches, pizza and seafood. Live music (marimbas, folk) attracts a lively crowd Wednesday to Sunday evenings.

La Fonda de Don Juan
PIZZERIA $$

(2a Calle 5-35; pizzas Q45-75; ☺24hr) The place for Huehue's night owls and early risers, La Fonda serves varied Guatemalan and international fare including good-value pizzas.

Museo del Café
CAFE

(www.cafemuseohuehue.com; 4a Calle 7-40; ☺7am-9:30pm Mon-Sat; ☎) This 'museum' serves some of Huehue's best coffee, and that's saying something. More than just a place to get a well-prepared cup, it also provides some background on this bewitching bean that has so influenced Guatemala's history. The various salons and delightful patio buzz with java hounds from early morning till late evening.

Besides examining antique coffee-processing paraphernalia and some diagrams demonstrating coffee production techniques, you can roast your own beans for purchase. Owner Manrique López, son of a small-scale producer from Barrillas, also organizes coffee plantation tours.

ⓘ Orientation & Information

The town center is 4km northeast of the Interamericana, and the bus station is off the road linking the two, about 2km from each. An **Inguat** (☎5768-7078; Parque Central; ☺8am-noon & 2-5pm) office is reportedly inside the *municipalidad* though it seems seldom occupied.

Banco Industrial (6a Av 1-26), a block west of the main plaza, has a reliable ATM. **Milenium Multimedia** (4a Av 1-54; ☺8am-6pm Mon-Sat & 9am-1pm Sun) offers internet access.

ⓘ Getting There & Away

The bus terminal is in Zona 4, 2km southwest of the plaza along 6a Calle. A number of companies ply the same routes, though information is not posted in any coherent fashion. Microbuses leave from the south end of the station. Another stop, for microbuses to Cobán and Barrillas, via Soloma and San Mateo Ixtatán, is by a gas station at El Calvario, at the corner of 1a Av and 1a Calle, four blocks northeast of the Parque Central.

Antigua Take a Guatemala City bus and change at Chimaltenango.

Aguacatán (Q8, one hour) Microbuses every 15 minutes.

Barrillas (Q50, seven hours) Microbuses hourly from 4:30am to 2:30pm.

Cobán (Q70, six hours) Microbus at 1:40pm daily from El Calvario gas station.

Gracias a Dios (Mexican border) (Q30, four hours) Four departures daily via Nentón.

Guatemala City (Q60, five hours) Various lines leave continuously until about 4pm, including Transportes El Condor, Díaz Álvarez and Velásquez. Two lines run Pullman buses from their own private terminals: **Transportes Los Halcones** (☎7765-7986; www.transportesloshalcones.com; 10a Av 9-12, Zona 1) (Q65) leaves at least five times a day, with deluxe service at 7am and 2pm; **Linea Dorada** (☎7768-1566; www.lineadorada.com.gt; 8a Calle 8-70) departs at 11pm (Q110).

La Mesilla (Q20, 2½ hours) Every 30 minutes from 3am to 6pm.

Nebaj Take a bus to Sacapulas from where there are frequent microbuses to Nebaj.

Panajachel Take a Guatemala City bus and change at Los Encuentros.

Quetzaltenango (Q20, two hours) Every 15 minutes from 3am to 6pm.

Sacapulas (Q20, two hours) Microbuses at 11:30am and 1pm.

Santa Cruz del Quiché (Q25, two hours) Frequent microbuses from 5am to 5pm.

Soloma (Q25, three hours) Hourly microbuses from 4:30am to 2:30pm from El Calvario gas station.

Todos Santos Cuchumatán (Q25, two hours) Microbuses hourly from 4:30am to 2:30pm from El Calvario gas station.

ⓘ Getting Around

City buses circulate between the bus station and the town center from 5am to around 9pm. Arriving in Huehue, leave the east side of the station through the gap between the Díaz Álvarez and Transportes Fortaleza offices; walk through the covered market opposite to the next street, where 'Centro' buses depart every few minutes (Q2). To return to the bus station from the center, catch the buses outside the Hotel La Sexta.

Around Huehuetenango

Except for Todos Santos Cuchumatán, the mountainous far northwest of Guatemala is little visited by travelers. The adventurous few will often be a novelty to the local Maya folks they meet. Spanish skills, patience and tact will pave the way in these parts.

Chiantla

POP 10,500 / ELEV 2056M

Just before the climb into the Cuchumatanes, you'll come across this village, the former seat of the municipality, now practically a suburb of Huehuetenango. Its church holds the **Virgen del Rosario**, a silver statue donated by the owner of a local mine. The virgin is believed to have mystical healing powers and people come from all over the country to seek her assistance. The main date for the pilgrimage is February 2, when the town packs out with supplicants and the infirm.

Also in the church are some interesting **murals** painted in the 1950s, showing local Maya having miraculous experiences while working in the silver mines.

Another 4km on from Chiantla, **El Mirador Juan Diéguez Olaverri** overlooks Huehuetenango from a point up in the Cuchumatanes. On a clear day it offers a great view of the entire region and many volcanoes. Mounted on plaques here is the poem, *A Los Cuchumatanes,* penned by the lookout point's namesake. Local kids will recite it to you for a tip. And thanks to the recently installed **Café del Cielo,** you can now savor a cup of Huehuetenango's fine coffee along with the views.

Any bus from Huehue heading for Todos Santos, Soloma or Barillas goes through Chiantla and past the turnoff for the Mirador.

Chancol

The Guatemalan- and French-run **Unicornio Azul** (☑ 5205-9328; www.unicornioazul. com; s/d/tr incl breakfast Q380/700/945) is a horseback-riding ranch at Chancol, about 25km by road northeast of Huehuetenango. It offers riding through the Cuchumatanes along trails used only by local inhabitants, camping out or staying in rural accommodations. Unicornio Azul also functions as a *posada rural,* with 10 simple but comfortable rooms in the estate home or a separate building.

Rides can range from one hour (Q130) to two, three or seven days (per person Q2300/3400/9500 with a minimum four riders). Among the options is a two-day journey to **Laguna Magdalena,** a turquoise lagoon nestled in the mountains, with massive boulders and ancient, gnarled trees scattered around. The seven-day option traverses the Cuchumatanes to the Mexican border through a number of different climatic zones and four distinct ethnic regions. The longer journeys are done only during the dry season (November to April). There are also one-day trips (Q620) for those who'd rather sleep at the *posada.*

To get to Chancol, take any bus heading for Todos Santos or Barillas and get off in

La Capellanía; the owners will come pick you up (Q45).

Chiabal

High in the Sierra Cuchumatanes (3400m) amid a rocky plateau dotted with maguey plants and sheep, Chiabal, 17km east of Todos Santos, welcomes visitors looking to experience rural life in a tiny **Mam community** (☑ 5381-0540; www.turismocuchumatanes. com). The villagers provide simple accommodations in four local houses and prepare hearty local fare (Q130 for three meals and a night's stay). A community-built 2.5km interpretive trail leads to the Piedra Cuache, an oddly shaped boulder at a 3666m-high lookout point. Guides can take you to various sites in the 18,000-hectare Todos Santos Forest Reserve, including the summit of La Torre. As compelling as the scenery is the chance to participate in community activities like herding llamas, weaving *huipiles* and planting potatoes while getting to know the local inhabitants.

Microbuses go directly to Chiabal (Q10) from the El Calvario gas station at the corner of 1a Av and 1a Calle in Huehuetenango. Otherwise, hop a Todos Santos bus and get off at Chiabal, 4km west of the turn off the Huehue–Barillas road.

Todos Santos Cuchumatán

POP 4109 / ELEV 2392M

Way up in the highlands, Todos Santos is as raw as Guatemalan village life gets – dramatic scenery, mud streets, beans and tortillas, and everything shut by 9pm. The community is nestled at the bottom of a deep valley and bordered by forested slopes, and the last 1¼ hours of the approach by bus are down a sporadically paved road that leaves the Huehuetenango–Soloma highway after a 1½-hour climb up from Huehue.

Traditional clothing is very much in use here and, unusually, it's the male costume that is the more eye-catching. Men wear red-and-white-striped trousers, little straw hats with blue ribbons, jackets with multicolored stripes and thick woven collars. Saturday is the main market day; there's a smaller market on Wednesday. The notorious post-market inebriation ritual has faded into history since dry laws took over (the November 1 celebrations now being the only permissible time to get smashed).

TODOS SANTOS' BIG DAY

Todos Santos Cuchumatán is renowned for its wildly colorful horse races, the highlight of a no-holds-barred annual celebration held on November 1 (El Día de Todos los Santos). It's the culmination of a week of festivities and an all-night spree of male dancing to marimbas and *aguardiente* (cane liquor) drinking on the eve of the races – which rather than a competitive event is a chance for *todosanteros* to ride up and down as fast as they can while getting progressively drunker the whole day long (with a break for lunch). The authentically indigenous event attracts throngs of inhabitants from surrounding communities who gather on a grassy hillside alongside the sand track or upon the rooftops opposite to observe the riders decked out in their finest traditional garb. Todos Santos, incidentally, is the only place in Guatemala where Day of the Dead is not observed on Nov 1 since that day is reserved for a celebration of autonomy within Huehuetenango province. Instead, the traditional visit to the cemetery is postponed to the following day, when graves are decorated and marimbas serenade groups of mourners as they arrive to pay their respects.

Reasons to visit Todos Santos include good walking in the hills, learning Spanish or Mam, and getting to know a traditional and close-knit but friendly community. Todos Santos suffered terribly during Guatemala's civil war when, by some accounts, 2000 area inhabitants were murdered. It is still very poor. To supplement their subsistence from agriculture, families travel in the early part of the year to work for meager wages on coffee, sugar and cotton plantations on the Pacific Slope. Working in the US is, however, proving a more lucrative alternative for some *todosanteros* today, as the amount of new construction in the valley demonstrates, not to mention the incorporation of urban elements into traditional clothing.

If you're coming to Todos Santos in the wet season (mid-May to November), bring warm clothes, as it's cold up here, especially at night.

◉ Sights & Activities

Tuj K'man Txun   MONUMENT
This ceremonial site, 500m up the uphill street beside the central plaza among trees on the left of the road, consists of a few grassy mounds and two crosses with indications of contemporary Maya offerings. The more recently installed cross commemorates the incidents of August 1982, when the army executed hundreds of alleged guerrilla collaborators, then torched many homes.

Museo Balam   MUSEUM
(admission Q5; ⊙8am-6pm) Todos Santos' museum is in a two-story house, along a sidestreet one block east of the plaza. The

collection of outfits and masks, traditional kitchen implements, archaeological finds and musical instruments comes to life when Fortunato, its creator and a community leader, is there to provide commentary.

Hiking
January to April are the best months for hitting the trails through Todos Santos' rugged countryside but you can usually walk in the morning, before the weather closes in, year-round. Get trail maps and info on hikes at Tienda Grupo de Mujeres, downstairs from Hotel Casa Familiar.

Rigoberto Pablo Cruz   HIKING
(☏5206-0916; rigoguiadeturismo@yahoo.com) Knowledgeable, easy-going and English-speaking *todosantero* Rigoberto leads walks of the area, including a climb to the peak of La Torre followed by a descent to La Maceta. Another of Rigo's hikes reaches the isolated mountain community of San Juan Atitán, where the women wear dazzling *huipiles*, in about five hours, returning by bus to Todos Santos.

In addition, Rigoberto leads two-day treks to Nebaj (Q800 per person with minimum of two), including food and lodging in community dwellings. He also offers classes in both Spanish and Mam.

La Torre   HIKING
One of the most striking destinations is La Torre (3837mm), the highest nonvolcanic point in Central America. Take a bus east up the valley to the hamlet of La Ventosa (Q10, one hour) from where it's a trail walk of 8km (about 1½ hours) through limestone and gnarly *huite* trees to the top.

At the summit (marked by a radio mast), the southern horizon is dotted with almost a dozen volcanoes from Tacaná on the Mexican border to Volcán Agua near Antigua.

Las Cuevas
HIKING

The walk to Las Cuevas, a sacred cave still used for Maya rituals, starts from La Maceta, a tree growing out of rock beside a football field, 15 minutes by bus up the Huehue road from Todos Santos (Q5).

Maya Sauna
HEALTH & FITNESS

Todos Santos' chilly climate makes a visit to the traditional Maya *chuj* especially inviting. This is a small adobe building with wooden boards covering the entrance. A wood fire burns in a stone hearth within, and water is sprinkled on the stones to provide steam. Also, check out the *chuj* at the Hotel Casa Familiar.

🛏 Sleeping & Eating

For long-term stays, local guide Rigoberto Pablo Cruz (p153) can arrange **rooms** (per person, per week Q250) with families. You'll get your own bedroom, and share the bathroom and meals with the family.

Hotel Tourist
HOTEL $

(☑4491-0220; r without bathroom Q50) This recently inaugurated option – perhaps constructed with tools from the hardware store below – is quite clean and well-maintained, with functional hot showers, quality mattresses and plenty of blankets for the evening chill. Around 200m east from the main square, turn left downhill by the Restaurante Bautista to find the solitary pink concrete structure.

Hotel Casa Familiar
HOTEL $

(☑7783-0656; adelamendozaj@yahoo.es; r without bathroom s/d/tr Q60/90/120) Only partially built, this central lodging just down from the main plaza has four cozy rooms with hardwood floors, traditional textile bedspreads, good hot showers and plenty of blankets. Have a breakfast bowl of *mosh* or fresh-baked banana bread at the cafe downstairs.

Hotelito Todos Santos
HOTEL $

(☑7783-0603; r Q125, s/d without bathroom Q45/90) South of the plaza, up a sidestreet that branches left, this backpackers' fave has small and bare but well-scrubbed rooms with tile floors and firm beds. The casual cafe here is noted for its pancakes.

Comedor Katy
GUATEMALAN $

(meals Q22) Women in traditional garb attend to great vats bubbling over glowing embers at this rustic cook shack just below the central plaza. There are tables on a terrace overlooking the market activity.

Comedor Evelín
GUATEMALAN $

(⊗6am-8pm Mon-Sat) This often busy eatery features two dining halls; you'll find the menu scrawled on a styrofoam board at the back. Lunchtime they serve classic traditional fare, such as *pepián de pollo* (chicken in pumpkin-seed sauce) and *caldo de res*. It's 100m east of the plaza, turning uphill at the bookstore.

🛍 Shopping

Tienda Grupo de Mujeres, downstairs from the Hotel Casa Familiar, has a great selection of *típica* clothing and accessories, all produced by a women's weaving cooperative.

ⓘ Orientation & Information

Todos Santos' main street is about 500m long. Towards its west end are the church and market, with the central plaza raised above street level on the south side.

The Grupo de Mujeres weaving shop at the base of the Hotel Casa Familiar functions as a de facto information center and they can give you a town map.

To make telephone calls look for signs saying 'Llamadas Nacionales y Internacionales' in the area around the church.

Banrural (Central Plaza) changes US dollars (cash or traveler's checks) and has an intermittently functional ATM.

ⓘ Getting There & Away

Buses and microbuses depart from the main street between the plaza and the church. About 10 buses leave for Huehuetenango (Q25, 2½ hours) between 4:30am and 2pm. Microbuses leave throughout the day, whenever they fill up. There are three buses northwest to Jacaltenango between 3pm and 5 pm. Another heads for La Mesilla at 11 am.

North to San Mateo Ixtatán

North of the Todos Santos turnoff, the paved road winds up between often mist-shrouded cliffs and a precipitous gorge. Out of the mists emerge a pair of massive fingers of granite, known as the **Piedras de Captzín**.

Soon after, you arrive in **San Juan Ixcoy**, where the women wear traditional white *huipiles* embroidered at the collar and hanging almost to their ankles. A rough 10km track leads to the **Pepajaú waterfalls** from the village of **San Lucas Quisil**, just north of San Juan. Their 250m drop is an impressive sight, particularly after the rains. Pickup trucks can get you to the trailhead at the Río Quisil, from where it's a delightful two- to three-hour walk to the falls.

Some 70km north of Huehuetenango, **Soloma** fills a valley and spreads up into the hills. This agricultural town is one of the biggest in the Cuchumatanes. The Maya here speak Q'anjob'al, but most of the *ladino* cowboys will greet you in English! Soloma's prosperity and its residents' language skills can be attributed to the migratory laborers who annually make the arduous trip to the US, working as cowhands, auto detailers or landscapers. On Sunday, market day, the town floods with people from surrounding villages. The pink-and-pastel **Hotel Don Chico** (☑7780-6087; 4a Av 3-65; s/d Q90/180; @), opposite the main Catholic church, is the most comfortable lodging in town.

Just over the hill from Soloma, the town of **Santa Eulalia** feels much more remote and traditional. It can get quite chilly here. This is sheep-farming territory, and you'll see shepherds wearing *capixays* (short woollen ponchos) in the fields. The town has a reputation for producing some of the finest marimbas in the country, with locally grown hormigo trees providing the wood for the keys. Factories and workshops producing marimbas line the streets around the plaza. If you're interested in the production process, wander in and ask to be shown around.

From Santa Eulalia the rough road keeps climbing through pasturelands and occasional pine forest – sit on the left and you can see all the way to Mexico – and after 30km reaches **San Mateo Ixtatán**, the logical place to break the journey if you're heading for Laguna Lachuá from Huehue. Perched on an aerie with the jagged peaks of the Cuchumatanes trailing off into the clouds, the town unfolds organically over the green slopes. (The mist can descend early here, wiping out visibility by early afternoon.) Quaint buildings with pillared verandas and painted designs on the doors line largely traffic-free paths.

The women of this small Chuj town wear captivating *huipiles*, lacy white affairs with concentric floral patterns embroidered on the neckline. San Mateo's church has a primitive charm. Beyond a rather dumpy facade is an austere interior with crude fruit motifs painted on the pillars. The real action seems to be out front in the atrium, where a smoking altar attests to the enduring Maya influence.

The newish **Hotel Magdalena** (☑5374-3390; s/d Q75/150) is easily the most comfortable option in town and the showers are scalding hot (but ask if the heater is on beforehand). From the park, go uphill and take the first street on the right; the yellow box is adjacent to the Banco Agromercantil. Right above the turnoff is spiffy **Los Picones al Chaz Chaz** (☺breakfast, lunch & dinner), where you can have fresh tamales with delicious salsas in the morning, as well as tacos and steaks.

Barillas-bound buses from Huehuetenango stop in Soloma, Santa Eulalia and San Mateo.

East to Playa Grande

Leaving San Mateo, the road drops and the weather becomes slightly kinder. After 28km, you'll reach **Barillas**, a prosperous coffee-growing town with a lowland feel. There are regular microbuses between the terminal and the town center (Q2, seven minutes). In town, the efficiently run **Hotel Villa Virginia** (☑7780-2236; cnr 3a Calle & 3 Av; r per person Q84) is right on the plaza, with a restaurant attached. There's a Banrural, with Cajero 5B ATM, at the corner of the park. Three restaurants are along 3a Calle within a block of the park; Restaurant El Café, opposite the Villa Virginia, does a mean *caldo de gallina*.

If you're moving on for Cobán or El Petén, get an early start. Pickups head for Playa Grande (Q60, four hours) hourly from 7am to 10am, departing from Mercado No 1 in the center of town. The road goes through the remote villages and forests of the Ixcán region, alternating between packed gravel and a tortuous exposed-boulder surface, but the trip is fascinating. Bad weather can extend the travel time by two or three hours. Ask around to see what conditions are like before committing to this trip.

Yalambojoch & Laguna Brava

In a lower-lying, more lushly vegetated zone between the Cuchumatanes and the Mexican border, the northwest corner of

Huehuetenango department has a distinctive culture where the Awakateco language is spoken. About 20km east of the border post at Gracias a Dios is the hamlet of Yalambojoch. Most of the inhabitants fled during the conflict of the 1980s, and have only recently returned to pick up the pieces of their lives. A European NGO has provided funding to resettle the community, constructing wells, houses, a school and a **cultural center** (per@cnl.nu), and ecotourism is being developed in the area.

One of the chief attractions for visitors is the **Laguna Brava** (also known as Laguna Yolnajab), 6.5km to the north, an extension of Mexico's Lagunas de Montebello. There's good swimming in the crystalline waters of the lagoon, reached by a two-hour descent on foot or horseback from Yalambojoch (best attempted from March to June). There's a Q25 entry fee to the lagoon, and guides charge Q75 to take you down, plus Q75 per day for horses.

East of Yalambojoch, a series of surprisingly intact **Maya pyramids** dating from the 10th century stand near the site of what used to be the village of San Francisco, the site of one of the civil war's most atrocious massacres, part of Rios Montt's scorched earth campaign.

Some visitors come here to experience rural life in a Chuj community, and volunteer opportunities are available teaching at the cultural center or working on reforestation projects.

Accommodations at Yalambojoch include a few comfortable cabins and a large but well-maintained dorm (Q50 per person). Guests have access to a well-equipped kitchen or can get meals at a pair of *comedores* for about Q20.

Buses by La Chiantlequita (Q30, six hours) depart for Yalambojoch from Huehuetenango at 4:45am and 1pm, returning at 4:45am and 9:30am. There is also transport from San Mateo Ixtatán.

West of Yalambojoch toward the border post at Gracias a Dios, is the Finca La Trinidad junction, where a paved road leads south to the Interamericana. Approximately 5km south of the Finca La Trinidad junction is the turnoff for **Posada Rural Finca Chaculá** (✆ 5205-9328; www.unicornioazul.com; s/d/tr incl breakfast QQ270/420/525), a community-tourism project started by returnees from five different ethnic groups who took refuge in Mexico during the civil war. Their 37-sq-km farm features a small lagoon, some Maya archaeological sites, a waterfall and abundant forest. The old estate house has been outfitted with three comfortable rooms with hot showers, and meals are served. Inguat-trained guides lead excursions to the Laguna Brava (Laguna Yolnajab) and Hoyo Cimarrón, a gigantic, almost perfectly cylindrical crater near the Mexican border. From Huehuetenango, buses bound for Yalambojoch and Gracias a Dios pass by here.

La Mesilla

The Mexican immigration post is a 100m walk from the Guatemalan border at La Mesilla. With an early start from Huehuetenango you should have no trouble getting through this border and onward to San Cristóbal de las Casas, Mexico. From the Mexican post, taxis charge 10 Mexican pesos for the 4km ride to Ciudad Cuauhtémoc, where there are connections to Comitán (80 pesos, every half hour), and onward to San Cristóbal (two hours).

The strip in La Mesilla leading to the border post has a variety of services, including a police station, a post office and a bank. There are also moneychangers who will do the deal – at a good rate if you're changing dollars, a terrible one for pesos or quetzals.

Entering Guatemala via La Mesilla, you'll find chicken buses leaving for Huehuetenango (Q20, two hours) every 20 minutes till 6pm, as well as transport to Quetzaltenango (Q40). Otherwise, Línea Dorada (p142) runs Pullmans to Guatemala City (Q170, eight hours) at 9pm.

The Pacific Slope

Best Places to Eat

➡ Taberna El Pelicano (p173)
➡ Cafetería La Luna (p161)
➡ Max Café (p160)
➡ Hotel Atelie del Mar (p173)

Best Places to Stay

➡ Takalik Maya Lodge (p163)
➡ Isleta de Gaia (p174)
➡ Hotel Pez de Oro (p173)
➡ Hotel Casa y Campo (p160)

Why Go?

Separated from the highlands by a chain of volcanoes, the flatlands that run down to the Pacific are universally known as La Costa. It's a sultry region – hot and wet or hot and dry, depending on the time of year – with rich volcanic soil good for growing coffee, palm-oil seeds and sugarcane.

Archaeologically, the big draws here are Takalik Abaj and the sculptures left by pre-Olmec civilizations around Santa Lucía Cotzumalguapa.

The culture is overwhelmingly *ladino* (mixed indigenous and European heritage), and even the biggest towns are humble affairs, with low-rise houses and the occasional palm-thatched roof.

Guatemalan beach tourism is seriously underdeveloped. Monterrico is the only real contender, helped along by a nature reserve protecting mangroves and their inhabitants. Sipacate is slowly developing as a surf resort, although serious surfers find more joy in Mexico or El Salvador.

When to Go

You can't escape the heat on the coast, although temperatures do get a little more moderate from November to March. Beaches pack out on weekends and places like Monterrico will often double their room rates. Guatemalans love the beach for the main vacation periods – Easter and Christmas – and booking accommodation around this time is a very good idea. The Pacific surf is rough at any time of year, but surfers find the best waves towards the end of hurricane season, late October through to November.

History

Despite it being one of the first settled areas in Guatemala, relatively little is known about the Pacific region's early history. Many archaeological sites are presumed overgrown by jungle; others have been destroyed to make way for agriculture.

What *is* known is that the Olmecs were among the first to arrive, followed by the Ocós and Iztapa, whose cultures appear to have flourished around 1500 BC.

Although these cultures were much more humble than those of their northerly counterparts, they developed a level of sophistication in stone carving and ceramics. It's also thought that the coastal region acted as a conduit, passing cultural advances (like the formation of writing and the Maya calendar) from north to south.

Between AD 400 and 900, the Pipil moved in, most likely displaced by the turmoil in the Mexican highlands, and began farming cacao, which they used to make a (rather bitter) chocolate drink. They also used cacao beans as currency.

Towards the end of the Postclassic period, the K'iche', Kaqchiquel and Tz'utujil indigenous groups began moving in as population expansion in Guatemala's highlands made food scarce and land squabbles common.

Pedro de Alvarado, the first Spaniard to land in Guatemala, arrived here in 1524, pausing briefly to fight the K'iche' as a sort of forerunner to a much larger battle around present-day Quetzaltenango.

Further agricultural projects (mostly indigo and cacao) were started around this time, but it wasn't until independence that the region became one of the country's main agricultural suppliers, with plantations of coffee, bananas, rubber and sugarcane.

In the languid tropical climate here, not much changes, particularly the social structure. The distribution of land – a few large landholders and many poorly paid, landless farm workers – can be traced back to these early post-independence days. You'll see the outcome as you travel around the region – large mansions and opulent gated communities alongside squalid, makeshift workers' huts.

Tilapita

Just south of the Mexican border, this little fishing village is the place to come for some seriously laid-back beach time. There's exactly one hotel here (and it's a good one) and it's a world away from the often hectic, scruffy feel of other towns along the coast.

The village, which sits on a sandbar cut off from the mainland by the Ocós estuary, is only reachable by boat from the town of Tilapa. There's some excellent swimming to be had here, although as with all the beaches along this coast, the undertow can be quite serious and there are no lifeguards. If you're not a strong swimmer, don't go too far out.

There's not a whole lot to do (which is kind of the point), but local fishermen offer fascinating boat tours of the estuary, mangroves and adjoining **Reserva Natural El Manchón** for Q100 per boat per hour. There are no guarantees, but local wildlife includes iguanas, crocodiles, white herons, egrets and kingfishers.

Back in Tilapita, the **Tortugario Tilapita**, across the path from Hotel Pacific Mar, is fighting an uphill battle to preserve the local sea turtle population, and would be quite happy for whatever help they can get if you're looking for some volunteer work.

One of the best accommodation deals along the coast, **Hotel Pacific Mar** (☏5914-1524; www.playatilapa.com; s/d Q60/100; ☒) is nothing fancy, but it has decent-sized, clean concrete rooms. Delicious meals (Q50) are served in an oversized thatched-roof *palapa* (thatched palm-leaf shelter), and generally consist of the catch of the day – shrimp, fish and *caldo de mariscos* (seafood stew) are always a good bet. The good-sized swimming pool is a welcome addition, as things can get slightly warm here.

Coming from Tecún Umán, you might luck onto a direct minibus (Q10, 45 minutes) to Tilapa – if not, take any bus heading out of town, get off at the Tilapa turnoff and wait for an onward bus there. A much more scenic option is to take a bus to Ocós (Q12, 30 minutes) and a *lancha* (small boat; around Q20, 45 minutes) to Tilapita from there. Coming in the other direction, direct buses run from Coatepeque to Tilapa (Q10, 1½ hours). Once you get to Tilapa, turn left down the side street and follow it to the dock, where you will find *lanchas* waiting. The 10-minute ride to Tilapita costs Q10 per person in a shared *lancha,* or you can hire a private one to make the trip for Q50. Tell the *lanchero* you are going to *el hotel* (although he will probably know that already). If you get stuck, there are cheap, not-so-lovely hotels in Tilapa.

Pacific Slope Highlights

1 Get away from absolutely everything at the one-hotel town of **Tilapita** (p157)

2 Investige the bridge in history between the Olmec and the Maya while strolling through the grassy **Parque Arqueológico Takalik Abaj** (p163)

3 Spot wildlife among the mangrove-lined canal and lagoons of the **Biotopo Monterrico-Hawaii** (p171)

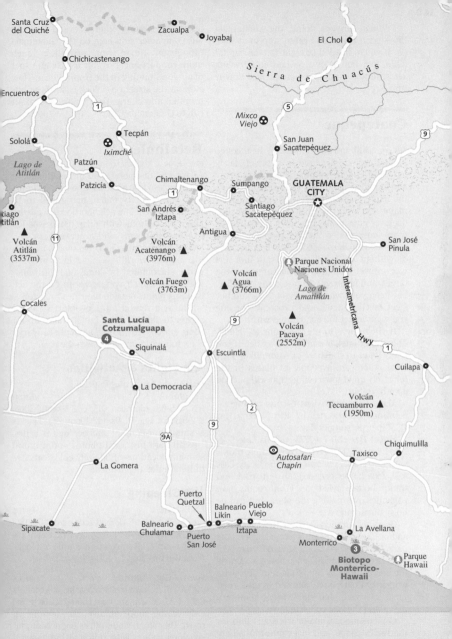

Santa Cruz del Quiché
Zacualpa
Joyabaj
El Chol
Chichicastenango
Sierra de Chuacús
Encuentros
1
Mixco Viejo
5
9
Sololá
Tecpán
San Juan Sacatepéquez
Iximché
Lago de Atitlán
Patzún
Patzicía
Chimaltenango
Sumpango
GUATEMALA CITY
1
Santiago Sacatepéquez
tiago titlán
San Andrés Iztapa
11
Volcán Atitlán (3537m)
Antigua
San José Pinula
Volcán Acatenango (3976m)
Parque Nacional Naciones Unidos
Volcán Agua (3766m)
Lago de Amatitlán
Cocales
Volcán Fuego (3763m)
9
Interamericana Hwy
Santa Lucía Cotzumalguapa
4
Siquinalá
Volcán Pacaya (2552m)
Escuintla
Cuilapa
1
La Democracia
2
Volcán Tecuamburro (1950m)
9
Chiquimulilla
9A
La Gomera
9
Autosafari Chapín
Taxisco
Puerto Quetzal
Balneario Likín
Pueblo Viejo
Sipacate
Balneario Chulamar
Puerto San José
Iztapa
La Avellana
Monterrico
Parque Hawaii
Biotopo Monterrico-Hawaii
3

④ Check out the big mysterious heads carved by the non-Maya Pipil culture around **Santa Lucía Cotzumalguapa** (p165)

⑤ Get wet at **Parque Acuático Xocomil** (p162) and dizzy at **Parque de Diversiones Xetulul** (p162), two fun parks near Retalhuleu

Pullman drivers doing the Guatemala City–Tecún Umán run often stop in at Tilapa. If you're headed straight for the capital (Q60, four hours) or anywhere in between, ask around to find out when the next departure is.

Coatepeque

POP 58,300

Set on a hill and surrounded by lush coffee plantations, Coatepeque is a brash, fairly ugly and chaotic commercial center, noisy and humid at all times. If you read the papers, the name Coatepeque should be familiar. A major stopover on the Colombia–Mexico drugs 'n' guns route, this town probably has more gang-related activity than any other outside of Guatemala City. Barely a day goes by without somebody getting shot in a turf war or revenge killing. Tourists are never the target, and rarely get caught in the crossfire, but keep your wits about you. It *is* another facet of Guatemala, and probably not one you want to get too acquainted with.

If you're here to see the ruins at Takalik Abaj, Retalhuleu is a much better bet. If you really want to stay here or (more likely) get stuck, there are a couple of places in the relatively quiet town center that will put you up admirably.

Maya Expeditions (p49) runs rafting expeditions on the nearby Río Naranjo for Q850 per person per day.

Hotel Baechli (⌨7775-1483; 6a Calle 5-45, Zona 1; s/d Q95/170; P) has cool, simple rooms with fan. **Hotel Europa** (⌨7775-1396; 6a Calle 4-01, Zona 1; r per person Q100) is a cool and tranquil older-style hotel. Front rooms have balconies overlooking the plaza, but can be noisy during the day.

Good restaurants (mostly in the steakhouse and/or Chinese vein) are scattered around the park. **Max Café** (4a Calle 3-52, Zona 1; mains Q35-75; ⊙7am-9pm Mon-Sat, 7am-1pm Sun) is vaguely hip and completely out of place in otherwise workaday Coatepeque, and serves up a good range of salads and sandwiches, some OK mains and the best coffee in town.

Coatepeque is a major transport hub for the Pacific Slope, and bus connections here are good. The bus terminal is 2km to the north of town, but most buses stop in the center. There are departures to El Carmen (Q25, two hours), Tecún Umán (Q25, two hours), Quetzaltenango (Q30, 2½ hours), Tilapa (Q10, 1½ hours) and Retalhuleu (Q10,

one hour), among others. Several Pullman bus companies stop here on the Guatemala City–Tecún Umán run, providing much more comfort and possibly a welcome spot of air-conditioning in the tropical heat. They stop on the street one block east of the bus terminal and charge Q60 for the four-hour run to Guatemala City.

Retalhuleu

POP 43,700 / ELEV 240M

Arriving at the bus station in Retalhuleu, or Reu (*ray*-oo) as it's known to most Guatemalans, you're pretty much guaranteed to be underwhelmed. The neighborhood's a tawdry affair, packed out with dilapidated wooden *cantinas* (canteens) and street vendors.

The town center, just five blocks away, is like another world – a majestic, palm-filled plaza, surrounded by some fine old buildings. Even the city police get in on the act, hanging plants outside their headquarters.

The real reason most people visit is for access to Takalik Abaj, but if you're up for some serious downtime, a couple of world-class fun parks are just down the road.

◉ Sights & Activities

Museo de Arqueología y Etnología MUSEUM

(6a Av 5-68; admission Q15; ⊙8:30am-12:30pm & 2-5:30pm Mon-Fri, 9am-12:30pm Sat) This is a small museum of archaeological relics. Upstairs are historical photos and a mural showing locations of 33 archaeological sites in Retalhuleu department.

⌸ Sleeping

La Estancia HOTEL $

(⌨7771-3053; 10a Calle 8-50, Zona 1; s/d Q100/180; P❅☎) The best budget deal in town are these simple, clean rooms a couple of blocks from the bus stop.

Hostal Casa Santa María HOTEL $

(⌨7771-6136; www.hostalcasasantamaria.com; 4a Calle 4-23, Zona 1; s/d from Q160/250; ❅☎❆) One of the more atmospheric options in town, this small hotel offers eight cool and spacious rooms with minimal but tasteful decorations. The small swimming pool in the courtyard is a good place for a dip.

Hotel Casa y Campo HOTEL $$

(⌨7771-3289; 3a Calle 4-73, Zona 1; s/d Q125/250; P❅☎) Comfortable, good-value rooms a

Retalhuleu

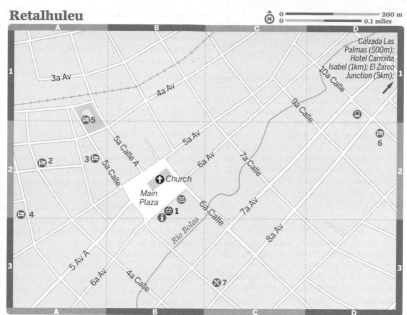

couple of blocks from the plaza. This one books up fast, so it's worth calling ahead.

Hotel Carmiña Isabel　　　　HOTEL **$$**
(☑7771-7217; Calz Las Palmas 2-71, Zona 2; s/d Q150/250; 🅿✳🌊) The Calzada Las Palmas used to be *the* place to live in Reu, and is still lined with stately mansions. This hotel is a fine example – rooms aren't huge but the grounds and pool area are lovely.

Hotel Posada Don José　　　HOTEL **$$**
(☑7771-0180; www.hotelposadadedonjose.com; 5a Calle 3-67, Zona 1; r from Q360; 🅿✳🛜🌊) A beautiful colonial-style hotel built around a huge swimming pool. Swan dives from the top balcony are tempting, but probably unwise. Rooms are spacious and comfortable – they're slowly remodeling here, so it's worth having a look at a few before deciding.

🍴 Eating

Reu seems to be slightly obsessed with pizza – 5a Av north of the plaza is almost wall-to-wall pizzerias. The dining rooms of the Posada Don José and the **Hotel Astor** (☑7771 2559; hotelastor@terra.com.gt; 5a Calle 4-60, Zona 1) both offer more refined dining options.

Retalhuleu

Cafetería La Luna　　　　GUATEMALAN **$**
(cnr 8a Av & 5a Calle, Zona 1; mains Q25-60; ⊗8am-10pm) In a new location a block off the plaza, this remains a town favorite for simple but filling meals in a low-key environment.

ℹ️ Orientation

The town center is 4km southwest of the Carretera al Pacífico, along Calzada Las Palmas, a grand boulevard lined with towering palms. The **main bus stop** is on 10a Calle between 7a and 8a Avs, northeast of the plaza. To find the plaza, look for the twin church towers and walk toward them.

❶ Information

There is no official tourist office, but people in the **municipalidad** (Town Hall; 6a Av), facing the east side of the church, will do their best to help.

Banco Industrial (cnr 6a Calle & 5a Av) changes US dollars and traveler's checks and has a Visa ATM. **Banco Agromercantil** (5a Av), facing the plaza, changes US dollars and traveler's checks and has a MasterCard ATM.

ReuXtreme (⏱5202-8180; www.reuxtreme. com; 4a Calle 4-23, Zona 1), operating out of the Hostal Casa Santa María, is the local tour operator, offering kayaking trips, bird-watching and nature walks, tours of local archaeological sites and shuttles to Antigua, Quetzaltenango and Panajachel, among others.

❶ Getting There & Away

Most buses traveling along the Carretera al Pacífico detour into Reu. Shared taxis (Q5) are the best way to get to El Asintal (for Takalik Abaj). Look for station wagons with 'Asintal' painted on the windscreen around the bus stop and plaza.

Champerico (Q10, one hour, every few minutes from 6am to 7pm)

Guatemala City (Q50 to Q80, three hours, every 15 minutes from 2am to 8:30pm)

Quetzaltenango (Q15, one hour, every 30 minutes from 4am to 6pm)

Santa Lucía Cotzumalguapa (Q25, two hours)

Tecún Umán (Mexican Border; Q15, 1½ hours, every 20 minutes from 5am to 10pm)

Around Retalhuleu

Parque Acuático Xocomil & Parque de Diversiones Xetulul

If you have children along, or the heat is simply getting to you, head out to the **Parque Acuático Xocomil** (⏱7772-9400; www.irtra.org. gt; Carretera CITO, Km 180.5; adult/child Q100/child Q100/50; ⊙9am-5pm Thu-Sun), a gigantic water park in the Disneyland vein, but with a distinct Guatemalan theme. Among the 14 water slides, two swimming pools and two wave pools are re-creations of Maya monuments from Tikal, Copán and Quiriguá. Visitors can bob along a river through canyons flanked with ancient temples and Maya masks spewing water from the nose and mouth. Three real volcanoes – Santiaguito, Zunil and Santa María – can be seen from the grounds. Xocomil is very well executed and maintained, and kids love it. It's at San Martín Zapotitlán on the Quetzaltenango road, about 12km north of Reu.

Next door to Xocomil on the same road is the even more impressive **Parque de Diversiones Xetulul** (⏱7722-9450; www.irtra.org. gt; Carretera CITO, Km 180.5; adult/child Q100/50; ⊙10am-6pm Thu-Sun). It's a theme park with representations of a Tikal pyramid, historical Guatemalan buildings and famous buildings from many European cities, plus restaurants and many first-class rides. You need a bracelet (extra Q50) for unlimited rides.

These two attractions are both run by **IRTRA** (Instituto de Recreación de los Trabajadores de la Empresa Privada de Guatemala; Guatemalan Private Enterprise Workers' Recreation Institute), which administers several fun sites around the country for workers and their families. Between them, Xocomil and Xetulul comprise the most popular tourist attraction in Guatemala, with over a million visitors a year.

If you'd like to stay close to all this action, there are a few hotels along this stretch of the highway, but none so nice as the IRTRA-run **Hostales** (⏱7722-9100; www.irtra.org.gt; Carretera CITO, Km 180; r with fan/air-con from Q400/440; ⓟ❄☰), right across the road. It's set on lush, tropical grounds that feature swimming pools, spa bath, various sports fields and probably the most impressive mini-golf course in the country. There are seven main buildings within the complex, each decorated in a different style – Colonial, Mediterranean, Asian, African, Maya – but rooms are spacious, modern and comfortable throughout. The best time to come is Sunday to Wednesday – otherwise the place packs out and prices rise considerably. There are a few restaurants (mains from Q50) on the premises, serving Guatemalan staples at reasonable prices.

Any bus heading from Retalhuleu toward Quetzaltenango will drop you at Xocomil, Xetulul or the Hostales.

Vuelo Extremo

Continuing towards Quetzaltenango from Retalhuleu, right by the roadside, you'll find this **zip line park** (⏱5908-8193; www.vuelo extremo.com; Carretera a Retalhuleu, Km 198; 3/4/11 cables Q75/100/150; ⊙6am-6pm). If you're into the whole zip line/canopy tour thing, this is one of the better-value ones in the country. It starts and ends with a terrifying 300m-long, 29m-high zip across the valley over the highway and then follows a circuit zigzagging down the hill on the other side. For the fainter of heart there are some nice walking trails (Q25), crossing swinging bridges and passing by small waterfalls.

Parque Arqueológico Takalik Abaj

About 25km northwest of Retalhuleu is the **Parque Arqueológico Takalik Abaj** (admission Q50; ☉ 7am-5pm), a fascinating archaeological site set on land now occupied by coffee, rubber and sugarcane plantations. Takalik Abaj was an important trading center in the late Preclassic era, before AD 250, and forms a historical link between Mesoamerica's first civilization, the Olmecs, and the Maya. The Olmecs flourished from about 1200 to 600 BC on Mexico's southern Gulf coast, but their influence extended far and wide, and numerous Olmec-style sculptures have been found at Takalik Abaj.

The entire 6.5-sq-km site spreads over nine natural terraces, which were adapted by its ancient inhabitants. Archaeological work is continuing outside the kernel of the site, which is the Grupo Central on terrace No 2, where the most important ceremonial and civic buildings were located. Classic-era baths and multicolored floors were discovered here in late 2005. The largest and tallest building is Estructura 5, a pyramid 16m high and 115m square on terrace No 3, above No 2. This may have formed one side of a ball court. Estructura 7, east of Estructura 5, is thought to have been an observatory. What's most impressive as you move around the park-like grounds, with temple mounds, ball courts and flights of steps paved with rounded river stones, is the quantity of stone sculpture dotted about, including numerous representations of animals and aquatic creatures (some in a curious pot-bellied style known as *barrigón*), miniature versions of the characteristic Olmec colossal heads, and early Maya-style monuments depicting finely adorned personages carrying out religious ceremonies.

Takalik Abaj, which had strong connections with the city of Kaminaljuyú (in present-day Guatemala City), was sacked about AD 300 and its great monuments, especially those in Maya style, were decapitated. Some monuments were rebuilt after AD 600 and the site retained a ceremonial and religious importance for the Maya, which it maintains to this day. Maya from the Guatemalan highlands regularly come here to perform ceremonies.

To reach Takalik Abaj by public transportation, catch a shared taxi from Retalhuleu to El Asintal (Q7, 30 minutes), which is 12km northwest of Reu and 5km north of the Carretera al Pacífico. Less frequent buses leave from a bus station on 5a Av A, 800m southwest of Reu plaza, about every half-hour from 6am to 6pm. Pickups at El Asintal provide transportation on to Takalik Abaj (Q5), 4km further by paved road. You'll be shown round by a volunteer guide, whom you will probably want to tip (Q20 per person is a good baseline). You can also visit Takalik Abaj on tours from Quetzaltenango (p135) and Retalhuleu (p162).

🛏 Sleeping

Takalik Maya Lodge HOTEL $$
(☑ 2334-7693; www.takalik.com; bungalow/farmhouse Q490/330) Set on the grounds of a working farm 2km past the entrance to Takalik Abaj (and on top of a large, unexcavated section of it) this is by far the most comfortable place to stay in the area. Accommodation options include the old farmhouse or newly constructed 'Maya-style' houses set in the middle of the forest.

Check the website for deals including accommodation, meals and tours of the coffee, macadamia and rubber plantation as well as guided horseback tours of the waterfalls on the property and the archaeological site. Any pickup from El Asintal passing Takalik Abaj will drop you at the entrance.

Nueva Alianza

This fair-trade **coffee farm** (☑ 5348-5290, in Quetzaltenango 4950-4283; www.comunidadnuevaalianza.org; dm Q65, d Q230, s/d without bathroom Q85/170; ⊚) was taken over by its ex-employees when the owner went bankrupt and ran off with their back wages. It now offers a range of tours (Q25 per person) around the farm and local countryside as well as workshops detailing the community's fascinating history and present. Set on a hillside overlooking the coast, the farm has gorgeous views, and the hike to the nearby waterfall comes with some very welcome swimming at the end of it. Various short- and long-term volunteer positions are available. The easiest way to get here is by contacting the office in Quetzaltenango and coming when a Spanish school comes on tour (most weekends). Otherwise it's easy enough from Retalhuleu. Buses leave at midday (but get there early) from the main terminal – look for the one that says 'Hochen' – and it's about a one-hour, Q10 ride out to the farm.

Champerico

POP 8700

Built as a shipping point for coffee during the boom of the late 19th century, Champerico, 38km southwest of Retalhuleu, is a tawdry, sweltering, dilapidated place that sees few tourists. Nevertheless, it's one of the easiest ocean beaches to reach on a day trip from Quetzaltenango, and heat-starved students still try their luck here. Beware of strong waves and an undertow if you go in the ocean, and stay in the main, central part of the beach: if you stray too far in either direction you put yourself at risk from impoverished, potentially desperate shack dwellers who live towards the ends of the beach. Tourists have been victims of violent armed robberies here.

Most beachgoers come only to spend the day, but there are several cheap hotels. With large clean rooms just across the road from the beach, the **Hotel Maza** (☑ 7773-7180; s/d Q150/250; ☀) is a good bet. All the seaside eateries offer a similar deal – fresh seafood for around Q40 to Q80 per plate. *Camarones al ajillo* (garlic shrimp) and *caldo de mariscos* (seafood stew) are the standout items. As always, the busiest place will have the freshest food. All other things being equal, **7 Mares** (mains from Q30; ☺ 8am-7pm) rates a mention for its shaded swimming pool, leafy dining area and upstairs deck which catches good breezes and views. The last buses back to Quetzaltenango leave at about 6pm, a bit later for Retalhuleu.

Mazatenango

POP 55,500 / ELEV 370M

Mazatenango, 23km east of Retalhuleu, is the capital of the Suchitepéquez department. It's a center for the farmers, traders and shippers of the Pacific Slope's agricultural produce. There are a few serviceable hotels if you need to stop in an emergency. Otherwise just keep on keeping on.

Tulate

Another beach town that's yet to make it onto the radar of most travelers is Tulate. The great thing about this beach is that, unlike others along the coast, the water gets deep very gradually, making it a great place to swim and just hang around and have some fun. The waves rarely get big enough to surf, but bodysurfers should be able to get a ride any time of the year. To get to the beach you have to catch a boat (Q5) across the estuary. Once on the other side, the water's 500m in front of you, straight down the only paved street. If you're heading towards the Paraíso or Iguana, avoid the long hot walk along the beachfront by taking the riverfront path to the left as soon as you get off the *lancha*. If you don't feel like walking, the *lancha* to the Paraíso/Iguana costs Q50/100.

There are three hotels in Tulate worth mentioning. All have restaurants, but the best, most atmospheric dining is at the little shacks right on the beachfront where good fresh seafood meals start at around Q35.

Buses run direct to Tulate from Mazatenango (Q15, two hours). Coming from the west, it's tempting to get off at Cuyotenango and wait for a bus there to avoid backtracking. The only problem with this is that buses tend to leave Mazatenango when full, so you might miss out on a seat.

🛌 Sleeping

Playa Paraíso   BUNGALOW $$
(☑ 7872-0626; bungalows Q350; ☀) This is a comfortable if slightly worn option about 1km down the beach to the left from the main street. The bungalows here have two double beds, a sitting room and laid-back little balconies out front. There are hammocks strung around the property and a good, if somewhat pricey, restaurant serves meals any time.

Things can get a little hectic on weekends, but midweek you may just have the place to yourself.

Hotel La Iguana   BUNGALOW $$
(☑ 2478-3135; iguanabungalows@yahoo.com; r midweek/weekend Q350/400; ☀) This has simple, pleasing rooms with a double bed and a bunk in each. It's a fair walk from the center, but simple meals (Q35) are available in the restaurant and bungalows come equipped with kitchen.

Villa Victoria   HOTEL $$
(☑ 4185-3605; www.turicentrosvillavictoria.com; r with fan/air-con Q250/300; ☀☀) On the main street, halfway between the boat landing and the beach, this is a reasonable deal. Rooms are fresh and simple, with two double beds. It also doubles as a Turicentro, meaning that local kids come and use the pool (which has an awesome waterslide, by the way) and they crank up the music ridiculously early on weekends.

Chiquistepeque

On a virtually untouched stretch of beach, this little fishing village is home to **Hamaca y Pescado Project** (☑7858-2700; www.hama caypescadous.blogspot.com; s/d Q100/150), a grassroots education and environmental awareness project. You can volunteer in the literacy program that they run, or just hang out on the beach. Accommodation is in comfortable rustic beachside *cabañas* (cabins), and home-cooked meals go for Q35 each.

If you've got a group together, you can rent out a house that sleeps five comfortably. If you're coming from Tulate, get off at La Máquina and change buses there. Otherwise, it's best to get to Mazatenango for one of the two daily buses (10:30am and 1:30pm) to Chiquistepeque (three hours, Q15).

Santa Lucía Cotzumalguapa

POP 111,700 / ELEV 356M

Another 71km eastward from Mazatenango is Santa Lucía Cotzumalguapa, an important stop for anyone interested in archaeology. In the fields and *fincas* (plantations) near the town stand great stone heads carved with grotesque faces and fine relief scenes, the product of the enigmatic Pipil culture that flourished here from about AD 500 to 700. In your explorations you may get to see a Guatemalan sugarcane *finca* in full operation.

The town, though benign enough, is unexciting. The local people around here are descended from the Pipil, an ancient culture that had linguistic and cultural links with the Nahuatl-speaking peoples of central Mexico. In early Classic times, the Pipil who lived here grew cacao, the money of the age. They were obsessed with the ball game and with the rites and mysteries of death. Pipil art, unlike the flowery, almost romantic style of the Maya, is cold, grotesque and severe, but still very finely done. When these 'Mexicans' settled in this pocket of Guatemala, and where they came from, is not known, though connections with Mexico's Gulf coast area, whose culture was also obsessed with the ball game, have been suggested.

◉ Sights

There are three main sites to visit, all outside town: El Baúl hilltop site, about 4.5km north; the museum at Finca El Baúl, 2.75km further north; and the Museo Cultura Cot zumalguapa, off the highway 2km northeast of town.

Taxi drivers in Santa Lucía's main square will take you around all three sites for about Q240 without too much haggling. In this hot and muggy climate, riding at least part of the way is the least you can do to help yourself.

El Baúl Hilltop Site   ARCHAEOLOGICAL SITE

This archaeological site has the additional fascination of being an active place of pagan worship for local people. Maya people regularly, and especially on weekends, make offerings, light fires and candles, and sacrifice chickens here. They will not mind if you visit as well, and may be happy to pose with the idols for photographs in exchange for a small contribution.

Of the two stones here, the great, grotesque, half-buried head is the most striking, with its elaborate headdress, beaklike nose and 'blind' eyes with big bags underneath. The head is stained with wax from candles, splashes of liquor and other drinks, and with the smoke and ashes of incense fires, all part of worship. People have been coming here to pay homage for more than 1400 years.

The other stone is a relief carving of a figure with an elaborate headdress, possibly a fire god, surrounded by circular motifs that may be date glyphs.

To get there you leave town northward on the road passing El Calvario church. From the intersection just past the church, go 2.7km to a fork in the road just beyond a bridge; the fork is marked by the entrance to the Ciudad España housing development (signposted from the center). Buses heading out to Finca El Baúl, the plantation headquarters, pass this sign. Take the right-hand fork, passing a settlement called Colonia Maya on your right. After you have gone 1.5km from the Los Tarros sign, a dirt track crosses the road: turn right here, between two concrete posts. Ahead now is a low mound topped by three large trees: this is the hilltop site. After about 250m, fork right between two more identical concrete posts, and follow this track round in front of the mound to its end after some 150m, and take the path up on to the mound, which is actually a great ruined temple platform that has not been restored.

Museo El Baúl   MUSEUM

(☺8am-4pm Mon-Fri, 8am-noon Sat) FREE About 2.75km on foot, or 5km by vehicle from the

THE PACIFIC SLOPE CHIQUISTEPEQUE

Santa Lucía Cotzumalguapa

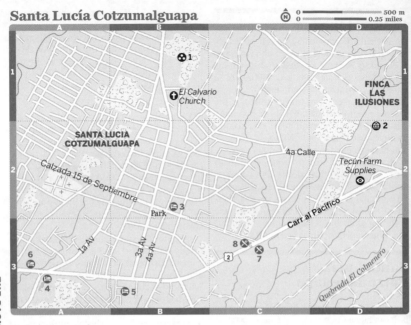

Santa Lucía Cotzumalguapa

◎ Sights
1 Bilbao Stones B1
2 Museo Cultura Cotzumalguapa D2

◎ Sleeping
3 Hospedaje Reforma............................... B2
4 Hotel El Camino A3
5 Hotel Internacional B3
6 Hotel Santiaguito A3

◎ Eating
7 Beer House C3
8 Robert's... C3

hilltop site is this museum comprising a very fine open-air collection of Pipil stone sculpture collected from around Finca El Baúl's sugarcane fields. A large stone jaguar faces you at the entrance.

Other figures include four humans or monkeys with arms folded across their chests, a grinning, blank-eyed head reminiscent of the one at the hilltop site, carvings of skulls, and at the back a stela showing a personage wearing an animal headdress, standing over a similarly attired figure on the ground: seemingly winner and loser of a ball game.

To get there, if driving, leave town northward on the road passing El Calvario church. From the intersection just past the church, go 2.7km to a fork in the road just beyond a bridge; take the left fork and follow the paved road 3km to the headquarters of the Finca El Baúl sugarcane plantation. Buses trundle along this road every few hours. (If you're on foot, you can walk from the hilltop site back to the crossroads with the paved road. Cross the road and continue along the dirt track. This will eventually bring you to the asphalt road that leads to the *finca* headquarters. When you reach the road, turn right.)

Approaching the *finca* headquarters (6km from Santa Lucía's main square), you cross a bridge at a curve. Continue uphill and you will see the entrance on the left, marked by a guard post and a sign 'Ingenio El Baúl Bienvenidos'. Tell the guards that you would like to visit the museo, and you should be admitted. Pass the sugar refinery buildings to arrive at the museum on the right.

Museo Cultura Cotzumalguapa MUSEUM

(admission Q25; ◎7am-1pm & 2-4pm Mon-Fri, 7am-1pm Sat) At the headquarters of another sugarcane plantation, Finca Las Ilusiones, you'll find this museum. The collection of sculptures found around Las Ilusiones' lands has some explanatory material and you'll probably be shown around by the caretaker.

It includes a reconstruction of a sacrificial altar with the original stones, and photos of some fine stelae that were removed to the Dahlem Museum in Berlin in 1880. The most impressive exhibit, Monumento 21, is actually a fiberglass copy of a stone that still stands in the fields of Finca Bilbao (part of Las Ilusiones' plantations), depicting what may be a shaman holding a sort of puppet on the left, a ball-game player in the middle with a knife in one hand, and a king or priest on the right holding what may be a heart. Another copy of this stone, along with one of Monumento 19, lies on the ground across the street from the museum. Along the road just before the bridge to the *finca* house are copies of some of the sculptures from the El Baúl museum.

About 1.5km east of the town center on Carretera al Pacífico (Hwy 2), shortly before the Tecún farm supplies depot, take a side track 400m to the left (north) to find the museum.

Bilbao Stones   ARCHAEOLOGICAL SITE
Monumento 21, whose copy is in the Museo Cultura Cotzumalguapa (p166), still stands with three other fine sculpted stones dotted about the Finca Bilbao cane fields to the northeast of El Calvario church, on the north edge of Santa Lucía town.

In the past, tourists have regularly visited these stones, often guided through the tall cane to Las Piedras (the Bilbao Stones) by local boys, but this is an isolated area and assaults on tourists are not unknown – ask around to find out what the current safety situation is.

🛌 Sleeping

The best hotels around are out on the entrance to town. You're not missing much by being out here.

Hotel Internacional   HOTEL $
(✆7882-5504; Callejón los Mormones; s/d Q110/160; P✻) Down a short lane (signposted) off Carretera al Pacífico is the best budget hotel in town. It has clean, good-sized rooms with a fan, cold showers and a TV. Air-con is Q70 extra.

Hospedaje Reforma   HOTEL $
(✆7882-1731; 4a Av 4-71; s/d Q70/120) This hotel has exactly three things going for it: it's

cheap, it's central and the patio is decorated with stuffed boars' heads. And if you like sleeping in dark and airless little concrete cells, make that four.

Hotel Santiaguito   HOTEL $$
(✆7882-5435; hsantiaguito@yahoo.com.mx; Carretera al Pacífico, Km 90.4; s/d Q330/440; P✻☀) On the highway on the west edge of town, the Santiaguito is fairly lavish for Guatemala's Pacific Slope, with spacious tree-shaded grounds and a nice swimming pool (open to nonguests for Q20). The large rooms have huge, firm beds and are set around a jungly patio/parking area.

The spacious restaurant is cooled by ceiling fans and serves up good cheeseburgers and slightly overpriced meals (Q30 to Q80).

Hotel El Camino   HOTEL $$
(✆7882-5316; Carretera al Pacífico, Km 90.5; s/d Q160/270; P✻🛜) About 200m east along the highway from the Santiaguito, Hotel El Camino's rooms are almost ridiculously large, with a few sticks of furniture like clothes racks and writing tables. You could organize a game of five a side with the rest of the floor space, but don't tell management it was our idea.

🍴 Eating

The Hotel Internacional (p167) (mains Q20 to Q40) and El Camino (p167) (mains Q40 to Q80) both have restaurants attached. Probably the nicest place to eat is **Robert's** (Carretera al Pacifico, Km 89; mains Q50-150; ⊘11:30am-10pm), a steak house with leafy outdoor seating. Across the highway is **Beer House** (Carretera al Pacifico, Km 89; mains Q40-80; ⊘1-11pm) which does good burgers and OK meals.

ℹ️ Getting There & Away

As Hwy 2 now bypasses Santa Lucía, a lot of buses along it do not come into town. Coming to Santa Lucía from the east, you will almost certainly need to change buses at Escuintla (Q11, 30 minutes). From the west you will probably have to change at Mazatenango (Q15, 1¼ hours). At Cocales, 23km west of Santa Lucía, a road down from Lago de Atitlán meets Hwy 2, providing a route to or from the highlands. Eight buses daily run from Cocales to Panajachel (Q28, 2½ hours, 70km, between about 6am and 2pm). Ask about the current situation, as there have been reports of robberies along this stretch of road in the past.

AGRITURISMO

With so many beautiful *fincas* (farms/plantations) in gorgeous rural settings, it was only a matter of time before agritourism started to take hold in Guatemala. This is seriously low-impact tourism – often you can stay in the original farmhouse and tours basically consist of walking around the property. Most *fincas* offering tours and accommodation still make most of their money from agriculture – they're not just sitting around waiting for you to show up. If you're planning on staying on a *finca*, get in touch a few days in advance to let them know you're coming.

Aldea Loma Linda (☑ 4996-2110; www.asodill.org; r without bathroom per person volunteers/visitors Q25/50) A beautiful little village set right on the southern foothills of the Santa María volcano. There are some great walks (Q50 to Q75 for around three hours) in the surrounding countryside, where an estimated 280 bird species (including the quetzal) make this place their home throughout the year.

Accommodations are basic but comfortable and meals (Q30/12 volunteers/visitors) are eaten with local families. Volunteers can work in the community's organic vegetable garden, the worm farm or in forest conservation. Buses for Loma Linda (Q8, two hours) leave from Retalhuleu at midday, 12:30pm, 1:30pm and 3pm.

Finca Santa Elena (☑ 7772-5294; www.fincasantaelena.com; Carretera a Quetzaltenango, Km 187; r without bathroom Q125-140 per person; 🐾) Set just off the main highway, this is one of the most easily accessible *fincas* in the region. Tours (Q60 to Q85 per person) are wonderfully informative – one takes you through the coffee production process, while the other plunges into the local forest, passing rivers, waterfalls, bamboo forest and a spot that thousands of butterflies naturally inhabit.

Accommodation is in the original farmhouse, a lovely wooden building, and most rooms have great views. Home-cooked meals cost around Q60. To get here, take any bus between Quetzaltenango and Retalhuleu and ask to be let off at the Entrada a Palmarcito (Km 187). The *finca* entrance is up the concrete road, 400m on the right.

Reserva El Patrocinio (☑ 5903-3603; www.reservapatrocinio.com; s/d Q437/636, campsites per person Q125) This working coffee, macadamia and rambutan (among other crops) farm has been converted into a private nature reserve. Sitting on 140 hectares, there are walks galore, canopy zip lines (Q120), informative tours through the plantations (Q25 to Q50, more for bird-watching) and a decent restaurant (meals Q50 to Q100) with panoramic views.

Accommodation is in a stylish, modern house set on the hillside overlooking the valley. If you're staying here, all meals and the above activities are included in the price. The reserve is 14km off the main road about 18km north of Retalhuleu – ask for transport options when making reservations.

La Democracia

POP 17,500 / ELEV 165M

La Democracia, a nondescript Pacific Slope town 10km south of Siquinalá, is hot day and night, rainy season and dry season. During the late Preclassic period (300 BC to AD 250), this area was home to a culture showing influence from southern Mexico. As you come into town from the highway, follow signs to the *museo,* which is on the plaza. You'll find a 5B ATM there, too.

◉ Sights

At the archaeological site of Monte Alto, on the outskirts of La Democracia, huge basalt heads and pot-bellied sculptures have been discovered. These heads resemble crude versions of the colossal heads that were carved by the Olmecs on Mexico's southern Gulf coast some centuries previously.

Today, these great Olmecoid heads are arranged around La Democracia's newly renovated main plaza, set in their own little roofed stands and illuminated at night.

Museo Regional de Arqueología   MUSEUM
(☑ 7880-3650; admission Q30; ◷ 8am-4pm Tue-Sat) Facing the plaza, along with the church and the modest Palacio Municipal, is this small, modern museum which houses some fascinating archaeological finds. The star of the show is an exquisite jade mask. Smaller

figures, yokes used in the ball game, relief carvings and other objects make up the rest of this small but important collection.

🛏 Sleeping & Eating

The flour tortillas stuffed with meat from the little roadside stands around the plaza are delicious, and a bargain at Q20.

Guest House Paxil de Cayala GUESTHOUSE $
(📞7880-3129; s/d without bathroom Q50/100) Half a block from the plaza, La Democracia's only place to stay is OK for the night, with big, mosquito-proofed rooms.

Burger Chops FAST FOOD $
(mains Q25-45; ⊙8am-9pm) Located just off the square, this is as close as the town gets to a restaurant.

🚍 Getting There & Away

The Chatía Gomerana company runs buses every half-hour from 6am to 4:30pm, from the Centra Sur terminal in Guatemala City to La Democracia (Q20, two hours) via Escuintla. From Santa Lucía Cotzumalguapa, catch a bus 8km east to Siquinalá (8km) and change there.

Sipacate

An hour and a half down the road from Santa Lucía is Guatemala's surf capital. Waves here average 6ft, the best time being between December and April. The town is separated from the beach by the Canal de Chiquimulilla. Oddly unexploited, the beach here has only a couple of hotels.

Budget **El Paredon** (📞4994-1842; www.paredonsurf.com; campsite/dm Q30/80, s/d from 240/320) is a rustic little surf camp to the east of the village. It's run by a couple of Guatemalan surfers. Board and kayak hire, surf lessons and good, simple meals (Q50 to Q80) are available. Book in advance. To get here you can catch the daily bus from Puerto San José (departs 1pm Monday to Friday, Q20) or a *tuk-tuk*/pickup to the El Escondite pier from Sipacate, then a boat (Q20 one way) to El Paredon.

Straight across the canal from Sipacate, **Rancho Carillo** (📞5517-1069; www.marmaya.com; r Q500, 6-person bungalow Q1000; ❋🛜🏊) is a short boat ride (Q10 return) from town. The only trouble you'll have sleeping is from the noise of crashing waves. Call ahead and you'll probably be able to get a better price – there's a 25% discount on weekdays. Surfboards are available for rent here.

Buses from Guatemala City's Centra Sur terminal (Q32, 3½ hours) pass through La Democracia en route to Sipacate every two hours.

Escuintla

POP 166,800

Surrounded by rich green foliage, Escuintla should be a tropical idyll where people swing languidly in hammocks and concoct pungent meals of readily available exotic fruits and vegetables. In fact, it's a hot, shabby commercial and industrial city that's integral to the Pacific Slope's economy but not at all important to travelers, except for making bus connections. Banks are located around the plaza. There's an ATM in the **Farmacia Herdez** (cnr 13a Calle & 4a Av), one block uphill from the bus terminal.

Escuintla's hotel and restaurant scene is limited. For budget digs, try the **Hotel Costa Sur** (📞7888-1819; 12a Calle 4-13; s/d with fan Q80/110, with air-con Q110/130; ❋), which has decent, cool rooms with TV and fan. More comfortable is the **Hotel Sarita** (📞7888-1959; Av Centro América 15-32; s/d Q380/480; ❋🛜🖳), behind the gloriously air-conditioned restaurant (mains Q50 to Q100) of the same name. It's a short walk from the bus terminal. Even closer is **Jacobo's** (4a Av 14-62; mains Q20-40; ⊙11am-10pm), which offers reasonable Chinese food in clean and tranquil surrounds.

All buses from the terminal pass along 1a Av, but if you really want to get a seat, head to the main bus station in the southern part of town, just off 4a Av. The station entrance is marked by a Scott 77 fuel station. Buses depart for Antigua (Q7, one hour, every half-hour from 5:30am to 4:30pm); Guatemala City (Q20, 1½ hours, every 20 minutes from 5am to 6pm), from the street outside the station; Puerto San José (Q5 to Q10, 45 minutes, every 20 minutes from 5am to 6pm), with some continuing to Iztapa; and Monterrico (Q25, one hour, 12:50pm and 4:50pm). Or catch a bus to Puerto San José or Iztapa and make a connection there.

Buses coming along the Carretera al Pacífico may drop you in the north of town, necessitating a sweaty walk through the hectic town center if you want to get to the main station.

Autosafari Chapín

About 25km southeast of Escuintla, **Autosafari Chapín** (☎ 2222-5858; www.autosafari chapin.com; Carretera a Taxisco, Km 87.5; adult/child Q60/50; ☺ 9:30am-5pm Tue-Sun) is a drive-through safari park and animal conservation project earning high marks for its sensitivity and success in breeding animals in captivity. Species native to Guatemala here include white-tailed deer, tapir and macaws. Around the grounds also roam non-native species such as lions, rhinos and leopards. There is a restaurant and pool, and it makes a good day if you're traveling with kids. It's more fun if you have your own vehicle, but if not, a 20-minute cruise through the park in a minibus is included in the admission price. Various companies run buses here (Q15, 1½ hours) from the Centra Sur terminal in Guatemala City. They leave every 10 minutes, from 4:30am to 5:30pm.

Iztapa

POP 6100

About 12km east of Puerto San José is Iztapa, Guatemala's first Pacific port, used by none other than Pedro de Alvarado in the 16th century. When Puerto San José was built in 1853, Iztapa's reign as the port of the capital city came to an end, and it relaxed into a tropical torpor from which it has yet to emerge.

Iztapa has gained renown as one of the world's premier **deep-sea fishing** spots. World records have been set here, and enthusiasts can fish for marlin, sharks and yellowfin tuna, among others. November through June is typically the best time to angle for sailfish.

THE ONE THAT DIDN'T GET AWAY

Somewhere between five and 40 miles off the coast of Iztapa, chances are that right now a sportfisher is hauling in a billfish. This area is recognized as one of the world's top sportfishing locations – the coastline here forms an enormous, natural eddy and scientists who have studied the area have concluded this might be the largest breeding ground for Pacific sailfish in the world.

Catches of 15 to 20 billfish per day are average throughout the year. During high season (October to May) this number regularly goes over 40.

Guatemala preserves its billfish population by enforcing a catch-and-release code on all billfish caught. Other species, such as dorado and tuna, are open game, and if you snag one, its next stop could well be your frying pan.

If you'd like lessons, or you're looking for an all-inclusive accommodation-and-fishing package, check www.greatsailfishing.com.

Fish here run in seasons. There's fishing all year round, but these are the best months:

May to October For dorado

June to September For roosterfish

September to December For marlin

September to January For yellowfin tuna

October For sea bass

October to May For sailfish

As in any part of the world, overfishing is a concern in Guatemala. The prime culprits here, though, are the commercial fishers, who use drag netting. Another concern, particularly for inland species and shrimp, is the practice of chemical-intensive agriculture. Runoff leeches into the river system, decimating fish populations and damaging fragile mangrove ecosystems.

It's estimated that Guatemala's Pacific coast has lost more than 90% of its original mangrove forests. The mangroves serve as nurseries for fish and shellfish and the trees maintain water quality and prevent erosion. They also provide food and income for local populations, but all along the Pacific coast, commercial shrimp farming is moving in. Over the past decade, commercial shrimp farms have consumed about 5% of all the remaining mangroves in the world.

B&B Worldwide Fishing Adventures (☎ toll-free in USA 888-479-2277; www.wheretofish.com) and **Fishing International** (☎ toll-free in USA & Canada 800-950-4242; www.fishinginternational.com) run all-inclusive deep-sea fishing tours to Iztapa from the USA. It is also possible to contract local boat owners for fishing trips, though equipment and comfort may be non-existent and catch-and-release could prove a foreign concept. The boat owners hang out at the edge of the Río María Linda – bargain hard. Yellowfin tuna will likely be out of reach for the local boats, as these fish inhabit the waters some 17km from Iztapa.

There's not much to do in Iztapa. The best thing to do is get a boat across the river to the sandbar fronting the ocean, where the waves pound and a line of palm-thatched restaurants offers food and beer.

🛏 Sleeping

Sol y Playa Tropical   HOTEL $$
(☎ 7881-4365; a Calle 5-48; s/d Q210/260; ✺ ▨)
This place has tolerable rooms with fan and a bathroom on two floors around a swimming pool that monopolizes the central patio. Air-con costs an extra Q50.

❶ Getting There & Away

The bonus about Iztapa is that you can catch a bus from Guatemala City all the way here (Q25, 1½ hours). They leave about every half-hour, from 5am to 6pm, traveling via Escuintla and Puerto San José. The last bus heading back from Iztapa goes around 5pm.

Most people will be just passing through here en route to Monterrico. If you're driving, follow the signs on the road east until you get to the new bridge (Q15 one way) across to Pueblo Viejo.

Monterrico

The coastal area around Monterrico is a totally different Guatemala. Life here is steeped with a sultry, tropical flavor – it's a place where hanging out in a hammock is both a major endeavor and a goal. Among the main cash crop here is *pachete* (loofah), which get as big as a man's leg. In season, you see them everywhere growing on trellises and drying in the sun. The architecture, too, is different, with rustic wooden slat-and-thatched roofed houses instead of the dull cinderblock, corrugated-tin models common elsewhere. When the sky is clear, keep your eyes peeled for the awesome volcanoes that shimmer in the hinterland. This part of Guatemala is also treated to sensational lightning storms from around November to April.

Monterrico is a coastal village with a few small, inexpensive hotels right on the beach, a large wildlife reserve and two centers for the hatching and release of sea turtles and caimans. The beach here is dramatic, with powerful surf crashing onto black volcanic sand at odd angles. This wave-print signals that there are rip tides; deaths have occurred at this beach, so swim with care. Strong swimmers, however, can probably handle and enjoy the waves. Behind the town is a large network of mangrove swamps and canals, part of the 190km Canal de Chiquimulilla.

Monterrico is probably the best spot for a weekend break at the beach if you're staying in Antigua or Guatemala City. It's fast becoming popular with foreigners. On weekdays it's relatively quiet, but on weekends and holidays it teems with Guatemalan families, and everything seems a bit harried.

◉ Sights & Activities

Biotopo Monterrico-Hawaii   WILDLIFE RESERVE
Sometimes called the Reserva Natural Monterrico, Biotopo Monterrico-Hawaii is administered by Cecon (Centro de Estudios Conservacionistas de la Universidad de San Carlos), and is Monterrico's biggest attraction. This 20km-long nature reserve of coast and coastal mangrove swamps is bursting with avian and aquatic life.

The reserve's most famous denizens are the endangered leatherback and ridley turtles, who lay their eggs on the beach in many places along the coast. The mangrove swamps are a network of 25 lagoons, all connected by mangrove canals.

Boat tours of the reserve, passing through the mangrove swamps and visiting several lagoons, take around 1½ to two hours and cost Q75 for one person, Q50 for each additional person. It's best to go just on sunrise, when you're likely to see the most wildlife. If you have binoculars, bring them along for bird-watching; January and February are the best months. Locals will approach you on the street (some with very impressive-looking ID cards), offering tours, but if you want to support the Tortugario (who incidentally has the most environmentally knowledgeable guides), arrange a tour directly through the Tortugario Monterrico (p172).

Some travelers have griped about the use of motorboats (as opposed to the paddled varieties), because the sound of the motor scares off the wildlife. If you're under no time pressure, ask about arranging a paddled tour of the canal.

Tortugario Monterrico   ECOTOUR

(admission Q50; ⊙7am-5pm) The Cecon-run Tortugario Monterrico is just a short walk east down the beach from the end of Calle Principal and then a block inland. Several endangered species of animals are raised here, including leatherback, olive ridley and green sea turtles, caimans and iguanas.

There's an interesting interpretative trail and a little museum with pickled displays in bottles. The staff offers lagoon trips, and night walks (Q50) from August to December to look for turtle eggs, and will accept volunteers. Around sunset nightly from September to January on the beach in front of the Tortugario, workers release baby turtles. For a Q10 donation you can 'buy' a turtle and release it. Despite what everybody else is doing, please refrain from using flash cameras and flashlights – the poor little things are probably already terrified and the flash may harm their eyes.

Parque Hawaii   WILDLIFE RESERVE

(☑4743-4655; www.arcasguatemala.com; ⊙8am-5pm) This nature reserve operated by Arcas (Asociación de Rescate y Conservación de Vida Silvestre; ☑7830-1374; www.arcasguatemala.com) comprises a sea-turtle hatchery with some caimans 8km east along the beach from Monterrico. It is separate from and rivals Cecon's work in the same field. Volunteers are welcome year round, but the sea turtle nesting season is from June to November, with August and September being the peak months.

Volunteers are charged Q580 a week for a room, with meals extra, and homestay options. Jobs for volunteers include hatchery checks and maintenance, mangrove reforestation, basic construction and data collection. See the website for the complete lowdown on volunteering here. Most of the egg collection happens at night. It's a way out of town, but there are usually other volunteers to keep you company and while you're here you can use the kayaks, go on village trips and go fishing in the sea and mangroves.

A bus (Q5, 30 minutes) leaves the Monterrico jetty every couple of hours during the week and every hour on weekends for the bumpy ride to the reserve. Pickups also operate on this route, charging Q30 per person.

Productos Mundiales   BOAT TOUR

(Map p50; ☑2366-1026; www.productos-mundiales. com; 11 Avenida 10-13, Zona 10, Guatemala City) This outfit offers marine wildlife-watching tours (six hours, from Q1560 per person), leaving from nearby Puerto Iztapa. Throughout the year you stand a pretty good chance of seeing pilot whales, bottlenose dolphins, spinner dolphins, olive ridley turtles, leatherback turtles, giant manta rays and whale sharks. From December to May, humpback and sperm whales can also be seen.

Reservations (five days in advance via bank account deposit) are essential – see the website for details.

🕮 Courses

Proyecto Lingüístico
Monterrico   LANGUAGE COURSE

(☑5475-1265; espanolmonterrico@yahoo.com; Calle Principal) About 250m from the beach, this place is quite professional. Classes are generally held outdoors in a shady garden area. You can study in the morning or afternoon, depending on your schedule. Twenty hours of study per week costs Q710, Q1100 with self-catering accommodation, or Q1200 with homestay.

Even if you're not studying here, the school is the best source of tourist information in town.

🛏 Sleeping

To save a difficult, hot walk along the beach, take the last road to the left or right before you hit the beach. All of these hotels either front or back onto it. Most hotels have restaurants serving whatever is fresh from the sea that day. Many places offer discounts for stays of three nights or more. Reservations on weekends are a good idea. Weekend prices are given here. Midweek, you'll have plenty more bargaining power.

🛏 Left of Calle Principale

Brisas del Mar   HOTEL $

(☑5517-1142; r per person with fan/air-con Q100/150; ⓟ ❄ ☀) Behind Johnny's, one block back from the beach, this popular newcomer offers good-sized rooms, a 2nd-floor dining hall with excellent sea views and a good-sized swimming pool.

Johnny's Place
HOTEL **$**

(☎5812-0409; www.johnnysplacehotel.com; dm/r Q45/160, s/d without bathroom Q70/140, r Q240-650, bungalows Q500-950; P☀) While Johnny's may not be everyone's cup of tea, it's easy enough to find – it's the first place you come to turning left on the beach, and one of the biggest operations here. It's got a decent atmosphere, though, and attracts a good mix of backpackers and family groups.

Every pair of bungalows shares a barbecue and small swimming pool. There's also a larger general swimming pool. The cheaper rooms are not glamorous but have fans and screened windows. Pay extra and things start to get very swish. The bar-restaurant overlooks the sea and is a popular hangout: the food is not gourmet but there are plenty of choices and imaginative *licuados* (fresh fruit drinks) and other long cool drinks.

Hotel Pez de Oro
BUNGALOW **$$**

(☎2368-3684; www.pezdeoro.com; s/d Q350/440; P☀) This is the funkiest looking place in town, with comfortable little huts and bungalows scattered around a shady property. The color scheme is a cheery blue and yellow, and the rooms have some tasteful decorations and big overhead fans. The excellent restaurant, with big sea views, serves up great Italian cuisine and seafood dishes.

Dos Mundos Pacific Resort
RESORT **$$$**

(☎7823-0820; www.dosmundospacific.com; bungalows from Q965; P☀☀☀) The biggest complex around is pushing resort status – manicured grounds, two swimming pools, and a gorgeous beachfront restaurant. The bungalows are spacious and simple but beautifully presented, with wide shady balconies out front.

Right of Calle Principale

Going in the opposite direction, heading right from Calle Principal, are more options.

Hostel El Gecko
HOSTEL **$**

(☎5251-3522; dm Q50; @) The first place you'll come to when you turn right from Calle Principal is this very basic hostel run by a couple of young Guatemalans. There are very few frills here, but it's a backpackers' favorite for the cheap beds and friendly atmosphere.

Hotel Atelie del Mar
HOTEL **$$**

(☎5752-5528; www.hotelateliedelmar.com; s/d with fan Q440/610; P☀☀☀) This is one of the most formal hotels in town, with lovely landscaped grounds and spacious, simple and beautiful rooms. It's got the best swimming pool around, along with the widest menu and an on-site art gallery. Prices include breakfast.

Café del Sol
HOTEL **$$**

(☎5810-0821; www.cafe-del-sol.com; s/d with fan from Q200/260, r with air-con from Q470; P☀☀) Set all under one big thatched roof, the 'economy' rooms here are a bit disappointing compared to the rest of the place. Across the road, the new annex offers 'standard' rooms that are a better deal – more spacious, with an on-site swimming pool.

The restaurant's menu has some original dishes and you can eat on the terrace or in the big *palapa* (thatched) dining area.

✗ Eating

There are many simple seafood restaurants on Calle Principal. For the best cheap eats, hit either of the two nameless *comedores* (basic, cheap eateries) on the last road to the right before the beach, where you can pick up an excellent plate of garlic shrimp, rice tortillas, fries and salad for Q40. All of the hotels have restaurants.

★Taberna El Pelicano
ITALIAN, SEAFOOD **$$**

(mains Q40-110; ☺12-2pm & 6-10pm Wed-Sun) By far the best place to eat in town, with the widest menu and most interesting food, like seafood risotto (Q80), beef *carpaccio* (Q75) and a range of jumbo shrimp dishes (Q140).

♟ Drinking

Las Mañanitas
BAR

(☺12pm-late) On the beachfront at the end of the main street, this little bar is what Monterrico really needed – plenty of hammock chairs looking out over the beach, a good range of drinks and low-key music playing in the background.

Playa Club
BAR

This venue, located at Johnny's Place, heats up on weekends, with plenty of reggaetón, house music and drinks specials keeping the crowd moving.

❶ Orientation & Information

From where you alight from the La Avellana boat, it's about 1km to the beach and the hotels. You pass through the village en route. From the *embarcadero* (wharf) walk straight ahead and then turn left. Pickups (Q5) meet scheduled boats or *lanchas*.

If you come by bus from Pueblo Viejo, from the stop walk about 300m toward the beach on Calle Principal.

Banrural, just off the main street on the road to Parque Hawaii, changes cash and may change traveler's checks. There's an ATM in the Supermercado Monterrico. The **post office** (Calle Principal) is on the main street.

❶ Getting There & Away

There are two ways to get to Monterrico. Coming from Guatemala City or Antigua, it's most logical to catch a bus which, with the new bridge at Pueblo Viejo, goes right through to Monterrico. The Pueblo Viejo–Monterrico stretch makes for a pretty journey, revealing local life at a sane pace.

The other option is to head to La Avellana, where *lanchas* and car ferries depart for Monterrico. The Cubanita company runs a handful of direct buses to and from Guatemala City (Q40, four hours, 124km). Alternatively, you reach La Avellana by changing buses at Taxisco on Hwy 2. Buses operate half-hourly from 5am to 4pm between Guatemala City and Taxisco (Q35, 3½ hours) and roughly hourly from 7am to 4:30pm between Taxisco and La Avellana (Q5, 40 minutes), although taxi drivers will tell you that you've missed the last bus, regardless of what time you arrive. A taxi between Taxisco and La Avellana costs around Q70.

From La Avellana catch a *lancha* or car ferry to Monterrico. The collective *lanchas* charge Q5 per passenger for the half-hour trip along the Canal de Chiquimulilla, a long mangrove canal. They start at 4:30am and run more or less every half-hour or hour until late afternoon. You can always pay more and charter your own boat. The car ferry costs Q85 per vehicle.

Shuttle buses also serve Monterrico. The most reliable leaves from outside the Proyecto Lingüístico Monterrico at 1pm and 4pm and charges Q70/150 to Antigua/Guatemala City. Book tickets and enquire for other destinations at the school (p172).

Around Monterrico

Isleta de Gaia

East down the coast from Monterrico, near Las Lisas, is the Guatemalan Pacific coast's best-kept secret – **Isleta de Gaia** (⌨ 7885-0044; www.isleta-de-gaia.com; 2-/4-person bungalow Q740/1360; @ 🛜 🔳) 🅿, a bungalow-hotel built on a long island of sand and named for the Greek earth goddess. Overlooking the Pacific on one side and mangroves on the other, this small, friendly, ecological, French-

owned resort is constructed from natural materials.

There are 12 bungalows, of one and two levels, with sea, lagoon or pool views. Each has good beds, fan, bathroom, balcony and hammock; decorations are Mexican and Costa Rican. The seafront restaurant (mains Q60 to Q120) offers Italian, Spanish and French cuisine, with fresh fish naturally the star. There are boogie boards and kayaks for rent and a boat for fishing trips. Reserve your stay in this little paradise by email four days in advance. The staff runs a shuttle service to and from Guatemala City and Antigua. From Monterrico there is no road east along the coast beyond Parque Hawaii, so you have to backtrack to Taxisco and take Carretera al Pacífico for about 35km to reach the turnoff for Las Lisas. From the turnoff it's 20km to Las Lisas, where you take a boat (Q100) to Isleta de Gaia.

Chiquimulilla & the El Salvador Border

Surfers found in this part of Guatemala will likely be heading to or from La Libertad in El Salvador. Most people shoot straight through Escuintla and Taxisco to Chiquimulilla and on to the Salvadoran border at Ciudad Pedro de Alvarado–La Hachadura, from where it is about 110km along the coast of El Salvador to La Libertad.

Buses leave Taxisco for the border every 15 minutes until 5pm. There are two serviceable *hospedajes* (guesthouses) in La Hachadura on the El Salvador side of the border, but the *hostales* (budget hotels) in Ciudad Pedro de Alvarado on the Guatemalan side are not recommended. Should you need to stop for the night before crossing the border, you could do worse than head to the friendly cowboy town of **Chiquimulilla** (population 15,100), some 12km east of Taxisco. There isn't much going on here, but it's a decent enough place to take care of errands and regroup. The **Hotel San Carlos** (⌨ 7885-0817; 2a Calle, Zona 2; s/d Q100/150; 🅿 🛜), a few blocks from the bus terminal, is a family-run setup offering reasonable rooms and an on-site restaurant. The new bus terminal is on the outskirts of town, but *tuk-tuks* will take you anywhere you want to go for Q4.

The other option for getting to El Salvador is to turn north from Chiquimulilla and take local buses through Cuilapa to the border at Valle Nuevo–Las Chinamas, traveling inland before veering south to La Libertad.

Cuilapa

POP 25,400

Surrounded by citrus and coffee plantations, the capital of Santa Rosa department isn't much of a tourist attraction in its own right, although the area's fame for woodcarvings, pottery and leather goods may turn up a couple of decent souvenirs.

People coming this way are usually headed for the border with El Salvador, but there are a couple of volcanoes just out of town that are easily climbed and afford some excellent views.

Dormant **Volcán Cruz Quemada** towers 1700m over the tiny village of Santa María Ixhuatán at its base. Coffee plantations reach about one third of the way up its slopes. The summit, littered with radio towers, offers excellent views of the land running down to the coast, the Cerro la Consulta mountain range and the nearby Tecuamburro volcanic complex. From Santa María it's an easy-to-moderate climb to the top that should take about three hours. The 12km hike is possible to do on your own, asking plenty of directions along the way. Alternatively, guides can be hired in Santa María – ask at the taxi stand on the main square. To get to Santa María, catch a minibus (Q5, 25 minutes) from Cuilapa.

The **Tecuamburro** volcanic complex comprises various peaks, including **Cerro de Miraflores** (1950m), **Cerro la Soledad** (1850m) and **Cerro Peña Blanca** (1850m). This last, which has several small vents releasing steam and sulfur, provides the most interesting climb, although its forested slopes mean no views until you're almost at the top. Buses and minibuses (Q15, 1½ hours) leave regularly for the village of Tecuamburro from Cuilapa. From there it's a two- to three-hour hike (14km) to the summit.

Cuilapa is connected by a good road with Guatemala City. Buses (Q25, 2½ hours) leave from the Centra Sur bus terminal in Guatemala City.

Lago de Amatitlán

Lago de Amatitlán is a placid lake backed by a looming volcano and situated a mere 25km south of Guatemala City, making it a good day trip. After suffering years of serious neglect, the lake is slowly being rejuvenated, thanks mainly to local community groups who hope to see it once again function as a tourist attraction. On weekends, people from Guatemala City come to row boats on the lake (its waters are too polluted for swimming) or to rent a hot tub for a dip. Many people from the capital own second homes here.

A **teleférico** (cable car; adult/child return Q15/5; ⊙9am-5pm Fri-Sun) heads out over the lakeshore then pretty much straight up the hillside. It's a half-hour ride with some stunning views of the surrounding countryside from the top.

Boat tours are about the only other thing to do here – rides cost Q70/10 in private/shared tours. If you're feeling energetic, rowboats rent from Q30 per hour.

A string of *comedores* along the lakefront offer fried fish, tacos and simple meals. For something a bit more refined, follow the signs up the hill to the right to **La Rocarena** (mains Q50-120; ⊙8am-9pm), which has lovely grounds, good views and a couple of warm-water swimming pools.

The lake is situated just off the main Escuintla–Guatemala City highway (Hwy 9). Coming from Guatemala City (one hour, Q5), just ask to be dropped at the *teleférico*. The waterfront is about half a kilometer from the signposted turnoff. Coming from Escuintla, or heading back to Guatemala City, buses stop on the main road, about 1km away. It's an easy 10- to 15-minute walk, and taxis are rare.

Central & Eastern Guatemala

Best Places to Eat

➡ Xkape Koba'n (p184)

➡ Antojitos Zacapanecos (p177)

➡ City Grill (p197)

➡ Hacienda San Lucas (p208)

Best Places to Stay

➡ Hotel Kangaroo (p211)

➡ Hotel Restaurant Ram Tzul (p180)

➡ Utopia (p188)

➡ Hotel Madrugada (p208)

Why Go?

Stretching from the steamy lowland forests of El Petén to the dry tropics of the Río Motagua valley, and from the edge of the Western Highlands to the Caribbean Sea, this is Guatemala's most diverse region.

The Carretera al Atlántico (Hwy 9) shoots eastward to the sea from Guatemala City, passing the turnoffs for the wonderfully preserved ruins of Copán in Honduras; Quiriguá, with its impressive stelae; and Río Dulce, a favored resting spot for Caribbean sailors and gateway to the wilds of the Refugio Bocas del Polochic (Bocas del Polochic Wildlife Reserve). While you're here don't miss the gorgeous boat ride down the Río Dulce to Lívingston, the enclave of the Garífuna people.

The north of the region is lush and mountainous coffee-growing country. The limestone crags around Cobán attract cavers the world over, and the beautiful pools and cascades of Semuc Champey rate high on Guatemala's list of natural wonders.

When to Go

Encompassing a huge area, measuring about one quarter of Guatemala's land mass, the climate is predictably diverse here – Cobán and the Alta Verapaz are best avoided in the cooler months from November to February, as many of the attractions involve swimming. Garífuna National Day in Lívingston at the end of November is worth putting on your calendar, as is Cobán's Rabin Ajau festival in July.

Bird-watchers hoping to see Guatemala's national bird, the quetzal, will have better luck during their laying period from March to June. Accommodation prices remain relatively stable throughout the year, with the usual exceptions of steep hikes during Christmas and Easter.

ALTA & BAJA VERAPAZ

Hwy 14 (also marked Hwy 17) leaves Hwy 9 at El Rancho, 84km from Guatemala City. It heads west through a dry, desertlike lowland area, then turns north and starts climbing up into the forested hills. After 47km, at the junction called La Cumbre Santa Elena, Hwy 17 to Salamá divides from Hwy 14 for Cobán. Descending the other side of the ridge, Hwy 17 winds down into the broad valley of the Río Salamá, and enters Salamá town, 17km from the highway.

Before the Spanish conquest, the mountainous departments of Baja Verapaz and Alta Verapaz were populated by the Rabinal Maya, noted for their warlike habits and merciless victories. They battled the powerful K'iche' Maya for a century but were never conquered.

When the conquistadors arrived, they too had trouble defeating the Rabinal Maya. It was Fray Bartolomé de Las Casas who convinced the Spanish authorities to try peace where war had failed. Armed with an edict that forbade Spanish soldiers from entering the region for five years, the friar and his brethren pursued their religious mission, and succeeded in pacifying and converting the Rabinal Maya. Their homeland thus was renamed Verapaz (True Peace) and is now divided into Baja Verapaz, with its capital at Salamá, and Alta Verapaz, which is centered on Cobán. The Rabinal Maya have remained among the most dedicated and true to ancient Maya customs, and there are many intriguing villages to visit in this part of Guatemala, including Rabinal itself.

Salamá & Around

A wonderful introduction to Baja Verapaz's not-too-hot, not-too-cold climate, the area around Salamá hosts a wealth of attractions, both post-Colonial and indigenous.

The town itself is known for its ornate church (complete with grisly depiction of Jesus), bustling Sunday market and the photogenic ex-sugar-mill-turned-museum and impressive stone aqueduct in the neighboring town of San Jerónimo.

Salamá has some fine accommodation options, including the **Posada de Don Maco** (☑7940-0083; 3a Calle 8-26; s/d Q110/140; ℗) and the **Hotel Real Legendario** (☑7940-0501; 8a Av 3-57; s/d Q140/150; ℗ ☎). There are restaurants and cafes around the plaza. The meat-stuffed flour tortillas at **Antojitos**

Zacapanecos (cnr 6a Calle & 8a Av; mains Q20; ⊙10am-9pm) are not to be missed. For caving, bird-watching, hiking, horseback riding and orchid trips, get in touch with **EcoVerapaz** (☑5722-9095; ecoverapaz@hotmail.com; 8a Av 7-12, Zona 1; 1-day tour per person Q350). Buses leave Salamá's downtown bus terminal frequently for Cobán (Q25, 1½ to two hours), Guatemala City (Q35 to Q50, three hours) and neighboring villages.

Salamá also marks the starting point for a back-roads route to Guatemala City, passing Rabinal, whose annual **fiesta of San Pedro** (January 19 to 25) is a beguiling mix of pre-Colombian and Catholic traditions, and Cubulco where the *palo volador* (flying pole) tradition is still observed. There are basic, adequate *pensiones* (family-run guesthouses) in both Rabinal and Cubulco.

From there it's 100km south to Guatemala City, passing the turn-off to **Mixco Viejo**, one of the least-visited and most spectacularly sited Maya sites in the country. The former Poqomam capital, it lies wedged between deep ravines with just one way in and one way out; the Poqomam further fortified the site by constructing impressive rock walls around the city. It took Pedro de Alvarado and his troops more than a month of concerted attacks to conquer it. When they finally succeeded, they furiously laid waste to this city, which scholars believe supported close to 10,000 people at its height. There are several temples and two ball courts here.

Salto de Chaliscó

What's claimed to be Central America's highest **waterfall** (admission Q15) lies 12km down a dirt road from a turnoff at Km 145 on Hwy 14 to Cobán. At 130m and surrounded by cloud forest, it's an impressive sight, especially if it's been raining and the fall is running at full force. Another waterfall, the **Lomo de Macho**, lies 8km away – an enjoyable walk, or you can hire a horse from the visitor center in town (about 5km from the falls). Previously, you could stay here as part of a **community tourism project** (☑5301-8928; per person Q75), in a rustic bunkhouse attached to the visitor center, but administrative problems saw the project suspended at the time of writing. It may be running again by the time you read this. Buses to Chaliscó leave every half hour from Salamá (Q15, 1½ hours), passing La Cumbre Santa Elena (Q10, 45 minutes) on Hwy 14.

MEXICO

Chajul

Río Salinas

Sayaxché (65km)

Cancuén

San Luís

Poptún (16km); Flores (128km);
Tikal (186km); Melchor de Menco
& Belize Border (218km)

Playa Grande

Barillas (75km)

Parque Nacional Laguna Lachuá

Tzetok

Rocjá Pomtilá

Parque Nacional Cuevas de Candelaria

Chisec

San Antonio Las Cuevas

Raxruhá

Fray Bartolomé de Las Casas

Las Conchas ❸

El Bistrot Frances

La Unión

Sepalau Cataltzul

Sebol

Chahal

Grutas de Lanquín ❶

El Pajal

Cahabón

Lanquín

Aldea Saquijá

San Pedro Carchá

Aldea Chajaneb

Semuc Champey ❶

Refugio Bocas del Polochic

To Huehuetenango (80km)

Cobán

Chicoj

San Juan Chamelco

San Cristóbal Verapaz

Tactic

Tucurú

Río Polochic

Panzós

Swamp

Purulhá

Biotopo del Quetzal (Biotopo Mario Dary Rivera)

Reserva de Biosfera Sierra de las Minas

Sierra de l

Salamá

Salto de Chaliscó

Cubulco

Rabinal

San Miguel Chicaj

San Jerónimo

Río Hondo

Valle Dora

Zacualpa

El Chol

La Cumbre Santa Elena

Teculután

Estanzuel

Joyabaj

Sierra de Chuacús

El Rancho

Zacapa

Mixco Viejo

El Progreso (Guastatoya)

Chiquimula

Vado Hondo

Montúfar

Sanarate

San Juan Sacatepéquez

GUATEMALA CITY

Jalapa

Ipala

Quetzaltepequ

Chimaltenango

Mataquescuintla

Volcán de Ipala (1650m)

Padre Miguel Junction

Volcán Acatenango (3976m)

Santiago Sacatepéquez

San José Pinula

Parque Ecoturístico Cascadas de Tatasirire

El Sauce

Antigua

Agua Blanca

Anguiatú

Volcán Fuego (3763m)

Volcán Agua (3766m)

Lago de Amatitlán

Volcán Pacaya (2552m)

Laguna de Ayarza

Volcán Suchitan

El Progreso

Central & Eastern Guatemala Highlights

❶ Splashing around the turquoise waters of **Semuc Champey** (p188) and getting deep in the caves at **Grutas de Lanquín** (p187)

❷ Admiring the impressive carvings at **Copán** (p199) and **Quiriguá** (p199) and relaxing in the Antigua-rivaling beauty of **Copán Ruinas** (p205)

❸ Going bush in the jungle hideaway of **Las Conchas** (p191), where waterfalls, jungle treks and village tours await

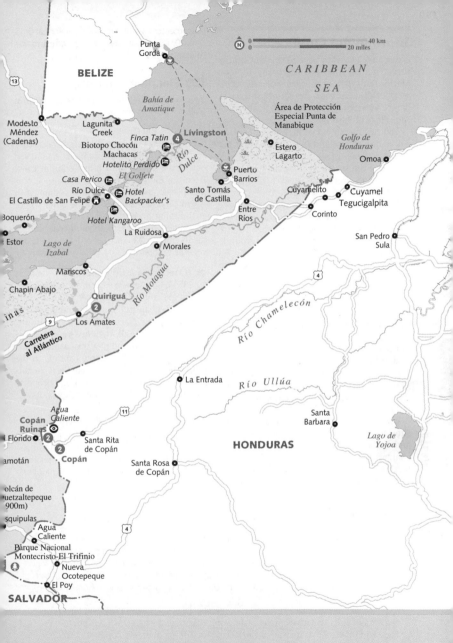

BELIZE

Punta
Gorda

*Bahía de
Amatique*

CARIBBEAN

SEA

Área de Protección
Especial Punta de
Manabique

*Golfo de
Honduras*

Modesto
Méndez
(Cadenas)

Lagunita
Creek

Finca Tatín
Biotopo Chocón
Machacas

Lívingston ④

*Río
Dulce*

Estero
Lagarto

Omoa

Hotelito Perdido

El Golfete

Casa Perico

Puerto
Barrios

Cuyamelito

Cuyamel
Tegucigalpita

Río Dulce

*Hotel
Backpacker's*

Santo Tomás
de Castilla

Corinto

El Castillo de San Felipe

Hotel Kangaroo

Entre
Ríos

Boquerón

La Ruidosa

San Pedro
Sula

Estor

*Lago de
Izabal*

Morales

Mariscos

Chapin Abajo

Río Motagua

Quiriguá ②

inas

Los Amates

Carretera
al Atlántico

La Entrada

Río Ullúa

Santa
Barbara

*Lago de
Yojoa*

Agua
Caliente

**Copán
Ruins** ②

Florido

HONDURAS

Santa Rita
de Copán

②
Copán

amotán

Santa Rosa
de Copán

olcán de
uetzaltepeque
900m)

squipulas

Agua
Caliente

Parque Nacional
Montecristo-El Trifinio

Nueva
Ocotepeque

El Poy

SALVADOR

0   40 km
0   20 miles

④ Getting down with the
Garífuna people in the unique
Caribbean town of **Lívingston**
(p218)

⑤ Taking in the natural
beauty of such little-visited
protected areas as **Parque
Nacional Laguna Lachuá**
(p186) and the **Refugio
Bocas del Polochic** (p215)

Biotopo del Quetzal

Along Hwy 14, 34km beyond the La Cumbre turnoff for Salamá, you reach the Biotopo Mario Dary Rivera nature reserve, commonly called **Biotopo del Quetzal** (Hwy 14, Km 161; admission Q40; ☺ 7am-4pm), just east of the village of Purulhá.

You need a fair bit of luck to see a quetzal, as they're rare and shy, though you have the best chance of seeing them from March to June. Even so, it's well worth stopping to explore and enjoy this lush high-altitude cloud-forest ecosystem that is the quetzal's natural habitat – and you may happen to see one. Early morning or early evening are the best times to watch out for them – they're actually more prevalent around the grounds of the nearby hotels.

Two excellent, well-maintained **nature trails** wind through the reserve: the 1800m Sendero los Helechos (Fern Trail) and the 3600m Sendero los Musgos (Moss Trail). As you wander through the dense growth, treading on the rich, spongy humus and leaf-mold, you'll see many varieties of epiphytes (air plants), which thrive in the reserve's humid atmosphere. Deep in the forest is **Xiu Gua Li Che** (Grandfather Tree), some 450 years old, which germinated around the time the Spanish fought the Rabinal in these mountains.

The reserve has a visitor center, a little shop for drinks and snacks, and a camping and barbecue area. The ruling on camping changes from time to time. Check by contacting **Cecon** (Centro de Estudios Conservacionistas de la Universidad de San Carlos; ☎ 2331-0904; biotoposcecon@gmail.com; Av La Reforma 0-63, Zona 10, Guatemala City), which administers this and other biotopes.

🛏 Sleeping & Eating

Two very good lodging places are within walking distance of the reserve.

Ranchitos del Quetzal   HOTEL **$**
(☎ 4494-3694;   ranchitosdelquetzal@yahoo.com; Hwy 14, Km 160.5; r per person Q100; **P**) Carved out of the jungle on a hillside 200m away from the Biotopo del Quetzal entrance, this place has good-sized simple rooms with warm (ie tepid) showers in the older wooden building and hot showers in the newer concrete one. Reasonably priced, simple meals (mains Q30) are served, and there are vegetarian options.

⭐**Hotel Restaurant Ram Tzul**   HOTEL **$$**
(☎ 2355-1904;   www.m-y-c.com.ar/ramtzul;   Hwy 14, Km 158; s/d Q250/350; **P** 🛜) Quite likely the most beautiful hotel in either of the Verapaces, this place features a restaurant/sitting area in a tall, thatched-roofed structure with fire pits and plenty of atmosphere. The rustic, upmarket theme extends to the rooms and bungalows, which are spacious and elegantly decorated. The hotel property includes waterfalls and swimming spots.

🛈 Getting There & Away

Any bus to or from Guatemala City will set you down at the park entrance. Heading in the other direction, it's best to flag down a bus or microbus to El Rancho and change there for your next destination.

COURTING THE QUETZAL

The resplendent quetzal, which gave its name to Guatemala's currency, was sacred to the Maya. Its feathers grace the plumed serpent Quetzalcoatl and killing one was a capital offense. In modern times it has enjoyed no such protection, and hunting (mostly for the male's long emerald-green tail feathers) and habitat loss have made the bird a rarity in Guatemala. You may well stand a much better chance of seeing one in Costa Rica or Panama.

However, the best place to look for a quetzal in Guatemala is in the cloud forests of the Alta Verapaz, especially in the vicinity of the Biotopo del Quetzal. Look out for avocado and fruit trees as they are the preferred food of the quetzal (along with insects, snails, frogs and lizards). But you'll have to look closely – the quetzal's green plumage is dull unless it's in direct sunlight, providing perfect camouflage, and it often remains motionless for hours.

The females lay two eggs per year, from March to June, and this is the best time to go looking, as the males' tail feathers grow up to 75cm long during this period. Keep an ear out for their distinctive call – sharp cackles and a low, burbling whistle: *keeeoo-keeeoo*.

Cobán

POP 68,900 / ELEV 1320M

Not so much an attraction in itself, but an excellent jumping-off point for the natural wonders of Alta Verapaz, Cobán is a prosperous city with an upbeat air. Return visitors will marvel at how much (and how tastefully) the town has developed since their last visit.

As you enter Cobán, a sign says 'Bienvenidos a Cobán, Ciudad Imperial,' referring to the city charter granted in 1538 by Emperor Carlos V.

The town was once the center of Tezulutlán (Tierra de Guerra, or 'Land of War'), a stronghold of the Rabinal Maya.

In the 19th century, when German immigrants moved in and founded vast coffee and cardamom *fincas* (plantations), Cobán took on the aspect of a German mountain town, as the *finca* owners built town residences. The era of German cultural and economic domination ended during WWII, when the USA prevailed upon the Guatemalan government to deport the powerful *finca* owners, many of whom had actively supported the Nazis.

Guatemala's most impressive festival of indigenous traditions, the national folklore festival of **Rabin Ajau** with its traditional dance of the Paabanc, takes place here in the latter part of July or in the first week of August. The **national orchid show** is hosted here every December.

◉ Sights

Orquigonia
GARDENS

(📞4740-2224; www.orquigonia.com; Hwy 14, Km 206; admission Q30; ⊗7am-4pm) Orchid lovers and even the orchid-curious should not miss the wonderfully informative guided tour of this orchid sanctuary just off the highway to Cobán. The 1½ to 2 hour tour takes you through the history of orchid collecting, starting with the Maya, as you wend your way along along a path in the forest.

To get here catch any bus from Cobán headed for Tontem and get off when you see the sign, about 200m up the dirt road off Hwy 14.

Parque Nacional Las Victorias
PARK

(3a Calle, Zona 1; admission Q10; ⊗8am-4:30pm, walking trails 9am-3pm) This forested 82-hectare national park, located right in town, has ponds, barbecue and picnic areas, children's play areas, a lookout point and kilometers of trails. The entrance is near the corner of 9a Av and 3a Calle. Most trails are very isolated – consider hiking in a group. You can camp here for Q40 per person.

Templo El Calvario
CHURCH

(3a Calle, Zona 1) You can get a fine view over the town from this church atop a long flight of stairs at the north end of 7a Av. Indigenous people leave offerings at outdoor shrines and crosses in front of the church. Don't linger here after 4pm, as muggings are not unknown in this area.

The **Ermita de Santo Domingo de Guzmán**, a chapel dedicated to Cobán's patron saint, is 150m west of the bottom of the stairs leading to El Calvario.

☞ Tours

Aventuras Turísticas
TOUR

(📞7951-2008; www.aventurasturisticas.com; 1a calle 4-25, Zona 1) Leads tours to Laguna Lachuá, the Grutas de Lanquín, Rey Marcos and Parque Nacional Cuevas de Candelaria, as well as to Semuc Champey, Tikal, Ceibal, and anywhere else you may want to go; it will customize itineraries. French, English and Spanish speaking guides are available.

Casa D'Acuña
TOUR

(📞7951-0484; www.casadeacuna.com; 4a Calle 3-11, Zona 2) Offering tours to Semuc Champey, the Grutas de Lanquín and other places further afield, the guides here have been repeatedly recommended.

Misterio Verde
TOUR

(📞7952-1047; 2a Calle 14-36, Zona 1; ⊗8:30am-5:30pm) Acts as a booking agent for various community tourism projects in the area, including the Chicacnab cloud forests (near Cobán) and the subtropical rainforests of Rocjá Pomtilá (near Laguna Lachuá) in which participants stay in villages with a Q'eqchi' Maya family. For Q320 to Q400 you get a guide, lodging for two nights, and four meals.

Your guide will take you on hikes to interesting spots. The men of the family are the guides, providing them an alternative, sustainable way to make a living. Reservations are required at least one day in advance. It also rents boots, sleeping bags and binoculars at reasonable prices, so you need not worry if you haven't come prepared for such a rugged experience. Participants should speak at least a little Spanish.

Cobán

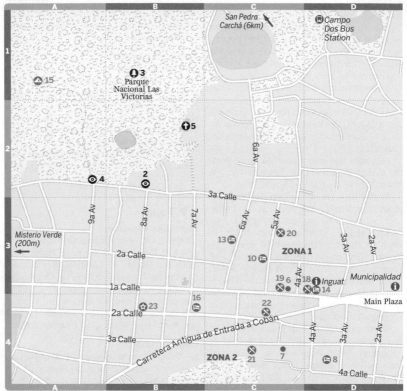

With a month's notice, this outfit also offers quetzal-viewing platforms.

Finca Santa Margarita
COFFEE TOUR

(☑ 7952-1586; 3a Calle 4-12, Zona 2; admission Q30; ⊙ guided tours 8:30am-11am & 2-4pm Mon-Fri, 8:30am-11am Sat) This working coffee farm in the middle of downtown Cobán offers stellar guided tours. From propagation and planting to roasting and exporting, the 45-minute tour will tell you all you ever wanted to know about these powerful beans. At tour's end, you're treated to a cup of coffee and you can purchase beans straight from the roaster.

The talented guide speaks English and Spanish.

Chicoj Cooperative
COFFEE TOUR

(☑ 5524-1831; www.coffeetourchicoj.com; tours Q50) Just 15 minutes out of town by bus, this is a community-tourism initiative offering 2km, 45-minute tours of its coffee farm. Halfway through there's the standard stop

for a canopy zip-line tour. The tour winds up with a cup of coffee made from beans grown and roasted at the farm.

Cobán tour operators offer this tour for Q160, but you can easily catch a bus from the stop near the police station on 1a Calle, which goes straight to the village of Chicoj.

🛏 Sleeping

When choosing a room in Cobán, you may want to ensure that the showers have hot water; it can be cold in these parts.

Hotel Central
HOTEL $

(☑ 7952-1442; 1a Calle 1-79, Zona 1; s/d Q120/170; 🅿 🗟) Reasonable-sized rooms and lovely outdoor sitting areas make this a decent choice. Try for a room at the back for better ventilation and views out over the town.

Casa Luna
HOSTEL $

(☑ 7951-3528; www.cobantravels.com/casaluna; 5a Av 2-28, Zona 1; dm/s/d without bathroom incl

N
0 ——————— 200 m
0 ——————— 0.1 miles

6a Calle
Transportes Martínez Cobán
1a Av
3a Av
5a Calle
Buses to Lanquín
Diagonal 1
4a Calle
ZONA 4
3a Calle
1a Av
3a Av
4a Av
Monja Blanca
5a Av
24
2a Calle
Buses to San Pedro Carchá
17
25 12
1a Calle
1a Av
2a Av
2a Calle
Central Market
3a Calle
ZONA 3
San Juan Chamelco (8km)
11
9

Cobán

◎ Sights
1	Cathedral	E4
2	Ermita de Santo Domingo de Guzmán	B2
3	Parque Nacional Las Victorias	B1
4	Parque Nacional Las Victorias Entrance	A2
5	Templo El Calvario	B2

◉ Activities, Courses & Tours
6	Aventuras Turísticas	C3
	Casa D'Acuña	(see 8)
7	Finca Santa Margarita	C4

⬤ Sleeping
8	Casa D'Acuña	D4
9	Casa Duranta	F4
10	Casa Luna	C3
11	Hostal de Doña Victoria	E4
12	Hotel Central	E3
13	Hotel La Paz	C3
14	Hotel La Posada	D3
15	Parque Nacional Las Victorias Camping	A1
16	Pensión Monja Blanca	B4
17	Posada de Don Antonio	F3

⊗ Eating
18	Café Fantasia	D3
19	Casa Chavez	C3
	El Bistro	(see 8)
20	El Peñascal	C3
21	Kardamomuss	C4
22	Xkape Koba'n	C4

✪ Entertainment
23	Bohemios	B4

⬤ Shopping
24	Mercado Terminal	E3
25	Supermarket	E3

breakfast Q50/75/150; @ 🛜) Modern rooms set around a pretty, grassy courtyard. Dorms have lockers and private rooms are well decorated. The shared bathrooms are spotless and breakfast is good.

Casa D'Acuña HOTEL $
(📞 7951-0482; www.casadeacuna.com; 4a Calle 3-11, Zona 2; dm/d without bathroom Q50/100; 🛜) This clean, very comfortable European-style hostel has four dormitories (each with four beds) and two private doubles, all with shared bathroom with good hot-water showers. Also here is a fabulous restaurant called El Bistro, a gift shop, laundry service and reasonably priced local tours.

Parque Nacional Las Victorias Camping CAMPGROUND $
(Parque Nacional Las Victorias; campsite per person Q40) Camping is available at Parque Nacional Las Victorias, right in town. Facilities include water and toilets but no showers.

Hotel La Paz HOTEL $
(📞 7952-1358; 6a Av 2-19, Zona 1; s/d Q45/75; 🅿) This cheerful, clean hotel, 1½ blocks north and two blocks west of the plaza, is an excellent deal. It has many flowers, and a good cafeteria next door.

Posada de Don Antonio HOTEL $$
(📞 7951-1792; www.hotelposadadedonantonio.com; 5a Av 1-51, Zona 4; s/d Q180/330; 🅿❄🛜) This atmospheric two-story place provides some of the best value in town. Rooms are spacious with two (or even three!) double beds, high ceilings and loving attention to detail. Breakfast (Q30 to Q50) in the lush patio area is a great way to start the day.

CENTRAL & EASTERN GUATEMALA COBÁN

Pensión Monja Blanca
HOTEL $$

(📞 7952-1712; 2a Calle 6-30, Zona 2; s/d Q170/225, without bathroom Q120/150; 🅿) This place is peaceful despite being on busy 2a Calle. After walking through two courtyards, you come to a lush garden packed with fruit and hibiscus trees around which the spotless rooms are arranged. Each room has an old-time feel to it and is furnished with two good-quality single beds with folksy covers, and has cable TV.

The hotel's central location and tranquil atmosphere make it a good place for solo women travelers.

Hostal de Doña Victoria
HOTEL $$

(📞 7951-4213; www.hotelescoban.com; 3a Calle 2-38, Zona 3; s/d Q150/215; 🅿🛜) This lovely hotel in a restored mansion more than 400 years old is jam-packed with eye-catching decorations varying from an old copper coffee machine to wooden masks to antique religious statues. Eight brightly painted comfortable rooms, with bathroom and TV, surround a central courtyard with lush plants and a restaurant-bar.

Casa Duranta
HOTEL $$

(📞 7951-4188; www.casaduranta.com; 3a Calle 4-46, Zona 3; s/d Q305/430; 🅿🛜) Some rooms at this carefully restored, eclectically decorated place are excellent value, while others are a bit cramped for the price. Have a look at the rooms if you can.

Hotel La Posada
HOTEL $$

(📞 7952-1495; www.laposadacoban.com; 1a Calle 4-12, Zona 2; s/d Q350/390) Just off the plaza, this colonial-style hotel is Cobán's best, though rooms streetside suffer from traffic noise. Its colonnaded porches are dripping with tropical flowers and furnished with easy chairs and hammocks. The rooms are a bit austere, with plenty of religious relics around the place, but they have nice old furniture, fireplaces and wall hangings of local weaving.

✖ Eating

Most of the hotels in Cobán come with their own restaurants. In the evening, food trucks (kitchens on wheels) park around the plaza and offer some of the cheapest dining in town. As always, the one to go for has the largest crowd of locals hanging around and chomping down.

★ Xkape Koba'n
GUATEMALAN $

(2a Calle 5-13, Zona 2; snacks Q20, mains Q40; 🕙10am-7pm) 🍴 The perfect place to take a breather or while away a whole afternoon, this beautiful, artsy little cafe has a lush garden out back. Some interesting indigenous-inspired dishes are on the small menu. The cakes are homemade, the coffee is delectable and there are some interesting handicrafts on sale.

Café Fantasia
CAFE $

(1a Calle 3-13, Oficinas Profesionales Fray Bartolomé de Las Casas; breakfast Q20-30; 🕙8am-7pm Mon-Sat) A good central cafe, offering several types of hot chocolate. It's a cozy little place in which to enjoy breakfasts, pastries and coffee or light meals, with a pleasant terrace away from the traffic.

Kardamomuss
FUSION $$

(3a Calle 5-34, Zona 2; mains Q40-90; 🕙8am-9pm; 🛜) The widest menu in town is at this chic new place a few blocks from the plaza. Billing itself as 'fusion' food, it takes a pretty good stab at Indian, Chinese and Italian dishes, with locally grown cardamom as the featured ingredient.

El Bistro
INTERNATIONAL $$

(4a Calle 3-11, Zona 2; mains Q60-120; 🕙7am-10pm) Casa D'Acuña's restaurant offers authentic Italian and other European-style dishes served in an attractive oasis of tranquility soundtracked to classical music. In addition to protein-oriented mains, there is a range of pastas (Q40 to Q65), salads, homemade breads, cakes and outstanding desserts.

Casa Chavez
INTERNATIONAL $$

(1a Calle 4-25, Zona 1; mains Q40-80; 🕙8am-8:30pm; 🛜) Set in a lovely old house, the menu here is ample if a little uninspired. Still, the location's great, and breakfast out back overlooking the garden and hills beyond is hard to beat.

El Peñascal
GUATEMALAN $$

(5a Av 2-61; mains Q55-90; 🕙11:30am-9pm) Probably Cobán's finest stand-alone restaurant, this one has plenty of regional specialties, Guatemalan classics, mixed meat platters, seafood and snacks in a relaxed, upmarket setting.

Nightlife

Bohemios
CLUB

(cnr 8a Av & 2 Calle, Zona 2; admission Q10-25; 🕙Thu-Sat) About as close as this town gets to a mega-disco, with balcony seating and bow-tied waiters.

❶ Orientation

Most buses will drop you at the terminal known as Campo Dos (p185), just north of town. It's a 15-minute walk (2km) or Q10 taxi ride to the plaza from there.

❶ Information

LAUNDRY

Lavandería Econo Express (7a Av 2-32, Zona 1; ⊙7am-7pm Mon-Sat) Laundry places are in short supply in Cobán – these folks wash and dry a load for Q40.

MONEY

The banks listed here change US-dollar cash and traveler's checks.
Banco G&T (1a Calle) Has a MasterCard ATM.
Banco Industrial (cnr 1a Calle & 7a Av, Zona 1) Has a Visa ATM.

POST & TELEPHONE

Post Office (cnr 2a Av & 3a Calle) A block southeast from the plaza.
Telgua On the plaza; has plenty of card phones outside.

TOURIST INFORMATION

Inguat (☑3176-7469; 1a Calle 3-13, Zona 1; ⊙8am-4pm Mon-Sat, 9am-1pm Sun) has an office, hidden away in a courtyard off the main street. If they can't help you, try the **Municipalidad** (Town Hall; ☑7951-1148, 7952-1305; 1a Calle, Zona 1; ⊙8am-4pm Mon-Sat), where some switched-on young staff work in an office behind the police office. Casa D'Acuña can also give you loads of information.

❶ Getting There & Away

BUS

The highway connecting Cobán with Guatemala City and Hwy 9 is the most traveled route between Cobán and the outside world. The road north through Chisec to Sayaxché and Flores is now paved all the way, providing much easier access to El Petén. The off-the-beaten-track routes west to Huehuetenango and northeast to Fray Bartolomé de Las Casas and Poptún are mostly unpaved and still provide a bit of an adventure (although this second one was being paved at the time of research). Always double-check bus departure times, especially for less frequently served destinations.

Buses leave from a variety of points around town. Minibuses, known as microbuses, are replacing or are additional to chicken buses (former US school buses) on many routes.

Buses leave from Cobán's **Campo Dos** (Campo Norte) bus terminal. Please be aware that the road to Uspantan and Nebaj is prone to landslides – get the latest before setting out.

Destinations not served by Campo Dos terminal include the following:
Cahabón (Q30; 4½ hours) Same buses as to Lanquín.
Guatemala City (Q50 to Q65; four to five hours) **Transportes Monja Blanca** (☑7951-3571; 2a Calle 3-77, Zona 4) has buses leaving for Guatemala City every 30 minutes from 2am to 6am, then hourly until 4pm.
Lanquín (Q25; 2½ to three hours) **Transportes Martínez** (6a Calle 2-40, Zona 4) has multiple departures throughout the day. Buses to Lanquin also depart from 7am to 4pm from the corner of 5a Calle and 3a Av, Zona 4, some continuing to Semuc Champey. Do check these times, though, as they seem to be fluid.
San Pedro Carchá (Q3; 20 minutes; every 10 minutes) Buses depart from 6am to 7pm from the lot in front of the Monja Blanca terminal.

Buses from Cobán
Biotopo del Quetzal (Q12, 1¼ hours)
Chisec (Q20, two hours)
Fray Bartolomé de Las Casas (Q40, four hours)
Nebaj (Q60, 5½ to seven hours)
Playa Grande, for Laguna Lachuá (Q50, three hours)
Raxruhá (Q30, 2½ to three hours)
Salamá (Q25, 1½ hours)
Sayaxché (Q65, four hours)
Tactic (Q8, 40 minutes)
Uspantán (Q35, 4½ hours)

CAR

Cobán has a couple of places that rent cars. Reserve your choice in advance. If you want to go to Grutas de Lanquín or Semuc Champey, you'll need a 4WD vehicle. Rental companies include **Inque Renta Autos** (☑7952-1994; inque83@hotmail.com; 3a Av 1-18, Zona 4) and **Tabarini Rent A Car** (☑7952-1504; www.tabarini.com; 7a Av 2-27, Zona 1).

Around Cobán

Cobán, and indeed all of Alta Verapaz, has become a magnet for Guatemalan adventure travel, both independent and organized. Not only are there scores of villages where you can experience traditional Maya culture in some of its purest extant forms, there are also caves running throughout the department, as well as waterfalls, pristine lagoons and many other natural wonders yet to be discovered. Go find them!

PARQUE NACIONAL LAGUNA LACHUÁ

This **national park** (📞4084-1706; entry fee adult/child Q50/25, campsite per adult/child Q25/12, bunk with mosquito net Q70/35, tent hire Q15) is renowned for the perfectly round, pristine turquoise lake (220m deep) for which it was named. Until recently, this Guatemalan gem was rarely visited by travelers because it was an active, violent area during the civil war and the road was in pathetic disrepair. Now it fills up quickly on weekends and public holidays, and if you're thinking about coming at these times, it's a good idea to call and reserve a space. Overnight visitors can use the cooking facilities, so come prepared with food and drink. There is only one shower. You can no longer rent canoes for exploring the lake, but there are about 4km of interpretative trails to explore. The Cobán tour outfits offer two-day and one-night trips for Q650 per person. If you don't want to stay in the park, there are hotels and restaurants in nearby Playa Grande. There's also a community tourism initiative in **Rocjá Pomtilá** (📞5381-1970; rocapon@yahoo.com; r for 2 nights, incl guide & 4 meals Q320-400) on the eastern edge of the park. Contact the community directly or Misterio Verde (p181) in Cobán to make arrangements.

A new road means you can get to the park entrance from Cobán in a bit over two hours by bus (Q55). Take a Playa Grande (Cantabal) bus from Cobán via Chisec and ask the driver to leave you at the park entrance, from which it's about a 2km walk to the lake. From Playa Grande there are buses and pickups leaving for Barillas (Q60, five hours), the first stop on the backdoor route to Huehuetenango in the Western Highlands.

San Cristóbal Verapaz is an interesting Poqomchi' Maya village set beside Lake Chicoj, 19km west of Cobán. During **Semana Santa** (Easter Week), local artists design elaborate *alfombras* (carpets) of colored sawdust and flower petals rivaled only by those in Antigua. Check out the town's excellent community website at www.sancrisav. net. In addition, San Cristóbal is home to the **Centro Communitario Educativo Pokomchi** (Cecep; 📞7950-4896), an organization dedicated to preserving traditional and modern ways of Poqomchi' life. To this end, Cecep inaugurated the **Museo Katinamit** (Calle del Calvario 0-33, Zona 3; admission Q10; ⏰8am-5pm Mon-Sat, 9am-12pm Sat), which re-creates a typical Poqomchi' house, with well-ordered displays of household items and everyday products. Other rooms feature art, tools and textiles still in daily use, and an introduction and orientation on the Poqomchi'. Cecep also offers volunteer and ethnotourism opportunities and houses the **Aj Chi Cho Language Center** (courses incl homestay per week Q1300) for teaching Spanish. **El Portón Real** (📞7950-4604; oscar_capriel@hotmail.com; 4a Av 1-44, Zona 1; s/d Q65/110) is a Poqomchi'-owned and -operated hostelry, a few blocks away from the museum and school.

Balneario Las Islas

At the town of San Pedro Carchá, 6km east of Cobán on the way to Lanquín, is the **Balneario Las Islas** (admission Q10; ⏰7am-4pm), a tributary of the river Cahabon coming down past rocks and into a natural pool that's great for swimming. It's a five- to 10-minute walk from the bus stop in Carchá; anyone can point the way. Buses operate frequently between Cobán and Carchá (Q3; 20 minutes).

Grutas Rey Marcos

Near Aldea Chajaneb, 12km east of Cobán, is the cave system **Grutas Rey Marcos** (📞7951-2756; www.grutasdelreymarcos.com.gt; admission Q25; ⏰8am-5pm). It's set in the **Balneario Cecilinda** (admission Q10; ⏰8am-5pm), which is, incidentally, a great place to go for a swim or a hike on scenic mountain trails. The caves themselves go for more than 1km into the earth, although chances are you won't get taken that far. A river runs through the cave (you have to wade through it at one point) and there are some impressive stalactites and stalagmites. Headlamps, helmets and rubber boots are included in the admission price to the cave. According to local legend, any wishes made in the cave are guaranteed to come true.

To reach the caves, take a bus or pickup (Q3, 15 minutes) from San Juan Chamelco towards Chamil and ask the driver to let you off at the turnoff. From there it's about a 1km walk to the entrance. Alternatively, hire a taxi from Cobán (Q100).

Lanquín

One of the best excursions to make from Cobán is to the pretty village of Lanquín, 61km to the east. People come for two reasons: to explore the wonderful cave system just out of town, and as a jumping-off point for visiting the natural rock pools at Semuc Champey. The Banrural on Lanquín's main square changes US dollars and traveler's checks, but at the time of writing did not have an ATM.

◉ Sights

Grutas de Lanquín   CAVE
(admission Q30; ⊙8am-6pm) These caves are about 1km northwest of the town, and extend for several kilometers into the earth. There is now a ticket office here. The first cave has lights, but do take a powerful flashlight (torch) anyway. You'll also need shoes with good traction, as inside it's slippery with moisture and bat droppings.

Though the first few hundred meters of the cavern have been equipped with a walkway and are lit by diesel-powered electric lights, most of this subterranean system is untouched. If you are not an experienced spelunker, you shouldn't wander too far into the caves; the entire extent has yet to be explored, let alone mapped.

As well as featuring funky stalactites, mostly named for animals, these caves are crammed with bats. Try to time your visit to coincide with sunset, when hundreds of them fly out of the mouth of the cave in formations so dense they obscure the sky. For a dazzling display of navigation skills, sit at the entrance while they exit. Please be aware that bats are extremely light-sensitive and tempting as it may be, flash photography can disorient and, in some cases, blind them.

The river here gushes from the cave in clean, cool and delicious torrents. You can swim in the river, which has some comfortably hot pockets close to shore.

🏃 Activities

Maya Expeditions (p49), based in Guatemala City, offers exciting one- to five-day rafting expeditions on the Río Cahabón.

Guatemala Rafting   RAFTING
(☑7983-3056; www.guatemalarafting.com) Operating out of El Retiro Lodge, this outfit has a variety of trips on offer, including kayaking on the river beneath Semuc Champey.

Travelers heading for Río Dulce or Flores may be interested in the two-day Adventure Route trip (from Q1380 per person), which takes you down the Río Cahabón and out to Hwy 13.

ADETES   RAFTING
(☑5069-3518; www.guaterafting.com) This excellent community-tourism initiative is based in Aldea Saquijá, 12km out of Lanquín. It offers rafting trips led by well-trained community members on the Río Cahabón. Prices range from Q160 to Q355 per person for a two- to five-hour trip. To get to the headquarters, catch any bus leaving Lanquín headed towards Cahabón.

🛏 Sleeping & Eating

Zephyr Lodge   HOSTEL $
(☑5168-2441; www.zephyrlodgelanquin.com; campsites per person Q30, dm Q40-50, r Q200-250) Lanquín's party hostel is all class – great rooms with spectacular views, OK dorms and some good hangout areas, including the big thatched-roof bar/restaurant. The river's a five-minute walk downhill.

El Retiro Lodge   BUNGALOW $
(☑4513-6396; www.elretirolanquin.com; dm Q45, r with/without bathroom Q200/100, cabin without bathroom s/d Q150/180; ℗@⊙) This sublimely located hotel is about 500m along the road beyond Rabin Itzam. Dorm rooms have only four beds. Individual decor includes some clever use of tiles, shells, strings of beads and local fabrics. *Palapa* (shelter with a thatched, palm-leaf roof and open sides) look down over the greenest of green fields to a beautiful wide river – the same one that flows out from the Lanquín caves.

It's safe to swim, and to inner-tube if you're a confident swimmer.

Rabin Itzam   HOTEL $
(☑7983-0076; s/d Q150/200, without bathroom Q50/100) A no-frills budget hotel in the center. The beds sag a bit, but rooms upstairs at the front (with shared bathroom) have good valley views.

El Recreo   HOTEL $$
(☑7823-4069; elrecreolanquin@gmail.com; s/d Q230/330, without bathroom Q75/150; ℗⊙▣) Between the town and the caves, this place has that 'made for tour groups' feel to it, but the bungalows set around forested grounds are a good deal – spacious and well decorated. The rooms set in the basement with

shared bathrooms might be a bit grim for some.

Restaurante Champey　　　GUATEMALAN $
(mains Q20-50; ☺ 8am-11pm) This large outdoor eatery halfway between town and El Retiro serves up good-sized plates of steak, eggs and rice and gets rowdy and beerish at night.

❶ Getting There & Away

Overnight tours to Grutas de Lanquín and Semuc Champey, offered in Cobán for Q300 per person, are the easiest way to visit these places, but it's really not that complicated to organize yourself. Tours take about two hours to reach Lanquín from Cobán; the price includes a packed lunch.

Buses operate several times daily between Cobán and Lanquín, continuing to Cahabón. There are eight buses to Cobán (Q30, three hours) between 6am and 5:30pm. Shuttles for Semuc Champey (Q30 return) leave at 9:30am (book at your hotel) and pickups (Q10 to Q15) leave whenever they are full, half a block from the main square.

If it's been raining heavily and you're driving, you'll need a 4WD vehicle. The road from San Pedro Carchá to El Pajal, where you turn off for Lanquín, is paved. The 11km from El Pajal to Lanquín is not. You can head on from Lanquín to Flores in 14 to 15 hours via El Pajal, Sebol, Raxrujá and Sayaxché. The road from El Pajal to Sebol was being paved at time of research. Or you can head on from Lanquín to Sebol and Fray Bartolomé de Las Casas and on to Poptún.

If you're heading towards Río Dulce, a back road exists, although it's unpaved for most of the way and gets washed out in heavy rains. Transportation schedules along here are flexible at best. Ask around to see what the current situation is. A daily shuttle (Q150, 6 hours) runs on this road and is the most reliable, easy option. Book at any of the hotels listed here.

Semuc Champey & Around

Eleven kilometers south of Lanquín, along a rough, bumpy, slow road, is **Semuc Champey** (admission Q50; ☺ 8am-6pm), famed for its great 300m-long natural limestone bridge, on top of which is a stepped series of pools with cool, flowing river water good for swimming. The water is from the Río Cahabón, and much more of it passes underground, beneath the bridge. Though this bit of paradise is difficult to reach, the beauty of its setting and the perfection of the pools, ranging from turquoise to emerald-green,

make it worth it. Many people consider this the most beautiful spot in all Guatemala.

If you're visiting on a tour, some guides will take you down a rope ladder from the lowest pool to the river, which gushes out from the rocks below. Plenty of people do this and love it, though it is a bit risky.

It's possible to **camp** (campsite per tent Q50) at Semuc Champey, but be sure to pitch a tent only in the upper areas, as flash floods are common down below. It's also risky to leave anything unattended, as it might get stolen. The place now has 24-hour security, which may reassure potential campers, but you should keep your valuables with you. A simple restaurant at the parking area serves OK meals (including *cack'ik* – turkey stew; Q45), but is a long way from the pools. It's a better idea to bring a picnic.

🏃 Activities

K'anba Caves　　　CAVE
(admission Q60; ☺ 9am-3pm, tours 9am, 10am, 1pm, 2:30pm & 3pm) About a kilometer before Semuc Champey, just before the large bridge crossing the river, you'll see a turnoff to the right for these caves, which many find to be much more interesting than Grutas de Lanquín. Bring a flashlight (torch) for the two-hour tour or you'll be stumbling around by candlelight.

A half hour of river tubing costs an extra Q10. There have been reports of serious overcrowding on these cave tours. If you can, arrive for the 9am tour, before the tour groups start showing up. And, as always, evaluate the conditions before setting out.

🛏 Sleeping

El Portal　　　HOSTEL $$
(📞 4091-7878; www.hostalelportaldechampey.com; dm Q40, r with/without bathroom Q200/100; 🅿🛜) About 100m short of the entrance to Semuc Champey, this is the obvious choice for convenient access to Semuc. There's only daytime electricity (thanks to a generator), but the well-spaced wooden huts built on the bank sloping down to the river are by far the best accommodation deal in the area. Meals and tours are available.

Utopia　　　HOSTEL, BUNGALOW $$
(📞 3135-8329; www.utopiaecohotel.com; camping per person Q25, hammock/dm Q30/45, r with/without bathroom Q400/150; 🛜) Set on a hillside overlooking the small village of Semil, 3km from Semuc Chapey, this is the most

impressive setup in the area. Every range of accommodation imaginable is available, from luxurious riverside cabins to campsites. The restaurant/bar (serving vegetarian family-style meals) has fantastic valley views and the stretch of river that it sits on is truly idyllic.

The turnoff to Semil is 2km before Semuc Champey. From there it's about 1km to the hotel. Call from Lanquín (or drop into the office at the crossroads where the bus arrives) for free transport out here.

❶ Getting There & Away

If you're into walking, the 2½-hour trip from Lanquín is a fairly pleasant one, passing through lush countryside and simple rural scenes. If not, there are plenty of transportation options. Pickups run from the plaza in Lanquín to Semuc Champey – your chances of catching one are better in the early morning and on market days: Sunday, Monday and Thursday. Expect to pay somewhere between Q10 and Q20. All the Lanquín hotels and hostels run shuttle services out here, too.

Chisec

POP 35,000

The town of Chisec, 66km north of Cobán, is becoming a center for reaching several exciting destinations. This is thanks to the paving of the road from Cobán to Sayaxché and Flores, which runs through here, and some admirable community tourism programs aiming to help develop this long-ignored region, the population of which is almost entirely Q'eqchi' Maya. The best source of information on these programs is the office of **Puerta al Mundo Maya** (📞5978-1465; www.puertamundomaya.com.gt; Lote 135, Barrio El Centro), which administers quite a few of them.

Hotel La Estancia de la Virgen (📞5514-7444; www.hotelestanciadelavirgen.com; Calle Principal; s/d with fan Q90/140, with air-con Q120/180; 🅿❄@🛜🏊), Chisec's best hotel, on the main road at the northern exit from town, has neat and sensible rooms, a restaurant and a swimming pool with some excellent waterslides in the shape of fallen tree trunks.

Hotel Nopales (📞5514-0624; Parque Central; s/d Q60/90; 🏊) has surprisingly large rooms (with smell) set around a courtyard dominated by a permanently empty (unless it's been raining) swimming pool.

Restaurante Bonapek (Parque Central; mains Q30-50; ⊗8am-9pm) is one of the few places you'd want to eat in town.

Buses leave Chisec for Cobán (Q20, two hours) eight times daily, from 3am to 2pm. Buses or minibuses to San Antonio and Raxrujá (one hour) go hourly, from 6am to 4pm. Some of these continue to Fray Bartolomé de Las Casas. There are also regular minibuses to Playa Grande (two hours), for the Parque Nacional Laguna Lachuá. Some Cobán–Sayaxché minibuses and buses pass through Chisec.

Around Chisec

Cuevas de B'ombi'l Pek   CAVE

(admission Q125; ⊗8am-4pm) A mere 3km north of Chisec, these painted caves remained undiscovered until 2001. They haven't been fully mapped yet, but some claim that they connect to the caves of Parque Nacional Cuevas de Candelaria. The community-run guide office is by the roadside. Pay the entrance fee and the guide will take you on the 3km walk through cornfields to the entrance.

The entire tour takes about four hours. The first, main cavern is the most impressive for its size (reaching 50m in height; you have the choice of rapelling or descending via a slippery 'jungle ladder' to enter), but a secondary cave – just 1m wide – features paintings of monkeys and jaguars. River tubing (Q60) is also possible, starting at the guide office.

Any bus running north from Chisec can drop you at the guide office.

Lagunas de Sepalau   OUTDOORS

(admission Q170; ⊗8am-5pm) Surrounded by pristine forest, these turquoise lagoons are 8km west of Chisec. Recently developed as a community ecotourism project by local villagers, tours of the area include a fair bit of walking and some rowboat paddling. The area is rich in wildlife: jaguars, tapir, iguanas, toucans and howler monkeys are all in residence.

There are three lagoons, the most spectacular of which is the third on the tour, Q'ekija, which is ringed by steep walls of thick jungle. From February to June the first two lagoons dry up.

Pickups leave Chisec's plaza for the village of Sepalau Cataltzul throughout the day and there's usually a bus (Q9, 45 minutes) at 10:30am. On arrival at the village, you pay the entrance fee and a guide will take you on the 3km walk to the first lagoon.

Raxruhá

POP 35,000

A sleepy little crossroads town, Raxruhá provides a good base for exploring the nearby attractions of Cancuén and Cuevas de Candelaria. Services are few – Banrural at the main intersection changes cash but not traveler's checks and the nearest ATMs are in Chisec or Fray Bartolomé. Reasonably fast internet access is available in the Hotel Cancuén.

The best hotel in town is a family-run affair just on the outskirts of town (a two-minute walk from the center). Rooms at **Hotel Cancuén** (☑7983-0720; www.cuevaslosnacimientos.com; s/d from Q100/140, without bathroom Q35/70; P✱) are clean and well decorated, and there's a good little *comedor* (cheap eatery) on-site. It has good information about visiting Cancuén. You can arrange walking/tubing tours (Q125 per person, four to six hours) of the nearby Cueva los Nacimientos, the northernmost point in the Candelaria complex.

With large, vaguely clean rooms around an oversized parking lot, **Hotel El Amigo** (☑5872-4136; r per person Q60; P✱✱) has great potential but is terribly rundown – it may have been fixed up by the time you get there.

Both of the hotels listed serve basic meals and there are good-value *comedores* around the market/bus terminal area. The best eating for miles around is oddly located a few kilometers west of town on the road to the Candelaria caves. The small French-inspired menu at **El Bistrot Frances** (Km 318; mains Q60-100, s/d from Q150/235; ⊙7am-8pm) offers decent variety and the daily special is always worth investigating. They also have extremely comfortable rooms and bungalows. Any bus heading to Chisec can drop you here.

Pickups and the occasional bus for La Union (to access Cancuén; Q10, one hour) leave from the stop one block uphill. There are at least five scheduled departures daily to both Sayaxché (Q30, 2½ hours) and Cobán (Q30, two hours) from Raxruhá.

Around Raxruhá

Parque Nacional Cuevas de Candelaria

Just west of Raxruhá, this 22km-long cave system, dug out by the subterranean Río Candelaria, boasts some monstrous proportions – the main chamber is 30m high, 200m wide and has stalagmites measuring up to 30m in length. Natural apertures in the roof allow sunlight in, creating magical, eerie reflections.

The caves were used by the Q'eqchi' Maya and you'll see some platforms and ladders carved into the stone. Community-run operations offer tours into the various entrances to the cave complex. You can walk, tube and spelunk the entire underground passage in about two days, but must do so with a guide. Prices depend on group size, but will probably average around Q2000 per person, not including food. Contact any of the organizations listed here or Maya Expeditions (p49) for details. The following are listed from north to south.

Located behind – and forming part of – the Complejo Cultural de Candelaria, the **El Mico** (www.cuevasdecandelaria.com; Km 316.5; tubing/walking tour Q40/75; ⊙9am-5pm) complex is is probably the most easily accessible and spectacular of the various cave tours. From the highway, look for the sign for the **Complejo Cultural de Candelaria** (☑4035-0566; www.cuevasdecandelaria.com; Km 316.5; s/d from Q300/400), which offers supremely comfortable accommodation in stylishly decorated cabins. Excellent French-influenced meals are included in the rates. Some slightly cheaper cabins with shared bathrooms may be available.

A couple of kilometers west on the same highway is the turnoff for **Comunidad Mucbilha'** (Km 315; tubing or walking tour Q75; ⊙8am-4pm). From the highway it's 2km along a dirt road to the parking lot, then another 1km to the visitor center, where you can walk or tube through the **Venado Seco cave**. The small **ecolodge** (dm Q85) here has bunk beds and shower facilities.

Another couple of caves can be visited nearby at the **Cuevas de Candelaria Camposanto** (Km 309.5; tubing or walking tours Q75; ⊙8am-4pm). Guides can be organized at the roadside *tienda* (store) for the short walk to the caves. With a couple of days notice, they will put on a Maya ceremony (Q35 per person) for visitors.

For more information about Muchilba' and Candelaria Camposanto, you can contact Puerta al Mundo Maya (p189) in Chisec.

Any bus running between Chisec and Raxruhá can drop you at any of these three places.

Cancuén

This large **Maya site** (admission Q75; ☺8am-4pm) hit the papers when it was 'discovered' in 2000, even though it had already been 'discovered' back in 1907. Excavations are still under way, but estimates say that Cancuén may rival Tikal for size.

It's thought that Cancuén was a trading center rather than a religious center, and the usual temples and pyramids are absent. In their place is a grand palace boasting more than 150 rooms set around 11 courtyards. Carvings here are impressive, particularly the grand palace, but also along the ball courts and the two altars that have been excavated to date.

Cancuén's importance seems to stem from its geographical/tactical position. Hieroglyphics attest to alliances with Calakmul (Mexico) and Tikal, and its relative proximity to the southern Highlands would have given it access to pyrite and obsidian, prized minerals of the Maya.

Artisans certainly worked here – their bodies have been discovered dressed, unusually, in royal finery. Several workshops have also been uncovered, one containing a 17kg piece of jade.

Casual visitors will need about an hour to see the main, partially excavated, sections of the site and another hour or two to see the rest.

You can camp here and eat in the *comedor* at Cancuén, but if you're planning on doing either, contact the community tourism office Puerta al Mundo Maya (p189) in Chisec a few days beforehand to let them know your plans.

Cobán tour companies make day trips to Cancuén. To get here independently, catch a pickup (leaving hourly) from Raxruhá to La Unión (Q10, 40 minutes), from where you can hire a boat (Q200 to Q350 for one to 16 people, round trip) to the site. You can also hire a guide (Q50 to Q150, depending on group size) to take you on the 4km walk to the site from La Unión, but in the rainy season this will be a very muddy affair. If walking or going by *lancha* (small motorboat), pay at the small store where the bus stops – the boat dock is an easy 1km walk from there. Pay your entrance fee at the site when you arrive. The last pickup leaves La Unión for Raxruhá at 3pm.

Fray Bartolomé de Las Casas

POP 9200

This town, often referred to simply as Fray, is a way station on the backdoor route between the Cobán/Lanquín area and Poptún on the Río Dulce–Flores highway (Hwy 13). This route is dotted with traditional Maya villages where only the patriarchs speak Spanish, and then only a little. This is a great opportunity for getting off the 'gringo trail' and into the heart of Guatemala.

Fray is substantial considering it's in the middle of nowhere, but don't let its size fool you. This is a place where the weekly soccer game is the biggest deal in town, chickens

---

WORTH A TRIP

LAS CONCHAS

From Fray you can visit Las Conchas (admission Q15), a series of limestone pools and waterfalls on the Río Chiyú, which some say are better than those at Semuc Champey. The pools are up to 8m deep and 20m wide and connected by a series of spectacular waterfalls, but aren't a turquoise-color like those at Semuc.

You can stay right by the pools at the rustic but charming **Oasis Chiyu** (☏4826-5247; www.naturetoursguatemala.com; r per person Q120) – make reservations well in advance, or in nearby Chahal at the clean and comfortable family-run **Villa Santa Elena** (☏5000-9246; www.hotelvse.com; Ruta 5, Km 365 ; s/d Q150/175, campsite per person Q10; [P][❄][@][☏]). Both of these hotels have restaurants.

Regular minibuses (Q12, one hour) leave Fray for Chahal when full. From there you must change buses for Las Conchas (Q8, one hour). If you're in your own vehicle, look for the marked sign to Las Conchas, 15km east of Chahal. If you're coming south from El Petén, get off in Modesto Mendez (known locally as Cadenas), catch a Chahal-bound minibus to Sejux (*Say*-whoosh) and walk or wait for another minibus to take you the remaining 3km to Las Conchas. Whichever direction you're coming from, travel connections are easiest in the morning and drop off severely in the late afternoon.

languish in the streets and siesta is taken seriously.

The town itself is fairly spread out, with the plaza and most tourist facilities at one end and the market and bus terminus at the other. Walking between the two takes about 10 minutes. Coming from Cobán, you'll want to hop off at the central plaza.

The post office and police station are just off the plaza. Nearby, Banrural changes US dollars and traveler's checks and has an ATM. The *municipalidad* (town hall) is on the plaza.

Hotel La Cabaña (☑7952-0352; 2a Calle 1-92, Zona 3; r per person with/without bathroom Q50/40) has the best accommodation in town. Eating options are limited here – try Comedor Jireh and Restaurante Doris on the main street. Otherwise, grab a steak (with tortillas and beans, Q15) at the informal barbecue shacks that open up along the main street at night.

At least two daily buses departs from the plaza for Poptún (Q35, five hours). Buses for Cobán leave hourly between 4am and 4pm. Some go via Chisec (Q40, 3½ hours). Others take the slower route via San Pedro Carchá.

EL ORIENTE

Heading east from Guatemala City brings you into the long, flat valleys of the region Guatemalans call El Oriente (the East). It's a dry and unforgiving landscape of stunted hillsides covered in scraggly brush. They breed 'em tough out here and the cowboy hats, boots, buckles and sidearms sported by a lot of men in the region fit well against this rugged backdrop.

Most travelers pass through on their way to Copán in Honduras, or to visit the pilgrimage town of Esquipulas. Further east, the landscape becomes a lot more tropical and you'll see plenty of fruit for sale at roadside stalls. If you've got some time in this area, a quick sidetrip to the ruins at Quiriguá is well worth your while.

Río Hondo

POP 10,500

Río Hondo (Deep River), 50km east of El Rancho junction and 130km from Guatemala City, is where Hwy 10 to Chiquimula heads south off the Carretera al Atlántico (Hwy 9). Beyond Chiquimula are turnoffs to Copán, just across the Honduras border; to Esquipulas and on to Nueva Ocotepeque

(Honduras); and the remote border crossing between Guatemala and El Salvador at Anguiatú, 12km north of Metapán (El Salvador).

The actual town of Río Hondo is northeast of the junction. Places to stay hereabouts may list their address as Río Hondo, Santa Cruz Río Hondo or Santa Cruz Teculután. Nine kilometers west of the junction are several attractive motels right on Hwy 9. By car, it's an hour from here to Quiriguá, half an hour to Chiquimula and 1½ hours to Esquipulas.

◉ Sights

Valle Dorado WATER PARK
(☑7943-6666; www.hotelvalledorado.com; Hwy 9, Km 149; r from Q480, aquatic park adult/child Q70/50; ◷ aquatic park 9am-5pm Wed-Sun) An attraction near Río Hondo is Valle Dorado, an aquatic park and tourist center. This large complex 14km past the Hwy 10 junction and 23km from the other Río Hondo hotels includes an aquatic park with giant pools, waterslides, toboggans and other entertainment. Check the website for promotional deals and make reservations on weekends.

Parque Acuatico Longarone WATER PARK
(Hwy 9, Km 126.5; adult/child Q60/45; ◷ 9am-5pm Fri-Sun) Río Hondo is home to the Parque Acuatico Longarone with giant waterslides, an artificial river and other water-based fun.

⌂ Sleeping

Nonguests can use the pools at all these places for around Q25 per person.

Hotel El Atlántico HOTEL $$
(☑7933-0598; www.hotelelatlanticoguate.com; Hwy 9, Km 126.5; s/d Q250/350; ⓟ❊@♠☀) The best-looking place in town has plenty of dark-wood fittings and well-spaced bungalows. The pool area is tranquil, with some shady sitting areas.

Hotel Nuevo Pasabién HOTEL $$
(☑7933-0606; www.hotelpasabien.com; Hwy 9, Km 126.5; s/d with fan Q100/200, with air-con Q200/350; ⓟ❊@☀) On the north side of the highway, this hotel is a good choice for families – kids will enjoy the three pools with all manner of fancy slides.

Hotel Longarone HOTEL $$$
(☑7933-0488; www.hotel-longarone.com; Hwy 9, Km 126.5; s/d from Q400/550; ⓟ❊@♠☀) Attached to Parque Acuatico Longarone, with

good-looking grounds, playgrounds for kids and a surprisingly fine Italian restaurant. Rooms are comfortable if somewhat dated.

Chiquimula

POP 55,400

Thirty-two kilometers south of Rio Hondo on Hwy 10, Chiquimula is a major market town for all of eastern Guatemala. For travelers it's not a destination but a transit point. Your goal is probably the fabulous Maya ruins at Copán in Honduras, just across the border from El Florido. There are also some interesting journeys between Chiquimula and Jalapa, 78km to the west. Among other things, Chiquimula is famous for its sweltering climate and its decent budget hotels (a couple have swimming pools).

🛏 Sleeping

Hotel Hernández   HOTEL $
(☎7942-0708; 3a Calle 7-41, Zona 1; s/d with fan Q80/120, with air-con Q140/200, without bathroom Q50/90; P❋☎☲) It's hard to beat the Hernández – it's been a favorite for years and keeps going strong, with its central position, spacious, simple rooms and good-sized swimming pool.

Hotel Posada Don Adan   HOTEL $
(☎7942-3924; 8a Av 4-30, Zona 1; s/d Q100/150; ☺until 10pm; P❋) The Don offers the best deal in this price range – neat, complete rooms with TV, fan, air-con, a couple of sticks of furniture and good, firm beds. They lock the doors at 10pm.

Posada Perla de Oriente   HOTEL $$
(☎7942-0014; 2a Calle 11-50, Zona 1; s/d with fan Q120/220, with air-con Q150/250; P❋☎☲) Surprisingly tranquil for its location just around the corner from the bus terminal, with some of the best-value rooms in town. They're large and unadorned, but the grounds are quiet and leafy and the big swimming pool is a bonus.

Hostal Maria Teresa   HOTEL $$
(☎7942-0177; 6a Calle 6-21, Zona 1; s/d Q190/350; P❋☎) Set around a gorgeous colonial courtyard with wide shady passageways, the single rooms are a bit poky, but the doubles are generous and all the comforts are here: cable TV, hot showers and air-con.

🍴 Eating & Drinking

There's a string of cheap *comedores* on 8a Av behind the market. At night, snack vendors and taco carts set up along 7a Av opposite the plaza, selling the cheapest eats in town.

Corner Coffee   CAFE $
(6a Calle 6-70, Zona 1; bagels Q30, breakfast Q25-30; ☺7am-10pm Mon-Sat, 3-10pm Sun) You could argue with the syntax of the name, but this air-con haven right on the lovely Parque Calvario serves up the best range of sandwiches, burgers and bagels in town.

OFF THE BEATEN TRACK

JALAPA

Jalapa is a small, friendly town 78km west of Chiquimula, and the route between the two is a stunning one: verdant gorges choked with banana trees alternate with fog-enveloped valleys. Jalapa isn't a tourist destination, but the hotel scene is more than adequate – **Hotel Recinos** (☎7922-2580; 2a Calle 0-80, Zona 2; s/d Q60/120), by the bus terminal, will appeal to budget-watchers, while the nearby **Posada de Don José Antonio** (☎7922-5751; Av Chipilapa A 0-64, Zona 2; s/d Q160/220; P@☎) offers several steps up in comfort. There's plenty of food on offer around the terminal, too, including good coffee and a wide menu at **Florencia** (Av Chipilapa 1-72, Zona 1; mains Q30-60; ☺7am-9pm).

While you're here, consider making a day trip to **Parque Ecoturístico Cascadas de Tatasirire** (☎5202-4150; www.cascadasdetatasirire.com; entry fee Q70, campsite per person Q70, r per person Q130; ☺8am-5pm), a lovely private nature reserve with waterfalls and walking trails just out of town. You can camp out here or stay in an extremely rustic 'eco-lodge'.

Buses leave regularly from Jalapa's central bus terminal for Chiquimula (Q23, 1½ hours) and Guatemala City (Q30/25 pullman/2nd class). For Esquipulas, change in Chiquimula.

DEM BONES

Most of the people you hear about who are digging stuff up in Guatemala these days are archaeologists. Or mining companies. But there's another group out there, sifting patiently through the soil in search of treasure – paleontologists.

While it's unclear whether dinosaurs ever inhabited what is now Guatemala, evidence shows that large prehistoric mammals – such as giant armadillos, 3m-tall sloths, mammoths and saber-toothed tigers certainly did. As they migrated southwards from North America they found they could not go much further than present-day Guatemala – back then the landmass stopped at northern Nicaragua, and 10 million years would pass before South and Central America joined, creating the American continents more or less as they are today.

Various theories seek to explain the disappearance of the dinosaurs and other large prehistoric mammals – the most widely accepted one being that a massive meteorite slammed into the Yucatán Peninsula, 66 million years ago, causing global climate change.

The great bulk of the fossil and bone evidence uncovered in Guatemala has been in the country's southeast corner, but giant sloth and mastodon remains have been found in what is now Guatemala City. Paleontologist Roberto Woolfolk Sarvia, founder of the **Museo de Paleontología, Arqueología y Geología** (Roberto Woolfolk Saravia Archeology & Paleontology Museum; Hwy 10, Estanzuela; ⊗8am-5pm Mon-Fri) **FREE**, claims to have collected more than 5000 fragments and skeletons, and he says there's a lot more out there, just that (you guessed it) the funding isn't available to dig it up.

If you have even a passing interest in prehistoric life, the museum makes for a worthy detour – it's been remodeled recently, and on display are remains of mastodons, giant sloths and armadillos, a prehistoric horse measuring 20in, and two molar teeth from a mammoth.

Charli's INTERNATIONAL $$
(7a Av 5-55; mains Q50-100; ⊗8am-9pm) Chiquimula's 'fine dining' option (tablecloths!) has a wide menu, featuring pasta, pizza, seafood and steaks, all served up amid chilly air-con, with relaxed and friendly service.

Parillada de Calero STEAKHOUSE $$
(7a Av 4-83; breakfast from Q30, mains Q50-100; ⊗8am-10pm) An open-air steakhouse, serving the juiciest flame-grilled cuts in town. This is also the breakfast hot spot – the Tropical Breakfast (pancakes with a mound of fresh fruit) goes down well in this climate.

ℹ Orientation & Information

Though it's very hot, Chiquimula is easy to get around on foot.

Banco G&T (7a Av 4-75, Zona 1; ⊗9am-8pm Mon-Fri, 10am-2pm Sat) Half a block south of the plaza. Changes US dollars and traveler's checks, and gives cash advances on Visa and MasterCard.

Post Office (10a Av) Between 1a and 2a Calles.

Telgua (3a Calle) Plenty of card phones; a few doors downhill from Parque Ismael Cerna.

ℹ Getting There & Away

Several companies operate buses and microbuses, arriving and departing from the bus station area on 11a Av, between 1a and 2a Calles. **Litegua** (☑7942-2064; 1a Calle, btwn Avs 10a & 11a), which operates buses to El Florido (the border crossing on the way to Copán) has its own bus station a half block north. For the Honduran border-crossing at Agua Caliente take a minibus to Esquipulas and change there. If you're headed to Jalapa, you'll need to go to Ipala to make the connection. For Río Dulce, take a Flores bus, or a Puerto Barrios bus to La Ruidosa junction and change there. If you're going to Esquipulas, sit on the left for the best views of the basilica housing the shrine of El Cristo Negro.

BUSES FROM CHIQUIMULA

Anguiatú, El Salvador border (Q15, one hour, leaves when full from 5am to 5:30pm)

El Florido, Honduras border (Q25, 1½ hours, leaves when full from 5:30am to 4:30pm)

Esquipulas (Q20, 45 minutes, every 20 minutes from 5am to 9pm)

Flores (Q100, seven to eight hours, two daily)

Guatemala City (Q40, three hours, every half hour from 3am to 3.30pm)

Ipala (Q6, 1½ hours, hourly from 5am to 7pm)

Puerto Barrios (Q45, 4½ hours, every 30 minutes from 3:30am to 4pm)

Quiriguá (Q30, two hours, every 30 minutes from 3:30am to 4pm)

Río Hondo (Q15, 35 minutes, every 15 minutes from 5am to 6pm)

Volcán de Ipala

The 1650m volcano, **Volcán de Ipala** (admission Q10), is notable for its especially beautiful clear crater-lake measuring nearly 1km around and nestled below the summit at 1493m. The dramatic hike to the top takes you from 800m to 1650m in about two hours, though you can drive halfway up in a car. There are trails, a visitor center and a campsite on the shores of the lake. To get there, take a bus from Chiquimula (1½ hours) or Jalapa (two hours) to Ipala and transfer to a microbus to Agua Blanca (Q6, every 15 minutes). The trailhead is at El Sauce just before Agua Blanca; look for the blue Inguat sign. You might luck on to a pickup to Aldea Chigüiton, where the road ends, 2km from the highway running south from Ipala. You may also be able to rent a horse in Chigüiton.

Of the very limited accommodation options in downtown Ipala, the **Hotel Peña** (☑7942-8064; 2a Calle 2-26, Ipala; s/d Q50/80; ℙ) is about the best, although it may be worth the 10-minute walk to the **Hotel Dorado** (☑7942-8334; Barrio El Rostro, Ipala; s/d with fan Q100/120, r with air-con Q150; ℙ❄), which offers new, vaguely modern rooms out on the highway to Agua Blanca. There are banks with ATM and *comedores* around the plaza. **Restaurante El Original** (2 Av 'A' 1-20, Ipala; mains Q40; ⊙11:30am-9pm Mon-Sat) is a down-home steakhouse which does a good flame-grilled chicken. Buses pull up a block away from Ipala's plaza, from where everything listed here is an easy walk.

Volcán de Quetzaltepeque

About 10km east of the village of Quetzaltepeque, this volcano tops out at 1900m. The walk to the top is tough going, through thick subtropical pine forest, and the trail disappears in sections, but if you have a car you can drive almost all the away to the top. From the summit are excellent views of the nearby Ipala and Suchítan volcanoes and the surrounding countryside. Due to the condition of the trail and some security concerns, you really need a guide to undertake this trek. Ask in the Quetzaltepeque **municipalidad** (Town Hall; ☑7944-0258; ⊙8am-4pm Mon-Sat) on the main plaza to be put in touch with a local guide. You can stay in Quetzaltepeque in the basic but functional **Hotel El Gringo** (☑7944-0186; 3a Av 2-25, Zona 2; r per person Q50), but you're probably better off in Esquipulas or Chiquimula.

Buses running between Chiquimula and Esquipulas pass through Quetzaltepeque.

Esquipulas

POP 27,400

From Chiquimula, Hwy 10 goes south into the mountains, where it's a bit cooler. After an hour's ride through pretty country, the highway descends into a valley ringed by mountains, where Esquipulas stands. Halfway down the slope, about 1km from the center of town, there is a *mirador* (lookout) from which to get a good view. The reason for a trip to Esquipulas is evident as soon as you catch sight of the place, dominated by the great Basílica de Esquipulas towering above the town, its whiteness shimmering in the sun. The view has changed little in over 150 years since explorer John L Stephens saw it and described it in his book *Incidents of Travel in Central America, Chiapas and Yucatan* (1841):

> Descending, the clouds were lifted, and I looked down upon an almost boundless plain, running from the foot of the Sierra, and afar off saw, standing alone in the wilderness, the great church of Esquipulas, like the Church of the Holy Sepulchre in Jerusalem, and the Caaba in Mecca, the holiest of temples... I had a long and magnificent descent to the foot of the Sierra.

History

This town may have been a place of pilgrimage before the Spanish conquest. Legend has it that the town takes its name from a noble Maya lord who ruled this region when the Spanish arrived, and who received them in peace.

With the arrival of the friars a church was built here, and in 1595 an image that came to be known as the Cristo Negro (Black Christ) was installed behind the altar. In response to the steady increase in pilgrims to Esquipulas, a huge new church was inaugurated in 1758, and the pilgrimage trade has been the town's livelihood ever since.

◉ Sights & Activities

Basílica de Esquipulas   BASILICA
(11a Calle) A massive pile of stone that has resisted the power of earthquakes for almost 250 years, the basilica is approached through a pretty park and up a wide flight of steps. The impressive facade and towers are floodlit at night.

Inside, the devout approach the surprisingly small El Cristo Negro (Black Christ) with extreme reverence, many on their knees. Incense, murmured prayers and the scuffle of sandaled feet fill the air. When there are throngs of pilgrims, you must enter the church from the side to get a close view of the famous shrine. Shuffling along quickly, you may get a good glimpse or two before being shoved onward by the crowd behind you. On Sundays, religious holidays and (especially) during the festival, the press of devotees is intense. On weekdays, you may have the place to yourself, which can be very powerful and rewarding. On weekends, you may feel very removed from the intensity of emotion shown by the majority of pilgrims, whose faith is very deep.

The annual **Cristo de Esquipulas festival** (January 15) sees mobs of devout pilgrims coming from all over the region to worship at the altar of El Cristo Negro.

Cruising the religious kitsch sold by the throngs of vendors around the basilica is an entertaining diversion. When you leave the church and descend the steps through the park and exit right to the market, notice the vendors selling straw hats that are decorated with artificial flowers and stitched with the name 'Esquipulas' – perfect for pilgrims who want everyone to know they've made the trip. These are very popular rearview mirror novelties for chicken-bus drivers countrywide.

Centro Turístico Cueva de las Minas CAVE
(admission Q15; ⊙ 8am-4pm) This has a 50m-deep cave (bring your own light), grassy picnic areas and the Río El Milagro, where people come for a dip and say it's miraculous. The cave and river are half a kilometer from the entrance, which is behind the basilica's cemetery, 300m south of the turnoff into town on the road to Honduras. Refreshments are available.

Parque Chatún   AMUSEMENT PARK
(✏ 7873-0909; www.parquechatun.com; adult/child from Q65/55 incl lunch; ⊙ 9am-6pm Tue-Sat) If you've got kids along (or even if you don't), this fun park 3km out of town should provide some light relief from all the religious business. There are swimming pools, a

---

EL CRISTO NEGRO

Attracting more than a million pilgrims from Mexico, Central America, the US and further afield every year, the Black Christ of Esquipulas is one of Guatemala's top tourist draws.

Myths surround the sculpture's color. It was long believed that the Spaniards who commissioned it in 1594 requested a Christ with a skin tone resembling Esquipulas' Ch'ortí natives, so that they would be easier to convert. Studies have shown, though, that it is made from a light wood, possibly cedar. Some believers say it turned black mysteriously overnight – others say that it happened as a result of human contact and the amount of incense burnt in the church over the centuries.

The Black Christ first gained widespread attention when the Archbishop of Guatemala recovered miraculously from a chronic illness after visiting Esquipulas in 1737, and the town got a healthy publicity kick when Pope John Paul II visited in 1996.

But the statue's popularity has also been explained by the syncretism of pre-Christian and Christian beliefs. All throughout the Americas, when the Spanish arrived, indigenous peoples soon discovered it was less painful to appear to accept the new religion, basically retaining their traditional beliefs and renaming the old gods accordingly. In Maya culture, black was the color of warriors, and associated with magic, death, violence and sacrifice. Accordingly, the Cristo Negro can be seen as a warrior Christ, defeater of death.

There are two authorized copies of Esquipulas' Cristo Negro in the United States. One in New York has come to represent the sufferings and hardships experienced by the Latino community there, while the one in Los Angeles (which was smuggled into the country, allegedly aided by bribed officials) has taken on a special significance for undocumented immigrants.

climbing wall, campgrounds, a petting zoo, a canopy tour and a mini bungee jump. Entry includes the use of all these except the canopy tour

If you don't have a vehicle, look for the minibus doing rounds of the town, or get your hotel to call it – it will take you out there for Q5.

Sleeping

Esquipulas has an abundance of places to stay. On holidays and during the annual festival, every hotel in town is filled, whatever the price; weekends are super-busy as well, with prices substantially higher. The rates given below are weekend prices. On weekdays (excluding the festival period), there are *descuentos* (discounts). For cheap rooms, look in the streets immediately north of the towering basilica.

Hotel Monte Cristo HOTEL $$
(7943-1453; 3a Av 9-12, Zona 1; s/d Q180/250, without bathroom Q80/100; P) Good-sized rooms with a bit of furniture and super-hot showers. A policy of not letting the upstairs rooms until the downstairs ones are full might see you on the ground floor.

Hotel La Favorita HOTEL $$
(7943-1175; 2a Av 10-15, Zona 1; r Q200, s/d without bathroom Q60/100; P) The real budget-watcher's choice, the rooms with shared bathroom here are a bit grim, but those with bathrooms are good enough.

Hotel Portal de la Fe HOTEL $$
(7943-4261; 11 Calle 1-70, Zona 1; s/d Q250/450; P ✴ @ 🛜 🛋) One of the few hotels with any real style in town. Subterranean rooms are predictably gloomy, but upstairs the situation improves considerably.

Hotel Mahanaim HOTEL $$
(7943-1131; 10a Calle 1-85, Zona 1; r Q350; P ✴ @ 🛜 🛋) This establishment is on three levels around a covered courtyard. Rooms are comfortable but plain. It wouldn't be such a good deal if it weren't for the big covered swimming pool out back.

Hotel Legendario HOTEL $$$
(7943-1824; www.hotellegendario.com; cnr 3a Av & 9a Calle, Zona 1; r Q850; P ✴ @ 🛜 🛋) The fanciest hotel downtown goes all out on the services, right down to a separate kids' swimming pool. Rooms are reasonable – big enough, with new beds, large windows

opening onto a grassy courtyard, and all the comforts you'd expect for the price.

Eating

Restaurant El Angel CHINESE $$
(7943-1372; cnr 11a Calle & 2a Av; mains Q45-60; ⊙11am-10:30pm) This main-street Chinese eatery does all the standard dishes, plus steaks and a good range of *licuados* (milkshakes). Home delivery is available.

Restaurante Calle Real GUATEMALAN $
(3a Av; mains Q30-60; ⊙8am-10pm) Typical of many restaurants here, this big eating-barn turns out cheap meals for the pilgrims. It has a wide menu, strip lighting and loud TV.

City Grill STEAKHOUSE $$
(cnr 2a Av & 10a Calle, Zona 1; mains Q40-120; ⊙8am-10pm) The best steakhouse in town (featuring some of the best steaks for miles around) also serves up some decent seafood and pasta dishes. The pizza is worth a look-in, too.

La Rotonda FAST FOOD $$
(11a Calle; mains Q50-100; ⊙8am-10pm) Opposite Rutas Orientales bus station, this is a round building with chairs arranged around a circular open-air counter under a big awning. It's a welcoming place – clean and fresh. There are plenty of selections to choose from, including pizza, pasta, and burgers.

ℹ Information

Post Office (6a Av 2-15) About 10 blocks north of the center.
Telgua (cnr 5a Av & 9a Calle) Plenty of card phones.

ℹ Getting There & Away

Buses to Guatemala City (Q50, four hours) arrive and depart hourly from 1:30am to 4:30pm from the **Rutas Orientales bus station** (7943-1366; cnr 11a Calle & 1a Av), near the entrance to town.

Minibuses to Agua Caliente (Honduran border; Q20, 30 minutes) arrive and depart across the street, leaving every half hour from 5am to 5pm; taxis also wait here, charging the same as minibuses, once they have five passengers.

Minibuses to Chiquimula (Q15, 45 minutes, every 15 minutes) depart from the east end of 11a Calle.

Transportes Guerra (cnr 5a Av & 10a Calle) goes to Anguiatú (El Salvador border; Q15, one hour, every 30 minutes).

GETTING TO EL SALVADOR

Between Chiquimula and Esquipulas (35km from Chiquimula and 14km from Esquipulas), Padre Miguel junction is the turnoff for Anguiatú, at the border with El Salvador, which is 19km (30 minutes) away. Minibuses pass by frequently, coming from Chiquimula, Quetzaltepeque and Esquipulas.

The border at Anguiatú is open 24 hours, but you're best crossing during daylight. Plenty of trucks cross here. Across the border there are hourly buses to the capital, San Salvador, passing through Metapán and Santa Ana.

There are three buses daily for Flores/Santa Elena (Q110, eight hours) from the **Transportes María Elena** (📞 7943-0957; 11 Calle 0-54, Zona 1) office. They pass Quiriguá (Q45, two hours), Río Dulce (Q60, four hours) and Poptún (Q90, six hours).

Quiriguá

POP 4800

From Copán it's only some 50km to Quiriguá as the crow flies, but the lay of the land, the international border and the condition of the roads make it a journey of 175km. Quiriguá is famed for its intricately carved stelae – the gigantic brown sandstone monoliths that rise as high as 10.5m, like ancient sentinels, in a quiet well-kept tropical park.

From Río Hondo junction it's 67km along Hwy 9 to the village of Los Amates, where there are a couple of hotels, a restaurant, food stalls, a bank and a small bus station. The village of Quiriguá is 1.5km east of Los Amates, and the turnoff to the ruins is another 1.5km to the east. The 3.4km access road leads south through banana groves. The most reliable accommodation in Quiriguá town is **Hotel y Restaurante Royal** (📞 7947-3639; s/d Q100/150; 🅿), which has simple clean rooms and serves OK food.

History

Quiriguá's history parallels that of Copán, of which it was a dependency during much of the Classic period. Of the three sites in this area, only the present archaeological park is of interest.

Quiriguá's location lent itself to the carving of giant stelae. Beds of brown sandstone in the nearby Río Motagua had cleavage planes suitable for cutting large pieces. Though soft when first cut, the sandstone dried hard in the air. With Copán's expert artisans nearby for guidance, Quiriguá's stone carvers were ready for greatness. All they needed was a great leader to inspire them – and to pay for the carving of the huge stelae.

That leader was K'ak' Tiliw Chan Yo'at (Cauac Sky; r 725–84), who decided that Quiriguá should no longer be under the control of Copán. In a war with his former suzerain, Cauac Sky took Uaxaclahun Ubak K'awil (King 18 Rabbit) of Copán prisoner in 737 and later had him beheaded. Independent at last, Cauac Sky commissioned his stonecutters to go to work, and for the next 38 years they turned out giant stelae and zoomorphs dedicated to his glory.

Cauac Sky's son Sky Xul (r 784–800) lost his throne to an usurper, Jade Sky. This last great king of Quiriguá continued the building boom initiated by Cauac Sky, reconstructing Quiriguá's Acrópolis on a grander scale.

Quiriguá remained unknown to Europeans until the explorer and diplomat John L Stephens arrived in 1840. Impressed by its great monuments, Stephens lamented the world's lack of interest in them in his book *Incidents of Travel in Central America, Chiapas and Yucatan* (1841):

Of one thing there is no doubt: a large city once stood there; its name is lost, its history unknown; and...no account of its existence has ever before been published. For centuries it has lain as completely buried as if covered with the lava of Vesuvius. Every traveler from Yzabal to Guatemala has passed within three hours of it; we ourselves had done the same; and yet there it lay, like the rock-built city of Edom, unvisited, unsought, and utterly unknown.

Stephens tried to buy the ruined city in order to have its stelae shipped to New York, but the owner, Señor Payes, assumed that Stephens (being a diplomat), was negotiating on behalf of the US government and that the government would pay. Payes quoted an extravagant price, and the deal was never made.

Between 1881 and 1894, excavations were carried out by Alfred P Maudslay. In the early 1900s all the land around Quiriguá was sold to the US-based United Fruit Company and turned into banana groves. The company is gone, but the bananas and Quiriguá remain. Restoration of the site was carried out by the University of Pennsylvania in the 1930s. In 1981 Unesco declared the ruins a World Heritage Site, one of only three in Guatemala (the others are Tikal and Antigua).

⊙ Sights

The beautiful parklike **archaeological site** (admission Q80; ⊙8am-4:30pm) has a small *tienda* near the entrance selling cold drinks and snacks, but you'll be better off bringing your own picnic. A small **museum** just past the entrance has a few information displays and a model of how the site (much of it unexcavated) would have looked in its heyday.

Despite the sticky heat and (sometimes) bothersome mosquitoes, Quiriguá is a wonderful place. The giant stelae on the **Gran Plaza** (Great Plaza) are all much more worn than those at Copán. To impede further deterioration, each has been covered

Quiriguá ⊙

Banana Grove
Carretera al Atlántico (Hwy 9) (3.4km)
Ticket Office & Snack Stand
Museum & Toilets
P
Stela A
Zoomorph B — Stela C
Stela D
Stela F
Stela E
Zoomorph G
Stela H
Gran Plaza
Altar L
Stela I
Altar M
Stela K
Zoomorph N
Stela J
Juego de Pelota
Grupo Oriental
Acrópolis
Zoomorph P
Zoomorph O
Trail
Grupo Sur

0 — 200 m
0 — 0.1 miles

by a thatched roof. The roofs cast shadows that make it difficult to examine the carving closely and almost impossible to get a good photograph, but somehow this does little to inhibit one's sense of awe.

Seven of the stelae, designated A, C, D, E, F, H and J, were built during the reign of Cauac Sky and carved with his image. **Stela E** is the largest Maya stela known, standing some 8m above ground, with another 3m or so buried in the earth. It weighs almost 60,000kg. Note the exuberant, elaborate headdresses; the beards on some of the figures (an oddity in Maya art and life); the staffs of office held in the kings' hands; and the glyphs on the sides of the stela.

At the far end of the plaza is the **Acrópolis**, far less impressive than the one at Copán. At its base are several **zoomorphs**, blocks of stone carved to resemble real and mythic creatures. Frogs, tortoises, jaguars and serpents were favorite subjects. The low zoomorphs can't compete with the towering stelae in impressiveness, but as works of art, imagination and mythic significance, the zoomorphs are superb.

❶ Getting There & Around

Buses running Guatemala City–Puerto Barrios, Guatemala City–Flores, Esquipulas–Flores or Chiquimula–Flores will drop you off or pick you up here. If you're heading for the hotel, make sure you get dropped at the *pasarela de Quiriguá* (the pedestrian overpass). They'll also drop you at the turnoff to the archaeological site if you ask.

From the highway it's 3.4km to the archaeological site – Q10 by *tuk-tuk* (three-wheeled motor taxi), but if one doesn't come, don't fret: it's a pleasant walk (without luggage) through banana plantations to get there.

If you're staying in the village of Quiriguá or Los Amates and walking to the archaeological site, you can take a shortcut along the railway branch line that goes from the village through the banana fields, crossing the access road very near the entrance to the archaeological site. A *tuk-tuk* from Quiriguá village to the site should cost around Q15.

Out on the main highway buses pass frequently for Río Dulce (Q25, two hours), Chiquimula (Q25, two hours) and Puerto Barrios.

COPÁN (HONDURAS)

Just over the border in Honduras is the ancient city of Copán, one of the most outstanding Maya achievements, ranking in splendor with Guatemala's Tikal, and

CROSSING THE BORDER

The Guatemalan village of El Florido, which has no services beyond a few soft drink stands, is 1.2km west of the border. At the border crossing is a branch of Banrural, the Litegua bus office and one or two snack stands. The border crossing is open 24 hours, but (as always) it's best to cross in daylight hours.

Mexico's Chichén Itzá and Uxmal. To fully appreciate Maya art and culture, you must visit Copán. This can be done on a long day-trip by private car, public bus, or organized tour from Antigua, but it's better to take at least two days, staying the night in the sweet little town of Copán Ruinas. There are two Copáns: the town and the ruins. The town is located about 12km east of the Guatemala-Honduras border. Confusingly, the town is named Copán Ruinas, though the actual ruins are just over 1km further east.

Copán Site

Get to the **site** (admission L300; ⊘ 8am-4pm) around opening time to avoid the heat and the crowds. Minivans coming from the border may take you on to the ruins after a stop in the town. If not, the *sendero peatonal* (footpath) alongside the road makes for a pretty 20-minute walk, passing several stelae and unexcavated mounds along the way to the Copán ruins and Las Sepulturas archaeological site, a couple of kilometers further.

History

Pre-Columbian

People have been living in the Copán Valley since at least 1200 BC; ceramic evidence has been found from around that date. Copán must have had significant commercial activity since early times, as graves showing marked Olmec influence have been dated to around 900 to 600 BC.

In the 5th century AD one royal family came to rule Copán, led by a mysterious king named Mah K'ina Yax K'uk' Mo' (Great Sun Lord Quetzal Macaw), who ruled from AD 426 to 435. Archaeological evidence indicates that he was a great shaman, and later kings revered him as the semidivine founder

of the city. The dynasty ruled throughout Copán's florescence during the Classic period (AD 250–900).

Of the subsequent kings who ruled before AD 628 we know little. Only some of their names have been deciphered: Mat Head, the second king (no relation to Bed Head); Cu Ix, the fourth king; Waterlily Jaguar, the seventh; Moon Jaguar, the 10th; and Butz' Chan, the 11th.

Among the greatest of Copán's kings was Smoke Imix (Smoke Jaguar; r 628–695), the 12th king. Smoke Imix built Copán into a major military and commercial power in the region. He may have taken over the nearby princedom of Quiriguá, as one of the famous stelae at that site bears his name and image. By the time he died in 695, Copán's population had grown substantially.

Smoke Imix was succeeded by Uaxaclahun Ubak K'awil (18 Rabbit; r 695–738), the 13th king, who willingly took the reins of power and pursued further military conquest. In a war with King Cauac Sky, his neighbor from Quiriguá, 18 Rabbit was captured and beheaded. He was succeeded by K'ak' Joplaj Chan K'awiil (Smoke Monkey; r 738–49), the 14th king, whose short reign left little mark on Copán. Smoke Monkey's son, K'ak' Yipyaj Chan K'awiil (Smoke Shell; r 749–63), was, however, one of Copán's greatest builders. He commissioned the city's most famous and important monument, the great Escalinata de los Jeroglíficos (Hieroglyphic Stairway), which immortalizes the achievements of the dynasty from its establishment until 755, when the stairway was dedicated. It is the longest inscription ever discovered in the Maya lands.

Yax Pasaj Chan Yopaat (Sunrise or First Dawn; r 763–820; also known as Yax Pac, Yax Pasaj Chan Yoaat and Yax Pasah), Smoke Shell's successor and the 16th king, continued the beautification of Copán. The final occupant of the throne, U Cit Tok', became ruler in 822, but it is not known when he died.

Until recently, the collapse of the civilization at Copán had been a mystery. Now, archaeologists have begun to surmise that near the end of Copán's heyday the population grew at an unprecedented rate, straining agricultural resources. In the end, Copán was no longer agriculturally self-sufficient and had to import food from other areas. The urban core expanded into the fertile lowlands in the center of the valley, forcing both agricultural and residential areas to spread onto the steep slopes surrounding the valley. Wide areas were deforested, resulting in massive erosion that further decimated food production and brought flooding during rainy seasons. Interestingly, this environmental damage of old is not too different from what is happening today – a disturbing trend, but one that meshes with the Maya belief that life is cyclical and history repeats itself. Skeletal remains of people who died during Copán's final years show marked evidence of malnutrition and infectious diseases, as well as decreased life spans.

The Copán Valley was not abandoned overnight – agriculturists probably continued to live in the ecologically devastated valley for maybe another one or two hundred years. But by the year 1200 or thereabouts even the farmers had departed, and the royal city of Copán was reclaimed by the jungle.

European Discovery

The first known European to see the ruins was a representative of Spanish King Felipe II, Diego García de Palacios, who lived in Guatemala and traveled through the region. On March 8, 1576, he wrote to the king about the ruins he found here. Only about five families were living here at the time, and they knew nothing of the history of the ruins. The discovery was not pursued, and almost three centuries went by until another Spaniard, Colonel Juan Galindo, visited the ruins and made the first map of them.

It was Galindo's report that stimulated John L Stephens and Frederick Catherwood to come to Copán on their Central American journey in 1839. When Stephens published the book *Incidents of Travel in Central America, Chiapas and Yucatán* in 1841, illustrated by Catherwood, the ruins first became known to the world at large.

Copán Today

The history of Copán continues to unfold today. The remains of 3450 structures have been found in the 27 sq km surrounding the Grupo Principal (Principal Group), most of them within about half a kilometer of it. In a wider zone, 4509 structures have been detected in 1420 sites within 135 sq km of the ruins. These discoveries indicate that at the peak of civilization here, around the end of the 8th century AD, the valley of Copán had more than 27,500 inhabitants, a population figure not reached again until the 1980s.

In addition to examining the area surrounding the Grupo Principal, archaeologists continue to make new discoveries in the Grupo Principal itself. Five separate phases of building on this site have been identified; the final phase, dating from AD 650 to 820, is what we see today. But buried underneath the visible ruins are layers of other ruins, which archaeologists are exploring by means of underground tunnels. This is how they found the Templo Rosalila (Rosalila Temple), a replica of which is now in the Museo de Escultura. Below Rosalila is yet another, earlier temple, Margarita, and below that, Hunal, which contains the tomb of the founder of the dynasty, Yax K'uk' Mo' (Great Sun Lord Quetzal Macaw). Two of the excavation tunnels, including Rosalila, are open to the public.

Copán Area

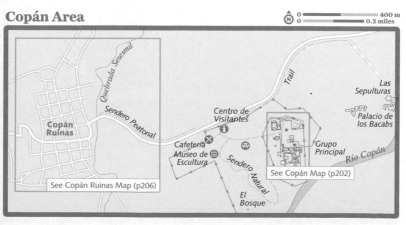

Copán

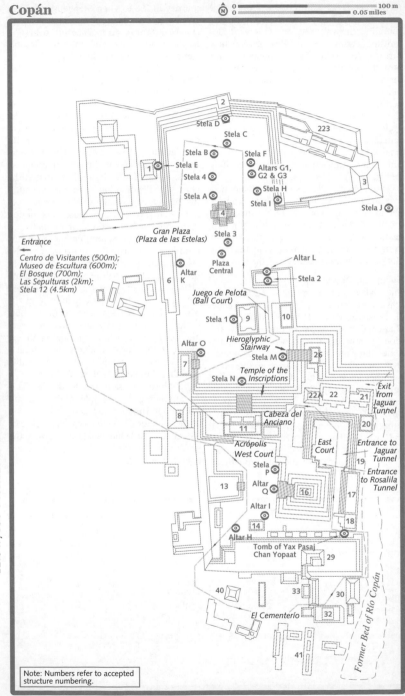

N 0 — 100 m
0 — 0.05 miles

2

Stela D

Stela C

223

Stela B

Stela F

Stela E

1

Altars G1, G2 & G3

Stela 4

Stela H

Stela A

3

Stela I

Stela J

4

Gran Plaza
(Plaza de las Estelas)

Stela 3

Entrance

Centro de Visitantes (500m);
Museo de Escultura (600m);
El Bosque (700m);
Las Sepulturas (2km);
Stela 12 (4.5km)

Plaza
Central

Altar L

Altar
K

6

Stela 2

Juego de Pelota
(Ball Court)

Stela 1

9

10

Altar O

Hieroglyphic
Stairway

Stela M

26

7

Temple of the
Inscriptions

Stela N

Exit
from
Jaguar
Tunnel

22A   22   21

Cabeza del
Anciano

20

8

11

East
Court

Entrance to
Jaguar
Tunnel

Acrópolis
West Court

19

Entrance
to Rosalila
Tunnel

Stela
P

Altar
Q

16

17

13

Altar I

14

18

Altar H

Tomb of Yax Pasaj
Chan Yopaat

29

40

33

30

El Cementerio

32

Former Bed of Río Copán

41

Note: Numbers refer to accepted
structure numbering.

⊙ Sights

⊙ Grupo Principal

The Principal Group of ruins is about 400m beyond the visitor center across well-kept lawns, through a gate in a fence and down shady avenues of trees. A group of resident macaws loiter along here. The ruins themselves have been numbered for easy identification and a well-worn path circumscribes the site.

⊙ Stelae of the Gran Plaza

The path leads to the **Gran Plaza** (Great Plaza; Plaza de las Estelas) and the huge, intricately carved stelae portraying the rulers of Copán. Most of Copán's best stelae date from AD 613 to 738. All seem to have originally been painted; a few traces of red paint survive on Stela C. Many stelae had vaults beneath or beside them in which sacrifices and offerings could be placed.

Many of the stelae on the Gran Plaza portray King 18 Rabbit, including stelae A, B, C, D, F, H and 4. Perhaps the most beautiful stela in the Gran Plaza is Stela A (AD 731); the original has been moved inside the Museo de Escultura, and the one outdoors is a reproduction. Nearby and almost equal in beauty are Stela 4 (731); Stela B (731), depicting 18 Rabbit upon his accession to the throne; and Stela C (782), with a turtle-shaped altar in front. This last stela has figures on both sides. Stela E (614), erected on top of Estructura 1 (Structure 1) on the west side of the Great Plaza, is among the oldest.

At the northern end of the Gran Plaza at the base of Estructura 2, Stela D (736) also portrays King 18 Rabbit. On its back are two columns of hieroglyphs; at its base is an altar with fearsome representations of Chac, the rain god. In front of the altar is the burial place of Dr John Owen, an archaeologist with an expedition from Harvard's Peabody Museum who died during excavation work in 1893.

On the east side of the plaza is Stela F (721), which has a more lyrical design than other stelae here, with the robes of the main figure flowing around to the other side of the stone, where there are glyphs. Altar G (800), showing twin serpent heads, is among the last monuments carved at Copán. Stela H (730) may depict a queen or princess rather than a king. Stela I (692), on the structure that runs along the east side of the plaza, is of a person wearing a mask. Stela J, further off to the east, resembles the stelae of Quiriguá in that it is covered in glyphs, not human figures.

⊙ Juego de Pelota

South of the Great Plaza, across what is known as the Plaza Central, is the Juego de Pelota (Ball Court; 731), the second largest in Central America. The one you see is the third one on this site; the two smaller courts were buried by this construction. Note the macaw heads carved atop the sloping walls. The central marker in the court is the work of King 18 Rabbit.

⊙ Escalinata de los Jeroglíficos

South of the ball court is Copán's most famous monument, the *Escalinata de los Jeroglíficos* (Hieroglyphic Stairway; 743), the work of King Smoke Shell. Today it's protected from the elements by a canvas roof. The flight of 63 steps bears a history (in several thousand glyphs) of the royal house of Copán; the steps are bordered by ramps inscribed with more reliefs and glyphs. The story told on the inscribed steps is still not completely understood because the stairway was partially ruined and the stones jumbled, but archaeologists are using 3D scanning technology to make a digital version of the original, with the hope of one day reading it in its entirety.

At the base of the Hieroglyphic Stairway is Stela M (756), bearing a figure (probably King Smoke Shell) dressed in a feathered cloak; glyphs tell of the solar eclipse in that year. The altar in front shows a plumed serpent with a human head emerging from its jaws.

Beside the stairway, a tunnel leads to the tomb of a nobleman, a royal scribe who may have been the son of King Smoke Imix. The tomb, discovered in June 1989, held a treasure-trove of painted pottery and beautiful carved jade objects that are now in Honduran museums.

⊙ Acrópolis

The lofty flight of steps to the south of the Hieroglyphic Stairway mounts the **Templo de las Inscripciones** (Temple of the Inscriptions). On top of the stairway, the walls are carved with groups of hieroglyphs. On the south side of the Temple of the Inscriptions is the **Patio Occidental** (West Court), with the **Patio Oriental** (East Court), also called the Patio de los Jaguares (Court of the Jaguars) to its east. In the West Court, check out Altar Q (776), among the most famous sculptures here; the original is inside the Museo de Escultura. Around its sides, carved in superb relief, are the 16 great kings of Copán, ending with its creator, Yax Pasaj Chan Yopaat. Behind the altar is a sacrificial vault in which archaeologists discovered the bones of 15 jaguars and several macaws that were probably sacrificed to the glory of Yax Pasaj Chan Yopaat and his ancestors.

This group of temples, known as the Acrópolis, was the spiritual and political core of the site – reserved for royalty and nobles, a place where ceremonies were enacted and kings buried.

The East Court also contains evidence of Yax Pasaj Chan Yopaat – his **tomb**, beneath Estructura 18. Unfortunately, the tomb was discovered and looted long before archaeologists arrived. Both the East and West Courts hold a variety of fascinating stelae and sculptured heads of humans and animals. To see the most elaborate relief carving, climb Estructura 22 on the northern side of the East Court. This was the **Templo de Meditación** (Temple of Meditation) and has been heavily restored over recent years.

Túnel Rosalila & Túnel de los Jaguares

In 1999, archaeologists opened up to **Túnel Rosalila & Túnel de los Jaguares** (admission L300), which allows visitors to get a glimpse of pre-existing structures below the visible surface structures. The first, Rosalila, is very short and takes only a few visitors at a time. The famous temple is only barely exposed, and behind thick glass. The other tunnel, Los Jaguares, was originally 700m in length, but a large section has been closed, reducing it to about 80m, running along the foundations of Temple 22. This tunnel exits on the outside of the main site, so you must walk around the base and rear of the main site to get back in again. While fascinating, it's hard to justify the extra you pay to get in.

Museo de Escultura

While Tikal is celebrated for its tall temple pyramids and Palenque is renowned for its limestone relief panels, Copán is unique in the Maya world for its sculpture. Some of the finest examples are on display at this impressive **museum** (Museum of Sculpture; admission L140), opened in August 1996. Entering the museum is an experience by itself: You go through the mouth of a serpent and wind through the entrails of the beast before suddenly emerging into a fantastic world of sculpture and light.

The highlight of the museum is a full-scale replica of the Rosalila Temple, which was discovered in nearly perfect condition by archaeologists in 1989 by means of a tunnel dug into Structure 16, the central building of the Acropolis. Rosalila, dedicated in AD 571 by Copán's 10th ruler, Moon Jaguar, was apparently so sacred that when Structure 16 was built over it, Rosalila was not destroyed but was left completely intact. The original Rosalila temple is inside the core of Structure 16.

El Bosque & Las Sepulturas

Excavations at El Bosque and Las Sepulturas have shed light on the daily life of the Maya in Copán during its golden age.

Las Sepulturas, once connected to the Gran Plaza by a causeway, may have been the residential area where rich and powerful nobles lived. One huge, luxurious residential compound seems to have housed some 250 people in 40 or 50 buildings arranged around 11 courtyards. The principal structure, called the **Palacio de los Bacabs** (Palace of the Officials), had outer walls carved with the full-sized figures of 10 males in fancy feathered headdresses; inside was a huge hieroglyphic bench.

To get to Las Sepulturas you have to go back to the main road, turn right, then right again at the sign (2km from the Gran Plaza).

The walk to get to El Bosque is the real reason for visiting it, as it's removed from the main ruins. It's a one-hour (5km) walk on a well-maintained path through foliage dense with birds, though there isn't much of note at the site itself save for a small ball court. Still, it's a powerful experience to have an hour-long walk on the thoroughfares of an ancient Maya city all to yourself. To get to El Bosque, go right at the hut where your ticket is stamped. There have been no reports of crimes against tourists here.

Information

Admission to Copán includes entry to Las Sepulturas archaeological site but not to Túnel Rosalila and Túnel de los Jaguares or Museo de Escultura.

The Centro de Visitantes (visitor center) at the entrance to the ruins houses the ticket office and a small exhibition about the site and its excavation. Nearby are a cafeteria, and souvenir and handicrafts shops. There's a picnic area along the path to the Principal Group of ruins. A **Sendero Natural** (Nature Trail) entering the forest several hundred meters from the visitor center passes by a small ball court.

Pick up a copy of the booklet *History Carved in Stone: A Guide to the Archaeological Park of the Ruins of Copán* by noted archaeologists William L Fash and Ricardo Agurcia Fasquelle; it's available at the visitors center for L100. It will help you to understand and appreciate the ruins. It's also a good idea to go with a guide, who can help to explain the ruins and bring them to life. Guides work for the cooperative **Asociación de Guías Copán** (☑ 2651-4108; www.asociacionguiascopan.com; 2hr tour for 1-9 people L500) and charge L500 for groups of up to nine and L600 for groups of 10 to 19. You can find them at the entrance to the parking lot. These prices are just for the main site – guides for the tunnels, Las Sepulturas or Museo de Escultura cost an additional L200 to L300 per site.

Copán Ruinas

POP 8500

The town of Copán Ruinas, often simply called Copán, is a beautiful place paved with cobblestones and lined with white adobe buildings with red-tiled roofs. There's even a lovely colonial church on the recently remodeled plaza. The Maya have inhabited this valley, which has an aura of timeless harmony, for about 2000 years. Copán has become a primary tourist destination, but this hasn't disrupted the town's integrity to the extent one might fear.

◎ Sights & Activities

Though the main attraction of the Copán region is the archaeological site, there are other fine places to visit in the area.

Museo de Arqueología Maya   MUSEUM
(☑ 2651-4437; Parque Central; admission L285; ◎ 9am-5pm) The Museo de Arqueología Maya is a little dated but still worth a visit. The exhibits include excavated ceramics, fragments from the altars and the supports of the Maya ruins, an insight into the Maya's sophisticated use of calendars and a recreation of a female shaman's tomb. Some descriptions have English translations.

Memorias Frágiles   GALLERY
(☑ 2651-3900; Parque Central; ◎ 8am-5pm Mon-Fri) FREE This permanent photo exhibition was a gift from Harvard University's Peabody Museum and features a worthwhile collection of rare photos detailing the first archeological expeditions to Copán at the turn of the 20th century. It's located inside the **Palacio Municipal** (City Hall). If the door's locked, ask someone to open it.

Mirador El Cuartel   LOOKOUT
The atmospheric ruins of the old town jail have a fine view of the town and surrounding countryside, making it worth the climb up here.

Macaw Mountain Bird Park   ZOO
(☑ 651-4245; www.macawmountain.com; admission L200; ◎ 9am-5pm) ✎ Around 2.5km out of town is an extensive private reserve aimed at saving Central American macaws. There's plenty of them in evidence, along with toucans, motmots, parrots, kingfishers and orioles, all flying around in spacious, humanely constructed cages. A favorite for many is the 'Encounter Center' where uncaged birds fly onto your shoulders or hands and you can pose for photos with them.

If caged birds give you the willies, bear in mind that nearly all of these birds have been donated to the park by owners who didn't want them anymore or were confiscated from bird smugglers. Even if you're not a bird freak, it's a lovely place to wander around, with plenty of walking trails weaving through the lush forest and over boardwalks to lookout points and swimming holes. The entrance ticket – which includes a guided tour in English – is valid for three days and there's a cafe-restaurant on the property. To get here, catch a *tuk-tuk* for L20 per person. If you buy your ticket in advance at Café ViaVia, they'll throw in the tuk-tuk for free.

Copán Ruinas

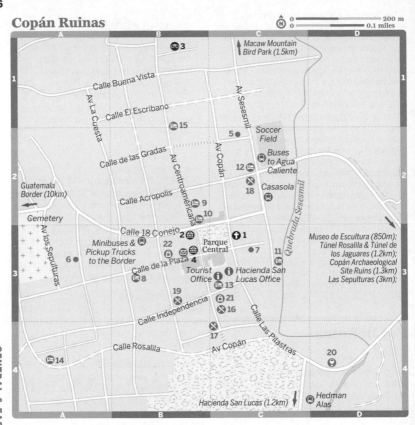

Los Sapos   ARCHAEOLOGICAL SITE
(Hacienda San Lucas; admission L30) The *sapos* (toads) are old Maya stone carvings in a location with a beautiful view over the town and the site is connected with Maya fertility rites. You can get there by horseback in about half an hour or walk in about an hour, all uphill.

From Los Sapos you can walk to Stela 10 – if you're planning on doing that, stop by Café ViaVia for a free map, as the trail is not well marked. Los Sapos is on the grounds of Hacienda San Lucas, a century-old farmhouse that has been converted into a B&B and restaurant. There are walking trails here, too.

Courses

Ixbalanque
Spanish School   LANGUAGE COURSE
(2651-4432; www.ixbalanque.com; Av Los Jaguares) Offers 20 hours of one-on-one instruc-

tion in Spanish for L4975 per week, including a homestay with a local family that provides three meals a day. Instruction only, for 20 hours per week, costs L2586.

Guacamaya
Spanish Academy   LANGUAGE COURSE
(2651-4360; www.guacamaya.com; Calle de las Gradas) Offers a package of 20 hours of one-on-one tuition for L2780. For L1700 more you can have full board and lodging with a local family.

Tours

A huge number of tours can be organized from Copán Ruinas. Local companies promote these widely. You can cave, tube a river, visit a Maya village and make tortillas or manufacture ceramics, plunge into hot springs, visit a coffee plantation or head off into the wilds of Honduras.

Copán Ruinas

Bird-watching tours are very popular in the area around Copán – it's said that there are more quetzals in the surrounding cloudforest than there are in the whole of Guatemala, where it is the national bird. One recommended, English-speaking bird-watching guide is **Alexander Alvarado** (☑9751-1680; birdinghonduras@gmail.com), who can also be contacted through the Macaw Mountain Bird Park.

Horseback riding (3-5hr tours L300-900) can be arranged by any of the town's tour companies and most hotels. You can ride to the ruins or make other, lengthier excursions. You will most likely be approached on the street by somebody wanting to rent you a horse. Unfortunately, there have been a number of incidents of payment without delivery, and it's recommended that you go through an agency. Hacienda El Jaral also offers horseback riding. Three- to five-hour rides out of Café ViaVia visit the hot springs, Hacienda San Lucas, Los Sapos and the small Ch'ortí village of La Pintada.

Yaragua Tours TOUR
(☑2651-4147; www.yaragua.com; cnr Calle de la Plaza & Av Copán; ☺8am-9pm) Leads hikes, horseback-riding trips, excursions to Lago de Yojoa and even some outings to nearby caves. Ask for Samuel, a well-respected and trusted local guide.

Base Camp Tours TOUR
(☑2651-4695; www.basecamphonduras.com; Calle de la Plaza) Located inside Café ViaVia, this outfit offers a range of original and adventurous tours around the local area on foot (L200 to L400) and horseback (L300, three

hours). Its highly recommended two-hour 'Alternative Copán' walking tour (L200) delves beneath the glossy surface of the town and investigates the reality of life for many Hondurans.

🛏 Sleeping

Hostel Iguana Azul HOSTEL $
(☑2651-4620; www.iguanaazulcopan.com; dm L150, s/d L270/320; ☎) This colonial style ranch home has eight comfy bunk beds in two rooms; the shared bathroom has terrific piping-hot water. Three private rooms sleep two and there's also a pretty garden. The common area has books, magazines, travel guides, a great bulletin board and lots of travel information. This is backpacking elegance at its finest.

Café ViaVia HOTEL $
(☑2651-4652; www.viaviacafe.com; Calle de la Plaza; s/d from L240/320; ☎) This small Belgian-run European-style hotel has five spotless rooms with private hot-water bathroom, tiled floors and great beds. There are hammocks, a small garden and enough space to chill out. It's a great place to come for tourist information, and has an art gallery and lively bar attached.

Hotel Patty HOTEL $
(☑2651-4021; hotelpatty@yahoo.com; cnr Avs Acrópolis & Sesesmil; s/d L300/400; ☐☎) The spacious rooms here come with a few colonial flourishes and are set upstairs, around a central parking lot/patio. There are good breezes on the communal balcony and it's run by a friendly family.

Hotel Madrugada HOTEL $

(☑2651-4092; Av Sesesmil; L470/570; ℗) Possibly the most atmospheric hotel in town, this beautiful little place is tucked away in a corner overlooking a babbling creek. Rooms are generously sized and fitted out with period touches such as four-poster beds. There are plenty of armchairs and hammocks on the wide wooden balcony.

Hotel Los Jaguares HOTEL $

(☑2651-4451; jaguares@copanhonduras.org; cnr Calle 18 Conejo & Av Centroamericana; s/d L490/588; ℗❉) A surprisingly good deal right on the plaza. The rooms don't have views, but are clean and cheery enough, without being overly stylish.

Hotel La Posada HOTEL $

(☑2651-4059; www.laposadacopan.com; Av Centroamericana; s/d L320/500; ☎) Good value, tranquil and comfortable, La Posada is only half a block from the plaza. Its 19 rooms with hot-water bathroom, fan and TV are set around two leafy patios. There's very tasty free black coffee first thing in the morning.

★La Casa de Café B&B B&B $$

(☑2651-4620; www.casadecafecopan.com; s/d incl breakfast L895/1150; ℗❉☎) This impeccably decorated B&B has rooms that are adorned with carved wooden doors and Guatemalan masks. The setting is stunning – the view over breakfast is of morning mists rising around the Guatemalan mountains. There's also an upscale house and townhouse available (L2000 to L2600 a night, negotiable for longer stays).

Hotel Yat B'alam BOUTIQUE HOTEL $$$

(☑2651-4338; www.yatbalam.com; Calle Independencia; r from L1770; ℗❉☎) Each of the four beautiful rooms here is spacious and comes with all the usual comforts as well as minibar and DVD player (the hotel has a selection of movies you can borrow). The whole place is pleasantly decorated with a mix of colonial and indigenous furnishings.

Terramaya BOUTIQUE HOTEL $$$

(☑2651-4623; www.terramayacopan.com; Av Centroamericana; s/d with breakfast L1700/1890; ❉☎) For comfort and style approaching upper midrange, this newcomer hovers somewhere between a B&B and boutique hotel offering six smartly appointed rooms, a lovely backyard garden and candlelit terrace with misty-eyed mountain views. Two upstairs rooms offer spectacular balconies with vistas out to the ruins and the mountains beyond.

Eating

The town's little food market is right by the Parque Central.

Café ViaVia INTERNATIONAL $

(Calle de la Plaza; breakfast L60-80, mains L80-140; ⏱7am-10pm; ☎☑) This terrific restaurant serves breakfast, lunch and dinner in a convivial atmosphere, with tables overlooking the street and a replica of Altar Q from the Acrópolis behind the bar. The organically grown coffee it prepares is excellent, bread is homemade and there's always a good selection of vegetarian and meat-based dishes on offer.

Picame INTERNATIONAL $

(Calle de la Plaza; mains L70-125 Wed-Mon) A cute little cafe-restaurant does a seriously full breakfast, yummy roast chicken and an assortment of burgers and sandwiches.

Café San Rafael CAFE, DELI $$

(Av Centroamericana; meals L100-200; ⏱9am-7:30pm; ☎) This cafe serves organic coffee grown at the *finca* of the same name, just out of town. There's also a yummy range of teas and homemade snacks and cheeses on offer.

★Hacienda San Lucas HONDURAN $$$

(☑2651-4106; www.haciendasanlucas.com; 5-course meal around L600) Set on farmland overlooking the town and archaeological site, this is the town's date-night favorite. The romance of dining by candlelight in the restored farmhouse can't really be exaggerated. Cuisine draws heavily on traditional ingredients and techniques and comes accompanied by fine South American wines. Reservations should be made two days in advance, either by phoning or dropping into the hacienda's downtown office (p210). A mototaxi here from town should cost L80 to L120 one way.

Carnitas Nia Lola HONDURAN $$$

(Av Centroamericana; mains L140-355; ⏱7am-10pm; ☎) Two blocks south of the plaza, this open-air restaurant has a beautiful view toward the mountains over corn and tobacco fields. It's a relaxing place with simple and economical food; the specialties are charcoal-grilled chicken and beef. Happy hour starts at 6:30pm.

Twisted Tanya's INTERNATIONAL $$$
(Calle Independencia; 2-/3-course meals L380/420; ⊙10am-10pm Mon-Sat) Set upstairs, with a lovely balcony sporting views out to the mountains, Tanya's serves up some good versions of Italian and Asian-influenced dishes. Cardboard Moroccan-style lampshades add an artistic flourish. The 'backpacker special' of a 3-course set meal for L120 is available between 4 and 6pm and is a good deal.

Drinking & Nightlife

Café ViaVia and the bar in Carnitas Nia Lola are happening spots in the evening.

Papa Chango CLUB
(Calle Las Pilastras; ⊙midnight-late, Thu-Sat) A popular, laid-back reggae bar. It heats up around midnight, when all the bars in the center are required by a town council ordnance to close. This area's a bit suspect – lone travelers (particularly women) are probably better off avoiding it, and if they decide to go, are advised to take a mototaxi, both to and from.

Orientation & Information

The town only introduced street names recently, but few people use them; most people know what street their own house or business is on, but everything else works by landmarks. There are no street numbers.

IMMIGRATION

Honduran Immigration Office (Av Centroamericana, Palacio Municipal; ⊙7am-4:30pm Mon-Fri) On the plaza; come here for visa matters.

MONEY

For US dollars, the banks give a better rate than the moneychangers at the border, but slightly less than banks elsewhere in Honduras. The following banks have ATMs that accept foreign cards.

Banco Atlántida (cnr Calle Independencia & Av Copán) Changes US dollars and traveler's checks. It also has an ATM.

Banco Credomatic (Calle de la Plaza) On the plaza.

Banco de Occidente (cnr Calle 18 Conejo & Av Copán) On the plaza, changes US dollars and traveler's checks, as well as Guatemalan quetzals, and gives cash advances on Visa and MasterCard.

POST

Post Office (Calle de la Plaza) A few doors from the plaza.

MOVING ON?

For tips, recommendations and reviews, head to shop.lonelyplanet.com to purchase a downloadable PDF of the Honduras chapter from Lonely Planet's *Central America On a Shoestring* guide.

TELEPHONE

Hondutel (⊙7am-9pm) Telephone office around the corner from the post office.

TOURIST INFORMATION

Tourist Office (☑2651-3829; www.copanhonduras.org; Calle Independencia; ⊙8am-5pm Mon-Fri, 8am-noon Sat) Run by the chamber of commerce; one block south of the plaza.

Getting There & Away

If you need a Honduran visa in advance, you can obtain it at the Honduran consulate in Esquipulas or the embassy (p298) in Guatemala City.

Several Antigua travel agencies offer weekend trips to Copán, which may include stops at other places, including Quiriguá. All-inclusive day trips from Antigua to Copán are very rushed.

BUS

Hedman Alas (☑2651-4037; Km 62, Carretera a San Lucas; ⊙6am-6:30pm) runs direct 1st-class services daily in both directions between Copán Ruinas and Guatemala City (from L1250, five hours), leaving its office in Copán Ruinas at 2:20pm and 6:30pm and Guatemala City at 5am and 8:30am. Coming from other places, you have to take a bus to Chiquimula, and change there for a connecting service to the border.

If you're coming from Esquipulas, you can get off the bus at Vado Hondo, the junction of Hwy 10 and the road to El Florido, and wait for a bus there.

Minivans and some pickups depart for Copán Ruinas from the Honduras side of the border regularly throughout the day. They should charge around L20, payable before you depart, for the 20-minute ride. Going the other way, they leave from one block west of the plaza. On the Guatemala side, buses to Chiquimula (Q25, 1½ hours) leave the border hourly from 5:30am to 4:30pm.

Buses serving points further afield in Honduras depart from a few different places in Copán Ruinas. Hedman Alas goes to San Pedro Sula (L520, three hours) and on to Tegucigalpa (L886, seven hours) twice daily.

CENTRAL & EASTERN GUATEMALA COPÁN RUINAS

Casasola (🖉 2651-4078; Av Sesesmil) offers semi-direct service to San Pedro Sula (L140) and La Ceiba (L280) at 5am, 6am and 7am.

If you're hoping to make it to the Bay Islands in one day, you really have to be on the 5am Casasola bus to San Pedro.

SHUTTLE MINIBUS

Base Camp Tours (p207) in Copán Ruinas and nearly every Antigua travel agency run shuttles between those two towns. Scheduled shuttles leave Copán for Antigua (L400, minimum four passengers, six hours) daily and can drop you in Guatemala City (five hours) en route. You can also get off at Río Hondo, or it can organize shuttle/Pullman combinations to Río Dulce and Flores.

Around Copán Ruinas

🏃 Activities

Finca El Cisne   TOUR
(🖉 2651-4695; www.fincaelcisne.com; r per person incl 3 meals, horseback tour & admission to thermal baths L1900) Visiting this working farm, 24km from Copán Ruinas, is more like an agro-eco experience than a tour. Founded in the 1920s and still operating, the *finca* mainly raises cattle and grows coffee and cardamom, but it also produces corn, avocados, beans, breadfruit and star fruit, among other things.

Day-long and overnight packages include guided horse riding through the forests and pastures (with a stop to swim in the Río Blanco) and tours of the coffee and cardamom fields and processing plants. If you come between February and October you can help with the harvest. Lodging is five simple, rustic rooms in the old workers quarters, with meals and a visit to nearby hot springs included. You can book tours in its office inside the Café ViaVia.

Agua Caliente   SWIMMING
(Av Sesemil; admission L40; ⊙ 8am-6pm) The attractively situated Agua Caliente is 23km north of Copán Ruinas via the road running north out of town (not to be confused with another Agua Caliente in Honduras, not far from Esquipulas). Here hot water flows and mingles with a cold river. There are change rooms, a basketball court and bathrooms plus a small shop selling soft drinks and snacks.

Frequent minibuses leave from in front of the football field in Copán Ruinas, passing right in front of the hot springs (L35).

Coming back, wait for one of the same buses, or you can hitch a ride in any passing pickup – most will happily give you a ride back into town.

Luna Jaguar Spa Resort   DAY SPA
(http://lunajaguarsparesort.com; admission L200; ⊙ 8am-5pm) Directly across the river from the hot springs, this is a high-concept Maya day spa, something like what the Maya kings would have done to relax if they had the chance. Thirteen 'treatment stations' (offering hot tub, herbal steam baths and so on) are scattered around the hillside, connected by a series of stone pathways.

The jungle here has been left as undisturbed as possible, and reproduction Maya sculptures dot the landscape. The water used in the hot tub and steam baths comes directly from the volcanic spring. It's an amazing and beautiful spot, and worth checking out even if you're not a spa junkie.

🛏 Sleeping

Hacienda San Lucas   HISTORIC HOTEL $$$
(🖉 2651-4495; www.haciendasanlucas.com; r from L2830; 🛜) 🅿 This is a magical place 3km south of town. Beautifully restored, utterly unique and with fabulous views of the valley, taking in the town and archaeological site, the place has to be seen to be believed. Phone beforehand or drop in to its **office** (🖉 2651-4495; Calle de la Plaza; ⊙ 9am-5pm) in Copán Ruinas.

The recently restored and expanded adobe hacienda is solar-powered, but the rooms are candlelit at night, adding to the serene atmosphere. The food here is highly praised, and many people come just for dinner. Los Sapos archaeological site is on the property.

CARIBBEAN COAST

This is a very different Guatemala – a lush and sultry landscape dotted with palm trees and inhabited by international sailors (around the yachtie haven of Río Dulce and the working port of Puerto Barrios) and one of the country's lesser-known ethnic groups, the Garífuna (around Lívingston).

A boat ride down the Río Dulce is pretty much mandatory for any visit to this region, and many visitors find a few days in Lívingston to be a worthy detour. Nature buffs will want to check out the huge wetlands reserves at Bocas del Polochic and Punta de Manabique.

Lago de Izabal

Guatemala's largest lake, to the north of Hwy 9, is starting to earn its place on the travelers' map. Most visitors checking out the lake stay at Río Dulce town, by the long, tall bridge where Hwy 13, heading north to Flores and Tikal, crosses the Río Dulce emptying out of the east end of the lake. Downstream, the beautiful river broadens into a lake called El Golfete before meeting the Caribbean at Lívingston. River trips are a highlight of a visit to eastern Guatemala. If you're looking for lakeside ambiance minus the Río Dulce congestion and pace, head to Chapin Abajo, north of Mariscos or El Estor near the west end of the lake, both of which give access to the rich wildlife of the Bocas del Polochic river delta. There are many undiscovered spots in this area waiting to be explored, so don't limit yourself.

Río Dulce

POP 5200

At the east end of the Lago de Izabal, this town still gets referred to as Fronteras – a hangover from the days when the only way across the river was by ferry, and this was the last piece of civilization before embarking on the long, difficult journey into El Petén.

Times have changed. A huge bridge now spans the water and El Petén roads are some of the best in the country. The town sees most tourist traffic from yachties – the US coast guard says this is the safest place on the western Caribbean for boats during hurricane season. The rest of the foreigners here are either coming or going on the spectacular river trip between here and Lívingston.

🖙 Tours

Ask around at any of the marinas for the latest on which sailboats are offering charter tours.

Aventuras Vacacionales　　　SAILING
(🖉7873-9221; www.sailing-diving-guatemala.com) This outfit runs fun seven-day sailing trips from Río Dulce to the Belize reefs and islands (from Q3200) and Lago Izabal (from Q1250, four-day trips). The office is in Antigua but you can also hook up with this outfit in Río Dulce. It makes the Belize and lake trips in alternate weeks.

🛏 Sleeping

Many places in Río Dulce communicate by radio, but all are reachable by telephone. The bar at Bruno's will radio your choice of place to stay if necessary.

ON THE WATER

The places listed here are out of town on the water, which is the best place to be. You can call or radio them and they'll come and pick you up. **Mansión del Río** (🖉2335-3516; www.mansiondelrio.com.gt; r Q940), just out of town, provides all-inclusive resort-style accommodation on the lakefront.

★**Hotel Kangaroo**　　　HOTEL $
(🖉5363-6716, in English 4513-9602; www.hotelkangaroo.com; dm Q60, r Q150-180, cabin Q220; @🛜) Located on the Río La Colocha, just across the water from the Castillo San Felipe, this beautiful, simple Australian/Mexican-run place is built on stilts in the mangroves. The whole place is constructed from wood, with thatched roofs, and windows are mosquito-netted – there's not a pane of glass in sight.

Wildlife is particularly abundant around here, with blue warblers, pelicans, a 7ft iguana and turtles making the surrounds their home. There's also a bar-restaurant. Drinks on the deck overlooking the river are a great way to start, finish or while away the day. The beguiling menu features some Aussie classics and probably the best Mexican food you're likely to find outside of Mexico. Call from Río Dulce or San Felipe and they'll come and pick you up for free, even if you're just dropping in for lunch.

Hotel Backpackers　　　HOSTEL $
(🖉7930-5480; www.hotelbackpackers.com; dm Q30, s/d Q100/120, without bathroom from Q60/120; @🛜) Across the bridge from Río Dulce town, this is a business run by Casa Guatemala and the orphans it serves. It's an old (with the emphasis on old) backpacker favorite, set in a rickety building with very basic rooms. The bar kicks on here at night.

If you're coming by *lancha* or bus, ask the driver to let you off here to spare yourself the walk across the bridge.

Hacienda Tijax　　　HOTEL $$
(🖉7930-5505; www.tijax.com; s Q170-530, d Q230-590; [P][❄][🛜][≋]) This 118-acre hacienda, a two-minute boat ride across the cove from Bruno's, is a special place to stay. Activities include horseback riding, hiking,

BANANA REPUBLIC

Bananas were first imported to the US in 1870. Few Americans had ever seen a banana, let alone tasted one. By 1898 they were eating 16 million bunches annually.

In 1899 the Boston Fruit Company and Brooklyn-born Central American railroad baron Minor C Keith joined forces, forming the United Fruit Company (UFC). The aim was to cultivate large areas of Central America, growing bananas that Keith would transport by rail to the coast for shipment to the USA.

Central American governments sold UFC large tracts of undeveloped jungle. The company created road and/or rail access to the land, cleared and cultivated it and built extensive port facilities.

By 1930, UFC – the largest employer in Central America – was capitalized at US$215 million and owned one of the largest private navies in the world. By controlling Puerto Barrios and the railroads, UFC effectively controlled Guatemala's international commerce, bananas or otherwise.

Local journalists began referring to UFC as El Pulpo, 'the Octopus', accusing it of corrupting government officials, exploiting workers and exercising influence far beyond its role as a foreign company in Guatemala.

On October 20, 1944, a liberal military coup paved the way for Guatemala's first-ever free elections. The new president was Dr Juan José Arévalo, who sought to remake Guatemala into a democratic, liberal nation. His successor, Jacobo Arbenz, was an even more vigorous reformer. Labor unions began clamoring for better conditions, with almost constant actions against UFC. The government demanded more equitable tax payments from the company and divestiture of large tracts of unused land.

The US government supported UFC. Powerful members of Congress and the Eisenhower administration were convinced that Arbenz was intent on turning Guatemala communist. Several high-ranking US officials had ties to UFC, and others were persuaded that Arbenz was a threat.

In 1954 a CIA-orchestrated invasion by 'anti-communist' Guatemalan exiles led to Arbenz' resignation and exile. His replacement was Carlos Castillo Armas, an old-school military man, who returned Guatemala to rightist military dictatorship.

A few years later, the US Department of Justice brought a suit against UFC for operating monopolistically. UFC was ordered to reduce its size by two-thirds within 12 years. It began by selling off its Guatemalan holdings and yielding its monopoly on the railroads.

UFC later became part of United Brands, which later sold its remaining land in Guatemala to the Del Monte Corporation, which is still active in Guatemala.

bird-watching, and walking and canopy tours around the rubber plantation and private nature reserve. Accommodation is in lovely little cabins connected by boardwalks. The pricier ones have kitchens and are well set-up for families.

Most cabins face the water and there's a very relaxing pool/bar area. Access is by boat or by a road that turns off the highway about 1km north of the village. The folks here speak Spanish, English and French, and they'll pick you up from across the river.

El Tortugal BUNGALOW $$
(☑ 7742-8847; www.tortugal.com; dm Q100, r without bathroom Q300, bungalow from Q300; 🛜) The best-looking bungalows on the river are located here, a five-minute *lancha* ride east from town. There are plenty of hammocks, the showers are seriously hot and kayaks are free for guest use.

IN TOWN

Bruno's HOTEL $$
(☑ 7930-5721; www.brunoshotel.com; dm Q50, s Q90-220, d Q125-300; P❄🛜☲) A path leads down from the northeast end of the bridge to this riverside hang-out for yachties needing to get some land under their feet. The dorms here are clean and spacious and the new building offers some of the most comfortable rooms in town, with air-con and balconies overlooking the river. They're well set up for families and sleep up to six.

Hotel Vista al Río HOTEL $

(☑ 7930-5665; www.hotelvistario.com; dm Q40, r from Q160, without bathroom Q100; ❄ ☎) Under the bridge just south of Bruno's, this little hotel/marina offers spacious, spotless rooms, the more expensive ones with river views. There's a good restaurant here, serving juicy steaks, Southern cooking and big breakfasts.

✖ Eating

All of the hotels listed above have restaurants. Bruno's and the Vista al Río serve good breakfasts and gringo comfort food and have full bars. Hacienda Tijax is a popular lunch spot – give them a call and they'll come pick you up.

★ **Sundog Café** INTERNATIONAL $

(sandwiches Q30, meals from Q35; ⊘ noon-9pm) Down a laneway opposite the Litegua bus office, this open-air riverfront bar-restaurant makes great sandwiches on homemade bread, a good selection of vegetarian dishes, tasty brick-oven pizzas and fresh juices. It's also the place to come for unbiased information about the area.

❶ Orientation & Information

Unless you're staying at Hotel Backpackers, get off the bus on the north side of the bridge. The Fuente del Norte and Litegua bus offices are both here, opposite each other. Otherwise you'll find yourself trudging over what is believed to be the longest bridge in Central America – it's a very hot 3.5km walk.

The main dock is now under the bridge on the opposite side of the main road from Bruno's – you'll see a side road leading down to it.

The local online newspaper *Chisme Vindicator* (ww.riodulcechisme.com) has loads of information about Río Dulce.

If you need to change cash or traveler's checks, hit one of the banks in town, all on the main road. There's a trustworthy Visa/Master-Card ATM inside the Despensa Familiar supermarket, also on the main street.

❶ Getting There & Away

Beginning at 9:30am, seven Fuente del Norte buses a day head north along a paved road to Poptún (Q35, two hours) and Flores (Q65, four hours). With good connections you can get to Tikal in a snappy six hours. There are also services to San Salvador (El Salvador; Q125) and San Pedro Sula (Honduras; Q135), both leaving at 10am.

At least 11 buses daily go to Guatemala City (Q65, six hours) with Fuente del Norte and Litegua. Línea Dorada has 1st-class buses departing at 1pm for Guatemala City (Q130) and 3pm for Flores (Q130). This shaves up to an hour off the journey times.

Minibuses leave for Puerto Barrios (Q25, two hours) when full, from the roadside in front of Hotel Las Brisas.

There's a daily shuttle to Lanquín (Q150, five hours), leaving from in front of the Sundog Café at 1:30pm.

Minibuses leave for El Estor (Q20, 1½ hours) from the San Felipe and El Estor turnoff in the middle of town, hourly from 7am to 6pm.

Colectivo lanchas go down the Río Dulce (from the new dock) to Lívingston, usually requiring eight to 10 people, charging Q125/200 per person one-way/round-trip. The trip is a beautiful one, making a 'tour' of it, with several halts along the way. Boats usually leave from 9am to about 2pm. There are regular, scheduled departures at 9:30am and 1:30pm. Pretty much everyone in town can organize a *lancha* service to Lívingston and most other places you'd care to go, but they charge more.

El Castillo de San Felipe

The fortress and castle of San Felipe de Lara, **El Castillo de San Felipe** (admission Q20; ⊘ 8am-5pm), about 3km west of the bridge, was built in 1652 to keep pirates from looting the villages and commercial caravans of Izabal. Though the fortress somewhat deterred the buccaneers, a pirate force captured and burned it in 1686. By the end of the next century, pirates had disappeared from the Caribbean, and the fort's sturdy walls served as a prison. Eventually, though, the fortress was abandoned and became a ruin. The present fort was reconstructed in 1956.

Today the castle is protected as a park and is one of the Lago de Izabal's principal tourist attractions. In addition to the fort itself, there are grassy grounds, barbecue and picnic areas, and the opportunity to swim in the lake. The place rocks during the **Feria de San Felipe** (April 30 to May 4).

⌁ Sleeping & Eating

Hotel Don Humberto HOTEL $

(☑ 7930-5051; s/d Q50/90; ℗) Near the Castillo, offering basic rooms with big beds and good mosquito netting. It's nothing fancy, but more than adequate for a cheap sleep.

Viñas del Lago
HOTEL $$

(☎7930-5053; www.vinasdelago.com; s/d Q165/260; P✻@🛜🏊) Near the Hotel Don Humberto, but much fancier, with 18 spacious rooms. The ones out the back have good views. The grounds are large and there's a restaurant (mains Q50 to Q100) with views of Lago de Izabal.

Hotel Monte Verde
HOTEL $

(☎5036-8469; hotelmonteverde@hotmail.com; s/d with fan Q100/150, with air-con Q200/250; P✻✻) One of the best deals for miles around – generously sized rooms, a huge pool set in a lush garden and an on-site bar-restaurant.

❶ Getting There & Away

San Felipe is on the lakeshore, 3km west of Río Dulce. It's a beautiful 45-minute walk between the two towns, or take a minivan (Q10, every 30 minutes). In Río Dulce it stops on the corner of the highway and road to El Estor; in San Felipe it stops in front of the Hotel Don Humberto, at the entrance to El Castillo.

Boats coming from Lívingston will drop you in San Felipe if you ask. The Río Dulce river tours usually come to El Castillo, allowing you to get out and visit the castle if you like, or you can come over from Río Dulce by private *lancha*.

Finca El Paraíso

On the north side of the lake, between Río Dulce and El Estor, **Finca El Paraíso** (☎7949-7122; admission Q10, cabin with fan/air-con Q200/250) makes a great day trip from either place. This working ranch's territory has an incredibly beautiful spot in the jungle where a wide, hot waterfall drops about 12m into a clear, deep pool. You can bathe in the hot water, swim in the cool pool or duck under an overhanging promontory and enjoy a jungle-style sauna. It also has accommodation and a restaurant (mains Q60 to Q120).

If you're coming for the waterfall, head north (away from the lake) where the bus drops you off – you pay the admission fee there, from where it's about a 2km walk to the falls. To get to the restaurant and hotel, head south (towards the lake) for about 3km.

A slightly humbler, but completely adequate overnight option can be found by turning right just before the *finca* house – follow the signs for **Brisas del Lago** (☎7958-0309; cabin per person Q100). There is a good restaurant here and plenty of hammocks strung around, catching the lake breezes.

The *finca* is on the Río Dulce–El Estor bus route, about one hour (Q10) from Río Dulce and 30 minutes (Q7) from El Estor. The last bus in either direction passes at around 4:30pm to 5pm.

El Boquerón

This beautiful, lushly vegetated canyon abutting the tiny Maya settlement of the same name is about 6km east of El Estor. Pay your Q5 entry fee, and for around Q15 per person, villagers will paddle you 15 minutes up the Río Sauce through the canyon, drop you at a small beach, where you can swim and if you like scramble up the rocks, and wait or return for you at an agreed time. Río Dulce–bound buses from El Estor will drop you at El Boquerón (Q7, 15 minutes), as will El Estor–bound buses from Río Dulce.

El Estor

POP 21,100

The major settlement on the northern shore of Lago de Izabal is El Estor, a friendly, somnolent little town with a lovely setting which provides an easy jumping-off point for Bocas del Polochic, a highly biodiverse wildlife reserve at the west end of the lake. The town is also a staging post on a possible route between Río Dulce and Lanquín.

🛏 Sleeping & Eating

Restaurante Típico Chaabil apart, the best place to look for food is around Parque Central, where **Café Portal** (mains Q30-50; ☉7am-9pm) serves a broad range of fare with some vegetarian options. On the other side of the park, **Restaurante del Lago** (mains Q40-80; ☉8am-8pm), on the 2nd floor, catches some good breezes and a bit of a lake view – it has the widest menu in town.

Hotel Villela
HOTEL $

(☎7949-7214; 6a Av 2-06; s/d Q75/150) The rooms are less attractive than the neat lawn and trees they're set around, but some are airier and brighter than others. All have fan and bathroom.

Restaurante Típico Chaabil
HOTEL $

(☎7949-7272; 3a Calle; r Q150; P) Although they go a bit heavy on the log-cabin feel, the rooms at this place, at the west end of the street, are the best deal in town. Get one upstairs for plenty of light and good views. The restaurant here, on a lovely lakeside terrace, cooks up delicious food, such as *tapado* (Garífuna seafood and coconut stew).

The water here is crystal clear and you can swim right off the hotel's dock.

Hotel Vista al Lago HOTEL **$$**
(✆7949-7205; 6a Av 1-13; s/d Q150/200) Set in a classic historic building down on the waterfront, this place has plenty of style, although the rooms themselves are fairly ordinary. Views from the upstairs balcony are superb.

ℹ Orientation & Information

Banrural (cnr 3a Calle & 6a Av; ⊙8:30am-5pm Mon-Fri, 9am-1pm Sat) Changes US dollars and Amex traveler's checks and has an ATM.

Café Portal (5a Av 2-65; ⊙6:30am-10pm) On the east side of Parque Central, this place provides information, tours, and transportation.

Municipal Police (cnr 1a Calle & 5a Av) Near the lakeshore.

ℹ Getting There & Away

El Estor is easily reached from Río Dulce.

The road west from El Estor via Panzós and Tucurú to Tactic, south of Cobán, once had a bad reputation for highway holdups and robberies, especially around Tucurú – ask around for current conditions. It's also prone to flooding during the wet season – another reason to enquire. You can get to Lanquín by taking the truck that leaves El Estor's Parque Central at 10:30am for Cahabón (Q40, four to five hours), and then a bus or pickup straight on from Cahabón to Lanquín the same day. Coming the other way currently involves ungodly departure times and staying the night in Cahabón.

Refugio Bocas del Polochic & Reserva de Biosfera Sierra de las Minas

The Refugio Bocas del Polochic (Bocas del Polochic Wildlife Reserve) covers the delta of the Río Polochic, which provides most of Lago de Izabal's water. A visit here provides great bird-watching and howler-monkey observation. The reserve supports more than 300 species of birds – the migration seasons, September to October and April to May, are reportedly fantastic – and many varieties of butterflies and fish. You may well see alligators and, if you're very lucky, glimpse a manatee. Ask at Café Portal in El Estor for boat guides.

The reserve is managed by the **Fundación Defensores de la Naturaleza** (✆7949-7130; www.defensores.org.gt; cnr 5a Av & 2a Calle, El Estor), whose research station, the **Estación Científica Selempim**, just south of Refugio Bocas del Polochic, in the Reserva de Biosfera Sierra de las Minas, is open for ecotouristic visits. Contact Defensores' El Estor office for bookings and further information.

You can get to the station on a local *lancha* service leaving El Estor at noon on Monday, Wednesday and Saturday (Q40 round trip, 1¼ hours each way) or by special hire (Q400 for a boatload of up to 12 people), and stay in a rustic wood-and-thatch *rancho* (per person Q40) or camp (per person Q20). There's no restaurant, but you can

---

MANATEES

In the days of New World exploration, reports of mermaid sightings were commonplace. Columbus' ship's log from January 1493 recorded: 'On the previous day when the Admiral went to the Rio del Oro he saw three mermaids which rose well out of the sea...' It's pretty much accepted now that what sailors were seeing were in fact manatees – who, along with the dugong, belong to the biological order Sirenia, a name taken from the Greek word for mermaid.

Distantly related to elephants, these huge (the largest recorded manatee weighed 1775kg, while newborns weigh around 30kg) vegetarian mammals seem destined to become an endangered species. They were hunted as far back as Maya times – their bones were used for jewelry and their meat (called *bucan*) was prized for its restorative properties. It's believed that the buccaneers (the original pirates of the Caribbean) were so named because they lived almost exclusively on *bucan* meat.

Some scientists claim that manatees were once sociable creatures who swam in packs and readily approached humans, but have adapted in response to human hunters, becoming the shy, furtive creatures they are today. You have to be extremely fortunate to see one in the wild – they scare easily, can swim in short bursts at up to 30km per hour, and can stay underwater for 20 minutes. In Guatemala, your best chance of seeing one is in the Bocas del Polochic or the Punta de Manabique. Good luck.

bring food and use the Estación Científica's kitchen. To explore the reserves you can use canoes free of charge, take boat trips (Q200 to Q300) or walk any of the three well-established trails.

The foundation also oversees another community tourism site at Chapín Abajo, on the other side of the lake where you can stay in a bit more comfort and make day trips to the reserve.

Chapín Abajo

To get right off the beaten track, make your way to this charming little village on the southwest shore of the lake. The **community tourism project** (☑ 4672-4773; www. turismocomunitarioguatemala.com/chapin_abajo. html) here offers accommodation in sweet wooden lakeside **bungalows** (☑ 4672-4773; s/d Q125/200, per person without bathroom Q75) with water views. Simple meals and boat tours (Q375, two hours) are available.

The village is 25 km west of Mariscos on an unmade but passable road. It's tricky getting here by road – catch any bus heading along Hwy 9 and get off at Trincheras junction (Km 218) – the turnoff for Mariscos, where minibuses (Q10) make the run into town. Coming from Los Amates or Quiriguá, there are direct minibuses to Mariscos. From Mariscos, pickups (Q20, one hour) make the run to Chapín Abajo but peter out around 10am. Hitchhiking is common along this stretch, but carries the usual risks.

The easy way to get here is on one of the *lanchas* (Q15, 20 minutes) from El Estor across the lake. One leaves at midday daily and there may be additional departures.

Puerto Barrios

POP 86,400

The country becomes even more lush, tropical and humid heading east from La Ruidosa junction toward Puerto Barrios.

Port towns have always had a reputation for being slightly dodgy, and those acting as international borders doubly so. Puerto Barrios has an edgy, somewhat sleazy feel; for foreign visitors, it's mainly a jumping-off point for boats to Punta Gorda (Belize) or Lívingston, and you probably won't be hanging around.

🛏 Sleeping

Hotel Ensenada　HOTEL $
(☑ 7948-0861; hotelensenadapuertobarrios@hot mail.com; 4a Av btwn Calles 10 & 11; s/d Q110/150; 🅿❄) Taking one step up in the budget category gets you these tidy little rooms with good bathrooms and OK beds. Get one upstairs to catch a breeze.

Hotel Europa　HOTEL $
(☑ 7948-1292; 3a Av btwn Calles 11a and 12a; s/d with fan Q75/120, with air-con Q110/150; 🅿❄🛜) The best of the budget options in the port area, this hotel, just 1½ blocks from the Muelle Municipal (Municipal Boat Dock), is run by a friendly family and has clean rooms with TV, arranged around a parking courtyard.

Hotel Lee　HOTEL $
(☑ 7948-0685; 5a Av btwn Calles 9a and 10a; s/d with fan Q60/100, d with air-con Q160; ❄) This is a friendly, family-owned place, close to the bus terminals. Typical of Puerto Barrios' budget hotels, it offers straightforward, vaguely clean rooms. The little balcony out front catches the odd breeze.

Hotel El Reformador　HOTEL $$
(☑ 7948-0533; reformador@intelnet.net.gt; cnr 7a Av & 16a Calle; s/d with fan Q113/173, with air-con Q158/228; 🅿❄🛜) Like a little haven away from the hot busy streets outside, the Reformador offers big, cool rooms set around leafy patios. Air-con rooms lead onto wide interior balconies. There is a restaurant (meals Q50 to Q80) here.

Hotel del Norte　HOTEL $$
(☑ 7948-2116; 7a Calle; s/d with fan Q90/160, with air-con Q160/270; 🅿❄@🛜) A large, classically tropical wooden building with mosquito-screened corridors, the century-old Hotel del Norte is in a class by itself. Its weathered and warped frame is redolent of history and the floorboards go off at crazy angles. Pick a room carefully – some are little more than a wooden box, others have great ocean views and catch good breezes.

Rooms with air-conditioning are in the newer, less atmospheric building, but are still an excellent deal. There's a swimming pool beside the sea.

Puerto Bello　HOTEL $$
(☑ 7948-0525; 8a Av btwn 18 & 19 Calle; s/d Q200/300; 🅿❄@🛜) By far the best-looking hotel in town, marred only by its slightly out

of the way location. The rooms are spacious and modern and the lovely garden and pool area is a blessing year-round.

Eating & Drinking

La Habana Vieja
CUBAN $$

(13 Calle btwn Avs 6a & 7a; mains Q40-80; ⊗11am-1pm) A good, wide selection of Cuban classics (including *ropa vieja* – a shredded beef stew) and some straightforward sandwiches. Also has a good bar if you're looking for a quiet drink.

Kaffa
CAFE $

(8a Av btwn Calles 7 & 8; sandwiches & breakfast Q30-50; ⊗8:30am-10pm) A hip coffee shop in Puerto Barrios? Well, why not? Let's see how long it lasts. The food's so-so, but the coffee and the breezy deck overlooking the park are both excellent.

Restaurante Safari
SEAFOOD $$

(☑7948-0563; cnr 1a Calle & 5a Av; seafood Q60-120; ⊗10am-9pm) The town's most enjoyable restaurant is on a thatch-roofed, open-air platform right over the water about 1km north of the town center. Locals and visitors alike love to eat and catch the sea breezes here. Excellent seafood of all kinds including the specialty *tapado* – that great Garífuna casserole.

Chicken and meat dishes are less expensive than seafood. There's live music most nights. If the Safari is full, the Cangrejo Azul next door offers pretty much the same deal, in a more relaxed environment.

Orientation & Information

Because of its spacious layout, you must walk or ride further in Puerto Barrios to get from place to place. For instance, it's 800m from the bus terminals by the market in the town center to the Muelle Municipal at the end of 12a Calle, from which passenger boats depart. Very few businesses use street numbers – most just label which street it's on, and the cross streets it's in between.

Banco Industrial (7a Av; ⊗9am-5pm Mon-Fri, 9am-1pm Sat) Changes US dollars and traveler's checks, and has an ATM.

Immigration Office (cnr 12a Calle & 3a Av; ⊗24hr) A block from the Muelle Municipal. Come here for your entry or exit stamp if you're arriving from or leaving for Belize. If you're leaving by sea, there is a Q80 departure tax to pay. If you are heading to Honduras, you can get your exit stamp at another immigration office on the road to the border.

Police Station (9a Calle)
Post Office (cnr 6a Calle & 6a Av)

Getting There & Around

BOAT
Boats depart from the Muelle Municipal at the end of 12a Calle.

Regular *lanchas* depart for Lívingston (Q35, 30 minutes, five daily) between 6:30am and 5pm. Buy your ticket as early as you can on the day (you can't book before your day of departure) – spaces are limited and sometimes sell out.

Outside of these regular times, *lanchas* depart whenever they have six people ready to go and cost Q50 per person.

Most of the movement from Lívingston to Puerto Barrios is in the morning, returning in the afternoon. From Lívingston, your last chance of the day may be the 5pm *lancha,* especially during the low season when fewer travelers are shuttling back and forth.

Lanchas also depart from the Muelle Municipal three times daily for Punta Gorda, Belize (Q200, one hour). The 10am departure arrives in time for the noon bus from Punta Gorda to Belize City. Tickets are sold at the dock. Before boarding you also need to get your exit stamp at the nearby immigration office (and pay Q80 departure tax).

If you want to leave a car in Puerto Barrios while you visit Lívingston for a day or two, there are plenty of *parqueos* (parking lots) around the dock area that charge around Q30 per 24 hours. All of the hotels listed here offer this service, too.

BUS & MINIBUS
Transportes Litegua (☑7948-1172; cnr 6a Av & 9a Calle) leaves for Guatemala City (Q65 to Q100, five to six hours), via Quiriguá and Río Hondo frequently. *Directo* services avoid a half-hour detour into Morales.

Minibuses for Chiquimula (Q45, 4½ hours), also via Quiriguá, leave every half-hour, from 3am to 3pm, from the corner of 6a Av and 9a Calle. Minibuses to Río Dulce (Q20, two hours) leave from the same location.

> ### GETTING TO HONDURAS
> Minibuses leave for the Honduran frontier (Q25, 1¼ hours) every 20 minutes, from 5am to 5pm, from 6a Av outside the market in Puerto Barrios. They stop en route to the border at Guatemalan immigration, where you may be required to pay Q10 for an exit stamp. Honduran entry formalities will leave you around L60 lighter.

Punta de Manabique

The Punta de Manabique promontory, which separates the Bahía de Manabique from the open sea, along with the coast and hinterland all the way southeast to the Honduran frontier, comprises a large, ecologically fascinating, sparsely populated wetland area. Access to the area, which is under environmental protection as the **Área de Protección Especial Punta de Manabique**, is not cheap, but the attractions for those who make it there include pristine Caribbean beaches, boat trips through the mangrove forests, lagoons and waterways, bird-watching, fishing with locals, and crocodile and possible manatee sightings. To visit, get in touch – a week in advance, if possible – with the **community tourism project** (☑ 5303-9822; www.turismocomunitario guatemala.com/estero_lagarto_turismo.html) at Estero Lagarto, on the south side of the promontory. You can stay in their ecolodge (room per person Q50, mains around Q60), take mangrove and laguna tours in wooden canoes to nearby Santa Isabel, on the Canal de los Ingleses – a waterway connecting the Bahía de Manabique with the open sea.

Lívingston

POP 26,300

Quite unlike anywhere else in Guatemala, this largely Garífuna town is fascinating in itself, but also has the attraction of a couple of good beaches and its location at the end of the river journey from Río Dulce.

Unconnected (for the moment) by road from the rest of the country (the town is called 'Buga' – mouth – in Garífuna, for its position at the river mouth), boat transportation is logically quite good here, and you can get to Belize, the Cayes and Puerto Barrios with a minimum of fuss.

The Garífuna people of Caribbean Guatemala, Honduras, Nicaragua and southern Belize trace their roots to the Caribbean island of St Vincent, where shipwrecked African slaves mixed with the indigenous Carib in the 17th century. It took the British a long time, and a lot of fighting, to establish colonial control over St Vincent, and when they finally succeeded in 1796, they decided to deport its surviving Garífuna inhabitants. Most of the survivors wound up, after many had starved on Roatán island off Honduras, in the Honduran coastal town of Trujillo. From there, they have spread along the Caribbean coast. Their main concentration in Guatemala is in Lívingston but there are also a few thousand in Puerto Barrios and elsewhere. The Garífuna language is a unique melange of Caribbean and African languages with a bit of French. Other people in Lívingston include the indigenous Q'eqchi' Maya (who have their own community a kilometer or so upriver from the main dock), *ladinos* (people of mixed indigenous and European heritage) and a smattering of international travelers.

◉ Sights & Activities

Beaches in Lívingston itself are disappointing, as buildings or vegetation come right down to the water's edge in most places. Those beaches that do exist are often contaminated; however, there are better beaches within a few kilometers to the northwest. You can reach **Playa Quehueche** by taxi (Q20) in about 10 minutes: this beach near the mouth of the Río Quehueche has been cleaned up by Exotic Travel. The best beach in the area is **Playa Blanca** (admission Q10), around 12km from Lívingston. This is privately owned and you need a boat to get there.

Rasta Mesa   CULTURAL BUILDING
(☑ 4459-6106; Barrio Nevago; ⊙ 10am-2pm & 7-10pm) This is a friendly, informal little cultural center where you can drop in for classes in Garífuna cooking (Q50 per person) and drumming (Q100 per person) or just get a massage (Q150). They also offer volunteering opportunities.

Los Siete Altares   WATERFALL
(The Seven Altars; admission Q20) About 5km (1½-hours' walk) northwest of Lívingston along the shore of Bahía de Amatique, Los Siete Altares is a series of freshwater falls and pools. It's a pleasant goal for a beach walk and is a good place for a picnic and swim.

Follow the shore northward to the river mouth and walk along the beach until it meets the path into the woods (about 30 minutes). Follow this path all the way to the falls. Boat trips go to the Seven Altars but if you're a walker, it's better to go by foot to experience the natural beauty and the Garífuna people along the way. About halfway along, just past the rope bridge is Hotel Salvador Gaviota, serving decent food and ice-cold beers and soft drinks. You can stay out here, too.

☞ Tours

A few outfits in Lívingston offer tours that let you get out and experience the natural wonders of the area. **Exotic Travel** (☎ 7947-0133; www.bluecaribbeanbay.com; Calle Principal, Restaurante Bahía Azul) and **Happy Fish Travel** (☎ 7947-0661; www.happyfishtravel.com; Calle Principal, Restaurante Happy Fish) are both well-organized operations. Happy Fish gets extra points for supporting community tourism initiatives in the area and their willingness to share information on how you can visit many of the local attractions without a guide.

The popular Ecological Tour/Jungle Trip (Q90 including lunch) takes you for a walk through town, out west up to a lookout spot and on to the Río Quehueche, where you take a half-hour canoe trip down the river to Playa Quehueche. Then you walk through the jungle to Los Siete Altares, hang out there for a while, and walk back down the beach to Lívingston. This is a great way to see the area, and the friendly local guides can also give you a good introduction to the Garífuna people who live here.

The Playa Blanca tour goes by boat first to Los Siete Altares and then on to Playa Blanca, the best beach in the area, for two or three hours. This trip goes with a minimum of two people and costs Q100 per person.

Happy Fish offers a return boat trip (Q200) just along the canyon section of Río Dulce (the most interesting and picturesque part) which gives you more time to enjoy the trails, bird-watching, etc than the 'tour' given on the public *lanchas*. They also run tours to Cueva del Tigre, a community-run tourism project 8km from Lívingston (Q160 for a tour, or they'll tell you how to get there on your own) and for transport to Lagunita Creek (p224), another community-operated tourism initiative.

Also popular are day/overnight trips to the Cayos Sapodillas (or Zapotillas), well off the coast of southern Belize, where there is great snorkeling (Q400/1000 for one/two days). A minimum of eight people is required and exit taxes and National Park fees (Q160 in total) are separate.

Río Dulce Tours

Tour agencies in town offer day trips up the Río Dulce to Río Dulce town (departing at 9:30am and 2:30pm), as do most local boatmen at the Lívingston dock. Many travelers use these tours as one-way transportation to Río Dulce, paying Q125/180 one way/round trip. It's a beautiful ride through tropical jungle scenery, with several places to stop on the way.

While a boat ride on the Río Dulce is not to be missed, if you're coming from Guatemala City or Puerto Barrios it makes much more sense to catch a boat from Puerto Barrios to Lívingston and do the tour on your way out.

CATCH THE RHYTHM OF THE GARÍFUNA

Lívingston is the heartland of Guatemala's Garífuna community, and it won't take too long before you hear some of their distinctive music. A Garífuna band generally consists of three drums (the *primera* takes the bass part, the other two play more melodic functions), a shaker or maraca, a turtle shell (hit like a cowbell) and a conch shell (blown like a flute).

The lyrics are often call and response – most often sung in Garífuna (a language with influences from Arawak, French and West African languages) but sometimes composed in Spanish. Most songs deal with themes from village life – planting time, harvests, things that happen in the village, honoring the dead and folktales of bad sons made good. Sometimes they simply sing about the beauty of the village.

Traditional Garífuna music has given birth to an almost bewildering array of musical styles, among them Punta Rock, Jugujugu, Calachumba, Jajankanu, Chumba, Saranda, Sambé and Parranda.

Punta Rock is by far the most widely known adaptation of traditional Garífuna rhythms, and you can hear 'Punta' in most discos throughout Central America. The dance that accompanies it (also called *punta*) is a frenzied sort of affair, following the nature of the percussion. The left foot swivels back and forth while the right foot taps out the rhythm. Perhaps coincidentally, this movement causes the hips to shake wildly, leading some observers to comment on the sexual nature of the dance.

If you're interested in learning more about Garífuna culture or want drumming lessons, drop in to Rasta Mesa (p218).

Lívingston

Rasta Mesa (560m);
Flowas (820m);
Vecchia Toscana (850m)

Calle al Cementerio

Calle Principal

Calle Minerva

Calle Principal

Muelle Municipal

Boats to Los Siete Altares, Playa Blanca, Punta Gorda

Bahía de Amatique

Boats to Puerto Barrios →

Boats to Finca Tatin, Hotelito Perdido, Roundhouse, Río Dulce Town

Calle Marcos Sánchez Díaz

Secondary Dock

Río Dulce

Shortly after you leave Lívingston, you pass the tributary Río Tatin on the right, then will probably stop at an **indigenous arts museum** set up by Asociación Ak' Tenamit (www.aktenamit.org) an NGO working to improve conditions for the Q'eqchi' Maya population of the area. The river enters a gorge called **La Cueva de la Vaca**, its walls hung with great tangles of jungle foliage and the humid air noisy with the cries of tropical birds. Just beyond that is **La Pintada**, a rock escarpment covered with graffiti. Fur-

Lívingston

ther on, a **thermal spring** forces sulfurous water out of the base of the cliff, providing a chance for a warm swim. The river widens into **El Golfete**, a lake-like body of water that presages the even more vast expanse of Lago de Izabal further upstream.

On the northern shore of El Golfete is the **Biotopo Chocón Machacas**, a 72-sq-km reserve established within the Parque Nacional Río Dulce to protect the beautiful river landscape, the valuable forests and mangrove swamps and their wildlife, which includes such rare creatures as the tapir and above all the manatee. A network of 'water trails' (boat routes around several jungle lagoons) provide ways to see other bird, animal and plant life of the reserve. You can stay here, at the community-run lodge Q'ana Itz'am (p224) in Lagunita Salvador but you will have to arrange transportation separately.

Boats will probably visit **Islas de Pájaros**, a pair of islands where thousands of waterbirds live, in the middle of El Golfete. From El Golfete you continue upriver, passing increasing numbers of expensive villas and boathouses, to the town of Río Dulce, where the soaring Hwy 13 road bridge crosses the river, and on to El Castillo de San Felipe on Lago de Izabal.

You can also do this trip starting from Río Dulce.

🎊 Festivals & Events

During **Semana Santa** Lívingston is packed with merrymakers. **Garífuna National Day** is celebrated on November 26 with a variety of cultural events.

🛏 Sleeping

Prices in Lívingston hit their peak from July to December – outside of these months many midrange and top-end places listed here halve their rates.

Hotel Ríos Tropicales   HOTEL $$
(☑ 5755-7571; www.mctropic.webs.com; Calle Principal; s/d Q150/200, without bathroom from Q60/120; 🗺) The Ríos Tropicales has a variety of big, well-screened rooms facing a central patio with plenty of hammocks and chill-out space. Rooms with shared bathroom are more spacious, but others are better decorated.

Casa de la Iguana   HOSTEL $
(☑ 7947-0064; www.casadelaiguana.com; Calle Marcos Sánchez Díaz; hammock/dm Q20/45, cabin with/without bathroom Q160/110; 🗺) A five-minute walk from the main dock, this party hostel offers good-value cabins. They're clean wooden affairs, with simple but elegant decoration. Happy hour here rocks on and you can camp or crash in a hammock.

Flowas   BUNGALOW $
(☑ 7947-0376; infoflowas@gmail.com; per person Q100) An extremely laid-back little backpacker enclave, this place offers rustic wood and bamboo cabins set up on the 2nd floor (catching the odd breeze) right on the beachfront. The atmosphere is relaxed and there's good, cheap food available. A taxi (Q15 from the dock) will drop you within 150m of the front gate.

Hotel Salvador Gaviota   BUNGALOW $$
(☑ 7947-0874; www.hotelsalvadorgaviota.com; Playa Quehueche; per person with/without bathroom Q140/70; ❷) Beautiful simple wood and bamboo rooms set back a couple of hundred meters from a reasonably clean beach. Daytrippers going to and from the Seven Altars drop in for meals (Q40 to Q80) and drinks here – otherwise you may have the place to yourself.

It's 500m from the swing bridge where the road ends – a taxi will charge about Q15 to get you there.

Posada El Delfín   HOTEL $$
(☑ 7947-0976; www.posadaeldelfin.com; Calle Marcos Sánchez Díaz; s/d from Q325/450; ❀ 🗺 ❀) Down by the waterfront, this is a big modern construction with reasonably sized, spotless

rooms and a great swimming pool overlooking the river. Don't expect views from your room – the recommended 2nd-floor restaurant steals them all.

Vecchia Toscana   HOTEL $$

(☑ 7947-0884;   www.vecchiatoscana-livingston. com; Barrio Paris; s/d from Q341/488; ✸ @ ⏀ ⩇)
This beautiful Italian-run place down on the beach has some of the best rooms in town. There are a variety of rooms on offer, going up to apartments that sleep eight comfortably. The grounds and common areas are immaculate and there's a good Italian restaurant with sea views out the front.

A taxi here from the dock will cost around Q10.

Hotel Villa Caribe   HOTEL $$$

(☑ 7947-0072;   www.hotelvillacaribeguatemala. com; Calle Principal; s/d Q830/1000, bungalows Q1300; ✸ @ ⏀ ⩇) The 45-room Villa Caribe is a luxurious anomaly among Lívingston's laid-back, low-priced Caribbean lodgings. Modern but still Caribbean in style, it has many conveniences and comforts, including extensive tropical gardens, a big swimming pool and a large poolside bar. Rooms are fan-cooled with modern bathrooms; little balconies overlook the gardens and river mouth. The bungalows are air-conditioned.

✖ Eating

Food in Lívingston is relatively expensive because most of it (except fish and coconuts) must be brought in by boat. There's fine seafood here and some unusual flavors for Guatemala, including coconut and curry. *Tapado,* a rich stew made from fish, shrimp, shellfish and coconut milk, spiced with cilantro, is the delicious local specialty. A potent potable is made by slicing off the top of a green coconut and mixing in a healthy dose of rum. Known as *coco locos,* they hit the spot.

Calle Principal is dotted with many open-air eateries.

Restaurante Gaby   GUATEMALAN $

(Calle Marcos Sánchez Díaz; mains Q30-50; ⊘ 8am-9pm) For a good honest feed in humble surrounds, you can't go past Gaby's. She serves up the good stuff: lobster, *tapado,* rice and beans and good breakfasts at good prices. The *telenovelas* (soap operas) come free.

Antojitos Yoli's   BAKERY $

(Calle Principal; baked goods Q10-30; ⊘ 8am-5pm) This is the place to come for baked goods.

Especially recommended are the coconut bread and pineapple pie.

Happy Fish   GUATEMALAN, SEAFOOD $$

(Calle Principal; mains Q40-100; ⊘ 7am-10pm; ⏀)
This bustling and breezy main street eatery is always busy with locals and tourists, keeping the food fresh and the service snappy. The requisite *tapado* is here, plus a good range of other options.

Restaurante Buga
Mama   GUATEMALAN, SEAFOOD $$

(Calle Marcos Sánchez Díaz; mains Q60-100; ⊘ 8am-9pm; ⏀) This place enjoys the best location of any restaurant in town, and profits go to the Asociación Ak' Tenemit (www.aktenamit.org), an NGO with several projects in the area. There's a wide range of seafood, homemade pasta, curries and other dishes on the menu, including a very good *tapado* (Q100).

Most of the waiters here are trainees in a community sustainable tourism development scheme, so service can be sketchy, but forgivable.

♟ Drinking & Nightlife

Adventurous drinkers should try *guifiti,* a local concoction made from coconut rum, often infused with herbs. It's said to have medicinal as well as recreational properties.

A handful of bars down on the beach to the left of the end of Calle Principal pull in travelers and locals at night (after about 10pm or 11pm). It's very dark down here, so take care. The bars are within five minutes' walk of each other, so you should go for a wander and see what's happening. Music ranges from punta to salsa, merengue and electronica. Things warm up on Friday but Saturday is the party night – often going until 5am or 6am.

Happy hour is pretty much an institution along the main street, with every restaurant getting in on the act. One of the best is at Casa de la Iguana.

☆ Entertainment

Quite often a roaming band will play a few songs for diners along the Calle Principal around dinnertime. If you like the music, make sure to sling them a few bucks. Several places around town have live Garífuna music, although schedules are unpredictable.

Café-Bar Ubafu LIVE MUSIC
(Calle al Cementerio; ⊘6pm-late) Probably the most dependable. Supposedly has music and dancing nightly, but liveliest on weekends.

Hotel Villa Caribe LIVE MUSIC
(www.hotelvillacaribeguatemala.com; Calle Principal) Diners in the hotel restaurant can enjoy a Garífuna show each evening at 7pm.

ℹ Information

After being here half an hour, you'll know where everything is. Though we use street names here for ease of orientation, in reality no-one uses them. For more on Lívingston, check out this community website, www.livingston.com.gt.
Banrural (Calle Principal; ⊘9am-5pm Mon-Fri, 9am-1pm Sat) Changes US dollars and traveler's checks and has an ATM.
Immigration Office (Calle Principal; ⊘6am-7pm) Issues entry and exit stamps for travelers arriving direct from or going direct to Belize or Honduras, charging Q80 for exit stamps. Outside business hours, you can knock for attention at any time.

DANGERS & ANNOYANCES

Lívingston has its edgy aspects and a few hustlers operate here – exercise normal precautions. Use mosquito repellent and other sensible precautions, especially if you go out into the jungle; mosquitoes here carry both malaria and dengue fever.

ℹ Getting There & Away

Frequent boats come downriver from Río Dulce and across the bay from Puerto Barrios. There are also international boats from Honduras and Belize.

Happy Fish and Exotic Travel operate combined boat and bus shuttles to La Ceiba (the cheapest gateway to Honduras' Bay Islands) for around Q450 per person, with a minimum of four people. Leaving Lívingston at 6am or earlier will get you to La Ceiba in time for the boat to the islands, making it a one-day trip, which is nearly impossible to do independently.

There's also a boat that goes direct to Punta Gorda daily at 7am (Q200, 1½ hours), leaving from the public dock. In Punta Gorda, the boat connects with a bus to Placencia and Belize City. The boat waits for this bus to arrive from Placencia before it sets off back for Lívingston from Punta Gorda at about 10:30am.

If you are taking one of these early international departures, get your exit stamp from immigration in Lívingston the day before.

Around Lívingston

Lanchas traveling between Río Dulce and Lívingston (or vice versa) will drop you at the Hotelito Perdido, Finca Tatín or Roundhouse. These places can also pick you up, charging around Q40 per person from Lívingston, more from Puerto Barrios or Río Dulce.

🛏 Sleeping

Roundhouse HOSTEL $
(☑4294-9730; www.roundhouseguatemala.com; dm/d without bathroom Q45/100; @🖾) ✎ The newest player on the river is this medium-sized party hostel. The first floor is a riverfront bar/restaurant/hammock area. On the second floor there's a spacious dorm and some good, simple private rooms. On offer are snorkel and sailing tours and the 8.5m pontoon boat used for booze cruises on the river.

Hotelito Perdido HOTEL $
(☑5725-1576; www.hotelitoperdido.com; dm Q45, bungalow s/d from Q150/200, without bathroom Q120/150) ✎ This beautiful, secluded hideout is a five-minute boat ride from Finca Tatín. The ambience is superb – relaxed and friendly. The whole place is solar powered and constructed in such a way as to cause minimal impact on the environment.

The two-story bungalows are gorgeous – simple yet well decorated, with a sleeping area upstairs and a small sitting area downstairs. It's a small, intimate place, so it's a good idea to book ahead. You can organize many of the activities available at Finca Tatín from here as well.

Finca Tatín BUNGALOW $
(☑4148-3332; www.fincatatin.com; dm Q50, s/d from Q140/180, without bathroom from Q75/120; 🔊) ✎ This wonderful, rustic B&B at the confluence of Ríos Dulce and Tatín, about 10km from Lívingston, is a great place to experience the forest. Four-hour guided walks and kayak trips, some visiting local Q'eqchi' villages, are offered. Accommodation is in funky wood-and-thatched cabins scattered through the jungle and some rather spiffy new riverfront ones with balconies overlooking the water.

There are trails, waterfalls and endless river tributaries that you can explore with one of the *cayucos* (indigenous fishing dugout) available for guest use (Q80 per day). Guided night walks through the jungle offer views of elusive nightlife, and cave tours are good for swimming and soaking in a natural sauna. You can walk to Lívingston from here in about four hours, or take a kayak and staff from Finca Tatin will come pick you up.

Q'ana Itz'am
CABIN **$$**

(☑ 5992-1853; www.lagunitasalvador.com; r Q185, bungalow Q350) 🍃 In the small Q'eqchi' community of Lagunita Salvador, this charming community tourism project offers simple accommodation in wooden bungalows connected by boardwalks in the mangroves. There's plenty to do here – bird-watching, jungle walks, kayaking and sampling delicious Q'eqchi' traditional cooking.

The villagers organize traditional dances on request and tours of the friendly village are offered to help give you a better understanding of the way of life in this curious little pocket of the world. Reservations are a must and transport is offered from Lívingston/Río Dulce Q100/125 per person.

Lagunita Creek
LODGE **$**

(☑ 4113-0103; dm Q80) Heading northwest from Lívingston brings you to the Río Sarstun, which forms the border between Belize and Guatemala. Ten kilometers upstream is the small community of Lagunita Creek, where a community-tourism project offers lodging in a simple ecolodge. Simple meals (Q50 to Q65) are available here, or you can bring your own food to cook.

Included in the price is use of kayaks to explore the beautiful, turquoise waters of the river and guided nature walks/bird-watching tours. Transport isn't complicated but it can be expensive – the only way to get here is by boat. *Lanchas* from Lívingston charge Q1200 per boatload (up to eight people), with a small discount for smaller groups. Happy Fish Travel in Livingston offers day/overnight tours here for Q280/480 but require a minimum of six people.

El Petén

Includes ➡

Best Least-Visited Ruins

Best Places to Stay

Why Go?

Vast, sparsely populated and jungle-covered, Guatemala's largest and northernmost department is ever ripe for exploration. Whether it's the mysteries of the Classic Maya, the biological bounty of the jungle or simply the chance to lounge lakeside that inspires you, it's all here in abundance. How deeply you choose to delve into the Maya legacy will depend on your level of interest/willingness to get your feet muddy. The towering temples of Tikal can be reached by tour from just about anywhere in the country, while more remote sites like El Mirador or Piedras Negras require days of planning and further days of jungle trekking. Wherever you go, you'll be serenaded by a jungle symphony – the forests are alive with parrots, monkeys and larger, more elusive animals. The Maya Biosphere Reserve covers virtually the entire northern third of El Petén, and together with its counterparts in Mexico and Belize forms a multinational wildlife haven that spans more than 30,000 sq km.

When to Go

If you're planning to do much jungle trekking to remote archaeological sites, late February to May are best: it's drier, less boggy and you won't have to wade through so much mud, though it can get rather hot and steamy toward late May. The rains begin in June and with them come the mosquitoes – bring rain gear, repellent and, if you plan on slinging a hammock, a mosquito net. September and October are peak hurricane and thunderstorm season, with the rains continuing into November, and are best avoided. December to February, with cool nights and mornings, can be quite a pleasant time to visit El Petén.

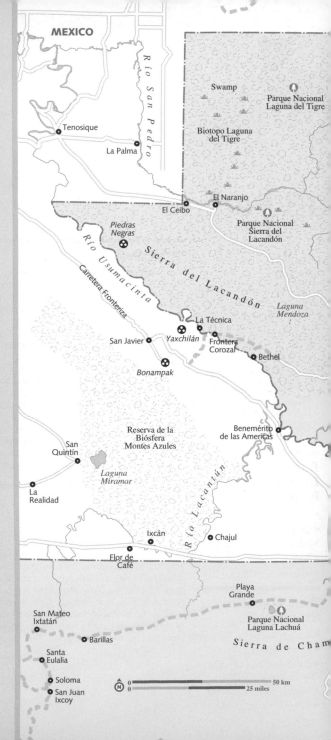

El Petén Highlights

1 Gazing over the jungle canopy from towering Temple IV at **Tikal** (p246)

2 Trekking through the jungle to the vast, though still scarcely excavated, Maya city of **El Mirador** (p260)

3 Awakening to the sound of howler monkeys at **Laguna Petexbatún** (p231)

4 Night cruising for crocodiles and spotting macaws at the **Estación Biológica Las Guacamayas** (p260)

5 Lounging lakeside over evening cocktails on the picturesque island/town of **Flores** (p234)

6 Admiring the sunset over **Lago de Petén Itzá** from laid-back El Remate (p244)

7 Breaking bread with fellow travelers at the rural retreat of **Finca Ixobel** (p233)

8 Rolling down the **Río de la Pasión** to **Ceibal** (p229), a remote riverside ruin with intricately carved stelae of past Maya rulers

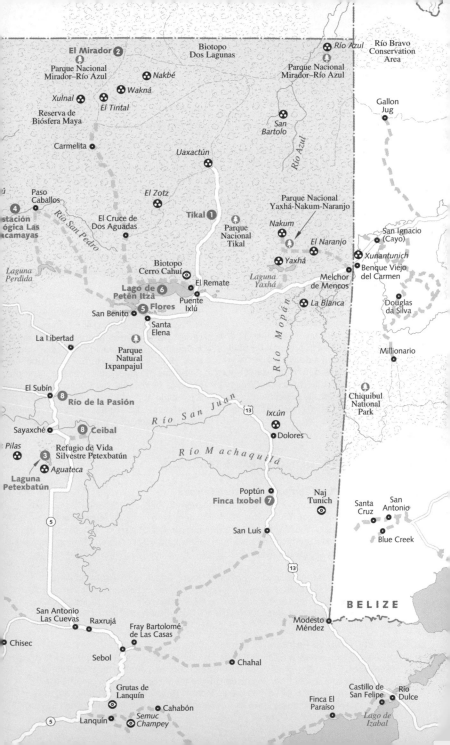

History

Often referred to as the cradle of Maya civilization, El Petén has historically been isolated from the rest of present-day Guatemala, a situation that continued until quite recently. The major Maya population centers – Tikal and El Mirador – had more contact with neighboring settlements in Belize and Mexico than with those down south.

The arrival of the Spanish changed little in this regard. The Itzá, who lived on the island now known as Flores, earned a reputation for cruelty and ferocity which, along with El Petén's impenetrable jungles and fierce wildlife, kept the Spanish at a distance until 1697, about 150 years after the rest of the country had been conquered.

Even after conquest, the Spanish had no great love for El Petén. The island of Flores was a penal colony before a small city was founded, mostly to facilitate the trade in chicle, hardwood, sugarcane and rubber that had been planted in the region.

The big change came in 1970, when the Guatemalan government saw the opportunity to market Tikal as a tourist destination and work began on a decent road network.

El Petén's population boom – largely a result of government incentives for farmers to relocate – has seen the population increase from 15,000 to a staggering 500,000 in the last 50 years.

Some of the new neighbors are not entirely welcome, however – large tracts of land, particularly in the northwest corner and in the Parque Nacional Laguna del Tigre, have been taken over by drug traffickers and people smugglers, capitalizing on the unpatroled border with Mexico.

❶ Getting There & Around

El Petén's main tourism node is at the twin towns of Flores and Santa Elena, about 60km southwest of Tikal. The main roads to Flores (from Río Dulce to the southeast, from Cobán and Chisec to the southwest, from the Belize border to the east and from the Mexican border to the northwest) are now all paved and in good condition, except for a few short stretches. Frequent buses and minibuses carry travelers along these routes. Santa Elena also has the only functioning civil airport in the country aside from Guatemala City.

Sayaxché

POP 13,700 / ELEV 133M

Sayaxché, on the south bank of the Río de la Pasión, 61km southwest of Flores, is the closest town to around 10 scattered Maya archaeological sites, including Ceibal, Aguateca, Dos Pilas, Tamarindito and Altar de Sacrificios. Besides its strategic position between Flores and the Cobán area, it has a riverside appeal all its own, with rickety motorboats and funky barges regularly floating passengers and trucks across the

---

MEXICAN BORDER (CHIAPAS & TABASCO)

Via Bethel/La Técnica & Frontera Coroza

Regular transportation service reaches the Mexican border at Bethel or La Técnica, on the eastern bank of the Río Usumacinta, from where there is regular ferry service to Frontera Corozal on the Mexican bank. Guatemalan immigration is in Bethel, but the crossing is quicker and much cheaper from La Técnica (Q10 per person). Microbus drivers will normally stop and wait for you to do the formalities in Bethel before proceeding to La Técnica.

Autotransporte Chamoán vans run hourly from Frontera Corozal *embarcadero* (wharf) to Palenque (M$100, 2½ to three hours), with the last departure at 3pm.

To visit the Maya ruins at Yaxchilán on the Mexican side of the river, Escudo Jaguar runs boats from M$950 to M$1300 (five to 10 people), round trip, with a two-hour wait at the ruins.

Via El Ceibo/La Palma

Further north, travelers may enter the Mexican state of Tabasco via a recently opened border post by El Ceibo, a village on the Río San Pedro. Immigration posts operate on both sides of the border from 9am to 6pm. From the Mexican side, taxis shuttle travelers to the terminal for buses to Tenosique, Tabasco (M$35, one hour, hourly 6am to 5pm), from where minibuses leave for Palenque (M$50, two hours) until 7pm.

broad waterway till sundown (pedestrian Q2, car Q15).

Banrural (⊙ 7:30am-4:30pm Mon-Fri, 7:30am-1pm Sat), two blocks up from Hotel Guayacán, then one block left, has a Cajero 5B and changes euros and American Express traveler's checks. Get online at **Zona X** (per hr Q6; ⊙ 8am-8pm Mon-Sat), three streets up from the dock on the left.

🛌 Sleeping

Hospedaje Yaxkin BUNGALOW **$**
(📞 4053-3484; bungalow per person Q50, without bathroom Q30) East of the center are these 15 cheery bungalows amid an impressive variety of plants and trees. A big open-air restaurant serves pasta, tacos and river fish (Q50). It's four blocks east and a block south of the church. Gregarious host Rosendo will pick you up at the dock if you phone ahead.

El Majestuoso Petén HOTEL **$**
(📞 7928-6166; s/d Q80/160, without bathroom Q50/100; ❄) This recently remodeled establishment has a peaceful setting overlooking a lazy stretch of the Río Petexbatún. Of the simply furnished rooms, the 'Tikal' and 'San José' have the best river views. From the dock, go up to the first intersection, then three blocks to the right to find the green building.

Hotel Del Río HOTEL **$$**
(📞 7928-6138; hoteldelriosayaxche@hotmail.com; d with fan/air-con Q175/250; 🅿 ❄) A few steps to the right of wharf (with your back to the river), this modern hotel is the cushy choice, with huge, sparkling rooms alongside an airy lobby and a terrace overlooking the river.

🍴 Eating

Café del Río GUATEMALAN **$**
(Calle del Ferry; mains Q40; ⊙ 6:30am-9pm) The most atmospheric eatery occupies a wooden dock on the north bank where you can enjoy river fish, sweet breezes and icy beer. It has its own boat to shuttle people over from the south side.

Café Maya GUATEMALAN **$$**
(Calle del Ferry; mains Q40-60; ⊙ 6:30am-9pm) About the best bet for grub is this casual, open-air hall, a popular gathering place both morning and evening. Aside from the usual fried chicken and grilled steak, there's river fish, served with abundant portions of salad, beans and rice, and fries.

ⓘ Getting There & Away

Southbound from Sayaxché, four microbuses head for Cobán (Q60, four hours) between 5am and 3pm. Every 25 minutes or so, Raxrujá-bound micros go to the San Antonio junction (Q30, 1½ hours), from where there are frequent departures for Cobán. Vehicles depart from a lot behind the Hotel Guayacán. From the north side of the Río de la Pasión, micros leave for Santa Elena every 15 minutes, from 5:45am to 6pm (Q23, 1½ hours).

For river transportation, inquire at **Viajes Don Pedro** (📞 4580-9389; servlanchasdonpedro@hotmail.com), the last building on the left when you're facing the dock. A trip all the way down the Río de la Pasión to Benemérito de las Américas (Mexico), with stops at the ruins of Altar de Sacrificios, should not cost more than Q3000 (3½ hours to ruins, up to four passengers).

Around Sayaxché

Of the archaeological sites reached from Sayaxché, Ceibal and Aguateca are the most interesting to the amateur visitor. Both are impressively restored and can be reached by boat trips along jungle-fringed waterways followed by forest walks. Most people arrive in the context of a tour but it is possible to make arrangements independently.

Ceibal

With its strategic position along the west bank of the Río de la Pasión, the independent kingdom of **Ceibal** (admission Q60; ⊙ 8am-4pm) amassed considerable power controlling commerce along this key stretch of the waterway. Though architecturally less amazing than some other sites, the river journey to Ceibal is among the most memorable, as is hiking below the jungle canopy with monkeys howling overhead.

Unimportant during most of the Classic Period, Ceibal (sometimes spelled Seibal) grew rapidly in the 9th century AD. It attained a population of around 10,000 by AD 900, then was abandoned shortly afterwards. Its low, ruined temples were quickly covered by a thick carpet of jungle. Excavation of the site is ongoing under the supervision of University of Arizona archaeologist Takeshi Inomata.

A one-hour ride up the Río de la Pasión from Sayaxché brings you to a primitive dock. After landing, you clamber up a narrow, rocky path beneath ceiba trees and

Ceibal

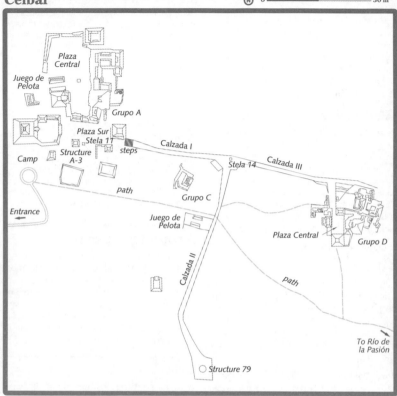

jungle vines to reach the archaeological zone, perched about 100m above the river.

There's a large scale model of the site by the entrance. The ceremonial core of the city covers three hills, connected over steep ravines by the original causeways. Smallish temples, many of them covered with jungle, surround two principal groups, A and D. In front of some temples, and standing seemingly alone on paths, are magnificent stelae, their intricate carvings still in excellent condition. It takes about two hours to explore the site. Bring mosquito repellent.

Most of the stelae appear at **Grupo A**, made up of three plazas at the site's highest point. At the best excavated of these, Plaza Sur, stands **Structure A-3**, a pyramidal platform with a stela on each side and one at the top. Some of the characters depicted here have distinctly non-Maya features and dress, which has led to speculation that foreigners once inhabited the area. According to one

hotly debated theory, the city was invaded by Putun Maya, a race of merchant-warriors from the Tabasco area of Mexico, around the mid-ninth century. This might account for the 'foreign' look of the moustachioed warrior on **stele 11**, for example, who stands on the east side of the platform.

Calzada I leads east to **Grupo D**, a more compact series of temples that backs up on a precipitous gorge. About midway is a turnoff south for Calzada II, just beyond which is the fantastically preserved stela 14, which may depict a tax collector. Proceeding down Calzada II to the south, you reach the intriguing **Structure 79**. Three stone steps surround the unusual ring-shaped structure, which stands alone in a clearing with a small altar in the shape of a jaguar's head. It is believed to have served as an astronomical observatory, from which the inhabitants studied planetary movements.

Café del Río (p229) in Sayaxché, on the north side of the river, runs *lanchas* (small motorboats) here (Q470 for up to three persons) and Viajes Don Pedro (p229) charges Q600 for up to five passengers. The fee should include a guide, who may actually be the boatman. In high season, ask the *lancheros* about joining a tour group.

Alternatively, Ceibal can be reached over land: get any bus, minibus or pickup heading south from Sayaxché on Hwy 5 (toward Raxrujá and Chisec) and get off after 9km at Paraíso, from where it's an 8km walk east down a dirt track to Ceibal. In the rainy season check first that this stretch is passable.

Laguna Petexbatún

Laguna Petexbatún is a 6km-long lake southwest of Sayaxché, approached by an hour's *lancha* ride up the Río Petexbatún, a tributary of the Río de la Pasión. The lake, river and surrounding forests harbor many birds, including kingfishers, egrets, vultures, eagles, cormorants and herons. Within reach of the waterways are five archaeological sites and a pair of jungle-hideaway accommodations.

What we know of the history of these archaeological sites has mostly been unraveled by archaeologists since the late 1980s. Dos Pilas was founded about AD 640 by a prince who left Tikal and later defeated it in two wars, capturing its ruler Nuun Ujol Chaak (Shield Skull) in 679, according to inscriptions at the site. Dos Pilas' second and third rulers carried out monumental building programs, waged wars of conquest and came to dominate most of the territory between the Pasión and Chixoy rivers, but in AD 761 their vassal Tamarindito rebelled and killed the fourth ruler, causing the Dos Pilas nobility to relocate to the naturally fortified site of Aguateca, which was already functioning as a twin capital. Aguateca in turn was abandoned in the early 9th century, around the same time as three defensive moats were cut across the neck of the Chiminos peninsula on the edge of Laguna Petexbatún. Archaeologists surmise that Punta de Chiminos was the last refuge of the Petexbatún dynasty founded at Dos Pilas.

Aguateca

The ruins of Aguateca stand on a hilltop at the far south end of Laguna Petexbatún. Defended by cliffs and split by a ravine, the city enjoyed military successes (including one over nearby Ceibal) up until about AD 735, according to data gleaned from carved stelae. The site is both the easiest to access and most immediately impressive within reach of Sayaxché.

It's fairly certain that rulers from Dos Pilas abandoned that city for the better-fortified Aguateca around AD 761, and that the city was finally overrun by unknown attackers around 790 – a wealth of arrowheads and skeletons have been found dating back to that time. The city was abandoned shortly afterwards.

A five-minute walk from the dock is the visitor center. Rangers can guide you round the site in about 1½ hours (a small tip is in order). Two main groups feature well-restored structures: the **Grupo del Palacio** where the ruler lived, and the **Plaza Mayor** (Main Plaza) to its south, where fiberglass copies of stelae showing finely attired rulers stand beside the fallen originals. The two groups are connected by a causeway over the ravine.

From the visitor center, you can skirt the cliff wall north to reach a **mirador** (lookout) with views over the rivers and swamplands toward the east. The trail then turns left and descends into the ravine, continuing 100m between two sheer limestone walls, then climbs back up to emerge onto the Grupo del Palacio. Proceed through the palatial complex back toward the entrance. At the lower end, turn right to take the causeway over the ravine (70m deep here) to reach the **Plaza Principal**.

Aguateca is a 1¼-hour *lancha* trip direct from Sayaxché, via the mangrove-fringed Río Petexbatún.

Dos Pilas

This fascinating site is a mere 16km from Sayaxché, but getting here is a serious undertaking. If you have the time, it's well worth considering for the fine carvings on display, particularly the **hieroglyphic staircase**, with five 6m-wide steps, each with two rows of superbly preserved glyphs, climbing to the base of the royal palace near the main plaza.

The city began life as a breakaway from the Tikal group when that city was taken by Calakmul. Dos Pilas appears to have been governed by a set of aggressive rulers – it clashed with Tikal, Ceibal, Yaxchilán and Motul all within 150 years, often ignoring

EXPLORE MORE OF EL PETÉN

The Petén region is literally brimming with archaeological sites in various stages of excavation. Some are harder than others to get to; tour operators in Flores and El Remate can help you reach them. Here are a few of the more intriguing ones that you might want to check out:

San Bartolo Discovered in 2003, this site features one of the best-preserved Maya murals with a depiction of the creation myth from the Popul Vuh. It's approximately 40km northeast of Uaxactún, near the Río Azul.

Piedras Negras On the banks of the Río Usumacinta amidst black cliffs, these remote ruins boast impressive carvings and a sizable acropolis complex. It was here that part-time archaeologist Tatiana Proskouriakoff deciphered the Maya hieroglyphic system.

La Blanca Located along the Río Mopan near the Belize border, this palatial complex may have been a trading center that flourished in the Late Classic period. The acropolis is notable for its remarkably preserved stone walls and an abundance of graffiti. Currently under excavation by a Spanish team. The Mayan Adventure (p235), based in Flores, leads tours here.

El Zotz This sprawling site occupies its own *biotopo* abutting Tikal National Park. Of the three barely excavated temples, one, the Pirámide del Diablo, can be scaled for views all the way to Tikal. Stick around till dusk to see how the place gets its name – 'The Bat' in Maya.

Río Azul Located up near the corner where the Belize, Guatemala and Mexico borders meet, this medium-sized site fell under the domain of Tikal in the early Classic period and became a key trading post for cacao from the Caribbean. Most notable are the tombs with vibrant painted glyphs inside. Hotel El Chiclero (p257) in Uaxactún leads a recommended excursion.

the traditional 'war season,' which finished in time for the harvest.

Many stelae at the site have been relocated to museums and replaced by crushed-rock and fiberglass replicas, in a pilot program designed to deter looters.

The best way to reach Dos Pilas is by tour from Sayaxché or by staying at the Posada Caribe (p232) and organizing a tour there. Either way, you'll be up for about 3½ hours of jungle trekking on foot or horseback from the *posada* (guesthouse), passing the sites of **Tamarandito** (which also features a hieroglyphic stairway) and the smaller site of **Arroyo de Piedra**, which has a plaza and some well-preserved stelae.

🛏 Sleeping & Eating

Posada Caribe   BUNGALOW $$
(☎ 5304-1745; www.posadacaribe.com; s/d Q385/ 475) Located at a lazy stretch of the river about halfway between Sayaxché and Laguna Petexbatún is this appealingly remote encampment managed by the ebullient don Julián Mariona and family. Seven humble, thatched bungalows with wood plank floors and lacy curtains are set back from the river-

bank. Meals are served for around Q100 each.

From here you can walk to the Dos Pilas ruins (p231) in about 3½ hours, including stops at the lesser ruins of Tamarindito and Arroyo de Piedra en route. Horses for the trip can be hired at Q120 each.

Chiminos Island Lodge   LODGE $$$
(☎ 2335-3506; www.chiminosisland.com; r adult/ child under 13 incl 3 meals Q1060/590) Jutting out from the western shore of Laguna Petexbatún, this magical lodge shares its promontory with a largely unexcavated Maya citadel. Five spare but elegantly furnished bungalows, with private bathroom, fan and porch, are spaced well apart from one another and reached along trails through the forest.

Built of natural hard woods and equipped with wraparound screened windows, they give the feeling of sleeping in the jungle without all those nasty bugs and bats. Naturally prepared food is served in an open-air restaurant/clubhouse, and folders full of absorbing archaeological information and articles about the area are available to peruse.

ℹ Getting Around

Getting to all of these places involves making arrangements with boatmen at Sayaxché, or taking a tour. Viajes Don Pedro (p229) offers a straightforward half-day return trip from Sayaxché to Aguateca, charging Q600 for up to five people. You could, for example, arrange to be dropped at one of the lodges afterwards and be picked up the next afternoon after making a trip to Dos Pilas. Martsam Travel (p235) and other outfits in Flores offer one-day tours to Aguateca, including lunch and guide.

Finca Ixobel

The **Finca Ixobel** (☑5410-4307; www.finca ixobel.com; Ⓟ@⌆) ⌀ is an ecological resort/bohemian hideaway amid pine forests and patches of jungle in southeast Petén, between Flores and Río Dulce. Its friendly, relaxed atmosphere makes it a great place to meet other travelers from around the globe, with a wide range of activities, accommodation options and lip-smacking homemade meals. American Carole DeVine founded this hideaway in the 1970s with her husband Michael, who was tragically murdered in 1990 during the civil war, when nearby Poptún was a training ground for the antiguerrilla forces called Kaibiles.

There's plenty to do around here. The grounds contain a natural pool for swimming, and horseback riding treks (from two hours to four days), cave trips, and innertubing on the Río Machaquilá (in the rainy season) are all organized on a daily basis. One of the most popular excursions is to the caves of Naj Tunich (p233) with their galleries of Maya painting; the cost of Q300 per person (minimum of four) includes admission, guide and lunch. Another trip combines a visit to ruins at Ixcún, with swimming at the waterfalls on the Río Mopán.

Among the numerous options for bedding down here are *palapas* (thatched palm-leaf shelters) for hanging hammocks, bungalows (single/double Q175/300) and 'treehouses' (single/double Q80/120) – most of which are actually cabins on stilts. The large, grassy camping area (per person Q30) has good bathrooms and plenty of shade. Assorted other accommodations include a couple of dormitories (Q40) and rooms with shared (single/double Q80/120) and private (single/double Q175/300) bathroom, all with fan, mosquito nets and screened windows.

Meals are excellent, including an eat-all-you-like buffet dinner. Finca Ixobel has its own bakery, grows its own salad ingredients and produces its own eggs. You can cook in the campground if you bring your own supplies. After dinner many people move to the poolside bar for reasonably priced cocktails and other drinks. Everything at Finca Ixobel works on the honor system: guests keep an account of what they eat and drink and the services they use.

There are often volunteer opportunities for fluent English and Spanish speakers in exchange for room and board. If the *finca* (farm) suits your style and you want to help/hang out for six weeks minimum, ask about volunteering.

ℹ Getting There & Away

The *finca* is 5km south of the regional commercial center of Poptún, from where you can take a taxi (Q30) or a *tuk-tuk* (three-wheeled motor taxi), which will cost Q20. Otherwise, any bus or minibus along Hwy 13 can drop you at the turnoff, from which it's a 15-minute walk to the *finca*. When leaving Finca Ixobel, most buses will stop on the highway to pick you up, but not after dark. The *finca* also offers shuttles to/from Flores for Q50.

Bus departures from Poptún include the following:

Flores/Santa Elena (two hours, 113km) Línea Dorada offers 1st-class service at 4am, 4.30am and 5pm among the sleepy passengers coming from Guatemala City. The best option is to take a minibus (Q30, every 10 minutes, 6am to 6pm).

Guatemala City (seven hours, 387km) First-class buses by Línea Dorada (Q150 to Q190) depart at 11:30am and 11pm. Fuente del Norte buses (Q80) pass through approximately every hour from 5:30am to midnight.

Río Dulce (Q50, two hours, 99km) All Guatemala City–bound buses make a stop in Río Dulce.

Around Finca Ixobel

◉ Sights

Naj Tunich   CAVE
(www.rutanajtunich.com; admission Q25; ◷8am-6pm) When they were discovered in 1979, these caves created a stir in the archaeological world. Measuring 3km long, they're packed with hieroglyphic texts and Maya murals depicting religious ceremonies, art education, ball games and even sex scenes – though whether they're of a gay nature is

a question that is still being disputed by anthropologists.

In all, there are 94 images, completed during the Maya Classic period. Scribes and artists traveled from as far away as Calakmul in Mexico to contribute to the murals.

The caves were closed in 1984, due to vandalism, reopened briefly, then closed permanently a decade later for conservation purposes. Fortunately, a superb replica has been created in a nearby cave. Reproductions of the murals were painted by local artists under the supervision of archaeological and cultural authorities.

Finca Ixobel (p233) runs tours to Naj Tunich, traveling by Land Rover to the nearby community of La Compuerta, then continuing on foot to the cave. Proceeds from the tour go to development projects in local communities.

Museo Regional del Sureste de Petén
MUSEUM

(☺8am-5pm) FREE Displaying some of the most significant finds from southern Petén sites, this museum is the main draw of Dolores (pop 22,203), a town 25km north of Poptún along the CA13. The collection features pottery, arrowheads and stelae dating from throughout the history of Classic Maya civilization.

Ixcún
ARCHAEOLOGICAL SITE

(admission Q30; ☺8am-5pm) The second-largest stela in the Maya world can be viewed amid a protected jungle zone at the remains of a late-Classic Maya kingdom, an hour's walk north of Dolores. Depicting a ruler wearing a headdress of quetzal feathers, it stands at one end of a large ceremonial center of three plazas, an unrestored temple and an acropolis.

Archaeologists speculate that the complex of structures on the Plaza Principal may have been used as an astronomical observatory. Ixcún's sister city, Ixtontón, a major trading center until the 11th century AD, is another 6km along the Río Mopán.

Flores & Santa Elena

POP FLORES 30,781, SANTA ELENA 29,000 / ELEV 117M

With its cubist houses cascading down from a central plaza to the emerald waters of Lago de Petén Itzá, the island town of Flores evokes a Mediterranean ambience. A 500m causeway connects Flores to its humbler sister town of Santa Elena on the lakeshore, which then merges into the even homelier community of San Benito to the west. The three towns actually form one large settlement, often referred to simply as Flores.

Flores proper is by far the more attractive place to base yourself. Small hotels and restaurants line the streets, many featuring rooftop terraces with lake views. Residents take great pride in their island-town's gorgeousness, and a lakeside promenade runs around its perimeter. Flores does have a twee, built-up edge to it, though, and some Tikal-bound shoestringers opt for the natural surrounds and tranquility of El Remate, just down the road.

Santa Elena is where you'll find banks, buses and a major shopping mall.

Flores feels different from its surroundings, more globalized in quality standards but also blander, and unless you're a big fan of Bob Marley, the party vibe could get on your nerves. Nevertheless, it is beautiful.

History

Flores was founded on an island *(petén)* by the Itzáes, who came here after being expelled from Chichén Itzá on Mexico's Yucatán Peninsula, probably in the mid-15th century. They called it Tah Itzá ('place of the Itzá'), which the Spanish later corrupted to Tayasal. Hernán Cortés dropped in on King Canek of Tayasal in 1525 on his way to Honduras, but the meeting was, amazingly, peaceable. Cortés left behind a lame horse, which the Itzáes fed on flowers and turkey stew. When it died, the Itzáes made a statue of it which, by the time a couple of Spanish friars visited in 1618, was being worshiped as a manifestation of the rain god Chac. It was not until 1697 that the Spaniards brought the Itzáes of Tayasal – by some distance the last surviving independent Maya kingdom – forcibly under their control. The Spanish soldiers destroyed its many pyramids, temples and statues, and today you won't see a trace of them, although the modern town is doubtless built on the ruins and foundations of Maya Tayasal.

◉ Sights

Museo Santa Bárbara
MUSEUM

(Isle of Santa Bárbara; admission Q15; ☺8am-noon & 2-5pm) On an islet to the west of Flores, this museum holds a grab bag of Maya artifacts from nearby archaeological sites, all crammed into a small room. There are over 9000 pieces, according to the caretaker who has a story about every one of them. From San Benito dock, phone (☑7926-0660) or whistle for the boatman, who'll take you across for Q10.

Some old broadcasting equipment was contributed by the caretaker's father, who was an announcer for 40 years at Radio Petén, which still broadcasts from an adjacent building. After browsing the museum, enjoy chilled coconuts at the cafe by the dock.

🏃 Activities

The Guatemalan NGO **Arcas** (Asociación de Rescate y Conservación de Vida Silvestre; ☑7830-1374; www.arcasguatemala.com) has a rescue and rehabilitation center for wildlife on the mainland northeast of Flores, where volunteers 'adopt' and feed animals that have been rescued from smugglers and the illegal pet trade, such as macaws, parrots, jaguars and coatis. The fee of Q1180 a week covers food and accommodation.

Language schools in San Andrés and San José provide the chance to get involved in community and environmental projects.

☞ Tours

Various travel agencies in Flores offer day tours to archaeological sites such as Tikal, Uaxactún, Yaxhá and Ceibal. Prices, with a guide and lunch, range from Q125 for a basic Tikal tour to Q1120 for a Ceibal excursion.

More demanding hiking-and-camping experiences to remote archaeological sites such as Nakum, El Perú, El Zotz, El Mirador, Nakbé and Wakná are also offered by the outfits listed here.

Maya Expeditions (p49), based in Guatemala City, offers mild (ie good for families or inexperienced rafters) one- to three-day raft-ing expeditions on the Río Chiquibul, with options to visit lesser-known sites like Yaxhá, Nakum and Topoxte for Q670 to Q3600 per person.

Hostel Los Amigos   ARCHAEOLOGICAL TOUR
(☑7867-5075; www.amigoshostel.com; Calle Central, Flores) Offers some of the lowest-cost tours to El Mirador and El Zotz.

Mayan Adventure   ARCHAEOLOGICAL TOUR
(☑5830-2060; www.the-mayan-adventure.com; Calle 15 de Septiembre, Flores) Coordinated by a German Mayanologist, this outfit offers 'scientific' tours to sites currently under excavation, with commentary by archaeologists working at the sites.

Explore   TOUR
(www.exploreguate.com; 2a Calle 04-68, Santa Elena) Professionally managed agency offering custom-designed tours and its own accommodations in Santa Elena.

Monkey Eco Tours   ARCHAEOLOGICAL TOUR
(☑5201-0759; www.nitun.com; San Andrés) Based at Ni'tun Ecolodge (p243) near San Andrés, this outfit offers adventure trips with transport in Land Cruisers and seasoned, English-speaking guides to such destinations as Ceibal, Yaxhá and Uaxactún. Prices range from Q1400 to Q1900 per person per day.

Martsam Travel   TRAVEL AGENCY
(☑7867-5377; www.martsam.com; Calle 30 de Junio, Flores) Central America–wide operator specializing in custom-designed tours; supports ecotourism initiatives and community involvement.

Lake Tours
Boats can be hired for lake tours at the *embarcaderos* (wharves) that are opposite Hotel Petenchel and beside the Hotel Santana in Flores, and in the middle of

TOURS TO LOCAL ARCHAEOLOGICAL SITES

The sample prices are per person for two/four/five-plus people, normally including food, water, sleeping gear and Spanish-speaking guide.

LOCATION	DURATION	COST
El Zotz & Tikal	3 days	Q3075/2140/2140
El Perú & Est Biológica Las Guacamayas	3 days	Q2995/1930/1725
El Mirador-Nakbé-Wakná	7 days	Q5915/4000/3815
Yaxhá & Nakum	2 days	Q1750/1170/1015
Dos Pilas, Aguateca & Ceibal	3 days	Q2840/1790/1635

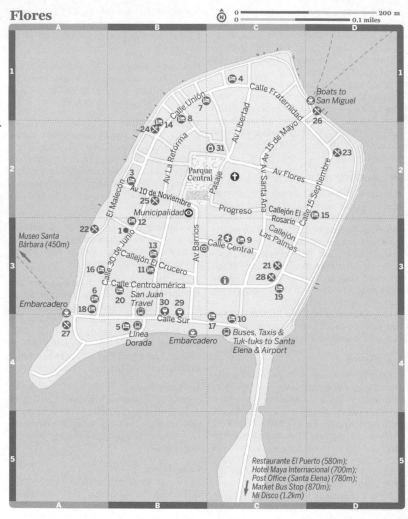

Flores

the Flores–Santa Elena causeway. Prices are negotiable. An hour-long jaunt runs around Q150. A three-hour tour, which might include the Arcas animal conservation preserve (p235), the Petencito Zoo, the isle of Santa Bárbara and its museum (p234) and the ruins of Tayazal should cost Q400 for three passengers, with stops and waiting time included.

🛏 Sleeping

Except for a few upscale properties along Santa Elena's waterfront, Flores makes a far

more desirable place to stay, unless you have a thing for traffic and dust.

Hostel Los Amigos   HOSTEL $
(☎7867-5075; www.amigoshostel.com; Calle Central, Flores; dm/r Q55/120; @) Flores' one true hostel, with a 10-bed dorm, hammocks and even a treehouse, has grown organically in its nine years of existence. All the global traveler's perks are here in abundance: nightly bonfires, happy hours, heaped helpings of organic food, yoga and cut-rate jungle tours. A new annex around the corner

Flores

is quieter, with seven originally designed rooms.

Hospedaje Doña Goya the 2nd   HOTEL $
(✆7867-5516; hospedajedonagoya@yahoo.com; Calle Unión, Flores; r with balcony Q160; ❋@🖤) Doña Goya's second effort is even spiffier than her first – this one's got a jungle theme, with banisters made to look like climbing vines. Rooms are plain, airy and well scrubbed, with screened windows, and most have some kind of view. And like its predecessor, DG2 features a hammock-slung terrace.

Hospedaje Doña Goya   HOSTEL $
(✆7867-5513; Calle Unión, Flores; dm Q35, s/d Q80/120, without bathroom Q70/90; 🖤) This family-run guesthouse makes a fine budget choice. Though ultra-basic, the sheets are clean, the fans work, the water's hot and the paint's fresh. Dorms, too, are spacious and spotless. Best of all is the roof terrace with a palm-thatched shelter and hammocks.

Hotel Mirador del Lago   HOTEL $
(✆7867-5409; Calle 15 de Septiembre, Flores; s/d Q60/90, r with rear view Q130/150; @🖤) The name is an exaggeration – only the units in the rear wing have views of lake. They're also in better shape than the rest, with nice wood-beam ceilings, soothing colors and cute balconies.

Hotel Petenchel   HOTEL $
(✆7867-5450; Calle Sur, Flores; s/d Q100/120, with air-con Q150/170; ❋) Eight spacious rooms, with firm beds and high arched ceilings, are set around a lush courtyard just off the causeway.

Hotel La Unión   HOTEL $
(✆7867-5531; gulzam75@hotmail.com; Calle Unión, Flores; s/d Q90/130, 🖤) Considering its location beside the waterfront promenade, this well-maintained property is quite a good deal, with relatively stylish decor in fan-cooled rooms.

Posada de la Jungla   HOTEL $
(✆7867-5185; www.posadadelajungla.com; Calle Centroamérica 30, Flores; s/d/tr Q100/150/200) Worth considering is this slender, three-story building with front balconies. Though a bit cramped, rooms are comfortably arranged, with quality beds.

Hotel El Peregrino   HOTEL $
(✆7867-5701; peregrino@itelgua.com; Av Reforma, Flores; s/d Q120/150, without bathroom Q70/125; ❋) El Peregrino is an older, family-run place with home cooking in the front *comedor* (basic and cheap eatery). Large rooms along plant-festooned corridors feature tile floors, powerful overhead fans and window screens.

Green World Hotel   HOTEL $
(✆7867-5662; greenworldhotel@gmail.com; Calle 30 de Junio; s/d Q110/160, with air-con Q190/260;

✳ @) This low-key shoreline property features an interior patio and an upstairs terrace overlooking the lake. Compact, low-lit rooms have safes, enormous ceiling fans and good hot showers – No 8, with its rear balcony, is by far the nicest.

Hotel Casablanca
HOTEL $

(☎ 5435-6592; Calle Sur, Flores; s/d Q80/120; 🛜) The first hotel you reach coming off the causeway is family-run with simple, spacious rooms and a terrace for lake-gazing. The steady flow of traffic from Santa Elena means you'll probably be up early.

Hotel La Mesa de los Mayas
HOTEL $$

(☎ 7867-5268; mesamayas@hotmail.com; Av La Reforma, Flores; s/d Q125/150, with air-con Q150/200; ✳🛜) Standing alongside a narrow alley, the Mesa's terrific value. Rooms are neatly furnished, with pyramidal headboards, checkered bedspreads and reading lamps; some feature plant-laden balconies.

Hotel Petén
HOTEL $$

(☎ 7867-5203; www.hotelesdepeten.com; Calle 30 de Junio, Flores; s/d/tr incl breakfast Q376/464/600; ✳@🛜❄) Rooms are cheerily decorated here with a dash of chintz. Definitely choose the lake balcony units as they cost no more than interior ones. A good-sized swimming pool straddles the courtyard and rear deck, and the popular restaurant-bar opens on a lakeside terrace.

Casa Amelia
BOUTIQUE HOTEL $$

(☎7867-5430; www.hotelcasamelia.com; Calle Unión, Flores; s/d Q220/340; ✳@🛜) Standing tall along Flores' western shore, the Amelia offers bright, stylish chambers with excellent lake views; rooms 301 and 302 are best, opening on the superb balustraded roof terrace.

Hotel La Casona de la Isla
HOTEL $$

(☎7867-5203; www.hotelesdepeten.com; Calle 30 de Junio, Flores; s/d/tr Q410/475/560; ✳@❄) Popular with package travelers, this has a Caribbean flavor. Smallish rooms line a long veranda facing a pool with a rock garden and adjacent lake-view deck for sunset dining. The most appealing units, 31, 303 and 304, have windows facing the lake.

Hotel Villa del Lago
HOTEL $$

(☎7867-5131; www.hotelvilladelago.com.gt; Calle 15 de Septiembre, Flores; s/d/tr Q290/340/385; ✳@🛜) Behind the odd Grecian facade there's a cool, breezy interior that's long on potted plants and patio furniture. Comfortable, airy rooms have bright decor and big ceiling fans; lake-view units are pricier. Breakfast is served on the delightful upper terrace.

Hotel Santana
HOTEL $$

(☎7926-0262; www.santanapeten.com; Calle 30 de Junio, Flores; r Q370-440; ✳@❄) An eclectic melange of concrete, wood, thatch and wickerwork the Santana holds a commanding presence at Flores' southwest corner, with its very own ferry dock. Rooms are generously sized with lime-green walls, and if you get one out back, you'll have a great balcony facing Isla Santa Barbara.

Casazul
BOUTIQUE HOTEL $$

(☎7867-5451; www.hotelesdepeten.com; Calle Unión, Flores; s/d/tr Q325/390/480; ✳🛜) As the name suggests, it's blue all over, from the plantation-style balconies to the nine individually decorated, spacious and comfortable rooms. A couple have their own balconies and everyone can enjoy the 3rd-floor terrace.

Gran Hotel de La Isla
HOTEL $$$

(☎7867-5549; www.granhoteldeflorespeten.com; Calle Sur, Flores; s/d Q560/640; P✳@🛜❄) This glossy business-class lodging holds a commanding presence at the southwest corner of the island. Along arched corridors with images of Maya royalty, the 45 rooms are luxuriously appointed. Leisure moments can be spent soaking in the outdoor or indoor pools or downing daiquiris in the Fisherman's Bar.

Hotel Maya Internacional
HOTEL $$$

(☎7926-2083; www.villasdeguatemala.com; Calle, Santa Elena; s/d Q585/829; P✳@🛜❄) One of the best reasons to stay in Santa Elena is this tropical-chic resort spreading over a landscaped marsh by the waterfront. The thatched big-top dining room is the center of activity; an adjacent wooden deck with a small infinity pool is great for sunset daiquiris. A boardwalk snakes through tropical gardens to reach the 26 rooms, thatch-and-teak affairs combining a jungly ambience with modern comforts. Rooms 49 to 54 have the best lake views.

🍴 Eating

As might be expected, Flores is rife with tourist-oriented joints pitching a bland melange of 'international' fare to the package crowd. Nevertheless, a few local gems rise above the pack.

Las Mesitas   GUATEMALAN $
(El Malecón; snacks Q5-10; ☺7-10pm) Every evening, but especially Sundays, there's a street party by the San Miguel ferry dock, as local families fix enchiladas (actually *tostadas* topped with guacamole, chicken salad and so on), tacos and tamales, and dispense fruity drinks from giant jugs. All kinds of cakes and puddings and served, too. Everyone sits on plastic chairs as the boats pick up and discharge passengers.

Café/Bar Doña Goya   CAFE $
(El Malecón; breakfast Q30-40; ☺6:30am-11pm) Doña Goya's is good for an early breakfast or sunset snack, with a pretty terrace facing the lake. Toward the weekend, it blends into the nightlife scene along this stretch of the promenade, with occasional live music.

Cool Beans   CAFE $
(Calle 15 de Septiembre, Flores; coffee & snacks Q8-25; ☺7am-10pm Mon-Sat; 📶) Also known as Café Chilero, this laid-back place is more clubhouse with snacks than proper restaurant, featuring salons for chatting, watching videos or laptop browsing. The lush garden with glimpses of the lake makes a *tranquilo* spot for breakfast or veggie burgers. Be warned – the kitchen closes at 9:01pm sharp.

★ Il Terrazo   ITALIAN $$
(Calle Unión, Flores; pasta Q65-75; ☺8am-10pm Mon-Sat) Inspired by a chef from Bologna, this Italian gourmet restaurant covers a romantic rooftop terrace. The fettuccine, tortellini and gnocchi are all produced in-house, the panini are amply stuffed, and the fruit smoothies are simply unbelievable. All this, and the service is the most attentive in town.

Café Arqueológico Yax-ha   CAFE $$
(www.cafeyaxha.com; Calle 15 de Septiembre, Flores; mains Q35-65; ☺6:30am-10pm) Apart from the usual egg-and-bean breakfasts, what's special here are the pre-Hispanic and Itzá items – pancakes with *ramón* seeds, yucca scrambled with *mora* (blackberry) herbs, chicken in *chaya* sauce.

Restaurante & Pizzería Picasso   PIZZERIA $$
(Calle 15 de Septiembre, Flores; pizza Q35-120; ☺2:30-10:30pm Sun-Fri) This long-standing, Italian-owned joint does primo wood-fired pizzas, and there is room to lounge in the courtyard.

Restaurante El Peregrino   GUATEMALAN $$
(📷7867-5115; Av La Reforma, Flores; mains Q40-60; ☺7am-10pm) This refreshingly nontouristy *comedor* serves heaping helpings of home-cooked fare such as pork-belly stew and breaded tongue. Ask for the daily lunch specials (Q25).

Capitán Tortuga   INTERNATIONAL $$
(Calle 30 de Junio, Flores; pizzas Q45-100; ☺8am-10:30pm) A barnlike venue with a pair of lakeside terraces, this places serves heaping helpings of comfort food – especially pizzas – at reasonable prices.

La Luna   MEDITERRANEAN $$
(cnr Calle 30 de Junio & Av 10 de Noviembre; mains Q60-120; ☺noon-11pm Mon-Sat) This deservedly popular restaurant cultivates a tropical ambience with low-lit patio dining. Aside from the usual steak and pasta dishes, Spanish cuisine is their strong suit (the owner hails from the *madre tierra*): go for the gazpacho.

Raíces   STEAKHOUSE $$
(Calle Sur, Flores; mains Q80-110; ☺4-10pm Sun-Thu, 4pm-1am Fri & Sat) A broad deck and a flaming grill are the main ingredients at this stylish lakefront restaurant-bar. Char-grilled meats and seafood are the specialty, and you can choose your grills by the pound or half-pound.

Restaurante El Puerto   SEAFOOD $$
(1a Calle 2-15, Santa Elena; mains Q100; ☺11am-11pm) Seafood is the star attraction at this breezy, open-air hall by the lakefront in Santa Elena, with a well-stocked bar at the front. It's an ideal setting to enjoy shellfish stews, *ceviches* (marinated seafood) or the famous *pescado blanco* – whitefish from the lake.

🍷 **Drinking & Entertainment**

Flores' little Zona Viva is traditionally the strip of bars along Calle Sur, but recently there's plenty of action around the bend, along the lakefront promenade north of Hotel Santana.

El Trópico   BAR
(Calle Sur, Flores; ☺4:30pm-1am Mon-Sat) The candlelit terrace here is a nice spot to start the night, as the lights of Santa Elena reflect pleasingly off the lake.

Casa de Palmas   BAR
(Calle Sur, Flores) Aside from drinking and conversing at the terrace tables, there's non-stop dancing on the crowded dance

floor. It's a mostly middle-class Guatemalan scene.

Mi Disco
DISCO

(cnr Calle Central & Av Santa Ana, Santa Elena; ☺ Mon-Sat) 'El Mi' is Santa Elena's major disco, a cavernous hall with a big stage for salsa combos. If you'd rather croon than dance, Monday to Wednesday evenings are reserved for karaoke.

🛍 Shopping

Castillo de Arizmendi
HANDICRAFTS

(Parque Central, Flores; ☺ 8am-9pm Mon-Sat) The 17th-century 'castle' on the main plaza's north side houses a series of shops with local handicrafts, particularly wood carvings by artists from El Remate working in mahogany, cedar and chicozapote.

ℹ Information

EMERGENCY

Hospital Privado de Petén (☎ 7926-1140; 3a Av 4-29, Zona 2, Santa Elena)
Proatur (Tourist Police; ☎ 5414-3594)

MONEY

Banrural (Av Flores, Flores), off the Parque Central, changes dollars and euros, cash or traveler's checks. There's a handy Banco Industrial **ATM** (Calle 30 de Junio, Flores) at the Fotomart convenience store, opposite Capitán Tortuga.There are plenty of other banks with ATMs along 4a Calle in Santa Elena.

Many travel agencies and places to stay will change US dollars and sometimes traveler's checks, though at poorer rates.

POST

Flores (Av Barrios, Flores)
Santa Elena (4a Calle & 4a Av, inside Centro Comercial Karossi, Santa Elena)

TOURIST INFORMATION

The official **Inguat office** (☎ 7867-5365; info-mun domaya@inguat.gob.gt; Calle Centroamérica; ☺ 8am-4pm Mon-Fri) provides basic information. There's an **info kiosk** (☎ 7926-0533) at the Aeropuerto Internacional Mundo Maya.

ℹ Getting There & Away

AIR

Aeropuerto Internacional Mundo Maya is on the eastern outskirts of Santa Elena, 2km from the causeway connecting Santa Elena and Flores. **Taca** (☎ 2470-8222) has two flights daily between here and Guatemala City (one way/return Q1255/2165). The Belizean airline **Tropic Air** (☎ 7926-0348; www.tropicair.com) flies twice a day to/from Belize City, charging Q1015 each way for the one-hour trip.

BUS & MICROBUS

Long-distance buses use the Terminal Nuevo de Autobuses in Santa Elena, located 1km south of the causeway along 6a Av. It is also used by a slew of microbuses, with frequent services to numerous destinations. Second-class buses and some microbuses make an additional stop at 5a Calle, in the **market area** (the 'old' terminal) before heading out. You can reduce your trip time by 15 minutes by going straight to the market, though the vehicle may be full by then.

Departures include the following (as always, schedules are highly changeable and should be confirmed before heading out):

Belize City (Q160, four to five hours, 220km) **Línea Dorada** (☎ 7924-8535) leaves at 7am, returning from Belize City at 1pm. This bus connects with boats to Caye Caulker and Ambergris Caye.

Bethel/La Técnica (Mexican border) (Q35/40, 4½ hours, 127km) **ACTEP** (☎ 7924-8215), with an office on the left side of the terminal, runs five microbuses to Bethel between 11am and 4:30pm, continuing on to La Técnica.

Carmelita (Q40, 4½ hours, 82km) Two Pinitas buses at 5am and 1pm from the market.

Cobán (six hours, 245km) Transportes Luna offers shuttle service from 9am (Q125), picking up passengers from their hotels; purchase tickets at Aventuras Turísticas. Or take a bus or minibus to Sayaxché, from where connecting microbuses leave for Cobán.

El Ceibo/La Palma (Mexican border) (Q35, four hours, 151km) El Naranjo–bound microbuses depart every 20 minutes, from 4:20am to 6pm, stopping at the El Ceibo junction, from where there are shuttles to the border (Q10, 15 minutes). Five of these go all the way to El Ceibo (Q40). At La Palma, on the Mexican side, you can find transportation to Tenosique, Tabasco (one hour).

El Remate (Q20, 40 minutes, 29km) Microbuses leave every half hour from 5am to 6pm. Buses and minibuses to and from Melchor de Mencos will drop you at Puente Ixlú junction, 2km south of El Remate.

Esquipulas (Q110, eight hours, 440km) **Transportes María Elena** (☎ 5850-4190) goes at 6am, 10am and 2pm via Río Dulce (Q60) and Chiquimula (Q100).

Guatemala City (eight to nine hours, 500km) Línea Dorada runs first-class buses at 10am and 10pm (Q150), plus a deluxe bus (Q190) at 9pm. **Autobuses del Norte** (☎ 7924-8131; www.adnautobusesdelnorte.com) has 1st-class (Q150) and deluxe (Q200) buses at 9pm and 11pm, respectively. All Línea Dorada and

CROSSING THE BELIZEAN BORDER

It's 100km from Flores to Melchor de Mencos, the Guatemalan town on the border with Belize. From the Tikal junction at Puente Ixlú, 27km from Flores, the road continues paved until 13km short of the border.

Officially there are no fees at the border for entering or leaving Guatemala, but in reality, immigration officials on the Guatemalan side charge a Q20 fee to enter or leave the country. Technically you don't have to pay it but most travelers fork over this de facto tip and move on. No fee is charged to enter Belize, but travelers leaving that country have to pay a B$30 departure tax and a B$7.50 protected areas conservation fee, in Belizean or US dollars.

There are moneychangers at the border for changing quetzals to Belize dollars, an exchange that is not performed by banks. Rates are better on the Guatemalan side. Taxis run between the border and the nearest town in Belize, Benque Viejo del Carmen, 3km away, for B$3. Authorized rates are posted for other destinations, including Belize International Airport (B$200). Buses run from Benque to Belize City (B$10, three hours) about every hour from 3:30am to 6pm.

Coming in the other direction, travelers bound for Flores or Tikal, after clearing immigration, should cross the bridge, where there's a microbus stop on the right side with departures to Santa Elena every half hour until 6pm. Red Asetur vans provide shuttle service to Yaxhá, Tikal and Flores with highly negotiable rates.

Most travelers pass through Melchor, though there is an actual town across the Río Mopán, with hotels, banks and businesses. There is a Cajero 5B ATM at the Texaco station 500m west of the bridge. There's little reason to linger but if you're done traveling for the day, Melchor has one fine place to stay, the **Río Mopan Lodge** ([2] 7926-5196; www.tikaltravel.com; s/d from Q100/150). Set back from the road in lush, jungly grounds, it's so tranquil that you'll find it hard to comprehend you're just 50m from the immigration booth. The rooms are big, cool and well decorated, with balconies overlooking the river, and the kitchen prepares good Mediterranean fare. It's between the bridge and Guatemalan immigration.

Autobuses del Norte buses pick up passengers in front of the Gran Hotel de la Isla an hour prior to the Santa Elena terminal departure.

Fuente del Norte ([2] 7926-2999) runs 16 buses between 3:30am and 10:30pm (Q110), plus deluxe buses at 10am, 2pm, 9pm and 10pm (Q160), although security problems have been reported by passengers using this line.

Melchor de Mencos (Belizean border) (two hours, 100km) Microbuses (Q25) go about every hour, 5:45am to 6pm. Línea Dorada Pullmans en route to Belize City depart at 7am (Q35).

Poptún (1¾ hours, 113km) Take a Guatemala City–bound Línea Dorada bus (Q40) or a microbus (Q25), going every 10 minutes, via Dolores, from 5am to 6:30pm.

Puerto Barrios (six hours) Take a Guatemala City–bound Fuente del Norte bus and change at La Ruidosa junction, south of Río Dulce.

Río Dulce (four hours, 212km) Take a Guatemala City–bound bus with Fuente del Norte (Q60) or Línea Dorada (Q100/125 *económico*/deluxe).

San Andrés/San José (Q7/10, 35/50 minutes, 22/25km) Microbuses depart around every 15 minutes, from 5am to 6:30pm, from the left side of the terminal entrance.

Sayaxché (Q20, 1½ hours, 60km) Microbuses depart about every 15 minutes from 5:45am to 6pm.

Tikal (Q50, 1¼ hours, 62km) Four microbuses by **Asociación de Transportistas Imperio Maya** (ATIM; [2] 4478-5996) between 6am and 3pm (Q30, 1½ hours), the last returning at 5pm. You could also take the Uaxactún-bound bus (Q35) at 2pm, which goes a bit slower. Autobuses del Norte provides Pullman service at 6am and 8am (Q80).

CAR & MOTORCYCLE

Several car-rental companies have desks at the airport.

Hertz ([2] 7926-0415; peten@rentautos.com.gt; Airport)

Tabarini ([2] 7926-0253; www.tabarini.com; Airport)

SHUTTLE MINIBUS

Aventuras Turísticas ([2] 4034-9550; www.aventurasturisticas.com; Av Barrios) offers a daily shuttle to Cobán at 9am (Q150, five hours) and Lanquín (seven hours). San Juan Travel operates shuttle minibuses to Tikal (Q60, 1¼ hours each way). They leave hourly from 5am to 10am. Most hotels and travel agencies can book these shuttles and they will pick you up where you're staying. Returns leave Tikal at 12:30pm, 2pm, 3pm, 4pm and 5pm. If you know which round-trip you plan to be on, ask your driver to hold a seat for you or arrange one in another minibus. If you stay overnight in Tikal and want to return to Flores by minibus, it's a good idea to reserve a seat with a driver when they arrive in the morning.

❶ Getting Around

A **taxi** from the airport to Santa Elena or Flores costs Q20. *Tuk-tuks* will take you anywhere between or within Flores and Santa Elena for Q5. Aventuras Turísticas (p241) rents mountain bikes for Q30 per day.

Around Flores

San Miguel & Tayazal

Covering the western end of the San Miguel peninsula, reached by frequent ferries from Flores, are the remains of **Tayazal** (admission Q5; ⊙6am-6pm), among the last of the Maya capitals. It was settled by the Itzáes, refugees from the destroyed city of Chichén Itzá in Yucatán, who held out against the Spanish until 1697. Scholars concur that Tayazal was actually centered on the island of Flores, but remnants of the Itzáes' reign are scattered around the peninsula. The chiefly Classic-era mounds are overgrown by vegetation, and a few pockmarked stelae have been recovered. The real draw, though, is the chance to wander the forested spine of the

peninsula, taking in panoramic views of the lake.

Colectivos (shared taxis or minibuses) cost Q5 per person and make the five-minute crossing to San Miguel village from the northeast side of Flores whenever they have a boatload. San Miguel itself is a quiet, slow-moving place. To reach the ruins, walk 250m to the left along the shore from where the boat drops you, then turn up the paved street to the right. After 300m, turn left at the 'Playa' sign, passing a football field on your right. About another 600m on, a trail on the right leads to **Playa El Chechenal**, a swimming beach with a dock extending over turquoise waters and a few picnic tables (admission Q5). Continue west another 300m to reach the main entrance to the site. From here it's a precipitous climb up the hillside – actually one of the pyramids of ancient Tayazal – to reach **El Mirador del Rey Canek**, an observation point with 360-degree views around Lago de Petén Itzá. The archaeological site can be visited by circling round the base of the tower and skirting the lake back toward the village. Around 800m further, go left up a hill (past a building foundation), then follow a dirt road left to reach the Gran Plaza, where you'll find some weathered stelae dating from the late Classic period.

Petencito Zoo

A couple of dozen native critters, including puma, ocelots, spider monkeys, crocodiles and macaws, dwell within this islet east of Flores, laced with **interpretive trails** (admission Q40; ⊙8am-5pm). Camping is permitted (Q25 with tent). Boatmen from Flores

Lago de Petén Itzá

charge Q200, including an hour's wait while you tour the zoo.

Cuevas de Ak'tun Kan

Try spelunking at the impressive limestone caverns of **Ak'tun Kan** (admission Q25; ⊙ 7am-6pm), which translates from Q'eqchi' Maya as 'Cave of the Serpent'. The cave-keeper provides the authorized interpretation of the weirdly shaped stalagmite and stalactite formations, including the Frozen Falls, the Whale's Tail, and the Gate of Heaven, the last within a great hall where bats flutter in the crevices.

If you haven't got a flashlight, you can rent one. Explorations take 30 to 45 minutes. It's 2km south of Flores; take a *tuk-tuk* there (Q10).

Hotel Villa Maya

At Laguna Petenchel, a small lake east of Santa Elena, this **hotel** (☑ 7931-8350; villasdeguatemala.com; s/d Q635/705; P @ 🛜 🕿) is among the finest in the area. Ensconced within its own wildlife refuge, the blissfully quiet accommodations include 10 two-to-three-level bungalows and 10 cabins. It's 4km north of the crossroads where the Guatemala City road diverges from the Tikal road, 8km east of Flores.

San José & San Andrés

POP 1601 / ELEV 202M

San Andrés and San José, a pair of small towns at the northwest corner of Lago de Petén Itzá, are just a few kilometers apart but are distinct in character. Each town has a language school, and their relative isolation makes it easier to learn Spanish as there are more chances to interact with locals.

In San Andrés, a jumble of mismatched houses covers a precipitous hillside interwoven with lushly overgrown paths, all imbued with the calming presence of the lake.

San José is peopled by Itzá Maya, descendants of the area's pre-Hispanic inhabitants. The extraordinarily neat and orderly village descends steeply from its little blue church to the lakefront, site of a waterslide park and a couple of seafood shacks.

🏊 Activities

Escuela Bio-Itzá　　LANGUAGE COURSE
(☑7928-8056; bioitza@yahoo.com) Community-owned Escuela Bio-Itzá is part of an asso-

NIGHT OF THE SKULLS

San José is a special place to be on the night of October 31, when perfectly preserved human skulls, normally housed in the church, are paraded around town on a velvet pillow followed by devotees in traditional dress, carrying candles. Throughout the night, the skulls make visits to predetermined houses, where blessings are sought, offerings made and a feast eaten.

ciation working to keep Itzá traditions and language alive. The group also manages a 36-sq-km nature reserve bordering the southern section of the Biotopo El Zotz, which is being outfitted for ecotourism. Students participate in community projects such as producing cosmetics from the medicinal plant garden, or helping the reserve rangers monitor wildlife.

Cost for the usual 20 hours of one-on-one Spanish classes is Q1260 per week to live with a local family, or Q1650 to stay on the reserve. Bio-Itzá also offers tours of the reserve to nonstudents with a focus on bird-watching, medicinal plants and the work of the *chicleros* who harvested the sap of the chicozapote tree for the production of chewing gum.

Eco-Escuela de Español　　LANGUAGE COURSE
(☑3099-4846; San Andrés) This community-owned school in San Andrés emphasizes ecological and cultural issues and organizes environmental trips and volunteer opportunities; Q1180 a week includes room and board with a local family.

🛏 Sleeping

Hotel Bahía Taitzá　　HOTEL $$
(☑7928-8125; www.taitza.com; s/d/tr Q400/500/600) West of San José, this is an elaborate spread where you can truly unwind. Eight well-designed rooms with high wood ceilings and lovely porches are in two buildings, facing the lake across a lawn dotted with ficus trees. Wood-fired pizzas, paellas and such are served under a beachfront *palapa*.

Ni'tun Ecolodge　　RESORT $$$
(☑5201-0759; www.nitun.com; s/d incl breakfast from Q1100/1770; P @) West of San Andrés and down a gravel road, Ni'tun is set on a

35-acre patch of protected secondary forest where six species of hummingbird nest year-round. Four spacious huts built of indigenous materials feature handcrafted furniture and wraparound screened windows. Superb meals are prepared in the open-air clubhouse with a lounge on the upper deck.

Bernie and Lorena, Guatemalan conservationists, built and operate the lodge and coordinate adventure excursions through their affiliated company, Monkey Eco Tours (p235).

Parque Natural Ixpanpajul

At **Parque Natural Ixpanpajul** (☑ 2336-0576; www.ixpanpajul.com; Zipline tour adult/child Q235/175; ☺ 7am-6pm) you can ride horses, mountain bikes or tractors, or zip-line your way through the jungle canopy. The big attraction is the **Skyway**, a 3km circuit of stone paths and six linked suspension bridges through the upper levels of the forest. Camping and cabins are available for overnight stays. It's 8km east of Flores. Call the park's **shuttle service** (☑ 5897-6766; Q40) to arrange transportation.

El Remate

This idyllic spot at the eastern end of Lago de Petén Itzá makes a good alternative base for Tikal-bound travelers – it's more relaxed than Flores, and closer to the site. Consisting of just two roads, really, El Remate has a ramshackle vibe all of its own.

El Remate begins 1km north of Puente Ixlú, where the road to the Belize border diverges from the Tikal road. The village strings along the Tikal road for 1km to another junction, where a branch heads west along the north shore of the lake.

El Remate is known for its wood carving. Some fine examples of the craft are sold from stalls along the main road.

You can change US dollars and euros, or check your email, at **Horizontes Mayas** (☑ 7928-8471; www.horizontesmayas.com), adjacent to Hotel Las Gardenias (p245).

🏃 Activities

Most El Remate accommodations can book two-hour boat trips for **bird-watching** or nocturnal **crocodile spotting** (each Q100 per person). Try Casa de Ernesto (p245) or Hotel Mon Ami; (p245) the latter also offers sunset lake tours with detours up the Ixlu and Ixpop rivers (Q150 per person).

Asunción, found by the second speed bump from the north shore junction, rents kayaks (Q35 per hour) and bicycles (per hour/day Q10/70). He also guides horseback rides to Laguna Sacpetén and a small archaeological site there (Q150 per person, 2½ hours).

Biotopo Cerro Cahuí   NATURE RESERVE
(admission Q40; ☺ 7am-4pm) Comprising a 7.3-sq-km swath of subtropical forest rising up from the lake over limestone terrain, this nature reserve offers mildly strenuous hiking and excellent wildlife watching, with paths to some brilliant lookout points. As a bonus, there's an adjacent lakeside park with diving docks for a refreshing conclusion to the tour.

More than 20 mammal species roam the reserve, including spider and howler monkeys, white-tailed deer and the elusive Mesoamerican tapir. Bird life is rich and varied, with the opportunity to spot toucans, woodpeckers and the famous ocellated turkey, a big bird resembling a peacock. Trees include mahogany, cedar, *ramón*, and cohune palm, along with many types of bromeliads, ferns and orchids.

A network of loop trails ascend the hill to two lookout points, affording a view of the whole lake and of Laguna Sacpetén to the east. The trail called Los Escobos (4km long, about 2¼ hours), through secondary growth forest, is good for spotting monkeys.

The admission fee includes the right to camp or sling your hammock under small thatch shelters inside the entrance. There are toilets and showers. The reserve is 1.75km west along the north-shore road from El Remate.

Project Ix-Canaan   VOLUNTEERING
(www.ixcanaan.com) This group supports the improvement of health, education and opportunities for rainforest inhabitants. Operating here since 1996, they runs a community clinic, women's center, library and research center. Volunteers work in the clinic, build and maintain infrastructure, and assist in various other ways.

👉 Tours

La Casa de Don David (p245) offers tours to Yaxhá (Q475 per person, minimum two people), and Tikal (Q490). Prices include an English-speaking guide and lunch but not admission to site. Horizontes Mayas (p244) has slightly cheaper tours and runs collective excursions to Yaxhá at 6:30am and 1pm (Q100 per person, minimum three people).

🛏 Sleeping

Most hotels are set up for swimming in – and watching the sun set over – the lake.

🛏 Along the Main Road

Posada Ixchel   HOTEL $
(📋7928-8475; hotelixchel@yahoo.com; s/d Q80/120, without bathroom Q50/60) This family-owned place near the village's main junction is a superior deal, with spotless, wood-fragrant rooms featuring newly tiled showers and handcrafted mosquito nets! The cobbled courtyard has inviting little nooks with tree log seats.

Hotel Sun Breeze   HOTEL $
(📋 7928-8044; sunbreezehotel@sunbreeze.net; Main Rd; s/d Q80/120) Nearest the junction is this excellent-value homey guesthouse. Rear units are best, with lake views through well-screened windows. It's a short stroll to the public beach.

Hotel Las Gardenias   HOTEL $
(📋7928-8377; www.hotellasgardenias.com; s/d from Q85/125; ❋@?) Right at the junction with the north shore road, this cordial hotel/restaurant/shuttle operator has two sections: the wood-paneled rooms at the front are bigger, those in the rear are appealingly removed from the road. All feature comfortable beds with woven spreads, attractively tiled showers and porches with hammocks.

Hotel La Mansión del Pájaro Serpiente   HOTEL $$
(📋5702-9434; Main Rd; s/d/ste from Q264/352/528; ❋❋) Dotted over a steep hillside, these 11 cottages all make the most of their perch, with wraparound windows and front lounges overlooking the lake. Peacocks strut around the landscaped grounds, which feature a pool with hammocks under nearby *palapa* shelters, and a reasonably priced restaurant-bar.

Hostal Hermano Pedro   HOSTEL $$
(📋4326-6253; www.hhpedro.com; dm/s/d Q96/152/208; ?) About 150m from the north shore junction, this two-level wooden structure has a relaxed environment, with plenty of hammocks in the patio and along the verandas. Recycled elements are cleverly incorporated into the decor of the spacious rooms, which feature big fans and lacy curtains. Guests can use the kitchen.

🛏 Along the North Shore Road

Casa de Ernesto   BUNGALOW $
(📋4915-8309; hotelcasadernesto@gmail.com; Jobompiche Rd; s/d Q100/150, without bathroom Q40/80; ❋) Ernesto and his clan offer cool and comfortable adobe huts in the woods plus four two-room blocks. Canoe rentals, horseback riding to Laguna Sacpetén and expeditions for the great white fish are among the activities offered.

Casa de Doña Tonita   HOSTEL $
(📋5767-4065; dm/s/d Q30/60/80) This friendly family-run place has four basic, adequately ventilated rooms, each with two single beds, in a two-story clapboard *rancho* (small house-like building), plus a dorm over the restaurant, which serves tasty, reasonably priced meals. There's just one shower. Across the road is a fine perch for sunset gazing.

★**Posada del Cerro**   BUNGALOW $$
(📋5376-8722; www.posadadelcerro.com; s/d Q220/330; P?❋) 🖊 This ecologically sound option blends brilliantly into its jungle setting, close enough to the Cerro Cahui nature reserve to hear the monkeys howl the evening in. Ten thoughfully furnished rooms occupy stone-and-hardwood houses and solitary huts scattered over the hillside; one is open to the woods with its own lake-view deck.

Herbs from the forest are stirred into local recipes in the neat, thatched-roof restaurant.

La Casa de Don David   HOTEL $$
(📋5306-2190; www.lacasadedondavid.com; Jobompiche Rd; s/d incl breakfast from Q235/360; ⊙restaurant 6:30am-9pm; ❋@?) Just west of the junction, this full-service outfit has spotless, modern rooms with Maya textiles for decor. All rooms feature verandas and hammocks facing the broad garden that's been cultivated into an incredible aviary. Drinks are conveyed to the new lakefront deck via the Toucan Express, invented by owner David Kuhn (the original Gringo Perdido).

Hotel Mon Ami   HOTEL $$
(📋7928-8413; www.hotelmonami.com; Jobompiche Rd; dm/s/d Q50/150/200; ?) A 15-minute walk from the Tikal road, Santiago's place maintains a good balance

between jungle wildness and Euro sophistication. Quirkily furnished cabins and dorms with hammocks are reached along candlelit paths through gardens bursting with local plant life. Fans of French cuisine will appreciate the open-air restaurant.

Gringo Perdido Ecological Inn   RESORT $$
(☑5804-8639; www.hotelgringoperdido.com; Jobompiche Rd; camping Q50, s/d Q150/300, with breakfast & dinner Q360/720; P) ✦ Ensconced in a paradisaical lakefront setting within the Cerro Cahui biosphere reserve, this jungly lodge offers a bank of rooms with full-wall roll-up blinds to give you the sensation of sleeping in the open air. A few lakeside bungalows offer a bit more seclusion. There's also a grassy campground with thatched-roof shelters for slinging hammocks, and a Maya sauna.

The Gringo Perdido is 3km along the north shore from the main Tikal road.

Pirámide Paraiso   HOTEL $$$
(www.hotelgringoperdido.com; Jobompiche Road; r Q1600; ☎) Built in time for the dawn of the new *baktún* is this glitzy addition to the Gringo Perdido Ecological Inn (p246), a smooth white structure that rises surreally from the forest like a Maya temple. Each of the eight huge, luxuriously decorated suites features its own exterior Jacuzzi.

🍴 Eating

Most hotels have their own restaurants and there are simple *comedores* scattered along the main road.

Mon Ami   FRENCH $$
(mains Q75-115; ◷7:30am-10pm) Down the north shore road, here's the French jungle bistro you've dreamt of, a peaceful palm-thatched affair. Try the lake whitefish or the big *ensalada francesa*.

La Casa de Don David   INTERNATIONAL $$
(mains Q45; ◷breakfast, lunch & dinner; ☑) This splendid open-air dining hall serves a good breakfast, including banana pancakes (Q30), fruit and granola, and a collection of *National Geographic* articles on Maya sites to browse over coffee. Nightly specials include vegetarian fare.

Las Orquideas   ITALIAN $$
(☑5819-7232; Jobompiche Rd; pasta Q55-80; ◷noon-9pm Tue-Sun) Almost hidden in the forest, a 10-minute walk down the north shore from the Tikal junction, is this marvelous open-air dining hall. The genial Italian owner-chef makes his own tagliatelle and *panzarotti* (smaller version of calzones), and there are tempting desserts, too.

ℹ Getting There & Around

El Remate is linked to Santa Elena by frequent microbus service (Q20) till around 7pm.

For Tikal, a collective shuttle departs at 5:30am, starting back at 2pm (Q30/50 one way/ round trip). Any El Remate accommodations can make reservations. Or catch one of the public shuttles (Q30) or **San Juan Travel shuttles** (☑5461-6010; Calle Playa Sur; Q50) passing through from Santa Elena to Tikal roughly hourly from 5am to 11am.

For taxis, ask at Hotel Sun Breeze (p245). A one-way ride to Flores costs about Q200; round trip to Tikal costs Q350.

For Melchor de Mencos on the Belizean border, get a minibus or bus from Puente Ixlú, 2km south of El Remate (Q25, 1¼ hours). Additionally, Horizontes Mayas (p244) offers daily departures to Belize City (Q160) at 5am and 7:30am.

Tikal

Towering pyramids poke above the jungle's canopy to catch the sun. Howler monkeys swing noisily through the branches of ancient trees as parrots and toucans dart to a cacophony of squawks. When the complex warbling of some mysterious jungle bird tapers off, the buzz of tree frogs fills the background and it will dawn on you that this is indeed hallowed ground.

Certainly the most striking feature of **Tikal** (☑2367-2837; www.parque-tikal.com; admission Q150; ◷6am-6pm) is its steep-sided temples, rising to heights of more than 44m. But what distinguishes Tikal is its setting, deep in the jungle. Its many plazas have been cleared of trees and vines, its temples uncovered and partially restored, but as you walk from one building to another you pass beneath the dense canopy of rainforest amid the rich, loamy aromas of earth and vegetation. Much of the delight of touring the site comes from strolling the broad causeways, originally built of packed limestone to accommodate traffic between temple complexes. By stepping softly you're more likely to spot spider monkeys, agoutis, foxes, ocellated turkeys and so on.

You can visit Tikal on a day trip from Flores or El Remate. But by spending a night here, you'll have a chance to visit the ruins both late afternoon and early morning, when there are fewer other tourists around and wildlife is more active.

History

Tikal is set on a low hill, which becomes evident as you ascend to the Gran Plaza from the entry road. Affording relief from the surrounding swampy ground, this high terrain may explain why the Maya settled here around 700 BC. Another reason was the abundance of flint, used by the ancients to make clubs, spear points, arrowheads and knives. The wealth of this valuable stone meant good tools could be made, and flint could be traded for other goods. Within 200 years the Maya of Tikal had begun to build stone ceremonial structures, and by 200 BC there was a complex of buildings on the site of the Acrópolis del Norte.

Classic Period

The Gran Plaza was beginning to assume its present shape and extent by the time of Christ. By the dawn of the early Classic period, around AD 250, Tikal had become an important religious, cultural and commercial city with a large population. King Yax Ehb' Xooc, in power about AD 230, is looked upon as the founder of the dynasty that ruled Tikal thereafter.

Under Chak Tok Ich'aak I (King Great Jaguar Paw), who ruled in the mid-4th century, Tikal adopted a brutal method of warfare, used by the rulers of Teotihuacán in central Mexico. Rather than meeting their adversaries on the plain of battle in hand-to-hand combat, the army of Tikal used auxiliary units to encircle the enemy and throw spears to kill them from a distance. This first use of 'air power' among the Maya of Petén enabled Siyah K'ak' (Smoking Frog), the Tikal general, to conquer the army of Uaxactún; thus Tikal became the dominant kingdom in El Petén.

By the middle of the Classic period, in the mid-6th century, Tikal's military prowess and its association with Teotihuacán allowed it to grow until it sprawled over 30 sq km and had a population of perhaps 100,000. But in 553, Yajaw Te' K'inich II (Lord Water) came to the throne of Caracol (in southwestern Belize), and within a decade had conquered Tikal and sacrificed its king. Tikal and other Petén kingdoms suffered under Caracol's rule until the late 7th century when, under new leadership, it

apparently cast off its oppressor and rose again.

Tikal's Renaissance

A powerful king named Jasaw Chan K'awiil I (682–734, also called Ah Cacao or Moon Double Comb), 26th successor of Yax Ehb' Xooc, restored not only Tikal's military strength but also its primacy in the Maya world. He conquered the greatest rival Maya state, Calakmul in Mexico, in 695, and his successors were responsible for building most of the great temples around the Gran Plaza that survive today. King Ah Cacao was buried beneath the staggering height of Templo I.

Tikal's greatness waned around 900, but it was not alone in its downfall, which was part of the mysterious general collapse of lowland Maya civilization.

Rediscovery

No doubt the Itzáes, who occupied Tayazal (now Flores), knew of Tikal in the late Postclassic period. Perhaps they even came here to worship at the shrines of old gods. Spanish missionary friars who moved through El Petén after the conquest left brief references to these jungle-bound structures, but their writings moldered in libraries for centuries.

It wasn't until 1848 that the Guatemalan government sent out an expedition, under the leadership of Modesto Méndez and Ambrosio Tut, to visit the site. This may have been inspired by John L Stephens' bestselling accounts of fabulous Maya ruins, published in 1841 and 1843 (though Stephens never visited Tikal). Like Stephens, Méndez and Tut took an artist, Eusebio Lara, to record their archaeological discoveries. An account of their findings was published by the Berlin Academy of Science.

In 1877 the Swiss Dr Gustav Bernoulli visited Tikal. His explorations resulted in the removal of carved wooden lintels from Templos I and IV and their shipment to Basel, where they are still on view in the Museum für Völkerkunde.

Scientific exploration of Tikal began with the arrival of English archaeologist Alfred P Maudslay in 1881. Others continued his work, Teobert Maler, Alfred M Tozzer and RE Merwin among them. Tozzer worked at Tikal on and off from the beginning of the 20th century until his death in 1954. The inscriptions at Tikal were studied and deciphered by Sylvanus G Morley.

Archaeological research and restoration was carried on by the University of Pennsylvania and the Guatemalan Instituto de Antropología e Historia until 1969. Since 1991, a joint Guatemalan-Spanish project has worked on conserving and restoring Templos I and V. The Parque Nacional Tikal (Tikal National Park) was declared a Unesco World Heritage Site in 1979.

◉ Sights & Activities

Gran Plaza

The path comes into the Gran Plaza around the **Templo I**, the Templo del Gran Jaguar (Temple of the Grand Jaguar). This was built to honor – and bury – Ah Cacao. The king may have worked out the plans for the building himself, but it was actually erected above his tomb by his son, who succeeded him to the throne in 734. The king's rich burial goods included stingray spines, which were used for ritual bloodletting, 180 jade objects, pearls and 90 pieces of bone carved with hieroglyphs. At the top of the 44m-high temple is a small enclosure of three rooms covered by a corbeled arch. The sapodilla-wood lintels over the doors were richly carved; one of them was removed and is now in a Basel museum. The lofty roofcomb that crowned the temple was originally adorned with reliefs and bright paint. When it's illuminated by the afternoon sun, it's possible to make out the figure of a seated dignitary.

Although climbing to the top of Templo I is prohibited, the views from **Templo II** just across the way are nearly as awe-inspiring. Templo II, also known as the Temple of the Masks, was at one time almost as high as Templo I, but it now measures 38m without its roofcomb.

Nearby, the **Acrópolis del Norte** (North Acropolis) significantly predates the two great temples. Archaeologists have uncovered about 100 different structures, the oldest of which dates from before the time of Christ, with evidence of occupation as far back as 600 BC. The Maya built and rebuilt on top of older structures, and the many layers, combined with the elaborate burials of Tikal's early rulers, added sanctity and power to their temples. The final version of the acropolis, as it stood around AD 800, had more than 12 temples atop a vast platform, many of them the work of King Ah Cacao. Look especially for the two huge, powerful wall masks, uncovered from an earlier structure and now protected by roofs. On the plaza side of the North Acropolis are two rows of stelae. These served to record the great deeds of the kings, to sanctify their memory and to add power to the temples and plazas that surrounded them.

Acrópolis Central

South and east of the Gran Plaza, this maze of courtyards, little rooms and small temples is thought by many to have been a palace where Tikal's nobles lived. Others think the tiny rooms may have been used for sacred rites and ceremonies, as graffiti found within them suggest. Over the centuries the configuration of the rooms was repeatedly changed, suggesting that perhaps this 'palace' was in fact a noble or royal family's residence and alterations were made to accommodate groups of relatives. A hundred years ago, one part of the acropolis provided lodgings for archaeologist Teobert Maler when he worked at Tikal.

Templo III

West of the Gran Plaza, across the Calzada Tozzer (Tozzer Causeway) stands Templo III, currently undergoing restoration. Only its upper reaches have been cleared. A scene carved into the **lintel** at its summit, 55m high, depicts a figure in an elaborate jaguar suit, believed to be the ruler Dark Sun. From this point, you can continue west to Templo IV along the Calzada Tozzer, one of several sacred byways between the temple complexes of Tikal.

Templo V & Acrópolis del Sur

Due south of the Gran Plaza, Templo V is a remarkably steep structure that was built sometime between the 7th and 8th centuries AD. Unlike the other great temples, this one has slightly rounded corners. A recent excavation of the temple revealed a group of embedded structures, some with geometric designs and Maya calendars on their walls. Rather than using the broad front stairs to scale the structure, you ascend via a steep wooden staircase on its left side. The view from the narrow platform at the top is wonderful, giving you a 'profile' of the temples on the Gran Plaza.

Excavation has hardly even begun on the mass of masonry just west of the temple, known collectively as the South Acropolis. The palaces on top are from late-Classic times (the time of King Moon Double

BIRD-WATCHING AT TIKAL

As well as howler and spider monkeys romping through the trees of Tikal, the plethora of birds flitting through the canopy and across the green expanses of the plazas is impressive. The ruined temple complexes present ideal viewing platforms for this activity, often providing the ability to look down upon the treetops to observe examples of the 300 or so bird species (migratory and resident) that have been recorded here. Bring binoculars and a copy of *The Birds of Tikal: An Annotated Checklist*, by Randell A Beavers, available at the visitor center shop. Tread quietly and be patient, and you'll probably see some of the following birds in the areas specified:

➡ Tody motmots, four trogon species and royal flycatchers around the Templo de las Inscripciones.

➡ Two oriole species, keel-billed toucans and collared aracaris in El Mundo Perdido.

➡ Great curassows, three species of woodpecker, crested guans, plain chachalacas and three tanager species around Complejo P.

➡ Three kingfisher species, jacanas, blue herons, two species of sandpiper, and great kiskadees at the Aguada Tikal (Tikal Reservoir) near the entrance. Tiger herons sometimes nest in the huge ceiba tree along the entrance path.

➡ Red-capped and white-collared manakins near Complejo Q; emerald toucanets near Complejo R.

Dedicated birding tours of the site are offered by **Roxy Ortíz** (☎5197-5173; tikalroxy.blogspot. com), an English-speaking naturalist who's studied wildlife at Tikal for a number of years.

Comb), but earlier constructions probably go back 1000 years.

Plaza de los Siete Templos

To the west of the Acrópolis del Sur is this broad grassy plaza, reached via a path to its southern edge. Built in late-Classic times, the seven **temples** with their stout roof combs line up along the east side of the plaza. They're currently the subject of an ongoing excavation project to restore them to their early splendor. On the south end stand three larger '**palaces**'; on the opposite end is an unusual **triple ballcourt**.

El Mundo Perdido

About 400m southwest of the Gran Plaza is El Mundo Perdido (Lost World), a complex of 38 structures with a huge **pyramid** in its midst, thought to be essentially Preclassic (with some later repairs and renovations). The pyramid, 32m high and 80m along the base, is surrounded by four mucheroded stairways, with huge masks flanking each one. The stairway facing eastward is thought to have functioned as a platform for viewing the sun's trajectory against a trio of structures on a raised platform to the east, a similar arrangement to the astronomical observatory at Uaxactún. Tunnels dug into the pyramid by archaeologists reveal four similar pyramids beneath the outer face; the earliest (Structure 5C-54 Sub 2B) dates from 700 BC, making this pyramid the oldest Maya structure at Tikal.

A smaller **temple** to the west, dating from the early Classic period, demonstrates Teotihuacán's influence, with its *talud-tablero* (stepped building) style of architecture.

Templo IV & Complejo N

Templo IV, at 65m, is the highest building at Tikal and the second-highest pre-Columbian building known in the western hemisphere, after La Danta at El Mirador. It was completed about 741, probably by order of Ah Cacao's son, Yax Kin, who was depicted on the carved lintel over the middle doorway (now in a museum in Basel, Switzerland), as the western boundary of the ceremonial precinct. A steep wooden staircase leads to the top. The view east is almost as good as from a helicopter – a panorama across the jungle canopy, with (from left to right) the temples of the Gran Plaza, Temple III, Temple V (just the top bit) and the great pyramid of the Mundo Perdido poking through.

Between Templo IV and Templo III is Complejo N, an example of the 'twin-temple' complexes erected during the late-Classic period. This one was built in 711 by Ah Cacao to mark the 14th *katun*, or 20-year cycle, of

Tikal

SURVEYING THE CLASSIC MAYA KINGDOM

Constructed in successive waves over a period of at least 800 years, Tikal is a vast, complicated site with hundreds of temples, pyramids and stelae. There's no way you'll get to it all in a day, but by following this itinerary you'll see many of the highlights. Before setting out be sure to stop by the visitor center and examine the scale model of the site, then admire the wealth of kings at the small **Museo Sylvanus G Morley 1** . Present your ticket at the nearby control booth and when you reach the posted map, take a left. It's a 20-minute walk to the solitary **Templo VI 2** . From here it's a blissful stroll up the broad Méndez causeway to the **Gran Plaza 3** , Tikal's ceremonial core, where you may examine the ancient precinct of the **North Acropolis 4** . Exit the plaza west, and take the first left, along a winding path, to **Templo V 5** . Round the rear to the right, a trail encircles the largely unexcavated South Acropolis to the **Plaza de los Siete Templos 6** . Immediately west stands the great pyramid of the **Mundo Perdido 7** . From here it's a quick stroll and a rather strenuous climb to the summit of **Temple IV 8** , Tikal's tallest structure.

Templo IV
Arrive in the late afternoon to get magically tinted photos of Temples I, II and III poking through the jungle canopy. If you're lucky you might also get a glimpse of an orange-crested falcon swooping around the treetops.

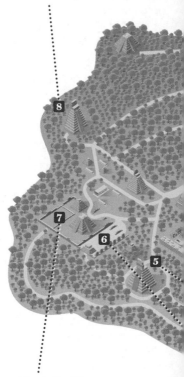

Mundo Perdido
The smaller temple to the west of the great pyramid may look familiar to those who've visited Teotihuacán near Mexico City, with its elegant stepped *talud-tablero* design, a vivid reminder of that distant kingdom's influence.

TOP TIPS

» Bring food and water.
» If you enter after 4pm, your ticket is good for the next day.
» Stay at one of the onsite hotels to catch the sunset/sunrise.
» To watch the sunset/sunrise from Temple IV, you'll need to purchase an additional ticket (Q100).
» Bring mosquito repellent.

Gran Plaza
Though the surreally tall Templo I, a mausoleum to the Late Classic ruler Ah Cacao, is off-limits to climbers, you're welcome to ascend the almost-as-tall Templo II across the plaza.

North Acropolis
Amid the stack of smaller and much older temples that rise up the hillside north of the plaza, take a peek beneath the two thatched shelters on a ledge to find a pair of fearsome masks.

Museo Sylvanus G Morley
Volumes have been written about the remarkably preserved Stela 31, a portrait of the ruler Stormy Sky crowning himself, flanked by spear-toting warriors in the attire of (ally or overlord?) Teotihuacán.

DANIEL SCHECHTER

Ticket Booth 1

Posted Map

Visitor Centre

Templo VI
The secluded temple has a lengthy set of glyphs inscribed on the back of its lofty roof comb, recording the lineage of successive kingdoms. Be patient: the contents of the weathered slab may take some effort to discern.

Plaza de los Siete Templos
even miniature temples line up along the east ide of this grassy courtyard. Climb the larger alace' at the south end to get a sightline along ne septet.

Templo V
As steep as it is massive, Tikal's second tallest temple has unusual rounded corners. Don't try climbing the broad front staircase but instead scale the almost vertical wooden ladder on the left.

DANIEL SCHECHTER

THE RESERVA DE BIÓSFERA MAYA

The Maya Biosphere Reserve, occupying 18,449 sq km stretched right across the north of El Petén, is part of the Unesco World Biosphere Reserve Network. As an innovative approach to conservation, the reserve is split into three spheres: a buffer zone where economic activities are permitted within a framework of environmental protection; a multiple-use zone, composed of tropical forest and supposedly dedicated to the sustainable harvest of *xate* (low-growing palm) ferns, chicle gum and timber; and the core area for scientific research, conservation of the natural environment and/or archaeological sites, and tightly controlled ecological and cultural tourism.

Unfortunately, the illegal harvesting of timber in the forests continues to occur on a massive scale, Maya tombs are desecrated by looters, and tourists (no matter how conscientious) have a negative impact on the fragile ecosystem. The buffer zone is rapidly changing from a forested landscape with scattered agricultural patches to an agricultural landscape with scattered forest patches. New roads meant to provide access to the core zones for researchers and tourists have fueled the migration and settlement of peasants from further south.

In fact, the most successful of the three zones, according to some conservationists, has been the one designated for multiple uses. This is because it is in the interest of the forest concessions to deter illegal activities, since the sustainable harvesting they engage in provides employment for their communities. These groups determinedly patrol their turf to ward off poachers, whom they see as competition, whereas violators in the core zones are less likely to face punitive action from the governmental agencies that are charged with managing them.

baktun 9. (A *baktun* equals about four centuries.) The king himself is portrayed on the remarkably preserved **Stela 16** in an enclosure just across the path. Beside the stele is **Altar 5**, a circular stone depicting the same king accompanied by a priestly figure in the process of exhuming the skeleton of a female ruler.

Templo de las Inscripciones (Templo VI)

One of the last temples to be erected at Tikal, Templo VI is also one of the few to bear written records. On the rear of its 12m-high roof comb is a long inscription – though it will take some effort to discern them in the bright sunlight – giving us the date AD 766, The sides and cornice of the roof comb bear glyphs as well. Its secluded position, about a 25-minute walk southeast of the Gran Plaza along the Calzada Méndez, make it a good spot for observing wildlife. From here, it's a 20-minute hike back to the main entrance.

Northern Complexes

About 1km north of the Gran Plaza is **Complejo P**. Like Complejo N, it's a late-Classic twin-temple complex that probably commemorated the end of a *katun*. **Complejo M**, next to it, was partially torn down by the late-Classic Maya to provide building materials for a causeway, now named after Alfred

Maudslay, which runs southwest to Templo IV. **Grupo H**, northeast of Complexes P and M, with one tall, cleared temple, had some interesting graffiti within its temples.

Complejo Q and **Complejo R**, about 300m north of the Gran Plaza, are very late-Classic twin-pyramid complexes with stelae and altars standing before the temples. Complex Q is perhaps the best example of the twin-temple type, as it has been partly restored. **Stele 22** and **Altar 10** are excellent examples of late-Classic Tikal relief carving, dated 771.

Museums

Museo Lítico   MUSEUM

(Stone Museum; admission Q10, also valid for Museo Morley; ☉9am-noon & 1-4:30pm) The larger of Tikal's two museums is in the visitor center. It houses a number of carved stones from the ruins. Outside is a model showing how Tikal would have looked around AD 800. The photographs taken by Alfred P Maudslay and Teobert Maler of the jungle-covered temples, in various stages of discovery, are particularly striking.

Museo Sylvanus G Morley   MUSEUM

(Museo Cerámico; admission Q10, also valid for Museo Lítico; ☉9am-5pm Mon-Fri, 9am-4pm Sat & Sun) This museum exhibits items recovered from excavations including carved jade, inscribed bones, ceramics and so on. Here you'll find the highly detailed Stela 31, dedicated to the ruler Stormy Sky-Double Comb, flanked by warriors from Teotihuacán, and at the rear the simulated tomb of King Moon Double Comb with the precious items unearthed from his burial site beneath Temple I.

CCIT
NOTABLE BUILDING

(Centro de Conservación e Investigación de Tikal; ⊙ 8am-noon & 1-4pm) Opened in July 2012, the Japanese-funded research center is devoted to the identification and restoration of pieces unearthed at the site. The 1300-sq-m facility has a huge cache of items to sort through, and you can watch the restorers at work.

Though not a museum per se, it features an excellent gallery on the different materials used by Maya craftsmen, with a good display of polychrome ceramics.

Tours

Canopy Tours Tikal
ADVENTURE TOUR

(☏ 5819-7766; www.canopytikal.com; admission Q235; ⊙ 8am-5pm) By the national park entrance this outfit offers a one-hour tour through the forest canopy, with the chance to ride a harness along a series of cables linking trees up to 300m apart and several hanging bridges. The fee includes transport from Tikal or El Remate.

Sleeping & Eating

Staying overnight enables you to relax and savor the dawn and dusk, when most of the jungle birds and animals can be seen and heard (especially the howler monkeys). Other than camping, there are only three places to stay, and tour groups often have many of the rooms reserved. One way of ensuring a room is to become a group tourist yourself. Almost any travel agency in Guatemala offers Tikal tours, including lodging, a meal or two, a guided tour and transportation.

There's no need to make reservations if you want to stay at Tikal's **campground** (campsite per person Q50, hammock with mosquito net Q85), behind the new research center. This is a large, grassy area with a clean bathroom block and *palapa* shelters for hanging hammocks.

Along the right-hand side of the access road stand a series of little *comedores,* offering bland versions of standards like grilled chicken or grilled steak (Q40 to Q50). All are open from 5am to 9pm daily. Another restaurant is in the Visitor Center, with pastas and hamburgers among the offerings.

Picnic tables beneath shelters are located just off Tikal's Gran Plaza, with soft-drink and water vendors standing by, but no food is sold. If you want to spend all day at the ruins without having to make the 20- to 30-minute walk back to the *comedores,* carry food and water with you.

★Tikal Inn
HOTEL $$

(☏ 7861-2444; www.tikalinn.com; s/d Q395/470, bungalow Q470/590; P @ ☎ ☒) Built in the late '60s, this resort-style lodging offers rooms in the main building and thatched bungalows alongside the pool and rear lawn, with little porches out front. All are simple, spacious and quite comfortable. The most secluded accommodations are the least expensive, in a handful of cabins at the end of a sawdust trail through the forest.

Jaguar Inn
HOTEL $$$

(☏ 7926-0002; www.jaguartikal.com; campsite per person Q25, with tent Q80, s/d Q395/590; P ✳ @ ☎) The inn of choice for youthful, independent travelers has duplex and quad bungalows with thatched roofs and hammocks on the porches, plus a smart little restaurant with a popular terrace out front. For those on a tight budget there are tents for rent on a platform.

Jungle Lodge
HOTEL $$$

(☏ 2477-0570; www.junglelodgetikal.com; s/d Q622/772, without bathroom Q298/338; P @ ☒) Nearest of the hotels to the site entrance, this was originally built to house archaeologists working at Tikal. Self-contained bungalows, plus a bank of cheaper units, are well spaced throughout rambling, jungly grounds. The restaurant-bar (mains Q80 to Q100) serves veggie pasta, crepes, pepper steak and other international dishes in a tropical ambience.

Orientation

The archaeological site is at the center of the 550-sq-km Parque Nacional Tikal. The road from Flores enters the park 19km south of the ruins. From the parking lot at the site, it's a short walk back to the junction where there's an information kiosk. Immediately south of this junction, a visitor center sells books, maps, souvenirs, hats, insect repellent, sun block and other necessities; it also houses a restaurant and museum (p252). Near the visitor center are Tikal's three hotels, a camping area, a few small *comedores* and a second museum.

It's a five-minute walk from the ticket control booth to the entry gate. Just beyond, there's a large map posted. From here, it's a 1.5km walk (20 minutes) southwest to the Gran Plaza. From the Gran Plaza west to Templo IV it's over 600m.

Information

Tickets are Q150 per person; if purchased after 4pm they're valid for the whole next day. Everyone must purchase a ticket at the entry gate on the road in. Those staying more than one day can purchase additional tickets at the ticket control booth along the path to the site entrance. Seeing the sunrise from Templo IV at the west end of the main site is possible from about October to March, but to enter the park before or after visiting hours you must purchase an additional ticket for Q100, presumably to pay the guide who must accompany you.

The core of the ancient city takes up about 16 sq km, with more than 4000 structures. To visit all the major building complexes, you must walk at least 10km, probably more, so wear comfortable shoes with good rubber treads that grip well. The ruins here can be very slick from rain and organic material, especially during the wet season. Bring plenty of water, as dehydration is a real danger if you're walking around all day in the heat. Please don't feed the coatis (pisotes) that wander about the site.

GUIDES

Multilingual guides are available at the information kiosk. These authorized guides display their accreditation carnet, listing the languages they speak. Before 7am, the charge for a half-day tour is Q100 per person. After that you pay Q300 for a group of up to four people, plus Q40 for each additional person.

MONEY

The Jaguar Inn (p253) will exchange US dollars and traveler's checks (at a poor rate) and provides internet access at Q50 per hour.

RESOURCES

For more complete information on the monuments at Tikal, pick up a copy of *Tikal – A Handbook of the Ancient Maya Ruins*, by William R Coe, which is available in Flores and at Tikal. A book you're best off finding before you come is *The Lords of Tikal*, by Peter D Harrison, a vivid, cogent summary of the city's history. Guards at the ticket booth sell you an 'official' site map (Q10) which is identical to the one posted at the site entrance.

ⓘ Getting There & Away

Four microbuses by Asociación de Transportistas Imperio Maya (p241) depart Flores between 6am and 3pm (Q30, 1½ hours), the last returning at 5pm. They return from Tikal at noon, 1:30pm, 3pm and 6pm. You could also take the Uaxactún-bound bus from Flores at 2pm, which goes a bit slower. Autobuses del Norte provides Pullman service to Tikal at 6am and 8am (Q80).

From El Remate a collective shuttle departs at 5:30am for Tikal, starting back at 2pm (Q30/50 one way/round trip). Any El Remate accommodations can make reservations.

If traveling from Belize, get a Santa Elena–bound microbus to Puente Ixlú, sometimes called El Cruce, and switch there to a northbound microbus for the remaining 36km to Tikal. But note that there is little northbound traffic after 11am. Heading from Tikal to Belize, start early and get off at Puente Ixlú to catch a bus or microbus eastward. Be wary of shuttles to Belize advertised at Tikal: these have been known to detour to Flores to pick up passengers!

Uaxactún

POP 963 / ELEV 175M

Uaxactún (wah-shahk-*toon*), 23km north of Tikal along an unpaved road through the jungle, was Tikal's political and military rival in late Preclassic times. It was conquered by Tikal's Chak Tok Ich'aak I (King Great Jaguar Paw) in the 4th century, and was subservient to its great sister to the south for centuries thereafter, though it experienced an apparent resurgence during the Terminal Classic, after Tikal went into decline.

Uaxactún village lies either side of a disused airstrip, a remnant of the age when planes were the only way to reach this inaccessible spot. The strip now serves as pasture and a football field. Villagers make an income from collecting chicle, *pimienta* (allspice) and *xate* (exported to Holland for floral arrangements) in the surrounding forest. In the *xate* warehouse on the west end of town, women put together bunches of the plants for export.

About halfway along the airstrip, roads go both left and right to the ruins. Village boys will want to guide you: you don't need a guide to find the ruins, but you might want to let one or two of them earn a small tip.

Much of the attraction here is the absolute stillness and isolation. Few visitors make it up this way. Uaxactún is off the power grid; evening church services and TV viewing are by generator only. At the time of writing there was still just one phone for public use, in an office on the south side of the airstrip,

Uaxactún

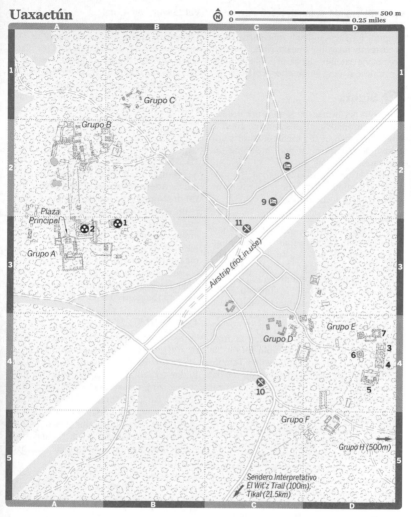

N

0 — 500 m
0 — 0.25 miles

Uaxactún

◎ **Sights**
Colección Dr Juan Antonio
Valdés..(see 9)
1 Palacio A-XVIII....................................... B3
2 Palacio V... A3
3 Templo E-I.. D4
4 Templo E-III... D4
5 Templo E-V.. D4
6 Templo E-VII-Sub.................................. D4
7 Templo E-X... D4

🛏 **Sleeping**
8 Aldana's Lodge......................................C2
9 Campamento, Hotel &
Restaurante El Chiclero......................C2

🍴 **Eating**
10 Comedor Imperial Okan Arin.................C4
11 Comedor Uaxactún.................................C3

open till around 6pm. To reach anyone in Uaxactún call ☎7783-3931, then wait a few minutes for them to fetch your party. There is currently no cell-phone coverage. Internet access, via satellite signal, is available Monday to Friday next to the **phone office**.

◉ Sights

Research performed by the Carnegie Institute in the 1920s and '30s laid the groundwork for much of the archaeological study that followed in the region, including the excavations at Tikal.

The fee of Q50 is collected at the gate to Tikal National Park, though there is no ticket control at the site itself.

Grupo E

The buildings here are grouped on five low hills. From the airstrip find the sign pointing to Grupo E between the Catholic and Evangelical churches on the right side, from where it's a 10- to 15-minute walk. The most significant temple here is **Templo E-VII-Sub**, among the earliest intact temples excavated, with foundations going back perhaps to 2000 BC. The pyramid is part of a group with astronomical significance: seen from it, the sun rises behind **Templo E-I** on the longest day of the year and behind **Templo E-III** on the shortest day. Also look for the somewhat deteriorated jaguar and serpent masks on this pyramid's sides.

Grupos B & A

About a 20-minute walk to the northwest of the runway are Grupo B and Grupo A, the latter featuring the more formidable structures around the city's main square. **Palacio V**, on the east side of the square, is considered a model for Tikal's North Acropolis. In 1916 the American archaeologist Sylvanus Morley uncovered a **stele** dating from the 8th *baktun* at Grupo A. Thus the site was called Uaxactún, meaning 'eight stone'. Behind Palacio V, along a path back toward the village, is the imposing **Palacio A-XVIII**, affording the most panoramic view of the site from its summit.

Stela 5, at Grupo B, displays Tikal's signature glyph, from which archaeologists deduced that Uaxactún was under that city's sway by the date inscribed, 358.

Colección Dr Juan Antonio Valdés

Though many of the objects unearthed at Uaxactún ended up in museums around the world, the **Colección Dr Juan Antonio Valdés** at the Hotel El Chiclero holds a remarkable wealth of Maya pottery from Uaxactún, Yaxhá and as far away as Oaxaca, Mexico. There are vases, cups, plates, bowls, incense burners and tall vessels for drinking chocolate. Caretaker Neria can tell you the history, origin, meaning and use of each one. A case contains some of the most precious finds: stone earrings, arrowheads and three plates showing the dance of the corn god.

🏃 Activities

A recently installed interpretive nature trail, the **Sendero Interpretativo El Wit'z**, runs 1.7km through the jungle, initiating from a point 200m beyond the Comedor Imperial and ending up at Grupo H of the Uaxactún archaeological site. Moving from cultivated to preserved sections of the forest, it is meant to demonstrate the effectiveness of conservation in preserving the environment. Chicozapote, *ramón* and other native trees grow in the protected part.

☞ Tours

Tours to Uaxactún can be arranged in Flores or at the hotels in El Remate and Tikal.

Hector Aldana Nuñez, from Aldana's Lodge (p256), is an English-speaking guide specializing in nature-oriented tours of the region. He leads three-day treks to El Zotz and Tikal for around Q1300 per person. He also offers survival training (Q350 per day), in which participants learn to find sustenance and shelter in the jungle; machetes are provided.

Hotel El Chiclero (p257) can organize trips to more remote sites such as El Mirador, Río Azul (three days), Xultún, Nakbé and San Bartolo.

⌷ Sleeping & Eating

A few basic *comedores* provide food, including Comedor Uaxactún and Comedor Imperial Okan Arin.

Aldana's Lodge   HUT $

(campsite per person Q20, r per person Q25) To the right off the street leading to Grupos B and A, the Aldana family offers half a dozen clapboard cabins, with thin mattresses on pallets. Father and son Alfido and Hector Aldaña lead tours to jungle sites, and Amparo prepares good meals.

Campamento, Hotel & Restaurante El Chiclero
HOTEL $

(☑ 7926-1095; campamentochiclero@gmail.com; campsites per person Q25, r per person Q50) On the north side of the airstrip, El Chiclero has 10 spartan, institutional green rooms underneath a thatched roof, with decent mattresses and mosquito-netted ceilings and windows. Clean showers and toilets are in an adjacent out-building; lights out at 9pm. Perky owner Neria does the best food in town (Q50 for soup and a main course with rice).

❶ Getting There & Away

A Pinita bus leaves Santa Elena for Uaxactún (Q35) at 2pm, passing through El Remate around 3pm and Tikal by 4pm, and starting back for Santa Elena from Uaxactún at 6am the following day. This means you'll need to spend two nights in Uaxactún to see the ruins. Otherwise, shuttles from El Remate to Uaxactún and back by La Casa de Don David (p245) cost Q624 for up to five people.

If you're driving, the last chance to fill your fuel tank as you come from the south is at Puente Ixlú, just south of El Remate. During the rainy season (from May to October, sometimes extending into November), the road from Tikal to Uaxactún can become pretty muddy. From Uaxactún, unpaved roads lead to other ruins at El Zotz (about 30km southwest), Xultún (35km northeast) and Río Azul (100km northeast).

Yaxhá

The Classic Maya sites of Yaxhá, Nakum and El Naranjo form a triangle that is the basis for a national park covering more than 37,000 hectares and bordering the Parque Nacional Tikal to the west. Yaxhá, the most visited of the trio, stands on a hill between two sizable lakes, Lago Yaxhá and Lago Sacnab. The setting, the sheer size of the site, the number of excellently restored buildings and the abundant jungle flora and fauna all make it particularly worth visiting. The site is 11km north of the Puente Ixlú–Melchor de Mencos road, accessed via unpaved road from a turnoff 32km from Puente Ixlú and 33km from Melchor de Mencos.

◉ Sights

Occupied as early as 600 BC, Yaxhá (translated as 'blue-green water') achieved its cultural apex in the 8th century AD, when it counted some 20,000 inhabitants and 500 buildings, including temples, palaces and residential complexes.

It takes about two hours to wander round the main groups of ruins, which have been extensively excavated and reconstructed. Cover the site in a clockwise fashion, traversing the original road network. The first group of buildings you come to, **Plaza C**, is one of a pair of astronomical observatories. Take the Calzada de las Canteras to the **South Acropolis**, a complex of palatial structures from which Yaxhá's aristocracy could watch the games going on in the **ball court** below. To the northwest stands one of Yaxhá's most ancient constructions, the **Greater Astronomical Complex (Plaza F)**. The arrangement is similar to the one at Uaxactún's Grupo E, with an observation tower (unexcavated) facing a three-part platform for tracking the sun's trajectory through the year. You can ascend the pyramidal tower (there's a wooden staircase alongside) for jaw-dropping views of the **North Acropolis** to the northeast, with a formidable temple rising above the jungle foliage. From here, take the Calzada de las Aguadas north to reach the **Plaza de las Sombras** (aka Grupo Maler), where archaeologists believe throngs of citizens once gathered for religious ceremonies. Return toward the entrance along the Calzada Este to reach the high point of the tour (literally), **Structure 216** in the East Acropolis. Also called the Temple of the Red Hands, because red handprints were discovered there, it towers over 30m high, affording views in every direction.

On an island near the far (south) shore of Laguna Yaxhá is a late Postclassic archaeological site, **Topoxté**, where the dense covering of ruined temples and dwellings may date back to the Itzá culture that occupied Flores island at the time the Spanish came. At the bottom of the Calzada del Lago is the **boat landing**, from where a boatman might be willing to take you to Topoxté for around Q250.

🛏 Sleeping & Eating

On the lake shore below the Yaxhá ruins is **Campamento Yaxhá** `FREE`, where you can camp for free on raised platforms with thatched roofs. Outbuildings have showers and toilets. Drinking water can be purchased at a store, but you must bring food.

Yaxhá

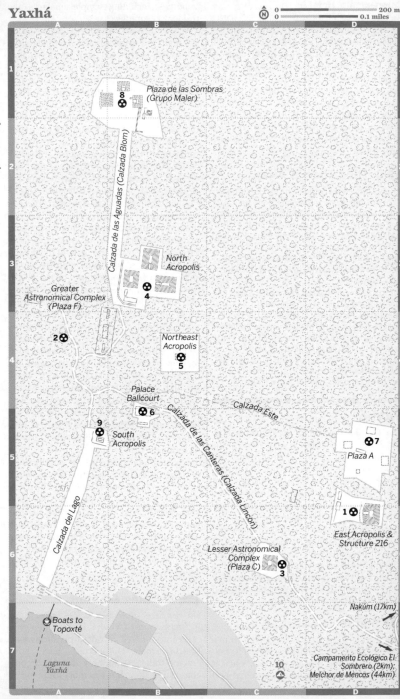

Yaxhá

Campamento Ecológico
El Sombrero   BUNGALOW $$
(☑4147-6830; ecosombreroinicio.tripod.com; s/d/tr
Q350/440/510, without bathroom Q120/200/545;
🅿) ✈ El Sombrero features solar-powered,
mosquito-netted bungalows amid gardens
overlooking the lake. The kitchen, overseen
by the Italian owner, is of a high standard,
and there's a small library on local archae-
ology. It's on the southern shore of Laguna
Yaxhá, 2km from the ruins and 250m off the
approach road; call ahead and they'll pick
you up from the bus stop.

You could also camp here or sling a ham-
mock for Q40. *Lancha* tours to Topoxté are
offered (Q250) as well as night crocodile ob-
servation tours, horseback riding and over-
night trips to Nakum, El Naranjo, Holmul
and other lesser-known Maya sites in the
vicinity.

⊙ Getting There & Away

Agencies in Flores and El Remate offer organized
trips to Yaxhá, some combined with Nakum and/
or Tikal. Horizontes Mayas (p244) in El Remate
runs shuttles (Q100 per person, minimum three
people) at 6:30am and 1pm, returning at 1pm
and 6:30pm. From Santa Elena's terminal, take
the daily 7am bus (Q25), returning at 1pm.

Nakum

A contemporary of Tikal, Nakum was a sig-
nificant port on the Holmul river during
the late Classic Period, when that waterway
linked Tikal with the Caribbean coast. It's
17km north of Yaxhá, a 1½ hour drive over
a rough road that's impassable from August
to January (though it was improved by the
crew of *Survivor Guatemala,* which was
shot here).

Remote as this spot is, it's particularly
exciting to find such a formidable group of
structures here. The excavated section is not
huge but it packs in a lot. Excavation is on-
going and you're likely to see the archaeol-
ogy crews at work. Archaeological research
focuses on the predominance of *talud-
tablero* type structures in the south section,
suggesting a connection with Teotihuacán
in Mexico, and seeks to understand why Na-
kum flourished during the Terminal Classic
at a time when its contemporaries were col-
lapsing all around it.

The site features two major architectural
groups, the North and South Sectors, con-
nected by a causeway; most of the excavated
structures are in the latter. The most inter-
esting of these, in the part dubbed the **Plaza
Central**, features an unusually well pre-
served roofcomb with a clearly visible mask.
In tandem with the pyramidal structure op-
posite, it presumably served as some kind of
astronomical observatory

Moving south from the Plaza Central,
you enter the **South Acropolis**, a walled
compound on a raised platform comprising
12 courtyards surrounded by 33 buildings,
which housed palatial residences. This ar-
rangement was in place around AD 900,
though there is evidence that the site had
been occupied for the previous 14 cen-
turies. What's unique about some of the
courtyards here, like **Patio 1**, is that they
were completely enclosed by buildings, a
layout not found elsewhere in the Maya
world. Outside the South Acropolis to the
east are **stelae** bearing dates from the 9th
century, among the latest recorded dates in
the Maya lowlands.

Campamento Ecológico El Sombrero
(p259) in Yaxhá can arrange horseback rides
with a night spent sleeping in hammocks
(Q150 per person). To get here independ-
ently, you'll need a 4WD. Should you wish
to spend the night, Nakum has a handful of
tent platforms, free of charge, but bring food
and water.

Parque Nacional Laguna del Tigre

A vast expanse of seasonally flooded forest cut through by slow-moving rivers, this 3340-sq-km park in the northwest corner of El Petén forms the largest protected wetlands area in Meso-America. Though its northwestern reaches are threatened by government-authorized petroleum extraction operations, it remains a haven for endemic wildlife.

El Perú (Waká)

Trips to El Perú are termed La Ruta Guacamaya (the Scarlet Macaw Trail), because the chances of seeing these magnificent birds are high, chiefly during their February-to-June nesting season. Several important Classic-period structures and stelae at the jungle site have led archaeologists to believe it may have allied with Calakmul, Tikal's great rival to the north.

El Perú is located 62km northwest of Flores in the Parque Nacional Laguna del Tigre. From the riverbank, it's a 20-minute walk to the site entrance, then a half-hour climb through primary-growth forest to the ruins. If you arrive independently, the resident rangers will set you up with a guide.

A number of stelae, in various states of deterioration, occupy four plazas. Stela number 16 in plaza 3 (the original lies under a thatched roof next to a fiberglass replica) portrays Siyaj K'ak', aka Smoking Frog, a warrior from Teotihuacán who arrived here in 378 and apparently allied with El Perú in a campaign to overthrow Tikal.

To get here independently, take the bus to Paso Caballos (Q25, 2½ hours from Flores), which leaves Santa Elena terminal at approximately 1:30pm, then travel an hour by boat down the Río San Pedro and its northern tributary, the Río San Juan. From Paso Caballos, *lanchas* charge Q550 to Q600. There are tent platforms at the ranger station if you'd like to camp out.

Estación Biológica Las Guacamayas

A scientific research center within the Parque Nacional Laguna del Tigre, the Scarlet Macaw Biological Station (📞 4890-9797; www.lasguacamayas.org) offers wildlife watching and archaeology tours, and the chance to tag along with researchers as they monitor macaws and butterflies. Overlooking the broad lazy river, it's a splendidly isolated spot and there is comfortable, ecofriendly accommodation in several thatched-roof houses.

One- to three-day tours consist of a visit to El Perú, 20 minutes north of the station up the Río San Juan, and nighttime observation of the endemic Morelet's crocodile, along with the chance to fish for the renowned *pescado blanco*.

Spacious rooms have wraparound screened windows and front porches. A separate building contains clean toilets and good showers; another has a *comedor,* where healthy meals are prepared. The rate per person on a two-day stay (with two persons) is Q1575, including accommodation, meals and transport.

Volunteering is also possible, with the chance to contribute to infrastructure, maintain trails, cultivate the butterfly garden or support environmental education projects among the Q'eqchi' community in Paso Caballos. There's a minimum two-week commitment, and volunteers pay Q625 per week for accomodation, food and transport to the site.

El Mirador

Buried within the furthest reaches of the Petén jungle, just 7km south of the Mexican border, the late-Preclassic metropolis at El Mirador contains the largest cluster of buildings of any single Maya site, among them the biggest pyramid ever built in the Maya world. Ongoing excavations have only scratched the surface, so many are still hidden beneath the jungle.

'The Lookout', the name given to the site by *chicleros* before its discovery by archaeologists, is due to the excellent views provided by some of the pyramids. La Danta (the Tapir) looms some 70m above the forest floor. Another pyramid, El Tigre, measures 55m high and its base covers 18,000 sq meters – six times the area of Tikal's biggest structure, Templo IV. La Danta, El Tigre and the other temples erected here display the unusual 'triadic' style, in which three pyramids crown a platform, with the one in the middle dominating the other two, which face each other at a lower level. The facades of these buildings were once embellished with carved masks.

You'll have to use your imagination to picture this city that at its height spread over 16 sq km and supported tens of thousands of citizens. It was certainly the greatest Maya city of the Preclassic era, far exceeding in size anything built subsequently in the Maya world. Within the complex, more than a dozen internal causeways link the main architectural complexes.

Scholars are still figuring out why and how El Mirador thrived (there are few natural resources and no water sources save for the reservoirs built by ingenious, ancient engineers) and what led to its abandonment in 150 AD. Some five centuries after that date, El Mirador appears to have been resettled, as suggested by the existence of Classic architecture among the older structures. Pottery unearthed from this era displays the highly refined codex-style of decoration, in which calligraphic lines are painted on a cream-colored surface, with designs believed to resemble Maya codices.

Richard Hansen, a professor from Idaho State University, is leading the effort to map the Mirador basin, a vast swath of northern El Petén comprising dozens of interconnected cities, with funding from an assortment of international and Guatemalan foundations and private sources. In March 2009, Dr Hansen and his crew made a significant discovery when they excavated a 4m frieze at the base of La Danta, dating from 300 BC, which they surmise decorated a royal pool. The carved images upon it depict the twin heroes Hunahpú and Ixbalnqué swimming through the underworld domain of Xibalbá, a tale that is related in the *Popul Vuh*. The finding underlines the importance of El Mirador in establishing the belief system of Classic era civilizations.

Getting to El Mirador

A visit to the site involves an arduous jungle trek of at least five days and four nights (it's about 60km each way), with no facilities or amenities aside from what you carry in and what can be rustled from the forest. During the rainy season, especially September to December, the mud can make it extremely difficult; February to June is the best period to attempt a trek.

The trip usually departs from a cluster of houses called Carmelita, 82km up the road from Flores. The **Comisión de Turismo Cooperativa Carmelita** (☎ 7861-2641; www.turismocooperativacarmelita.com), a group of 16 Inguat-authorized guides, can make all arrangements for a trek to El Mirador, with optional visits to the Preclassic sites of Nakbé, El Tintal, Wakná and Xulnal. Travelers who participate in these treks should be in good physical shape, able to withstand high temperatures (average of nearly 100 degrees) and humidity (average 85 percent) and be prepared to hike or ride long distances (up to 30km per day).

On the first day of a typical six-day itinerary, you'll hike six hours through mostly agricultural country to El Tintal, where you'd camp for the night. On the second day, after a look around El Tintal, you proceed through denser forests to El Mirador and set up camp there. The next day is reserved for exploring El Mirador. On Day 4, you hike

---

THE MIRADOR BASIN

The 2169 sq km of tropical forest surrounding El Mirador harbors dozens of other substantial cities that flourished during the middle- and late-Preclassic eras as well. At least six major causeways connected El Mirador to these satellites, an engineering feat that enabled it to become what was possibly the New World's first political state. The four largest cities in the vicinity are all within a day's walk of El Mirador.

El Tintal (23km southwest of El Mirador) One of the largest and most important Preclassic cities, with a moat surrounding the civic center and one of the biggest ball courts in El Petén.

Wakná (15km south) Built around what is possibly the largest astronomical observatory in the Maya world, with Preclassic murals and a series of internal causeways.

Nakbé (13km southeast) Established around 1200 BC, it grew to be one of the most important Preclassic sites. El Mirador was probably modeled upon this predecessor. All the characteristic features of Maya civilization – monumental architecture, palaces, causeways and ball courts – had appeared here by 600 BC.

Xulnal (7km west of El Tintal) Discovered in 2001. Pottery found here is evidence of some of the earliest occupation in the Mirador Basin.

four hours southeast to arrive at Nakbé and camp there. The next day the expedition begins the return south via an eastern trail, stopping for the night at the site of La Florida. On Day 6, you head back to Carmelita.

For a five-day trip, the cooperative charges Q2760/2800/3680 per person in groups of four/three/two persons; six-day trips cost Q3280/3380/4520. The fee includes tents, hammocks and mosquito netting; all meals and drinking water; Spanish-speaking guide; mules and muleskinners; and first-aid supplies.

Two buses daily travel from Flores to Carmelita. In Carmelita, **Comedor Pepe Toño** (☎ 7783-3812) is about it for accommodation, with two very basic thatched huts containing five lumpy, mosquito-netted beds each, and primitive bathroom facilities. Some local families may also provide lodging; ask around.

It's also possible to get here from Uaxactún, a longer but gentler approach, since there are fewer *bajos* (seasonal swamps) and it's less affected by agricultural clearing so you're underneath the jungle canopy from the outset. Hotel El Chiclero (p257) offers a six-day tour at Q1000 per person per day. The first leg of the journey you're driven in a monster truck to a campground at the former *chiclero* camp of Yucatán, a five-hour journey. The next morning the group is outfitted with mules and proceeds to another camp, La Leontina, a 3½-hour tramp through the jungle. The following day it's a 1½-hour walk to Nakbé. After visiting that site, the expedition continues to El Mirador. The journey back follows the same route in reverse.

If expense is not a concern, you can go the easy way: by helicopter (Q4380 per person, minimum four passengers). The website **Mirador Park** (www.miradorpark.com) has details for arranging one- and two-day 'heli-tours' to El Mirador from Flores, arriving in just half an hour at the site.

Understand
Guatemala

Guatemala Today

Guatemalans are struggling. Over half the population lives below the poverty line and gang membership is rising as an overwhelmed and under-resourced police force struggles to maintain order. Against this increasingly bleak backdrop, scores of grass-roots organizations have sprung up, tirelessly combatting Guatemala's many problems. While successive governments continue to make promises, it is Guatemalans themselves who are delivering solutions.

Best on Film

Aquí me Quedo (2010; Rodolfo Espinoza) Subtle political commentary, black comedy and satire abound in this story of a kidnapping, shot in and around Quetzaltenango.

When the Mountains Tremble (1983; Pamela Yates & Newton Thomas Sigel) Documentary featuring Susan Sarandon and Rigoberta Menchú, telling the story of the civil war.

Capsulas (2011; Verónica Riedel) A look at greed, corruption and the drug trade from one of Guatemala's few female directors.

El Norte (1983; Gregory Nava) Young indigenous siblings flee their village and begin the tortuous journey to enter the US as illegal immigrants.

Best in Print

The President (Miguel Ángel Asturias; 1946) Nobel Prize–winning Guatemalan author takes some not-too-subtle jabs at the country's long line of dictators.

A Mayan Life (Gaspar Pedro Gonzáles; 1995) The first published novel by a Maya author is an excellent study of rural Guatemalan life.

The Art of Political Murder (Francisco Goldman; 2008) Meticulously-researched account of the assassination of Bishop Gerardi.

The More Things Change...

In mid-January 2012, Otto Fernando Perez Molina was sworn in as Guatemala's president. Molina is a former army general who served during Efraín Ríos Montt's dictatorship and was stationed in the Ixíl region, where many of the worst human rights abuses and massacres of the civil war took place.

During his successful campaign, Molina offered Guatemalans the two things that polls consistently say they want – security and jobs. In one of his first moves as president, Molina announced a plan that would put 7000 soldiers on the streets in the country's most dangerous and criminally active areas. While arrest rates skyrocketed, crime rates remained steady.

Recent years have shown that often the worst criminal excesses are committed by security forces. In just one month in early 2012, four police officers were charged with assault, conspiracy and unlawful association while various members of the Secret Service were accused of being members of a countrywide kidnapping gang.

Molina's own anti-corruption credentials were called into question as he came under fire for defending three members of his government who had each racked up over Q800,000 (over US$100,000) in travel expenses in a three month period. The trips were defended by Molina as being necessary to avoid becoming 'isolated'. Meanwhile Congress opened up the way to grant themselves whatever pay rises they feel like, whenever.

A Question of Security

One very touchy subject in rural Guatemala has to do with large (often foreign-administered) projects such as hydroelectric dams and mineral mines. Opponents to Molina's mobilization of troops claim that the security argument is a smokescreen and that the soldiers are really there to protect the interests of these projects. As if to prove them right, troops were sent in to 'restore order' at various anti-mining and anti-dam protests around the country. In late 2012 soldiers shot into crowds at a protest outside of Totonicapán, killing seven and wounding 40, a result characterized by Foreign Minister Harold Caballeros to the international media as 'not a big deal'.

Guatemala still struggles with violence. The National Gun Registry campaign started off well, but is faltering. While a little over 125,000 guns were registered and turned in, it's estimated that nearly twice that amount are unregistered, leaving more than 250,000 illegal weapons in circulation.

Global Policy

Global policy continues to affect Guatemala. A possibly unforeseen consequence of the move to renewable fuels has seen corn tortilla prices double in Guatemala as the United States uses up to 40 percent of its corn crop to make biofuel. Corn is a staple in Guatemala, nearly the one ingredient you are guaranteed to see at every meal and despite widespread plantations the country imports nearly half of its corn.

The Slow Road to Recovery

Guatemala is on the slow road to recovery from its civil-war wounds. While this is in part due to the passing of generations who lived through the war, official recognition of some atrocities has been an important step in the recovery process. Though President Molina has stated he does not believe the killings amounted to genocide, a campaign is underway to exhume clandestine cemeteries used by the military to bury 'disappeared' dissidents and the legal processes have at last begun, with some war criminals being brought to justice. So far the heftiest penalty to be handed down was to ex-Military Commissioner Lucas Tecún, who was sentenced to 7710 years in prison.

In March 2012, in a move that shocked many hardened cynics, a Guatemalan judge removed the final obstacle barring former dictator Efraín Ríos Montt from facing trial on charges of genocide. It will be the first time that a former Latin American head of state has faced such charges in a national court.

Grass Roots Movement

In the face of official indifference and/or inability to deal with the country's myriad problems, many community-based organizations and NGOs are moving in to fill the void. Large segments of the Guatemalan population are becoming active in volunteer work, focusing on everything from neighborhood-watch–type programs in areas unpatrolled by police to larger efforts focusing on food security and housing for the poor. This community spirit is also evident after natural disasters hit the country, as citizens band together to deliver aid to affected families.

POPULATION: **14,100,000**

AREA: **108,889 SQ KM**

GDP: **US$46.15 BILLION**

INFLATION: **6.2%**

POPULATION BELOW POVERTY LINE: **54%**

RATIO OF CELL PHONES TO LANDLINES: **13 TO 1**

if Guatemala were 100 people

59 would be Mestizo
40 would be Maya
1 would be Other

Guatemalan diaspora

(% of migrating population)

84 — USA
10 — Mexico
1.6 — Canada
4.4 — Other

population per sq km

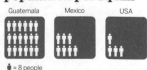

Guatemala   Mexico   USA

👤 ≈ 8 people

History

Tumultuous barely begins to describe the series of events that this small piece of land has seen over the past few millennia. Great empires have risen and fallen, conquerors have come and gone, and the population has repeatedly found itself trapped in the crossfire of war.

The Ancient Maya, by Robert J Sharer, is a 1990s update of Sylvanus G Morley's classic 1940s tome of the same name, and is admirably clear and uncomplicated.

Preclassic Period (2000 BC–AD 250)

The Preclassic period is generally thought to have coincided with the emergence of stable social structures and early forms of agriculture, pottery and tool-making in what is now Mexico and Guatemala. The improvement in the food supply led to an increase in population, a higher standard of living and developments in agricultural and artistic techniques. Decorative pots and healthier, fatter corn strains were produced. Even at the beginning of the Preclassic period, people in Guatemala spoke an early form of the Maya language.

By the middle Preclassic period (800–300 BC) there were rich villages in the Copán Valley, and villages had been founded at what would become the majestic city of Tikal, amid the jungles of El Petén. Trade routes developed, with coastal peoples exchanging salt and seashells for highland tribes' tool-grade obsidian.

As the Maya honed their agricultural techniques, including the use of fertilizer and elevated fields, a noble class emerged, constructing temples which consisted of raised platforms of earth topped by thatch-roofed shelters. The local potentate was buried beneath the shelter, increasing the site's sacred power. Such temples have been found at Uaxactún, Tikal and El Mirador. Kaminaljuyú, in Guatemala City, reached its peak from about 400 BC to AD 100, with thousands of inhabitants and scores of temples built on earth mounds.

In El Petén, where limestone was abundant, the Maya began to build platform temples from stone. As each succeeding local potentate demanded a bigger temple, larger and larger platforms were built over existing platforms, eventually forming huge pyramids. The potentate was buried deep within the stack of platforms. El Tigre pyramid at El Mirador,

TIMELINE	3114 BC	1100 BC	c 250 BC
	The Maya creation story says that the world was created on August 13 of this year, which corresponds to the first date on the Maya Long Count Calendar.	Proto-Maya settlements begin to appear in the Copán Valley. By 1000 BC settlements on the Guatemalan Pacific coast show early signs of developing a hierarchical society.	Early Maya cities El Mirador and Kaminaljuyú flourish between 250 BC and 100 AD due to tactical and commercial advantages. Agricultural techniques are refined as the trade in obsidian and jade booms.

18 stories high, is believed to be the largest ever built by the Maya. More and more pyramids were built around large plazas. The stage was set for the flowering of Classic Maya civilization.

Classic Period (AD 250–900)

The Classic Maya were organized into numerous city-states. While Tikal began to assume a primary role around AD 250, El Mirador had been mysteriously abandoned about a century earlier. Some scholars believe a severe drought hastened this great city's demise.

Each city-state had its noble house, headed by a priestly king who placated the gods by shedding his blood by piercing his tongue, penis or ears with sharp objects. As sacred head of his community, the king also had to lead his soldiers into battle against rival cities, capturing prisoners for use in human sacrifices.

A typical Maya city functioned as the religious, political and market hub for the surrounding farming hamlets. Its ceremonial center focused on plazas surrounded by tall temple pyramids and lower buildings with warrens of small rooms. Stelae and altars were carved with dates, histories and elaborate human and divine figures.

In the first part of the Classic period, most of the city-states were probably grouped into two loose military alliances centered on Calakmul, in Mexico's Campeche state, and Tikal.

In the late 8th century, trade between Maya states waned and conflict grew. By the early 10th century the cities of Tikal, Yaxchilán, Copán, Quiriguá and Piedras Negras had reverted to minor towns or even villages, and much of El Petén was abandoned. Many explanations, including population pressure, drought and ecological damage, have been offered for the collapse of the Classic Maya period.

Postclassic Period (900–1524)

Some of the Maya who abandoned El Petén must have moved southwest into the highlands of Guatemala. In the 13th and 14th centuries they were joined by Maya-Toltecs from the Tabasco or Yucatán areas of Mexico. Groups of these newcomers set up a series of rival states in the Guatemalan highlands: the most prominent were the K'iche' (or Quiché; capital, K'umarcaaj, near modern Santa Cruz del Quiché), the Kaqchiquels (capital, Iximché, near Tecpán), the Mam (capital, Zaculeu, near Huehuetenango), the Tz'utujil (capital, Chuitinamit, near Santiago Atitlán), and the Poqomam (capital, Mixco Viejo, north of Guatemala City). Another group from the Yucatán, the Itzáes, wound up at Lago de Petén Itzá in El Petén, settling in part on the island that is today called Flores.

The Maya, by Michael D Coe, is probably the best single-volume, not-too-long telling of the ancient Maya story. Coe's *Breaking the Maya Code* recounts the modern decipherment of ancient Maya writing, and his *Reading the Maya Glyphs* will help you read ancient inscriptions.

The Blood of Kings: Dynasty & Ritual in Maya Art, by Linda Schele and Mary Ellen Miller, is a heavily and fascinatingly illustrated guide to the art and culture of the ancient Maya.

AD 230	682	900	c 13th century
El Mirador begins to decline in importance. King Yax Ehb' Xooc of Tikal establishes the dynasty that will make Tikal the dominant city of the southern Maya world.	King Moon Double Comb, or Lord Chocolate, ascends Tikal's throne and begins remodeling and reconstructing Tikal's grand plazas and temples that had been destroyed by Caracol and Calakmul.	The collapse of Classic Maya civilization begins, and the Postclassic era starts. A century-long exodus from Tikal commences, after which the city will never be inhabited again.	Ruthlessly organized Toltec-Maya migrants from southeast Mexico establish kingdoms in Guatemala. Highlands Maya organize into competing kingdoms, establishing language and cultural groupings that survive today.

Spanish Conquest

Spaniards under Hernán Cortés defeated the Aztec Empire based at Tenochtitlán (modern Mexico City) in 1521. It only took a couple of years for the conquistadors to turn to Guatemala in their search for wealth. Pedro de Alvarado, one of Cortés' most brutal lieutenants, entered Guatemala in 1524, forging temporary alliances with local Maya groups while murdering and subjugating their rivals. And then laying waste to them.

And so it went throughout Guatemala as Alvarado sought fortune and renown. The one notable exception was the Rabinal of present-day Baja Verapaz, who survived with their preconquest identity intact and remain one of Guatemala's most traditional groups to this day.

Alvarado moved his base to Santiago de los Caballeros (now called Ciudad Vieja) in 1527, but shortly after his death in 1541, Ciudad Vieja was destroyed by a flood. The Spanish capital was relocated under the same name to a new site nearby, known today as Antigua.

> Archaeologists estimate that only 10% of Tikal – one of the country's biggest and most famous Maya sites – has been uncovered.

Colonial Period (1524–1821)

The Spanish effectively enslaved Guatemala's indigenous people to work what had been their own land for the benefit of the Spanish, just as they did throughout the hemisphere. Refusal to work meant death. The colonists believed themselves omnipotent and behaved accordingly.

Enter the Catholic Church and Dominican friar Bartolomé de Las Casas. Las Casas had been in the Caribbean and Latin America since 1502 and had witnessed firsthand the near complete genocide of the indigenous populations of Cuba and Hispaniola. Horrified by what he had seen, Las Casas managed to convince Carlos V of Spain to enact the New Laws of 1542, which technically ended the system of forced labor. In reality, forced labor continued, but wanton waste of Maya lives ceased. Las Casas and other friars went about converting the Maya to Christianity.

A large portion of the church's conversion success can be attributed to its peaceful approach, the relative respect extended to traditional beliefs, and the education provided in indigenous languages.

> Returning from the Americas, Christopher Columbus introduced Europeans to a whole range of foods they'd never seen before – including tomatoes, sweet potatoes, squash, potatoes, avocados, corn and cocoa.

Independence

By the time thoughts of independence from Spain began stirring among Guatemalans, society was already rigidly stratified. Only the European-born Spaniards had any real power, but the *criollos* (Guatemalan-born Spaniards) lorded it over the *ladinos* (of mixed Spanish and Maya blood), who in turn exploited the indigenous population who still remain on the bottom rung of the socioeconomic ladder.

Angered at being repeatedly passed over for advancement, Guatemalan *criollos* successfully rose in revolt in 1821. Independence changed

1523	1527	1542	1609–1821
Spaniard Pedro de Alvarado begins the conquest of Guatemala. Alvarado quickly conquers much of the country, although parts of the highlands hold out for years and El Petén is not subdued for another 170 years.	Alvarado establishes his capital at Santiago de los Caballeros (modern Ciudad Vieja, near Antigua). When he dies in Mexico, 14 years later, his wife decrees the entire city be painted black.	Spain enacts the New Laws, officially banning forced labor in its colonies. Catholic influence becomes more institutionalized and traditional Maya social structures are transformed.	The Captaincy General of Guatemala comprises what are now Costa Rica, Nicaragua, Honduras, El Salvador, Guatemala and the Mexican state of Chiapas, with its capital at Antigua, then Guatemala City.

little for Guatemala's indigenous communities, who remained under the control of the church and the landowning elite.

Mexico, which had recently become independent, quickly annexed Guatemala, but in 1823 Guatemala reasserted its independence and led the formation of the United Provinces of Central America (July 1, 1823), along with El Salvador, Nicaragua, Honduras and Costa Rica. Their union lasted only until 1840 before breaking up into its constituent states. This era brought prosperity to the *criollos* but worsened the lot of the Guatemalan Maya. The end of Spanish rule meant that the crown's few liberal safeguards, which had afforded the Maya a minimal protection, were abandoned. The Maya, though technically and legally free, were enslaved by debt peonage to the big landowners.

The Liberals & Carrera

The ruling classes split into two camps: the elite conservatives, including the Catholic Church and the large landowners, and the liberals, who had been the first to advocate independence and who opposed the vested interests of the conservatives.

A short succession of liberal leaders ended when unpopular economic policies and a cholera epidemic led to an indigenous uprising that brought a conservative *ladino* pig farmer, Rafael Carrera, to power. Carrera held power from 1844 to 1865, undoing many liberal reforms and ceding control of Belize to Britain in exchange for construction of a road between Guatemala City and Belize City, a road that was never built.

Liberal Reforms of Barrios

The liberals returned to power in the 1870s, first under Miguel García Granados, next under Justo Rufino Barrios, a rich young coffee plantation owner who held the title of president, but ruled as a dictator (1873–79). Barrios modernized Guatemala's roads, railways, schools and banking system and favored the burgeoning coffee industry disproportionately. Under Barrios' successors a small group of landowning and commercial families came to control the economy, while foreign companies were given generous concessions, and political opponents were censored, imprisoned or exiled.

Estrada Cabrera & Minerva

Manuel Estrada Cabrera ruled from 1898 to 1920, bringing progress in technical matters but placing a heavy burden on all but the ruling oligarchy. He fancied himself a bringer of light and culture to a backward land, styling himself the 'Teacher and Protector of Guatemalan Youth'.

In reaction to Cabrera's doublespeak, the *Huelga de Dolores* (Strike of Sorrows) began around this time. Students from Guatemala City's

Guatemala finally recognized Belizean independence in 1992, but the exact border remains in dispute. An agreement to take the matter to the International Court of Justice was signed in 2008.

Mesoweb (www .mesoweb. com) is a great resource on the Maya, past and present.

1697	1773	1823–40	Feb 2, 1838
The Spanish conquest of Guatemala is completed as the island of Tayasal (present-day Flores) – home of the Itza, the last remaining unconquered tribe – is defeated.	Antigua, a jewel in the colonial crown, complete with a university, printing press, schools, hospitals and churches, is destroyed by an earthquake. The new capital is founded at present-day Guatemala City.	Guatemala, El Salvador, Honduras, Nicaragua and Costa Rica form the United Provinces of Central America. Liberal reforms are enacted, and vehemently opposed by conservative groups and the Catholic Church.	Much of southwestern Guatemala declares independence, becoming the sixth member of the United Provinces. The new state, called Los Altos, has its capital at Quetzaltenango. It will secede, briefly, in 1844, 1848 and 1849.

San Carlos University took to the streets during Lent – wearing hoods to avoid reprisals – to protest against injustice and corruption. The tradition caught on in university towns across the country, culminating with a parade through the main streets on the Friday before Good Friday, a tradition that continues to this day.

La Hija del Puma (The Daughter of the Puma), directed by Ulf Hultberg, is a powerful 1994 film, based on a true story, about a K'iche' Maya girl who survives the army massacre of her fellow villagers and sees her brother captured. She escapes to Mexico but then returns to Guatemala in search of her brother.

Jorge Ubico

Estrada Cabrera was overthrown in 1920 and Guatemala entered a period of instability, ending in 1931 with the election of General Jorge Ubico as president. Ubico insisted on honesty in government, and modernized the country's health and social welfare infrastructure. His reign ended when he was forced into exile in 1944.

Arévalo & Arbenz

Just when it appeared that Guatemala was doomed to a succession of harsh dictators, the elections of 1945 brought a philosopher – Juan José Arévalo – to the presidency. Arévalo, in power from 1945 to 1951, established the nation's social security system, a bureau of indigenous affairs, a modern public health system and liberal labor laws. He also survived 25 coup attempts by conservative military forces.

Arévalo was succeeded by Colonel Jacobo Arbenz, who continued Arévalo's policies, instituting agrarian reforms designed to break up the large estates and foster productivity on small, individually owned farms. He also expropriated vast, unused lands conceded to the United Fruit Company during the Estrada Cabrera and Ubico years. Compensation was paid at the value declared for tax purposes (far below its real value), and Arbenz announced that the lands were to be redistributed to peasants and put into cultivation for food. The announcement set off alarms in Washington and in 1954 the US, in one of the first documented covert operations by the CIA, orchestrated an invasion from Honduras. Arbenz stepped down, and the land reform never took place.

In *Silence on the Mountain,* Daniel Wilkinson uncovers in microcosm the social background to the civil war as he delves into the reasons for the burning of a coffee estate by guerrillas.

Arbenz was succeeded by a series of military presidents. More covert (but well documented) support came from the US government, in the form of money and counterinsurgency training. Violence became a staple of political life, land reforms were reversed, voting was made dependent on literacy (disenfranchising around 75% of the population), the secret police force was revived and military repression was common.

In 1960, left-wing guerrilla groups began to form.

The Civil War Begins

Guatemalan industry developed fast, but the social fabric became increasingly stressed as most profits flowed upwards. Labor unions organized, and migration to the cities, especially the capital, produced urban

1840	1870s	1901	1940s
Rafael Carrera seizes power and declares Guatemala fully independent and re-incorporates Los Altos into Guatemala. He sets about dismantling many of the liberal reforms of the United Provinces.	Liberal governments modernize Guatemala but turn indigenous lands over to coffee plantations. European newcomers are given preferential treatment, further disenfranchising the Maya.	President Manuel Estrada Cabrera courts the US-owned United Fruit Company to set up shop in Guatemala. United Fruit soon takes on a dominant role in national politics.	Bowing to pressure from the US (buyers of 90% of Guatemala's exports at the time), President Jorge Ubico expels German landowners from the country. Their lands are redistributed to political and military allies.

sprawl and slums. A cycle of violent repression and protest took hold and by 1979 Amnesty International estimated that 50,000 to 60,000 people had been killed during the political violence of the 1970s alone.

A severe earthquake in 1976 killed about 22,000 people and left around a million homeless. Most of the aid sent for those in need never reached them.

1980s

In the early 1980s four disparate guerilla groups united to form the URNG (the Guatemalan National Revolutionary Unity) and military suppression of antigovernment elements in the countryside peaked, especially under the presidency of General Efraín Ríos Montt, an Evangelical Christian who came to power by coup in March 1982. Huge numbers of people – mainly indigenous men – from more than 400 villages were murdered in the name of anti-insurgency, stabilization and anticommunism.

It was later estimated that 15,000 civilian deaths occurred as a result of counterinsurgency operations during Ríos Montt's term of office alone, not to mention the estimated 100,000 refugees (again, mostly Maya) who fled to Mexico. The government forced villagers to form Patrullas de Autodefensa Civil (PACs; Civil Defense Patrols), who were later accused of some of the worst human rights atrocities committed during Ríos Montt's rule.

As the civil war dragged on and both sides committed atrocities, more and more rural people came to feel caught in the crossfire.

In August 1983 Ríos Montt was deposed by General Oscar Humberto Mejía Victores, but the abuses continued. Survivors were herded into remote 'model villages' surrounded by army encampments. The ongoing reports of human rights violations and civilian massacres led the US to cut off military assistance to Guatemala, which in turn resulted in the 1986 election of a civilian president, Marco Vinicio Cerezo Arévalo of the Christian Democratic Party.

There was hope that Cerezo Arévalo's administration would temper the excesses of the powerful elite and the military, and establish a basis for true democracy. But armed conflict festered in remote areas and when Cerezo Arévalo's term ended in 1990, many people wondered whether any real progress had been made.

Early 1990s

President Jorge Serrano (1990–93) from the conservative Movimiento de Acción Solidaria (Solidarity Action Movement) reopened a dialogue with the URNG, hoping to bring the decades-long civil war to an end. When the talks collapsed, the mediator from the Catholic Church blamed both sides for intransigence.

Searching for Everardo, by US attorney Jennifer K Harbury, tells how she fell in love with and married a URNG guerrilla leader who then disappeared in combat, and of her dedicated and internationally publicized struggles with the US and Guatemalan governments – including a hunger strike outside the White House – to discover his fate.

1945–54	1954	1950s–1960s	1967
Juan José Arévalo, elected with 85% of the popular vote, comes to power, ushering in an era of enlightened, progressive government that is continued by his successor Jacobo Arbenz.	Effecting the country's first serious attempt at land reform, Arbenz appropriates Guatemalan lands of the US-owned United Fruit Company. He is soon deposed in a US-orchestrated coup.	Military dictators rule the country, reversing liberal reforms of previous governments. Crackdowns lead to the formation of left-wing guerrilla groups. The civil war begins.	Guatemalan writer and diplomat Miguel Ángel Asturias, credited as a pioneer of modernist Latin American literature, is awarded the Nobel Prize for Literature for his political novel *El Señor Presidente*.

RIGOBERTA MENCHÚ TUM

Of all the unlikely candidates for the Nobel Prize throughout history, a rural indigenous Guatemalan woman would have to be near the top of the list.

Rigoberta Menchú was born in 1959 near Uspantán in the highlands of Quiché department and lived the life of a typical young Maya woman until the late 1970s, when the country's civil war affected her tragically and drove her into the left-wing guerrilla camp. Her father, mother and brother were killed in the Guatemalan military's campaign to eradicate communism in the countryside.

Menchú fled to exile in Mexico, where her story *I, Rigoberta Menchú: An Indian Woman in Guatemala* was published and translated throughout the world, bringing the plight of Guatemala's indigenous population to international attention. In 1992 Rigoberta Menchú was awarded the Nobel Prize for Peace, which provided her and her cause with international stature and support. The Rigoberta Menchú Tum Foundation (www.frmt.org), which she founded with the US$1.2 million Nobel Prize money, works for conflict resolution, plurality, and human, indigenous and women's rights in Guatemala and internationally.

Guatemalans, especially the Maya, were proud that one of their own had been recognized by the Nobel committee. In the circles of power, however, Menchú's renown was unwelcome, as she was seen as a troublemaker.

Anthropologist David Stoll's book *Rigoberta Menchú and the Story of All Poor Guatemalans* (1999) contested the truth of many aspects of Menchú's book, including some central facts. The *New York Times* claimed that Menchú had received a Nobel Prize for lying, and of course her detractors had a field day.

Menchú took the controversy in her stride, not addressing the specific allegations, and the Nobel Institute made it clear that the prize was given for Menchú's work on behalf of the indigenous, not the content of her book. More than anything, the scandal solidified support for Menchú and her cause while calling Stoll's motives into question.

In 1994 Menchú returned to Guatemala from exile. Since then her work with the Foundation has continued, alongside efforts to promote greater access to low-cost, generic pharmaceuticals and a stint as a UN goodwill ambassador for the Peace Accords. In 2007 she decided to run for president. The problematic, often fragmented nature of indigenous politics was highlighted when the World Indigenous Summit of that year chose not to support her. Menchú's party won a little over 3% of the popular vote in the presidential elections.

Human-rights abuses continued during this period despite the country's return to democratic rule. In one dramatic case in 1990, Guatemalan anthropologist Myrna Mack, who had documented army violence against the rural Maya, was fatally wounded after being stabbed dozens of times. Former head of the Presidential Guard, Colonel Juan Valencia Osorio,

1976	Feb 1982	1982–83	1990
Earthquake kills 22,000 in Guatemala. Reconstruction efforts help to consolidate leftist opposition groups. The Carter administration bans military aid to Guatemala.	Four powerful guerrilla organizations unite to form the URNG (Guatemalan National Revolutionary Unity). An estimated half a million people actively support the guerrilla movement.	State terror against rural indigenous communities peaks during the rule of General Efraín Ríos Montt. Peasants, particularly in the highlands, begin an exodus to Mexico to escape violence from both sides.	The army massacres 13 Tz'utujil Maya (including three children) in Santiago Atitlán. Outraged, the people of Santiago fight back, becoming the first town to succeed in expelling the army by popular demand.

was found guilty of masterminding the assassination and sentenced to 30 years imprisonment, but went into hiding before he could be arrested.

Serrano's presidency came to depend more on the army for support. In 1993 he tried to seize absolute power, but after a tense few days was forced to flee into exile. Congress elected Ramiro de León Carpio, an outspoken critic of the army's strong-arm tactics, as president to complete Serrano's term.

Peace Accords

President de León's elected successor, Álvaro Arzú of the center-right Partido de Avanzada Nacional (PAN; National Advancement Party), took office in 1996. Arzú continued negotiations with the URNG and, finally, on December 29, 1996, 'A Firm and Lasting Peace Agreement' was signed. During the 36 years of civil war, an estimated 200,000 Guatemalans had been killed, a million made homeless, and untold thousands had disappeared.

Guatemala Since the Peace Accords

Any hopes for a truly just and democratic society have looked increasingly frayed in the years since 1996. International organizations regularly criticize the state of human rights in the country and Guatemalan human rights campaigners are threatened or simply disappear on a regular basis. The major problems – poverty, illiteracy, lack of education and poor medical facilities (all much more common in rural areas, where the Maya population is concentrated) – remain a long way from being resolved.

The 1999 presidential elections were won by Alfonso Portillo of the conservative Frente Republicano Guatemalteco (FRG). Portillo was seen as a front man for FRG leader, ex-president General Efraín Ríos Montt. At the end of his presidency Portillo fled the country in the face of allegations that he had diverted US\$500 million from the treasury to personal and family bank accounts. Having evaded prosecution for years, Portillo was finally charged by the United States for laundering money using US banks, and looks set to be extradited and put on trial there.

Ríos Montt was granted permission by Guatemala's constitutional court to stand in the 2003 elections, despite the fact that the constitution banned presidents who had taken power by coup in the past, as Ríos Montt had in 1982.

In the end Guatemala's voters dealt Ríos Montt a resounding defeat, electing Oscar Berger of the moderately conservative Gran Alianza Nacional as president. Berger managed to stay relatively untouched by political scandal, critics saying this was because he didn't really do *anything*, let alone anything bad.

Guatemala: Nunca Mas (1998), published by ODHAG and REMHI, details many of the human-rights abuses committed during Guatemala's civil war, and includes moving testimonials.

1992	1996	1998	2000–04
Indigenous rights and peace activist Rigoberta Menchú is awarded the Nobel Prize for peace. Menchú receives the award while living in exile in Mexico, returning to Guatemala two years later.	After nearly a decade of talks, the Peace Accords are signed, bringing to an end the 36-year civil war in which an estimated 200,000 Guatemalans died.	The true nature of peace is questioned as Bishop Gerardi, author of a paper blaming the army for the overwhelming amount of civil-war deaths, is found bludgeoned to death in his home.	Presidency of Alfonso Portillo of the FRG party, led by Efraín Ríos Montt. Portillo begins by prosecuting those responsible for the death of Bishop Gerardi, but is soon mired in corruption allegations.

The Central America Free Trade Agreement (CAFTA; TLC or Tratado de Libre Comercio, in Spanish) was ratified by Guatemala in 2006. Supporters claim it frees the country up for greater participation in foreign markets, while detractors state that the agreement is a bad deal for the already disenfranchised rural poor.

Another round of elections was held in late 2007, bringing to power Álvaro Colom of the center-leftist Unidad Nacional de la Esperanza. Colom followed Berger's example of steady, minimalist governance and spearheaded some much needed improvements to the country's infrastructure. Unfortunately, his entire presidency was dogged by corruption claims, from straight-out vote buying to backroom deals granting contracts to companies who had contributed to his campaign fund.

But probably the most bizarre twist of the Colom presidency happened as he was leaving office. The Guatemalan constitution prohibits members of the president's family from running for the subsequent presidency (supposedly an anti-dictatorship measure), so Colom and his wife filed for divorce in the lead-up to the 2011 elections in an attempt to make her a valid candidate. The Constitutional Court banned her candidature anyway, leaving the door open for hardline ex-civil war general Otto Pérez Molina to take office in early 2012.

For the latest on human rights in Guatemala, visit the Guatemala Human Rights Commission/USA website (www.ghrc-usa.org) or click on 'Human Rights' on the website of the US embassy in Guatemala City (http://guatemala.usembassy.gov).

2006	May 2011	Jan 14, 2012	Dec 21, 2012
CAFTA, a free-trade agreement between the US and Central America, is ratified. Massive street protests and seemingly endless media discussion have little effect on the final document.	First Lady Sandra Torres announces she will divorce the president in order to run for upcoming elections, or in her words, 'marry the people'. The move is slammed as electoral fraud by the opposition.	Ex-civil war general Otto Perez Molina takes office as president, having won the election promising a reign of 'mano dura' (iron fist) as a solution to Guatemala's burgeoning crime problems.	Despite end-of-the-world predictions from non-Mayans, Baktun 13 ends without major incidents and a new Great Cycle of the Mayan Long Count calendar begins.

Guatemalan Way of Life

The usual socio-economic dividers aside, the way you live in Guatemala depends largely on where you live – the differences between the coast and the highlands, big cities and small villages are so marked that sometimes it feels like that one-hour bus ride has taken you into another country. Some things are common to all Guatemalans, though – a set of national characteristics that when taken together largely define the essence of *ser Chapín* (being Guatemalan).

Bright Lights, Big City

Around half of all Guatemalans live in what are classified as 'urban environments', but it's important to remember that by international standards, Guatemala City is the country's only really big city – while the capital has more than 4 million inhabitants, Quetzaltenango (the second largest city) is yet to hit 200,000.

Life in the capital (and even in the larger cities) resembles life in any big city in many ways. There are slums, middle-class neighborhoods and exclusive gated communities. Overcrowding and an ever-growing car culture make for traffic jams that wouldn't be out of place in London or New York. Guatemala City in particular has a bad reputation for street crime and it's rare to see people out walking at night. Also here you'll see the most fortified homes – razor wire, barred windows, closed circuit camera surveillance; people tend to take as many measures as they can afford to guard against burglars and home invasion.

The standard of living in Guatemala City is slowly improving, thanks largely to the efforts of ex-President and four-time mayor Álvaro Arzú, whose initiatives to open up public spaces and create pedestrian-only streets have earned him the nickname 'El Jardinero' (the gardener) from critics.

Life on the Mountain

Guatemala's mountainous regions also happen to be the most indigenous. As a result, Maya culture and tradition is much stronger in the mountains than on the coastal plain and in the capital. Even in larger cities you'll see many more women (and even some men) dressed in traditional Maya clothing, and no doubt you'll hear locals speaking in their dialect. Many people from these regions, particularly from older generations, speak Spanish as a second language, and some don't speak it at all.

The cold is a factor in the mountains – towns like Quetzaltenango and Todos Santos regularly register below-freezing temperatures in December. Another sight you're likely to see is men chopping and hauling firewood, which is used for both heating and cooking in many traditional homes.

The highlands rich volcanic soil also makes for some of the best farmland in the country. Vegetables grown in the Western Highlands are exported as far away as Belize, while the Cobán region has become a leading exporter of cardamom – much of it going as far away as India and the Middle East. Many mountain-dwellers work in agriculture, either tending small subsistence plots or working on larger commercial farms.

Down on the Coast

The pace of life on the coast – where midday temperatures regularly hit 104°F (40°C) – slows right down. There's very little industry in these parts, and economic opportunities are few. The big employers on the coast are the sugar cane, chicle and African palm farms, which provide seasonal work. It's hardly cushy employment (imagine cutting cane with a machete in 104°F heat) and many coastal-dwellers migrate to the cities in search of better opportunities.

Fishing is another income source. There are a few large industrial operations, but the bulk of fishermen (Guatemalan fisherwomen are extremely rare) either work independently, selling the day's catch at market, or in small cooperatives.

Housing on the coast is radically different to the rest of the country. Due to the extreme heat, cinderblock is not the popular construction material it is in the rest of the country, nor is corrugated iron for roofing. The classic coastal house will be open plan, often with wooden walls and a thatched roof. Doors will always be open and windows often lack glass, instead just having wooden shutters to keep out the monsoonal downpours of the rainy season.

Village Life

Guatemala's rural areas, while undoubtedly her most picturesque, are the epicenter for many of the country's persistent problems. Life in many villages has barely changed over the last hundred years, as subsistence farmers eke out a daily existence on tiny plots of land. The precariousness of this life is emphasized with every flood, drought, plague or crop failure – the smallest of any of these being enough to place entire families in danger of starvation.

Guatemalan governments have ignored villages, and infrastructure levels can be dire. Many children have to travel for hours to attend the local school and what they call a school may not be something that you recognize as such. Access to health care is equally limited – at best a village will have a small medical clinic, capable of dealing with minor complaints. Patients requiring hospitalization may need to be transported several hours away. Many smaller villages don't even have a doctor, and medical care is provided by *curanderas* (healing women), *comadres* (mid-wives) and maybe a pharmacist.

Despite all of these drawbacks, Guatemalan villages are often stunningly beautiful – surrounded by lush countryside, with dirt roads winding between adobe huts. An old colonial church on the plaza and chickens and horses roaming about, as barefoot children play in the streets in a carefree way unseen in the rest of the country.

Being Guatemalan

Despite these huge regional differences, there is such a thing as *ser Chapín*. With a few unfortunate exceptions, you'll be amazed when you first reach Guatemala by just how helpful, polite and unhurried Guatemalans are. Everyone has time to stop and chat and explain what you want to know. This is apparent even if you've just crossed the border from Mexico, where things aren't exactly rushed either. Most Guatemalans like to get to know other people without haste, feeling for common ground and things to agree on, rather than making blunt assertions and engaging in adversarial dialectic.

RURAL LIFE

While many rural houses now have running water, the village *pila* (communal laundry trough) remains a place to get together and exchange gossip.

GETTING ALONG WITH GUATEMALANS

While Guatemalans tend to give foreigners a fair amount of leeway, at least trying to adapt to local ways is bound to make your travels run more smoothly.

➡ Even in such routine situations as entering a store or taking a bus seat, a simple greeting is often exchanged: *buenos días* or *buenas tardes* and a smile is all that's needed.

➡ When leaving a restaurant, it is common to wish other diners *buen provecho* (*bon appétit*).

➡ In general, the Maya are a fairly private people and some communities are still recovering from the nightmare of the civil war. People may be willing to share their war stories, but don't dig for information – let your hosts offer it.

➡ Referring to a Maya person as *indio* (Indian) is considered racist. The preferred term is *indígena*.

➡ When dealing with officialdom (police, border officials, immigration officers), try to appear as conservative and respectable as possible.

➡ Dress modestly when entering churches or attending family gatherings.

What goes on behind this outward politeness is harder to encapsulate. Few Guatemalans exhibit the stress, worry and hurry of the 'developed' nations, but this obviously isn't because they don't have to worry about money or employment. They're a long-suffering people who don't expect wealth or good government but make the best of what comes their way – friendship, their family, a good meal, a bit of good company.

The tales of violence – domestic violence, civil-war violence, criminal violence – that one inevitably hears in Guatemala sit strangely with the mild-mannered approach you will encounter from nearly everybody. Whatever the explanation, it helps to show why a little caution is in order when strangers meet.

Religion

Guatemalans are a religious bunch – atheists and agnostics are very thin on the ground. People will often ask what religion you are quite early in a conversation. Unless you really want to get into it, saying 'Christian' generally satisfies.

Orthodox Catholicism is gradually giving way to Evangelical Protestantism amongst the *ladinos*, with the animist-Catholic syncretism of the traditional Maya always present. The number of new Evangelical churches, especially in indigenous Maya villages, is astonishing. Since the 1980s Evangelical Protestant sects, around 58% of them Pentecostal, have surged in popularity, and it is estimated that 30% to 40% of Guatemalans are now Evangelicals.

Catholicism's fall can be attributed in part to the civil war. On occasion, Catholic priests were (and still are) outspoken defenders of human rights, attracting persecution (and worse) from dictators at the time, especially from the Evangelical Ríos Montt.

Catholicism is fighting back with messages about economic and racial justice, papal visits and new saints – Guatemala's most venerated local Christian figure, the 17th-century Antigua-hospital-founder Hermano Pedro de San José de Bethancourt, was canonized in 2002 when Pope John Paul II visited Guatemala.

Catholicism in the Maya areas has never been exactly orthodox. The missionaries who brought Catholicism to the Maya in the 16th century wisely permitted aspects of the existing animistic, shamanistic Maya

THE BIGGEST PARTY IN TOWN

It's Friday night in any small town in Guatemala. The music's pumping, there's singing and hands are clapping. Have you just stumbled onto a local jam session? Sorry to disappoint, but what you're most likely listening to is an Evangelical church service.

The Evangelicals are the fastest-growing religion in Latin America – one estimate puts the number of new Latino converts at a staggering 8000 per day.

The Catholic Church is worried – this is their heartland, after all, and the reasons that they're losing their grip aren't all that easy to identify.

Some say it's the Evangelicals' use of radio and TV that brings them wider audiences; for some it's their rejection of rituals and gestures and customs in favor of real human contact. Others say it's the way the newcomers go to the roughest barrios and accept anybody – including 'the drunks and the hookers', as one priest put it.

For some, they're just more fun – they fall into trances and speak in tongues, heal and prophesize. And then there's the singing – not stale old hymns, but often racy pop numbers with the lyrics changed to more spiritual themes.

One thing's for sure – an Evangelical makes a better husband: drinking, smoking, gambling and domestic violence are all severely frowned upon. Maybe, once again in Guatemala, it's the wives who are really calling the shots.

To get a handle on Maximón and shamanism around Lago de Atitlán, check out *Scandals in the House of Birds: Shamans and Priests on Lake Atitlán*, by anthropologist and poet Nathaniel Tarn.

religion to continue alongside Christian rites and beliefs. Syncretism was aided by the identification of certain Maya deities with certain Christian saints, and survives to this day. A notable example is the deity known as Maximón in Santiago Atitlán, San Simón in Zunil and Rilaj Maam in San Andrés Itzapa near Antigua, who seems to be a combination of Maya gods, the Spanish conquistador Pedro de Alvarado and Judas Iscariot (see the boxed text, p105).

Family Life

Despite modernizing influences – education, cable TV, contact with foreign travelers, international popular music, time spent as migrant workers in the USA – traditional family ties remain strong at all levels of society. Large extended-family groups gather for weekend meals and holidays. Old-fashioned gender roles are strong too: many women have jobs to increase the family income but relatively few have positions of much responsibility.

Cynics say that much of this closeness has more to do with economics than sentiment – that it's hard to be distant when there are three generations living under the same roof. But this doesn't really play out. You see the strong bonds of family amongst middle- and upper-class Guatemalans, and one of the questions you're bound to get asked at least once (and possibly many more times) while on your travels here is if you miss your mother.

Despite this closeness, it's rare to meet a family who doesn't have at least one member who has emigrated to the United States to work – the couple of hundred dollars that these emigrants send back per month are some families sole income, and, when totalled, equal around 40% of what Guatemala earns from exports.

Women in Guatemala

One of the goals of the 1996 Peace Accords was to improve women's rights in Guatemala. By 2003 the Inter-American Commission on Human Rights had to report that laws discriminating against women had yet to be repealed. Women got the vote and the right to stand for election in 1946, but in 2013 only 13% of congressional deputies were women.

Women's leaders repeatedly criticize Guatemala's *machista* culture, which believes a woman's place is in the home. The situation is, if anything, worse for indigenous women in rural areas, who also have to live with most of the country's direst poverty.

The international organization Human Rights Watch reported in 2002 that women working in private households were persistently discriminated against. Domestic workers, many of whom are from Maya communities, lack certain basic rights, including the rights to be paid the minimum wage and to work an eight-hour day and a 48-hour week. Many domestic workers begin working as young adolescents, but Guatemalan labor laws do not provide adequate protection for domestic workers under the age of 18.

Probably of greatest concern are the reports of escalating violence against women, accompanied by a steadily rising murder rate. These victims were once brushed off as being 'just' gang members or prostitutes, but it is now clear that murder, rape and kidnapping of women is a serious issue. The international community has begun to put pressure on Guatemala to act, but the realities of *machista* society mean that crimes against women are seldom investigated and rarely solved.

For information on Guatemalan women's organizations (and much, much more) visit www.entremundos.org.

Education in Guatemala

Education is free and in theory compulsory between the ages of seven and 14. Primary education lasts for six years, but the average school-leaving age is 11 years, according to UN statistics. Secondary school begins at age 13 and comprises two cycles of three years each, called *básico* and *magisterio*. Not all secondary education is free – a major deterrent for many. Some people continue studying for their *magisterio* well into adulthood. Completing *magisterio* qualifies you to become a school teacher yourself. It's estimated that only about 34% of children of the 13-to-18 age group are in secondary school. Guatemala has five universities.

Overall, adult literacy is around 69% in Guatemala, but it's lower among women (63%) and rural people. Maya children who do seasonal migrant work with their families are least likely to get an education, as the time the families go away to work falls during the school year. A limited amount of school teaching is done in Maya languages – chiefly the big four, K'iche', Mam, Kaqchiquel and Q'eqchi' – but this rarely goes beyond the first couple of years of primary school. Spanish remains the necessary tongue for anyone who wants to get ahead in life.

Sport (aka Futból)

If there's one thing that unites almost all Guatemalans, it is their passion and enthusiasm for football (soccer). If you'd like a universal talking point, you could do worse than brush up on your soccer teams. Many Guatemalans keep a keen eye on their local team, the Guatemalan national team and at least one European team (Barcelona being by far the most popular Spanish side). Although Guatemalan teams always flop in international competition, the 10-club Liga Mayor (Major League) national competition is keenly followed by reasonably large crowds. Two seasons are played each year: the Torneo de Apertura (Opening Tournament) from July to November, and the Torneo de Clausura (Closing Tournament) from January to May. The two big clubs are Municipal and Comunicaciones, both from Guatemala City. The 'Classico Gringo' is when teams from Quetzaltenango and Antigua (the two big tourist towns) play.

For up-to-the-minute news on the football scene in Guatemala, log on to www.guatefutbol.com.

Maya Heritage

The ancient Maya constructed a civilization that was vastly impressive, complex and fruitful. While some legacies, such as the archaeological sites, are obvious, scholars are still working to put together the various pieces of how Maya society worked. Here we present a summary of some of the things we do know about the Maya, from traditions long lost to rituals still carried out in modern times.

Ancient Maya Beliefs

Maya priests used a variety of drugs during divination rituals – ranging from fermented maize and wild tobacco to hallucinogenic mushrooms.

The date of creation that appears in inscriptions throughout the Maya world is 13.0.0.0.0, 4 Ahaw, 8 Kumk'u, or August 13, 3114 BC on our calendar. On that day the creator gods set three stones in the dark waters that covered the primordial world. These formed a cosmic hearth at the center of the universe. They then struck divine fire by means of lightning, charging the world with life.

This account of creation is echoed in the first chapters of the Popol Vuh, a book compiled by members of the Maya nobility soon after the Spanish conquest.

> This is the account of when all is still silent and placid. All is silent and calm. Hushed and empty is the womb of the sky. These then are the first words, the first speech. There is not yet one person, one animal, bird, fish, crab, tree, rock, hollow, canyon, meadow, or forest...

> All alone are the Framer and the Shaper, Sovereign and Quetzal Serpent, They Who Have Borne Children and They Who Have Begotten Sons... There is also Heart of Sky [a lightning god], which is said to be the name of the god...

> Then they called forth the mountains from the water. Straightaway the great mountains came to be. It was merely their spirit essence, their miraculous power, that brought about the conception of the mountains.

The Creation of Humankind

The gods made three attempts at creating people before getting it right. First they made deer and other animals, but not being able to speak properly to honor the gods, the animals were condemned to be eaten.

Next was a person made from mud. At first, the mud person spoke, 'but without knowledge and understanding,' and he soon dissolved back into the mud.

The gods' third attempt was people carved from wood. These too were imperfect and also destroyed. The Popol Vuh says that the survivors of these wooden people are the monkeys that inhabit the forests. The gods finally got it right when they discovered maize, and made mankind:

> Thus their frame and shape were given expression by our first Mother and our first Father. Their flesh was merely yellow ears of maize and white ears of maize...

MAYA BEAUTY

The ancient Maya considered flat foreheads and crossed eyes beautiful. To achieve these effects, children would have boards bound tight to their heads and wax beads tied to dangle before their eyes. Both men and women made cuts in their skin to gain much-desired scar markings, and women sharpened their teeth to points, another mark of beauty – which may also have helped them to keep their men in line!

The Maya Cosmovision

For the ancient Maya, the world, the heavens and the mysterious under-world called Xibalbá were one great, unified structure that operated according to the laws of astrology, cyclical time and ancestor worship.

The towering, sacred ceiba tree symbolized the world-tree, which united the heavens (represented by the tree's branches and foliage), the earth (the trunk) and the nine levels of Xibalbá (the roots). The world-tree had a sort of cruciform shape, so when the Franciscan friars came bearing a cross and required the Maya to venerate it, the symbolism meshed easily with established Maya beliefs.

Each point of the compass had a color and a special religious sig-nificance. Everything in the Maya world was seen in relation to these cardinal points, with the world-tree at the center.

Blood-letting ceremonies were the most important religious ceremo-nies for the Maya – a way for humans to link themselves to the under-world – and the blood of kings was seen as the most acceptable for these rituals. Maya kings often initiated blood-letting rites to heighten the re-sponsiveness of the gods.

Maya ceremonies were performed in natural sacred places as well as their human-made equivalents. Mountains, caves, lakes, cenotes (natural limestone cavern pools), rivers and fields were – and still are – sacred. Pyramids and temples were thought of as stylized mountains. A cave was the mouth of the creature that represented Xibalbá, and to enter it was to enter the spirit of the secret world. This is why some Maya temples have doorways surrounded by huge masks: as you enter the door of this 'cave' you are entering the mouth of Xibalbá.

Ancestor worship was very important to the ancient Maya, and when they buried a king beneath a pyramid or a commoner beneath the floor or courtyard of a *na* (thatched Maya hut), the sacredness of the location was increased.

Mayan Folktales, edited by James D Sexton, brings together the myths and legends of the Lago de Atitlán area, translated into English.

The Ball Game

The recreation most favored by the Maya was *juego de pelota* (a ball game), courts for which can still be seen at many archaeological sites. It's thought that the players had to try to keep a hard rubber ball airborne using any part of their body other than their hands, head or feet. In some regions, a team was victorious if one of its players hit the ball through stone rings with holes little larger than the ball itself.

The Maya Counting System

The Maya counting system's most important use – and the one you will encounter during your travels – was in writing dates. It's an elegantly simple system: dots are used to count from one to four; a horizontal bar signifies five; a bar with one dot above it is six, a bar with two dots is seven, and so forth. Two bars signifies 10, three bars 15. Nineteen, the highest common number, is three bars stacked up and topped by four dots.

MAYA WRITING

During the Classic period, the Maya lowlands were divided into two major linguistic groups. In the Yucatán Peninsula and Belize people spoke Yucatec, and in the eastern highlands and Motagua Valley of Guatemala they spoke a language related to Chol. People in El Petén likely spoke both languages. Scholars have suggested that the written language throughout the Maya world was a form of Chol.

Long before the Spanish conquest, the Maya developed a sophisticated hieroglyphic script which is partly phonetic (glyphs representing sounds), and partly logographic (glyphs representing words).

To signify larger numbers the Maya stack numbers from zero to 19 on top of each other. Thus the lowest number in the stack shows values from one to 19, the next position up signifies 20 times its face value, the third position up signifies 20 times 20 times its face value. The three positions together can signify numbers up to 7999. By adding more positions one can count as high as needed. Zero is represented by a stylized picture of a shell or some other object.

The Maya Calendar

To translate a date using the Maya calendar, visit the Maya Date Calculator at www.mayan-calendar.com/calc.html.

The ancient Maya's astronomical observations and calculations were uncannily accurate and time was, in fact, the basis of the Maya religion. Perhaps the best analog to the Maya calendar is the gears of a mechanical watch, where small wheels mesh with larger wheels, which in turn mesh with other sets of wheels to record the passage of time.

Tzolkin, Cholq'ij or Tonalamatl

The two smallest wheels were two cycles: one of 13 days and another of 20 days. As these two 'wheels' meshed, the passing days received unique names. The two small 'wheels' thus created a larger 'wheel' of 260 days, called a *tzolkin, cholq'ij* or *tonalamatl*.

Vague Year (Haab)

Another set of wheels in the Maya calendar comprised 18 'months' of 20 days each, which formed the basis of the solar year or *haab* (or *ab'*). Eighteen months, each of 20 days, equals 360 days, a period known as a *tun;* the Maya added a special omen-filled five-day period called the *uayeb* at the end of this cycle in order to produce a solar calendar of 365 days.

Calendar Round

The Foundation for the Advancement of Mesoamerica Studies website (www.famsi.org) is incredibly detailed, with information ranging from current and past research to studies on writing, educational resources, linguistic maps and more.

The huge wheels of the *tzolkin* and the *haab* also meshed and repeated every 52 solar years, a period called the Calendar Round. The Calendar Round was the dating system used not only by the Maya but also by the Olmecs, Aztecs and Zapotecs of ancient Mexico.

Long Count

The Calendar Round has one serious limitation: it only lasts 52 years. Hence the Long Count, which the Maya developed around the start of the Classic period.

The Long Count uses the *tun*, but ignores the *uayeb*. Twenty *tuns* make a *katun* and 20 *katuns* make a *baktun*. Curiously for us today, 13 *baktuns* (1,872,000 days, or 5125 Gregorian solar years) form something called a Great Cycle, and the first Great Cycle began on August 11, 3114 BC which means it ended on December 23 (or 25), AD 2012. The end of a Great Cycle was a time fraught with great significance – you may have noticed a little (non-Maya) end-of-the-world panic around Christmas 2012.

Maya Architecture

Ancient Maya architecture is a mixed bag of incredible accomplishments and severe limitations. The Maya's great buildings are both awesome and beautiful, with their aesthetic attention to intricately patterned facades, delicate 'combs' on temple roofs, and sinuous carvings. These magnificent structures, such as the ones found in the sophisticated urban centers of Tikal, El Mirador and Copán, were created without beasts of burden (except for humans) or the luxury of the wheel. Once structures were completed, experts hypothesize, they were covered with stucco and painted red with a mixture of hematite and most probably water.

Although formal studies and excavations of Maya sites in Guatemala have been ongoing for more than a century, much of their architectural how and why remains a mystery. For example, the purpose of *chultunes,* underground chambers carved from bedrock and filled with offerings, continues to baffle scholars. And while we know that the Maya habitually built one temple on top of another to bury successive leaders, we have little idea how they actually erected these symbols of power. All the limestone used to erect the great Maya cities had to be moved and set in place by hand – an engineering feat that must have demanded astronomical amounts of human labor.

Mary Ellen Miller's well-illustrated Maya Art and Architecture paints the full picture from gigantic temples to intricately painted ceramics.

Modern Maya Rituals

Many sites of ancient Maya ruins – among them Tikal, Kaminaljuyú and K'umarcaaj – still have altars where prayers, offerings and ceremonies continue to take place today. Fertility rites, healing ceremonies and sacred observances to ring in the various Maya new years are still practised with gusto. These types of ceremony are directed or overseen by a Maya priest known as a *tzahorín* and usually involve burning candles and copal (a natural incense from the bark of various tropical trees), making offerings

THE MAYA BURY THEIR DEAD

It is the night before the funeral, and the shaman is in the house of the deceased, washing candles in holy water. If he misses one, a family member could go blind or deaf. He has counted off the days, and divined that tomorrow will be propitious for the burial.

He prays to the ancestral spirits, asking for the health of the family and the absence of disaster. The list is long and detailed. Personal objects are placed in the coffin; if they're not, the man's spirit might return home looking for them.

Members of the *cofradía* (fraternity) bear the coffin to the cemetery, a trail of mourners following. Four stops are made on leaving the house: at the doorway, in the yard, on entering the street, and at the first street corner. At each stop, mourners place coins on the coffin – in reality to buy candles, symbolically so that the spirit can buy its way out of purgatory and into heaven.

As the coffin is lowered into the ground, mourners kiss handfuls of dirt before throwing them on top. Once the coffin is buried, women sprinkle water on top, packing down the soil and protecting the corpse from werewolves and other dark spirits.

Every All Soul's Day (November 2) the family will come to the cemetery to honor their dead. Sometimes this will stretch over three days (beginning on the first). They will come to clean and decorate the grave, and set out food such as roasted corn, sweet potatoes, vegetable pears (*chayote* or chokos), and other fresh-picked fruit of the field. The church bells will ring at midday to summon the spirits, who feast on the smells of the food.

to the gods and praying for whatever the desired outcome may be – a good harvest, a healthy child or a prosperous new year, for example. Some ceremonies involve chicken sacrifices as well. Each place has its own set of gods – or at least different names for similar gods.

Visitors may also be able to observe traditional Maya ceremonies in places such as the Pascual Abaj shrine at Chichicastenango, the altars on the shore of Laguna Chicabal outside Quetzaltenango, or El Baúl near Santa Lucía Cotzumalguapa, but a lot of traditional rites are off-limits to foreigners.

Arts & Architecture

Guatemala's contributions to the artistic world have been few, but important. The enduring legacy of Maya architecture and weaving cannot be denied, and the country has produced writers and musicians who have gone on to attain international fame.

Literature

Guatemala's first great literary figure was poet and Jesuit priest Rafael Landivar, whose collection of poetry *Rusticatio Mexicana*, containing 5348 verses in Latin, was published in 1781.

A great source of national pride is the Nobel Prize for Literature that was bestowed on Guatemalan Miguel Ángel Asturias (1899–1974) in 1967. Best known for *Men of Maize,* his magical-realist epic on the theme of European conquest and the Maya, and for his thinly veiled vilification of Latin American dictators in *The President,* Asturias also wrote poetry. He served in various diplomatic capacities for the Guatemalan government.

Other celebrated Guatemalan authors include short-story master Augusto Monterroso (1921–2003), who is credited as having written the shortest story in published literature, *El Dinosaurio.* Look also for his published work *The Black Sheep and Other Fables.* Luis Cardoza y Aragón (1901–92) is principally known for his poetry and for fighting in the revolutionary movement that deposed dictator Jorge Ubico in 1944. Gaspar Pedro Gonzáles' *A Mayan Life* is claimed to be the first novel written by a Maya author.

Guatemalan-born Arturo Arias is an author and professor of Spanish-American Literature at the University of Texas. His most famous works include *Itzam Na* (1981), *Jaguar en llamas* (1990) and *The Rigoberta Menchú Controversy* (2001), in which he examines the heated debate that ensued after Menchú won the Nobel Prize (see the boxed text, p272).

Born in the US to a Guatemalan mother, Francisco Goldman is probably the most famous author writing about Guatemala in modern times. Primarily a novelist, Goldman's non-fiction account of the assassination of Bishop Gerardi, *The Art of Political Murder,* won him international and critical acclaim and a good selection of enemies from within Guatemala's power structure.

One of Central America's largest literary competitions, the Juegos Florales Hispanoamericanos, is held in Quetzaltenango in September to coincide with Independence Day celebrations.

For an extensive, searchable database of photographs of pre-Columbian ceramics, have a look at www.mayavase.com.

Painting

Precolonial

No discussion of painting in Guatemala would be complete without a mention of the fabulous mural work that the Maya created long before the Spanish arrived. Most have been severely worn by time and vandals, but a few archaeological sites such as San Bartolo and Río Azul have paintings that remain surprisingly vivid.

Early Postcolonial

One of the earliest postcolonial painters of note was Tomás de Merlo, widely credited as the father of the 'Antigua Baroque' movement. You can see many of his works in the National Museum of Colonial Art, in Antigua and hanging on church walls in Antigua, too.

Modern Maya Painting

One truly Guatemalan genre of painting, dubbed 'Maya naïve art' was spearheaded by Andrés Curruchich, a native of San Juan Comalapa near Lago de Atitlán. Curruchich's works depicted the simple rural scenes of the Guatemalan countryside you can still see today. There is a permanent exhibition of Curruchich's work in the Ixchel museum in Guatemala City. While the artist died in 1969, his legacy continues – there are an estimated 500 artists working in San Juan Comalapa today, many of them trained by Curruchich himself. Juan Sisay was another Maya primitivist painter from the Atitlán region to gain international fame (see the boxed text, p106).

Efraín Recinos

Of all modern Guatemalan artists, the architect, muralist, painter and sculptor Efraín Recinos is probably the most famous. His murals grace Guatemala City's National Music Conservatory and he is also responsible for the facade of the National Library and the design of the Centro Cultural Miguel Ángel Asturias, both also in Guatemala City. Recinos was awarded Guatemala's highest honor, the Order of the Quetzal, in 1999, and the country went into mourning when he died in 2011.

Music

To find out about up-and-coming Guatemalan rock bands, the best place to go is www.rock republik.net.

Folk Music

Guatemalan festivals provide great opportunities to hear traditional music featuring instruments such as cane flutes, square drums and the *chirimía,* a reed instrument of Moorish roots related to the oboe.

The other popular form of 'folk' music is made by the Garífuna people who live around the country's Caribbean coast (see the boxed text, p219). Completely different from traditional Maya music, the Garífuna's most popular style is *punta*, variants of which you can hear in dance clubs around the country.

Modern Music

Guatemalan tastes in pop music are greatly influenced by the products of other Latin American countries. Reggaetón is huge – current favorites being Pitbull, Wisin & Yandel, and Daddy Yankee.

THE MARIMBA

The marimba is considered the national instrument, although scholars cannot agree whether this xylophone-type instrument already existed in Africa long before and was brought to Guatemala early on by slaves. Marimbas can be heard throughout the country, often in restaurants or in plazas in the cool of an evening.

The earliest marimbas used a succession of increasingly large gourds as the resonator pipes, but modern marimbas are more commonly fitted with wooden pipes, though you may see the former type in more traditional settings. The instrument is usually played by three men and there is a carnival-like quality to its sound and compositions.

Jazz buffs should be familiar with the sound of the marimba – the instrument became hip in the 1940s when jazz greats such as Glenn Miller started to include it in their compositions.

The only record label seriously promoting new Guatemalan artists (mostly in the urban/hip hop vein) is Guatemala City–based UnOrthodox Productions (www.uoproductions.com).

Guatemalan rock went through its golden age in the '80s and early '90s. Bands from this era like Razones de Cambio, Bohemia Suburbana and Viernes Verde still have their diehard fans. The most famous Guatemalan-born musician is Ricardo Arjona.

Architecture

Modern Guatemalan architecture, apart from a few flashy bank and office buildings along Av La Reforma in Guatemala City and the work of Efraín Recinos, is chiefly characterized by expanses of drab concrete. Some humbler rural dwellings still use a traditional wall construction known as *bajareque*, where a core of stones is held in place by poles of bamboo or other wood, which is faced with stucco or mud. Village houses are increasingly roofed with sheets of tin instead of tiles or thatch – less aesthetically pleasing but also less expensive. For a discussion on traditional Maya architecture, see p283.

Colonial Architecture

During the colonial period (the early 16th to early 19th centuries) churches, convents, mansions and palaces were all built in the Spanish styles of the day, chiefly Renaissance, baroque and neoclassical. But while the architectural concepts were European-inspired, the labor used to realize them was strictly indigenous. Thus, Maya embellishments – such as the lily blossoms and vegetable motifs that adorn Antigua's La Merced – can be found on many colonial buildings, serving as testament to the countless laborers forced to make the architectural dreams of Guatemala's newcomers a reality. Churches were built high and strong to protect the elite from lower classes in revolt.

Guatemala does not have the great colonial architectural heritage of neighboring Mexico, partly because earthquakes destroyed many of its finest buildings. But the architecture of Antigua is particularly striking, as new styles and engineering techniques developed following each successive earthquake. Columns became lower and thicker to provide more stability. Some Antigua buildings, including the Palacio de los Capitanes and Palacio del Ayuntamiento on the central plaza, were given a double-arch construction to strengthen them. With so many colonial buildings in different states of grandeur and decay, Antigua was designated a World Heritage Site by Unesco in 1979.

After the 1776 earthquake, which prompted the relocation of the capital from Antigua to Guatemala City, the neoclassical architecture of the day came to emphasize durability. Decorative flourishes were saved for the interiors of buildings, with elaborate altars and furniture adorning churches and homes. By this time Guatemalan architects were hell-bent on seeing their buildings stay upright, no matter how powerful the next earthquake. Even though several serious quakes have hit Guatemala City since then, many colonial buildings (such as the city's cathedral) have survived. The same cannot be said for the humble abodes of the city's residents, who suffered terribly from the devastating quake of 1976.

Handicrafts

Guatemalans make many traditional handicrafts, both for everyday use and to sell to tourists and collectors. Crafts include basketry, ceramics and wood carving, but the most prominent are weaving, embroidery and other textile arts practiced by Maya women. The beautiful *traje* (traditional clothing) made and worn by local women is one of the most awe-inspiring expressions of Maya culture.

Well-illustrated books on Maya textiles will help you to start identifying the wearers' villages. Two fine works are *Maya of Guatemala – Life and Dress*, by Carmen L Pettersen, and *The Maya Textile Tradition*, edited by Margot Blum Schevill.

Weaving

The most arresting feature of traditional clothing is their highly colorful weaving and embroidery, which makes many garments true works of art. It's the women's *huipil*, a long, sleeveless tunic, that receives the most painstaking loving care in its creation. Often entire *huipiles* are covered in a multicolored web of stylized animal, human, plant and mythological shapes, which can take months to complete. Each garment identifies the village from which its wearer hails (the Spanish colonists allotted each village a different design in order to distinguish their inhabitants from each other) and within the village style there can be variations according to social status, as well as the creative individual touches that make each garment unique.

Maya men now generally wear Western clothing, except in places such as Sololá and Todos Santos Cuchumatán, where they still sport colorful *trajes*. Materials and techniques are changing, but the pre-Hispanic backstrap loom is still widely used. The warp (long) threads are stretched between two horizontal bars, one of which is fixed to a post or tree, while the other is attached to a strap that goes round the weaver's lower back. The weft (cross) threads are then woven in. Throughout the highlands you can see women weaving in this manner outside the entrance to their homes. Nowadays, some *huipiles* and *fajas* are machine made, as this method is faster and easier than weaving by hand.

TEXTILES

For a wonderful collection of photos of *huipiles* and other Maya textiles, see the website of Nim Po't (www .nimpot.com).

Yarn is still hand-spun in many villages. For the well-to-do, silk threads are used to embroider bridal *huipiles* and other important garments. Vegetable dyes are not yet totally out of use, and red dye from cochineal insects and natural indigo are employed in several areas. Modern luminescent dyes go down very well with the Maya, who are happily addicted to bright colors, as you will see.

The colorful traditional dress is still generally most in evidence in the highlands, which are heavily populated by Maya, though you will see it in all parts of the country. The variety of techniques, materials, styles and designs is bewildering to the newcomer, but you'll see some of the most colorful, intricate, eye-catching and widely worn designs in Sololá and Santiago Atitlán, near Lago de Atitlán; Nebaj, in the Ixil Triangle; Zunil, near Quetzaltenango; and Todos Santos and San Mateo Ixtatán in the Cuchumatanes mountains.

You can learn the art of backstrap weaving at weaving schools in Quetzaltenango, San Pedro La Laguna and other towns. To see large collections of fine weaving, don't miss the Museo Ixchel in Guatemala City or the shop Nim Po't in Antigua.

Other Handicrafts

The Maya, particularly in the highlands, have a long tradition of skilled artisanry, products of which you can see in nearly every market in the country. The small town of Totonicapán has dozens of tiny workshops that are open to visitors where you can see tinsmiths, potters, wood carvers and instrument makers at work.

Jade was a sacred stone to the Maya and remains a popular material for jewelers. To see the finest pieces you can tour the workshops and showrooms in Antigua.

One of the most popular Guatemalan souvenirs are the wooden masks used for village festivals. Many display a curious mixture of pre- and post-Columbian influences, such as the very devilish-looking masks used to depict the Spanish colonizers. Again, masks are in markets everywhere but to see the best selection, go to Chichicastenango and for the best prices head to Panajachel or Antigua.

Land & Wildlife

Even 'city people' will have to admit that some of the best parts of Guatemala are in the countryside. The ever-changing terrain takes in the balmy coast, the harsh high-lands, cool cloud forest, lush jungle and desert-like savannah. Many animals have, quite frankly, been eaten, but there are still enough exotic critters and creatures around to keep most wildlife-spotters happy.

The Land

Guatemala covers an area of 109,000 sq km – a little less than the US state of Louisiana, a little more than England. Geologically, most of the country lies atop the North American tectonic plate, but this abuts the Cocos plate along Guatemala's Pacific coast and the Caribbean plate in the far south of the country. When any of these plates gets frisky, earth-quakes and volcanic eruptions ensue. Hence the major quakes of 1773, 1917 and 1976 and the spectacular chain of 30 volcanoes – some of them active – running parallel to the Pacific coast from the Mexican border to the Salvadoran border. North of the volcanic chain rises the Cuchuma-tanes range.

North of Guatemala City, the highlands of Alta Verapaz gradually decline to the lowland of El Petén, occupying northern Guatemala. El Petén is hot and humid or hot and dry, depending on the season. Central America's largest tracts of virgin rainforest straddle El Petén's borders with Mexico and Belize, although this may cease to be true if conservation efforts are not successful.

Northeast of Guatemala City, the valley of the Río Motagua (dry in some areas, moist in others) runs down to Guatemala's short, very hot Caribbean coast. Bananas and sugarcane thrive in the Motagua valley.

Between the volcanic chain and the Pacific Ocean is the Pacific Slope, with rich coffee, cotton, rubber, fruit and sugar plantations, cattle ranches, beaches of black volcanic sand and a sweltering climate.

Guatemala's unique geology also includes tremendous systems of caves. Water coursing for eons over a limestone base created aquifers and conduits that eventually gave way to subterranean caves, rivers and sinkholes when the surface water drained into underground caverns and streams. This type of terrain (known as karst) is found throughout the Verapaces region and makes Guatemala a killer spelunking destination.

Wildlife

Guatemala's natural beauty, from volcanoes and lakes to jungles and wetlands, is one of its great attractions. With its 19 different ecosystems, the variety of fauna and flora is great and, if you know where to go, opportunities for seeing exciting species are plentiful.

Tajumulco (4220m), west of Quetzaltenango, is the highest peak in Central America. La Torre (3837m), north of Huehuetenango, is the highest nonvolcanic peak in Central America.

Les D Beletsky's *Belize & Northern Guatemala: The Ecotravellers' Wildlife Guide* is a comprehensive, all-in-one guide to flora and fauna in the region. The book features hundreds of illustrations and photos and some welcome splashes of humor.

SNAKE IN THE GRASS

The Central American or common lancehead, also called the fer-de-lance (locally known as *barba amarilla*, 'yellow beard') is a highly poisonous viper with a diamond-patterned back and an arrow-shaped head. The *cascabel* (tropical rattlesnake) is the most poisonous of all rattlers. Both inhabit jungles and savannah.

Animals

Estimates point to 250 species of mammals, 600 species of birds, 200 species of reptiles and amphibians, and many species of butterflies and other insects.

The national bird, the resplendent quetzal (for which the national currency is named), is small but exceptionally beautiful. The male sports a bright-red breast, brilliant blue-green neck, head, back and wings, and a blue-green tail several times as long as the body, which stands only around 15cm tall. The female has far duller plumage. The quetzal's main habitat is the cloud forests of Alta Verapaz.

Exotic birds of the lowland jungles include toucans, macaws and parrots. If you visit Tikal, you can't miss the ocellated turkey (also called the Petén turkey), a large, multicolored bird reminiscent of a peacock. Tikal is an all-round wildlife hot spot: you stand a good chance of spotting howler and spider monkeys, coatis (locally called *pisotes*) and other mammals, plus toucans, parrots and many other birds. Some 300 endemic and migratory bird species have been recorded at Tikal, among them nine hummingbirds and four trogons. Good areas for sighting waterfowl – including the jabiru stork, the biggest flying bird in the western hemisphere – are Laguna Petexbatún and the lakes near Yaxhá ruins, both in El Petén, and the Río Dulce between Lago de Izabal and Lívingston.

Guatemala's forests still host many mammal and reptile species. Petén residents include jaguars, ocelots, pumas, two species of peccary, opossums, tapirs, kinkajous, agoutis (*tepescuintles;* rodents 60cm to 70cm long), white-tailed and red brocket deer, and armadillos. Guatemala is home to at least five species of sea turtle (the loggerhead, hawksbill and green ridley on the Caribbean coast, and the leatherback and olive ridley on the Pacific) and at least two species of crocodile (one found in El Petén, the other in the Río Dulce). Manatees exist in the Río Dulce, though they're notoriously hard to spot.

Endangered Species

Guatemala's wildlife faces two major threats. The first is the loss of habitat, as more land is turned over to farming. The second threat is hunting, which is mostly done for food, but also takes place for the collection of skins and other products, as is the case for deer, turtles and some reptiles. Endangered mammals include jaguars, howler monkeys, manatees, several species of mice and bats, and the Guatemalan vole.

More than 25 bird species native to the region are listed as endangered, including the Atitlán grebe (found only in Guatemala) and the national bird, the resplendent quetzal. Many reptiles, including the Morelet's crocodile are likewise disappearing.

Plants

Guatemala has more than 8000 species of plants in 19 different ecosystems ranging from mangrove forests and wetlands on both coasts to the tropical rainforest of El Petén and the pine forests, open grasslands and

Bird-lovers must get hold of either *The Birds of Tikal: An Annotated Checklist,* by Randell A Beavers, or *The Birds of Tikal,* by Frank B Smithe. If you can't find them elsewhere, at least one should be on sale at Tikal itself, and both are useful much further afield.

Jonathon Maslow's *Bird of Life, Bird of Death* begins as a story about a naturalist's search for the quetzal, but quickly develops into a terrifying portrait of Guatemala during the civil war.

---

cloud forests of the mountains. The cloud forests, with their epiphytes, bromeliads and dangling old-man's-beard, are most abundant in Alta Verapaz department. Trees of El Petén include the sapodilla, wild rubber trees, mahogany, several useful palms and Guatemala's national tree for its manifold symbolism to the Maya, the ceiba (also called the kapok or silk-cotton tree in English). Cities such as Antigua become glorious with the lilac blooms of jacaranda trees in the early months of the year.

The national flower, the *monja blanca* (white nun orchid), is said to have been picked so much that it's now rarely seen in the wild; nevertheless, with 550 species of orchid (one third of them endemic to Guatemala), you shouldn't have any trouble spotting some. If you're interested in orchids, be sure to visit the Vivero Verapaz orchid nursery at Cobán and try to land in town for their annual orchid festival, held every December.

Domesticated plants, of course, contribute at least as much to the landscape as wild ones. The *milpa* (maize field) is the backbone of agricultural subsistence everywhere. *Milpas* are, however, usually cleared by the slash-and-burn method, which is a major factor in the diminution of Guatemala's forests.

Parks & Protected Areas

Guatemala has more than 90 protected areas, including *reservas de biosfera* (biosphere reserves), *parques nacionales* (national parks), *biotopos protegidos* (protected biotopes), *refugios de vida silvestre* (wildlife refuges) and *reservas naturales privadas* (private nature reserves). Even though some areas are contained within other, larger ones, they amount to 28% of the national territory. Tikal National Park is the only such area on the Unesco World Heritage list in Guatemala, and owes half its listing to the archaeological site found within.

Many of the protected areas are remote and hard to access for the independent traveler; the table shows those that are easiest to reach and/or

To see rare scarlet macaws in the wild, the place to head is La Ruta Guacamaya (the Scarlet Macaw Trail) of El Perú ruins in El Petén.

Find out about the Yaxhá Private Reserve and what you can do to protect it at www.yaxhanatural.org.

DON'T LET YOUR MOM READ THIS

We don't want to worry you, but Guatemala, along with being the Land of the Eternal Spring, the Land of Smiles, and the Land of the Trees also seems to be the Land of the Natural Disaster. Don't panic – there are really only three biggies you have to worry about:

➡ **Earthquakes** Sitting on top of three tectonic plates hasn't really worked out that well for Guatemala. The present-day capital was founded after Antigua got flattened, but Guatemala City still got pummeled in 1917, 1918 and 1976. This last one left 23,000 people dead.

➡ **Hurricanes** Nobody likes a hurricane. They're windy and noisy and get mud and water everywhere. Guatemala has two coastlines, so theoretically the hit could come from either angle, although it's statistically more likely to come from the Pacific side. 2005's Hurricane Stan was the worst the country's seen, killing more than 1500 and affecting nearly half a million people. Hurricane season runs June to November – for the latest news, you can check with the National Hurricane Center & Tropical Prediction Center (www.nhc.noaa.gov).

➡ **Volcanoes** Great to look at, fun to climb, scary when they erupt. Guatemala has four active volcanoes: Pacaya, Volcán de Fuego, Santiaguito and Tacaná. The nastiest event to date was back in 1902, when Santa María erupted, taking 6000 lives. In recent years Pacaya and Fuego (both outside of Antigua) have been acting up, with increased lava flow and ash. Fuego's 2012 eruption led to over 5000 people being evacuated from nearby communities. If you feel you need to keep an eye on it, log on to the Humanitarian Early Warning website (www.hewsweb.org/volcanoes).

PARKS & PROTECTED AREAS

PROTECTED AREA	FEATURES	ACTIVITIES	BEST TIME TO VISIT
Área de Protección Especial Punta de Manabique	large Caribbean wetland reserve; beaches, mangroves, lagoons, birds, crocodiles, possible manatee sightings	boat trips, wildlife observation, fishing, beach	any
Biotopo Cerro Cahuí	forest reserve beside Lago de Petén Itzá; Petén wildlife including monkeys	walking trails	any
Biotopo del Quetzal (Biotopo Mario Dary Rivera)	easy-access cloud forest reserve; howler monkeys, birds	nature trails, bird-watching, possible quetzal sightings	any
Biotopo San Miguel La Palotada	within Reserva de Biosfera Maya, adjoins Parque Nacional Tikal; dense Petén forest with millions of bats	jungle walks, visits to El Zotz archaeological site and bat caves	any, drier Nov–May
Parque Nacional Grutas de Lanquín	large cave system 61km from Cobán	bat-watching; observation of the nearby Semuc Champey lagoons and waterfalls	any
Parque Nacional Laguna del Tigre	remote, large park within Reserva de Biosfera Maya; freshwater wetlands, Petén flora and fauna	wildlife-spotting, including scarlet macaws, monkeys, crocodiles; visiting El Perú archaeological site; volunteer opportunities at Las Guacamayas biological station	any, drier Nov-May
Parque Nacional Laguna Lachuá	circular, jungle-surrounded, turquoise lake, 220m deep; many fish, occasional jaguars and tapir	camping, swimming	any
Parque Nacional Mirador–Río Azul	national park within Reserva de Biosfera Maya; Petén flora and fauna	jungle treks to El Mirador archaeological site	any, drier Nov–May
Parque Nacional Río Dulce	beautiful jungle-lined lower Río Dulce between Lago de Izabal and the Caribbean; manatee refuge	boat trips	any
Parque Nacional Tikal	diverse jungle wildlife among Guatemala's most magnificent Maya ruins	wildlife-spotting, seeing spectacular Maya city	any, drier Nov–May
Refugio de Bocas del Polochic	delta of Río Polochic at western end of Lago de Izabal; Guatemala's second-largest freshwater wetlands	bird-watching (more than 300 species), howler monkey observation	any
Refugio de Vida Silvestre Petexbatún	lake near Sayaxché; water birds	boat trips, fishing, visiting several archaeological sites	any
Reserva Natural Monterrico-Hawaii	Pacific beaches and wetlands; birdlife, turtles	boat tours, bird-watching and turtle-watching	Jun–Nov (turtle nesting)
Reserva de Biosfera Maya	vast 21,000-sq-km area stretching across northern Petén; includes four national parks	jungle treks, wildlife-spotting	any, drier Nov–May
Reserva de Biosfera Sierra de las Minas	cloud-forest reserve of great biodiversity; key quetzal habitat	hiking, wildlife-spotting	any

most interesting to visitors (but excludes volcanoes, nearly all of which are protected, and areas of mainly archaeological interest).

Environmental Issues

Environmental consciousness is not enormously developed in Guatemala, as the vast amounts of garbage strewn across the country and the choking clouds of diesel gas pumped out by its buses and trucks will quickly tell you. Despite the impressive list of parks and protected areas, genuine protection for those areas is harder to achieve, partly because of official collusion to ignore the regulations and partly because of pressure from poor Guatemalans in need of land.

Guatemala's popularity as a tourist destination leads to a few environmental problems – the question of sewerage and trash disposal around Lago de Atitlán being a major one, and some inappropriate development in the rainforests of El Petén being another. Infrastructure development in Guatemala is moving at such a pace, though, that these problems seem minor compared to some of the other challenges that environmentalists face.

Deforestation is a problem in many areas, especially El Petén, where jungle is being felled not just for timber but also to make way for cattle ranches, oil pipelines, clandestine airstrips, new settlements and new maize fields cleared using the slash-and-burn method.

Oil exploration is a concern all over the country – Guatemalans are scrambling to start drilling in El Petén, as the Mexicans have been doing for years, tapping into a vast subterranean reserve that runs across the border. In his short stint in office, then-president Alfonso Portillo proposed drilling for oil in the middle of Lago de Izabal. The plan was shelved after massive outcry from international and local environmental agencies and some not too subtle pressure from Guatemala's trading partners. It's a project that's gone but not forgotten.

Large-scale infrastructure projects are being announced with regularity, often in environmentally sensitive areas. The most controversial of these is the almost complete Northern Transversal, a strip of highway consolidating existing roads that will stretch from the Mexican border at Gracias a Dios, pass Playa Grande and eventually connect up to Modesto Méndez, where a new border crossing for Belize is planned. Concerns with the project are many, as the road passes through sites of archaeological, environmental and cultural significance. Local environmental groups fear its construction will facilitate oil exploration in the Ixcán. One component of the plan is the construction of the Xalalá dam, a hydroelectric project. Despite claims that the dam will produce 886 GWh of hydroelectric energy per year, thus reducing the country's energy deficit and reliance on fossil fuels, the project has run into stiff opposition, as detractors claim that construction will displace local communities, affect water quality downstream and alter the ecology of the area through habitat loss

Transnational mining companies are moving in, most notably in San Marcos in the Western Highlands and the Sierra de las Minas in the southeast. Without the proper community consultation called for by law, the government has granted these companies license to operate open-cut mines in search of silver and gold. Chemical runoff, deforestation, eviction of local communities and water pollution are the main issues here. Police have been used to forcibly evict residents and quash community groups' peaceful protests.

Environmental Organizations

Despite such a dire-sounding list of obstacles, a number of Guatemalan organizations are doing valiant work to protect the country's environment

Timber, Tourists, and Temples, edited by Richard Primack and others, brings together experts on the forests of Guatemala, Mexico and Belize for an in-depth look at the problems of balancing conservation with local people's aspirations.

For information about the spectacular Chelemhá cloud forest, check out www .chelemha.org.

and biodiversity. The following are good sources of information for finding out more about Guatemala's natural and protected areas:

➡ Alianza Verde (www.alianzaverde.org; Parque Central, Flores, Petén) Association of organizations, businesses and people involved in conservation and tourism in El Petén; provides information services such as *Destination Petén* magazine, and Cincap, the Centro de Información Sobre la Naturaleza, Cultura y Artesanía de Petén, in Flores.

➡ Arcas (Asociación de Rescate y Conservación de Vida Silvestre; ☎7830-1374; www.arcasguatemala.com; Calle Hillary, Km 30, Lote 6, Casa Villa Conchita, San Lucas Sacatepéquez, Guatemala) NGO working with volunteers in sea turtle conservation and rehabilitation of Petén wildlife.

➡ Asociación Ak' Tenamit (www.aktenamit.org) Maya-run NGO working to reduce poverty and promote conservation and ecotourism in the rainforests of eastern Guatemala. Branches in Guatemala City (☎2254-1560; 11a Av A 9-39, Zona 2) and Río Dulce (☎5908-3392).

➡ Cecon (Centro de Estudios Conservacionistas de la Universidad de San Carlos; ☎2331-0904; biotoposcecon@gmail.com; Av La Reforma 0-63, Zona 10, Guatemala City) Manages six public *biotopos* and one *reserva natural*.

➡ Fundación Defensores de la Naturaleza (☎2310-2900; www.defensores.org. gt; 2a Av 14-08, Zona 14, Guatemala City) NGO that owns and administers several protected areas.

➡ ProPetén (Map p236; ☎7867-5296; www.propeten.org; Calle Central, Flores, Petén) NGO that works in conservation and natural resources management in Parque Nacional Laguna del Tigre.

Ecotravels in Guatemala (www .planeta.com/ guatemala.html) has arresting articles, good reference material and numerous links.

Survival Guide

Directory A–Z

Accommodations

Hotels, Hostels & Guesthouses

Guatemalan accommodations range from luxury hotels to budget hotels to ultrabudget guesthouses called *hospedajes, casas de huéspedes* or *pensiones*.

Accommodations options are listed in order of price range, and within that price range by author preference. Places at the lower end of the budget range are generally small, dark and not particularly clean. Security may not be the best in such places. At the upper end of the budget range you should expect a clean, sizable and airy room, with a bathroom, TV and, in hot parts of the country, a fan (and possibly air-con).

Hostels are becoming more prevalent throughout the country, particularly in tourist hotspots like Antigua, Flores and Lanquín. While sleeping arrangements in these places can be fairly bare-bones (a bunch of bunk beds crammed into a room) facilities often include on-site bars and restaurants, tour services, swimming pools and other top-shelf amenities. They're also a great place to meet other travelers.

Midrange rooms are almost always comfortable: private hot-water bathroom, TV, decent beds, fan and/or air-con are standard. Good midrange hotels have attractive public areas such as dining rooms, bars and swimming pools.

Top-end accommodations in Guatemala mainly consists of Guatemala City's international-class business-oriented hotels, Antigua's very finest hostelries, and a few resort hotels elsewhere. These places offer all the comforts (and many more) that you would expect for the price.

Room rates often go up in places popular with tourists during Semana Santa (the week leading up to Easter Sunday), Christmas–New Year and July and August. Semana Santa is the major Guatemalan holiday period, and prices can rise by anything from 30% to 100% on the coast and in the countryside – anywhere Guatemalans go to relax. At this time advance reservations are a very good idea.

SLEEPING PRICE RANGES

The following price ranges refer to a double room with bathroom in high (but not absolute peak) season. Unless otherwise stated, taxes of 22% are included in the price.

$	less than Q180
$$	Q180-500
$$$	more than Q500

Regardless of your budget, if you're planning on staying for longer than a few days, it's worth asking for a discount.

Be aware that room rates are subject to two large taxes – 12% IVA (value-added tax) and 10% to pay for the activities of the Guatemalan Tourism Institute (Inguat), although there is discussion about eliminating this second tax. All prices listed include both taxes. Some of the more expensive hotels forget to include them when they quote their prices.

Camping

Camping in Guatemala can be a hit-or-miss affair as there are few designated campgrounds and safety is rarely guaranteed. Where campsites are available, expect to pay from Q20 to Q50 per person per night.

Homestays

Travelers attending Spanish school have the option of living with a Guatemalan family. This is usually a pretty good bargain – expect to pay between Q300 and Q600 a week on top of your tuition for your own room, shared bathroom, and three meals a day except Sunday. It's important to find a homestay that gels with your goals – some families host several students at a time, creating more of an international hostel atmosphere than a family environment.

Children

For general information on traveling with children, have a look at Lonely Planet's *Travel with Children*.

Facilities such as safety seats in hired cars are rare but nearly every restaurant can rustle up something resembling a high chair. If you are particular about brands of diapers and creams, bring what you can with you and stock up in supermarkets. Fresh milk is rare and may not be pasteurized – again, supermarkets are your best bet. Packet UHT milk and milk powder are much more common. If your child has to have some particular tinned or packaged food, bring supplies with you. Public breastfeeding is not common among urban, non-indigenous women and, when done, is done discreetly.

Customs Regulations

Normally customs officers won't look seriously in your luggage and may not look at all. Guatemala restricts import/export of pretty much the same things as everybody else (weapons, drugs, large amounts of cash, etc).

Electricity

120V/60Hz

120V/60Hz

Climate

Guatemala City

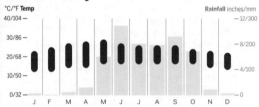

Huehuetenango

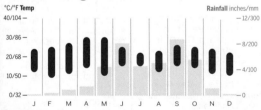

Río Dulce

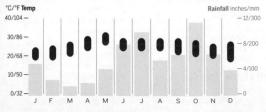

Embassies & Consulates

New Zealand and Australia do not have embassies in Guatemala. The Canadian embassy can be of some assistance, but otherwise you'll have to go to Mexico City.

Belizean Embassy (☎2367-3883; www.embajadadebelize.org; 5a Av 5-55, Europlaza 2, Office 1502, Zona 14, Guatemala City)

Canadian Embassy (☎2363-4348; www.guatemala.gc.ca; 13a Calle 8-44, 8th fl, Edificio Edyma Plaza, Zona 10, Guatemala City)

French Embassy (☎2421-7370; www.ambafrance-gt.org/; 5a Av 8-59, Zona 14, Guatemala City)

German Embassy (☎2364-6700; www.guatemala.diplo.de; Avenida La Reforma 9-55, Zona 10, Guatemala City, Edificio Reforma 10, 10th fl)

Honduran Embassy (☎2366-5640; embhond@intelnet.net.gt; 19a Av 'A' 20-19, Zona 10, Guatemala City)

Irish Honorary Consulate (☎2384-9442; irelandgua@gmail.com; 7a Av 14-44, Edificio La Galería, Office 15A, Zona 9, Guatemala City)

Mexican Embassy (☎2420-3400; www.sre.gob.mx/guatemala/; 2a Av 7-57, Zona 10, Guatemala City)

Netherlands Embassy (☎2381-4300; www.embajadadeholanda-gua.org; 16a Calle 0-55, 13th fl, Torre Internacional, Zona 10, Guatemala City)

Salvadoran Embassy (☎2245-7272; Embajada Guatemala@rree.gob.sv; Av Las Américas 16-40, Zona 13, Guatemala City)

UK Embassy (☎2380-7300; www.ukinguatemala.fco.gov.uk; 16a Calle 0-55, 11th fl, Torre Internacional, Zona 10, Guatemala City)

US Embassy (☎2326-4501; http://guatemala.usembassy.gov; Av La Reforma 7-01, Zona 10, Guatemala City)

Food

The following price ranges refer to a standard main course, including taxes but not including tip. For useful words and phrases, see the Food Glossary (p317).

$	less than Q40
$$	Q40–130
$$$	more than Q130

Gay & Lesbian Travelers

Few places in Latin America are outwardly gay-friendly and Guatemala is no different. Technically, homosexuality is legal for persons over 18 years, but the reality can be another story, with harassment and violence against gays too often poisoning the plot. Don't even consider testing the tolerance for homosexual public displays of affection here.

Though Antigua has a palatable – if subdued – scene, affection and action are still kept behind closed doors; the chief exception is the gay-friendly club La Casbah. In Guatemala City, Genetic and the Black & White Lounge are the current faves. Mostly, though, gays traveling in Guatemala will find themselves keeping it low-key and pushing the twin beds together.

Gay.com (www.gay.com) has a personals section for Guatemala and **The Gully** (www.thegully.com) usually has some articles and information relevant to Guatemala. The best site, **Gay Guatemala** (www.gayguatemala.com), is in Spanish.

Health

Staying healthy in Guatemala involves some common-sense precautions and a few destination-specific ones.

Before You Go

Step number one would be getting the recommended vaccines. Discuss these with your doctor, but the vaccines that are usually recommended for travel to Central America are hepatitis A & B and typhoid. If you are planning to spend time handling animals or exploring caves, consider getting vaccinated for rabies.

Mosquitoes

Mosquitoes can transmit two serious diseases – malaria and dengue fever. Malaria tablets are available and recommended if you are planning to travel in rural areas at altitudes lower than 1500m, especially in the rainy season (June to November). It's worth noting that there is no malaria risk in Antigua or around Lake Atitlán. The best prevention against mosquito-borne diseases is to avoid getting bitten. In high-risk areas this means a DEET-based insect repellent (bring one from home), long sleeves and pant legs, avoiding being outside around sunrise and sunset and checking window screens and mosquito nets in hotel rooms for holes where mosquitoes can enter.

Healthy Eating

By far the most common health issue that travelers to Guatemala experience is stomach-related. This can range from serious diseases like cholera to simple cases of diarrhea. Watch what you eat, drink and generally put in your mouth. Here are a few simple guidelines to keep you out of the bathroom and on the road:

➡ Wash your hands thoroughly before eating or touching your face.

➡ Eat only in places that appear to be clean (conditions in the dining room are sometimes a good indicator of what's going on in the kitchen).

➡ To ensure the food you eat is fresh and freshly cooked, eat only in busy places around mealtimes.

➡ Peel, cook or disinfect fruits and vegetables.

➡ Be very selective when it comes to street food.

➡ Avoid tap water unless it has been boiled thoroughly or disinfected. Ice in more expensive restaurants is made from purified water, but order drinks without it if you want to be really cautious.

➡ If you do get sick and it lasts longer than a few days, take a stool sample to the laboratory (even the smallest towns have them) for analysis. You'll get a possibly alarming readout of exactly what kinds of bugs you have. Any pharmacist will be able use the readout to prescribe the appropriate medicine.

Health Care in Guatemala

Larger towns have both public (cheap, with long waiting times) and private (expensive, but faster) hospitals, often with doctors who speak at least a little English. In smaller towns there will be a health clinic and in villages there is usually a doctor. Guatemala City naturally has the best range of health services in the country.

Health care is relatively cheap in Guatemala (around Q25 for a standard doctor's consultation). Despite low costs, it is generally recommended that travelers to Guatemala take out travel insurance, which almost always covers medical costs. Check your policy carefully to see what is and is not covered before buying.

While 'medical tourism' is taking off in Guatemala (dentistry, for example, is a serious bargain compared to what you will pay elsewhere), if you have a serious complaint that does not require immediate attention, consider returning to your country to get treated.

Insurance

Getting travel insurance to cover theft, loss and medical problems is recommended.

Some policies specifically exclude dangerous activities, which can include scuba diving, motorcycling, and even trekking.

You may prefer a policy that pays doctors or hospitals directly, rather than you having to pay on the spot and claim later. If you have to claim later, ensure you keep all documentation.

Check that the policy covers ambulances or an emergency flight home.

Worldwide travel insurance is available at www.lonelyplanet.com/travel_services. You can buy, extend and claim online anytime – even if you're already on the road.

Internet Access

Most travelers make constant use of internet cafes and free web-based email. Most towns have cybercafes with fairly reliable connections. Internet cafes typically charge between Q5 and Q10 an hour.

Wi-fi is becoming readily available across the country, but can only really be counted on in large and/or tourist towns. Most (but not all) hostels offer wi-fi, as do many hotels in the midrange and up category. The best reliable source of wi-fi around the country is at Pollo Campero restaurants – they're in pretty much every town of any size and all offer free, unsecured access.

Language Courses

Guatemala is celebrated for its many language schools. A spot of study here is a great way not only to learn Spanish but also to meet locals and get an inside angle on the culture. Many travelers heading south through Central America to South America make Guatemala an early stop so they can pick up the Spanish skills they need for their trip.

Guatemalan language schools are some of the cheapest in the world, but few people go away disappointed. There are so many schools to choose from that it's essential to check out a few before deciding.

You can start any day at most schools, and study for as long as you like. If you're coming in peak season and hoping to get into one of the more popular schools, it's a good idea to book ahead, although many schools charge around Q300 for phone or internet reservations. All decent schools offer a variety of elective activities from salsa classes to movies to volcano hikes. Many schools offer classes in Maya languages as well as Spanish.

Where to Study

Antigua is the most popular place to study. Quetzaltenango is second, perhaps attracting a more serious type of student; Antigua has a livelier students' and travelers' social scene. Outside of those areas, there are Spanish schools scattered across the country. On average, schools charge Q900 to Q1200 for four hours of one-on-one classes five days a week and accommodation with a local family.

Studying in a small town has its pros and cons. On the upside, you may be the only foreigner around, so you won't be speaking any English. On the downside, Spanish may be the second language of the inhabitants of the village (including your teacher), meaning that you could pick up all sorts of bad habits.

Choosing a School

Choosing between the mass of Spanish schools in Guatemala can be tough. Many schools don't have in-house teacher training programs, so there aren't so many 'good schools' as there are 'good teachers'. It's best to pay for as little time as possible (a week, usually) so you can change if you're really unhappy. You should be completely up-front about what your goals (conversation, grammar, vocabulary etc) are when starting, as well as any specialized interests that you have (politics, medical, legal etc) so the school can design a curriculum and assign you a teacher to best suit your needs. If you end up liking like the school, but not the teacher, ask for a new teacher as soon as possible – personality conflicts occur, and four or five hours of one-on-one with someone you don't like can soon turn into hard work.

Here are some questions to think about when you're looking at schools. Some you can find out just by turning up, some you should ask the school, others you'll have to talk to current and ex-students to get a feel for.

➡ Where do the classes take place – on a quiet, shaded patio or in hot classrooms with buses roaring along the street outside?

➡ What experience and qualifications do the teachers have in teaching a second language?

➡ Is Spanish your teacher's first language?

➡ What afternoon and evening activities are available?

➡ Many schools offer gimmicks to get you in, like a half hour of free internet per day, which ends up saving you around Q2.50 per day – should these little perks really sway your judgment?

➡ What is the general atmosphere of the school? Serious students probably won't fit in at a school whose activities include all-night bar crawls, and party animals may feel out of place at schools with names like the Christian Spanish Academy.

➡ Does the school offer opportunities for voluntary work – eg visiting hospitals?

➡ If the school claims to be involved in social/community projects, is it a serious commitment, or just a marketing ploy?

For (completely unverified) reviews of some of Guatemala's Spanish schools by ex-students, check out www.guatemala365.com.

REPORTING A CRIME

Reporting a crime is always a toss-up in Guatemala. If you're the victim of something really serious, of course you should take it to the police – the phrase you're looking for here is '*Yo quisiera denunciar un crimen*' ('I'd like to report a crime'). If you've been robbed, get a statement filed so you can show your insurance company.

If it's a minor thing, on the other hand, you might want to consider whether or not it's really worth your while reporting it to the police.

Specially trained tourist police (often English speaking) operate in some major tourist areas – you can call them in **Antigua** (☎5978-3586) and **Guatemala City** (☎2232 0202; 11 Calle 12-06).

Outside of those areas (and normal office hours) your best bet is to call **Proatur** (☎in English 1500), which operates a 24-hour nationwide toll-free hotline in English and Spanish. It can give you information and assistance, help deal with the police and even arrange a lawyer if need be.

Legal Matters

You may find that police officers in Guatemala might, at times, be somewhat unhelpful. Generally speaking, the less you have to do with the law, the better.

Whatever you do, don't get involved in any way with illegal drugs – even if the locals seem to do so freely. As a foreigner, you are at a distinct disadvantage, and you may be set up by others. Drug laws in Guatemala are strict, and though enforcement may be uneven, penalties are severe. If you do get caught doing something you shouldn't, your best line of defence is to apologize, stay calm and proceed from there.

Money

Guatemala's currency, the quetzal (ket-*sahl,* abbreviated to Q), was fairly stable at around Q7.5 = US$1 for years, but in recent years it has been hovering around Q8. The quetzal is divided into 100 centavos.

Many banks give cash advances on Visa cards, and some on MasterCard. You can pay for many purchases with these cards or with American Express (Amex) cards, but always ask if there is a *recargo* (transaction fee).

Cash

Cash is king in Guatemala, although carrying too much of it makes getting robbed a bigger pain than it would otherwise be. Some towns suffer from change shortages: always try to carry a stash of small bills. Keep a small supply of low-denomination US dollars (which are accepted pretty much anywhere, at various rates of exchange) as an emergency fund.

Currencies other than the US dollar are virtually useless, although a small handful of places now change euros.

ATMs

You'll find ATMs (cash machines, *cajeros automáticos*) for Visa/Plus System cards in all but the smallest towns, and there are MasterCard/Cirrus ATMs in many places too, so one of these cards is the best basis for your supply of cash in Guatemala. The 5B network is widespread and particularly useful, as it works with both Visa and MasterCard cards.

Be aware that card skimming is as rife in Guatemala as it is in the rest of the world. Avoid ATMs that are left unguarded at night (ie those in the little room out front of the bank) and look for one that is in a secure environment (such as those inside supermarkets, shopping malls etc). Failing that, keep your hand covered when entering your PIN and check your balance online.

Tipping

A 10% tip is expected at restaurants and automatically added to your bill in places such as Antigua – a practice that is spreading to other tourist towns as well. In small *comedores* (basic, cheap eateries) tipping is optional, but follow local practice and leave some spare change. Tour guides are generally tipped, around 10%, especially on longer trips.

Traveler's Checks

If you're not packing plastic, a combination of Amex US-dollar traveler's checks and some US dollars is the way to go. Take some of these as a backup even if you do have a card. Many banks change US-dollar traveler's checks, and tend to give the best rates. Amex is easily the most recognized traveler's check brand. Few businesses will accept traveler's checks as payment or change them for cash.

Opening Hours

Guatemalan shops and businesses are generally open from 8am to noon and 2pm to 6pm, Monday to Saturday, but there are many variations. Banks typically open 9am to 5pm Monday to Friday (again with variations), and 9am to 1pm Saturday. Government offices usually open 8am to 4pm, Monday to Friday. Official business is always better conducted in the morning.

Restaurant hours are typically 7am to 9pm, but can vary by up to two hours either way. Most bars open from 11am to midnight. The *Ley Seca* (dry law) stipulates that bars and *discotecas* must close by 1am, except on nights before public holidays. It is rigidly adhered to in large cities and universally laughed at in smaller towns and villages.

If restaurants or bars have a closing day, it's usually Sunday. Typical shopping hours are 8am to noon and 2pm to 6pm Monday to Saturday.

Photography

Ubiquitous film stores and pharmacies sell film, though you may not find the brand you like without a hunt. There are quick processing labs in the main cities. Most internet cafes have card readers *(lectores de tarjeta),* so you can upload your digital photos or burn them onto CD. For tips on taking professional-grade travel pics, hunt down a copy of Lonely Planet's *Travel Photography*.

Photographing People

Photography is a sensitive subject in Guatemala. Always ask permission before taking portraits, especially of Maya women and children. Don't be surprised if your request is denied. Children often request payment (usually Q1) in return for posing. In certain places such as the church of Santo Tomás in Chichicastenango, photography is forbidden. Maya ceremonies (should you be so lucky to witness one) are off-limits for photography unless you are given explicit permission to take pictures. If local people make any sign of being offended, put your camera away and apologize immediately, both out of decency and for your own safety. Never take photos of army installations, men with guns or other sensitive military subjects.

Post

The Guatemalan postal service was privatized in 1999. Generally, letters and parcels take eight to 10 days to travel to the US and Canada and 10 to 12 days to reach Europe. Almost all cities and towns (but not villages) have a post office where you can buy stamps and send mail. If you want to get a package couriered to you, make sure the courier company has an office in the town where you are staying; otherwise you will be charged some hefty 'handling fees.'

Public Holidays

The main Guatemalan holiday periods are Semana Santa, Christmas–New Year and July and August. During Semana Santa room prices rise in many places and it's advisable to book all accommodations and transport in advance.

Guatemalan public holidays include the following:

New Year's Day (Año Nuevo) January 1

Easter (Semana Santa; Holy Thursday to Easter Sunday inclusive) March/April

Labor Day (Día del Trabajo) May 1

Army Day (Día del Ejército) June 30

Assumption Day (Día de la Asunción) August 15

Independence Day (Día de la Independencia) September 15

Revolution Day (Día de la Revolución) October 20

All Saints' Day (Día de Todos los Santos) November 1

Christmas Eve afternoon (Víspera Navidad) December 24

Christmas Day (Navidad) December 25

New Year's Eve afternoon (Víspera de Año Nuevo) December 31

Safe Travel

While crime definitely happens in Guatemala, and definitely happens to tourists, these days the most frequently reported type of nasty incident involves robbery on walking trails.

The days of robbers targeting buses and tourist shuttles out on the open highway seem to be thankfully in the past, although some tourists in rental cars have been targeted. This information is incredibly fluid – if you're planning on driving yourself around, check with **Proatur** (⌨ in English 1500) for the latest.

The crime you're most likely to become a victim of involves pickpocketing, bag-snatching, bag-slitting and the like in crowded bus stations, buses, streets and markets, but also in empty, dark city streets.

In short, use your street smarts and you should stay out of trouble.

It's best to travel and arrive in daylight hours. If that's not possible, travel at night using 1st-class buses and catch a taxi to your hotel once you arrive.

Tips

➡ Only carry the money, cards, checks and valuables that you need. Leave the rest in a sealed, signed envelope in your hotel's safe, and obtain a receipt for the envelope.

➡ Don't flaunt jewelry, cameras or valuable-looking watches. Keep your wallet or purse out of view.

➡ On buses keep your important valuables with you, and keep a tight hold on them.

GOVERNMENT TRAVEL ADVICE

The following government websites offer travel advisories and information on current hot spots. Please bear in mind that these sites are updated occasionally and are obliged to err on the safe side – many, many travelers visit Guatemala and don't experience any of these problems.

➡ **Australian Department of Foreign Affairs** (www.smarttraveller.gov.au)

➡ **British Foreign Office** (www.fco.gov.uk)

➡ **Canadian Department of Foreign Affairs** (www.dfait-maeci.gc.ca)

➡ **US State Department** (http://travel.state.gov/)

➡ Use normal precautions when using ATMs (and be aware that card skimming is a reality here).

➡ Hiking in large groups and/or with a police escort reduces the risk of robbery.

➡ Resisting or trying to flee from robbers usually makes the situation worse.

Hiking on active volcanoes obviously has an element of risk. Get the latest story before you head out. In the wet season, hike in the morning before rain and possible thunderstorms set in.

Be careful, especially in rural areas, when talking to small children, always ask permission to take photographs and generally try not to put yourself in any situation that might be misinterpreted.

Scams

One common scenario is for someone to spray ketchup or some other sticky liquid on your clothes. An accomplice then appears to help you clean up the mess and robs you in the process. Other methods of distraction, such as dropping a purse or coins, or someone appearing to faint, are also used by pickpockets and bag snatchers.

Regrettably, ATM card cloners have moved into Guatemala, targeting Guatemalans and foreigners alike.

They operate by attaching a card reading device to the ATM (often inside the slot where you insert your card) and once they have your data, proceed to drain your account. There have been reports of card cloning in all the major tourist destinations. The only way to avoid it is to use ATMs that cannot be tampered with easily (inside supermarkets or shopping malls). The ATMs most prone to tampering are the ones in the little unlocked room at the front of a bank.

You should *never* have to enter your PIN number to gain access to an ATM room.

Telephone

Guatemala has no area or city codes. Calling from other countries, you just dial the international access code (00 in most countries), then the Guatemala country code (502), then the eight-digit local number. Calling within Guatemala, just dial the eight-digit local number. The international access code from Guatemala is 00.

Many towns and cities frequented by tourists have privately run call offices where you can make international calls for reasonable rates.

Many travelers use an account such as Skype. If an internet cafe does not have Skype installed, it can usually be downloaded in a matter of minutes. If you're planning on using internet cafe computers to make calls, buy earbuds with a microphone attached before you leave – you can plug them into the front of most computers in the country.

The most common street phones are those of Telgua, for which you need to buy a Telgua phone card (tarjeta telefónica de Telgua) from shops, kiosks and the like. Card sales points may advertise the fact with red signs saying 'Ladatel de Venta Aquí'. The cards come in denominations of Q20, Q30 and Q50: you slot them into a Telgua phone, dial your number, and the display will tell you how much time you have left.

Don't use the black phones placed strategically in tourist towns that say 'Press 2 to call the United States free!' This is a bait and switch scam; you put the call on your credit card and return home to find you have paid between US$8 and US$20 per minute.

Telgua street phones bear instructions to dial ✍147110 for domestic collect calls and ✍147120 for international collect calls.

Cell Phones

Cell phones are widely used. It's possible to bring your cell phone from home, have it 'unlocked' for use in Guatemala (this costs around Q50 in Guatemala), then substitute your SIM card for a local one. This works on some phones and not others and there doesn't appear to be a logic behind it. Guatemalan phone companies work on either 850, 900 or 1900 MHz frequencies – if you have a tri- or quad-band phone you should be OK. Compatibility issues, and the possibility of theft (cell phones are a pickpocket's delight) makes buying a cheap prepaid phone on arrival the most popular option.

Prepaid phones are available pretty much everywhere and cost around Q100 to Q150, often coming with Q100 or so in free calls. Cards to restock the credit on your phone are sold in nearly every corner store. Calls cost Q1.50 per minute anywhere in the country, the same for the US (depending on the company you're with) and up to five times that for the rest of the world.

At the time of writing, Movistar had the cheapest rates (with coverage limited not much further than major cities) and Tigo and Claro had the best coverage.

Time

Guatemala runs on North American Central Standard Time (GMT/UTC minus six hours). The 24-hour clock is often used, so 1pm may be written as 13 or 1300. When it's noon in Guatemala, it's 1pm in New York, 6pm in London, 10am in San Francisco and 4am the next day in Sydney. For more time conversions, see www.time anddate.com/worldclock.

Toilets

You cannot throw *anything* into Guatemalan toilets, including toilet paper. Bathrooms are equipped with some sort of receptacle (usually a small wastebasket) for soiled paper. Toilet paper is not always provided, so always carry some. If you don't have any and need some, asking a restaurant worker for *un rollo de papel* (a roll of paper), accompanied by a panicked facial expression, usually produces fast results.

Public toilets are rare. Use the ones at cafes, restaurants, your hotel and archaeological sites. Buses rarely have toilets on board and if they do, don't count on them working.

Tourist Information

Guatemala's national tourism institute, **Inguat** (www .visitguatemala.com), has information offices in major tourist areas. A few towns have departmental, municipal or private-enterprise tourist information offices. **Proatur** (✍in English 1500), a joint private-government initiative, operates a 24-hour toll-free advice and assistance hotline.

Travelers with Disabilities

Guatemala is not the easiest country to negotiate for travelers with a disability. Although many sidewalks in Antigua have ramps and cute little inlaid tiles depicting a wheelchair, the streets are cobblestone, so the ramps are anything but smooth and the streets worse!

Many hotels in Guatemala are old converted houses with rooms around a courtyard; such rooms are wheelchair accessible, but the bathrooms may not be. The most expensive hotels have facilities such as ramps, elevators and accessible toilets. Transportation is the biggest hurdle for travelers with limited mobility: travelers in a wheelchair may consider renting a car and driver as the buses will prove especially challenging due to lack of space.

Mobility International USA (www.miusa.org) advises travelers on mobility issues, runs exchange programs (including in Guatemala) and publishes some useful books. Also worth consulting are **Access-Able Travel Source** (www.access-able.com) and **Accessible Journeys** (www.disabilitytravel.com).

Antigua-based **Transitions** (www.transitionsfoundation.org) is an organization aiming to increase awareness and access for people with disabilities in Guatemala.

Visas

Citizens of the US, Canada, EU countries, Norway, Switzerland, Australia, New Zealand, Israel and Japan are among those who do not need a visa for tourist visits to Guatemala. On entry into Guatemala you will normally be given a 90-day stay. (The number 90 will be written in the stamp in your passport.)

In August of 2006 Guatemala joined the Centro America 4 (CA-4) trading agreement with Nicaragua, Honduras and El Salvador. Designed to facilitate the movement of people and goods around the region, it has one major effect on foreign visitors – upon entry to the CA-4 region, travelers are given a 90-day stay *for the entire region*. You can get this extended once, for an additional 90 days, for around Q120. The exact requirements change with each government, but just for kicks, here's how it was working at the time of writing: you needed to go to the **Departamento de Extranjería** (Foreigners' Office; ☑2411-2411; 6a Av 3-11, Zona 4, Guatemala City; ◷8am-2:30pm Mon-Fri), with *all* of the following:

➡ One black and white passport-sized photo on matte paper

➡ A valid passport

➡ Two photocopies of the first page of your passport and one of the page where your entry visa was stamped

➡ A credit card with a photocopy of both of its sides (or photocopy of US$400 worth of travelers' checks)

➡ A ticket out of the country or proof of flight reservation (on Travel Agency letterhead, signed and sealed by a Travel Agent)

Extensions can take up to a week to process, but this period is also very flexible – it's worth asking about before you start the process.

Citizens of some Eastern European countries are among those who do need visas to visit Guatemala. Enquire at a Guatemalan embassy well in advance of travel.

Visa regulations are subject to change – it's always worth checking with a Guatemalan embassy before you go.

If you have been in the CA-4 for your original 90 days and a 90-day extension, you must leave the region for 72 hours (Belize and Mexico are the most obvious, easiest options), after which you can return to the region to start all over again. Some foreigners have been repeating this cycle for years.

Volunteering

If you want to get to the heart of Guatemalan matters, consider volunteer work. Opportunities abound, from caring for abandoned animals to writing grant applications to tending fields. Travelers with specific skills such as nurses, doctors, teachers and website designers are particularly encouraged to investigate volunteering in Guatemala.

Most volunteer posts require basic or better Spanish skills and a minimum time commitment. Depending on the organization, you may have to pay for room and board for the duration of your stay. Before making a commitment, you may want to talk to past volunteers and read the fine print associated with the position.

An excellent source of information on volunteer opportunities is Quetzaltenango-based **EntreMundos** (Map p136; ☑7761-2179; www.entremundos.org; 6a Calle 7-31, Zona 1; ◷2-5pm Mon-Thu). You only have to visit their websites to see the huge range of volunteer opportunities that exist. Many language schools have close links to volunteer projects and can introduce you to the world of volunteering. The best worldwide site

for volunteer positions (with many Guatemala listings) is www.idealist.org.

Women Travelers

Women should encounter no special problems traveling in Guatemala. The primary thing you can do to make it easy for yourself while traveling here is to dress modestly. Modesty in dress is highly regarded, and if you practice it, you will usually be treated with respect.

Specifically, shorts should be worn only at the beach, not in town, and especially not in the highlands. Skirts should be at or below the knee. Going braless is considered provocative. Many local women swim with T-shirts over their swimsuits.

Women traveling alone can expect plenty of attention from talkative men. Often they're just curious and not out for a foreign conquest. It is, of course, up to you how to respond, but there's no need to be intimidated. Consider the situation and circumstances, and stay confident. Try to sit next to women or children on the bus. Local women rarely initiate conversations, but usually have lots of interesting things to say once the ball is rolling.

While there's no need to be paranoid, the possibility of rape and assault does exist. Use your normal traveler's caution – avoid walking alone in isolated places or through city streets late at night, and skip hitchhiking.

Work

Some travelers find work in bars, restaurants and places to stay in Antigua, Panajachel or Quetzaltenango, but the wages are just survival pay. If you're looking to crew a yacht, there's always work being offered around the Río Dulce area, sometimes for short trips, sometimes to the States and further afield. Check noticeboards for details.

Transportation

GETTING THERE & AWAY

Entering the Country

When you enter Guatemala – by land, air, sea or river – you should simply have to fill out straightforward immigration and customs forms. In the normal course of things you should not have to pay a cent.

However, immigration officials sometimes request unofficial fees from travelers. To determine whether these are legitimate, you can ask for *un recibo* (a receipt). You may find that the fee is dropped. When in doubt, try to observe what, if anything, other travelers are paying before it's your turn (Q10 is the standard, nonstandard fee).

To enter Guatemala, you need a valid passport.

Air

Airports & Airlines

Guatemala City's **Aeropuerto La Aurora** (www.dgacguate.com) (GUA) is the country's major international airport. The only other airport with international flights (from Cancún, Mexico, and Belize City) is Flores (FRS). The Guatemalan national airline, Aviateca, is part of the regional Grupo TACA, along with El Salvador's Taca and Costa Rica's Lacsa.

There are direct flights from the USA with a variety of airlines. **AeroMexico** (www.aeromexico.com) and **Interjet** (www.interjet.com.mx) fly direct to Mexico City. **Grupo TACA** (www.taca.com) has flights to most Central American capitals. If you are coming from elsewhere, you will almost certainly be changing planes in one of those places.

Land

It's advisable to get through all borders as early in the day as possible. Onward transportation tends to wind down in the afternoon and border areas are not always the safest places to hang around late. There is no departure tax when you leave Guatemala by land, although many border officials will ask for Q10. If you're willing to argue and wait around, this may be dropped, but most travelers take the path of least resistance and simply pay up.

Border Crossings

Guatemala has official border crossings with all of its neighboring countries.

BELIZE

➧ Melchor de Mancos (GUA) – Benque Viejo del Carmen (BZE)

EL SALVADOR

➧ Ciudad Pedro de Alvarado (GUA) – La Hachadura (ES)

➧ Valle Nuevo (GUA) – Las Chinamas (ES)

➧ San Cristóbal Frontera (GUA) –San Cristobal (ES)

➧ Anguiatú (GUA) – Anguiatú (ES)

HONDURAS

➧ Agua Caliente (GUA) – Agua Caliente (HND)

➧ El Florido (GUA) – Copán Ruinas (HND)

➧ Corinto (GUA) – Corinto (HND)

MEXICO

➧ Tecún Uman (GUA) – Ciudad Hidalgo (MEX)

DEPARTURE TAX

Guatemala levies a departure tax of US$30 on outbound air passengers, which is mostly (but not always) included in your ticket price. If it's not, it has to be paid in cash US dollars or quetzals at the airline check-in desk. For some time there was a separate US$3/Q25 airport security tax, but that seems to have been dropped.

CLIMATE CHANGE & TRAVEL

Every form of transport that relies on carbon-based fuel generates CO_2, the main cause of human-induced climate change. Modern travel is dependent on airplanes, which might use less fuel per kilometer per person than most cars but travel much greater distances. The altitude at which aircraft emit gases (including CO_2) and particles also contributes to their climate change impact. Many websites offer 'carbon calculators' that allow people to estimate the carbon emissions generated by their journey and, for those who wish to do so, to offset the impact of the greenhouse gases emitted with contributions to portfolios of climate-friendly initiatives throughout the world. Lonely Planet offsets the carbon footprint of all staff and author travel.

➡ El Carmen (GUA) – Talisman (MEX)

➡ La Mesilla (GUA) – Ciudad Cuauhtémoc (MEX)

Bus

Bus is the most common way to enter Guatemala by land, though you can also do so by car, river or sea.

Most first-class international buses run nonstop from Guatemala City to their destinations – see Guatemala City's Getting There & Away section (p59) for details.

First-class buses for Belize also depart from Flores/Santa Elena. For cheaper, local transportation, see town sections closest to the border you will be crossing. On first-class buses (particularly to Honduras and El Salvador) the driver may take your passport and complete border formalities for you. Going to Belize or Mexico, you will be required to do them yourself. Second-class buses tend not to cross the border.

Car & Motorcycle

The mountain of paperwork and liability involved with driving into Guatemala deters most travelers. You will need the following documents, all clear and consistent, to enter Guatemala with a car:

➡ current and valid registration

➡ proof of ownership (if you don't own the car, you'll need a notarized letter of authorization from the owner that you are allowed to take it)

➡ your current and valid driver's license or an International Driving Permit (IDP), issued by the automobile association in your home country

➡ temporary import permit available free at the border and good for a maximum 90 days

Insurance from foreign countries is not recognized by Guatemala, forcing you to purchase a policy locally. Most border posts and nearby towns have offices selling liability policies. To deter foreigners from selling cars in Guatemala, the authorities make you exit the country with the vehicle you used to enter it. Do not be the designated driver when crossing borders if you don't own the car, because you and it will not be allowed to leave Guatemala without each other.

Gasoline is readily available in all but the tiniest of villages. If you see a young kid waving a funnel at you, it means he is selling cheap contraband Mexican gas – some people swear by it, others claim that its high sediment content ruins engines.

Mechanics are also everywhere. Authorized agencies can only be found in the larger cities. Generic parts are easy to come by, but if you're looking for originals, Toyota is by far the most popular make in the country, followed (distantly) by Mazda and Ford.

River

There are two possible crossings from Mexico's Chiapas State to El Petén – the most commonly used one crosses at the Mexican town of Frontera Corozal to either La Técnica or Bethel in Guatemala. Frontera Corozal has good transport connections to Palenque in Mexico and there are regular buses from La Técnica and Bethel to Flores/Santa Elena, Guatemala.

The other river route from Mexico into Guatemala's Petén department is up the Río de la Pasión from Benemérito de las Américas, south of Frontera Corozal, to Sayaxché, but there are no immigration facilities or reliable passenger services along this route.

Sea

Public boats connect Punta Gorda in Belize with Lívingston and Puerto Barrios in Guatemala. The Punta Gorda services connect with bus services to/from Belize City.

There is a Q80 departure tax when leaving Guatemala by sea.

GETTING AROUND

Air

At the time of writing the only scheduled internal flights were between Guatemala City and Flores, a route operated daily by **Grupo TACA** (www.taca.com) and **TAG** (www.tag.com.gt).

Bicycle

Guatemala's mountainous terrain and occasionally terrifying road conditions make for hard going when it comes to intercity pedalling. That said, if you have your wits about you, cycling is a great way to get around smaller towns – Antigua, Quetzaltenango and San Pedro La Laguna are among the towns where you can rent reasonable mountain bikes (you don't want skinny wheels here) by the hour, day, week or longer. There are bike shops in almost every town where you can buy a new bike starting from around Q800.

Boat

The Caribbean town of Lívingston is only reachable by boat, across the Bahía de Amatique from Puerto Barrios or down the Río Dulce

from the town of Río Dulce – both great trips. In Lago de Atitlán fast fiberglass launches zip across the waters between villages – by far the best way to get around.

Bus, Minibus & Pickup

Buses go almost everywhere in Guatemala. Guatemala's buses will leave you with some of your most vivid memories of the country. Most of them are ancient school buses from the US and Canada. It is not unusual for a local family of five to squeeze into seats that were originally designed for two child-sized bottoms. Many travelers know these vehicles as chicken buses, after the live cargo accompanying many passengers. They are frequent, crowded and cheap. Expect to pay Q10 (or less!) for an hour of travel.

Chicken buses will stop anywhere, for anyone. Helpers will yell '*hay lugares!*' (eye loo *gar* ays), which

literally means 'there are places'. Never mind that the space they refer to may be no more than a sliver of air between hundreds of locals mashed against one another. These same helpers will also yell their bus's destination in voices of varying hilarity and cadence; just listen for the song of your town. Tall travelers will be especially challenged on these buses. To catch a chicken bus, simply stand beside the road with your arm out parallel to the ground.

Some routes, especially between big cities, are served by more comfortable buses with the luxury of one seat per person. The best buses are labeled 'Pullman,' '*especial*' or '*primera clase*'. Occasionally, these may have bathrooms (but don't count on them working), televisions and even food service.

Pullman routes always originate or end in Guatemala City. See Guatemala City's Getting There & Away section (p59) for route information.

A CHICKEN BUS IS HATCHED

If you rode the bus to school 10 years ago or more in the US, you might just end up meeting an old friend in Guatemala, resurrected and given new life as a 'chicken bus'. Love 'em or hate 'em, chicken buses (*camionetas* or *parrillas* to Guatemalans) are a fact of life in traveling around Guatemala. A lot of times there is no alternative.

As you can probably tell by the signs that sometimes remain in these buses ('anyone breaking the rules will lose their bus riding privileges'), these buses really did once carry school kids. In the US, once school buses reach the ripe old age of 10 years, or they do 150,000 miles, they're auctioned off. This is just the first step in the long process that results in the buses hitting the Guatemalan road. They then get towed through the States and Mexico, taken to a workshop here where they are refitted (bigger engine, six-speed gearbox, roof rack, destination board, luggage rack, longer seats) and fancied up with a paint job, CD player and chrome detailing.

Drivers then add their individual touches – anything from religious paraphernalia to stuffed toys and Christmas lights dangling around the dashboard area.

Thus, the chicken bus is ready to roll, and roll they do. The average bus works 14 hours a day, seven days a week – more miles in one day than it covered in a week back on the school run.

If you've got a choice of buses to go with, looks *are* important – chances are that if the paint is fresh and the chrome gleaming, the owner also has the cash to spend on new brakes and regular maintenance. And, with a conservative estimate of an average of one chicken-bus accident per week in Guatemala, this is something you may want to keep in mind.

In general, more buses leave in the morning (some leave as early as 3am) than the afternoon. Bus traffic drops off precipitously after about 4pm; night buses are rare and not generally recommended. An exception are the overnight buses from Guatemala City to Flores, which have not experienced (to our knowledge) any trouble of note in several years (we hope we're not tempting fate here).

Distances in Guatemala are not huge and, apart from the aforementioned Guate–Flores run, you won't often ride for more than four hours at a time. On a typical four-hour bus trip you'll cover 175km to 200km for Q50 to Q80.

For a few of the better services you can buy tickets in advance, and this is generally worth doing as it ensures that you get a place.

On some shorter routes minibuses, usually called 'microbuses', are replacing chicken buses. These are operated by the same cram-'em-all-in principle and can be even more uncomfortable because they have less leg room. Where neither buses nor minibuses roam, pickup (picop) trucks serve as de facto buses; you hail them and pay for them as if they were the genuine article.

At least a couple of times a month, a chicken bus plunges over a cliff or rounds a blind bend into a head-on collision. Newspapers are full of gory details and diagrams of the latest wreck, which doesn't foster affectionate feelings toward Guatemalan public transportation.

Car & Motorcycle

You can drive in Guatemala with your home-country driver's license or with an International Driving Permit (IDP). Guatemalan driving etiquette will probably be very different from what you're used to back home: passing on blind curves, ceding the right of way to vehicles coming uphill on narrow passes and deafening honking for no apparent reason are just the start. Expect few road signs and no indication from other drivers of what they are about to do. Do not pay any attention to turn signals – they are rarely used and even more rarely used to indicate a turn in the direction they would seem to be. Hazard lights mean that the driver is about to do something foolish and/or illegal.

A vehicle coming uphill always has the right of way. *Túmulos* are speed bumps that are generously (sometimes oddly) placed throughout the country, usually on the main drag through a town. Use of seat belts is obligatory, but generally not practiced.

In Guatemala driving at night is a bad idea for many reasons, not the least of which are armed bandits, drunk drivers and decreased visibility.

Every driver involved in an accident that results in injury or death is taken into custody until a judge determines responsibility.

If someone's car breaks down on the highway (particularly on curvy mountain roads), they'll warn other drivers by putting shrubs or small branches on the road for a few hundred meters beforehand. Annoyingly, they rarely pick them up afterwards, but if you're driving and you see these, it's best to be cautious and slow down.

Rental

While car hire is certainly possible, if you're sticking to the main sights, logistically it is rarely a good idea – Antigua is best seen on foot, the villages around Lake Atitlán are best visited by boat, and the distance from either of those to Tikal makes it a much better idea to catch a bus or fly. That said, for freedom and comfort, nothing beats having your own wheels.

There are car hire places in all the major tourist cities. To rent a car or motorcycle you need to show your passport, driver's license and a major credit card. Usually, the person renting the vehicle must be 25 years or older. Insurance policies accompanying rental cars may not protect you from loss or theft, in which case you could be liable for hundreds or even thousands of dollars in damages. Be careful where you park, especially in Guatemala City and at night. Even if your hotel does not have parking, they will know of a secure garage somewhere nearby.

Motorcycles are available for rent in Antigua and around Lake Atitlán. Bringing safety gear is highly recommended.

Hitchhiking

Hitchhiking in the strict sense of the word is generally not practiced in Guatemala because it is not safe. However, where the bus service is sporadic or nonexistent, pickup trucks and other vehicles may serve as public transport. If you stand beside the road with your arm out, someone will stop. You are expected to pay the driver as if you were traveling on a bus and the fare will be similar. This is a safe and reliable system used by locals and travelers, and the only inconvenience you're likely to encounter is full to overflowing vehicles – get used to it.

Local Transportation

Bus

Public transportation within towns and cities outside of Guatemala CIty is chiefly provided by newish, crowded minibuses. They're useful to travelers chiefly in the more spread-out cities such as Quetzaltenango and Huehuetenango. Guatemala City has its own forms of bus services – the old red buses that are not recommended for safety reasons and the newer fleets of TransMetro and TransUrbano buses. See Guatemala City's Getting Around section (p61) for details.

Tuk-tuk

If you've spent any time in Asia, you'll be very familiar with the *tuk-tuk*, a three-wheeled minitaxi nominally seating three passengers and a driver, but obviously capable of carrying twice that amount.

Named for the noise their little lawn-mower engines make, *tuk-tuks* are best for short hops around town – expect to pay somewhere between Q3 and Q5 per person. Hail them the way you would a normal taxi.

Shuttle Minibus

Shuttle minibuses run by travel agencies provide comfortable and quick transport along the main routes plied by tourists. You'll find these heavily advertised wherever they are offered. With a few notable exceptions, they're much more expensive than buses (anywhere between five and 15 times as expensive), but more convenient – they usually offer a door-to-door service, with scheduled meal and bathroom breaks. The most popular shuttle routes include Guatemala City airport–Antigua, Antigua–Panajachel, Panajachel–Chichicastenango and Lanquín–Antigua.

Taxi

Taxis are fairly plentiful in most significant towns. A 10-minute ride can cost about Q50, which is relatively expensive – expect to hear plenty of woeful tales from taxi drivers about the price of gasoline. Except for some taxis in Guatemala City, they don't use meters: you must agree upon the fare before you set off – best before you get in, in fact.

If you feel reluctant to take on the Guatemalan roads, an interesting alternative to car hire can be to hire a taxi driver for an extended time. This often works out only slightly more expensive than renting and gives you all the freedom and comfort without the stress of having to drive.

Language

There are around 20 Maya indigenous languages used in Guatemala, but Spanish is the most commonly spoken language.

SPANISH

Latin American Spanish pronunciation is easy, as most sounds have equivalents in English. Note that kh is a throaty sound (like the 'ch' in the Scottish *loch*), v and b are like a soft English 'v' (between a 'v' and a 'b'), and r is strongly rolled. There are some variations in spoken Spanish across Latin America, the most notable being the pronunciation of the letters *ll* and *y*. In our pronunciation guides they are represented with y because they are pronounced as the 'y' in 'yes' in most of Latin America. Note, however, that in some parts of the continent they sound like the 'lli' in 'million'. If you read our colored pronunciation guides as if they were English, you'll be understood. The stressed syllables are indicated with italics in our pronunciation guides.

The polite form is used in this chapter; where both polite and informal options are given, they are indicated by the abbreviations 'pol' and 'inf'. Where necessary, both masculine and feminine forms of words are included, separated by a slash and with the masculine form first, eg *perdido/a* (m/f).

Basics

| Hello. | *Hola.* | o·la |
| Goodbye. | *Adiós.* | a·dyos |

WANT MORE?

For in-depth language information and handy phrases, check out Lonely Planet's *Latin American Spanish Phrasebook*. You'll find it at **shop.lonely planet.com**, or you can buy Lonely Planet's iPhone phrasebooks at the Apple App Store.

How are you?	*¿Qué tal?*	ke tal
Fine, thanks.	*Bien, gracias.*	byen gra·syas
Excuse me.	*Perdón.*	per·don
Sorry.	*Lo siento.*	lo syen·to
Please.	*Por favor.*	por fa·vor
Thank you.	*Gracias.*	gra·syas
You are welcome.	*De nada.*	de na·da
Yes./No.	*Sí./No.*	see/no

My name is ...
Me llamo ... me ya·mo ...

What's your name?
¿Cómo se llama Usted? ko·mo se ya·ma oo·*ste* (pol)
¿Cómo te llamas? ko·mo te ya·mas (inf)

Do you speak English?
¿Habla inglés? a·bla een·gles (pol)
¿Hablas inglés? a·blas een·gles (inf)

I don't understand.
Yo no entiendo. yo no en·tyen·do

Accommodations

I'd like a single/double room.
Quisiera una kee·sye·ra oo·na
habitación a·bee·ta·syon
individual/doble. een·dee·vee·dwal/do·ble

How much is it per night/person?
¿Cuánto cuesta por kwan·to kwes·ta por
noche/persona? no·che/per·so·na

Does it include breakfast?
¿Incluye el desayuno? een·kloo·ye el de·sa·yoo·no

campsite	*terreno de cámping*	te·re·no de kam·peeng
guesthouse	*pensión*	pen·syon
hotel	*hotel*	o·tel
youth hostel	*albergue juvenil*	al·ber·ge khoo·ve·neel

Signs

Abierto	Open
Cerrado	Closed
Entrada	Entrance
Hombres/Varones	Men
Mujeres/Damas	Women
Prohibido	Prohibited
Salida	Exit
Servicios/Baños	Toilets

air-con	*aire acondi-cionado*	ai·re a·kon·dee·syo·na·do
bathroom	*baño*	ba·nyo
bed	*cama*	ka·ma
window	*ventana*	ven·ta·na

Directions

Where's ...?
¿Dónde está ...?   don·de es·ta ...

What's the address?
¿Cuál es la dirección?   kwal es la dee·rek·syon

Could you please write it down?
¿Puede escribirlo,   pwe·de es·kree·beer·lo
por favor?   por fa·vor

Can you show me (on the map)?
¿Me lo puede indicar   me lo pwe·de een·dee·kar
(en el mapa)?   (en el ma·pa)

at the corner	*en la esquina*	en la es·kee·na
at the traffic lights	*en el semáforo*	en el se·ma·fo·ro
behind ...	*detrás de ...*	de·tras de ...
in front of ...	*enfrente de ...*	en·fren·te de ...
left	*izquierda*	ees·kyer·da
next to ...	*al lado de ...*	al la·do de ...
opposite ...	*frente a ...*	fren·te a ...
right	*derecha*	de·re·cha
straight ahead	*todo recto*	to·do rek·to

Eating & Drinking

Can I see the menu, please?
¿Puedo ver el menú,   pwe·do ver el me·noo
por favor?   por fa·vor

What would you recommend?
¿Qué recomienda?   ke re·ko·myen·da

Do you have vegetarian food?
¿Tienen comida   tye·nen ko·mee·da
vegetariana?   ve·khe·ta·rya·na

I don't eat (red meat).
No como (carne roja).   no ko·mo (kar·ne ro·kha)

That was delicious!
¡Estaba buenísimo!   es·ta·ba bwe·nee·see·mo

Cheers!
¡Salud!   sa·loo

The bill, please.
La cuenta, por favor.   la kwen·ta por fa·vor

I'd like a table for ...	*Quisiera una mesa para ...*	kee·sye·ra oo·na me·sa pa·ra ...
(eight) o'clock	*las (ocho)*	las (o·cho)
(two) people	*(dos) personas*	(dos) per·so·nas

Key Words

bottle	*botella*	bo·te·ya
breakfast	*desayuno*	de·sa·yoo·no
(too) cold	*(muy) frío*	(mooy) free·o
dinner	*cena*	se·na
fork	*tenedor*	te·ne·dor
glass	*vaso*	va·so
hot (warm)	*caliente*	kal·yen·te
knife	*cuchillo*	koo·chee·yo
lunch	*comida*	ko·mee·da
plate	*plato*	pla·to
spoon	*cuchara*	koo·cha·ra

Meat & Fish

beef	*carne de vaca*	kar·ne de va·ka
chicken	*pollo*	po·yo
duck	*pato*	pa·to
lamb	*cordero*	kor·de·ro
pork	*cerdo*	ser·do
prawn	*langostino*	lan·gos·tee·no
salmon	*salmón*	sal·mon
tuna	*atún*	a·toon
turkey	*pavo*	pa·vo
veal	*ternera*	ter·ne·ra

Fruit & Vegetables

apple	*manzana*	man·sa·na
banana	*plátano*	pla·ta·no
beans	*judías*	khoo·dee·as
cabbage	*col*	kol
capsicum	*pimiento*	pee·myen·to
carrot	*zanahoria*	sa·na·o·rya
cherry	*cereza*	se·re·sa
corn	*maíz*	ma·ees
cucumber	*pepino*	pe·pee·no
grape	*uvas*	oo·vas
lemon	*limón*	lee·mon
lettuce	*lechuga*	le·choo·ga

mushroom	champiñón	cham·pee·*nyon*
nuts	nueces	*nwe*·ses
onion	cebolla	se·*bo*·ya
orange	naranja	na·*ran*·kha
peach	melocotón	me·lo·ko·*ton*
peas	guisantes	gee·*san*·tes
pineapple	piña	*pee*·nya
plum	ciruela	seer·*we*·la
potato	patata	pa·*ta*·ta
spinach	espinacas	es·pee·*na*·kas
strawberry	fresa	*fre*·sa
tomato	tomate	to·*ma*·te
watermelon	sandía	san·*dee*·a

Other

bread	pan	pan
butter	mantequilla	man·te·*kee*·ya
cheese	queso	*ke*·so
egg	huevo	*we*·vo
honey	miel	myel
jam	mermelada	mer·me·*la*·da
pepper	pimienta	pee·*myen*·ta
rice	arroz	a·*ros*
salt	sal	sal
sugar	azúcar	a·*soo*·kar

Drinks

beer	cerveza	ser·*ve*·sa
coffee	café	ka·*fe*
(orange) juice	zumo (de naranja)	*soo*·mo (de na·*ran*·kha)
milk	leche	*le*·che
red wine	vino tinto	*vee*·no *teen*·to
tea	té	te
(mineral) water	agua (mineral)	*a*·gwa (mee·ne·*ral*)
white wine	vino blanco	*vee*·no *blan*·ko

Emergencies

Help!	*¡Socorro!*	so·*ko*·ro
Go away!	*¡Vete!*	*ve*·te
Call ...!	*¡Llame a ...!*	*ya*·me a ...
a doctor	un médico	oon *me*·dee·ko
the police	la policía	la po·lee·*see*·a

I'm lost.
Estoy perdido/a.   es·*toy* per·*dee*·do/a (m/f)

I'm ill.
Estoy enfermo/a.   es·*toy* en·*fer*·mo/a (m/f)

I'm allergic to (antibiotics).
Soy alérgico/a a   soy a·*ler*·khee·ko/a a
(los antibióticos).   (los an·tee·*byo*·tee·kos) (m/f)

Where are the toilets?
¿Dónde están los   *don*·de es·*tan* los
baños?   *ba*·nyos

Shopping & Services

I'd like to buy ...
Quisiera comprar ...   kee·*sye*·ra kom·*prar* ...

I'm just looking.
Sólo estoy mirando.   *so*·lo es·*toy* mee·*ran*·do

Can I look at it?
¿Puedo verlo?   *pwe*·do *ver*·lo

I don't like it.
No me gusta.   no me *goos*·ta

How much is it?
¿Cuánto cuesta?   *kwan*·to *kwes*·ta

That's too expensive.
Es muy caro.   es mooy *ka*·ro

There's a mistake in the bill.
Hay un error   ai oon e·*ror*
en la cuenta.   en la *kwen*·ta

ATM	cajero automático	ka·*khe*·ro ow·to·ma·*tee*·ko
internet cafe	cibercafé	see·ber·ka·*fe*
market	mercado	mer·*ka*·do
post office	correos	ko·*re*·os
tourist office	oficina de turismo	o·fee·*see*·na de too·*rees*·mo

Time, Dates & Numbers

What time is it?	*¿Qué hora es?*	ke *o*·ra es
It's (10) o'clock.	*Son (las diez).*	son (las dyes)
It's half past (one).	*Es (la una) y media.*	es (la *oo*·na) ee *me*·dya
morning	mañana	ma·*nya*·na
afternoon	tarde	*tar*·de
evening	noche	*no*·che

Question Words

How?	*¿Cómo?*	*ko*·mo
What?	*¿Qué?*	ke
When?	*¿Cuándo?*	*kwan*·do
Where?	*¿Dónde?*	*don*·de
Who?	*¿Quién?*	kyen
Why?	*¿Por qué?*	por ke

yesterday	ayer	a·yer
today	hoy	oy
tomorrow	mañana	ma·nya·na

Monday	lunes	loo·nes
Tuesday	martes	mar·tes
Wednesday	miércoles	myer·ko·les
Thursday	jueves	khwe·ves
Friday	viernes	vyer·nes
Saturday	sábado	sa·ba·do
Sunday	domingo	do·meen·go

1	uno	oo·no
2	dos	dos
3	tres	tres
4	cuatro	kwa·tro
5	cinco	seen·ko
6	seis	seys
7	siete	sye·te
8	ocho	o·cho
9	nueve	nwe·ve
10	diez	dyes
20	veinte	veyn·te
30	treinta	treyn·ta
40	cuarenta	kwa·ren·ta
50	cincuenta	seen·kwen·ta
60	sesenta	se·sen·ta
70	setenta	se·ten·ta
80	ochenta	o·chen·ta
90	noventa	no·ven·ta
100	cien	syen
1000	mil	meel

Transportation

boat	barco	bar·ko
bus	autobús	ow·to·boos
plane	avión	a·vyon
train	tren	tren

A ... ticket, please.	Un billete de ..., por favor.	oon bee·ye·te de ... por fa·vor
1st-class	primera clase	pree·me·ra kla·se
2nd-class	segunda clase	se·goon·da kla·se
one-way	ida	ee·da
return	ida y vuelta	ee·da ee vwel·ta

first	primero	pree·me·ro
last	último	ool·tee·mo
next	próximo	prok·see·mo

bus stop	parada de autobuses	pa·ra·da de ow·to·boo·ses
cancelled	cancelado	kan·se·la·do
delayed	retrasado	re·tra·sa·do
ticket office	taquilla	ta·kee·ya
timetable	horario	o·ra·ryo
train station	estación de trenes	es·ta·syon de tre·nes

I want to go to ...
Quisiera ir a ...   kee·sye·ra eer a ...

Does it stop at ...?
¿Para en ...?   pa·ra en ...

What stop is this?
¿Cuál es esta parada?   kwal es es·ta pa·ra·da

What time does it arrive/leave?
¿A qué hora llega/sale? a ke o·ra ye·ga/sa·le

Please tell me when we get to ...
¿Puede avisarme   pwe·de a·vee·sar·me
cuando lleguemos a ...? kwan·do ye·ge·mos a ...

I want to get off here.
Quiero bajarme aquí.   kye·ro ba·khar·me a·kee

I'd like to hire a ...	Quisiera alquilar ...	kee·sye·ra al·kee·lar ...
bicycle	una bicicleta	oo·na bee·see·kle·ta
car	un coche	oon ko·che
motorcycle	una moto	oo·na mo·to

helmet	casco	kas·ko
mechanic	mecánico	me·ka·nee·ko
petrol/gas	gasolina	ga·so·lee·na
service station	gasolinera	ga·so·lee·ne·ra

Is this the road to ...?
¿Se va a ... por   se va a ... por
esta carretera?   es·ta ka·re·te·ra

(How long) Can I park here?
¿(Cuánto tiempo)   (kwan·to tyem·po)
Puedo aparcar aquí?   pwe·do a·par·kar a·kee

The car has broken down (at ...).
El coche se ha averiado el ko·che se a a·ve·rya·do
(en ...).   (en ...)

I have a flat tyre.
Tengo un pinchazo.   ten·go oon peen·cha·so

I've run out of petrol.
Me he quedado sin   me e ke·da·do seen
gasolina.   ga·so·lee·na

MODERN MAYA

Since the pre-Columbian period, the two ancient Maya languages, Yucatec and Cholan, have subdivided into more than 20 separate Maya languages (such as Yucatec, Chol, Ch'orti', Tzeltal, Tzotzil, Lacandón, Mam, K'iche' and Kakchiquel). Indigenous languages are seldom written, but when they are, the Roman alphabet is used. Most Maya speakers will only read and write Spanish – they may not be literate in Maya.

Maya pronunciation is pretty straightforward. There are just a few rules to keep in mind: **c** is always a hard 'k' sound, as in 'cat'; **j** is similar to the 'h' in 'half'; **u** is pronounced as in 'prune', but at the beginning or end of a word, it's like English 'w'; and **x** is pronounced like the 'sh' in 'shoes'. The consonants followed by an apostrophe (**b', ch', k', p', t'**) are pronounced more forcefully and explosively. Vowels followed by an apostrophe (') indicate a glottal stop (like the sound between the two syllables in 'uh-oh'.) Stress usually falls on the last syllable.

K'iche'

K'iche' is spoken throughout the Guatemalan highlands, from around Santa Cruz del Quiché to the area around Lago de Atitlán and Quetzaltenango. There are around two million K'iche' Maya in Guatemala.

Good morning.	Saqarik.
Good afternoon.	Xb'eqij.
Good evening/night.	Xokaq'ab'.
Goodbye.	Chab'ej.
See you soon.	Kimpetik ri.
Excuse me.	Kyunala.
Thank you.	Uts awech.
What's your name?	Su ra'b'i?
My name is ...	Nu b'i ...
Where are you from?	Ja kat pewi?
I'm from ...	Ch'qap ja'kin pewi ...
Where is a/the ...?	Ja k'uichi' ri ...?
bathroom	b'anb'al chulu
bus stop	tek'lib'al
doctor	ajkun
hotel	jun worib'al
Do you have ...?	K'olik ...?
boiled water	saq'li
coffee	kab'e
rooms	k'plib'al
bad	itzel
blanket	k'ul
closed	tzapilik
cold	joron
good	utz
hard	ko
hot	miq'in
open	teb'am
sick	yiwab'
soft	ch'uch'uj
vegetables	ichaj
north (white)	saq
south (yellow)	k'an
east (red)	kaq
west (black)	k'eq
1	jun
2	keb'
3	oxib'
4	kijeb'
5	job'
6	waq'ib'
7	wuqub'
8	wajxakib'
9	b'elejeb'
10	lajuj

Mam

Mam is spoken in the department of Huehuetenango. This is the language you'll hear in Todos Santos Cuchumatán. Note that many Mam words have been in disuse for so long that the Spanish equivalent is used almost exclusively. The numbers from one to 10 are the same as in K'iche', and for numbers higher than 10, Spanish words are used.

Good morning/	Chin q'olb'el teya. (sg inf)
afternoon/evening.	Chin q'olb'el kyeyea. (pl inf)
Goodbye.	Chi nej.
See you soon.	Ak qli qib'.
Excuse me.	Naq samy.
Thank you.	Chonte teya.
How are you?	Tzen ta'ya?
What's your name?	Tit biya?
My name is ...	Luan bi ...
Where are you from?	Jaa'tzajnia?
I'm from ...	Ac tzajni ...
Where is a/the ...?	Ja at ...?
bathroom	bano
doctor	medico/doctor
hotel	hospedaje

Is there somewhere we can sleep?	*Ja tun kqta'n?*
Where is the bus stop?	*Ja nue camioneta?*
How much are the fruit and vegetables?	*Je te ti lobj?*
Do you have ...?	*At ...?*
boiled water	*kqa'*
coffee	*café*
rooms	*cuartos*
I'm cold.	*At xb'a'j/choj.*
I'm sick.	*At yab'.*

bad	*k'ab'ex/nia g'lan*
closed	*jpu'n*
good	*banex/g'lan*
hard	*kuj*
hot	*kyaq*
open	*jqo'n*
soft	*xb'une*
north (white)	*okan*
south (yellow)	*eln*
east (red)	*jawl*
west (black)	*kub'el*

GLOSSARY

Apartado Postal – post-office box; abbreviated Apdo Postal

Ayuntamiento – often seen as H Ayuntamiento (Honorable Ayuntamiento) on the front of town hall buildings; translates as 'Municipal Government'

barrio – district, neighborhood

billete – bank note

boleto – ticket (bus, train, museum etc)

bolo – colloquial term for drunk (noun)

cabañas – cabins

cacique – Maya chief; also used to describe provincial warlord or strongman

cafétería – literally 'coffee-shop,' but refers to any informal restaurant with waiter service; not usually a cafeteria in the North American sense of a self-service restaurant

cajero automático – automated teller machine(ATM)

callejón – alley or narrow or very short street

camión – truck or bus

camioneta – bus or pickup truck

cardamomo – cardamom; a spice grown extensively in the Verapaces and used as a flavor enhancer for coffee and tea

casa de cambio – currency exchange office; offers exchange rates comparable to those of banks and is much faster to use, though uncommon in Guatemala

cenote – large, natural limestone cave used for water storage (or ceremonial purposes)

cerveza – beer

Chac – Maya god of rain

chac-mool – Maya sacrificial stone sculpture

chapín – slang term for citizen of Guatemala

charro – cowboy

chicle – sap of the sapodilla tree; used to manufacture chewing gum

chicleros – men who collect chicle

Chinka' – small, non-Maya indigenous group living on the Pacific Slope

chuchkajau – Maya prayer leader

chuj – traditional Maya sauna; also known as *tuj*

chultún – artificial Maya cistern

cigarro – cigarette

cocina – kitchen; also used for a small, basic one-woman place to eat, often located in or near a municipal market, and in the phrases *cocina económica* (economical kitchen) or a *cocina familiar* (family kitchen)

cofradía – religious brotherhood, most often found in the highlands

colectivo – jitney taxi or minibus (usually a Kombi or minibus) that picks up and drops off passengers along its route

comal – hot griddle or surface used to cook tortillas

comedor – basic and cheap eatery, usually with a limited menu

completo – full; a sign you may see on hotel desks in crowded cities

conquistador – explorer-conqueror of Latin America from Spain

copal – tree resin used as incense in Maya ceremonies

correos – post office

corte – Maya wraparound skirt

costumbre – traditional Maya rites

criollos – people born in Guatemala of Spanish blood

cruce – crossroads, usually where you make bus connections; also known as *entronque*

cuadra – a city block

curandero – traditional indigenous healer

damas – ladies; the usual sign on toilet doors

dzul, dzules – Maya for foreigners or 'townsfolk'

faja – Maya waist sash or belt

ferrocarril – railroad

finca – plantation, farm

galón, galones – US gallons; fluid measure of 3.79L

glyph – symbolic character or figure; usually engraved or carved in relief

gringo/a – a mildly pejorative term applied to a male/female North American visitor; sometimes applied to any visitor of European heritage

gruta – cave

guayabera – man's thin fabric shirt with pockets and appliquéd designs on the front, over the shoulders and down the back; often worn in place of a jacket and tie on formal occasions

hacienda – estate; also 'treasury,' as in Departamento de Hacienda, Treasury Department

hay – pronounced like 'eye,' meaning 'there is' or 'there are'; you're equally likely to hear no hay, meaning 'there isn't' or 'there aren't'

hombre/s – man/men

huipil – Maya woman's woven tunic; often very colorful and elaborately embroidered

IVA – *impuesto al valor agregado* or value-added tax; on hotel rooms it is 12%

juego de pelota – ball game

kaperraj – Maya woman's all-purpose cloth; used as a head covering, baby sling, produce sack, shawl and more

Kukulcán – Maya name for the Aztec-Toltec plumed serpent Quetzalcóatl

ladino – person of mixed indigenous and European race; a more common term in Guatemala than *mestizo*

lancha – motorboat used to transport passengers; driven by a *lanchero*

larga distancia – long-distance telephone

lavandería – laundry; a *lavandería automática* is a coin-operated laundry

leng – in the highlands, a colloquial Maya term for coins

libra – pound; weight measurement of 0.45kg

lleno – full (fuel tank)

machismo – maleness, masculine virility

malecón – waterfront boulevard

manglar – mangrove

manzana – apple

mariachi – small group of street musicians featuring stringed instruments, trumpets and often an accordion; sometimes plays in restaurants

marimba – Guatemala's xylophone-like national instrument

mestizo – person of mixed indigenous and European blood; the word *ladino* is more common in Guatemala

metate – flattish stone on which corn is ground with a cylindrical stone roller

milla – mile; distance of 1.6km

milpa – maize field

mirador – lookout, vista point

mochilero – backpacker

mordida – 'bite'; small bribe paid to keep the wheels of bureaucracy turning

mudéjar – Moorish architectural style

mujer/es – woman/women

na – thatched Maya hut

onza – ounce; weight of 28g

palacio de gobierno – building housing the executive offices of a state or regional government

palacio municipal – city hall; seat of the corporation or municipal government

palapa – thatched shelter with a palm-leaf roof and open sides

panza verde – literally 'green belly,' a nickname given to Antigua residents who are said to eat lots of avocados

parada – bus stop; usually for city buses

picop – pickup truck

pie – foot; measure of 0.30m

pisto – colloquial Maya term for money, quetzals

posada – guesthouse

propino, propina – a tip, different from a *mordida*, which is really a bribe

punta – sexually suggestive dance enjoyed by the Garífuna of the Caribbean coast

puro – cigar

Quetzalcóatl – plumed serpent god of the Aztecs and Toltecs; see also Kukulcán

rebozo – long woolen or linen scarf covering the head or shoulders

refago – Maya wraparound skirt

retablo – ornate, often gilded altarpiece

retorno – 'return'; used on traffic signs to signify a U-turn or turnaround

sacbé, sacbeob – ceremonial limestone avenue or path between great Maya cities

sacerdote – priest

sanatorio – hospital, particularly a small private one

sanitario – literally 'sanitary'; usually means toilet

secadora – clothes dryer

stela, stelae – standing stone monument(s); usually carved

supermercado – supermarket; anything from a corner store to a large, US-style supermarket

taller – shop or workshop

taller mecánico – mechanic's shop, usually for cars

teléfono comunitario – community telephone; found in the smallest towns

tepezcuintle – edible jungle rodent the size of a rabbit

tienda – small store that may sell anything from candles and chickens to aspirin and bread

típico – typical or characteristic of a region; particularly used to describe food

tocoyal – Maya head covering

traje – traditional clothing worn by the Maya

tzut – Maya man's equivalent of a *kaperraj*

viajero – traveler

vulcanizadora – automobile tire repair shop

zonas – zones

zotz – bat (the mammal) in many Maya languages

FOOD GLOSSARY

a la parrilla – grilled, perhaps over charcoal
a la plancha – grilled on a hotplate
aguacate – avocado
ajo – garlic
almuerzo – lunch
antojitos – snacks (literally 'little whims')
arroz – rice
atole – a hot gruel made with maize, milk, cinnamon and sugar
aves – poultry
azúcar – sugar

bebida – drink
bistec or bistec de res – beef steak

café (negro/con leche) – coffee (black/with milk)
calabaza – squash, marrow or pumpkin
caldo – broth, often meat-based
camarones – shrimps
camarones gigantes – jumbo shrimp
carne – meat
carne asada – grilled beef
cebolla – onion
cerveza – beer
ceviche – raw seafood marinated in lime juice and mixed with onions, chilies, garlic, tomatoes and cilantro (coriander leaf)
coco – coconut
chicharrón – pork crackling
chile relleno – bell pepper stuffed with cheese, meat, rice or other foods, dipped in egg whites, fried and baked in sauce
chuchito – small tamal
chuletas (de puerco) – (pork) chops
churrasco – slab of thin grilled meat

ensalada – salad

filete de pescado – fish fillet
flan – custard, crème caramel
fresas – strawberries

frijoles – black beans
frutas – fruits

guacamole – avocados mashed with onion, chili sauce, lemon and tomato
güisquil – type of squash

hamburguesa – hamburger
helado – ice cream
huevos fritos/revueltos – fried/scrambled eggs

jamón – ham
jícama – a popular root vegetable resembling a potato crossed with an apple
jocón – green stew of chicken or pork with green vegetables and herbs

leche – milk
lechuga – lettuce
legumbres – root vegetables
licuado – milkshake made with fresh fruit, sugar, and milk or water
limón – lemon
limonada – drink made from lemon juice

mantequilla – butter
margarina – margarine
mariscos – seafood
mesa – table
melocotón – peach
miel – honey
milanesa – crumbed, breaded
mojarra – perch
mosh – oatmeal/porridge

naranja – orange
naranjada – like a *limonada* but made with oranges

pacaya – a squash-like staple
papa – potato
papaya – pawpaw
pastel – cake
pato – duck
pavo – turkey

pepián – chicken and vegetables in a piquant sesame and pumpkin seed sauce
pescado – fish (fried in butter and garlic)
piña – pineapple
pimienta – pepper (black)
plátano – plantain (green banana), edible when cooked (usually fried)
plato típico – set meal
pollo (asado/frito) – (grilled/fried) chicken
postre – dessert
propina – tip
puerco – pork
puyaso – a choice cut of steak

queso – cheese

refacciones – snacks; see *antojitos*

sal – salt
salchicha – sausage
salsa – sauce made with chilies, onion, tomato, lemon or lime juice, and spices
sopa – soup

taco – a soft or crisp corn tortilla wrapped or folded around meat and salsa
tamal – corn dough stuffed with meat, beans, chilies or nothing at all, wrapped in banana leaf or corn husks and steamed
tapado – a seafood, coconut milk and plantain casserole
tarta – cake
tenedor – fork
tocino – bacon
tomate – tomato
tostada – flat, crisp tortilla topped with meat or cheese, tomatoes, beans and lettuce

vaso – glass
verduras – green vegetables

zanahoria – carrot

Behind the Scenes

SEND US YOUR FEEDBACK

We love to hear from travelers – your comments keep us on our toes and help make our books better. Our well-traveled team reads every word on what you loved or loathed about this book. Although we cannot reply individually to postal submissions, we always guarantee that your feedback goes straight to the appropriate authors, in time for the next edition. Each person who sends us information is thanked in the next edition – the most useful submissions are rewarded with a selection of digital PDF chapters.

Visit **lonelyplanet.com/contact** to submit your updates and suggestions or to ask for help. Our award-winning website also features inspirational travel stories, news and discussions.

Note: We may edit, reproduce and incorporate your comments in Lonely Planet products such as guidebooks, websites and digital products, so let us know if you don't want your comments reproduced or your name acknowledged. For a copy of our privacy policy visit lonelyplanet.com/privacy.

OUR READERS

Many thanks to the travelers who used the last edition and wrote to us with helpful hints, useful advice and interesting anecdotes:

Sadik Ahmad, Xavier Alcober, Santiago Alvarez, Erin Ball, Thilo Ball, Tom Banbury, Elodie Bedin, Christian Behrenz, Matthew Bell, Tom De Bock, Sofie Bryder Nielsen, Charlotte Bushnell, Annalisa Cavallini, Tina Coffield, Clay Derouin, Annie Dupont, Goretty Elustondo, Joel Fentin, Alessandra Furlan, Roberto Giunchi, Luisa Fernanda González Pérez, Patti Gorman, Marianne Marita Hansen, Jussi Haunia, Fred Hembree, David Holman, Fanny Honguer, Frank Ihle, Eva Kalny, Alicia Kamm, Philippe Le Voyageur, Mike Lubing, Marjorie Macieira, Allegra Marshall, Carolina Mense, Bruce Morris, Scott Murphy, Daniel Musikant, Katharina Nickoleit, Conor O'Brien, Joep Peters, Charlotte Piwowar, Sarah Poynter, Brandee Smith, Paul Spizman, Eddie Stiel, Jane Taylor, Marleen ter Haar, Nina Thinggaard, Karin Troch, Kathrin Weber, Janice Westenhouse, Christian Wirsig

AUTHOR THANKS

Lucas Vidgen

Thanks firstly to the Guatemalans, for making my adopted country such an amazing place to live, work and travel. To all the travelers and tourism people along the way, especially Brenda Orantes in Guate, Thomas Ansems in Lanquín, and Geert Van Vaeck in Copán. At Lonely Planet, thanks to Jonathan Ricketson for whatever patience he has left with me, and to all the grease monkeys in the author pool – it's been quite a ride and the support was much appreciated.

Daniel C Schechter

Heartfelt *gracias* go to the numerous Guatemala denizens who contributed info and insights, including Christian Behrenz, Stefanie Zecha, Eduardo Orozco, Richard Morgan, Ana San Sebastián, David Mercer, Carolina C McCabe and Dolores Ratzán around Lago de Atitlán; Alida Pérez (mother and daughter) and Inguat rep Norman Raxón in Antigua; Rigoberto Pablo Cruz in Todos Santos Cuchumatán; Inguat reps Ángel Quiñones and Jorge

Grijalba in Xela; Kelsey Kuhn in El Remate; the unflappable Julián Mariona in Sayaxché; as well as fellow travelers Anna Knecht, Paulina Naser and Meli Kepfer.

ACKNOWLEDGMENTS

Climate map data adapted from Peel MC, Finlayson BL & McMahon TA (2007) 'Updated World Map of the Köppen-Geiger Climate Classification', *Hydrology and Earth System Sciences, 11, 163344.*

Illustration on p250 by Michael Weldon.
Cover photograph: Bus in Panajachel, with Lago de Atitlán in the background; Kelly Chang Travel Photography/Getty Images.

THIS BOOK

This 5th edition of Lonely Planet's Guatemala guidebook was researched and written by Lucas Vidgen (coordinating author) and Daniel C Schechter. The previous edition was also researched and written by Lucas Vidgen and Daniel C Schechter. The 3rd edition was written by Lucas Vidgen, the 2nd by John Noble and Susan Forsyth, and the 1st by Conner Gorry. This guidebook was commissioned in Lonely Planet's Oakland office, and produced by the following:

Commissioning Editor Catherine Craddock-Carrillo

Coordinating Editors Carolyn Boicos, Lauren Hunt

Coordinating Cartographers Rachel Imeson, Andy Rojas

Coordinating Layout Designer Clara Monitto

Managing Editor Bruce Evans

Senior Editors Andi Jones, Catherine Naghten, Martine Power

Managing Cartographers Anita Banh, Alison Lyall

Managing Layout Designer Jane Hart

Assisting Editors Kate Daly, Jeanette Wall

Cover Research Jennifer Mullins

Internal Image Research Aude Vauconsant

Illustrator Michael Weldon

Language Content Branislava Vladisavljevic

Thanks to Penny Cordner, Ryan Evans, Larissa Frost, Chris Girdler, Genesys India, Jouve India, Trent Paton, Raphael Richards, Dianne Schallmeiner, Kerrianne Southway, Gerard Walker

Index

Map Legend

Sights
- Beach
- Bird Sanctuary
- Buddhist
- Castle/Palace
- Christian
- Confucian
- Hindu
- Islamic
- Jain
- Jewish
- Monument
- Museum/Gallery/Historic Building
- Ruin
- Sento Hot Baths/Onsen
- Shinto
- Sikh
- Taoist
- Winery/Vineyard
- Zoo/Wildlife Sanctuary
- Other Sight

Activities, Courses & Tours
- Bodysurfing
- Diving/Snorkelling
- Canoeing/Kayaking
- Course/Tour
- Skiing
- Snorkelling
- Surfing
- Swimming/Pool
- Walking
- Windsurfing
- Other Activity

Sleeping
- Sleeping
- Camping

Eating
- Eating

Drinking & Nightlife
- Drinking & Nightlife
- Cafe

Entertainment
- Entertainment

Shopping
- Shopping

Information
- Bank
- Embassy/Consulate
- Hospital/Medical
- Internet
- Police
- Post Office
- Telephone
- Toilet
- Tourist Information
- Other Information

Geographic
- Beach
- Hut/Shelter
- Lighthouse
- Lookout
- Mountain/Volcano
- Oasis
- Park
- Pass
- Picnic Area
- Waterfall

Population
- Capital (National)
- Capital (State/Province)
- City/Large Town
- Town/Village

Transport
- Airport
- Border crossing
- Bus
- Cable car/Funicular
- Cycling
- Ferry
- Metro station
- Monorail
- Parking
- Petrol station
- Subway/Subte station
- Taxi
- Train station/Railway
- Tram
- Underground station
- Other Transport

Note: Not all symbols displayed above appear on the maps in this book

Routes
- Tollway
- Freeway
- Primary
- Secondary
- Tertiary
- Lane
- Unsealed road
- Road under construction
- Plaza/Mall
- Steps
- Tunnel
- Pedestrian overpass
- Walking Tour
- Walking Tour detour
- Path/Walking Trail

Boundaries
- International
- State/Province
- Disputed
- Regional/Suburb
- Marine Park
- Cliff
- Wall

Hydrography
- River, Creek
- Intermittent River
- Canal
- Water
- Dry/Salt/Intermittent Lake
- Reef

Areas
- Airport/Runway
- Beach/Desert
- Cemetery (Christian)
- Cemetery (Other)
- Glacier
- Mudflat
- Park/Forest
- Sight (Building)
- Sportsground
- Swamp/Mangrove

OUR STORY

A beat-up old car, a few dollars in the pocket and a sense of adventure. In 1972 that's all Tony and Maureen Wheeler needed for the trip of a lifetime – across Europe and Asia overland to Australia. It took several months, and at the end – broke but inspired – they sat at their kitchen table writing and stapling together their first travel guide, *Across Asia on the Cheap*. Within a week they'd sold 1500 copies. Lonely Planet was born. Today, Lonely Planet has offices in Melbourne, London and Oakland, with more than 600 staff and writers. We share Tony's belief that 'a great guidebook should do three things: inform, educate and amuse'.

OUR WRITERS

Lucas Vidgen

Coordinating Author, Guatemala City, The Pacific Slope, Central & Eastern Guatemala Born and raised in Melbourne, Australia, Lucas has been living in Quetzaltenango, Guatemala, for nearly 10 years. He first arrived with the idea of studying Spanish for a couple of weeks and the rest is too much history to fit into this space. Lucas has contributed to a variety of Lonely Planet titles over the last decade, mostly in Central and South America. When not writing for Lonely Planet, he divides his time between other writing projects and working with two Quetzaltenango-based NGOs, as Vice President of EntreMundos and Managing Director of Solidaridad y Desarrollo. Lucas also wrote the Plan Your Trip, Understand Guatemala and Survival Guide sections.

Daniel C Schechter

Antigua, The Highlands, El Petén A native New Yorker, Daniel called Mexico home for more than a decade. During that time he spanned the Mundo Maya on various forays from the capital, discovering and writing about such places as Campeche, Calakmul and Tikal and cultivating an enduring interest in Classic Maya history. It seemed fitting to revisit the territory for this edition at the dawn of the new *baktún*. Daniel currently resides in the Netherlands.

Published by Lonely Planet Publications Pty Ltd
ABN 36 005 607 983
5th edition – September 2013
ISBN 978 1 74220 011 8
© Lonely Planet 2013   Photographs © as indicated 2013
10 9 8 7 6 5 4 3 2 1
Printed in China

Although the authors and Lonely Planet have taken all reasonable care in preparing this book, we make no warranty about the accuracy or completeness of its content and, to the maximum extent permitted, disclaim all liability arising from its use.